Studies in Eighteenth-Century Culture

VOLUME 33

Studies in Eighteenth-Century Culture

VOLUME 33

Edited by

Catherine Ingrassia
Virginia Commonwealth University

and

Jeffrey S. Ravel
Massachusetts Institute of Technology

Published by The Johns Hopkins University Press for the
American Society for Eighteenth-Century Studies

The Johns Hopkins University Press
Baltimore and London

The Johns Hopkins University Press
2715 North Charles Street
Baltimore, Maryland 21218-4363
www.press.jhu.edu

ISBN 0-8018-7873-X
ISSN 0360-2370

Articles appearing in this annual series are abstracted and
indexed in *Historical Abstracts* and *America: History and Life*.

Editorial Readers for Volume Thirty-Three

MAUREEN HARKIN / English / Reed College
ELIZABETH HECKENDORN COOK / English / University of California, Santa Barbara
CARLA HESSE / History / University of California, Berkeley
EMILY HIPCHEN / English / University of Wisconsin-Whitewater.
TIMOTHY ERWIN / English / University of Nevada, Las Vegas
LOFTUS JESTIN / English / Central Connecticut State University
GEORGE JUSTICE / English / University of Missouri
ROBERT JONES / English / University of Leeds
GARY KATES / History / Pomona College
BRIDGET KEEGAN / English / Creighton University
CHARLES KNIGHT / English / University of Massachusetts, Boston
ELIZABETH KOWALESKI-WALLACE / English / Boston College
SUSAN LANSER / Comparative Literature / Brandeis University
DEVONEY LOOSER / English / University of Missouri
ALFRED LUTZ / English / Middle Tennessee State University
MICHAEL LYNN / History / Agnes Scott College
LAURA MANDELL / English / Miami University
ALLEN MICHIE / English / Iowa State University
HELENE MOGLEN / Literature and Women's Studies / University of California, Santa Cruz
CLAUDIA MOSCOVICI / Romance Languages / University of Michigan
ANNA NEILL / English / University of Kansas
JOHN O'BRIEN / English / University of Virginia
ROSALIND O'HANLON / History / Cambridge University, Clare College
ANTHONY PAGDEN / Political Science / University of California, Los Angeles
JULIE ANNE PLAX / Art History / University of Arizona
DAVID PORTER / English / University of Michigan
ADAM POTKAY / English / College of William and Mary
WILLIAM RAY / French / Reed College
JESSICA RISKIN / History / Stanford University
CHRISTINE ROULSTON / French / University of Western Ontario
JULIE SHAFFER / English / University of Wisconsin, White Water
ALAN SINGERMAN / French / Davidson College
GEOFFREY SILL / English / Rutgers University
MONA SCHUERMANN / English / Oakton Community College
PATRICK SPEDDING / English / University of Monash
PHILIP STEWART / Romance Studies / Duke University
FELICIA STURZER / French / University of Tennessee, Chattanooga

KATHRYN TEMPLE / English / Georgetown University
DOWNING THOMAS / French / University of Iowa
HANS TURLEY / English / University of Connecticut
ENID VALLE / Romance Languages / Kalamazoo College
ANNE C. VILA / French / University of Wisconsin, Madison
ROXANNE WHEELER / English / Ohio State University
CHRISTINE WIESENTHAL / English / University of Alberta
MELVIN WILLIAMS / English / American International College
AURORA WOLFGANG / French / California State University, San
    Bernardino

Contents

Meditations on Beauty

Editor's Note

The directions of scholarship in eighteenth-century studies are quite exciting, as the essays in this volume suggest. These pieces, all presented at a regional or national meeting of the American Society for Eighteenth-Century Studies, draw on unusual archival materials, discuss a variety of non-"literary" or extra-textual materials, employ new theoretical approaches, or offer innovative discussions of canonical texts. Like our field of study, which embraces multiple disciplines, this volume creates vibrant conversation, a heterogeneous mix of approaches, texts, and languages.

The "novel" as a genre remains a dominant focus, and a number of essays in this volume offer new perspectives on the genre or new readings of canonical texts. Neil Saccamano reads dramatizations of sentimental attachments in relation to discussions of political authority in Laclos's *Les Liaisons dangereuses*. Barbara Benedict explores the ways early advertising discourse, like early fiction of Eliza Haywood and Daniel Defoe, commodifies desire, and the implications of that parallel on the novel. In her discussion of Burney's *Cecilia*, Susan Greenfield redefines "madness" as a kind of heroic quixotism, and explores the interesting intersections between madness and imagination. The connection between prison reform efforts and the English Jacobin novel is the focus of Alexander Pitofsky's essay. Though Casanova's *Histoire de ma vie* is not a novel, that autobiography is often compared to one; within the text, suggests Ted Emery, Casanova critiques the novel's construction of feminine subjectivity. Laurence Mall distinguishes the tragic exoticism of the Abbé Prévost's *Histoire de M. Cleveland* from the ancillary exoticism of the baroque novel that preceded it and the aesthetically charged exoticism of the Romantics that followed. These pieces share a concern with situating fictional discourses into a wider cultural field.

A number of essays use unusual or little-known sources or materials. Melissa Downes discusses *The Jamaica Lady*, a novel published long ago in William McBurney's *Four Before Richardson* (1963) but infrequently discussed since. She reveals how deeply imbricated the conversation about the West Indies—both in terms of finance and race—is with the anxieties emerging from the South Sea Bubble. April Shelford similarly focuses on the Caribbean as the context for her discussion of an unidentified eighteenth-century British sailor's previously uncovered journal and the journals of Edward Thompson. Laura Schattschneider examines the narratives implicitly created by "tokens"—or "infant's petitions"—left with foundlings at the foundling hospital, and their intersections with contemporaneous novels. These three essays demonstrate how archival work and unusual sources invigorate our discipline. The volume also includes essays that explore notions of "author"-ity. Geoffrey Turnovsky suggests how the dystopic representation of commercial publishing and so-called "marginal" writers redefine both the literary marketplace and the construction of authorship in eighteenth-century France. Discussing the poetry of Stephen Duck, James Mulholland examines the use of singing, as differentiated from other types of orality, and its relation to class, gender, and poetic authority in the pastoral. Caroline Weber explores the representations of statuary in eighteenth-century French painting and literature, and focuses on their implications for subjectivity, sociability, and gender. Samuel Johnson's commitment in his moral writing to the ancient Stoic and Baconian principle that learning and happiness derive from attempting difficulties and registering mistakes is the subject of Jeffrey Barnouw's essay. George Haggerty reconsiders the correspondence between Horace Walpole and William Cole, usually considered in terms of antiquarianism, in terms of homosocial interaction.

Finally, the volume contains a cluster of essays that meditate on "beauty" in the eighteenth century. The first three of these four essays were drawn from the 32nd annual meeting of the Midwestern ASECS which was organized around the theme of beauty. Downing Thomas, program chair, hoped to encourage the discussion of eighteenth-century creations and preoccupations within the aesthetic frameworks of the period, but also in light of recent critical concerns with the category of the aesthetic and the renewed interest in beauty that has emerged at the turn of the millennium. All three essays from the conference frame the recent return of interest in beauty in light of the complex discourses that grappled with the subject throughout the eighteenth century. The fourth essay, though not part of the original conference, is consonant both in the concerns and approach.

David Porter interweaves Hogarth's *Analysis of Beauty*, eighteenth- and twentieth-century appraisals of it, Hogarth's illustrations for *The Rape of the Lock*, and the contemporary fascination with chinoiserie; the author explores the exotic and erotic components of Hogarth's post-classicist aesthetic. The second essay, "The Ecliptic of the Beautiful," revisits the eighteenth-century disjunction of the sublime and the beautiful, proposing a new reading of these foundational aesthetic figures through a blend of visual and textual examples. Timothy Erwin reveals that the opposition between the beautiful and the sublime, in fact co-dependants, is played out in contest between work and image. Peter Sonderen advances a paradoxical thesis: that the firm connection between beauty and art is a modern phenomenon, first arising in the eighteenth century. The essay sheds light on the subsequent disjunction of art and beauty and the latter's "return" at the close of the twentieth century. Finally, Adam Komisaruk uses a "dirty picture," Thomas Rowlandson's "Pygmalion and Galatea," to trace the aesthetic developments in the latter part of the century.

This journal is definitely a collaborative project. It emerges from the ongoing dialogues initiated at ASECS sessions all over the country, continued between authors and anonymous readers of many manuscripts, and, we hope, extended between readers of the journal and the authors represented within. The efforts of the editorial board make the (relatively) smooth evaluation of manuscripts possible. All five members worked diligently to secure readers and make decisions about essays; particular recognition must be extended to the two board members whose terms have ended— Downing Thomas and Mary Trouille. Their long service and exemplary work has been an enormous benefit to this publication and the ASECS organization as a whole. Additionally, Jeff Ravel, the volume's associate editor, has offered careful opinions, great support, and unfailing enthusiasm. I would also like to thank Timothy Erwin, a past editor of this journal, for his generosity with his wealth of editorial knowledge. The unflappable, patient, and multi-talented (and, doubtless, multi-tasking) Vickie Cutting makes sure all the pieces come together in a timely manner. Finally, it is worth remembering that this journal is made possible only through the efforts of the members of ASECS who are its readers, writers, and subscribers.

Catherine Ingrassia
Virginia Commonwealth University

Studies in Eighteenth-Century Culture

VOLUME 33

"Le plus fort lien": Sentimental Fixation and Spectacles of Suffering in *Les Liaisons dangereuses*

NEIL SACCAMANO

This essay has its origin in an invitation to join a continuing discussion of the relationship between British and French literary culture in the eighteenth century, specifically with reference to the novel.[1] For all of their obvious reciprocal influences and citations, English and French eighteenth-century novels often appear to have elicited relatively independent and even discrepant critical discourses in their respective national fields of scholarship. In an effort not to define but to perform these different critical practices with the aim of marking or perhaps narrowing the gap between them, I have consented to represent the English side of the channel in a reading of a major French novel. I take it as my task to raise critical concerns that have some currency in British scholarship but that also acknowledge the cultural crossings between these two nations of letters during the period. Left unattempted in this essay is any effort to formalize critical discourses so that one might then be able to identify a reading, for instance, that belongs recognizably to British studies. In fact, I am uncertain even of the "representativeness" of my reading since, in preparing it, I found myself in the odd situation of having first to objectify and then self-consciously assume a position within the discipline of English that I presumably already occupy in practice and on account of which I was asked to participate in this project.

1

In light of this invitation and the questions of disciplinary identity it entails, my essay perhaps unsurprisingly takes its point of departure in the cultural politics of dialogue as a critical and collaborative practice and then proceeds primarily to address the disciplinary or ideological constitution of social subjects in philosophical and novelistic discourses of sentiment. Laclos's *Les Liaisons dangereuses* is a productive text to investigate in this context not only, of course, because it itself reads both English and French novels, but also because it invokes reflection on the claims made for both epistolary "dialogue" and the dynamics of sentiment as means to found an ethical society in which the consent or desire of subjects replaces force and mere obedience to law. Through Laclos's presentation of "epistolary subjects" and especially of libertinism, the novel takes aim at one of the basic presuppositions of liberal political theory in the seventeenth and eighteenth centuries: the claim, as Carole Pateman puts it, that "consent, contract, agreement, commitment, or promises, or more broadly, . . . the voluntary actions of individuals . . . give rise to political obligation," that "political obligation is a form of self-assumed obligation, or a moral commitment freely entered into by individuals and freely taken upon themselves by their own actions."[2]   By reading Laclos's dramatizations of sentimental attachment in relation to liberal legitimations of political authority through self-binding subjects, the novel allows us to consider, we shall see, not only the failure of such a project of legitimation but also the dependence of even an affective sociality on the forceful negativity of law that such an ethical society hopes to supersede.

As Jürgen Habermas has shown in his early work on the bourgeois public sphere that has been resuscitated in British studies, the epistolary novel of the eighteenth century participates in the more general liberal appeal to a dialogue and critical debate oriented toward consensus in both cultural and political spheres. The privileging of this ethical and political understanding of "dialogue" in the novel is evident, for example, in Richardson's *Clarissa*, in which we are told that the letters between Clarissa and Anna Howe abound with "affecting Conversations; many of them written in the dialogue or dramatic way," and these letters themselves perform a critical function ascribed to dialogue.[3]   This critique aims to unsettle the dogmatic or unconditional authority Richardson associates with both aristocratic and patriarchal power by introducing a formal equality. To refuse to enter into dialogue would be, Clarissa reassures the outspoken Anna, "to put myself into the inconvenient situation of royalty: that is to say, *out of the way* of ever being told of my faults; of ever mending them: and *in the way* of making the sincerest and warmest friendship useless to me" (1:L89,455). Clarissa seeks consent through dialogue as the ethical alternative to force and thus continually gives an account of herself to Lovelace in an effort to convince him of the justness of her actions and to deflect his recourse to compulsion. In fact, she puts herself in the position of being tricked by Lovelace to flee her family only because she insists on delivering one letter to him and promising subsequent ones with "further reasons" that "will convince [him] that [she] ought not to go." When the aristocrat responds by imperiously asserting, "Nothing, madam, can convince me" and by attempting to abduct her, she rises indignant at being "thus compelled" and reiterates her "resolve not to go," while, however, continuing to insist: "I will convince you that I *ought* not" (1: L94,477). Once under his constraint, she still imagines that dialogue can counter the threat of force: "We have had warmer dialogues than ever yet we have had. At fair argument I find I need not fear him," she writes [2:L22,75]). Similarly, in resisting her father's command to marry the unappealing Mr. Solmes, Clarissa hopes to reach a consensus which, however, can only qualify absolute paternal authority, as her mother reminds her: "Am I to be questioned and argued with? You know this won't do somewhere else. . . . Condition thus with your father. Will *he* bear, do you think, to be thus dialogued with?" (1: L16, 73). Dialogue here offers the promise of a discursive practice that allows the subject to condition or limit patriarchal and political authority and thus to legitimate her subjection to its commands. Hence the insistence of both Clarissa and Madame de Tourvel on a critical self-accounting—Tourvel too, engages in epistolary dialogue with Valmont because, as she remarks, "I wish to convince you [je veux vous convaincre] that I have done everything for you I could do" so as to remove "any subject of complaint [aucun sujet de plainte] against me"—is not just vanity or pride: it is the sign of an ethico-political will to rationalize and moralize a decision by eliciting the assent of those affected by or subject to it.[4] As it is also remarked in the *Liaisons*, only "despotism . . . judges without hearing" and thus rules the subject as a "prisoner before his judge, [a] slave before his master" (L91, 254; 202).

Of course, that it is Valmont who makes this last remark as part of his effort to subdue Tourvel already points to the way in which the *Liaisons* could be analyzed as marking the limits of an appeal to the progressive potential of critical debate. By reciting the prevailing *doxa* concerning the ethico-political value of dialogue as part of a strategy of seduction, Valmont troubles the presumption that force and consent could be discursively separated, as liberal or bourgeois political theory in the seventeenth and eighteenth centuries continually claims in its critique of absolutism. Madame de Merteuil's advice to Cécile on how to write letters states, in this respect, an always possible challenge to such a discursive legitimation of power: "when you write to someone it is for him and not for yourself; you ought then to try less to say what you are thinking than to say what will please him more [ce qui lui plaît davantage]" (L105, 293; 240). To affirm in epistolary dialogue that power is legitimated (rationalized, justified, or moralized) through dialogue is perhaps only to perform a rhetorical ploy to move others. That the letters in the *Liaisons* are always shadowed by the possibility of such rhetorical ends–addressed to readers both in and of the novel—might suggest another interpretation of why Clarissa's siblings prevent her from speaking or writing to their father: what she considers the consent attained through dialogue cannot in principle be distinguished from an act of seduction accomplished by her "bewitching," "insinuating address," as her sister Bella calls it, and a "knack at writing [and] . . . making everyone do what you would when you wrote" (1:L42, 214–15; 4:L32, 82).

As in *Clarissa*, the plot of Tourvel's seduction in the *Liaisons* goes forward according to the terms dictated by a liberal self-understanding: the legitimate exercise of power must have some reference to the subjectivity—the will, the affects, the disposition—as well as to the enforceable juridical position, of the subject. To have recourse to an act of sexual violence on an unconscious female body is, by the terms Richardson has Lovelace adopt, to fail where Valmont succeeds with Tourvel: in eliciting desire. While the legitimate operation of power becomes contingent upon the consent of the subject, this consent is in turn contingent upon its solicitation; consent as voluntary decision cannot be separated from the conditions that move or impel the subject's consent.[5] Violence to the body is a last resort. In this context, the ideological stakes of love in the *Liaisons* are evident. As in the British novel, "love" in the *Liaisons* raises the question of the moral basis of the institution of marriage, the question posed by the bourgeoisie in the critique of the hegemony of aristocratic social arrangements by which they sought to legitimate themselves. Although Laclos subordinates class conflict to an explicit gender conflict in the *Liaisons* (Tourvel's seduction is not explicitly played up as a struggle against the bourgeoisie and its notions of marital virtue), nonetheless, as Pierre Campion has recently reminded us, Laclos rehabilitates the nobility of love to challenge a fallen aristocracy through "une bourgeoise": it is Tourvel "who proposes a vision of peace [through love] to the degenerate descendent of a noble family."[6] As Madame de Volanges describes a similar vision in a letter (98) in which she momentarily imagines her daughter wedded to her lover instead of compelled "to marry one [man] and to love another": "I compare my daughter, happy with the husband her heart has chosen, only knowing her duties by the pleasure she finds in carrying them out [ne connaissant ses devoirs que par la douceur qu'elle trouve à les remplir]." In this vision of a marriage where each spouse "find[s] happiness in the other's happiness," the issue of subjection seems to have been entirely superseded by the reciprocity of the desire to please–as if the necessity and negativity of the "ought" of duty had been canceled, as if an amorous marriage were not also a stratified institution regulated by law (L98, 269; 217). As Rousseau imagines the Genevans obeying their magistrates, so here women who know their duties in marriage solely through their pleasures are imagined not subject to the law as to sheer force, since desire takes its place.[7]

Laclos, of course, does not simply endorse (or simply discredit) the sentimental vision of marriage. Although rigorous in sustaining the reciprocally qualifying double-perspective of the libertines and their enemies, Laclos nonetheless questions this sentimental vision through the libertines' dismissal of it as a mere illusion, and, more interestingly perhaps, through the general understanding of the characters in the novel that what is at stake is how to "bind," "attach," or "fix" subjects. When Tourvel echoes Volanges's vision of happiness through love, for instance, she does so in a way that stresses the effective force of sentiment: "the happiness one creates is the strongest bond, the only one which really binds [le plus fort lien, le seul qui attache véritablement]" (L132, 354–55; 303). Similarly, in the preceding letter Merteuil parries Valmont's insistence on returning to her by reminding him that "pleasure, which is indeed the sole motive for the union of the two sexes, is not sufficient to form a bond [liaison] between them"; "love alone" binds, she says, but one cannot compel oneself to "feel it at will [en a-t-on quand on veut?]" (L131, 352; 300). (Indeed, Merteuil had broken off with her lover Belleroche the moment he was bound by his "tenderness" to want to "hold [fixer]" her in "an exclusive right [droit exclusif]" [L113, 313; 260].) To which Valmont (lamely) replies: "Yes, of course, you will hold me [vous me fixerez]. . . . Our ties [liens] were loosened, not broken" (L133, 357; 305–306). Whether a question of sex or love, what is at stake is the fixing or binding of subjects of desire as such and to each other.

In other words, to recall Louis Althusser's discussion of interpellation, what Laclos analyzes in these "liaisons" is the ideological formation of subjects who imagine themselves as free subjectivities who can therefore freely subject themselves by accepting their identities. In contrast to repressive state apparatuses, which operate by the negativity of force or violence, ideological state apparatuses such as the family, the church, or the school operate by soliciting identifications and inserting individuals into practices that constitute their lived experiences. An ideological state institution works by obtaining from individuals "the *recognition* that they really do occupy the place it designates for them as theirs in the world, a fixed residence [une résidence fixe]: 'It is really me, I am here.'"[8] For Althusser, such institutions are in the last instance delegates of the ruling class's power and hence what he calls a "bad subject" might occasionally "provoke the intervention of one of the detachments of the (repressive) State apparatus" (the police and courts)—violence being always the last resort; but the "vast majority of (good) subjects work all right 'all by themselves' [des (bons) sujets marchent bien 'tout seuls'], i.e., by ideology" (181; 35). And if we follow Althusser's suggestion that novels, which for him belong to the ideological rituals of culture (143; 13), nonetheless enable us to see or perceive *"from the inside,* by an *internal distance,* the very ideology in which they are held" (223), we might read the rhetorical undecidability of the *Liaisons* about sentimental fixation versus libertine critique as the mode by which we are given ideology to see.

Moreover, if we also recall Foucault's discussion of subject formation in the *History of Sexuality* and consider sexual identity as a kind of disciplinary (if not state-ideological) subjection, we can easily read the *Liaisons'* representation of the binding force of love as what fixes heterosexual identity in the novel and thus "recognizes" the normativity of the heterosexual family. From the eighteenth century onward, Foucault argues, sexuality as a discursive system concerned with inciting and managing the pleasures, passions, and sensations of the body gets and stays propped onto the family as a system of alliance concerned with the transmission of property and with reproduction as regulated by moral-juridical law; an institutional medium of exchange, the family "conveys [transporte] the law and the juridical dimension in the deployment of sexuality, and it conveys the economy of pleasure and the intensity of sensation in the regime of alliance."[9] In the *Liaisons*, the libertines who resist sentimental fixation also exhibit sexual *practices* that exceed the disciplinary function of the family. One need only think, for instance, of Merteuil's comment that Cécile's growing desire for Danceny is a "ravishing spectacle [un spectacle ravissant]" eliciting from her a "true passion" that would make her Dancency's rival—if she were "less moral [si j'avais moins de moeurs]," she says (L20; 97; 51). Or one might also cite Valmont's pleasure in kissing Vressac (L71) or his witty vaunt after dictating Cécile's love letter to Dancency: "I shall have been at once [Danceny's] friend, his confident, his rival, and his mistress!" (L115, 319; 267). In these instances, Laclos suggests a mobility in desire that crosses and thus discloses the normative limits of the heterosexual family freely bound together by sentimental attachments.

Of course, I do not mean to suggest that the libertines are so completely disidentified, so liberated from such fixed identity positions, that they should be considered as either "not-yet" or "no-longer" subjects. They do not embody a free-floating potential that anticipates or outlives practices of cultural and social subjectivation. They have not become merely "human beings" abstracted from any effects of binding. On the one hand, the libertines do clearly identify themselves as socially disidentified. As Merteuil proudly asserts in her autobiographical letter, the principles of other women are contingent upon social conditions, "given at hazard, accepted without reflection, and followed from habit [données au hasard, reçus sans examen et suivis par habitude]," whereas she claims to have "created" her own and therefore herself: "I can say that I am my own work [je suis mon ouvrage]" (L81, 223; 172). If other women are at risk as subjects by chance, Merteuil is distinguished by an autonomy resulting from a dialectically enlightened self-mastery that counters the contingent social constitution of identity. In misrecognizing her fixed residence in the social order, Merteuil seems to figure the possibility of critical detachment from and engaged resistance to sexual ideology, especially given her commitment to a "revolutionary" politics of subverting the teachings of the convent and enslaving the male tyrant (L81, 222; 171).

On the other hand, Laclos does not present the *soi-disant* autonomous libertine as a non-subjectivated or ideologically free individual. If the possibility of some maladjusted relation to social regulation appears in the departure from chance toward self-production, this very possibility itself occurs apparently only by chance and cannot be grasped as anything more than a contingent event, too—what Theodor Adorno calls a costly "stroke of undeserved luck."[10] By what chance does Merteuil escape the chance that subjects all other women? The condition of Merteuil's liberation from social conditions of gender and sexual identity remains occluded or presupposed at the origin of her autobiographical narrative in Letter 81. (Another way of putting this might be to say that narrative takes the place of an account of this chance of misrecognition, that this chance is a narrative presupposition.) Moreover, Laclos clearly undercuts the claim of absolute autonomy to which Merteuil ascribes her liberation. William Ray has noted, for instance, that Merteuil "aspires to nothing short of virtual cultural transcendence" but that this aspiration is contradicted by her correspondence with Valmont and her desire to have him corroborate her mastery: her sense of independence still depends on the recognition of at least one other and thus remains socially mediated.[11] In addition, what we could call the libertines' disidentification and mobility is, in turn, owing to and determined by the heroic sexual ideology of "conquer or perish," to which they bind themselves in refusing to be bound by sentiment at any cost. In their rigorous self-regulation—"When have you seen me depart from the rules I have prescribed for myself or lose my principles [m'écarter des règles que je me suis prescrites]?" Merteuil triumphantly asks (L81, 223; 172)—the libertines are as rule-bound as those whose apparently conventional or normalized lives they seek to undo. Such a conception of liberation as self-subjection in the service of domination over others mirrors the ideology of law as conflated with a reciprocal desire to please others in love. Furthermore, the conflicts among these ruly individuals and their corresponding ideologies are formally conditioned in the epistolary novel by the absence of any transcendental authorial position—an omniscient narrator, certainly, even an ironic and satirical one, but also an editor or a publisher—that Laclos could employ to decide, reconcile, or sublate them for us. In deflecting our potential identification with a figure that could subsume these competing ideologies through some general perspective, the epistolary novel in Laclos's hands becomes a form that gives, if anything, only a negative presentation of community, figuring it in its absence.[12]

Yet, through the libertines' critical (though not unbound) perspective, Laclos's novel nonetheless gives us a chance to see the ideological workings of sentiment as the fixing of subjects—and not only for the institution of the family, via love, but for the entire social field, via sympathy. In the works of Shaftesbury, Burke, Rousseau, and other philosophical discourses of sentiment in the eighteenth century, love and sympathy rank among the most essential passions because they are regarded as the affective springs of society and thus as moral sentiments tending toward the public good. The *Liaisons,* however, discloses and troubles the ideology of sympathy as the basis for an ethical community to the extent that this moral affection must be elicited by the spectacle of others' suffering. Indeed, while insisting on Laclos's "resolutely undecidable" stance as a defensive maneuver, Joan DeJean has divided most other interpretations of the novel according to those readers who either privilege the libertines' "mythology of intelligence," the supposition of superior knowledge and thus mastery most explicitly represented by Merteuil in Letter 81, or those who privilege sentiment to affirm the "moral placement of Laclos's fiction" and who, following

Diderot's reading of Richardson, believe "that the author wants [them] to 'associate' [themselves] with those who suffer."[13]   In his "Eloge de Richardson," we should recall, Diderot divides the characters in Richardson's work (as well as in the world) into two classes, "those who enjoy [jouissent] and those who suffer," and he finds himself having been insensibly "associated" by the author with those who are afflicted—"C'est toujours à ceux-ci qu'il m'associe; et sans que je m'en aperçoive, le sentiment de la commisération s'exerce et se fortifie"—and who undergo the "self-sacrifice" demanded of virtue: "Qu'est-ce que la vertu? C'est, sous quelque face qu'on la considère, un sacrifice de soi-même."[14]   What interests me is how Laclos unsettles this division in the *Liaisons*: not so much by showing that those who enjoy might also suffer, or by soliciting our "association" with both the libertines and their victims, but by suggesting that suffering and enjoying (*jouir*) are co-constitutive. Put simply, the libertines are on the side of moral *law* in this novel to the extent that they demystify the sentimental basis of ethical sociality by exposing its violence. To associate with them is perhaps to break with "affection" as constitutive of the social link, or at least to acknowledge a certain negativity of affection.

As an example, let me turn to Merteuil's response to the letter in which Madame de Volanges entertains the possibility of allowing Cécile to marry her lover and thus to know her duties through her pleasures. Merteuil's plot against Gercourt requires, of course, that she dissuade Volanges from acting on this possibility, and in this letter (104) she mimes or cites the same kind of arguments against love as an illusory passion that Rosemonde offers to Tourvel in letter 130. In contrast to Tourvel's affirmation of the binding happiness of love's desire to please, the disenchanted Rosemonde rejects such notions as "deceitful ideas [idées chimériques]" imposed upon our imaginations by love and educates the younger woman about the nonreciprocal, asymmetrical gender dynamics of sentiment: "Man enjoys the happiness he feels, woman the happiness she gives" (L130, 350; 299). In her letter to Volanges, Merteuil offers a similar critique of love presumably as a strategy to preserve her morally austere character, but her position here also converges in certain respects with her various objections to sentimental binding in her letters to Valmont. Both Merteuil the virtuous friend and Merteuil the libertine plotter insist on the necessity of law as force versus law as desire. She writes to Volanges: "It is not that I have any disapproval of a soft and virtuous sentiment which should embellish the conjugal tie [le lien conjugal] and soften, as it were, the duties imposed by it [les devoirs qu'il impose]; but the sentiment should not form the tie [ce n'est pas à lui qu'il appartient de le former]; the illusion of a moment should not govern [régler] our choice for life" (L104; 288, 236). And as if citing Diderot on Richardson, she asks: "What would virtue be without the duties it imposes? Its cult is in our sacrifices, its rewards in our hearts" (L104; 286, 234). In these remarks and others in this letter, Meteuil repeats her critique of affection as insufficiently binding for the institution of marriage.[15] At best, sentiment may supplement the duties imposed by the institution, but virtue requires sacrifice to law and should not be imagined as indistinguishable from pleasure. The illusory effect of love in marriage, in other words, is to occult violence and repression—the necessity of the force of moral-juridical law and its sacrificial logic.

Moreover, in so doing, the novel exposes the necessary element of cruelty in morality, even in the disciplinary function of sentimental attachment. For we should remember that the event that prompts Volanges's denunciation of marriages of "convenience" is the pathetic sight of her daughter's suffering. Consistently sustaining a double perspective, Laclos somewhat undercuts the sentimental drama of this scene by staging it after Cécile, surprised by sex, has yielded to Valmont. Although we are invited to read what Volanges calls Cécile's "dangerous melancholy" (L98, 268; 216) as the pathological symptom of a conflicted self-identity—the discovery of her sexual passion contradicting her self-understanding as the virtuous lover of Danceny—Volanges reads it as literally the life-threatening effect of self-sacrifice in obedience to parental law. Imagining herself to be the author of the law and the agent of its execution, Volanges responds to her daughter's sobs ("elle pleura aux sanglots") with her own tears: "I cannot tell you how much it pained me," she tells Merteuil; "the tears came into my eyes at once [Je ne puis vous rendre la peine qu'elle m'a faite; les larmes me sont venues aux yeux tout de suite]" (268; 216). Cécile's pain induces her mother's pain. In taking pity on Cécile, Volanges also pities herself, since her own pain is the result of a conflict with the law which demands she repress her own sentiments: she would need to "stifle [j'étoufferais] the natural sentiment which makes us desire the happiness of our children" (268; 216–17). In this sentimental scene, the spectacle of suffering is doubled in its spectator, and both entail the sacrifice of sentiment to the law.

In one perspective, this scene can be interpreted as Laclos's staging of the cruelty of a sacrificial ethics in contrast to a moral affection that conditions sociality. We would then associate ourselves with those who suffer, and our pained response to "sanglots" would differentiate us from those, like Merteuil, whose superior critical knowledge and commitment to gender-political struggle might enable her to look on suffering with *sang-froid.* And we would then also, perhaps, take Laclos to support Rousseau's attack on the emergence of philosophical reflection as the demise of pre-reflective, natural pity—the "first sentiment of humanity" that "takes the place of laws": "Philosophy is what isolates [man] and what moves him to say in secret, at the sight of a suffering man, Perish if you will; I am safe and sound [C'est la Philosophie qui l'isole; c'est par elle qu'il dit en secret, à l'aspect d'un homme souffrant, peris si tu veux, je suis en sureté]."[16] But this reading would overlook two issues at stake in the dissolution of law into affect. One is the necessity of pain for the enactment of virtue as sentiment: someone needs to suffer in order for the social bond to be formed through moral affection, and so a question arises concerning the cause of this suffering. As William Blake cunningly puts it: "Pity would be no more /If we did not make somebody Poor /And Mercy no more could be, /If all were as happy as we."[17] Another is the necessity of a certain pleasure in the sight of suffering, and so a question arises concerning the aesthetic nature of sympathy and, by extension perhaps, sociality. These issues are interrelated and exposed as such in the *Liaisons.*

Both of these questions may be posed with regard to the lingering spectacle of Valmont's seduction of Tourvel. Following up on Peggy Kamuf's emphasis on the irreducibility of deferral in the novel, we should note that both libertines tend to defer their reunion, although in somewhat different ways: Merteuil explicitly delays it until Valmont fulfills certain conditions (L20), and Valmont, while explicitly requesting permission (or issuing barely veiled threats) to return, practically postpones it by continuing to indulge himself with Tourvel.[18] Yet, when it comes to their strategies and preferences more generally, the libertines part company: Merteuil respects and takes pride in brilliantly calculated, speedily executed plots of seduction—"a sharp and well-conducted [vive and bien faite] attack, where everything is carried out [se succède] with order but with rapidity" (L10, 81; 35; see also the Prévan affair)—whereas Valmont prefers to tarry in the role of sentimental lover. The Marquise wants to proceed directly to a narratorial position from which to vaunt that she has already conquered, that her mastery is secure since the combat is past and she can give an account of it as if she were writing an episode in the orderly succession of her war memoirs. Hence Merteuil occasionally taunts Valmont about the slow pace of his seduction of Tourvel, claiming to spy a sign of weakness in what she scorns as his desire "less to triumph than to combat [vous désirez moins de vaincre que de combattre]" (L33, 119; 73).[19] Valmont, however, seems unperturbed by these challenges; he parries them as simply signs of a difference in taste: "I do not want to talk to you about Madame de Tourvel; her slow advance displeases you. You only like completed affairs [les affaires faites]. Drawn-out scenes weary you; but I have never tasted the pleasure I now enjoy in this supposed tardiness [Les scènes filées vous ennuient; et moi, jamais je n'avais goûté le plaisir que j'éprouve dans ces lenteurs prétendues]" (L96,260; 208).[20] Reminding us that it is Lovelace in Richardson's *Clarissa* who "love[s] to write to the *moment*" (2:L125, 498) and who exploits the resources of epistolary fiction, Valmont takes pleasure in the dynamics of unfolding passion and wants to assume the position of a spectator so as to give a blow-by-blow account of the experience of witnessing a tragedy. What pleases Valmont is not just the mastery of being a conqueror—or a retrospective narrator of *les affaires faites qui se succèdent avec ordre quoique avec rapidité*—but the arresting spectacle of subjectivity in conflict with itself over the sacrifice of passion demanded by the law. To behold this spectacle, Valmont must elicit that very passion and also provoke Tourvel to exhibit her struggling subjectivity to him, even in her letters—a practice Merteuil considers the absurdity of seduction through writing and cautions to avoid.[21] In this respect, Valmont wants repeatedly to expose the violence of law in relation to desire, to expose that desire is repressed and that repression is the law of desire.

Yet, at the same time, the libertine who is in complicity with the violence of the law in this drama is also moved by the spectacle of suffering he has produced. And it is precisely in the way that Valmont describes his affection for such a spectacle that Laclos problematizes the ethics of sympathy. Valmont's most elaborate affirmation of his specular pleasure in response to Merteuil's disdain for his lingering with Tourvel occurs in Letter 96, directly following his rejoinder about their differences in taste:

> Yes, I like to see, to watch [j'aime à voir, à considérer] this prudent woman impelled, without her perceiving it, upon a path which allows no return, and whose deep and dangerous incline [pente rapide et dangereuse] carries her on in spite of herself and forces her to follow me. There terrified by the peril she runs, she would like to halt and cannot check herself [s'arrêter et ne peut se retenir]. Her exertions and her skill may render her steps shorter, but they must follow one upon the other [il faut qu'ils se succèdent]. . . . At least leave me the time to watch these touching struggles between love and virtue [laissez-moi du moins le temps d'observer ces touchants combats entre l'amour et la vertu].
>
> What! Do you think that very spectacle [ce même spectacle] which makes you rush eagerly to the theatre, which you applaud there wildly, is less interesting [moins attachant]

in reality? You listen with enthusiasm to the sentiments of a pure and tender soul, which dreads the happiness it desires and does not cease to defend itself even when it ceases to resist; should they be of value less for him who gives birth to them? But these, these are the delicious enjoyments [délicieuses jouissances] this heavenly woman offers me every day; and you reproach me for lingering over their sweetness [d'en savourer les douceurs]! Ah! The time will come only too soon when, degraded by her fall, she will be nothing but an ordinary woman to me.

But in speaking to you of her I forget that I did not wish to speak of her. I do not know what power attaches me to her [m'y attache], ceaselessly brings me back to her [m'y ramene], even when I insult it [l'outrage]. (L96, 260–61; 208–209)

Valmont elides the distinction between theater and life to argue that in both cases the tragic spectacle of suffering—the moment to moment struggle of a subjectivity that moves or is moved backward and forward, in fits and starts, to flee or embrace a final fall—elicits the spectator's "enjoyment [jouissance]." In so doing, he underscores not only the arresting time of dramatic passion that postpones the presumably inevitable narrative climax, but also the spectator's pleasure of self-affection that is explicitly ascribed to the workings of sympathy as a socially binding sentiment by various eighteenth-century writers. For it is the spectacle of female subjectivity riven by law and desire that "attaches" the spectator by delightfully "touching" and leading him back *there* (the unaccountable power of the "spectacle" undifferentiated from Tourvel herself), just as Tourvel's combat entails that she be repeatedly moved to return, despite herself, to her passion. What potentially "binds" Valmont and other social subjects is the pleasurable fixation on the dramatic suffering of others.

I want to stress that the pleasure taken in another's suffering is not a perversion of sympathy but its essence as a social affection—at least for some moral philosophers, if not for Rousseau. Laclos's most influential French predecessor does not quite elaborate a psychological calculus of pleasure and pain, an analytics of passional subjectivity, to explain the operation of pity. Rather, as we have briefly noted, Rousseau in the *Discourse on the Origin of Inequality* tends simply to presume that the sight of another's distress naturally elicits commiseration as a "sentiment that puts us in the position of the one who suffers" and, through this identification, we are impelled to relieve the distress. Self-reflective philosophy and self-interested reasoning or prudence in the social state thwart the natural motion of pity, but Rousseau cites the example of tragic theater to argue that pity cannot be entirely eradicated even by "the most depraved mores [moeurs]": "everyday one sees in our theaters [spectacles] someone affected and weeping at the ills of some unfortunate person, and who, were he in the tyrant's place, would intensify the torments of his enemy still more" (54; 155). Of course, that theater can turn into a refuge for the declining virtue of pity signifies the disastrous progress of sociality in Rousseau, since, as this example suggests, the pity elicited there (if at all) remains solely a theatrical or aesthetic sentiment that has no moral source in or effect on social life, which is organized around self-interest and self-distinction. The *Letter to M. D'Alembert* puts it even more derisively: "[W]hat is this pity [elicited by tragedy]? A fleeting and vain emotion which lasts no longer than the illusion which produced it; a vestige of natural sentiment soon stifled by the passions; a sterile pity which feeds on a few tears and which has never produced the slightest effect [le moindre acte] of humanity."[22] Hence, for Rousseau, the pity we feel at a play should be distinguished from the moral sentiment elicited by the sight of those suffering off stage, which requires "works [des travaux]" from us that demand "at least the sacrifice of our indolence [qui coûteraient du moins à notre indolence]" as detached spectators (25; 78). This theatrical passion not only takes the place of moral action but may even be prompted by an unjust identification with those who inflict, instead of undergo, suffering: "[M]urder and parricide are [not] always hateful in the theatre. With the help of some easy suppositions, they are rendered permissible or pardonable" so that Agammenon, Orestes, Phaedra and other murderers might become "figures who arouse sympathy [ne laissent pas d'être des personnages intéressants]" (33; 91).[23]

What Rousseau does not elaborate, however, is the role of pleasure in pity, even in the obvious and traditional case of the aesthetics of tragedy. In fact, Rousseau insists in the *Letter* on countering the Abbé Du Bos's stress on the condition of the spectator's pleasure—a pleasure that Du Bos concedes is felt in "spectacles of horror" such as gladiatorial combat and public executions, as well as in the theater—by arguing that tragedy often "move[s] [spectators] to the point of discomfort [au point d'en être incommodés]" (25; 79, n.).[24] In so doing, he erases pleasure as precisely a mark of the nonidentity of the spectator and the sufferer that Du Bos and certain British philosophers emphasize in their psychological accounts of sympathy both inside and outside the theater of tragedy. For if the sight of another's pain induced *only* pain or horror, these philosophers argue, if the spectator and the sufferer felt identically, then aversion would result, not the desire to attend a tragedy or the impulse to compassionate or relieve another's distress. David Hume, for instance, explains the affective puzzle of a pity derived from sympathetic pain by insisting on a moment of self-reflection: "Now as we seldom judge of objects from their intrinsic value, but form our notions of them from a comparison with other objects; it follows, that according as we observe a greater or less share of happiness or misery in others, we must make an estimate of our own, and feel a consequent pain or pleasure. The misery of another gives us a more lively idea of our happiness, and his happiness of our misery. The former, therefore, produces delight; and the latter uneasiness."[25] The reflex of self-reference allows for the doubling of pain with delight; otherwise, as Hume remarks elsewhere, the response to this suffering would be a sympathy "related to anger and to hatred, upon account of the uneasiness it conveys to us" (387).

Closer in one respect to Valmont's account of his "delicious enjoyments," however, is that given by Edmund Burke in *A Philosophical Enquiry.* Burke affirms that we are all "united by the bond of sympathy"; yet in contrast to Hume, for whom the delightful effects of aesthetic form predominate over the pains felt in the tragic theater, Burke, like Valmont, does not differentiate between representation and life.[26] If sympathy is to be regarded a moral sentiment that binds an ethical community, the essential condition for Burke does not concern whether one enjoys the suffering of others—on or off-stage—but whether one has been the author of that suffering. In citing the public's delight in executions, he writes in direct opposition to Hume: "I believe that this notion of our having a simple pain in the reality, yet a delight in the representation, arises from hence, that we do not sufficiently distinguish what we would by no means chuse to do, from what we should be eager enough to see if it was once done. We delight in seeing things, which so far from doing, our heartiest wishes would be to see redressed" (44). In other words, our pleasure in violence remains moral as long as we have not staged the spectacle of suffering. The crucial factor in the moral status of such delight for Burke is teleological agency. Not only must the spectator be exempt from danger (like Rousseau's philosopher as well as any spectator of fictitious or staged violence) so as not to become in turn a spectacle of suffering for others, but, above all, the spectator cannot have produced the spectacle of violence with the end of being touched, of touching oneself, by means of the scene. This would be malice, in Hume's definition: "the unprovok'd desire of producing evil to another, in order to reap a pleasure from the comparison" (377). Hence we might rush in good conscience to enjoy the pleasures of a public execution, for example, because we only observe the force of law in operation. Or as Laurence Sterne's Yorick puts it in *A Sentimental Journey* as he imagines his travels culminating in the spectacle of a woman's suffering: "with what a *moral delight* will it crown my journey, in sharing the sickening incidents of a tale of misery told to me by such a sufferer [and] to see her weep."[27]

Yet, as Sterne's novel performs for us, the distinction between "passion" and "action" on which hangs the moral status of sympathy is by no means secure. When Yorick, for instance, draws a portrait of a prisoner in order to "figure to [himself] the miseries of confinement" in the Bastille, he shuttles between being the spectator and the agent of this pain:

> "I took a single captive, and having first shut him up in his dungeon, I then look'd through the twilight of his grated door to take his picture. I beheld his body, half wasted away with long expectation and confinement, and felt what kind of sickness of heart it was which arises from hope deferr'd. . . . But here my heart began to bleed, and I was forced to go on with another part of the portrait. . . . As I darkened the little light he had, he lifted up a hopeless eye towards the door. . . . I heard his chains upon his legs. . . . I saw the iron enter into his soul—I burst into tears" (73).

Yorick's sympathetic tears here—and his subsequent rousing of himself to escape a similar fate–depend on his identification first and foremost with the jailer. Yorick invites his readers to become spectators and sympathetically view with and through him the prisoner's affliction, yet the sentimental scene is entirely conditioned by the force of law. The "I" of this passage signifies Yorick the writer-artist as indistinguishably the executor of the law who both inflicts violence and beholds its effects, who becomes both the agent and spectator of affliction, who violently lays hands on the captive only to find himself touched by this resulting spectacle of misery—which he continues to produce: "my heart began to bleed. . . . I was forced to go on." We, like Yorick, cannot simply assume a passive position as spectators of a scene of violence, since the spectator also inflicts suffering on the prisoner with whom we also sympathetically identify. The agent or executor of the law is the sentimental spectator.

My sense, then, is that the complexities of "action" and "passion" in this admittedly fictional passage enable us to locate the ideological problems at work in the claim to found an ethical society on a self-binding affection presented as an ethical alternative to the force of law.[28] And when Laclos gives us the drama of Tourvel's affliction at the hands of

Valmont as both the author and the moved spectator of this tragedy, his novel, too, brings to the fore the element of enjoyment in another's suffering entailed in a certain understanding of sympathy. Of course, Valmont explicitly violates Burke's moral condition by not remaining content to happen upon suffering and, instead, by giving birth to his own sentimental attachments. But if we insist on distinguishing such a perversion of sentiment in Laclos from those instances of its normative operation, we should recall that in one of the most prominent instances of ethical pity in the novel—Mme. Volanges's for Cécile—the agent and spectator of affliction are imagined as identical: the mother believes herself the author of the sacrificial demand whose painful effects on her daughter she finds so moving. The novel shows that a sacrificial logic of virtue must be repeatedly affirmed so as to produce the touching spectacle of suffering; indeed, Valmont insists that his plot absolutely depends on his tragic heroine's moral "prejudices," which he by no means seeks to eliminate as a project of public enlightenment: "Far be it from me to wish to destroy the prejudices which torture her! . . . Let her believe in virtue, but let her sacrifice it to me" (L6, 75; 29). And in reading Laclos alongside certain British moral philosophers, we find the novel also suggesting that sympathy itself is an impure or mixed sentiment that binds the social field through a negative delight—the pleasure in spectacles of pain that signals, perhaps, an irreducible cruelty at the heart of this liberal notion of sociality.

NOTES

1.   A version of this essay was presented at the 2002 ASECS Conference in the session organized by Carole Martin, "Closing the Gap: French Readings of the English Novel versus English Readings of the French Novel."

2.   Carole Pateman, *The Disorder of Women: Democracy, Feminism, and Political Theory* (Stanford: Stanford University Press, 1989), 58. Pateman's own critique centers on the attempt of liberal political theory from Hobbes and Locke onward to justify political domination, especially of women, by transforming the relationship between individual subjects and the state through voluntarism "from one of mere *obedience*, however engendered, into one of *obligation*, into a relationship in which individuals are bound by their own free acts" (60).

3.   Samuel Richardson, *Clarissa*, 4 vols. (London and New York: Dent and Dutton, 1962), 1: xiv. See Habermas's *The Structural Transformation of the*

Public Sphere, trans. Thomas Burger and Frederick Lawrence (Cambridge, MA: MIT Press, 1989). See especially the discussion of domestic drama and the psychological-epistolary novel as derived from and representing the subjectivity of private persons in the conjugal family, pp. 43–51. I have discussed Habermas's understanding of cultural politics at some length in "The Consolations of Ambivalence: Habermas and the Public Sphere," *MLN* 106 (1991): 685–698.

4. Pierre Ambrose Choderlos de Laclos, *Les Liaisons Dangereuses*, trans. Richard Aldington (London and New York; Routledge and Kegan Paul, 1987); *Les Liaisons dangereuses* (Paris: Garnier-Flammarion, 1964), L67, 186; 136. Hereafter, page references to the French edition will follow those to the English edition in the body of the text.

5. In an article whose concerns with conjugal relations and political obligation my own essay closely shares, Victoria Kahn forcefully articulates the tensions in consensual or contractual political theory between rational and psychological understandings of the will that prompted an appeal to the passions in seventeenth-century political theory: "Particularly in materialist theories of human nature, the passions seemed to offer a new psychology of political obligation and thus a solution to the antinomies of contract [between rationalism and voluntarism, voluntarism and determinism]. According to this psychology, the passions are at once caused and volitional, but this fact is less of a problem than a virtue, for the passions so conceived become a way of imagining a consent that is also compelling, a coercion that is also willed. . . . the subjects of contract are imagined as binding themselves rather than as submitting to purely external coercion" ("'The Duty to Love': Passion and Obligation in Early Modern Political Theory," *Representations* 68 [1999]: 85–86).

6. Pierre Campion, "La catégorie de l'ennemi dans *Les Liaisons dangereuses*," *Poétique* 26, 101 (1995): 118.

7. "[C]e Peuple équitable et genereux se fait un plaisir de son devoir, . . . il aime naturellement à vous honorer," "Dédicace" to the magistrates of Geneva, *Discours sur l'origine de l'inégalité,* in *Oeuvres complètes*, 4 vols (Paris: Editions Gallimard, 1964), 3: 118. English edition: *The Basic Political Writings of Jean-Jacques Rousseau*, trans. Donald A. Cress (Indianapolis: Hackett, 1987), 31.

8. Louis Althusser, *Lenin and Philosophy* (NY: Monthly Review Press, 1971), 178; "Idéologie et Appareils Idéologiques d'Etat," *La Pensée*, n.151 (1970): 33.

9. Michel Foucault, *The History of Sexuality: An Introduction* (New York: Vintage Books,1980), 108; *Histoire de la sexualité: La volonté de savoir* (Paris: Editions Gallimard, 1976), 143.

10. Theodor W. Adorno, *Negative Dialectics*, trans. E.B. Ashton (NY: Continuum, 1997): a "stroke of undeserved luck has kept the mental composition of some individuals not quite adjusted to the prevailing norms—a stroke of luck they have often enough to pay for in their relations with the environment" (41); *Negative Dialektik* (Frankfurt: Suhrkamp Verlag, 1973), 51.

11. William Ray, *Story and History: Narrative Authority and Social Identity in the Eighteenth-Century French and English Novel* (Cambridge, MA and Oxford: Basil Blackwell, 1990), 330.

12. Ray, somewhat differently, interprets the negativity of the *Liaisons* as Laclos's "willing renunciation of control": the author "counters the text's negation of narrative mastery" by extend[ing] to the reader the authority he declines, thus enacting the "historical imbrication of the reader" (*Story and History*, 345–46). Also, for a different reading of Althusser on interpellation, see Slavoj Zizek's "Class Struggle or Postmodernism? Yes, Please!" (in Judith Butler, Ernesto Laclau, and Zizek's *Contingency, Hegemony, and Universality* [New York: Verso, 2000], especially 101–104, 114–115), for whom such disidentification and mobility *is* the work of interpellation and for whom, as with Althusser, the ideology of the capitalist ruling class is also the ultimate determining instance. In terms of an ideological reading of the *Liaisons*, we can see the difficulties here: mobility is a value of the aristocratic libertines who attempt to resist what they consider the sentimental fix required for the ethical status of the bourgeois family. Contrast with Defoe's Moll Flanders, however, for whom mobility is essential to survive in a market society and fixity is the equivalent of death: "I was now fix'd indeed," she proclaims the moment she is imprisoned in Newgate, and soon laments, "I was no more the same thing that I had been, than if I had never been otherwise than what I was now" (Daniel Defoe, *Moll Flanders* [New York: Oxford University Press, 1981], 273, 279).

13. Joan DeJean, *Literary Fortifications: Rousseau, Laclos, Sade* (Princeton: Princeton UP, 1984), 208, 231.

14. Denis Diderot, *Oeuvres esthétiques* (Paris: Editions Garnier, 1968), 33, 31.

15. For example, Merteuil's enlightened psychological analysis here diagnoses love as a pathological condition, a "dangerous disorder [mal dangereux]" suffered by delusional women who unwittingly substitute cause for effect in projecting "illusory perfections [perfections chimériques]" onto the thus deified love object: "they are duped by their own handiwork [leur propre ouvrage] and prostrate themselves to adore it" (288; 236). Similarly, in her autobiographical Letter 81 Merteuil distinguishes herself from other, "unbalanced women who rave of their 'sentiment' [ces femmes à délire, et qui se disent *à sentiment*],. . . who, having never reflected, always confuse love with the lover; . . . who, being truly superstitious, give the priest the respect and faith which is due only to the divinity" (222; 171). (Since love is not just illusory for the libertines but fictitious, the invention of novels and romances, the failure to read love as a literary-cultural phenomenon and to read oneself as having identified with and become a novelistic character—Valmont calls the amorous Danceny "that fine novel-hero [ce beau héros de roman]" [L57, 167; 118]—gives point to the pun on *dé-lire*.) As evinced by her own claim of self-constitution through work, Merteuil consistently understands "passion" to be a deluding, misread (*dé-lire*) figure of "action"; "it was sufficient to want to

resist [passion] in order to be able to do so [pour résister, il suffisait de le vouloir]," she tells Volanges [L104; 286; 234], echoing her earlier expression of contempt to Valmont for Danceny's excuse of the involuntariness of sentiment: "as if it did not cease to be involuntary, the moment one ceases to oppose it!" (L51, 158;109). The insistence on exposing all apparent passivity as the dialectical misrecognition of action and therefore of the priority of the will leads Merteuil to question the possibility of rape (L10, 81;35). Also, Rosemonde's gendering of happiness resembles Merteuil's stress on the nonreciprocity of love's fix to Valmont, reminding us that Merteuil declines to reunite with Valmont because she refuses (as he well knows) to play the part of the woman whose happiness lies only in desiring to please, even if she adds deception as a counterweight: "indeed, one enjoys the happiness of loving, the other that of pleasing [l'un jouit du bonheur d'aimer, l'autre de celui de plaire], a little less animated it is true, but I add to it the pleasure of deceiving, which makes a balance. . . . But tell me, Vicomte, which of us will undertake to deceive the other?" (L131, 352; 300).

16. Rousseau, *Discours sur l'origine de l'inégalité,* in *Oeuvres complètes,* 3: 156–57; *Basic Political Writings,* 55, 54. Rousseau specifically counters Bernard Mandeville's *Fable of the Bees* in this section.

17. William Blake, "The Human Abstract," *Songs of Innocence and Experience,* in the Oxford Authors edition of Blake's work (New York: Oxford University Press, 1988), 275. From the perspective of "experience" in Blake, sympathy is not simply a "natural" moral sentiment but refers to a political relation to the social and introduces the question of agency (versus "natural" suffering); hence, suffering is the result of direct human action or of the refusal of humans to alter the social conditions that produce it. For critical readings of sentimentality, especially in Laurence Sterne, that take a similar approach, see John Mullan's *Sentiment and Sociability: The Language of Feeling in the Eighteenth Century* (Oxford: Clarendon Press, 1988), which stresses the "private and idiosyncratic" justifications of social sentiment that has no public consequences (e.g., 8, 197), and Robert Markley's "Sentimentality as Performance: Shaftesbury, Sterne, and the Theatrics of Virtue" (in *The New Eighteenth Century,* ed. L. Brown and F. Nussbaum [New York: Routledge, 1987], 210–230), which more explicitly spells out Blake's point: "Sterne's theatrics of bourgeois virtue . . . are devoted paradoxically to demonstrating the sensitivity of a culture that shies away from acknowledging its responsibility for inflicting upon its victims the very injuries that it mourns and pities but does little to alleviate" (223).

18. Peggy Kamuf, *Fictions of Feminine Desire: Disclosures of Héloise* (Lincoln and London: University of Nebraska Press, 1982), 123–147.

19. Merteuil's taunts begin as early as Letter 10, where she accuses Valmont of no longer being himself: "How long is it since you began to travel by short stages and side-tracks [à petites journées et par des chemins de traverse]? My friend, when you want to get somewhere—post-horses and the main road!" (82; 35).

20. Valmont had earlier explained his preference for leisurely taking "chemins de traverse" in terms of the psychology of love as a novel pleasure for libertines: "the heart, surprised by an unknown sentiment, hesitates [s'arrête] as it were at every step to enjoy [jouir] the charm it feels, and because this charm is so powerful upon a fresh heart [un coeur neuf] that it forgets every other pleasure. This is so true, that a libertine in love—if a libertine can be in love—becomes at that very moment less eager to enjoy [moins pressé de jouir]" (L57, 168; 119).

21. To Merteuil's objections to writing in Letter 33—that one cannot foresee where it will lead, that one cannot verisimilarly mime love so as to move the reader and produce the intoxication of love, or that one will not be at hand to profit from it, even if one could—Valmont retorts that these are rudimentary lessons of seduction: everyone already knows that "[t]o advance rapidly in love it is better to speak than to write," but he claims that he has no choice, at the moment, except to correspond with Tourvel (L34; 121–22; 74–75). Valmont's concessions, however, do not address the pleasures of dramatic subjectivity that the epistolary form also makes possible. Nor do they account for his stated preference for arresting the narrative progress of seduction and prolonging the moment.

22. Jean-Jacques Rousseau, *Letter to M. D'Alembert on the Theater*, in *Politics and the Arts*, trans. Allan Bloom (Ithaca, NY: Cornell University Press, 1973), 24; *Lettre à M. D'Alembert* (Paris: Garnier-Flammarion, 1967), 78.

23. See David Marshall's astute discussion of the *Lettre à M. D'Alembert* in *The Surprising Effects of Sympathy: Marivaux, Diderot, Rousseau and Mary Shelley* (Chicago: University of Chicago Press, 1988), 135–177, for a reading that shows the necessity of reflection and comparison even in Rousseau's understanding of pity and hence the difficulty of distinguishing pity and self-love (especially 148–151). Also see Suzanne Gearhart's similar analysis in *The Open Boundary of History and Fiction: A Critical Approach to the French Enlightenment* (Princeton: Princeton University Press, 1984), especially 260–271, where she shows that Rousseau's examples of natural pity already presuppose the spectatorial distance that characterizes the theatrical scene he condemns as the degradation of pity in an entirely theatrical social world.

24. See Jean-Baptiste Du Bos, *Critical Reflections on Poetry, Painting, and Music*, trans. Thomas Nugent, 5th edition (London, 1748); *Réflexions critiques sur la poésie est sur la peinture,* 4th edition (Paris, 1740), Part 1, section 2, for spectacles of affliction, and section 3, for the priority of the spectator's self-command: "The painter and the poet afflict us only inasmuch as we desire it ourselves; they make us fall in love with their heroes and heroins [sic], only because it is thus agreable [sic] to do so [Le Peintre & le Poëte ne nous affligent qu'autant que nous le voulons, ils ne nous font aimer leurs Heros & leurs Heroïnes qu'autant qu'ils nous plaît]" (25–26; 30). Du Bos also emphasizes the transience of the "artificial passions" elicited in the theater as what allows the spectator to indulge them in pleasure, stresses the condition of

the spectator's safety from danger, which extends to aesthetic representations and the sentiments they evoke, and proposes something like a psychophysiology of passion as producing pleasure through sheer (e)motion that arouses and diverts the soul from solitude or indolence, regardless of the pains associated with that which moves us.

25. David Hume, *A Treatise of Human Nature* (Oxford: Oxford University Press, 1978), 375.

26. Edmund Burke, *A Philosophical Enquiry into the Origin of our Ideas of the Sublime and the Beautiful* (New York: Oxford University Press, 1990), 42. Compare Hume: "The force of imagination, the energy of expression, the power of numbers, the charms of imitation; all these are naturally, of themselves, delightful to the mind: And when the object presented lays also hold of some affection, the pleasure still rises upon us, by the conversion of this subordinate movement into that which is predominant. The passion . . . when excited by the simple appearance of a real object, it may be painful; yet is so smoothed, and softened, and mollified by the finer arts, that it affords the highest entertainment" ("Of Tragedy," *Essays Moral, Political, and Literary* [Indianapolis: Liberty Classics, 1987], 222–223).

27. Laurence Sterne, *A Sentimental Journey* (New York: Oxford University Press, 1984), 43 (my italics).

28. One might object to my reading of Yorick's portrait that it is explicitly a fictional or imaginative representation and, thus, a kind of fantasy that knows itself as such and thus that must not be confused with the actual infliction of such violence. But, aside from the fact, as I have shown, that the problem of pleasure in spectacles of affliction is not restricted to fictions or representations, Sterne's novel elsewhere shows that fancy cannot be so easily quarantined. See, for example, the utter inability of Yorick to distinguish between fancy and perception in the scene where he imagines and then sees the face of Madame de L at the remise door. First, imaginative projection explicitly takes the place of sight: "I had not yet seen her face—'twas not material; for the drawing was instantly set about and . . . *Fancy* had finished the whole head"; however, once Yorick can "see the original," his fancy still reads its lines as, of course, signs of suffering: "I fancied it wore the characters of a widow'd look . . . I felt benevolence for her" (17).

Ladies of Ill-Repute:
The South Sea Bubble,
The Caribbean,
and *The Jamaica Lady*

MELISSA K. DOWNES

England's power in the early eighteenth century depended heavily on its imperialist adventures, and particularly upon a series of islands—the Caribbean. The Caribbean was of central economic importance to England in the eighteenth century, particularly in its reliance on slaves and its production of sugar.[1] Indeed, various historians argue the important role of the Caribbean in developing English commercial power. For example, historian W.T. Selley remarks, "The West Indies occupied a place of supreme importance in the first British Empire." He notes their strategic value during the great conflicts of the century where "the possession of the Islands was constantly at stake in these struggles." The islands functioned as naval bases and strengthened England's maritime growth and power, both commercially and in terms of military capability. The Caribbean also served as a source of tropical goods for England and functioned as a place for exporting English goods. By the end of the century, the West Indies accounted for about a quarter of all British import and export trade, a very high proportion.[2] In terms of export, import, taxation, maritime growth, British industries and manufacture, and the slave trade, the Caribbean was essential to the British economy (and culture). I would argue the centrality of the Caribbean to both the English culture and economy, in part because the two—economy and culture—are so entangled within the early eighteenth century. I would suggest further that the Caribbean plays a significant part in the developing discourses of imperialism, trade, Englishness, and the South Sea Bubble.

The Bubble was the economic scandal of the British early eighteenth century, and around it much of the anxiety over luxury, credit, empire, sexuality and women coalesced. The majority of early eighteenth-century British writers, both the canonical and the Grub Street variety, were taken up with the convulsions of a more fully urbanized and commercialized England. Not only did human anxiety about the tumult of the time insist upon comment, but the literary market insisted that, for a writer to be published, those comments must be made. Topical events were the frequent subject of both celebration and satiric attack, and the South Sea Bubble was the central event.

The South Sea Company was established to alleviate the national debt crisis and, simultaneously, to cash in on the immense wealth and trading possibilities of Spanish possessions in the Americas. The Company was set up to counter and compete with the "whiggish Bank of England and East India Company."[3] But corruption soon set in. The stocks rose to extreme heights before the Bubble burst. When it did, "the fire of London or the plague ruined not the number of people that are now undone."[4] There were devastating bankruptcies, mass panic, and a general outcry to hang the directors.

The purpose of this essay is twofold: first, to bring the Caribbean, trade, and the institution of slavery back into discussions of the South Sea Bubble and, second, to read *The Battle of the Bubbles* and *The Jamaica Lady* as Bubble texts within that context of trade, slavery, and the Caribbean. I am suggesting that representations of the Caribbean in early eighteenth-century literature enter into the anxieties about the domestic market and the changing economic identity of England, with particular reference here to the moment of greatest anxiety, the South Sea Bubble.

To discuss narratives surrounding the scandal of the South Sea Bubble is, judging by surface appearance, to enter a realm far away from the Caribbean. The South Seas appear to have nothing to do geographically with the Caribbean. We have come to think of the South Seas as Pacific space. However, modern understanding of the South Seas differs somewhat from early eighteenth-century discourse. As John Carswell notes:

> The £9 million worth of unfunded government securities were
> to be exchanged compulsorily for shares at par in a joint

stock company to be set up under the Act to carry on "the sole trade and traffic, from August 1, 1711, into unto and from the Kingdoms, Lands etc. of America, on the east side from the river Aranoca, to the southernmost part of the Terra del Fuego, on the west side thereof, from the said southernmost part through the South Seas to the northernmost part of America, and into unto and from all countries in the same limits, reputed to belong to the Crown of Spain, or which hereafter shall be discovered."[5]

The original design of the South Sea Company clearly included not only Pacific space, but Caribbean and Atlantic space as well.

I am arguing that we must see the Caribbean as part of a geographic and economic interactive system with the South Seas and the South Sea trade. Certainly, when it came to the primary form of trade—slavery—that was gained by the South Sea Company, the Caribbean was essential. One of the few forms of power the company held at the end of the scandal was the power it was granted by the Treaty of Utrecht, that of the *asiento*, the power to transport and trade slaves with the Spanish colonies of South America. Some might argue that the *asiento* trade was not important.[6] However, though the trade was often inefficient and ineffective (and always protested by the British Caribbean as deleterious to Caribbean economic health), the profits and power gained by England should not be belittled and the slave trade's influence on the imagination of investors in South Sea stock should not be denied.[7] Laura Brown emphasizes the importance of the *asiento* and the slave trade to England:

> The Peace of Utrecht of 1713, concluding the war of the Spanish succession with France, intensified and in some cases codified these trends . . . [England] attained equality with France in trade with Spain and supplanted France in holding the Asiento grant, a monopoly contract to supply 4,800 slaves a year to the Spanish New World. As a result of these gains, England replaced Holland as the major European slave-trading nation. . . . [8]

As the data from Colin Palmer's *Human Cargoes: The British Slave Trade in Spanish America, 1700–1739* suggest, the Caribbean was a primary site in the interactive system of South Sea slaving. Not only were slaves sent to Spanish Caribbean islands[9] but, as Palmer found, "Most of the slave voyages to Spanish America originated in Jamaica. . . . Of 390 ships for which the point of origin is available, 231 (59 percent) sailed from Jamaica."

Further, the English Caribbean as a whole accounted for 303 slave ships, or 83.9 percent.[10] Thus the Caribbean would be an essential part of the South Sea Company's endeavors.

More than one scholar has argued for a discontinuity between any reality of actual trade in the Caribbean/South Seas and the financial fiasco called the South Sea Bubble. For example, Glyndwr Williams argues: "The financial manipulation and chicanery which led to the crisis had little to do with the overseas trade, actual or potential, of the South Sea Company."[11] But I would suggest, instead, that imperialist relations with the Caribbean are inextricably bound to the gendered and sexualized narratives about commerce and the Bubble in early eighteenth-century England. Indeed, as Antonio Benítez-Rojo implies, the whole history of the British eighteenth century cannot exist without the Caribbean: "[W]ithout deliveries from the Caribbean womb, Western capital accumulation would not have been sufficient to effect the move, within a little more than two centuries, from the so-called Mercantilist Revolution to the Industrial Revolution. In fact, the history of the Caribbean is one of the main strands in the history of capitalism, and vice versa."[12] I would suggest, further, that the emergent capitalist manipulations of the South Sea Bubble could not exist without the Caribbean:

> Situated in a tropical island world easily accessible to sea-going vessels, the sugar colonies supplied Europeans with a variety of exotics in growing demand, took off European manufactures, gave employment to ships and seamen, provided raw materials for processing and manufacturing industries, generated a variety of auxiliary trades ranging from African slaves to Newfoundland codfish, were favorably situated for a lucrative entrepôt trade with Spanish America, provided a field for fortune hunters, yielded revenue to European governments, and gave rise to wealth and income which revived the image of the Indies as a source of fabulous riches after the precious metal mines of New Spain began to falter.[13]

As Richard Sheridan articulates, the Caribbean enabled British capitalism in numerous, diverse ways.

One of the most potent forms of commerce fueling British imperial and economic power was the slave trade in general. As Brown suggests, "the slave trade was a crucial source of English prosperity."[14] The *asiento* was an important part of this developing prosperous slave trade. The Caribbean was the "lucrative entrepôt" that made possible the South Sea Company and the functioning of the *asiento*. The interactive Caribbean system of slavery both financed the "financial manipulations and chicanery" and, to a degree, inspired investments in South Sea stock with those "prospects of glittering profits."[15] It should also be noted that the South Sea Company was set up to take over major portions of a national debt largely incurred through wars over trading rights and territory that included the Caribbean.[16]

Beyond the factual links of the South Sea Company with the Caribbean, discussions of commerce and credit are always already bound to trade and imperialism in a mercantilist, burgeoning, consumer society like that of early eighteenth-century England. And Caribbean slavery helped finance that society. Thus, I am suggesting that the background to any contemporary discussion of commerce, credit, or the Bubble was at least partially Caribbean. And there was frequent and vociferous discussion of these topics, and those discussions were both heavily gendered and highly sexualized.

In the early eighteenth century, numerous writers used representations of women's bodies, behaviors, and beings in discourses on trade and imperialism. In fact, trade, credit, and even England itself were variously represented as female.[17] Woman was also a primary emblem of the South Sea Bubble. As Sandra Sherman suggests: "A female figure, embodying credit as instantiated in the notorious South Sea Company, is savaged in drama, poetry, and tracts which insist that this apparent 'fine lady' was a whore in masquerade."[18]

Laura Brown has provided a useful pattern for understanding these often contradictory representations and functions of women in discourses on trade and empire, in her now-famous argument that women were primarily represented within texts in terms of fetishization and/or difference.[19] Yet, while misogynist discourse focused on fetishization and difference was common currency within discussions of trade, credit, and the South Sea Bubble (as well as the Caribbean) during the early eighteenth century, I am interested in the specific cultural work done by such misogyny (and by a related ethnocentrism) within two texts: the clearly Caribbean text, *The Jamaica Lady*, and the clearly Bubble text, *The Battle of the Bubbles*. In these works, we can see a similarity of discourse: a sexualized misogynist imagery that plays on infection and cannibalism (and/or cannibalistic female sexual appetite), as well as witchcraft and the grotesque. Tied to this misogynistic imagery, we can also see an overt horror of transgressive mixing—particularly racial and ethnic sexual intermixing. This horror at intermixing is linked to a deep concern over shifting unstable identities, to an anxiety over lost "appropriate" hierarchies and boundaries, and to a recurrent fear of the specter of foreign infestation and reverse colonization. Both these texts, through this discourse, allow condemnation of the crisis of the Bubble while displacing responsibility for that crisis and for the violence of eighteenth-century trade away from English men and onto foreigners and women. Such rhetoric protects trade, credit, and English investment in a mercantile self-image by allowing a sense of cultural and moral superiority, yet allows for the expression of deep fear—and deep excitement—about trade at the same time. Such a displacement is paradoxical, of course: both economic and imperial expansion rely upon contact and exchange with foreigners, yet both *The Battle of the Bubbles* and *The Jamaica Lady* depend upon the foreign (and the female) as the scapegoat for the dangers and violence of such expansion and for the disaster of the South Sea Bubble.

   The Battle of the Bubbles, a combination of political tract and allegory, begins by associating the arrival of the Bubble horde with a series of disasters:

> In the self-same Year, wherein the Plague raged in *France*. . . .
> In the Year wherein Old Women were very much given to
> Marriage; and wherein the Inhabitants of *England*, and the
> Dominions thereunto belonging, ran Mad, and Transfer'd all
> their Wealth and Substance to Foreigners and Strangers—In
> that Year (No. 1720) was the aforesaid Kingdom of England
> Infested with numerous and monstrous Beasts, of uncommon
> Nature. . . . Men call'd them BUBBLES. [20]

While in this passage the South Sea Bubble is associated with transgressive women, with madness, and with a disruption of appropriate hierarchies, the overwhelming sense is one of potential invasion of English borders: the dangerous influence and infiltration of foreigners and strangers, the threatening possibilities of plague (and, possibly, Mississippi Bubbles) in nearby France, and the infestation of (or infection by) unnatural, bestial women/economic practices. I would suggest that anxieties about borders and containment in *The Battle of the Bubbles* are tied, in part, to a concern over English identity under the shifting possibilities of a new domestic economy dependent on, and deeply involved in, foreign space and foreign trade.

   This discomfort with inappropriate female sexuality, foreign contact, and the transgression of borders is further emphasized when the anonymous author of *The Battle of the Bubbles* argues that the transgressive mating of "the Renown'd *Avaritia*, a *Dutch* Woman" with "_____ *Trickster*, an

Englishman" (*BB* 8–9) brings forth unholy, monstrous female offspring. The eldest of these offspring is Oceana, the South Sea Bubble. Oceana's genealogy ensures her corruption: "such as both their Names are, such was both their natures, and such their Offspring also . . . " (*BB* 9). Avarice/ Avaritia's Dutch heritage may evoke the economic scandal of Tulipmania; further, it brings to mind the Netherlands' deep involvement in trade. What is most important in this passage is that economic contact and exchange are rewritten as a frighteningly fruitful sexual relationship between ethnicities. The inappropriate liaison of two criminals from separate ethnic backgrounds assures the inevitable production and invasive presence of "the Grand Monster," Oceana, and her 365 "Sister Monsters" (*BB* 18). Here, the borders of "appropriate" English identity are threatened by (sexual) commerce among nations. England is invaded by (and, thus, not fully responsible for) Bubble mania.

The Battle of the Bubbles evokes another invasive foreign presence, as well, in its utilization of the most obvious of Caribbean references: cannibalism. The imagery of cannibalism has been used to denote the Other since classical times.[21] However, in analyzing the colonial discourse surrounding the Caribbean, Peter Hulme reminds us that: "Discursively the Caribbean is a special place partly because it has been seen as the location, physically and etymologically, of the practice that, more than any other, is the mark of unregenerate savagery—cannibalism."[22] And, after the publication of Defoe's widely read *Robinson Crusoe* (1719), the association of cannibalism with Caribbean space would have been fixed firmly in the English cultural imagination. And these "Sister Monsters" are certainly cannibals, as *The Battle of the Bubbles* makes very clear:

> [T]hey were All equally given to Rapine, and Plunder, and Murther; so given, that, rather than suffer their Savageness to be unemploy'd, they tore to pieces, and devoured, one another. . . . These Things, compar'd with a joint Insatiableness of Appetite, and an Unmercifulness of Unrelenting Temper, tho' they had swallow'd You up, and All that you had, may make one conclude that they were All Genuine Brethren. . . .
> (*BB* 7–8)

Just as images of invasive foreign elements, sexual intermixing, and infection are tied to larger issues of boundaries and hierarchies, so, too, is a fear of bodily consumption and of eating or being eaten. Further, the metaphor of cannibalism serves as a vehicle to express contradictory anxieties about being consumers and being consumed: Oceana and her savage sisters, emblems of the potential dangers of the new economy—an economy dependent on domestic consumption and upon a voracious imperialism—not only swallow you up; they also swallow all that you have. England, English fortunes, and an English male identity are always in danger of dismemberment and objectification; in the arena of economic and imperial contact, there is a sense that Others of an "unrelenting temper" might literally do unto England as England has done unto them. Thus the writer of *The Battle of the Bubbles* exclaims against this female/financial corruption: "Deform'd! devouring! uncompassionate! multifarious Monsters!" (*BB* 5). The Bubble disaster is scripted as a horde of grotesque, cannibalistic women preying upon English men.

The author of *The Battle of the Bubbles* links cannibalistic savagery to insatiable sexual appetite, as well as to witchcraft:

> Of *Oceana*, the Eldest Brute (for so she was call'd, for other Reasons, besides the Place of her Birth;) many strange and surprizing Things are told, as, that she was magically Begotten; and that her Mother became Impregnate by the wafting of a certain Caballistical Rod over her Womb, the night whereon—whereby the unintelligible Art of Amuletts, Fascination, and Charms, was infus'd into her with the first Speck of Life: Accordingly, she bewitch'd Thousands to fall in Love with her, and so spend their whole Fortunes upon her: And what is monstrous in her, is, that tho' she has reduc'd 'em all to Skin and Bone, yet her Lust is not one Bit abated; and she runs whoring after new Lovers every Day. . . .
> (*BB* 10)

Oceana's most outstanding characteristic is her femaleness-as-aggressive-sexuality.[23] The use of cannibalism in *The Battle of the Bubbles* evokes not only the "savage" Caribbean and the dangers of invaded borders, but also female sexual appetite and woman's perceived place within the new economy. Even Oceana's sexual practices reduce men to skin and bone. And with their bodies, they also give up their fortunes. Certainly, eighteenth-century stereotypical imagery of female sexual appetite was frequently linked to an assumed feminine appetite for imperial goods and luxuries. In *The Battle of the Bubbles*, this stereotypical hunger is transferred to Oceana, the feminized emblem of the circulation of imperial trade and domestic speculation, who threatens to invade and consume England, whole.

Further, Oceana's sexual desirability and appetite are both linked to witchcraft.[24] This link heightens the sense of her instability and tainted bloodline; not only is she the result of inappropriate sexual intermixing, but her existence and sexuality are based on the dangerous, irrational practices of witchcraft and fortune-telling. She is able to seduce, deceive, and destroy by a series of "unintelligible Arts." Here, this undependable, unreadable magic seems to refer to the terrifying uncertainties of a market economy and the dangers of speculation. Thus, witchcraft is linked not only to the corporeal, insatiable, cannibal women, but also to the fetishized woman and commerce.[25]

The "unintelligible" practices of the South Sea Bubble, developing capitalism, and witchcraft tap into a primary anxiety about the new economy—an anxiety which reached amazing heights during the crisis of the Bubble. Issues of identity, both national identity and self identity, became central concerns.[26] In *The Battle of the Bubbles* we can see this preoccupation with identity, not only in doubts about mixed-blood children, but in the mutability of the female Bubbles. While all distinctly monstrous and cannibalistic, the sister bubbles are difficult to identify or to control: "their Looks were so *Naturally* Artificial, that Nothing Sure or Certain was ever to be guess'd at, or concluded from them" (*BB* 7). These women are unpardonably natural (and thus associated with flesh, corruption, and death) and blatantly false (and thus connected with lack, luxury, and lies). The anxiety surrounding issues of identity and sexuality is further emphasized by the changeability of Oceana's reproductive organs: "As to her Members, and Joints, and Parts, she chang'd and vary'd them almost every Day; . . . and you'd see a young innocent Maiden's *All*, brush, in an Instant, into the Spot of an arrant old Bawd's. . . . " (*BB* 11). Oceana is grotesque, desirable, and dangerously unstable.

Expressions of anxiety about consumption and identity in the new economy frequently focused on women's clothing.[27] In the early eighteenth century, with the combined rise of capitalism, mercantilist consumer society, imperialism, and individualism, status and class are marked more and more clearly by possessions and by the ability to display and consume possessions. There is a particular fear when "lower" groups gain access to possession, consumption, and display, since this destabilizes categories of readable identity.[28] Thus it is not surprising that *The Battle of the Bubbles* makes a correlation between the sexual mutability of Oceana and an English woman transformed by rich dress (and prostitution) until she "knew not her self":

> So, have I seen a tender Nymph from *Northampton* . . . on her
> first Appearance in Town, humbly content with moderate

> Gain and Shew. . . . But when the Heroes, at *Garaways*, had
> once singled her out, and became Rivals and Bidders for her
> Love, and extoll'd her Beauty, and enhaunc'd her Price, the
> sawcy Slut step'd out Dutchess all at once. . . . Her Callico
> grew into Damask; her Damask was metamorphos'd into a
> Brocade; and so Madam knew not her self; not what she
> came from....but, lo! the Gentry grow sick and weary; Madam
> is discover'd to be false at Heart, and unsound at Bottom. . . .
> (*BB* 13–14)

Placed on the market with "bidders for her love," the simple country maid loses her identity and her virtue as she gains imported luxuries. In her disruption of rank ("step'd out Dutchess") and her involvement in sexual commerce she becomes both false and sexually diseased ("unsound at bottom"). Thus Oceana is potentially like all women: each can potentially metamorphose into a savage, seductive, whorish, sexually-diseased cannibal. The South Sea Bubble, designed by English men and predominantly invested in by English men, becomes the responsibility of grotesque, unstable, fortune-telling prostitutes and female foreigners, threatening to invade, infect, and consume orderly, appropriate English identity, English men, and English trade.

The Jamaica Lady, a short novel possibly authored by William Pittis, [29] draws together these issues that we have discussed in a clearly Caribbean context. While relying on stereotypical representations of the Caribbean current in the eighteenth century, the text also applies to the Caribbean and to the female characters in *The Jamaica Lady* images and associations that are similar to those used in discourses surrounding the South Sea Bubble: invasion and reverse colonization; grotesque corporeality; disease (including sexual infection); sexual transgression and other transgressive mixings that break down hierarchies and threaten established identities; insatiable appetite; witchcraft; and, finally, falseness, cheating and bubbling. A reading of *The Jamaica Lady* as South Sea Bubble text can make explicit the misogynistic, xenophobic, erotic rhetoric bound to the Caribbean that underlies many Bubble texts. Most telling about *The Jamaica Lady* is the difference between its date of publication and its moment of narration. Published in 1720, the year of greatest movement in the South Sea schemes and the year of the Bubble, it is set at the time just after the signing of the Treaty of Utrecht. The journey of invasive corruption from Jamaica to England begins at the moment when the granting of the *asiento* consolidates the South Sea Company.[30]

The novel opens with a disparate group of civilians leaving Jamaica for

England on a naval ship, just after the conclusion of the War of the Spanish Succession. These passengers include the doctor Pharmaceuticus and his unnamed wife. Also included is Holmesia, a woman of mixed English and African ancestry who is accompanied by her slave, Quomina. Pharmaceuticus has presented Holmesia in a pleasant and wealthy light to Captain Fustian, insuring Pharmaceuticus' own passage on the naval vessel. The other passenger is the frighteningly ugly Bavia, the daughter of a Scottish father and an English mother, who has also sent an emissary to tell a false tale, so that she, too, might be allowed on board. During the voyage, various sexual intrigues take place which are very disturbing to the Captain. One involves his son, Compy-boy, and others involve his lieutenant Frutesius, "a man of much cupidity, a great admirer not only of the fair but of the female sex. . . . "[31] Pharmaceuticus worries that his wife may be involved in the sexual transgressions taking place on the ship. It is important to note that she was a virtuous wife in England, but seems to have slipped somewhat in Jamaica (*JL* 110–111). In order to reassure Pharmaceuticus, the Irish surgeon Phlebotomus tells him the tale of his own cuckoldom. This stereotypical representation of the 'comic' foolish (emasculated) Irish colonial reemphasizes how much this text is about trade and empire and their risks and does so by telling yet another tale of sexual transgression. The voyage also allows the telling of the "true" tales of Holmesia and Bavia. When the ship comes to harbor in England, there is a brief adventure where Holmesia and Quomina are mistaken for gypsies. The rest of the text hurries through the continued loss of power and reputation for Holmesia and Bavia, until they are successfully expelled from England and exiled back to colonial space. All these interwoven stories balance and reemphasize the dangerous possibilities of female sexuality and power, the threat to male sexuality and control, and the threatening possibilities of foreign, torrid climes.

While the various narratives of the two women's pasts and their antics are primary to the tale, the space in which those antics take place is important. Most of the story takes place on a ship crossing the Atlantic from Jamaica to England. Naval warfare in the Caribbean was an essential part of trade. The English man-of-war is both a military/national and a mercantile/national space. Lord Haversham said as much in 1707: "Your fleet and your trade have so near a relation, and such a mutual influence upon each other they cannot be well separated; your trade is the mother and nurse of your seamen; your seamen are the life of your fleet, and your fleet is the security and protection of your trade, and both together are the wealth, strength, security and glory of Britain."[32] Naval space is also an intensely male space.[33] The women disrupt this space mightily. Captain Fustian comments on this disruption: "I thought, Lieutenant, you had been a man of better principles than to make a brothel of the Queen's ship, though you spent every night on shore to your loose woman at Jamaica. I passed it by without notice, but this is such an affront to her Majesty that I am obliged to resent it" (*JL* 109). The "Queen's ship" works, in part, as a miniature England. Enacted on the ship we already see the invasive, disruptive possibilities for England of these tainted foreign female imports.

Holmesia and Bavia must be compared to understand the text. Looking at their stories, one of a mixed-race woman and the other of a product of cross-ethnic sexual relations (Scotland/England)[34] brings forth the dangerous similarities of sexual power in women and the seductive, disruptive empowering of women within the Caribbean. A comparison of Bavia and Holmesia's textual representations emphasizes the ties between this text, South Sea Bubble texts, and, specifically, *The Battle of the Bubbles*. The brief mention of Quomina at various intervals further emphasizes and complicates these comparisons.

Our first introduction to Bavia and Holmesia, after the initial false tales, is indicative of a fascinated male gaze. The aspects of Bavia's grotesque appearance are listed in detail; in her own body her corruption can be read: "She was of dead wainscot complexion with large pobble walleyes, bottle-nose, very wide mouth with great blubber-lips, her teeth broad, long and yellow, with space enough betwixt each one to fix one of a moderate size, and one of her legs was much shorter than the other" (*JL* 102). Bavia's appearance is marked by an absolute difference from contemporary European aesthetics, and the emphasis on her mouth and lips links her to caricatured representations of Africans. The gap teeth, of course, denote sexual appetite, as they have since Chaucer's time. Her disability is written as deformed monstrosity, a particular fascination of the early eighteenth century. But the text is quite ready to point out that she has grown more monstrous by her stay in the Caribbean:

> She never was tolerably handsome, or indeed passable, which, though the West-India climate has something altered her for the worse, may easily be discerned by her features. . . . This defect of corporeal perfection was not the only fault appeared in her, for she had as great a carity of virtuous fundamentals, as she had of formosity, her vicious inclinations being visible to the minutest observer without the help of a microscope. (*JL* 122)

Already marked as terrifyingly different, Bavia's contact with a foreign center of trade makes her more monstrous. The passage also implies a correlation between her looks and her lack of virtue.

While Bavia is ineradicably marked as monstrous by her appearance, as well as by her behavior, Holmesia is disguised, her true identity masked; her corruption is hidden by her demureness: "Holmesia was at the seaside with only one Negro woman-slave, named Quomina, who was to attend her the voyage. She herself was a Creole and consequently of a pale yellow complexion, of stature tall and meager, very demure and precise in her carriage but haughty withal, and, when moved, of an implacable, revengeful temper, yet a great pretender of piety and virtue" (*JL* 94). Like the sister Bubbles, Holmesia is of an "unrelenting temper." The greatest evidence of her temper is given when she beats Quomina severely for a misdemeanor. Captain Fustian exclaims "a Negro had better live in Hell than with a Jamaica termagant" (*JL* 112). Thus, Holmesia is also represented as a stereotypical creole woman, as described by Wylie Sypher in his "The West Indian as 'Character'": "Such, then, are the marks of the West-Indian 'creole': a yellowish complexion, lassitude of body and mind, fitful spells of passion or energy, generosity bordering on improvidence, sentimentality combined with a streak of haughtiness and cruelty to subordinates, and a certain exotic grace, especially in the creole girl."[35] Holmesia clearly bears the worst of these characteristics. Added to this combination of laziness, unpredictability, and cruelty is a sexual transgressiveness far more marked in the female West Indian than in the male: J.P. Moreton (1790) notes that, morally, creole women "are pliable as wax, and melt like butter."[36] Holmesia's career as prostitute, adulteress, and unfaithful mistress confirms this stereotype.

Genealogies are sexual. They emphasize inappropriate liaisons or further legitimate appropriate ones. Both Holmesia and Bavia are marked by geography (and Bavia by her dangerous mobility) and by genealogies; they are both as "bad as bad can be" because of their mixed ethnic heritage. Bavia is the result of a marriage between an English woman and a Scottish man; Holmesia is the product of a liaison between a white female criminal and a "mulatto" sailor (*JL* 115). Bavia's mixed ethnic birth as well as Holmesia's "mustee" status are important to the text and to the cultural commentary enacted in *The Jamaica Lady*. That uneasy creature, Oceana, is the result of a mixed marriage. And like Oceana, the women of *The Jamaica Lady* are corrupt threats to English identity and stability from birth. Holmesia's genealogy marks her as an illegitimate child, the daughter of a lower-class criminal, and the product of miscegenation. Bavia, too, is tainted by her Scottish blood. Her Scottishness also potentially links her to the Scottish John Law, often considered responsible for the financial fiasco of the Mississippi scheme, the bubble in France that preceded the South Sea Bubble. Holmesia, of course, is tainted by absolute Caribbeanness.

Bavia, too, is involved in the violence and sexual transgression that is marked as essentially Caribbean. Her actions also play on the fears, not only of climate and character, but of miscegenation:

> Bavia had not been long at the plantation before, by false suggestions she whispered into her master's and mistress's ears, she made each jealous of the other's having too familiar a converse with the slaves, which caused such a disturbance in the family that, instead of peace and quietness, as usual, there was nothing but fighting and scratching amongst them. The master whipped the men, and the mistress the women, and then went to't themselves. (*JL* 128–129)

The woman of mixed heritage increases the violence of the slave trade by implicating slave owners in transgressive sexual acts. The dangers of the South Sea Bubble and trade, particularly the slave trade, are rewritten as sexual contact, a sexual contact that might bring forth new "non-English" progeny.

This image of the sexual depravity of the Caribbean and the invasive threat of the foreign is further emphasized by Holmesia's eventual infection by venereal disease (*JL* 117). Like Oceana, Holmesia is "unsound at bottom." She is not only infected, but also infecting, corrupting, and disruptive. The Caribbean and the women who come from it are generally marked as a pestilence. Venereal disease was often considered an outcome of the discovery of the Caribbean; the text reaffirms the medico-historical alignment of the Caribbean world with sexual disease, a dangerous corrupting import.[37] The use of sexual infection also strengthens the links between this representation of the Caribbean and South Sea Bubble literature. This use of venereal disease to mark bodily corruption and sexual transgression can be read, like *The Battle of the Bubbles'* plague in France and like Defoe's plague, as a symbol of the infectious nature of the South Sea Bubble.[38]

While Holmesia's infection is physical and sexual, Bavia's infectious possibilities are shown as social and moral by the ship's mate who tells her "true" story: "Bavia, sir, was a liar from her cradle, and so great a sower of dissension that there was scarce a family in the whole town in which she was admitted as a frequent visitor or intimate acquaintance but she raised a dissension. So that in a short time her company was as much avoided as a person infected with the pestilence" (*JL* 122). In each place that she lives, Bavia commits both sexual and financial transgressions and continually disrupts orderly hierarchies.

The direction of the ocean passage, from Jamaica to England, further raises the fear of reverse colonization. These fears are linked both to anxiety about the colonial Other as a constant, potentially invasive presence and to tensions about the transgression of appropriate sexual, racial, and class borders. Thus there is blending of anxieties about dangerous female sexuality and power and about the invasive colonial Other which reverses the historical facts of the violence and transgression that were a systemic part of English imperial endeavors, and scapegoats the colonized as the violent and transgressive. That such fears should arise in a text about the Caribbean at this time should not be surprising. As Carol Barash notes:

> Soon after England inherited the transatlantic slave trade from Spain with the Treaty of Utrecht in 1713, there were for the first time significant numbers of slaves (as well as some free black people) in London and other English trading centers. Concomitantly, narrative constructions of Jamaica (and Jamaican women) as culturally distinct come to suggest English fears about the entanglement of Jamaican slave culture within structures of English bourgeois life.[39]

The realities of slavery and Caribbean life are reversed again and again in this text, as a variety of colonial Others are scapegoated via the specter of reverse colonization. First, Holmesia is the daughter of a "mulatto" sailor and a lower-class white woman transported to the islands. Most mixed-race births in the Caribbean were, in actuality, the result of white male property owners having sexual relations with enslaved women of color. Secondly, the history of Holmesia and her mother states that they set up in prostitution and procuring by choice and without a sponsor. However, the prostitution of women of color in the Caribbean was primarily a business concern run by West Indian slaveholders.[40] Thirdly, the violence enacted against the African slave, Quomina, is performed by her "mustee" mistress, Holmesia. The white and male realities of a large portion of the violence of slavery are therefore displaced and absent.

The Jamaica Lady bears a general and overt animus to almost all things colonized and foreign. Few ethnicities escape being at least briefly vilified in this short work. For example, Captain Fustian, forgetting his knowledge of Bavia's ancestry, calls her "Sclavonian" and links Eastern Europe into a web of witchcraft. Relatedly, Gypsy culture in England is invoked briefly as Holmesia and Quomina are mistaken for fortunetellers, and threatened. The hated Bavia is of Scottish and English ancestry. The uneducated Irish doctor is a cuckold, a fool, and has attained his status via a cheat.

Interestingly—and hardly accidentally, I think—two women of the lower classes and of mixed-blood, the Scottish-English woman and the English-African woman, both further tainted by Jamaica, are the focus of this text. In a text riddled with grotesque Others, they are the greatest Others of all, "the Grand Monster[s]." Holmesia and Bavia are two different visions of horrific femaleness, tainted by foreignness. Bavia is monstrous. Holmesia is demure and yellow, but her body is marked as a site carrying infection. Bavia "glories in her guilt" while Holmesia believes that "dishonour lay in discovery and not in the act." Holmesia is a prostitute, selling her body for wealth. Bavia is more horrible than Holmesia in some ways, not only in her appearance, but because, instead of being a regular whore, she must pay Irish men to be her gallants (*JL* 126). She is like the old and ugly women of many South Sea texts, but Bavia does not even marry the men she prostitutes. Out of this corrupt transfiguration of the economy of "appropriate" male and female sexuality, she becomes morally and financially bankrupt, for all her bubble schemes. Neither Bavia nor Holmesia is specifically associated with cannibalism (as Oceana is and as the Caribbean is); they are, however, both associated with corrupt corporeality and excessive female appetites. Both are corrupt and corrupting. Both are overwhelmingly associated with difference: they embody colonial Otherness and transgressive sexuality. They also endanger male power and sexuality: disrupting appropriate order and hierarchies and turning men into cuckolds, male prostitutes, and/or lascivious pursuers of lust and money, rather than love.

While the two women are clearly marked as in and of the corrupt body and their diseased transgressive sexuality is very much a site of terrifying difference, both Bavia and Holmesia are clearly aligned with issues of identity, commercialization, and trade, as well. This fetishization is emphasized in their association with witchcraft and fortune-telling, with luxurious dress and with trade in general, and with false status, false stories, and bubbles. As in *The Battle of the Bubbles*, this fetishization is linked to deep anxieties with stability and identity.

As mentioned earlier, necromancy, sorcery, magic, and witchcraft are important to *The Battle of the Bubbles* and in representations of the South Sea Bubble. In *The Battle of the Bubbles*, witchcraft and fortune-telling further taint Oceana's bloodline and empower her sexual desirability and disruption. They also emphasize the uneasy issue of identity in relation to the economy of the Bubble. While *The Jamaica Lady* shares some of these readings of witchcraft, the association of Quomina with the devil takes us into new territory. In *The Jamaica Lady*, the references to fortune-telling, magic and witchcraft are quite numerous. Bavia, like Oceana, is assumed to gain her seductive power from magic implements (*JL* 136). Furthermore, much of Bavia's financial success in bubbles and cheats is founded in fortune-telling. Both her sexual and financial power rely on what are perceived to be irrational, unintelligible mysteries and/or lies. For all her solid corporeality, her power to invade and disrupt is based on the terrifying insubstantial.

While Bavia is the primary character associated with witchcraft, there are other incidents relating to other women. The Irish surgeon's cuckoldom is achieved by sham fortune-telling, and both Holmesia and Quomina, once in England, are mistaken for gypsy fortune-tellers because of their language and color: "Don't think your gibberish shall save you! We know you are a pack of counterfeits and stroll about only to cheat the country under pretense of telling fortunes" (*JL* 143). Like Captain Fustian's misreading of Bavia as a Sclavonian witch, this incident is tied to a constant attempt to fix and understand the identities of these dangerously mixed and mobile women.

Most interesting is Fustian's correlation of Quomina with witchcraft, as the devil's mistress. Quomina is hidden and passive in much of this text: the shadow and interpreter of her mistress or the subject Holmesia's cruel temper. She does not participate in the sexual transgression and disruptions on board. Her most notable action is to catch Fustian's head accidentally in the door as she attempts to "screen" her mistress (and Holmesia's sexual misconduct) from the Captain's view. But her passive existence does not stop Captain Fustian from marking her as the very essence of sexualized witchcraft. The Captain, mistakenly believing that one of his sailors has been consorting with Quomina comments: "[W]hat do you there, you rascal? Have you been caterwauling too? If you must have a scout, stay till you come to England. Go to hell in the common road and be damned. Don't make a cuckold of the Devil, you dog" (*JL* 111).[41] An African slave, the object of trade that lies at the heart of the South Sea Bubble and a domestic economy based on empire, is also at the heart of images of absolute fetish and absolute transgressive sexuality. It should be noticed that this representation of Quomina as aligned with fetishization and transgression again transforms and reverses the realities of trade, slavery, and sexual violence against enslaved women.

Witchcraft is not the only link between trade, commercialization, identity, *The Jamaica Lady*, and other Bubble texts. As noted earlier, both Holmesia and Bavia pretend to a class status above their rank, threatening social order and appropriate hierarchies when they do so. Both of them achieve this false status though deceit and through dress, thus bringing us back to the issues of commercialization and luxury. Bavia is associated with clothing and the cloth trade in a variety of ways—as seamstress, in the transport and sale of blackmarket cloth, and in her own dressing up and masquerading as a lady of quality.[42] Holmesia, too, is associated with luxurious dress, and this dress is specifically associated with her transgressive sexuality:

> [Holmesia] brought much custom to her mother and much money to herself, all which she bestowed on fine clothes, and those drew more admirers, so that the more her finery, the more her followers, and the greater her extravagance, the greater her gains. She outshined the greatest merchant or planter's wife or daughter of the whole country, and became as famous among the women for her rich gowns and petticoats as infamous for her manner of obtaining them. (*JL* 116)

Here the cultural anxieties about British indulgence in luxury, already displaced onto women, are further displaced onto the Caribbean and its women. This textual moment brings out several key concerns about dress: Firstly, a "vicious" woman is made more desirable by luxurious dress, thus enhancing transgressive sexual commerce. Secondly, her extravagant dress undoes hierarchies. If, in the discourse surrounding the Bubble we find maids in fancy dresses mistaken for their ladies or a whore parading as a Duchess, in Jamaica we have a prostitute who "outshine[s]" planter's wives.

It is easy to see that both fortune-telling and luxurious dress in *The Jamaica Lady* are tied to falsity and cheats. False narratives and bubbles are fundamental issues in this text. Such concerns over identity and falsity are clearly tied to the Bubble, since bubbles are so "Naturally Artificial" that you can not tell any type of truth from observing them. References to falsity, broken promises, bubbles, and broken reputations litter the text: Holmesia is "a great pretender of piety"; Frutesius "counterfeit[s] a sort of passion" (*JL* 103); the colonel whom Bavia has aided by telling false fortunes so he could seduce a neighboring maiden avoids paying Bavia and offers only "fair promises and put-offs" (*JL* 131). Bavia, "a liar from her cradle," is busy contriving bubbles, when not maliciously causing disorder or glorying in other transgressive acts (*JL* 124, 126). But, beyond these continual references to falsity and unstable identity, the structure of the text itself relies on questions of identity and falsity. Its entire plot and structure depends on the construction of false narratives. These false narratives are "speculative" and mobile, and, as such, are related to the shifting economy and to the fetishization of women. The male characters are fascinated by these stories, repeatedly attempting to discover the "true" stories of these women. Thus, Holmesia and Bavia are clearly associated with the "problems of identity and knowledge, artifice and reality, dissembling and truth, where the effort of seeing past the objects of accumulation becomes a kind of cultural obsession."[43]

While Bavia and Holmesia are delineated as the "Grand Monster[s]" *par excellence*, attempting to corrupt all they touch, the novel affirms that they are potentially like all women in the Caribbean, as Oceana is like all English women:

> [T]hat woman is of greatest reputation in Jamaica who manages her intrigues with the most prudence and not she who has the greatest share of modesty; for that the scandal does not lie in the action but in the discovery, and that they are as great enemies to virute [sic] as to public vice. And...that should such a prodigy happen, as a virtuous woman to land and reside in the island, she is sure to be the subject of the whole sex, shall have amours and meetings made for her and reported in all companies, and the more her innocence, the more scandal shall be heaped on her, till they have brought her to be like themselves, and then she may sin on as quiet and undisturbed as the rest of the frail, frippery fry of Satan's emissaries. (*JL* 117)

The Caribbean and its sinful females transform even innocent women into whores.

The Jamaica Lady represents Jamaica as a transgressive space, where England has banished its corrupt and disruptive elements. The Caribbean is also represented as a place voluntarily sought by transgressive women. In *The Jamaica Lady*, the return of these female transgressors to England signals the perceived threat of the colonies to the homeland. Thus the most transgressive, disruptive "lady" in this text is potentially the Caribbean itself, aligned as it is with infection, filth, disorder, and all the supposed attendant evils of a torrid climate.

Captain Fustian even denies the Caribbean its traditional seductive Edenic qualities in his condemnation of it: "But he inquired how she came into that cursed country, for he said none but mad people and fools, when possessed of a plentiful fortune or even of a moderate competency in England, in Paradise, would leave it to go to Jamaica, the sink of sin and receptacle of all manner of vices, a place so intolerably hot and suffocating that he swore there was only a brown paper betwixt it and hell" (*JL* 95). Fustian suggests an almost scientific connection between hot climates and "sinful" living. This view of the sexualized tropics is an important key to understanding the eroticization of the Caribbean. This repeated "scientific" discourse about climate clearly helps construct perceptions of the islands.[44] Wylie Sypher cites Francis Alexander Stanislaus, who believes that the creole exemplifies "the astonishing power of what is called the influence of climate. The relaxation which the excessive heat produces on the organs of the body, is equally extended over the faculties of the mind. There is an indolence of thought, as well as action."[45] It was believed that the tropics rendered people lazy, temperamental, and both physically and morally degenerate—the perceived West Indian character. This "character" was not only considered inherent to the natives of torrid climes. The Caribbean could infect the most virtuous of women, as Pharmaceuticus fears it has infected his wife:

> It is true, indeed, he had caught her tripping at Jamaica, but that he thought was not so much the fault of the woman as of the climate, believing that cursed malevolent planet which predominates in that island and so changes the constitution of its inhabitants that if a woman land there as chaste as a vestal, she becomes in forty-eight hours a perfect Messalina, and that 'tis as impossible for a woman to live at Jamaica and preserve her virtue as for a man to make the journey to Ireland and bring back his honesty . . . her now having lived five years in Jamaica was time long enough not only to tincture but to change her whole mass of blood and totally alter her nature, and that a disease so long growing was not to be presently eradicated. (*JL* 110–111)

These two commentaries on the Caribbean as essentially corrupt and corrupting come from the two most authoritative characters in the text, the two most concerned with maintaining order. They are also the two most concerned with "true language" and "true stories." According to them, the Caribbean is the sexually dangerous "Grand Monster" of them all.

If we overlay the narrative of *The Jamaica Lady* onto the events and texts of the South Sea Bubble, the comparison is telling and its relationship to *The Battle of the Bubbles* seems clear. Bavia and Holmesia are equal to Oceana in their association with witchcraft, disorder, disease, sexual transgression and appetite, and bubbles. *The Jamaica Lady* also partakes in a discourse that continually transfigured women into desirable/corrupt markers of credit and empire with its focus on luxury, dress, and the danger of false narratives. These parallels between the texts can make clear the links between the South Sea Bubble and the actual Caribbean in the early eighteenth-century world. In both *The Battle of the Bubbles* and *The Jamaica Lady*, the transgression of borders, hierarchies and identities by invasion, infection, sexual transgression, disruption, and pretense works to marshal anxiety and hatred outward toward the foreign. This similarity in discourse suggests that the Caribbean (and other sites of foreign trade) was implicated in, even central to, the anxiety provoked by changes ongoing in England. Stereotypical representations of the Caribbean were tied to the fear that England, too, might be tainted with a corrupt corporeality, marked as the site of sexual transgression, and represented as wallowing in luxury, avarice, and lust. Further, under the influence of England's growing economy and identity as a trading nation, this possible internal corruption and transgression might be threatening "appropriate" gender, racial, and class positions. It is no surprise that to refute these possibilities the women of *The Jamaica Lady* are exiled back to colonial space. The figuration of women, the foreign, and the Caribbean as overdetermined markers of corruption, infection, transgressive mixing, and invasion in relation to the socioeconomic changes occurring in the early eighteenth century helped legitimate the domination and regulation of women, the economy, and the Caribbean. The displacement of the scandal of the South Sea Bubble and the violence of a trading empire onto the foreign and the female legitimates an English identity based on cultural and moral superiority. This displacement also legitimizes the imposition of violence onto the foreign and the female in order to protect English trade, English masculinity, and English identity. To maintain a sense of English stability and superiority in the midst of a destabilizing crisis, the dangerously desirable must be possessed and controlled; the dangerously corrupt must be exiled.

NOTES

1.   Richard Sheridan in his overview of historical approaches to the Caribbean sees a division in both contemporaneous and current stances to the

importance of the West Indies. One stance, which he terms "neo-Smithian," decries the importance of the Caribbean to the formation, cultural or economic, of England. The other "neo-Burkian" stance emphasizes the absolute importance of the Caribbean to the English economy, if not culture. *Sugar and Slavery: An Economic History of the British West Indies, 1623–1775* (Baltimore: Johns Hopkins UP, 1974), 5–11.

2. W.T. Selley, *England in the Eighteenth Century*, 2nd ed. (London: Adam and Charles Black, 1949), 285–288. Selley emphasizes the value of the Caribbean without ever fully discussing slavery. For a discussion of the Anglo-Caribbean slave system and its importance to England, see particularly Richard Sheridan, *Sugar and Slavery*, Eric Williams, *Capitalism and Slavery* (New York: Capricorn Books, 1966), and Richard S. Dunn, *Sugar and Slaves: The Rise of the Planter Class in the English West Indies, 1624–1713* (New York: Norton, 1973).

3. W.A. Speck, *Stability and Strife: England, 1714–1760* (Cambridge MA: Harvard UP, 1977), 198. For a further discussion of the Bubble see John Carswell, *The South Sea Bubble*, rev. ed. (Phoenix Mill UK: Alan Sutton Publishing Ltd., 1993); P.G.M. Dickson, *The Financial Revolution in England: A Study in the Development of Public Credit, 1688–1756* (London: Macmillan, 1967); and Larry Neal, *The Rise of Financial Capitalism: International Capital Markets in the Age of Reason* (Cambridge: Cambridge UP, 1990).

4. Sir John Perceval in Speck 198.

5. Carswell 45.

6. For example: "In 1720, the assets of the South Sea Company consisted of monopoly rights on British trade with the South Seas—that is, the Spanish colonies of South America—and its holdings of government debt. It was well known that British trade with the South Americas was effectively blocked by the Spanish, so only the holdings of government debt are important to the economic story." Peter M. Garber, "Famous First Bubbles," in *Speculative Bubbles, Speculative Attacks, and Policy Switching*, ed. Robert P. Flood and Peter Garber (Cambridge: MIT, 1994), 44.

7. John Carswell emphasizes the importance of slavery in the construction of the South Sea Company: "The British trader was not wholly ignorant of South America. There was one loophole for the foreigner, through which he was able to glimpse its possibilities. Partly, at any rate, because of the protection given by the Church to its native peoples, South America had an inexhaustible appetite for African slaves." Carswell 45.

8. Laura Brown, *Alexander Pope* (Oxford: Basil Blackwell, 1985), 16–17.

9. Colin Palmer, *Human Cargoes: The British Slave Trade in Spanish America, 1700–1739* (Urbana: U of Illinois P, 1981), 28, 60.

10. Palmer 28–29.

11. Glyndwr Williams, "'The Inexhaustible Fountain of Gold': English Projects and Ventures in the South Seas, 1670–1750," in *Perspectives of Empire*, ed. John E. Flint and Glyndwr Williams (London: Longman, 1973), 45.

12. Antonio Benítez-Rojo, *The Repeating Island: The Caribbean and the*

Postmodern Perspective, trans. James E. Maraniss (Durham NC: Duke UP, 1992), 5.

13. Sheridan 11.

14. Brown, *Pope* 16.

15. Speck 198.

16. The War of the Spanish Succession was such a war, as L. Brown notes. *Pope* 22–23.

17. Catherine Ingrassia's *Authorship, Commerce and Gender in Early Eighteenth-Century England: A Culture of Paper Credit* (Cambridge: Cambridge UP, 1998), Laura Mandell's *Misogynous Economies: The Business of Literature in Eighteenth-Century Britain* (Lexington: UP of Kentucky, 1999), and Laura Brown's *Ends of Empire* (Ithaca: Cornell UP, 1993) are just three of a number of texts which have focused attention on the myriad uses of the female figure and the "feminine" in the discursive formations of imperialism and rising capitalism. A text of particular importance to my work is Charlotte Sussmann's *Consumer Protest, Gender, and British Slavery, 1713–1833* (Stanford UP, 2000).

18. Sandra Sherman, *Finance and Fictionality in the Early Eighteenth Century: Accounting for Defoe* (Cambridge: Cambridge UP, 1996), 53.

19. Brown, *Ends* 18. Brown's definitions of fetishization and difference are included below.

> First, through an association with trade, commodification, and consumption generated by the economic devaluation of women's labor, woman takes a central position in the representation of such fundamental dimensions of cultural experience as character, identity, and value. The female figure is associated with the mystifying process of fetishization, and with the related problems of identity and knowledge, artifice and reality, dissembling and truth, where the effort of seeing past the objects of accumulation becomes a kind of cultural obsession. In this role the woman typically acts as a proxy for male acquisition or a scapegoat of male violence. The corruption assigned to the female body and the murderousness attributed to the militarized female figure can be understood as a reversal of agent and object characteristic of the process by which capitalist alienation or imperialist violence is occluded. . . . (18)

> The second major function of the figure of the woman arises from the connection between gender and difference—the radical heterogeneity of sexual, racial, or class dissimilarities. . . .This second function is represented in terms of the female body and of sexuality, both male and female. As figures of difference, women are connected with sexual instability, class instability, natives, the colonized, and the potentially threatening, unassimilable other. (18–19)

20. *The Battle of the Bubbles* (London, 1720), 3–4. *The Battle of the Bubbles* will be cited parenthetically throughout the rest of this essay as *BB*.

21. Anthony Pagden, *The Fall of Natural Man: The American Indian*

and the Origins of Comparative Ethnology (Cambridge: Cambridge UP, 1982), 80–81. Several valuable studies have dealt with the weight of the term linguistically, historically, and in light of desires of empire in the Caribbean in the period from 1492 to the middle and late eighteenth century in European countries. See, in particular, Peter Hulme, *Colonial Encounters: Europe and the Native Caribbean, 1492–1797* (London/New York: Routledge, 1986) and Philip P. Boucher, *Cannibal Encounters: Europeans and the Island Caribs, 1492–1763* (Baltimore/London: Johns Hopkins UP, 1992). Other studies have dealt with the metaphorical and psychological possibilities of the act. See, for example, Mervyn Nicholson, "Eat—or Be Eaten: An Interdisciplinary Metaphor," *Mosaic* (Special issue on "Diet and Discourse") 24. 3–4 (1991) and Maggie Kilgour, *From Communion to Cannibalism: An Anatomy of Metaphors of Incorporation* (Princeton: Princeton UP, 1990). See also the essays in Francis Barker, Peter Hulme, and Margaret Iversen, ed., *Cannibalism and the Colonial World*, (Cambridge: Cambridge UP, 1998).

22. Hulme 3.

23. Ingrassia notes that Oceana "brings men to a state of frenzied arousal. Sexually insatiable, Oceana seduces, emasculates, and, in a sense, devours a succession of male lovers to satisfy her own desires. . . ." (8).

24. Loretta Collins has noted this recurrent combination of cannibalism and witchcraft in European discourse: "Often perceived as orgiastic sabbaths or scenes of demoniacal possession, the cannibalistic feast was repeatedly inscribed...according to European discursive tropes of witchcraft." Loretta Collins, letter to the author, n.d., 9.

25. For example, Patrick Brantlinger, commenting on the use of dangerous seductive female icons such as Fortuna and Luxuria, notes their association with both commerce and witchcraft. *Fictions of State: Culture and Credit in Britain, 1694–1994* (Ithaca: Cornell UP, 1996), 64.

26. As J.G.A. Pocock notes: "The emergence of classes whose property consisted not of land or goods or even bullion, but of paper promises to repay in an undefined future, was seen as entailing the emergence of new types of personality, unprecedentedly dangerous and unstable"; *Virtue, Commerce, and History* (Cambridge: Cambridge UP, 1985), 235.

27. As Laura Brown suggests, relying on Neil McKendrick's excellent work, there is an "implicit cultural designation of dress as synecdoche for commercialization." Brown *Ends of Empire* 113. See Neil McKendrick, John Brewer, and J.H. Plumb, *The Birth of a Consumer Society: The Commercialization of Eighteenth-Century England* (Bloomington: Indiana UP, 1988), particularly McKendrick's chapter on "The Commercialization of Fashion"; and John Sekora, *Luxury: The Concept in Western Thought, Eden to Smollett* (Baltimore: Johns Hopkins UP, 1977).

28. Julian Hoppit notes this general discomfort with the loss of appropriate hierarchies and identities in the new commercial system. "Attitudes to Credit in Britain, 1680–1790," *The Historical Journal* 33.2 (1990), 310–311.

29. William H. McBurney, introduction, *Four Before Richardson: Selected*

English Novels, 1720–1727, ed. William H. McBurney (Lincoln: U of Nebraska P, 1963), xx.

30. Little has been written about *The Jamaica Lady*. William H. McBurney includes a brief analysis of the novel in his introduction to the text, and Carol Barash provides a valuable consideration of it in her "Character of Difference: The Creole Woman as Cultural Mediator in Narratives about Jamaica," *Eighteenth-Century Studies* 23 (1990): 406–424, while Erin Mackie studies the importance of the representation of witchcraft and magic in the text in "Jamaica Ladies," West Indians at Home and Abroad Session, ASECS Convention, Sheraton Society Hill, Philadelphia, 15 April 2000.

31. *The Jamaica Lady* in *Four Before Richardson: Selected English Novels, 1720–1727*, ed. William H. McBurney (Lincoln: U of Nebraska P, 1963), 93. *The Jamaica Lady* will be cited parenthetically throughout the rest of this essay as *JL*.

32. During this period, though Scotland and England had "united" in 1707, the Scottish were still viewed as a feared Other, as Linda Colley notes. *Britons: Forging the Nation, 1707–1837* (New Haven: Yale UP, 1992), 373.

33. Wylie Sypher, "The West-Indian as 'Character,'" *Studies in Philology* 36 (1939): 504.

34. Moreton in Sypher "West Indian" 507.

35. Claude Quétel, *The History of Syphilis*, trans. Judith Braddock and Brian Pike (Baltimore: Johns Hopkins UP, 1992), 34–40.

36. Maxmillian E. Novak, "Defoe and the Disordered City," *PMLA* 92 (1977): 241–252.

37. Haversham in Colley 65.

38. Marcus Rediker, "Liberty beneath the Jolly Roger," in *Iron Men, Wooden Women: Gender and Seafaring in the Atlantic World, 1700–1920*, ed. Margaret S. Creighton and Lisa Norling (Baltimore: Johns Hopkins UP, 1996), 8.

39. Barash 416.

40. Hilary McD. Beckles, "Property Rights in Pleasure: The Marketing of Slave Women's Sexuality in the West Indies," in *West Indies Accounts: Essays on the History of the British Caribbean and the Atlantic Economy in Honour of Richard Sheridan*, ed. Roderick A. McDonald (Kingston, Jamaica: PU of the West Indies, 1996), 174–179.

41. Mackie argues that these numerous references to witchcraft are linked to fears about the various forms of African religion practiced by slaves in the Caribbean, particularly the power of those religions to incite rebellion and threaten the violently imposed orderliness of slavery. She also suggests in her comparison between representations of witchcraft in *The Jamaica Lady* and representations of *obeah* in *Wide Sargasso Sea* that this disruptive magic is most closely associated with women, with slaves, and with transgressive sexuality. Comments on Erin Mackie's arguments are based on my notes from her presentation.

42. Barash 418.

43. Brown *Ends* 18.

44. For further discussion of eighteenth-century theories about tropical climate, see Felicity Nussbaum, *Torrid Zones: Maternity, Sexuality, and Empire in Eighteenth-Century Narratives* (Baltimore: Johns Hopkins UP, 1995).

45. Stanislaus in Sypher 503–504.

Money or Mind?
Cecilia, the Novel, and the Real Madness of Selfhood

SUSAN C. GREENFIELD

A man, apparently depressed by his economically constrained and repetitive life, compulsively reads romances. He then dons his forefathers' rusty armor, devises a helmet out of cardboard, changes his own name and status (as well as that of his horse), and sets off on an adventure about the problem of material reality. Designated mad because he sees windmills as giants, sheep as soldiers, and prostitutes as ladies, Don Quixote is famous because he fathoms absent bodies in mundane objects—because the presence of romances makes him long for the nonexistent. If, as many have argued, Cervantes's work influenced eighteenth-century English writers and helped inaugurate the modern realist novel, then perhaps this is partly because the narrative exposes the very problem of reality. What is realistic about *Don Quixote* is the painful inadequacy of a world that cannot begin to accommodate the mind. Psychological survival ironically depends on the mad act of imagining the missing.

Frances Burney's *Cecilia* (1782) makes several references to *Don Quixote,* and among the knight errant's many descendants, I would count the eponymous heroine who is briefly but decidedly insane toward the novel's end.[1] Though Cecilia's madness marks her involuntary reaction to social victimization whereas Quixote thinks it "beaut[iful]" to go mad "without a cause,"[2] they share the calamity of absence and the fantasies it provokes. Don Quixote performs feats for his imagined lady Dulcinea, and Cecilia heroically raves to her missing husband: "Oh beloved of my heart! . . . I will snatch thee from destruction!" (899). In both cases, madness signals the mind's detachment from the real world and the centrality of fantasy on the spectrum of thought.

This essay considers the historical and psychoanalytic value of understanding the early modern English novel in general, and Frances Burney's *Cecilia* in particular, in terms of this paradigm. I am interested in how the novel problematizes the relationship between reality and the mind. And I am interested in how what is unreal or immaterial (like Don Quixote's giants or Cecilia's "beloved" husband) shapes the delusions that define the novel's thinking self. "Reality" is, of course, notoriously difficult to define. I use it only in the restricted sense as that which "actually exist[s]" and which is in "implicit or explicit contrast with [the] *imaginary*" or fictitious.[3]

To the countless debates about the novel's "formal realism" I would add that novels are themselves often concerned with what is not real or not materially certain. Even a text steeped in such physical detail as *Robinson Crusoe* devotes far more space to Crusoe's fear of the cannibals he does not see for fifteen years than it does to their eventual appearance; the seemingly endless pages of *Clarissa* consist of letters between distant people about characters who rarely meet and a rape that defies physical description; and Tristram Shandy spends a good third of his "autobiography" discussing the years before his existence and the birth that nearly killed him. As I will suggest more specifically about *Cecilia*, in each of these novels, thought exists in tension with material reality and is often enriched by what is missing.

At the essay's end, I speculate about how modern theories of psychological subjectivity are premised on a distinction between the mind and reality and on the roles literal loss and existential absence play in self-development. In *The Ego and the Id,* for instance, Freud aligns the difference between "what is real and what is psychical" with that "between the external . . . and the internal world."[4] Stressing the dominance of fantasy, distorted memories and unrealizable desires, psychoanalysis implies that thought passes in a mind organized around the missing. Even the fetishism of an object marks the displacement or absence of the "normal sexual" one in Freud's early work and the substitute for the lost maternal phallus (that never really existed) in his essay on the subject.[5]

My purpose below is to sketch the early modern history of such unreality and the role the novel may have played in defining it as mental life. While a single essay can hardly do justice to the cultural and intellectual complexity of the topic, it can, I hope, contribute to the lively scholarly conversation about the development of both the novel and the self.[6] The current critical interest in commercial culture has invigorated this conversation, influencing, for instance, Deidre Lynch's brilliant account of how the "world of moving objects" in and beyond the novel shaped the very psychological depth to which commodities seem opposed.[7] I understand the novel's simultaneous attention to absent objects and material indeterminacy as a complementary concern for a market culture in which the crowded circulation of goods was tied to the uncertainties of new money; in which the credit that fueled object consumption was feared for its absent center, for its lack of real referent. The mind, prone to the immateriality of imagination and madness, was often described in analogous terms. *Cecilia* provides an especially fertile example of how these shared anxieties could unfold.

Madness and Money

The epistemological question of whether the mind's objects are connected to the world of real objects is "as old as the history of philosophy."[8] What I will offer is a particular consideration of its early modern appearance in discourses about madness and money, both of which frame my interpretation of *Cecilia*. But I also want to raise the broad possibility that the evolution of Cartesian dualism and of empiricism gave epistemological problems greater urgency and scope. When in *Essay Concerning Human Understanding* (1690) John Locke insists that all knowledge is empirically derived from sensory experience, he inevitably (if unwittingly) raises the skeptical possibility that "man's grasp on reality [is] doomed to be precarious."[9] Tellingly, Locke begins the *Essay* by apologizing for his frequent dependence on the word "idea" to describe objects of the mind (a relatively new and unfamiliar usage). That he then defines idea as "whatever is meant by *phantasm, notion, species*" indicates its incorporeality and potential kinship with mere fancy.[10] Hume is more explicit, arguing that "'Tis absurd . . . to imagine the senses can ever distinguish betwixt ourselves and external objects" and that the mind invariably confuses its "perceptions" with "the real body or material existence."[11]

In representations of madness and money such problems are especially pronounced. Thus, in *Don Quixote* and *Cecilia* madness occurs when fantastic thoughts supersede the external world—when the mind privileges what is absent to material evidence, giving the "value of truth to the image" of imagination.[12] Money evokes material detachment both in its endless capacity to be absent or lost, and in the way its symbolic value far exceeds its literal worth as paper. Existing at several levels of remove from real property, money, like a mad thought, has no indisputable foundation—there is potentially nothing there.

The skeptical possibilities raised by Lockean empiricism had important implications for eighteenth-century discussions of mental illness and were linked to what many scholars have called the first "Psychiatric Revolution." In tying knowledge to a mind whose accumulated ideas were possibly illusory, empiricism made madness a logical inevitability. Reason could not exist without its reverse, not simply in the linguistic sense that all concepts are defined by and dependent on opposition; but also because reason and fantasy were simply different and sometimes even indistinguishable forms of mental work on the same continuum of thought.[13]

Significantly, in the early modern period, madness was increasingly understood as the loss of reason and the substitution of fantasy for reality. The definition may seem timeless to us, but previously the insane tended to be likened to animals or seen as the victims of diabolic forces.[14] By contrast, when Dr. Johnson told Frances Burney's stepmother that "madness . . . is occasioned by too much indulgence of imagination," he assumed that insanity originated in the mind and was the consequence, as Imlac tells Rasselas, of "fictions begin[ning] to operate as realities."[15] Locke had already offered this definition in the *Essay*: Madmen are those who "by the violence of their imaginations . . . [take] their fancies for realities."[16]

Such standards made a certain degree of insanity the routine consequence of human existence. If madness marked the tension between reality and thought—and thought depended on ideas that were at least partly "phantasms"—then what thinking person could be spared? Little wonder that after defining madness as the "opposition to reason" Locke admits that "there is scarce a man free from it," and Imlac notes that "if we speak with rigorous exactness, no human mind is in its right state."[17]

For the English, the possibility of madness implicit in dualism and empiricism was compounded by the population's reputation for derangement. Since at least the sixteenth century, Roy Porter notes, England was viewed "as a hotbed of wrongheads, crack-brains and suicides." This was a "national joke" on the continent that English writers like Dr. George Cheyne did little to dispute. Titling his treatise on "nervous Distempers, Spleen, Vapours, and Lowness of Spirits" *The English Malady* (1733), Cheyne confesses that he named the book after the sadly legitimate "Reproach universally thrown on this Island by Foreigners"; as Dr. William Rowley noted in 1788, "England . . . produces and contains more insane than any other country in Europe, and suicide is more common."[18]

Such a national propensity was often attributed to the imperial expansion, changing economy, and general prosperity that accompanied what P.G.M. Dickson has famously called the English "Financial Revolution." The Bank of England was founded in 1694 along with a policy of government borrowing and credit designed to finance both "the capture of empire" and "the growth of internal capital market."[19] For many concerned about English derangement, the new wealth born of global and local trade was fundamentally infectious, and "nervous disorders . . . were the price of progress."[20] Both Dr. Cheyne and Dr. Rowley, for instance, blame the increase in madness on the luxuries and freedom of trade. "The Wealth and Abundance of [English] inhabitants (from their universal Trade) . . . have brought forth a Class and Set of Distempers, with atrocious and frightful Symptoms, scare known to our Ancestors"; "in those kingdoms where the greatest luxuries, refinements, wealth, and unrestrained liberty abound, are the most numerous instances of madness."[21] Even Daniel Defoe, generally a defender of new capitalist practices and of empire, lamented that "the Storms and Vapours of Human Fancy" created "A Sort of Lunacy in Trade."[22] Meanwhile, what had widely become known as the "Trade in Lunacy" transformed insanity itself into a new source of private profit for those homeowners who accepted and routinely advertised for mentally-ill boarders.[23]

The closeness between "Trade" and "Lunacy" suggested by the easy reversibility of the terms is only one of countless examples of the interdependence of ideas about money, madness and mind. The mental and monetary connotations of "interest," "speculation," "credit," "worth," and "ruin" record the kinship as does the idea of "loss," which can describe an economic or a psychological state. Mary Poovey highlights these kind of linguistic overlaps in *A History of the Modern Fact*, which notes that "(what we call) psychological attitudes have always had material . . . ramifications."[24] All I would add is that the semantic relationship between money and mind was arguably based (at least in part) on the way new financial practices raised the same problem of fantasy and reality commonly associated with thought.

As scholars routinely note, to support its debt to private investors the government issued paper promises of return in the form of stocks and public funds that themselves became marketable commodities. In general, "the practice and recording of payment and exchange through various kinds of paper document developed exponentially" in England's increasingly commercial society.[25] Whereas property had long been defined in very material terms as the ownership of land or *real*-estate, the new paper-money economy—maintained by "a promise to repay at a future date" and founded on the mental exercise of risk and faith—was infinitely less concrete. J.G.A. Pocock's assessment is oft-repeated: "property—the material foundation of both personality and government—[had] ceased to be real and [had] become not merely mobile but imaginary."[26]

It is typical of money's potential lack of real referent that in his *Second Treatise* (1688) Locke writes: "Gold, Silver . . . Diamonds," and the general *"Invention of Money"* are "things that Fancy or Agreement hath put the Value on, more than real Use."[27] Though Locke was generally supportive of new capitalist practices (and was, in fact, among the earliest stockholders of the Bank of England[28]), his description of invented money differs little from the much more critical political economist Charles Davenant who in 1698 complained that "of all beings that have existence only in the minds of men, nothing is more   fantastical . . . than Credit."[29]

The consistent return to fantasy in discussions of both madness and money indicates that the problem of human access to reality had become a preoccupation of early modern life. Even if the tension was as old as epistemology itself, newer philosophical, psychological and financial concerns may well have intensified it. Pocock argues that by the early eighteenth century, "the subversion of real by mobile property had entered a phase in which reality was seen as endangered by fiction and fantasy." Dr. Johnson offers an analogous definition of madness in *Rasselas*: "to indulge the power of fiction, and send imagination out upon the wing, is often the sport of those who delight too much in silent speculation."[30] In both cases, fantasy is a form of fiction and risk that poses a profound challenge to the material foundation of human comprehension.[31]

Cecilia

Published toward the end of the eighteenth century, Burney's *Cecilia* bears witness to the anxiety about such fictions even as its own status as fiction necessarily exacerbates it. Like Richardson's Clarissa, Cecilia is an heiress who discovers that a woman's fortune is ephemeral and incapable of promoting her benevolent ideals. Swept into the commercial vortex of London society despite her better feelings, understanding and principles, she must learn the difference between mind and matter—not in a dualistic privileging of the former—but in the slow and degrading recognition that her personal interests are irrelevant. To its own questions about whether the mind can either know or influence the material world, the novel responds pessimistically. As the plot proceeds, Cecilia's thought breaks from a reality it can neither comprehend nor affect.

And yet, because the point of view remains attentive to Cecilia's mind—because much of the text is rendered from her well-intentioned, mystified, humiliated, and at one point entirely deranged perspective—the outcome of the novel is ambiguous. Paraphrasing Addison in her canceled preface to the novel, Burney writes, "the Mind of Man . . . is 'Dark & Intricate,/ Filled with wild Mazes, & perplexed with *Error*'" (945). By placing a premium on the "dark," "intricate," and often mistaken thoughts the social world preempts, the narrative romanticizes the mind's separateness (even as the tropes used to describe this are often indebted to market culture).

The tension between reality and the mind, played out between plot and point of view, is well summarized in a debate that occurs late in the novel. The debate involves Mr. Monckton—Cecilia's trusted advisor who secretly lusts after her wealth and periodically maligns her so as to prevent her marrying anyone but himself—and Mr. Belfield—a likable but irresponsible dilettante who has wasted his small inheritance on romantic claims to social status. As befits his own materialism, Mr. Monckton insists on the force of socioeconomic reality and the irrelevance of personal goodness or intent. Evoking the contemporary discourse about fantasy, he calls "independence" the "vision of a heated brain," suggesting that the very belief in mental authority is a form of madness.[32] "Who is there in the whole world . . . that can pretend to assert, his thoughts, words, and actions are exempt from controul?" A great lover of literature who strongly identifies with Don Quixote, Belfield counters that an individual is not merely an "Automaton" but a "being of feeling and understanding . . . with nerves to tremble."[33] In explicitly revolutionary rhetoric, he asks: "May [a person] not claim the freedom of his own thoughts? may not that claim be extended to the liberty of speaking and the power of being governed by them?" (734–37).[34]

The novel's most obvious answer to this question is "no," as, time and again, it "subordinates" individual striving to a "socioeconomic process that works steadily against simple choice and personal agency."[35] Thus, the mind is dwarfed in the "commercial city" of London where the "exchange . . . and constant traffic among [the] inhabitants" (44) convert people into commodities. This is especially true for Cecilia, whose status as object trumps her belief in the personal "freedom and power" supplied by her inheritance (55), exposing both the paradox of female ownership and the faultline of individualism. A mob of nauseating men relish her as "future property" (9), from Mr. Monckton who impatiently awaits his wife's death so he can marry her, to Mr. Harrel who tries to sell her in marriage as payment for his gambling debts (433; also see 367, 447, 467). Symptomatic not just of sexism, but of the warped priorities of a "money-mad world,"[36] such dehumanization propels the glee with which the bankrupted are declared "Poor soul[s]!" as a crowd scrambles to enjoy the auction of their property (31, 43–44). It accounts for why Mr. Harrel can heartlessly tell the impoverished mother of a dead child "so much the better, there's one the less of you" (85) and then be subject to the same economic logic when his creditors seize his "dead body" to force payment from his relatives (463).

In such a world, the sense of "DUTY" and charity that "rul[e] . . . [Cecilia's] mind" (55) *is* "the vision of a heated brain" (734). Although she is able to offer some help to the Hill family, Cecilia must learn that her grander plans for the poor and unfortunate are "scenes . . . [of] fancy" (55), "promissory enjoyment[s]" for a "delighted imagination" (711).[37] Like the value of money itself, her ideals are fantastic and as unreal as the inheritance from her father and uncle on which they depend. Both portions are unavailable until Cecilia comes of age. The bequest from her father, in the dubious form of stocks (766), is quickly swallowed in the debt she accrues for Mr. Harrel. And her uncle's provision of a landed estate and annual income, which only *promises* financial independence if Cecilia remains single or if her husband takes her surname, is sacrificed when she marries Mortimer Delvile, who refuses the terms. By the novel's end Cecilia has lost the fortune she never even had.

Especially important is the way Cecilia's loss for Mr. Harrel confirms countless critiques of the Financial Revolution by stressing the absent center of a credit economy. To support his habits of lavish consumption and excessive gambling, Mr. Harrel borrows on the false promise of return, first from creditors and then, when they threaten an execution of his property, from Cecilia to pay them back. To her horror, Cecilia can help only by becoming indebted to a Jew, the stereotypical figure of unredemptive and nationally debilitating interest.[38] That she willingly does so involves several layers of delusion: her beliefs that she is promoting Mr. Harrel's reformation, that he has a monetary basis for repayment, and that she can prevent his suicide all prove utterly fantastic.[39] The effect of her lending exactly opposes her intent as she becomes the "tool of the extravagance I abhor!" and is made "responsible for the luxury I condemn!" (271–72).

Such failures of thought are reiterated in the countless tropes that stress the mind's infection by economic formulations. Cecilia's credit problems, for instance, derive from her crediting the credibility of the very man she should mistrust.[40] She dwells on her difference from Mrs. Harrel, whose "mind [is] devoid of all genuine resources" (537).[41] But her belief in "the well regulated purity of her mind" (251) proves almost as groundless as her hope that the Harrels will exert "new regulations" in their "expenses"

(300) or that she can properly manage "the regulation of her fortune" (741). As the romance plot gains momentum in the wake of Mr. Harrel's suicide, Mortimer Delvile exacts Cecilia's reluctant consent to a secret marriage. Believing their "transaction" (576; also 190, 622, 637) and her "promise" (576; also 617, 618) are as immoral as those performed for the Harrels, Cecilia feels as if she is "at war with my own actions and myself" (618). Her sense of unreality is so profound that "truth from imagination she scarcely could separate; all was darkness and doubt, inquietude and disorder!" (576).

Even as they emphasize Cecilia's personal powerlessness and confusion, however, passages like these have a complex effect. They forward the plot of Cecilia's mental inefficacy, while paradoxically privileging the point of view of her thoughts. Cecilia's inner "war," "darkness and doubt" (like the "'Dark . . . & perplexed'" "Mind of Man" evoked in the canceled preface [945]) become important in their own right, and her mind's perspective, however materially useless, remains central to the narrative. Indeed, phrases like the following are so routine they become a litany: Cecilia's "mind was [not] . . . at liberty to attend to any emotions but its own" (65); "her mind was now occupied by new ideas" (251); "reflections such as these . . . were . . . so humiliating" (283); "Cecilia [tried] to drive Delvile . . . from her thoughts" (338); "her mind [was] depressed by what was passed, and in suspense with what was to come" (458); "every thing she thought conspired to punish [her]" (633); all that "distinguished" her journey was "what passed in her own mind" (833).

It is a testament to the fertility of the difference between point of view and plot, mind and external world, that it underwrites the narrative technique of free indirect discourse, the development of which Burney clearly influenced. Free indirect discourse allows for a third-person rendition of a character's free associations. Jane Austen, a great fan of Burney, is generally credited with perfecting the technique.[42]   Simultaneously recording and satirizing individual perception, Austen's narrators can capture both the weight of thought and its incapacity to measure reality. Thus Elizabeth Bennet is comically mystified by the attraction Darcy's frequent visits to Hunsford reveal: "Why Mr. Darcy came so often to the Parsonage, it was . . . difficult to understand. It could not be for [her] society"; and readers suspect Emma will do the exact opposite when, having failed so spectacularly in matching Harriet and Mr. Elton, she resolves to be "humble and discreet, and [to repress] imagination all the rest of her life."[43]

Though Burney's use of point of view is never as sophisticated as Austen's, her mental perspective begins to afford the illusion of personal depth on which so much of the modern self depends. It is precisely because there is an assumed and often ironic dissonance between thought and reality that the mind can be cordoned off as an inner space worthy of extended probing. The problem of desire is particularly productive in this context, for the work of longing is dependent on lack, loss or the general inadequacy of what is actually available. "Absence makes the heart grow fonder" when the failure of real access underwrites the compulsion of thought.[44]

Consider, for instance, two scenes that recount Cecilia's desire for Mortimer Delvile, one appearing toward the middle, the other near the end of the book. In each the romantic hero has just left her and she grows motionless in her seat, experiencing a solitary pain to which the reader has intensely personal access.

> Lost in thought and in sadness, [Cecilia] continued fixed to her seat; and looking at the door through which [Delvile] had passed, as if, with himself, he had shut out all for which she existed. (519)

> When not all the assistance of fancy could persuade her she still heard the footsteps of Delvile, she went to the chair upon which he had been seated, and taking possession of it, sat with her arms crossed, silent, quiet, and erect, almost vacant of all thought. (851)

In these extraordinary narrative moments, the reader, like Cecilia, attends to what has disappeared. We enter a mind cut off from the world, preoccupied not with the crowded craze of exchange, but with what is missing—so much so that even physical objects—the door through which Delvile passed, the chair on which he sat—record his absence and Cecilia's utter isolation. When, in the second passage, fancy fails and her mind mirrors the loss it cannot explain, Cecilia's static loneliness becomes the surest mark of her material detachment.[45]

Like so many other terms in the novel, the psychological "loss" evoked in these passages can, in other contexts, mark the overlap between money and mind. "Loss" refers to the "diminution of . . . wealth" (195) that plagues so many characters. Mr. Harrel "los[es] all he had gained" at a gaming table (369), and Cecilia cannot help but "murmur at her loss of fortune" in the novel's last paragraph (941). Loss also refers to the diminution of reason—the loss of sense—that prompts madness. Insanity can accompany lost money, as when Belfield squanders his inheritance and appears "for ever lost!" (246) or when Mr. Harrel shoots "out his brains without paying any body a souse" (727). Or reason can be lost with love, as when Cecilia experiences her desire for Mortimer as a "loss of mental freedom" (252). His endless physical absences (517, 546, 646, 797, 868) prompt her to bewail "his loss" (521). "Losing its object" Cecilia's "heroism . . . los[es] its force" (678) until she herself is lost in a crowd and loses her mind toward the novel's end. Marking the conversion of losses in all senses of the word, Cecilia's madness follows directly upon her financial ruin (she has lost her father's money and been evicted from her uncle's estate for losing her surname in marriage) and erupts when Delvile abandons her under the mistaken impression that she is unfaithful.

To the extent that Cecilia's madness is driven by her economic ruin, she appears to fall prey to the "English Malady" that is the price of financial, commercial and urban excess and has reached epidemic proportions, infecting Albany, Mr. Belfield, Mrs. Belfield, Mr. Harrel, Mrs. Delvile, and Mortimer himself. Thus, like the word "loss," "melancholy" (often used as a harbinger of madness) is one of the most oft repeated in the text.[46] In Dr. Cheyne's treatise, madness is blamed on greed and glut as well as on "the present Custom of Living, so much in great, populous, and over-grown Cities [like] London (where nervous Distempers are most frequent, outrageous, and unnatural)."[47] Those who go mad in *Cecilia* regularly do so in London (Cecilia goes mad among an urban mob) and are to varying extents debilitated by luxury and wealth or their loss.

Moreover, like the "lunacy in trade," the "trade in lunacy" is pervasive in the novel. Not only are there several references to the private mad-houses that had become so profitable (291, 487, 897), but when Cecilia is deranged "her pockets" are "rifled" after which a pawn-broker and his wife lock her up and advertise her in the hope of a "reward" (898, 899). While waiting for payment from Cecilia's "keepers" (898), they treat her dreadfully. "Shut up in a place of confinement, without light, without knowledge where she was, and not a human being near her" (898), Cecilia suffers the kind of cruelty for which private asylums were notorious and which led to the first act of Parliament "for regulating Madhouses" in 1774.[48] The ubiquity, anonymity and commercialism of madness suggest that the force of market culture and greed has cost Cecilia whatever remained of her "freedom of . . . thoughts" (735).

Yet to the extent that lunacy marks the infestation of fantasy, it arguably represents "mental freedom" (252) at its most extreme.[49] As an "English Malady," madness is an anonymous social disease that signals the failure of personal meaning or worth. But as an experience of mind (the view that shaped modern psychiatry and appears to have influenced the doctor who cures Cecilia [932; also see 690]), madness marks the divorce from social reality that gives thought the illusion of integrity. In this respect Cecilia's lunacy is distinguished from that of the other mad characters, all of whom suffer from their own worldly values; Cecilia alone is innocent and victimized by the world from which she finally loses connection.

Burney suggests the ironic value of such loss when employing free indirect discourse to describe Cecilia at her most deranged. Abandoned by Delvile, wrongly convinced that he will be killed in a duel over her honor, Cecilia runs alone and lost, afraid that "Delvile [will] be lost to her" (895). The point of view requires the reader's complete intimacy as

> Delvile's danger took sole possession of her brain, though all connection with its occasion was lost . . . . She called aloud upon Delvile as she flew to the end of the street. No Delvile was there!—she turned the corner; yet saw nothing of him . . . . [S]he forced herself along by her own vehement rapidity . . . . Delvile, bleeding . . . was the image before her eyes . . . . She scarce touched the ground; she scarce felt her own motion. (896–97)

"No Delvile was there!" we are told directly from the mind whose solitude we share, whose fantasy of that man's bloody body we are encouraged to conjure.[50] In this instance it is not the socioeconomic flurry of English maladies, but the privacy of absence that prevails. The mind detaches from external reality, and madness, precisely because it represents such independence, becomes the absurd sign of individuality. While recounting Cecilia's failure to feel "her own motion" and noting that "all trace" of her body is "lost" to her friends, the narrative offers one of its most complete conceptions of the space of inner self.[51]

Book Bills and Freud

In *Cecilia* it is their very retreat from reality that makes the heroine's thoughts seem realistic. I would suggest the paradigm is characteristic of the early modern novel. Granted, the claim is implicit in Ian Watt's "formal realism." Watt himself calls the contrast between "inner life" and the external space of "physical objects" a central feature of realism. "What interests the realist," Michael Seidel writes, is how even a deluded "mind [like Don Quixote's or Cecilia's] reads experience."[52] Some of the most effective recent interrogations of Watt—Deidre Lynch's *The Economy of Character* and William Warner's *Licensing Entertainment*—document the material and commercial conditions that complicate or belie the novel's "inner self." Lynch's aim, for instance, is to demystify interiority by "apprehending [it] as an effect of public and social discourses."[53]

But I confess I remain compelled by the insularity of interiority even as I try to be wary of its fictions. In this respect, I am struck by how the very pressures of economic change—the rise of a commodity culture and of commercialism—may have driven the desire to imagine a mind beyond materiality.[54] But I am also struck by how often money itself is seen as immaterial, unreal and dangerous for just this reason. In some contexts (like the scenes of Cecilia's madness) thought seems to thrive on the lost or nonexistent, and the mind's apparent detachment from market culture makes the self an individual. On the other hand, the language of unreality and loss on which the inner self depends is also the language of finance.

From a psychological perspective what we see in Cecilia's mad interiority is the prototype of the psychoanalytic mind. For Freud, subjectivity exists in complex relation with loss. The subject emerges with the loss of the original "love-object" of the mother, from whom the child must detach to individuate during the oedipal period.[55] Freud's unconscious is, among other things, a storehouse of lost memories and inaccessible thoughts.[56] In *Mourning and Melancholia*, Freud suggests that the melancholic suffers from an "object-loss which is withdrawn from consciousness." His great insight in *The Ego and the Id* is that melancholic loss (which includes the loss of awareness of loss) is fundamental to the normal "character of the ego." In fundamental tension with the here and now of material reality, the ego is itself "a precipitate of abandoned object-cathexes." As Judith Butler summarizes Freud, "the lost object continues to haunt and inhabit the ego as one of its constitutive foundations"; and Adam Phillips writes that the "making of identities" thus becomes a process of "our making ourselves up through loss."[57]

Surely something similar could be said of the evolution of Cecilia, whose mind is plagued by "melancholy" and most complete when most lost. It might even be said of the evolution of the novel, which features Tristram Shandy with his deadly birth and truncated name and nose; Emma Woodhouse who discovers her love for Mr. Knightley only when "threatened with [his] loss"[58]; and Jane Eyre whose deprivation of family and status certify her right to tell her story.

Dominick LaCapra warns that the theoretical inclination to view "loss related to melancholia as originary or constitutive of the subject" can be inaccurate and ahistorical, simply another secular version of "the fall or original sin." He cautions readers to avoid conflating historical and literal loss (the Holocaust, for instance) with transhistorical and metaphysical absence (existential angst and the problem of "ultimate foundations" or "divinity").[59] This is a difficulty I cannot pretend to resolve. But I would suggest that Cecilia's melancholic madness is historically situated both in its imbrication in eighteenth-century commerce and in its difference from that of earlier novel characters. As I indicated at the essay's opening, both Robinson Crusoe and Clarissa anticipate Cecilia's struggles with reality (and, I would here add, with commerce). Defoe's protagonist is lost on an island and Richardson's is lost when she is raped and both are prone to delusion (Clarissa even suffers a brief bout of madness). But unlike Cecilia, Crusoe and Clarissa recover through religion. Though it underscores their mental experience, loss is also attributed to original sin, enabling each character to believe that suffering is superintended by a God who unifies the self and world in ways beyond human comprehension.

Cecilia never does anything wrong in the religious sense. She does not disobey her father (like Crusoe) or flee his garden (like Clarissa). Her pain cannot be explained as deserved retribution, and there is no promise whatsoever that it is part of a divine plan. Instead all Cecilia has to escape the commerce that degrades her and everyone else is her lunatic mind; and mind, for all its profound limitations, is the only redemptive alternative in the modern world. "Paradise absent is [not] paradise lost," LaCapra writes, and it is perhaps this very difference that distinguishes Cecilia from her forebears. What is historically specific about her loss is its basis in a new existential absence.[60]

The irony of *Cecilia* is that it locates such angst in a commercial infection of mind even as it romanticizes the mind's detachment from commercialism to sell itself. The privileging of madness to market implicit in Cecilia's final breakdown is one version of the superiority of fantasy to social reality on which the novel genre's own market success depends. For regardless of whether they represent paradise absent or paradise lost, novels work by persuading readers that the solitary act of imagining nonexistent characters and places is meaningful and filling.[61] Though *Cecilia* makes no sustained reference to novel-reading, it several times suggests that books are the most reliable antidote to melancholy and the only realistic and morally sustainable form of imaginative relief. Early in the novel, when she grows lonely at the Harrels and recognizes the futility of searching for a "companion she . . . expected not to find," Cecilia gets "together her books, arrang[ing] them to her fancy, and secur[ing] to herself . . . [an] exhaustless fund of entertainment" (31). As the "mind's first luxury," books provide "a source of entertainment so fertile and delightful that [they leave her] nothing to wish" (103). Direct substitutes for real relationships, books are valued for their "exhaustless" and "fertile" difference from human companions. Leaving Cecilia "nothing to wish," they circumvent "melancholy" by forcing "new images . . . in her mind" (790).[62]

But we never actually read of Cecilia's reading a book. Her greatest interest seems rather in assembling them as commodities, a habit of "luxury" (103) which, if less insidious than the gambling and greed that ruin so many others, nevertheless involves Cecilia in personal debt. Determined to "furnish herself with a well-chosen collection" Cecilia "confined not her acquisitions . . . , but, as she was laying in a stock for future as well as immediate advantage, she was restrained by no expence" (103). The consequence is that she accumulates bills that make her anxious and go unpaid until near the novel's end (766).[63]

Though they relieve the "heaviness of [Cecilia's] mind" (722), books prove just as dubious a "luxury" and "stock" (103) as any other empty "promise" of "pleasure" (722). They are, after all, at least as prone to fiction and fantasy as money or madmen. Like the book-loving heroine and the novel that bears her name, the consolation of reading replicates the very unreality and emptiness it pretends to resolve.[64] Indeed, if Cecilia (like Don Quixote) is a lunatic when she sees the bloody body of a man who is not there, how different is she from the reader who consumes one thousand pages of printed text in conjuring Cecilia?

N O T E S

I thank Eve Keller, John Richetti, Stuart Sherman, and the anonymous readers for *SECC* for their generous help with earlier versions of this essay.

1.   A good summary of *Don Quixote*'s popularity in eighteenth-century England can be found in Ronald Paulson, *Don Quixote in England: The Aesthetics of Laughter* (Baltimore: Johns Hopkins Univ. Press, 1998), ix and in Frances Burney, *Cecilia, or Memoirs of an Heiress*, ed. Peter Sabor and Margaret Anne Doody (Oxford: Oxford Univ. Press, 1999), 967n. Hereafter *Cecilia* is cited parenthetically in the text. Mr. Belfield dresses as Don Quixote at the masquerade (108–111; also see 736).

2.   Miguel de Cervantes, *Don Quixote*, trans. John Rutherford (New York: Penguin, 2000), 208.

3.   Raymond Williams, *Key Words: A Vocabulary of Culture and Society* (New York: Oxford Univ. Press, 1985), 258.

4.   Sigmund Freud, *The Ego and the Id*, ed. James Strachey (New York: Norton, 1989), 32. See also *The Interpretation of Dreams*: "Real and imaginary events appear in dreams at first sight as of equal validity; and that is so not only in dreams but in the production of more important psychical structures" (*The Interpretation of Dreams*, ed. James Strachey [New York: Avon, 1965], 323). To benefit from psychoanalysis, Freud writes in *Beyond the Pleasure Principle*, a patient must "recognize that what appears to be reality is in fact only a reflection of a forgotten past" (*Beyond the Pleasure Principle*, ed. James Strachey [New York: Norton, 1989], 19).

5.   Sigmund Freud, *Three Essays on the Theory of Sexuality* in *The Standard Edition of the Complete Psychological Works of Sigmund Freud*, ed. James E. Strachey, 24 vols. (London: Hogarth Press, 1981), 2:153 and "Fetishism," in *Sexuality and the Psychology of Love*, ed. Philip Rieff (New York: Collier Books, 1963), 205.

6.   My interest in unreality and mind in the novel is clearly indebted to the tradition of scholarly attention to the metaphysics of fiction (as it concerns what is imagined, invented or untrue) in prose fiction. One need only consider a few major texts of the last few decades to recognize the emphasis. In *Imagining a Self*, Patricia Spacks suggests that the novel's self is caught in the intricate "relation between language, illusion and 'the real'" (*Imagining a Self: Autobiography and Novel in Eighteenth-Century England* [Cambridge, M.A.: Harvard Univ. Press, 1976], 27). Michael McKeon argues that the novel's generic problem "registers an epistemological crisis . . . in attitudes toward how to tell the truth in narrative" (*The Origins of the English Novel, 1600–1740* [Baltimore: Johns Hopkins Univ. Press, 1987], 20). And Catherine Gallagher's *Nobody's Story* explores how "nothingness . . . , disembodiment" and the basic problem of "referent in the material world" are central to defining eighteenth-century prose "fiction" (as well as the related terms of "woman," "author," and "marketplace") (*Nobody's Story: The Vanishing Acts of Women Writers in the Marketplace, 1670–1820* [Berkeley: Univ. of California Press, 1994], xviii–xix). The more general problem of realism and the novel was, of course, initiated by Ian Watt's *The Rise of the Novel: Studies in Defoe, Richardson and Fielding* (Berkeley: Univ. of California Press, 1957). At the end of this essay, I comment on how my reading returns to Watt. Watt's paradigm has been questioned and challenged in countless ways. On the ancient roots of the novel see Margaret Anne Doody, *The True Story of the Novel* (New Brunswick, N.J.: Rutgers Univ. Press, 1996). On the amorphous nature of early English novels, the complexity or fallacy of defining their origin, and/or the problem of nationality, see, for instance, Homer Obed Brown, "Prologue: Why the Story of the Origin of the (English) Novel is an American Romance (If Not the Great American Novel)" in *Cultural Institutions of the Novel*, ed. Deidre Lynch and William B. Warner (Durham: Duke Univ. Press, 1996): 11–43; Lennard J. Davis, *Factual Fictions: The Origins of the English Novel* (New York: Columbia Univ. Press, 1983); J. Paul Hunter, *Before Novels: The Cultural Context of Eighteenth-Century Fiction* (New York: Norton, 1990); Michael McKeon; and John Richetti, "Introduction:

Twenty Years On" in his *Popular Fiction Before Richardson: Narrative Patterns, 1700–1739* (New York: Oxford Univ. Press, 1992): xi–xxix. Drawing especially on prose fiction's imbrication in material and print culture, Deidre Shauna Lynch's *The Economy of Character: Novels, Market Culture, and the Business of Inner Meaning* (Chicago: Univ. of Chicago Press, 1998) and William Warner's *Licensing Entertainment: The Elevation of Novel Reading in Britain, 1684–1750* (Berkeley: Univ. of California Press, 1998) offer powerful and persuasive challenges to basic assumptions about the novel's "inner self." Though less at odds with Watt, John Richetti argues that "the ideology of individualism . . . is precisely what" the novel interrogates (*The English Novel in History, 1700–1780* [London: Routledge, 1999], 3, 16). *Reconsidering the Rise of the Novel*, a special volume of *Eighteenth-Century Fiction* 12 (2000), offers an array of newer and older approaches to the genre.

7. Lynch, *The Economy of Character*, 4–8.

8. John W. Yolton, *Realism and Appearances: An Essay in Ontology* (Cambridge: Cambridge Univ. Press, 2000), 1.

9. Roy Porter, *Mind-Forg'd Manacles: A History of Madness in England from the Restoration to the Regency* (Cambridge, M.A.: Harvard Univ. Press, 1987), 189. For more on the skeptical problems Locke raises see Stephen D. Cox, *"The Stranger Within Thee": Concepts of the Self in Late-Eighteenth-Century Literature* (Pittsburgh: Univ. of Pittsburgh Press, 1980), 15; Porter, *The Creation of the Modern World: The Untold Story of the British Enlightenment* (New York: Norton, 2000), 63–65; Yolton, *Perceptual Acquaintance: From Descartes to Reid* (Oxford: Basil Blackwell, 1984), 94.

10. John Locke, *An Essay Concerning Human Understanding*, ed. Roger Woolhouse (London: Penguin, 1997), 1.1.8. On Locke's original use of "idea" see Porter, *Creation*, 63–64 and Yolton, *Perceptual*, ix, 4.

11. David Hume, *A Treatise of Human Nature*, ed. Ernest C. Mossner (London: Penguin, 1985), 240, 257. A good summary of Hume's skepticism, including its possible relation to his mental breakdown, can be found in Porter, *Creation*, 89–90, 176–79; also see Mary Poovey, *A History of the Modern Fact: Problems of Knowledge in the Sciences of Wealth and Society* (Chicago: Univ. of Chicago Press, 1998), 198–99. Yolton suggests that "Hume strives to retain a material world independent of perceivers" (*Realism*, 3).

12. Michel Foucault, *Madness and Civilization: A History of Insanity in the Age of Reason*, trans. Richard Howard (London: Routledge, 1989), 88. Madness, Foucault suggests, "form[s] the unreal unity of hallucination" (87; also see 88–98). Though *Don Quixote* pre-dates Descartes and Locke, for many later "English readers . . . the world against which Quixote knocks his head—and loses part of an ear and several grinders—began as the world of the senses posited by empiricism" (Paulson, 8). Quixote's madness, Michael McKeon writes, "is the first and indispensable step in the dialectical generation of extreme skepticism" (282). In the early modern period, madness could also be defined as a corporeal (as opposed to an exclusively mental or epistemological) problem. In *Cecilia*, for instance, Mortimer Delvile's depression is accompanied

by extreme physical illness, and when Lady Delvile has her maddest moment she bursts a blood vessel in her brain; Cecilia's own derangement is accompanied by the "inflammation of fatigue, heat" and "high fever" (897, 900). On the late eighteenth-century interest in the biology of the mind, see Alan Richardson, *British Romanticism and the Science of the Mind* (Cambridge: Cambridge Univ. Press, 2001).

13. As Porter puts it, "the distinction between sanity and madness seemed one not of kind but of degree" (*Mind*, 280).

14. Porter, *Mind*, 81; Foucault, 208–9.

15. James Boswell, *Boswell's Life of Johnson*, ed. George Birkbeck Hill, rev. L.F. Powell, 6 vols. (Oxford: Clarendon Press, 1934), 4:208 and Samuel Johnson, *Rasselas: Prince of Abissinia*, ed. J.P. Hardy (London: Oxford Univ. Press, 1968), 105.

16. Locke, *Essay*, 2.11.13. Michael DePorte quotes Locke's journal entry from January 22, 1678: "[The ideas of imagination are sometimes so clear that they] make impressions as strong and as sensible as those Ideas which come immediately by the senses from externall objects soe that the minde takes one for tother its own imaginations for realitys." "When this happens," DePorte adds, "a man goes mad" ("Vehicles of Delusion: Swift, Locke, and the Madhouse Poems of James Carkesse" in *Psychology and Literature in the Eighteenth Century*, ed. Christopher Fox [New York: AMS Press, 1987], 72).

17. Locke, *Essay*, 2.33.4; Johnson, *Rasselas*, 104.

18. Porter, *Mind*, 82; George Cheyne, *The English Malady* (Delmar, N.Y.: Scholars' Facsimiles & Reprints, 1976), i; William Rowley, *A Treatise of Female Nervous, Hysterical, Hypochondriacal, Bilious, Convulsive Diseases*, qtd. in Porter, *Mind*, 82.

19. P.G.M. Dickson, *The Financial Revolution in England: A Study in the Development of Public Credit, 1688–1756* (London: Macmillan, 1967), 12. Also see J.G.A. Pocock, *The Machiavellian Moment: Florentine Political Thought and the Atlantic Republican Tradition* (Princeton: Princeton Univ. Press, 1975), chapters 13 and 14 and *Virtue, Commerce, and History: Essays on Political Thought and History, Chiefly in the Eighteenth Century* (Cambridge: Cambridge Univ. Press, 1985).

20. Porter, *Mind*, 83.

21. Cheyne, i–ii; Rowley, qtd. in Porter, *Mind*, 82.

22. Daniel Defoe, *A Review of the State of the English Nation* (London, 1704–13), edited in 22 facsimile books by A.W. Secord (New York: Columbia Univ. Press, 1938), III, no. 126, 503 (facsimile book 8).

23. See William Ll. Parry-Jones, *The Trade in Lunacy: A Study of Private Madhouses in England in the Eighteenth and Nineteenth Centuries* (London: Routledge, 1972).

24. Poovey, 27. Also See Raymond Williams on "interest": "It seems probable that this now central word for attention, attraction and concern is saturated with the experience of a society based on money relationships" (173).

25. Colin Nicholson, *Writing and the Rise of Finance: Capital Satires of*

the Early Eighteenth Century (Cambridge: Cambridge Univ. Press, 1994), 6.

26. Pocock, *Virtue*, 112. Catherine Ingrassia offers an excellent summary of the fictive, intangible and unstable qualities of speculative finance in *Authorship, Commerce and Gender in Early Eighteenth-Century England: A Culture of Paper Credit* (Cambridge: Cambridge Univ. Press, 1998), 4–7, 22–26, 46–53, 141.

27. John Locke, *Two Treatises of Government*, ed. Peter Laslett (New York: New American Library, 1963), 342–43.

28. Pocock, *Machiavellian*, 451; also see Nicholson, 19.

29. Qtd. in Pocock, *Machiavellian*, 439.

30. Pocock, *Machiavellian*, 451; Johnson, *Rasselas*, 105.

31. Thomas Laqueur comments on the widespread fear of imaginative excess and unreality in his "Credit, Novels, Masturbation," in *Choreographing History*, ed. Susan Leigh Foster (Bloomington: Indiana Univ. Press, 1995). In the eighteenth century, he suggests, "it was precisely the fictional quality of the characters in a novel or masturbatory fantasy" that seemed to make them more dangerously "compelling . . . than so called real characters or real sexual partners" (125); and money was seen as "the same sort of fetish as the masturbatory [or novelistic] object of desire" (126).

32. The word "brain" appears several times in the novel's allusions to madness; Mr. Harrel shoots "out his brains" (727); Mrs. Delvile screams "My brain is on fire!" and bursts a blood vessel (680); "Delvile's danger" takes "sole possession of [Cecilia's] brain" (896). Such references suggest the mind's corporeality and anticipate the Romantic era's treatment of the brain as "the organ of thought" (Richardson, 1).

33. On Burney's interest in—and the historical significance of—the "automaton" see Lynch, *Economy of Character*, 192–93.

34. On the revolutionary implications of Belfield's response to Monckton in an earlier and similar debate see Margaret Anne Doody, *Frances Burney: The Life in the Works* (New Brunswick, N.J.: Rutgers Univ. Press 1988), 112.

35. Richetti, *English Novel*, 231. For a similar point about *Cecilia* see Doody, *Frances Burney*, 118. Although he does not discuss *Cecilia*, Paulson suggests that eighteenth-century sentimental novels generally feature a feminized Quixote whose delicate imagination comes "into contact with a real, unsentimental world" (175).

36. Doody, Introduction, in Burney, *Cecilia*, xxi.

37. Because of her debts for the Harrels, Cecilia cannot help the poor as much as she wants. At the novel's end, when she acquires an inheritance from Mortimer's aunt, she is less interested in "unbounded" benevolence than before (939). Catherine Keohane offers an excellent reading of Cecilia's confusion about charity and debt in "'Too Neat for a Beggar': Charity and Debt in Burney's *Cecilia*," *Studies in the Novel* 33 (2001): 379–401.

38. For the novel's Anti-Semitic rhetoric see 189–92 and 267; on the way Jews were typically scapegoated in critical attacks on stock-jobbing see Dickson, 34.

39. In this way Cecilia evokes the popular image of credit itself, which "stood for fantasy, fiction, and social madness," and which was often represented as a female figure of a delicate and volatile constitution (Pocock, *Machiavellian*, 458, 455–56). Keohane's reading of how Cecilia's mistakes with Mr. Harrel reflect her confused entanglement in the new credit economy is very helpful; see 391–95.

40. On how the "cluster of related terms" from "credit to credulity . . . takes us from activities that seem to be merely economic to attitudes that seem exclusively psychological," see Poovey, 27.

41. The passage anticipates Emma Woodhouse's declaration that her "active, busy mind" has a "great many independent resources" (Jane Austen, *Emma*, ed. R.W. Chapman [London: Oxford Univ. Press, 1971], 85).

42. As is oft-noted, the title *Pride and Prejudice* is a direct quotation from *Cecilia* (930).

43. Jane Austen, *Pride and Prejudice*, ed. R.W. Chapman (London: Oxford Univ. Press, 1965), 180 and *Emma*, 142. Ironically, what is unrealistic is Emma's idea that the unreality of imagination can be controlled.

44. In the psychoanalytic account of desire absence or loss is a staple component. Thus, Mikkel Borch-Jacobsen writes that "if desire is always already 'staged' in fantasy, it is doubtless understandable that its object will be forever elided from that stage where it is (only) represented in absentia" (*The Freudian Subject*, trans. Catherine Porter [Stanford: Stanford Univ. Press, 1988], 25).

45. Cecilia's nearly comatose disconnection here anticipates her later lunacy. Significantly, in both passages she is seated, one of the most classic positions in popular images of the mentally ill; see Sander L. Gilman, *Seeing the Insane* (New York: John Wiley & Sons, 1982), 12. The posture shapes the rhetoric of madness: Belfield's "mind was . . . the seat of his disease" (248); Mortimer cannot "conceal . . . that the seat of his disorder was his mind" (690).

46. See, for instance, 502, 523, 576, 623, 711, 903, 940, 941.

47. Cheyne, 38.

48. The act cited the "many great and dangerous Abuses frequently aris[ing] from the present State of Houses kept for the Reception of Lunaticks" as evidence of the need for legal change (qtd. in Richard Hunter and Ida Macalpine, *Three Hundred Years of Psychiatry, 1535–1860* [London: Oxford Univ. Press, 1963], 455). On both the significance and limitations of this act see Hunter and Macalpine, 451–56.

49. Foucault suggests that madness represents "that threatening space of absolute freedom" (79).

50. I am impressed with Julia Epstein's reading of the narrative, historical and psychological implications of this passage: "The reader is inside the disintegrating mind of the heroine . . . , following her through the streets of London controlled by a maniacal mental image. The narrator neither judges nor sympathizes. In Burney's most important narrative departure in *Cecilia*, she experiments with a vocally rich and multilayered third-person omniscient narrator. . . . Burney experiments in *Cecilia* with pre-Austenian irony . . . . No

one had written like this before Burney" (*The Iron Pen: Frances Burney and the Politics of Women's Writing* [Madison: Univ. of Wisconsin Press, 1989], 170).

51. On the moral importance and paradox of disembodiment in *Cecilia* see Gallagher, especially 233–37. Gallagher suggests that Cecilia wants to be "Nobody *in particular*" (236) and that the "suspended identity" she achieves in her pawnshop madness, represents a "bizarre fulfillment of [her] fantasy of freedom" (247).

52. Ian Watt, "Flat-Footed and Fly-Blown: The Realities of Realism," *Eighteenth-Century Fiction* 12 (2000): 157–58; Michael Seidel, "The Man Who Came to Dinner: Ian Watt and the Theory of Formal Realism," *Eighteenth-Century Fiction* 12 (2000): 208. Gallagher's summary of the paradox implicit in Watt's use of realism is eloquent: "'formal realism' [is] not a way of trying to hide or disguise fictionality; realism [is], rather, understood to be fiction's formal sign" (xvi–xvii).

53. Lynch, *Economy of Character*, 168.

54. As Lynch writes, the fiction of inner life may "have been serviceable to readers anxious to personalize their reading experience" and to believe that "characters have been redemptively set apart from the market" ("Personal Effects and Sentimental Fictions," *Eighteenth-Century Fiction* 12 [2000]: 365).

55. Freud stresses the loss of the mother in several works, including *Beyond the Pleasure Principle*, 14; *The Ego and the Id*, 27; "Some Psychological Consequences of the Anatomical Distinction Between the Sexes" (in *Sexuality and the Psychology of Love)*, 176; "Female Sexuality" (in *Sexuality and the Psychology of Love*), 187. The necessity of the mother's loss is tied to the castration complex, another threat of loss. Jacques Lacan famously adds that the loss of the mother creates the need for speech to make "presence . . . of absence" ("The Function and Field of Speech and Language in Psychoanalysis," in *Ecrits: A Selection*, trans. Alan Sheridan [New York: Norton, 1977], 65). Separation inaugurates the child's entrance into language which is itself predicated on the gap between referent and word. On maternal loss in the early novel and in psychoanalysis see my *Mothering Daughters: Novels and the Politics of Family Romance, Frances Burney to Jane Austen* (Detroit: Wayne State Univ. Press, 2002).

56. The forgotten memories of infancy leave "the deepest (unconscious) impressions" on "our minds and have a determining effect upon the whole of our later development" (*Three Essays*, 189, 175). But the unconscious is unavailable to the very individual it helps construct. Thus, the "scandalous" and most "fundamental hypothesis of psychoanalysis" is the idea that "the subject is not conscious of all 'its' thoughts" (Borch-Jacobsen, 3).

57. Freud, "Mourning and Melancholia" in *On Metapsychology: The Theory of Psychoanalysis,* ed. Angela Richards (London: Penguin, 1984), 254; Freud, *Ego and Id*, 24; Butler, *The Psychic Life of Power: Theories in Subjection* (Stanford: Stanford Univ. Press, 1997), 134; Adam Phillips, "Melancholy Gender/ Refused Identification: Keeping it Moving," in Butler, *Psychic Life of Power*,

157.

58. Austen, *Emma*, 415; For more on loss in *Emma* see my *Mothering Daughters*, 145–68.

59. Dominick LaCapra, "Reflections on Trauma, Absence, and Loss" in *Whose Freud? The Place of Psychoanalysis in Contemporary Culture*, ed. Peter Brooks and Alex Woloch (New Haven: Yale Univ. Press, 2000), 193, 179.

60. LaCapra, 190. In this sense *Cecilia* epitomizes Georg Lukacs's classic characterization of the novel as "the epic of a world that has been abandoned by God" (*The Theory of the Novel*, trans. Anna Bostock [Cambridge, M.A.: MIT Press, 1996], 88).

61. Laqueur describes this absence as one of the conceptual links between novels and masturbation in the eighteenth century: "novelism, like onanism, is dangerous because its protagonists are not really there and are all the more stimulating for their absence" (126).

62. Though this last passage (790) does not directly refer to Cecilia's use of books, it captures their supposed effect on her mind.

63. For a similar account of Cecilia's book bills and the relationship between reading and debt see Gallagher, 243–44.

64. See Catherine Ingrassia on the "keen insubstantiality" (6) that links the problems of "speculative investment and the emergence of the novel" (2).

The Infants' Petitions: An English Poetics of Foundling Reception, 1741–1837

LAURA SCHATTSCHNEIDER

Narratives about foundlings, or abandoned children, have appeared in literary fiction at least since Sophocles's *Oedipus Tyrannos* and the Hebrew Bible's Moses narrative. Foundling narratives typically hinge upon two scenes of discovery. In one, which sets the narrative in motion, the child is discovered in a public place and is taken in by strangers. In the other, which ends the narrative, the child's blood kin are discovered or revealed. Thus the entire narrative might be said to have originated with the parents who abandoned the child at its outset. Parents stage abandonment, and thus author the narrative; when they finally appear in its closing recognition scene it is more a long-awaited return than an entrance. Nevertheless, parents in foundling narratives, like all authors, keep their audience of receivers in mind as they "publish" their children, for it is receivers who ensure that the narrative progresses past the first moment of discovery, by preserving the life of its central figure, the foundling. Indeed, one element in the literary trope of foundling discovery is the note parents attach to their abandoned child, entreating receivers to care for the child. Real foundling discoveries in European culture followed a similar cultural convention. Parents often staged a kind of scene, leaving their infants in ways designed to inspire charity, and often leaving notes, before absenting themselves.[1] It is hard to say whether literature inspired this practice, or vice versa.

Because the social practice of foundling reception and its literary representation work in tandem, foundling narratives have preserved this basic structure over time, but the elements of their plots acquire different meanings as real reception practices change. In the seventeenth and eighteenth centuries, innovations in older modes of reception occurred throughout Europe. In England, France, and Germany, older religious foundling hospitals were made secular or national institutions, and new ones were established in a wave of charitable reform inspired by Enlightenment humanitarianism and mercantilist political economy.[2] When children were brought to foundling hospitals, institutions often cited parental notes, or enclosed them as evidence in records of the child's reception.[3] Fictional reception scenes in the eighteenth-century English vogue for foundling narratives[4] demand to be examined in the context of these innovations. Specifically, the foundation of the London Foundling Hospital, a private charitable corporation established in 1739, changed the cultural context of English foundling narratives profoundly. The institutionalization of written tokens took a unique form in England. The London hospital devised an intake form called the "billet" (whose name evokes the parents' notes), and required parents to submit tokens. After 1763, the hospital also required petitions from women who wished to leave children there. Thus, this hospital subjected mothers' disclosures to increasing scrutiny and control. Similarly, in English foundling narratives, by the end of the eighteenth century, male receivers were depicted as mediators of mothers' authority in the narratives of foundling lives. As a result, foundlings came to represent their mothers' stories, and foundling narratives in England mitigated, rather than explored, the potential for scandal caused by the reception of illegitimate children.

In this article, I will look at the ways a consistent trope in English eighteenth- and early-nineteenth-century fiction—the scene of a foundling's discovery and reception—changes in accord with the evolution in the ways the London Foundling Hospital solicited, reframed, and co-opted the evidence of its charges' origins. I will pay particular attention to the token objects and notes parents left with foundlings before their disclosures were constrained by the hospital's official expectations. What this juxtaposition of literary texts and social practices reveals is that the scene of a foundling's reception in eighteenth-century England, be it lived or written, not only preserved an infant's life, but also invoked a particular story about sexual transgression, maternal authority, and redemption that pervaded eighteenth- and early nineteenth-century English culture.[5] After the modes of foundling reception practiced at the London Foundling Hospital changed in 1763, the plots of English foundling narratives also changed. Mid-eighteenth-century works such as Eliza Haywood's *The Fortunate Foundlings* (1744) and Henry Fielding's *Tom Jones* (1749) emphasize the universal humanity of the foundling, and grant mothers almost unquestioned discretion and authority over their own stories. However, in later texts such as Frances Burney's *Evelina* (1778) and Charles Dickens's *Oliver Twist* (1837), men mediate the disclosure of women's secret histories.

From Infants' to Mothers' Petitions: London Foundling Reception, 1741–1836

The London Foundling Hospital, a private charity intended to supplement the scanty provisions made for children by the poor laws, began taking in abandoned or exposed children in 1741. It cared for the children, if they survived, until they were old enough to be apprenticed or go into domestic service, or, in rare cases, until their parents reclaimed them.[6] Until 1756, children might be brought to the hospital by anyone, not just their mothers. Those who brought children were not subject to any form of interrogation, but the number of children admitted was limited by lottery. In part as a result of a new focus in political economy on increasing the population, from June 1756 to late March 1760 the hospital received funds from Parliament so that it could take in all comers indiscriminately (a period known as the General Reception). The numbers of foundlings received shot up dramatically, and their parents remained unexamined. However, from 1741, although they were not interrogated, parents were asked to "affix on each child some particular writing, or other distinguishing mark or token, so that the children may be known hereafter if necessary."[7] This measure also prevented women from being charged with infanticide: after presenting their tokens, they were given a certificate attesting to the reception of their child at the Foundling.[8] Tokens continued to be required during the period of indiscriminate admission.

The sea change in the hospital's reception protocols occurred after the period of indiscriminate admission ended ignominiously: extraordinary mortality rates culled the large numbers of children admitted from 1756 to 1760, the practice of receiving illegitimate children was criticized as immoral, and the hospital suffered financially.[9] No foundlings, with the exception of some soldiers' orphans, were taken in from 1760 to 1763. After 1763, the number of foundlings continued to decrease: one hundred were taken in during 1763–1764, after which only vacancies were filled. Despite small increases to the total number of foundlings in 1767 and 1768, by 1786 the number of admissions had shrunk to ten per year. After 1801, children were admitted only to fill vacancies in the hospital, where the number of all children present was held steady at 420 (1801) or 430 (1803).[10] As the number of children admitted decreased, the "objects" of the charity were subjected to more intense scrutiny. After 1763, the Hospital's governors required petitions of the mothers and other people who brought them foundling infants. The facts stated in the petitions were investigated by hospital administrators, and the number of applicants whose petitions were successful was further limited by ballot. By 1801, the governors agreed that certain tales, those provided by unwed mothers, and those that followed the sentimental narratives of seduction and desertion made so popular by the period's literary authors, were more acceptable.[11] In 1815, they finally required that petitions be submitted by mothers rather than any other person, but this seems to have been the most common mode of admission well before this date.[12] By 1836, they had gone so far as to outline which maternal history would be "ideal"—one that followed the outline of a Richardsonian plot of virtue betrayed.[13]

Tokens, both written notes and objects, are present in the collections of the London Foundling Hospital archive from 1741 to approximately 1799, but in varying numbers. Despite a 1757 advertisement that promised that tokens would continue to be carefully preserved during the period of indiscriminate admission, in this period official documents from parishes predominate, rather than personal items from parents. Markedly fewer tokens appear in the archives from 1763 to 1801, in part because far fewer infants were admitted. It was also during this later period that petitions began to be required of abandoning mothers, but interrogation of mothers was not yet based on an official "ideal case." From 1763, the trend seems to be toward "official" documentation of foundling reception, and away from personal notes that could be written in any way parents wanted, notes that could disclose only as much as parents wished about their circumstances.[14]

Historians who work in the archives of the London Foundling Hospital have typically chosen to focus on the mothers' petitions submitted after 1763 and have rarely commented upon the written tokens.[15] Perhaps the tokens frustrate historians because they are so cryptic, and reveal little about the parents who produced them. But for this very reason, they offer to the literary scholar fascinating insight into scenes of reception in mid- to late-eighteenth-century English fiction. Written tokens are often derivative— they include citations from Latin or English poets (including verses from Ovid's *Heroides* and Matthew Prior's *Solomon on the Vanity of the World*).[16] They are also frequently very short—many, possibly provided by vicars after foundling children had been privately baptized, do little more than provide names of child and parent, and sometimes give a date of baptism. Nevertheless, several are unusually discursive and poetic, written in verse form.[17] Several of the most interesting of these longer token poems are written from the first-person perspective of the child, and appeal to benefactors by emphasizing that both benefactor and foundling are human. Such notes often imply a parental history, but do not fully disclose its particulars. These tokens thus create a conceit of the foundling's "speaking" body that invokes in the reader's imagination the full scene of its discovery: we as readers are placed in the position of its receivers, just as the foundling's body becomes a ventriloquist for the thoughts of its parent-authors. Simply put, by means of this conceit, the foundlings and their texts are made interchangeable: they are both productions of their mothers.

Indeed, all the tokens might be better considered as objects than as texts, or considered as texts only if one keeps in mind their peculiar status as objects. Many other tokens kept by the hospital are, in fact, actual objects. Coins, ribbons, snowflake-like[18] or otherwise ornate paper cutouts (see fig. 1, a Valentine), pieces of needlework, and other items are commonplace. Writing appears in some of these objects in conjunction with embroidery, which could be considered a particularly feminine medium.[19] Even those tokens written in the more usual media (scrawled in pencil on scraps of paper, or folded and sealed like letters) possess a poignant immediacy, affiliated as they are with a particular human body. They are preserved together with the "billet" form I discuss above, upon which administrators could list other distinguishing marks on the child, as well as make a careful inventory of his or her clothing. Thus, like the foundlings' bodies they accompanied, written tokens bear witness to a secret romantic history about which the Foundling's governors became increasingly curious as the century progressed. But despite the fact that unlike foundlings themselves, the tokens "speak," only rarely do they divulge any of the details of this secret romantic history.

Twenty-seven tokens in the overview of billet books I discuss in note 14 are written from the first-person point of view of the child and styled as its prayer for assistance. Several short notes in the first person, as in "my name is John Newman" (5 June 1741) are present in the earliest billet books. The earliest longer poem in the first person appears to be "Pray use me well & you shall find/my Father will not prove unkind/Unto that Nurse who's my protector/Because he is a Benefactor," from the first day of admission on 17 April 1741.[20] Other longer poems in the first person date from the 1750s. I have transcribed five longer poems in the appendix to this article and will refer to them below by their order in the appendix. In these tokens, the author responsible for both child and note—the parent,

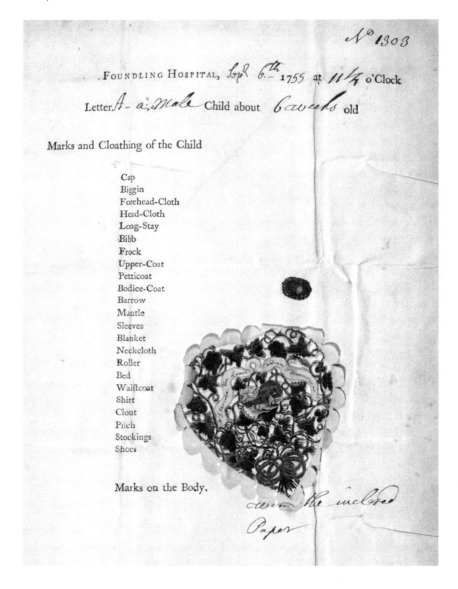

Figure 1. London Metropolitan Archive A/FH/A09/001/201/1303. An elaborately decorated Valentine. The text reads: "Sapientiae Veni Lumen Cordium L Mansuetudinis (Come light of wisdom, [sc. light?] of the kindness of hearts)." Thanks to Scott McGill (Classics, Rice University) for the translation. The image at the center is a country church. Reproduced by permission of the *Coram Family*.

often figured as the mother, whether or not she wrote the note—conceals herself (or himself) behind the fictive eloquence of the foundling "speaker." As the author of poem 4 puts it: "Here I am brought without a name/Im' sent to hide my mother's shame." Indeed, several of these poems, if they make reference to their origins at all, point to the story without telling it. A note from 6 April 1751 (poem 1) describes poverty and fate "forcing" an infant from its "tender Mother," whereas tokens from 6 September 1755 and 2 August 1757 (poems 3 and 4) mention a "Stol'n Embrace" and "mattrymony" being "Laid a side." Nevertheless, all withhold the details of the story, the tokens in poems 3 and 4 going so far as to obscure their importance. "My helpless Situation loudly Cries" in poem 3 could refer both to child and mother, but is clearly fixed as the child's plaint and plight in the next line ("extend Compassion to an Infant's Sighs"). "[I]tt tis, no matter whos my Mother" claims the token in poem 4, given that "I am a son" and "you are my Brother."

Instead of presenting themselves as somebody's child, then, these infant "speakers" extend the conceit that gives them a voice, while hiding their authors, who have recast them as kin to everybody, or as exceptional in ways that are socially worthy rather than scandalous. The speaker in poem 3 entreats his receivers to "search but Antiquity" to find heroic examples of illegitimates whose "acts Ennoble History," and makes specific reference to the founders of Rome. More common is a reference to Heaven as both the origin of the speaker and (by implication) of all people, including the receivers. In A/FH/A09/001/201/2026 (1756), entitled "Soliloquy of Richard Bower/ a Foundling Infant," the speaker, after seeking "kindred help" "In Vain" from sublunary fellow creatures in the second stanza, tries a different tack, saying "Imediate at my Birth I knew/From Heaven the Breath of Life I drew," and finally finding a place that recognizes this birthright in stanzas 4 and 5, when he hears Handel's *Messiah* "swift echoing from yon rising Ground" (that is, the Foundling Hospital, where it was performed frequently from 1750 on). Even in the much less sophisticated verses of poem 4, "Increas and multiply was heavens Command/and thats a text my Mother understands." This rhetorical strategy distracts the reader's focus from a specific origin by citing one that is common to all people, and thereby puts the infant "speaker" and his or her audience on a common footing, the better to inspire charitable actions from receivers.

The fifth poem in the appendix, a very late token from 18 May 1799, is entitled "The Infant's Petition," in what must be read as a deliberate reference to the petition submitted by the foundling's mother. It provides the most fully developed example of the conceit common to tokens written from the infant's first-person perspective.[21] This speaker distinguishes a fallible human law from the infallible and inexorable law of reproduction when he turns to the "crime" of his conception in stanza three, as did the speakers of earlier tokens, like poem 4. "Increas and multiply" in the earlier token is apparently a command that takes precedence over the authority of "men that make and Break the Law," to whom "poor Woman" can "nere say None."[22] In "The Infant's Petition," our infant narrator also implies that the fortuitousness of his arrival carries with it a kind of divine authority—"By Laws divine, unask'd, unsought, I came." The legitimacy of this authority is unquestionable, and thus generally applicable to all people, but its applicability to this particular illegitimate infant must nevertheless be argued. The best argument in its favor, the poem implies, is not so much the ventriloquized rhetoric with which our infant speaker "pleads" his case, but his puny, helpless (and universally human) body. Thus, this body's particular origin is hidden, in order to foreground the divine origin from which all people come. This strategem is most clear in the fourth stanza, in a passage that coyly refuses to reveal the secret history the child so obviously betokens: "If you enquire who sent me here to live/ Or by what Pow'r this vital Spark was giv'n/ Why truly, Sirs, no Answer can I give,/ But 'tis my All, and 'tis the Gift of Heaven." The mute presence of the infant's "All" both pleads and argues without "giving an Answer," and so the poem rests upon a conceit whereby the child becomes a kind of text. Its body, supplemented by this note, makes its mother's case for its reception, yet it does so without telling her tale. Instead, in the ensuing stanzas it makes an extended plea for sympathy and shelter that is based upon the argument of the child's resemblance to a desired benefactor: the child asks the reader to imagine sharing his predicament.

In part because of the conceit of voice they share, this group of written tokens poses significant problems when it comes to assessing both their authorship and their audience. Their authors are concealed behind the point of view of the infant. Did the mothers of the children write them? How many were commissioned as set pieces from schoolmasters, vicars, or stationers?[23] How many were written by fathers? "The Infant's Petition" was likely written by a mother, given that an annotation appears on the page of the billet book in which it appears that identifies it with "Elizabeth Hardy's child." Several of the tokens bear marks of a female perspective or are written from the point of view of an abandoned woman, but this alone does not indicate feminine authorship, especially given men's adoption of a female perspective in the history of epistolary fiction and poetry, linked by many scholars to imitations and rewritings of Ovid's *Epistolae Herodium*.[24] In fact, token A/FH/A09/001/011/866 (7 December 1751) provides a direct link to this tradition, quoting "sit tibi cura mei, sit tibi cura tui" ("if you would care for me, care for yourself"), from the 13th Heroid, *Laodamia to Protesilaus*. The fact that several other tokens are written in (often incorrect) Latin suggests an educated woman, or the hand of a man who poorly remembers his school Latin.[25] Nevertheless, whether the tokens were written by women, or written by men on behalf of women, or written by (perhaps repentant) fathers, many partially disclose the sufferings of a particular type of literary female character, the abandoned woman.

The tokens also typecast their audience. For whom did the billet writers write? Because the tokens were advertised as a means to recognizing the child later if the parent wished to reclaim it, the authors wrote first on behalf of, and perhaps to, their children. However, these tokens are also clearly addressed to the Hospital's governors. Whether the Hospital's governors read them at the time of admission is unlikely. It seems they piled up in the archives unexamined for several decades: Brownlow says that "fifty years ago [circa 1800], the Governors being curiously inclined, appointed a committee to inspect these tokens, with the view of ascertaining their general nature," and Nichols and Wray concur: a committee appointed in 1806 to investigate the tokens left there from 1741 to 1790 discovered "over 18000 to examine."[26] Nevertheless, many notes are addressed specifically to the governors, or to an indeterminate benefactor.

Tokens, then, have as phantom authors the stereotype of the "fallen" woman, and are written to an imagined audience of benevolent gentlemen. If it is impossible to identify their real authors and readers (whether these be stationers and receiving nurses, or debauched university students and their grown offspring), the rhetorical situation the tokens depict is one familiar to readers of English foundling narratives: notes written by "fallen" women to male benefactors. Thus, because of the way that the tokens both reveal and conceal secret romantic histories, they participate in a cultural trope of feminine secrecy about illegitimate birth and paternity common to all regions of Europe that administered charity under the common-law system, where officials attempted to discover the parents of abandoned children and make them financially responsible for their offspring. This trope of feminine secrecy is common to the literary fictions of these same regions. It is associated with the figure of a proud woman who refuses to name the father of her child, and who claims this knowledge is hers alone to keep or to divulge.[27]

Indeed, it is this female figure and her history, embodied in her child, that proved a troubling (and titillating) reminder of sexual transgression to both real benefactors and the readers of fictional texts.[28] This fact may account for the trend toward requiring more regulated and greater disclosure of women's stories. Women could not be allowed to keep their secrets and hide their shame with the complicity of the foundling hospital. Women's disclosures, in petitions that had been carefully investigated, would defuse the potentially scandalous implications of foundling reception by ensuring that women who turned to the Foundling for help would be deserving, repentant, "objects of charity." The transition was thus one from a situation in which receivers took in foundlings and their secrets without requiring a full account of their conception and birth, to one in which receivers took in foundlings and a full account from the mother of her story. At the same time, the fact that only a select few—the Hospital's administrators—were privy to maternal secrets meant that women would not be publicly exposed or humiliated, and that foundlings did not entirely lose the cachet of mystery that made them compelling objects of charity. Instead, this mystery was given social sanction because it was mediated and examined by the Foundling Hospital.[29] The post-1763 mode of reception might thus best be described as "confidential."

Thus, even though tokens were still produced after 1763 in addition to the narratives present in the petitions, by the early 1800s they seem archaic throwbacks to an earlier mode of reception. The 1799 poem "The Infant's Petition" self-consciously sets itself up as a supplement to the mother's petition that would have accompanied it, and it is necessary because it provides an alternate narrative of the child's origin. Without reading too much into this late token, it seems clear that it was a necessary supplement because a particular way of seeing foundling infants as deserving of charity was being lost.[30] Instead of making an appeal through the voice and body of an innocent infant to the generic attributes of all people, the authors of the petitions presented themselves as a typecast character, one to whose secrets only a select few were privy.

An example of how the rhetoric of confidential reception works appears in a passage from John Brownlow's 1858 edition of his history. Brownlow describes the Hospital's chief object as "...a woman, with a sense of honour, [who] finds herself the unsuspecting victim of treachery, with the witness of her disgrace hanging about her neck, in the person of her child . . . ."[31] Brownlow's metaphoric use of the foundling child in this passage plays upon the paradoxical ways children used to "witness" their mothers' disgrace in the written tokens: by "testifying," as well as by serving as objects of evidence. The child is "the witness of [its mother's] disgrace" both before and after 1763, but after 1763, its number in the records refers not only to it, but also to its mother's written history of "her disgrace." Like the tokens, the Foundling Hospital's institutional mediation gives the mother's shame a safely cryptic representation (one that is not scandalous, because its particulars are not publicized). Nevertheless, in confidential reception the mother's secret "disgrace" is embodied not in the child's impossible voice, but in the child's institutional identity. The Hospital's governors were able to convert children and their texts from witnesses to shame into the innocent objects of their corporate charity, thus defusing the potentially scandalous act of reception, but they did so by co-opting the authority of abandoning mothers.

"Authors of their Being": Mothers and Benefactors in English Fiction, 1744–1837

The trend visible in the history of the Foundling Hospital from blind, no-questions-asked reception to confidential reception can also be seen in fictional foundling narratives, as novels by Eliza Haywood and Henry Fielding give way to texts by Frances Burney and Charles Dickens. In the earlier texts, mothers retain control over the exposure of their infants and the disclosure of their secrets, whereas in the latter two, benefactors know the facts of the foundling's origin and are active participants in its discovery, and mothers are passive, dead victims of circumstance.

Why does this evolution in the dynamic between "mother" authors and "benefactor" readers occur in both fictional and nonfictional texts, however? The circumstances of the Hospital's publicity in the eighteenth century may have inspired the same poetic and rhetorical choices in the writers of private tokens and the authors of published works. The Hospital's publicity may also explain why so many written tokens share the same formal idiosyncrasies, despite the fact that none were published until Brownlow's 1847 history. The London Foundling Hospital was an institution with an exemplary place in the eighteenth- and nineteenth-century cultural and literary imagination. It inspired artists and musicians, including Hogarth and Handel, who donated works to the museum. Samuel Johnson, Henry Fielding, and other writers discussed it in print.[32] Because of the Foundling's wide-ranging effect on English culture, it seems likely that any author who read widely enough in the London journals would have been familiar with its reception protocols.[33] Indeed, the Hospital's pre-1763 reception protocols lent a new metaphoric image to the old trope of text as child, as witnessed by the collections of anonymous poems, tales, essays and satires, organized on the principle of (disingenuous) fortuitous discovery, called *The Foundling Hospital for Wit* and the *New Foundling Hospital for Wit*.[34] Moreover, in England, the situation in which the "fallen" woman both conceals and reveals her story is one that figures forth the coy publicity characteristic of the fictionality of the eighteenth-century novel (especially the epistolary novel) and its characters.[35] The Hospital's reception procedures, in short, were metaphorically rich in ways that resonated across the culture. Conversely, the culture's representations of foundling reception in the episodes from the novels I discuss here may have inspired some of the authors of the tokens at the Hospital.

Because the longer written tokens I discuss above are poems, it may seem strange to juxtapose them with scenes from prose fiction. However, because of the circumstances of their production and preservation, written tokens can be argued to be the emblems of narratives that remain untold. In each of the novels I will discuss, foundlings at the moment of their discovery possess "speaking bodies"; that is, they are represented as icons of loss or need. As such, the depiction of such moments is akin to narrative moments of *ekphrasis*, in the sense that the action of the plot pauses, and narrative becomes dramatic or poetic, because emphasis is placed on the display of an object or tableau—in this case, the foundling's body as emblem of human vulnerability—rather than upon the telling of a tale. Thus, the poetic form of the token is preserved in a static moment within these prose narratives. Represented in this way, foundling characters begin to look like their institutional tokens: riddles, puzzles, or ciphers; keys to the deciphering of a complicated plot.

Like everybody else, foundlings possess generic attributes capable of inspiring sympathy, as well as the particular marks of bloodline, capable of inspiring intrigue. In the case of foundlings, however, these particular marks of bloodline are often unreadable, because a key to their significance is not provided by a parental story. Foundlings might thus be described as "Hieroglyphics," as one foundling character is called in Edward Moore's 1748 play, *The Foundling*; that is, encoded messages requiring a deciphering reader.[36] In mid-eighteenth-century narratives, mothers at first downplay the particular marks that enabled the child to be recognized as blood kin to *somebody* in favor of the child's generic resemblance to *everybody*. Later, under circumstances of their choosing, they reveal their identities and stories. In late-eighteenth-century and nineteenth-century narratives, benefactors know mothers' secrets and use them to interpret and manipulate the particular marks of bloodline in ways beneficial to the foundlings. Whereas the benefactors in the earlier texts decipher the story of a common human origin, the benefactors in later texts discover and disclose a woman's secret romantic history. Thus, from the early part of the century to its end, we can perceive a shift in benevolent ways of making foundlings' bodies and texts signify.

In Eliza Haywood's late novel, *The Fortunate Foundlings*, published in 1744, two foundlings are discovered in "the ever memorable year 1688" by Dorilaus, a gentleman who "to avoid interesting himself on either side" of the Succession question "forbore coming to London" and remained instead at his country seat.[37] There, he is given "an opportunity of exercising the benevolence of his disposition" (2) when he discovers a basket containing a twin boy and girl, complete with a note which reads,

> *To the generous D O R I L A U S:*
> Irresistible destiny abandons these helpless infants to your care.—They are twins, begot by the same father, and born of the same mother, and of a blood not unworthy the protection they stand in need of; which if you vouchsafe to afford, they will have no cause to regret the misfortune of their birth, or accuse the authors of their being.—Why they seek it of you in particular, you may possibly be hereafter made sensible.— In the mean time content yourself with knowing they are already baptized by the names of Horatio and Louisa. (3)

This note is just as cryptic as the real tokens about the circumstances that led to the foundlings' birth and abandonment. "Irresistible destiny," not a mother in anything but a figurative sense, abandons the children. Hence, Dorilaus's reaction to the foundlings is typical of most benefactors in this period's reception scenes. The infants' physical needs cause him to take them in without considering too greatly whether he would be thereby embroiled in any kind of scandal. Indeed, had he not arrived in the country sooner, he would have been suspected of being the children's father (like Allworthy in *Tom Jones*) (4). Nevertheless, in a moment common across the literature, he determines that "To what person so ever…I am indebted for this confidence, it must not be abused.—Besides, whatever stands in need of protection, merits protection from those who have the power to give it" (3). Dorilaus thus decides upon reception out of a general concern for humanity, his studious cultivation of which will only redound to his own fame: "he was looked upon as a prodigy of charity and goodness" (4).

Once he is given a chance to catch his breath, Dorilaus turns his mind to the letter in a vain attempt to determine the foundlings' origin (a question that seems to have supplanted his efforts at political decision-making):

> He read the letter over and over, yet still his curiosity was as far to seek as ever.—The hand he was entirely unacquainted with, but thought there was something in the stile that shewed it wrote by no mean person: the hint contained in it, that there was some latent reason for addressing him in particular

> on this account, was very puzzling to him...all his endeavours to give him any farther light into it being unsuccessful; he began to imagine the parents of the children had been compelled by necessity to expose them and had only wrote in this mysterious manner to engage a better reception . . . .
> (4–5)

Dorilaus thus is presented with a note just as mysterious as the foundlings themselves, a note the particulars of which fail to signify much that can be relied upon despite his best efforts at deciphering it. What he is left with is a conclusion much the same as that he made during his encounter with the infants' bodies: the fact that they were deposited on his property is a mark of honor. He "explains" this "seeming riddle" by reasoning that he is single and wealthy and thus can bear the expense of Horatio and Louisa's care (5). But most strikingly, he explains the very mysteriousness of the note as an effort on the part of the "authors" of the children's "being" to ensure their safe reception. This is a blind act of reception that realigns the particulars of the note to refer to the general humanity linking Dorilaus to his new charges, so that he may exercise the exemplary "benevolence of his disposition."

The narrative that follows this opening scene twists through a series of trials and tribulations for both foundlings, notable for a remarkable depiction of Dorilaus's developing passion for Louisa (who flees his estate in a flurry of confusion and guilt at what she interprets as her ingratitude for refusing him). It closes with the revelation that Dorilaus is in fact Horatio and Louisa's father. Their mother Matilda and her nurse, who appear in the last pages of the novel, had engineered the scene of their discovery, and written the letter that accompanied them. This revelation makes it possible for Dorilaus and his wards to be reconciled, and permits the foundlings to marry their respective paramours and settle happily in France. Thus, because Dorilaus cannot read the earlier "hint" of the letter, recognition is not engineered by his sudden interpretation of a mysterious mark or clue, but by a woman's chosen disclosure of her secret history, a secret history that was guarded unseen (like a sealed letter, or like the stories of foundlings' mothers at the London Foundling Hospital before the institution of petitions) by Dorilaus's benevolence. An unquestioned feminine authority governs this plot, a legible but unidentifiable hand with "something in the stile that shewed it wrote by no mean person." As such, the novel records reception much as did the London Foundling Hospital before 1763.

In *Tom Jones,* Allworthy, unlike Dorilaus, legally pursues the authors of Tom's being.[38] Nonetheless, his failure to do so accurately, combined with the novel's famous failure to legitimize Tom, provides a very clever take on the tradition of female secretiveness. The discovery scene begins as Allworthy is abstracted in contemplation of the infant Tom, who is "in a sweet and profound Sleep"[39] rather than "want[ing] immediate Succour" and crying, as was the case with Horatio and Louisa (Haywood 3):

> He stood some Time lost in Astonishment at this Sight; but, as Good-nature had always the Ascendant in his Mind, he soon began to be touched with Sentiments of Compassion for the little Wretch before him. He then rang his Bell, and ordered an elderly Woman Servant to rise immediately and come to him, and in the mean Time was so eager in contemplating the Beauty of Innocence, appearing in those lively colours with which Infancy and Sleep always display it, that his Thoughts were too much engaged to reflect that he was in his Shirt, when the Matron came in. (29)

Allworthy thus focuses almost exclusively on the general characteristic of Innocence, portrayed by the equally generic conditions Infancy and Sleep, rather than preoccupying himself with the questions of scandal, shame, and illegitimacy Mrs. Wilkins brings into the picture (along with her horror at Allworthy's nakedness—Allworthy's mental abstraction here comically mirrors Tom's naked, generic abstraction). Allworthy's memory is forever imprinted with this scene, and that which immediately follows it, in which Tom's infant hand "outpleads" Deborah Wilkins's fear of scandal (31), a scene which is repeated in his memory shortly after he discovers the bank bills in possession of Black George: "I have considered him as Child sent by Fortune to my Care. I still remember the innocent, the helpless Situation in which I found him. I feel the tender Pressure of his little Hands at this Moment" (715). Given the narrative longevity of this scene of discovery, and the lively impression the grown Tom has made on all he encounters, the final recognition of Tom's "true" identity does little to dispel the identity that readers have already received as Tom's own, and which Allworthy takes in out of a recognition, not of any particular parental origin, but of the generic attribute of Innocence Tom's infant body represents and literally impresses upon him.[40] The novel thus chronicles the affective history of Allworthy's unpopular and unconventional decision to ameliorate the consequences of illegitimate birth for Tom.

Moreover, despite his best efforts, Allworthy cannot discover the truth of Tom's identity. Tom thus embodies a maternal secret just as do his real London counterparts. At the end of the novel, we discover the real author of Tom's being and the real engineer of the novel's plot—Brigid.[41]

Confessing her subterfuge to Allworthy in book 18, chapter 7, the erstwhile Jenny Jones describes the feminine education in secrecy she has received from Brigid, an education that enables her to keep Tom's identity in confidence for years: "At last she began to catechise me on the Subject of Secrecy, to which I gave her such satisfactory Answers, that, at last, having locked the Door of her Room, she took me into her Closet, and then locking that Door likewise, she said, she should convince me of the vast Reliance she had on my Integrity, by communicating a Secret in which her Honour, and consequently her Life was concerned" (727–728). The utility of this principle of secrecy is best summed up in Jenny's description of Brigid's authorial pride. She "was highly rejoiced that her Plot had succeeded so well, and that you had of your own Accord Taken such a Fancy to the Child, that it was yet unnecessary to make any express Declaration" (729). Thus, Jenny, not Allworthy, is the repository of Brigid's secret, and Fielding's narrator is her accomplice, saying during Allworthy's investigation of Partridge that "if the Historic-Muse has entrusted me with any secrets, I will by no means be guilty of discovering them till she shall give me leave" (76). In Haywood's *Fortunate Foundlings*, this maternal secret has unquestioned authority over the plot. Fielding's view of this authority seems more ambiguous, and the discovery of Brigid's secret is delayed due to circumstances beyond her control. Nevertheless, although Fielding allows other characters to call this feminine authority an error, he does not displace it from its sovereign position.

If Dorilaus and Allworthy, however generous, can also be seen as dupes of Matilda and Brigid, the same cannot be said of benefactors in later foundling narratives. Both Evelina "Anville" and Oliver Twist are aided by benefactors who mediate the disclosure of maternal stories in ways apparently conditioned by the Foundling Hospital's confidential rhetoric of reception after 1763. In neither text does a mother willingly relinquish her child to another's care. Instead, the mothers are dead—not lurking behind the scenes, proudly viewing the success of their plots. Frances Burney and Charles Dickens were both familiar with the Foundling Hospital. Burney's father wanted to teach the foundlings music.[42] Dickens had a pew at the Foundling, and must have been aware of the real John Brownlow, given his homage to him in the benefactor figure in *Oliver Twist*, and the similarities between that plot and the one of Brownlow's own novel, *Hans Sloane*.[43]

In Burney's text, Evelina, like the infants at the Foundling Hospital, is portrayed as a "cypher" for her mother's story.[44] However, Caroline Evelyn presents her daughter and her story to two receivers. Belmont must recognize Evelina as his legitimate child. Villars, entrusted with Caroline's confidence, her letter to Belmont, and her infant when she dies, must raise

Evelina to be virtuous, and ensure that Caroline's story is told only when it will be heard sympathetically (by a reformed Belmont). The novel thus presents us with two ways of legitimizing Evelina: by means of Belmont's legal recognition, and by means of Villars's moral education. If Belmont's recognition makes Evelina socially legible, Villars ensures that she behaves virtuously (if awkwardly) in public. Like her infant counterparts at the London Foundling Hospital, Evelina is the bearer of her mother's story in the form of the letter to Belmont. However, Evelina's face, which closely resembles Caroline's, supplements the letter: her body also references Caroline's story, and according to Villars, she should need no other "certificate of her birth" (337).[45] Whereas the letter to Belmont seems more like a Foundling Hospital petition, Evelina and her words in the letters that compose the novel take on some qualities of the Foundling Hospital's tokens. However, Evelina could be argued to be an equal production of Caroline and Villars: Villars's "Berry Hill philosophy" (376) makes Evelina's evocative person eminently "publishable," because it conditions her comportment to ensure that Caroline's words have their full effect. If not Evelina's "real parent" in a legal sense, Villars is her true reader.[46] Villars's role thus aligns the novel with the rhetoric of confidential reception characteristic of the post-1763 procedures at the Foundling Hospital.

In *Oliver Twist*, the role of the receiver is even more important, given Oliver's illegitimacy and the fact that Agnes Fleming has even less control over her child's future than Caroline Evelyn. Like Caroline, Agnes has left the marks of her resemblance in Oliver's face.[47] However, unlike Caroline, Agnes leaves no other token behind. Her locket and ring, the only other proofs of Oliver's identity, are intercepted and destroyed by Oliver's brother Monks before they can be of use (254). It falls to Brownlow, the privileged confidant of Oliver's father, to notice Oliver's resemblance to Agnes, and engineer the discovery of Oliver's identity. In the end, Brownlow adopts Oliver, thereby supplanting both his parents.[48]

The absence of written tokens in *Oliver Twist*, which makes the foundling's face his only maternal legacy, represents the endpoint of a shift in narrative authority in the later novels from mother to receiver. Whereas notes preserve the words, and attempt to convey the intentions, of the mothers who have written them, foundlings' faces can only point to a history that those who encounter them—receivers, not mothers—must discover and recount. Moreover, the faces in the later narratives clearly refer to mothers' histories, unlike the equally mute body of Tom Jones, which signified something more universal to Allworthy.[49] Thus, after 1763, when reception at the London Foundling Hospital changed from blind to confidential, the balance of power in literary texts between mother's story and benefactor's narrative also changed. In mid-eighteenth-century foundling narratives, benefactors focus on the generic attributes that make all people kin to one another, and mothers' texts remain sealed within the terms of their own poetic figures. In later texts, receivers decipher the particular marks of maternal history to help author the recognition scene that gives foundling narratives their conventional resolution, and this process gives the foundling a sanctioned, "publishable" identity. By the 1830s, therefore, reception becomes the end, as well as the beginning, of the English foundling plot.

Appendix: Written Tokens from the London Foundling Hospital
1. LMA A/FH/A09/001/010/735 (6 April 1751)
     <u>Poverty thou Enemy</u> to my Tender Mother
     Has forced me from her and brought me hether
     weand from her Breast tho not from her Hart
     fate Direct us <u>that wee thus do part</u>.
                    S—— S—dh—m
2. LMA A/FH/A09/001/010/745 (1 June 1751)
     An Outcast, to these friendly Gates I Press
     To Seek a Timely Shelter from Distress
     O May the Snowy Ball, propitious, Give [reference to lottery system
                                                  of admission]
     A Foundling, right within this Dome to Live
     Sim, licet Exposita, et utroque Deserta Parente [Although exposed and
                                                  deserted by both parents]
     Te precor Auxilio Numen Adesso Meo. [I prithee, divinity, be present
                                                  for/as my aid]
     This Child is Christned her Name Anne Edwardson + has been Dry
     Nursed
[Thanks to James Ker (Classics, Harvard University) for the translation.]
3. LMA A/FH/A09/001/018/1315 (6 September 1755)
     My helpless Situation loudly Cries
     Extend compassion to an Infant's Sighs
     Despise me not————Search but Antiquity
     Heroes whose Acts Ennoble History
     Owe to a Stol'n Embrace their Births like me
     A Foundling ——Sprung from the fair Vestal Maid
     The first Foundation of Rome's Empire Laid
     And wou'd you Listen to a Babes request
     Grant me (unweaned) my Native Food————the Breast.
4. In book LMA A/FH/A09/001/201/1– [unnumbered, before 1303] (2
     August 1757)
     To the Hon[ble] Gentlemen of the Foundalen Hospital—
     The Erand Boys Brest Plat

Sir,
Here I am brought without a name
Im' sent to hide my mother's shame,
I hope youll say, Im' not to Blame—
Itt, seems my mothers' twenty five
and mattrymony Laid a side
Why, what is to be Done
poor woman thatt Can nere say None[?]
to men that make and Break the Law
twas by that Law I Came—
Increas and multiply was heavens Command
and thats a Text my mother understands
I am a son, you are my Brother—
itt tis, no matter whos my mother
in mattremony she was born—
tho now itt seems, tis held in scorn
Unless she has a mony^d purse
to give for better, or for worse
I am, but young, and cannot chew
Who shall be Chancellor, or I rewe[?]
if I could speak, i^{de} tell you who
I^{de} Chuse, for King and Country to
make me a man and I will fight
both for my King, and Country's Right:
Which every Inglish man should do
for his, own Rights, and Countrys to
Blame not the woman that is week
When mon^{n}arks are afraid to speak
there minds in truth, and so we find
that all mankind is of one mind.

Yours [initials, ruled out]

Born 1st August 1757

5.   Token A/FH/A09/001/201/12919 (18 May 1799), "token of Elizabeth
Hardy's Child"

The Infant's Petition
to the Governors of the
Foundling Hospital
          1
Pity the cravings of a puny Wretch
Oh Ye, whose Ears these slender Cries assail
To you, kind Sirs, these helpless hands I stretch
Oh take me in, and hear my piteous Tale!

2

Late, whilst the busy Scenes of Life you trod
In silent Stillness, and in Night I lay,
'Till from these Slumbers, summon'd by my God,
I woke, and lo! am usher'd into Day.

3

The Child of Crimes, (so call'd by human Laws)
By Laws divine, unask'd, unsought, I came
Say, will ye let me stay, to plead my Cause,
Ah me! indeed, indeed, I'm not to blame.

4

If you enquire who sent me here to live
Or by what Pow'r this vital Spark was giv'n
Why truly, Sirs, no Answer can I give
But 'tis my All, and 'tis the Gift of Heaven.

5

That Curse which visits by divine Command
The Sinner's Children, Oh! if strictly true!
What Mortal could the awful Doom withstand,
That Curse alas! might visit some of you!

6

If ye, benighted, shipwreck'd, cast on Shore
Some Cottage found, and thus your Host began
"Go! get ye forth —to brave the Tempest's roar"—
Would you not call him, cruel, savage Man?

7

I was benighted, shipwreck'd, and at Sea
Nor know I, whence I came, or whither bound,
You will not then, less hospitable be—
His was a Cottage—I, a World have found.

8

A spacious world!—'twill surely hold us all,
Ye'll not be crowded by a tiny Elf
Which ye yourselves a little Foundling call,
Then hard's my Fate, if I have lost myself.

9

If ye reject me, friendless must I die
This providence foresaw, + Widom [sic] plan'd
And plac'd you here, to listen to my Cry
The Instruments of Heaven's protecting hand

10

The Ways of God are just, tho' unexplor'd
Weakness on me, on you he Strength bestows
The grov'ling Ivy is to Health restor'd
And by its kindred Oak supported grows.

11

Haply, some distant year, mysterious Fate
With Fortune's Gifts may crown the life you save
And drive your Orphan Ofspring [sic] to my Gate
To bless the Hand which snatch'd me from the Grave.

12

Pity the Cravings of a puny Wretch
A little food + Raiment will suffice
To you, these Infant, helpless hands I stretch
To you, my Friends, I lift these suppliant Eyes

13

That Smile, speaks Comfort, from a gentle Mind
You've snatch'd a shipwreck'd Wand'rer from the flood
—do tell the Nurse, that if she prove as kind
Indeed I will be very, very good!

N O T E S

I would like to thank the London Metropolitan Archive, Rhian Harris and Janet Broadhurst at the Coram Family, the Stadtarchiv Nürnberg, and the Deutsche Akademische Austauschdienst for help with the archival research that went into this article. Catherine Gallagher, Sarah Ellenzweig, Alessa Johns, Leah Middlebrook, two anonymous reviewers for *SECC*, and the audiences at the panel "The Abandoned Child" at ASECS 2002 and at a meeting of the Andrew W. Mellon Seminar at the UCLA Humanities Consortium in May 2002 provided valuable responses to earlier drafts. James Ker and Scott McGill provided translations for Latin tokens. I owe special thanks to Catherine Ingrassia: her faith in this essay sustained my own.

1. Leaving notes with foundlings was probably a social practice from ancient times. See John Boswell, *The Kindness of Strangers: The Abandonment of Children in Western Europe from Late Antiquity to the Renaissance* (New York: Vintage Books, 1990), p. 126. For France, see Isabelle Robin and Agnès Walch, "Les billets trouvés sur les enfants abandonnés à Paris aux XVIIᵉ et XVIIIᵉ siècles," in *Enfance abandonnée et société en Europe: XIVᵉ–XIXᵉ siècle: Actes du colloque international organisé par la Società italiana di demografica storica, la Société de démographie historique, l'École des hautes études en sciences sociales, l'École française de Rome, le Dipartimento di Scienze demografiche (Università di Roma-La Sapienza), le Dipartimento statistico (Università di Firenze), Rome, 30 et 31 janvier 1987* (Rome: École française de Rome, 1991), pp. 981–991. For northern Germany, see Markus Meumann, *Findelkinder, Waisenhäuser, Kindsmord: Unversorgte Kinder in der frühneuzeitlichen Gesellschaft* (Munich: R. Oldenbourg Verlag, 1995), pp.

149–150. In southern Germany, several notes exist in the records of the Findelhaus present in the Nuremberg city archive (research conducted June 2000), and the practice of leaving notes seems to have been widespread enough that a probably spurious "Mägdlein-Brief" (maiden's note) was included with the documents found on the person of the mysterious foundling Kaspar Hauser in 1828 (cited in several eyewitness accounts, including P.J.A. Feuerbach, *Beispiel eines Verbrechens am Seelenleben des Menschen* [Waldkirch: Waldkircher Verlagsgesellschaft, 1981], p. 33).

2. See *Enfance abandonnée*; Rachel Ginnis Fuchs, *Abandoned Children: Foundlings and Child Welfare in Nineteenth-Century France* (Albany, NY: SUNY Press, 1984); Meumann; and Otto Ulbricht, "The Debate about Foundling Hospitals in Enlightenment Germany: Infanticide, Illegitimacy, and Infant Mortality Rates," *Central European History* 18 (1985): 211–256.

3. See Laura Schattschneider, "'Received into the Arms of Civil Society': Foundling Narratives in England, France, and Germany, 1740–1840," Ph.D. diss., University of California, Berkeley, 2000, pp. 39–62. Examples of institutional documents from Paris are cited by Léon Lallemand, *Histoire des enfants abandonnés et délaissés: Études sur la protection de l'enfance aux diverses époques de la civilization* (Paris, 1885), p. 235, n. 1; pp. 732–740.

4. The vogue for foundling narratives, or at least, for foundling characters, may be traced from the mid-eighteenth century into the 1830s through such well-known texts and characters as Eliza Haywood's *The Fortunate Foundlings* (1744), Edward Moore's 1748 play *The Foundling*, Henry Fielding's *Tom Jones* (1749) and *Joseph Andrews* (1742), Miss Mancel in Sarah Scott's *Millenium Hall* (1762), Tobias Smollett's *Humphry Clinker* (1771), Clara Reeve's *The Old English Baron* (1778), Mary Robinson's *The Natural Daughter* (1799), William Combe's *Johnny Quae Genus* (an 1822 sequel to his comic poem about Dr. Syntax), John Brownlow's *Hans Sloane* (1831), and Dickens's *Oliver Twist* (1837). A partial list of more ephemeral foundling narratives includes (with English Short Title Catalog [ESTC] numbers where I have them): "The Foundling's Lamentation" (London, 175-?); *The Female Foundling: or, Virtue, Truth, and Spirit, Opposing Every Difficulty* (translated from the French) (London: T. Waller, 1751, ESTC T108462); *The History of Benjamin St. Martin, A fortunate foundling, interspersed with curious anecdotes and narratives of the love affairs of some persons in High Life* (London: J. Coote, 1759, ESTC N30530); Henry Lemoine, *The Kentish Curate; or, the history of Lamuel Lyttleton, a foundling* (London: J. Parsons, 1786, ESTC T106128); *Lady Sophia, or, the embarrassed wife. Containing, The History of Mira, the new foundling. A novel. By a Lady.* (London: G. Allen, 1788, ESTC N46408); N. N. *The History of Maria Farrell; or, the beautiful foundling* (London, 1790?, ESTC T224632); E. Miles, *Violet Hill, or Memoirs of a Fair Foundling* (London, 1791, ESTC T226255). Also of note are the two collections of anonymous, miscellaneous, tales, verses, satires, and political observations, collected in *The Foundling Hospital for Wit* and *The New Foundling Hospital for Wit* (see note 34 below for full details). I should note that I limit myself here to characters specifically

denoted as foundlings or whose origins are obscured in ways that make them akin to foundling infants. Were I to add a list of other unassisted, orphaned, or illegitimate children in English literature of the eighteenth and nineteenth centuries, this list would comprise many other novels in the canon.

5. For another view of the social implications of this story, see Toni Bowers's discussion of "narratives of maternal failure" in Augustan England, in *The Politics of Motherhood: British Writing and Culture, 1680–1760* (Cambridge: Cambridge University Press, 1996). Bowers discusses Hogarth's work for the Foundling Hospital on pp. 1–14.

6. My historical account of the London Foundling Hospital is derived from various sources. The most important are those compiled by two of the recording secretaries of the hospital. John Brownlow, himself a foundling, was the recording secretary in the mid-nineteenth century, and wrote a history of the Hospital in 1847, *Memoranda, or Chronicles of the Foundling Hospital including Memoirs of Cpt. Coram.* I will cite throughout from a later edition: *The History and Design of the Foundling Hospital, with a Memoir of the Founder* (London, 1858). R. H. Nichols, the recording secretary in the early to mid-twentieth century, began a history of the hospital that is almost entirely a collage of citations from the records, with very little narrative retelling, that was completed after his death by F. A. Wray: R. H. Nichols and F. A. Wray, *The History of the Foundling Hospital* (London: Oxford University Press, 1935). The definitive modern history of the hospital is Ruth K. McClure's *Coram's Children: The London Foundling Hospital in the Eighteenth Century* (New Haven: Yale University Press, 1981). Other discussions of the hospital include Donna T. Andrew's account of it in *Philanthropy and Police: London Charity in the Eighteenth Century* (Princeton, NJ: Princeton University Press, 1989); Françoise Barret-Ducrocq, *L'amour sous Victoria* (Paris: Plon, 1989); R. B. Outhwaite, "'Objects of Charity': Petitions to the London Foundling Hospital 1768–72," *Eighteenth-Century Studies* 32, no. 4 (1999): 497–510; and Bernd Weisbrod's "How to Become a Good Foundling in Early Victorian London," *Social History* 10, no. 2 (1985): 193–209.

7. Citation of the advertisement posted by the Hospital in 1741, from Brownlow, p. 7.

8. Nichols and Wray mention cases where mothers were cleared of such accusations with the aid of tokens, p. 125.

9. See Andrew, pp. 156–158.

10. Figures from the 1760s are from McClure 1981, pp. 137 and 141. Later figures are from Nichols and Wray, pp. 90, 92, and 94. One exception to this intake policy came as a result of the Hanway Act of 1767, which proposed a scheme whereby infants would be farmed out from parish workhouses to the Foundling Hospital (where they would be more likely to survive), yet their upkeep would still be paid for by the parish. This scheme was not very successful and was finally stopped in 1795 (Nichols and Wray, pp. 65–66; McClure 1981, pp. 144–148).

11. Nichols and Wray note that from 1801, "the illegitimacy of a child. . .

became an almost invariable condition of admission" (92–93).

12. Nichols and Wray cite the change in instructions to petitioners in 1815, p. 96, but also note that a petition from a father, dated 1763, was "unusual" (84). See also McClure 1981, p. 140: "most applications that resulted in admissions [in the 1760s] came from destitute, unmarried women seduced by lovers under a promise of marriage and then deserted."

13. "The most meritorious case, therefore, would be one in which a young woman, having no means of subsistence, except those derived from her own labour, and having no opulent relations, previously to committing the offence bore an irreproachable character, but yielded to artful and long-continued seduction, and an express promise of marriage; whose delivery took place in secret, and whose shame was known to only one or two persons; as, for example the medical attendant and a single relation; and lastly, whose employers or other persons were able and desirous to take her into their service, if enabled again to earn her livelihood by the reception of her child" (Report to Parliament in 1836, cited by Nichols and Wray, p. 99, and by Brownlow, p. 24).

14. My research at the archive is ongoing: of the billet books present in the London Metropolitan Archive (A/FH/A09/001/001 to 200, and A/FH/A09/001/201 to 203), this essay is based on billet books 1–15, 18, 20, 39, 60, 79, 90, 119, 138, 160, 171, 177, 179, 190, 200, and 201. Based on examination of billet books 1 through 15, excluding billet books 9 (Dec 1750 through June 1756) and 15 (June 1753 through July 1756), which are catchall books with gaps in the intake record, written tokens were produced for approximately 42 percent of the total of children admitted from 1741 to 1756. In contrast, although documentation of the foundlings' origins from parishes accompanies most foundlings after 1756, only three unofficial notes are recorded in billet book 160 (1759, during the period of indiscriminate admission), and none are recorded in the last billet book, 200 (1809 to 1811). However, at some point in time it appears that either the governors or the recording secretary collected exemplary tokens (including several from 1756 and 1757, the beginning of indiscriminate admission) in three billet books called books of "strays" in the archives (A/FH/A09/001/201 to 203), so these figures are perhaps hard to state with complete assurance. Nevertheless, the trend away from these "free" verses toward "official" documentation of foundling reception is clear both from the institutional record and from the work of the historians listed in note 6.

15. Nichols and Wray, and McClure 1981, list and describe tokens but refrain from interpreting them as literary texts. Historians who have focused on the petitions (but not the tokens) include Françoise Barret-Ducrocq and R. B. Outhwaite, both of whom use the petitions as first-person accounts of working-class women's lives in the late nineteenth and late eighteenth centuries, respectively. Bernd Weisbrod considers nineteenth-century petitions but does not discuss the tokens.

16. Ovid is cited in London Metropolitan Archive A/FH/A09/001/011/866 (7 December 1751). See discussion of this token in the text. Lines 235–241 of *Solomon on the Vanity of the World* are cited by London Metropolitan Archive

A/FH/A09/001/201/734 (6 April 1751) (Matthew Prior, *The Literary Works of Matthew Prior*, ed. H. Bunker Wright and Monroe K. Spears, vol. 1 [Oxford: The Clarendon Press, 1959], p. 367). McClure 1981 also notes the citation of Prior, p. 85.

17. These discursive tokens, especially those written in verse, may be unique, or at least characteristic, to England. Neither Robin and Walch, nor Meumann, nor Lallemand, mentions poems or notes written from the infant's first-person perspective appearing in France or Germany. None of the notes at the Nuremberg city archive, with the exception of legal documents, says much more than name and date of birth or baptism.

18. See London Metropolitan Archive A/FH/A09/001/009/1596 (8 June 1756).

19. A/FH/A09/001/003/166 (9 December 1743), A/FH/A09/001/009/1589 (1756?), A/FH/A09/001/011/878 (7 December 1751), and A/FH/A09/001/018/1386 (8 May 1756) are examples of embroidered tokens.

20. "My name is John Newman" is London Metropolitan Archive A/FH/A09/001/002/105. Similar tokens include A/FH/A09/001/002/118 and A/FH/A09/001/002/134 (both from 19 February 1742). "Pray use me well. . ." is London Metropolitan Archive A/FH/A09/001/001/038.

21. London Metropolitan Archive A/FH/A09/001/201/12919.

22. See also London Metropolitan Archive A/FH/A09/001/201/12719 (10 May 1759) ("Hard is my lot in deep distress"), which complains, "Sure Nature meant her sacred Laws/Should Men as strong as Women bind . . . ."

23. That mothers in later periods turned to professional writers is something that concerned the hospital's governors. Nichols and Wray cite a case in which they responded to a letter of complaint sent to the *Morning Chronicle* in 1829, in which a mother claimed her written petition had not been accepted, by explaining that use of a pre-printed form was preferred at that time, "to prevent the last shilling of the unfortunate being wrung from them by men who made a Trade of writing Petitions, and to relieve the unsuspecting Mother from the necessity of detailing her misfortunes to those persons, who too frequently had taken the most cruel advantages of disclosures made to them" (Governors' response to a letter of April 30, 1829 to the *Morning Chronicle*, cited by Nichols and Wray, p. 97).

24. The *Heroides* were translated or adapted several times by English authors including George Turberville (1567), Michael Drayton (*England's Heroical Epistles*, 1597), Dryden et al. (1680), and Pope (*Eloisa to Abelard*, 1717). On the Tudor translations/adaptations, see Deborah S. Greenhut, *Feminine Rhetorical Culture: Tudor Adaptations of Ovid's* Heroides (New York: Peter Lang, 1988). Notable analyses of the influence of the *Heroides* upon English epistolary fiction include Robert Adams Day, *Told in Letters* (Ann Arbor, MI: The University of Michigan Press, 1966), pp. 11–13; Janet Gurkin Altman, *Epistolarity: Approaches to a Form* (Columbus, OH: Ohio University Press, 1982), pp. 13–16; and Christina Marsden Gillis, *The Paradox of Privacy* (Gainesville, FL: University of Florida Press, 1984), pp. 126–131. William C.

Dowling discusses the effects of the *Heroides* on eighteenth-century verse in *The Epistolary Moment: The Poetics of the Eighteenth-Century Verse Epistle* (Princeton, NJ: Princeton University Press, 1991), pp. 27–29. In so doing, he relies heavily upon Gillian Beer's analysis of the effects of the rhetorical situation of Ovid's abandoned women upon the Gothic novel in her essay "'Our unnatural No-voice': The Heroic Epistle, Pope, and Women's Gothic," in Leopold Damrosch, ed. *Modern Essays on Eighteenth-Century Literature* (New York: Oxford University Press, 1988), pp. 379–411. Tempting as it might be to compare the tokens I analyze here with the *Heroides*, there are significant formal differences between them and the Ovidian verse epistle, primarily because the Ovidian tradition epitomizes the mode of first-person complaints of abandoned women (and does not couch these complaints in the conceit of infants' words).

25. Other tokens in Latin include A/FH/A09/001/201/1303 (figure 1), London Metropolitan Archive A/FH/A09/001/003/232 (1746), A/FH/A09/001/010/745 (poem 2 in the appendix), A/FH/A09/001/011/863 (7 December 1751).

26. Brownlow, p. 18; Nichols and Wray, pp. 125–126. This may have been the committee that created the billet books of "strays" I mention in note 14, which collect tokens of unusual interest from various periods, out of chronological order.

27. For a literary example of this trope from the Continent, see Goethe's 1775 poem "Vor Gericht," which is written from the first-person perspective of a woman who refuses to name the father of her child. Much as is the case in the English tokens, the woman aligns the child with her "Schatz"—the treasure that comprises her feelings of love, her lover, her child, and her secret. Johann Wolfgang Goethe, "Vor Gericht," *Sämtliche Gedichte*, vol. 1 (Zürich: Artemis-Verlag, 1949), pp. 128–129.

28. See McClure 1981, pp. 108–109; and McClure, "Johnson's Criticism of the Foundling Hospital and its Consequences," *Review of English Studies* 27, no. 105 (1976): 18, on eighteenth-century critiques of the effect the London Foundling Hospital might have on public morality. See also the 1760 doggerel verse "Joyful news to Batchelors and Maids: Being a Song, In Praise of the Fondling Hospital...Shewing how, young Maids may safely take a Leap in the dark with their Sweethearts. . ." (Brit. Lib. 1876.f.1 [166]).

29. Indeed, both Weisbrod and Jenny Bourne Taylor describe this post-1801 process as one of a symbolic "legitimation" (Weisbrod, p. 194; and Taylor, "Nobody's Secret: Illegitimate Inheritance and the Uncertainties of Memory," *Nineteenth-Century Contexts* 21, no. 4 [2000]: 586–587).

30. Outhwaite argues that the petitions from 1763 to 1801 were not as circumscribed by the administrators' expectations but does admit that successful petitions may have been "in accord with the principles adumbrated by the Governors." Outhwaite, p. 499, p. 501. The most striking difference between the petitions from 1760 to 1801 and those submitted after the turn of the century seems to be that married women are no longer eligible petitioners after 1801 (Outhwaite, p. 499). Cf. Nichols and Wray, and McClure 1981, as cited in note 12 above.

31. Brownlow, p. 3.

32. On the cultural impact of the Foundling, in addition to Brownlow, McClure 1976 and 1981, and Nichols and Wray, see Michael Cohen, "Addison, Blake, Coram, and the London Foundling Hospital: Rhetoric as Philanthropy and Art," *The Centennial Review* 31, no. 4 (1990): 540–566. Fielding praised the Foundling Hospital in Number 44 of the *Covent-Garden Journal* (2 June 1752) (*The Covent-Garden Journal and A Plan of the Universal Register-Office*, ed. Bertrand A. Goldgar [Middletown, CT: Wesleyan University Press, 1988], p. 251); his benefactor the Duke of Bedford headed the Foundling's corporation (ibid., p. 251, n. 3).

33. On numerous occasions the texts cited by Nichols and Wray make reference to repeated advertisement of the Hospital's reception procedures. When indiscriminate admission began in 1756, the notes of the General Committee call for advertisement of procedures in the *Daily Advertiser* and *Publick Advertiser* (cited by Nichols and Wray, pp. 51–52). Upon the cessation of indiscriminate admission, Nichols and Wray mention that "public notices were printed and circulated" advertising the change (ibid., 81). In the General Committee minutes of January 10, 1770, an advertisement about the particulars required in petitions is directed to be posted at the hospital's gates (cited by Nichols and Wray, p. 87), and Nichols and Wray close their citation of this document by commenting that "notices as to admission by ballot were thenceforth advertised at stated intervals in the newspapers" (ibid., 87–88).

34. These collections were subtitled "intended for the reception and preservation of such brats of wit and humour, whose parents chuse to drop them." In a recent article, Donald Nichol has resurrected their significance to eighteenth-century political culture. He explains that they were first published by Hanbury Williams, a friend to Henry Fielding, under the pseudonyms "Timothy Silence" and "Samuel Silence" in the 1740s. The conceit was revisited by the radical publisher John Almon in the "New Foundling Hospital for Wit," which was published in several volumes and editions from 1768–1774. Nichol surmises that John Wilkes had a hand in editing the later version. Although Nichol is aware of the Hospital, he seems not to be aware of the practice of leaving tokens at the Foundling: this practice arguably influenced the two collections' titles. (Donald W. Nichol, "The New Foundling Hospital for Wit: From Hanbury Williams to John Wilkes," *Studies in the Literary Imagination* 34, no. 1 [2001]: 101–119.) Fielding did not like the collections, judging from a comment in the *Jacobite's Journal* (*The Jacobite's Journal and Other Writings*, ed. W. B. Coley [Great Britain: Oxford University Press, 1975]), p. 294.

35. The history of this dynamic, and its relevance to the conventions of feminine authorship, has been investigated and described by Catherine Gallagher in chapters on Charlotte Lennox and Frances Burney in *Nobody's Story* (Berkeley: University of California Press, 1994). On the ways epistolary fiction both reveals and conceals the private lives of its characters, see Altman; Gillis; Leo Braudy, "Penetration and Impenetrability in Clarissa," in Leopold Damrosch, ed., *Modern Essays on Eighteenth-Century Literature* (New York:

Oxford University Press, 1988); and, on the political implications of the ways the epistolary mode negotiates publicity and privacy, see Elizabeth Heckendorn Cook, *Epistolary Bodies* (Stanford, CA: Stanford University Press, 1996). Richardson's heroines certainly haunt many of the narratives I discuss here.

36. The story of the origin of Fidelia/Harriet, the foundling heroine of Moore's play, is called a Hieroglyphic in 1.1 by her dodgy benefactor, the rake Belmont (Edward Moore, *The Foundling and the Gamester,* ed. Anthony Amberg [Newark, DE: The University of Delaware Press, 1996]). Of course, according to the dynamic I describe, the appellation applies equally to her person. Moore's play bore striking similarities to Steele's *Conscious Lovers,* which was itself modeled on Terence's *Andria.* "Hieroglyphic" also used to refer to the emblem of a holy mystery in seventeenth-century poetry. See Joseph H. Summers, *George Herbert: His Religion and Art* (Cambridge, MA: Harvard University Press, 1954), chapter VI (cited in *George Herbert and the Seventeenth-Century Religious Poets,* ed. Mario A. Di Cesare [New York: W. W. Norton & Company, 1978], pp. 255–270.)

37. Eliza Haywood, *The Fortunate Foundlings* (New York: Garland Publishing, 1974), p. 1. All subsequent references are to this edition and appear parenthetically in the text.

38. Kirsten T. Saxton argues that *The Fortunate Foundlings* "anticipates *Tom Jones*…with which it shares many innovative narrative strategies" in her introduction to *The Passionate Fictions of Eliza Haywood: Essays on Her Life and Work,* ed. Saxton and Rebecca P. Bocchicchio (Lexington, KY: The University of Kentucky Press, 2000), p. 9. John Richetti, in the same volume, discusses the ways Haywood's texts competed with Fielding's for popularity, and at the same time underlines Fielding's distaste for "romances" ("Histories by Eliza Haywood and Henry Fielding," in Saxton and Bocchicchio, pp. 241, 243–6).

39. Henry Fielding, *Tom Jones,* ed. Sheridan Baker (New York: W. W. Norton & Company, Inc., 1973), p. 29. All subsequent references are to this edition and will appear parenthetically in the text.

40. Homer Obed Brown's description of a narrative principle of "misattribution" in *Tom Jones* could thus be viewed as a pattern of reception, especially given that Allworthy keeps the boy even after Partridge is incorrectly labeled the child's father. Reception implies that misattribution has become a deliberate act, one that overlooks the particular ties of blood kinship in favor of the general ties that link all people. See chapter 3 of Homer Obed Brown, *Institutions of the English Novel from Defoe to Scott* (Philadelphia, PA: University of Pennsylvania Press, 1997), especially pp. 110–115. Brown links the foundling plot in *Tom Jones* to the Jacobite crisis of the 1740s as well. Thus, both this novel and Haywood's are foundling narratives concerned with the legitimacy issues surrounding that crisis.

41. Sheridan Baker's defense of Brigid as the repository of all Fielding's skill in plotting is cogent here. See "Bridget Allworthy: The Creative Pressures of Fielding's Plot," *Papers of the Michigan Academy of Science, Arts, and*

Letters 52 (1967): 345–356.

42. See Brownlow's citation of Burney's memoir of her father (Brownlow, pp. 80–89).

43. See David Paroissen, *The Companion to Oliver Twist* (Edinburgh: Edinburgh University Press, 1992), pp. 39 and 228. *Hans Sloane*'s plot involves tokens, with which Brownlow would only have been too familiar.

44. Evelina calls herself a "cypher" on p. 340 of Fanny Burney, *Evelina* (Oxford: Oxford University Press, 1968). All subsequent references are to this edition and will appear in the text parenthetically. The novel references earlier foundling narratives: the phrase "Author of my being!" in the novel's frontispiece also appears in Haywood's text, and the character John Belmont shares a surname with the rake benefactor in Moore's play.

45. Belmont is struck by the resemblance on 372 and 385. See Susan C. Greenfield's compelling reading of this moment in "'Oh Dear Resemblance of Thy Murdered Mother': Female Authorship in *Evelina*," *Eighteenth-Century Fiction* 3, no. 4 (July 1991): 301–320; and in her revision of this article as chapter 1 of *Mothering Daughters* (Detroit: Wayne State University Press, 2002). Although Greenfield makes a very good case for Caroline's control of Evelina's future from beyond the grave, she shortchanges Villars in his capacities as Evelina's reader and the receiver of Caroline's legacy. Greenfield argues that Villars, motivated by a desire to perpetuate his relationship with Evelina, hinders rather than facilitates the reunion with Belmont by keeping her identity secret for so long. However, although it gives her imposter an opportunity, Evelina's seclusion ensures her virtuous behavior (which within this novel's world is a higher end than swift legitimation). Additionally, by the end of the novel, although Villars's authority over Evelina is superseded by first Belmont's, then Orville's, their emotional bond is intact: the novel closes with her en route to his arms (Burney, p. 406).

46. See Burney, p. 350 for Evelina's nomination of Villars as her "real" parent.

47. Brownlow discovers the resemblance on p. 86 of Charles Dickens's *Oliver Twist* (New York: W. W. Norton & Company, 1993). All subsequent references are to this edition and will appear in the text parenthetically.

48. For a more in-depth discussion of this novel, see Laura Schattschneider, "Mr. Brownlow's Interest in Oliver Twist," *Journal of Victorian Culture* 6, no. 1 (2001): 46–60.

49. See Deidre Shauna Lynch, *The Economy of Character* (Chicago: The University of Chicago Press, 1998), chapter 2, on the ways characters' faces in the mid-eighteenth century become generic.

Marginal Writers and the 'Literary Market': Defining a New Field of Authorship in Eighteenth-Century France

GEOFFREY TURNOVSKY

Scholars of literary culture in eighteenth-century France have long identified the expansion of the Book Trade and commercial publishing, on the one hand, and the establishment of a stable regime of intellectual property rights, on the other, as key developments for the "modernization" of authorship, especially after 1750.[1] These related developments have, in turn, coalesced in many accounts around the concept of the "literary market," invoked as new type of cultural space in which the conditions and possibilities for the most essential transformations in authorial practice were to be found. Roger Chartier situates "les conditions d'une possible indépendance pour les hommes de lettres" within "les contours d'un marché littéraire."[2]

In line with much eighteenth-century cultural historiography, Chartier here puts a positive spin on the "market," depicting it as a field of liberation for *gens de lettres* who discover in it the new economic opportunities and legal prerogatives that will enable them to break with their traditional bonds to courts and patrons in order to adopt "modern" authorial comportments as autonomous, unaligned critics of society. Other accounts, though, have proposed starkly different views of the "market" and its repercussions for writers. In her readings of Diderot and Rousseau, Julia Simon underscores "the alienating effects of the *literary* market," identifying new authorial strategies that were rooted, above all, in a resistance to its "commodification."[3] Similarly, Robert Darnton's influential research into the "low-life" of the Parisian "literary underground" represents the "literary market" as an arena of cruel exploitation, in which writers were sociologically and psychologically transformed by the "rampant capitalism" of the late eighteenth-century Book Trade.[4]

My paper discusses this latter, dystopic representation of commercial publishing and the Book Trade, particularly insofar as such a model of the late eighteenth-century cultural field might shed light on how authorial practices evolved in this period and became "modern." The former, positive image has probably been more prevalent in studies of eighteenth-century literary life, where it draws on a long-standing topos in Enlightenment scholarship of a progression among *gens de lettres* towards greater and greater "independence" and "autonomy." The "market" has thus been viewed as one of the principle institutions through which this liberation took place: the "gradual progress of the writer towards independence," writes John Lough, is a function of the growing feasibility "in the last decades of the *Ancien régime* [. . .] to earn a comfortable living with [the] pen."[5] But the negative image of the "literary market" has undoubtedly offered a more enduring model of how authorship was transformed in its contact with the commercial practices and the values of the Book Trade. The liberating "market" ultimately appears as somewhat of an historical oddity, pertinent mainly to a few decades in which *gens de lettres* might have imagined and desired for themselves greater intellectual freedom, yet continued to have to adapt their literary activities to the exigencies of a patronage system that still determined both realistic possibilities and plausible expectations. By contrast, the image of the "literary market" as a sphere of authorial pain and suffering, in which the personal, aesthetic, and ethical priorities of writers continually and inexorably clashed against the cold, hard calculations of profiteering publishers, suggests a more obvious link with Romanticism and beyond. Darnton implies that the underpaid hacks of the Parisian gutters and garrets were indeed the forebears of the struggling poets later "romanticized" by Balzac.[6] Looking back from the other side of the divide, Pierre Bourdieu sees in this same "société des écrivains et des artistes" an early manifestation of the anti-commercial, anti-bourgeois culture of mid-nineteenth-century Bohemianism, albeit "à une échelle sans doute beaucoup plus restreinte."[7]

A number of questions of precision, though, must be raised regarding such a genealogy, especially insofar as it might appear to be established retrospectively. Indeed, how much does the reference to a cut-throat model of the "literary market," greatly inspired by the nineteenth century, tell us about how the eighteenth-century cultural field was modified by the expansion of the Book Trade and by the growing significance of commercial publishing for the average literary life? Correlatively, how helpful is it to invoke stridently anti-economic authorial postures that appear similarly drawn from the cultural imaginary of Romanticism in the effort to explain how the comportments and strategies of Enlightenment *gens de lettres* were consequently transformed? Or to ask the question yet another way, how analogous are the experiences of Darnton's "poor devils," who "smolder[ed] helplessly and expire[d] down and out in Paris,"[8] to those of, say, Lucien de Rubempré, Balzac's famous protagonist, or of any other Romantic anti-hero who, like Lucien, entered the fray with the loftiest of artistic, cultural, and social aspirations only to be spectacularly crushed by what Georg Lukács called "the capitalist debasement and prostitution of literature itself"?[9]

The language and stock images on which nineteenth-century authors relied to represent their experiences in the various spaces of literary commerce are, in fact, not so prevalent in the writings of Enlightenment-era *gens de lettres*, who, in their discussions of literary life, remained beholden to the vocabulary and sensibilities of the early modern era. Moreover, this latter group of authors inhabited a quite different cultural world, one in which traditional distinctions and aristocratic protectors continued to play dominant roles in the social trajectories of writers. This is not to say that the genealogy is invalid or lacking in relevance. But it does suggest the need for a more nuanced, careful account of how certain types of authorial practice emerged in the second part of the eighteenth century—those, in particular, that seem impelled by the growth of the Book Trade—which, in hindsight, appear to point forward to some of the most essential characteristics of "modern" authorship. How precisely did eighteenth-century *gens de lettres*, whose desires, anxieties, and expectations had been shaped by the institutions and customs of Old Regime literary culture, conceptualize a new authorial space that was defined and regulated by the commercial interests of entrepreneurs, and in which new forms of authorship might be undertaken, in particular, ones that hinged on a vilification of and resistance to those interests, as well as on the formulation of other "purer" or "artistic" motives, which were understood and articulated in opposition to them?

This paper outlines a more specific historical characterization of the "literary market" as a model for better understanding how certain eighteenth-century authors came to adopt "modern" anti-commercial postures. It does so, first, through a subjective approach that explores the "market" not so much as an external reality that was defined by concrete, objective conditions—the rising prices paid for manuscripts, the defense of intellectual property rights, or negatively, the underpayment of writers and the pervasiveness of counterfeiting—but as a product of the perception of an external reality by *gens de lettres* who began to discern in its opportunities and pitfalls decisive factors for their own careers. Studies of eighteenth-century cultural practices have generally presumed the "market" to be more or less the same thing as the "Book Trade." As a result, its effects on the "modernization" of authorship have been sought primarily in the changing variables of the commercial publishing business; above all, of course, in the rising income of authors seeking to publish and in the legal protection of their literary property rights, objective facts that have then tended to monopolize critical attention on this question.[10]

I would suggest, though, that the "literary market" is not simply the "Book Trade" or the sector of "commercial publishing"; rather, it is the Book Trade or commercial publishing as these were conceived by *gens de lettres* to constitute a cultural field in which they might seek to establish particular identities as authors and build for themselves literary lives. In other words, the Book Trade becomes the "literary market" only once aspiring writers have invested its positive and negative possibilities with a specific significance for their *authorial* selves. Thus, writers do not discover the "market" merely by selling their manuscripts to *libraires*. Rather, they envision the "market" to the extent that their decisions to sell their works are driven by the expectation that success (or failure) in the publishing sphere would have a concrete impact on their cultural status as Authors. By the same token, the "literary market" is more than an objectively cut-throat commercial arena in which writers are often underpaid and mistreated by greedy publishers. Instead, I would contend that the "market," as a modern field of authorship, has more to do with the conceptualization and representation of the mistreatment of writers by publishers as a distinct "fact of literary life," which, as "exploitation" or "commodification," is then increasingly identified and decried as a grave moral affront against Authors and Literature, as well as that against which Authors seek essentially to define themselves socially and culturally.

This conceptual approach to the "market" can, I hope, help to illuminate some of the specific experiences of eighteenth-century *gens de lettres* before the new possibilities of the Book Trade, along with the specific effects that these experiences had on their views, strategies, and comportments. Indeed, one crucial characteristic of this authorial field immediately comes into focus, which is that the Enlightenment "literary market" was imagined and represented by writers as a relative and derivative space, one that was perceived to exist only on the outer fringes of the cultural world of the Old

Regime. In this respect, it was quite distinct from the "market" of the nineteenth century, engaged by poets, novelists, and journalists as the dominant field in which—or against which—to construct a career in letters. This essay will argue that the defining negativity of the eighteenth-century "literary market," as a transformative realm of authorial suffering for *littérateurs*, lay precisely in the sense of cultural exile and exteriority, rather than of economic injustice and exploitation, that was experienced by writers who found themselves toiling in the marginal reaches of the Book Trade. These writers reacted against their lot, but not simply by railing bitterly against greedy publishers; for they launched a more profound attack against the Old Regime cultural establishment that had expelled them, in the course of which they redefined the traditional spaces of literary practice—the courts, academies, and salons from which they had been excluded—as corrupt and debased. In so doing, they also reconceptualized their own ex-centric positions in the literary field as ones, by contrast, of moral "purity" and cultural superiority, positions that were, in turn, buttressed rather than undermined by abuse at the hands of publishers. The "literary market" emerged in the aspirations of these writers as an authorial space in which they could not only project their exclusion, but also publish an elevating, and ultimately even a liberating indifference to this "exploitation."

"Il ne vit que de ses ouvrages . . .": The Book Trade and Exteriority

Enlightenment historiography has consistently evoked the "literary market" in a pointed contrast with the established institutions and spaces in which literary life in eighteenth-century France was played out. One of the best-known and most emphatic examples of this pattern is Darnton's research on the "literary underground," in which writing for the Book Trade is rendered through a stark opposition to any cultural activity performed within the more traditional framework of academic posts or sinecurial jobs, and sponsored by state or aristocratic patronage.[11] In a similar vein, Daniel Roche names the "literary market" as one of "deux systèmes de rémunération," coexisting with the institution of "patronage perpétué et la rétribution indirecte," but fundamentally differing in its logic and operation.[12] Henri-Jean Martin, too, divides the eighteenth-century literary world into two divergent sectors: on the one hand, "un patronage perpétué, fondé sur la rétribution indirecte, en places et recommendations, de services et mérites de plumes," and on the other, "un marché littéraire, régi par les lois de l'offre et de la demande, qui considère les textes aussi comme des marchandises et les prise en fonction de leur possible débit."[13]

By this antithesis, Roche and Martin represent the "literary market" as essentially an alternative for eighteenth-century *gens de lettres* who thought to look elsewhere than to the traditional institutions for their livelihood. In fact, it is not so obvious that this latter group actually shared the historians' vision of the Old Regime Book Trade as a separate and distinct "system of remuneration." They did, however, perceive economic dependence on publishing primarily as a social condition that was defined more by the writer's distance from the centers of eighteenth-century literary life than by any of the experiences of commercial publishing in and of themselves. Seen as a field in which to build a literary career, the Book Trade was a secondary and marginal space rather than a fully autonomous professional field, one in which the presence of the writer implied, first and foremost, his or her absence and exclusion from more significant cultural *milieux*.

For evidence of this, we might briefly look into some of the files on active *gens de lettres* that were compiled between 1748 and 1753 by Joseph d'Hémery, official inspector of the Book Trade, and which are now housed in the *departement des manuscrits* of the Bibliothèque nationale.[14] Among the numerous details that he recorded in the dossiers, along with age, height and current address, d'Hémery notes for certain, though not all, of his authors where and how they made their livings. Most did so, of course, in the standard ways, through positions at court, in the Church, in aristocratic households, or in some part of the public sector, many as lawyers. A quite small number, however, perhaps not more than 8 or 10 writers, are observed by the inspector to support themselves through the commercial publication of their works, often by some variant on the expression "vivre de."[15] Thus, in one representative case, a 28 year-old lawyer from Senlis named Gaillard, "à présent, [. . .] vit de ses ouvrages."[16]

Straightforward as this might sound, though, one does not "live off one's works" in d'Hémery's records as a simple matter of personal choice. Rather, it is invariably the end result of an unlucky social trajectory by which the author has fallen out of more established positions, or been locked out of them from the beginning. Gaillard "lives off his works" only after having been "sous Bibliothequaire au College de quatre nations, place de peu de consequence, et qu'il a quitté pour etre gouverneur d'enfans ou M. de Voltaire l'avoit placé, il n'y a resté que six mois." The Norman author de la Barre "a été revetu d'une charge de Controlleur de l'extraordinaire des guerres, qu'il a été obligé de vendre par des malheurs, de façon qu'il est presentement dans une misere affreuse." As a result, "n'ayant aucune ressource, il s'est adonné entierement à La Billiot [his bookseller-publisher], qui le fait vivre, et pour laquelle il fait de tems en tems quelques petits ouvrages que La Billiot vend."[17] And in his dossier on the two brothers Parfaict, "gentilshommes" who "n'ont point de bien," d'Hémery documents that the would-be novelists and playwrights "ne vivent que de leurs ouvrages," employing in this case the restrictive French construction "ne . . . que" to bolster an image of living off one's published works as a condition that was, in essence, a last desperate resort: they do not live, except off their works.[18]

D'Hémery's evocations of writing for the Book Trade consistently reveal a professional field seen to absorb *gens de lettres* only once they did not have something more substantial on which to rely in a more established place—a respectable job in an aristocratic household or the government, a pension, or an honorary post. As a result, in the contemporary perception of the inspector, the Book Trade became a plausible authorial field only insofar as it was presumed to be a realm of failure and rejection. Such a depiction must, of course, be clearly differentiated from a more modern notion of writing for the commercial press as, for example, "selling out" for economic gain or immediate renown. The "literary market" of the eighteenth century seemingly offered no benefit at all to the aspiring author other than that of brute survival in the cultural field when all other possibilities had fallen through.

Does this "survivalist" image of commercial publishing then imply that the "market," as a field of authorship, was inevitably experienced by writers as a sphere of crushing poverty in which they were abused and exploited by powerful *libraires* who were only too pleased to take advantage of their desperation? One might initially be inclined to answer "yes." Again, in the files of d'Hémery, we find the dossier of François-Vincent Toussaint, "avocat au Parlement qui n'exerce point," and thus a writer who grew somewhat dependent on the sale of his manuscripts: "Il travaille beaucoup pour les Libraires, ce qui fait qu'il n'est pas trop a son aise," noted the inspector.[19] And on the whole, it is by no means difficult to find in eighteenth-century France statements to the effect that *gens de lettres* did not live particularly well any reliance on income earned through the publication of their works. "Quand un livre réussit, c'est le libraire qui met l'argent dans sa poche," wrote Louis-Sébastien Mercier, who about authors remarked: "[d]e leur vivant, on les laisse dans l'indigence."[20] The *Mémoires secrets* recorded the appearance in 1769 of a vitriolic pamphlet that portrayed those who cultivate letters, "avec non moins de vérité que d'énergie, gémissant sous le joug des libraires, travaillant en vils esclaves au champ fécond de la littérature, tandis que ces maîtres durs recueillent tout le fruit de leurs sueurs, et vivent à leurs dépens dans l'abondance et dans le luxe."[21]

Yet, too quick an affirmative answer risks oversimplifying the matter by assuming that authorial poverty was the self-evident result of authorial dependence on the Book Trade when the causal relationship may, in fact, have been the reverse: a prior poverty was the cause rather than the effect of the writer's dependence on the sales of manuscripts. Moreover, there is ample reason to be cautious in generalizing about real-life conditions in the Book Trade based on a tendency in late eighteenth-century rhetoric on *gens de lettres* and *libraires* to depict the latter as the "maîtres durs" of the former. D'Hémery's papers identify another writer who "vend lui-même [ses ouvrages] et n'a que cela pour vivre."[22] The deprecating "ne . . . que" might, however, be misleading in this case for the writer in question is the abbé de la Porte who would become notorious for his widely disparaged, though extremely profitable publishing ventures. Grimm's *Correspondance littéraire* estimated in 1769 that de la Porte earned about 5–6000 livres a year as the producer of such varied Book Trade ephemera as compilations, dictionaries, almanacs, and travel journals.[23] Seven years later, Pidansat de Mairobert upped that figure to 10–12000 livres.[24] These sums were easily competitive with the most generous pensions that writers could hope to obtain from the State or other non-commercial sources.[25]

To be sure, d'Hémery's report was from twenty years earlier, and it is obviously the case that de la Porte, in his mid-thirties and having recently quit the Jesuits to make a life for himself in letters, was faring less remarkably well in the early years of his career. Indeed, according to Pidansat de Mairobert, the abbé had left the *Compagnie* "nud comme un ver."[26] Still, it is hard to dismiss the striking disparity between the unmistakably positive shape of his career in the "literary market" and the essentially negative formulation of the abbé's dependence on income from the Book Trade in the file of d'Hémery: "il n'a que cela pour vivre." For one thing, de la Porte's success came relatively quickly. He might have entered the fray with nothing at all, but he apparently did not spend too many years toiling for pittance as the "vil esclave" of publishers. About the time that the inspector was recording his impressions around 1749 or 1750, de la Porte enjoyed a modest breakthrough with his first work of criticism, the *Voyage au séjour des ombres*, published in 1749, with subsequent re-editions in 1751 and 1753, and mentioned by d'Hémery himself in the dossier.[27] For another, even at the height of his commercial success, de la Porte continued to be widely scorned as a literary non-entity, who inhabited only the outer fringes of the Old Regime cultural universe: "L'abbé de la Porte est mort, il y a quelque temps, sans qu'on fît beaucoup plus d'attention à sa mort qu'on n'en avait fait à sa vie," wrote La Harpe in 1780. "C'est pourtant un homme qui a fait imprimer quantité de livres."[28]

De la Porte's file calls for more precision in defining the eighteenth-century Book Trade as an authorial field. It calls, in my view, for a shift in emphasis away from images of indigence and "exploitation," assumed in and of themselves to characterize the condition of writing for commercial publication, and onto the evolving expectations of writers for whom the Book Trade was less about distinct economic outcomes—be they negative or, as have argued Elizabeth Eisenstein and Rémy Saisselin, actually improving for *gens de lettres* in this period[29]— than about exteriority with respect to the cultural order of the traditional field. Dependence on the Book Trade placed the writer in an authorial space defined not primarily by either financial self-sufficiency or exploitation, but instead by a lack of qualitative distinction, by a void of symbolic rather than of economic richness. "Ne vivant que de ses ouvrages," the writer fell out of the important networks, and therefore abandoned all hope of finding prestige, renown, or, as a respectable *philosophe* like Charles Duclos would call it, *considération*.[30] In this respect, the "market," as a field of authorship, was an inevitably barren space where pensions were pointedly not to be acquired; sinecurial posts not to be secured; and important contacts not to be made. Conversely, the acquisition of a pension or a position instantaneously drew the writer back into the fold of meaningful Old Regime cultural practices where he or she could once again "appartient a d'honnetes gens," as in the case of de la Barre, whose story ends with his happy reintegration, recorded a year later by d'Hémery: "M. Bouyer lui a fait avoir une petite commission a la Gazette de France chez M. des Meslée."[31]

The question of the rise of the "market" as a literary institution in which *gens de lettres* "modernized" their comportments must, therefore, be placed not only in the context of changing economic or demographic conditions in the cultural field, but also in that of changing attitudes towards this exteriority. The evolution of authorial practices was about more than experiencing and reacting to rising prices, deteriorating conditions, or "overpopulation."[32] It was also about the growing willingness of writers to construct authorial identities that were based on representations of themselves as, precisely, excluded and marginal, and hence, as pitifully dependant on earnings from manuscript sales. D'Hémery's files show the Book Trade as a space in which *gens de lettres* essentially lost their identities, becoming visible in the cultural sphere only as unimportant nobodies who lacked the pensions, connections, or positions needed to establish and legitimize themselves. These writers adopted new kinds of attitudes and strategies, I would suggest, not only in their anger and bitterness at their irrelevance, but more significantly, in their efforts to transform this loss of public identity into the basis of a new kind of authorial self-representation that was built upon images of themselves as failures, rejected by the primary institutions in which Old Regime literary activity found its distinction and value. Studies of how the comportments of *gens de lettres* were transformed in their contacts with the Book Trade, influenced by the angry denunciations of the writers themselves, have tended to emphasize the effects of a purely negative state. But perhaps more essential to the history of authorship is how that negative state came to be imagined and valorized in and through a *positive* exercise of identity construction.[33]

"Je vivrai dans l'oubli": Social Rebuff and Authorship

It did so, I would argue, as part of a new model of authorship that specifically represented itself against traditionally sociable or courtly models, which, in turn, for their emphasis on pleasing elites, were disparaged as vacuous, frivolous, and false. By contrast, the new authorial posture was rooted in an image of the writer as sincere, serious, and moral, qualities assumed both to be inimical to the refined and contrived sociability of *le monde*—in a "Dissertation sur la littérature" with which he prefaced an early poem on "Le Génie, Le Goût et l'Esprit," Mercier lamented that "tout ouvrage qui paroît sérieux, est aussitôt rejetté" by the "Monde littéraire"[34] —and to exclude any graceful social capacities on the part of the writer. In an account in the *Tableau de Paris* of a meeting with Crébillon *fils* as the latter performs his functions as Royal Censor, Mercier develops a representation of authorship that is pointedly opposed to, rather than based on, any mastery of the codes of civility.[35] Invited to stay "jusqu'à [. . .] l'heure que les poètes arrivent pour [lui] apporter leurs manuscrits," Mercier describes two visits. The first by an author who is "vif et sémillant; il se présente avec assez de grâce, parle de même; [. . .] La conversation s'engage, et notre auteur dit des choses spirituelles." His book? Crébillon unexpectedly predicts: "il parle avec facilité; il a de l'esprit. Voulez-vous gager avec moi que son ouvrage n'a ni rime ni raison?" Soon afterwards, the second author arrives:

> il ne sait ni entrer, ni parler, ni s'asseoir; il est gauche, et tout d'une pièce; il manque de renverser une petite table où était le déjeuner de son censeur. C'est un opéra de le faire asseoir; il recule à chaque instance; enfin il est assis; il veut parler, et il bégaie; il répond mal à ce qu'on dit. Après avoir regardé pendant six minutes sa poche gonflée de son manuscrit, il le tire gauchement, laisse tomber sa canne et son chapeau en le présentant, cherche de l'oeil son parasol, comme si on le lui avait volé, blesse ma jambe du bout de son épée [. . .].

Mercier assumes that his writing would reflect his graceless, unpleasing manner: "Quel loudard! m'écriai-je; et cela écrit!" But he is quite wrong: "Voulez-vous gager avec moi que son oeuvre n'est pas sans mérite?" replies Crébillon, defying Mercier's typically Old Regime presupposition that literary expression was, at its core, an extension onto paper of social comportment.[36]

To the contrary, meritorious literary production was now defined in opposition to the breezy interaction of elite society, in an emerging conceptualization of authorship that rested on a two-fold representational strategy. On the one hand, the writer cultivated an image of self as too earnest, too preoccupied, and too passionate to participate capably in *le monde*. In his *Mémoires*, Jacques-Pierre Brissot offers a portrait of himself in his early years through a contrast with his friend and "concitoyen Guillard," a poet "répandu dans les sociétés les plus brillantes."[37] Speaking to Brissot of the "agréments de la vie d'un homme de lettres," Guillard proposes to introduce the former into these "sociétés," particularly that of the playwright Favart, "chez qui l'on trouvait beaucoup de poètes et d'auteurs." But Brissot's conscientiousness precludes him from doing anything but refuse: "Je n'allai là et dans d'autres réunions de ce genre que très rarement, bien déterminé de me consacrer à la solitude, d'y poursuivre mes études, et de ne paraître en public que lorsque j'aurais un amas considérable de connaissances et de travaux." Recalling those moments when Guillard, "rentrant de ses petits soupers, à une heure du matin, me trouvait souvent mon dictionnaire grec à la main," the future revolutionary highlights his inherent unsuitability, precisely *because* he is an *homme de lettres*, for life in elite society. Similarly, Rousseau's autobiographical writings develop an image of the author in which not simply his lack of interest, but his repeated failures to adopt the language and behavior necessary to be accepted in "sociétés" become integral, defining characteristics, signaling his difference, his transcendence, and his extraordinary ardor, indeed exactly those qualities that would distinguish him as an author, though pointedly not as a member of salon society: "Si peu maître de mon esprit seul avec moi-même, qu'on juge de ce que je dois être dans la conversation" he writes in the *Confessions*, "[. . .] Je ne sais si ceci tient à ma mortelle aversion pour tout assujetissement; mais c'est assez qu'il faille que je parle pour que je dise une sottise infailliblement."[38]

On the other hand, the traditional, sociable centers of cultural activity were reconceptualized as too frivolous, too hermetic, and too depraved to accept and integrate this new type of "serious" and "moral" author. The seventeenth century had portayed the "court" as a site of correct and reasoned judgment in all matters literary and linguistic; Vaugelas identified the "bon usage" of the French language with "la façon de parler de la plus saine partie de la cour."[39] Mercier, however, reimagined the court as an institution that reflected outmoded and misguided opinion: "On casse les jugements de la Cour; on dit nettement, elle n'y entend rien, elle n'a point d'idées là-dessus, elle ne saurait en avoir."[40] He did the same for government pensions: "Les pensions que le gouvernement accorde aux *gens de lettres* ne se donnent [pas . . .] à ceux qui ont le plus utilement travaillé. Les plus souples, les plus intrigants, les plus importuns, enlèvent ce que d'autres se contentent d'avoir mérité au fond de leur cabinet"; as well as for the *Académie française*: "Ce goût exclusif qu'elle s'arroge est d'ailleurs bien fait pour éveiller le ridicule."[41] Principally responsible for both the social identification and maintenance of *gens de lettres*, these dominant Old Regime cultural bodies shared, in Mercier's rendering of literary life, a systematic incapacity to discern those worthy of preeminent cultural status.[42]

In a pamphlet seeking to discourage "la Jeunesse" from choosing a career in letters, the lawyer Simon-Nicolas-Henri Linguet extended a view of the traditional spheres of cultural success as irremediably debased, casting doubt, like Mercier, on the possibility that "le mérite seul suffise" to acquire a reputation there.[43] Reputations were dependent on the "Public," which had been envisioned since the seventeenth century as an elite gathering of the most refined, competent judges of poetic expression:

> Je viens, pour commencer entre nous ce beau noeud,
> Vous montrer un sonnet que j'ai fait depuis peu,
> Et savoir s'il est bon qu'au public je l'expose,

Oronte asked Alceste, seeking the misanthrope's preliminary critique before submitting his poem to the public's trenchant and unquestionably reasonable appraisal.[44] Linguet recast this public as a "prodigieuse foule de gens oisifs qui soulagent leur ennui par des conversations frivoles [. . .]. Leur désoeuvrement les rend assez propres à devenir les trompettes de la renommée." To be recognized and celebrated, "il faut les faire sonner en bien ou en mal. C'est ce fracas, cet éclat flatteur, qui met le sceau aux réputations." Thus one cannot simply write well. Rather, "[l]'assiduité à faire sa cour à je ne sais quelles femmes, à je ne sais quels hommes, la patience à souffrir leurs rebuts, leurs plaisanteries, voilà les degrés de la gloire." An author who has attained some visibility in the established centers of literary life has, according to Linguet, "presque toujours commencé par être le jouet des sociétés mêmes qui l'ont ensuite le plus prôné. [. . .] Qui croirait pourtant que ces singeries boufonnes deviennent le fondement solide d'une réputation?"[45]

This radical devalorization of the traditional signs of cultural distinction

—pensions, academic posts, or reputations at court and in *le monde*— had the counter-effect of valorizing the invisibility, ex-centricity, exclusion, and the consequent suffering of the writer, assertions of which became essential, self-defining gestures: "Et moi, moi, malheureux! j'aurai bien travailler,/ Je vivrai dans l'oubli," wrote Nicolas Gilbert, one of several late Enlightenment poets who, in their authorial anguish, have been portrayed as early precursors to Romanticism.[46] "Pourquoi mettre au jour un Ouvrage rejetté par l'Académie Française?" he asked in the first line of the preface to his 1772 poem "Le Génie aux prises avec la fortune," aggressively positioning himself from the onset as an afflicted outsider.[47] In 1767, having had his tragedy, *Virginie*, rejected by the *Comédie française*, Mercier went against convention and published it anyway, asking in the *Avertissement au lecteur*, "si cette pièce est bonne, pourquoi n'a-t-elle pas été représentée; et si elle est mauvaise, pourquoi est-elle imprimée?"[48] Such vexatious questions were not merely indictments of the difficulties endured by a certain population of unestablished *gens de lettres*—the "intellectual proletariat" evoked by Darnton, Martin, Roche, and others[49]—, but were acts of authorial self-representation, by which writers constructed personae in a stark opposition to the dominant cultural spaces, simultaneously reconfigured as corrupt, frivolous, and misguided. The lack of a pension, a position, or any visibility in Society—all marks, that is, of non-inclusion, non-distinction, and as a result, the stigmata of a specific kind of authorial pain—was thus revalorized as a sign of the seriousness, morality, and honorability of the *littérateur*, qualities that were then themselves reinvented as fundamental, defining attributes of an Author. "La pauvreté de l'homme de lettres," wrote Mercier, "est à coup sûr un titre de vertu, et preuve du moins qu'il n'a jamais avili ni sa personne, ni sa plume. Ceux qui ont sollicité et obtenu des pensions, n'en peuvent pas dire autant devant leur conscience."[50] For Linguet, the merit that is "réduit à attendre du tems une considération tardive, dont il est bien rare que la mort le laisse jouir" is "le mérite réel, dont la sombre fierté a éloigné les protecteurs, et [. . . n'a] pu flatter par des complaisances."[51]

Moreover, this new image of the Author was caught in a spiraling symbolic logic: the more debased the established cultural spaces were made out to be, the more undistinguished and decentralized writers became, and thus, the more profound their anguish. For refusing the "singeries bouffones" required for "considération" in elite society, the lot of *gens de lettres* was, according to Linguet, "une obscurité pénible."[52] And the more manifest the suffering of obscure writers in such a hostile context, the more clearly ardent, sincere, and virtuous they had to be, and hence, the more they became recognizable, unmistakably, as Authors. Indeed, if an eighteenth-century writer such as Nicolas Gilbert can be considered an early Romantic, it would have to be in the degree to which he invested himself, precisely as an Author, in a representational intensification of his own marginality vis-à-vis the governing cultural spaces, to the point where the evocation of the poet's own death could become, in a sense, the most quintessentially authorial act insofar as it figured at a basic level this defining excruciating exteriority:

> Vous ne me verrez plus! Mon dernier jour s'avance,
> Mes yeux se fermeront sous un ciel inhumain.
> Amis!. . . vous me fuyez?. . . cruels! je vous implore,
> Rendez-moi ces pinceaux échappés de ma main. . . .
> Je meurs . . . ce que je sens, je veux le peindre encore.[53]

Needless to say, the rising authorial stakes of such *gens de lettres* as Gilbert, Linguet, Mercier, Rousseau, and Brissot in images of themselves as "suffering outsiders," and of the dominant spaces of cultural activity as hermetic, unjust, and corrupt, raise significant questions about the possibility of deducing from their portrayals of the Enlightenment cultural sphere the real-life conditions that prevailed there, particularly for these outsiders.[54]

Inventing the Eighteenth-Century "Literary Market"

If a concept such as the "literary market" can be useful for understanding how these writers of the eighteenth century, in an acute sense of their own exclusion, evolved in the direction of "les générations modernes,"[55] it is not only for giving a name to the "alternative" system in which they were able to construct new kinds of literary identities. It is also for allowing some precision in defining the decisive, but far from obvious role of the Book Trade in their literary lives. Dependence on income from publishing was an integral aspect of their images as authors, though not so much as the outcome of a necessarily and self-evidently catastrophic socio-economic scenario. Instead, this dependence had a more important symbolic function as being what essentially marked these writers as excluded, and consequently, as "pure" and untainted by such base delegitimizing priorities as their own social ascension in *le monde*.

Indeed, insofar as the public repudiation of social aspiration, as a signal of legitimacy, increasingly came to identify the writer as an Author, the "literary market" was, to this extent, reinvented as an authorial field, that is, as a space into which the writer entered with the desire and expectation of constructing a legitimate literary self. Moreover, it was in this respect, rather than as a source of revenues, that the "market" could become a field of authorial "liberation" and "independence," in which writers could repudiate patronage and its humiliations. Lough associates the "independence" of Enlightenment *gens de lettres* with the rising income that they could earn by selling their manuscripts to publishers; yet, there is actually little in their writings to indicate that eighteenth-century *littérateurs* themselves made the same connection. In the opening pages of his *Mémoires*, Brissot asserts that: "Voulant vivre indépendant je ne me reposais que sur ma plume," transforming d'Hémery's nullifying "ne . . . que" now into a declaration of his intellectual freedom and moral dedication.[56] But Brissot scarcely saw this independence to lie in the kind of social and economic autonomy that a figure such as Voltaire, with his tremendous affluence, would be seen to incarnate. On the contrary, self-professed self-supporting writers like Brissot almost invariably distinguished their own circumstances from those of the wealthy *philosophes* of the previous generation, who had initially grounded their cultural activities in strong and novel conceptions of themselves as intellectually "liberated": "Helvétius et Montesquieu étaient riches," wrote Brissot just prior to confessing his own chosen path to independence via the Book Trade, "et ne retiraient aucun livre de leurs importantes productions. Il leur était facile de prendre le temps nécessaire pour les rendre parfaits."[57] Mercier similarly observed: "Quelle différence de cultiver les lettres, comme M. de Voltaire, avec cent mille livres de rentes [. . .], ou d'avoir à combattre les plus pressants besoins et de retomber sur ses propres infortunes, lorsqu'on devrait jouir d'un esprit libre, dégagé de toute inquiétude, pour mieux s'abandonner, et tout entier, à la méditation de son art!"[58] Gilbert, too, rendered his misery in a stark contrast with the prosperous, and as a result, unallied and critical *homme de génie*,

> Qui, placé dans l'aisance et cultivant les arts,
> N'a plus besoin d'appui pour fixer nos regards!
> Il vole à tire-d'aile au Temple de Mémoire:
> Semblables aux beautés qui vont baissant les yeux
> A l'aspect d'un soleil brûlant et radieux,
> Les grands le craindront tous, éblouis de sa gloire.[59]

Considered as a specifically authorial strategy, the decision to situate oneself in the "literary market" did not ultimately have much to do with the desire to make money in order to become materially self-sufficient, no more than the simple desire to become rich through the publication of works could constitute a viable authorial strategy, as the career of an abbé de la Porte, notoriously uninterested in any of the cultural distinctions of Authorship, shows: "celui-ci n'élève pas en effet ses prétentions si haut. Il n'est ni homme à bonnes fortunes, ni curieux de renommée. Il vise au solide, à amasser de l'argent. [. . .] en un mot, c'est un fripier de la littérature dans toute la valeur du terme," wrote Pidansat de Mairobert.[60] Instead, what we retrospectively identify as the "literary market" existed for eighteenth-century writers, first and foremost, as a space in which they could construct themselves as independent, and thus "pure," in and through images of themselves as living off the commercial sales of their works. Brissot's intellectual autonomy rested not on his economic self-sufficiency. More exactly, it consisted in an authorial *prise de position* by which the writer, in his self-representations, proclaimed his dependence on the Book Trade as a strategy for clearly positioning himself externally to the Old Regime cultural field, thereby laying claim to his transcendence as an Author whose pronouncements on society, morality, and politics would, by this very distance from the corrupt spaces of traditional literary life, resonate with legitimacy and seriousness.[61]

Furthermore, not only was this dependence hardly a socially, legally, or economically liberating state, but to the contrary, the writer had a clear stake in intensifying the dependence, rendering it as severely and as negatively as possible. This enhanced the image that the writer sought to project. Brissot thus elaborates on his own experience of "vivre indépendent," so unlike that of, say, Montesquieu: "Cependant aucun auteur, je crois, n'a eu pour ses intérêts privés l'abandon que j'ai témoigné pour les miens. Je vendais à vil prix, à peine étais-je payé de la moitié, et le plus souvent par des arrangements qui achevèrent de me ruiner."[62] His *Mémoires* are scattered with recurrent allusions to his bad fortunes in the Book Trade, as well as to the terrible conditions that, he claims, were imposed on him by his publishers; about some brochures that he had composed in the early stages of his career: "Je m'adressai à un libraire qui me promit, et ne tint rien, qui vendait et gardait tout."[63] In 1781, he undertook a 10-volume compilation entitled *Bibliothèque philosophique des lois criminelles*, for which his *libraire* paid him 1000 livres: "mais les frais d'impression absorbèrent les deux tiers, et l'autre ne me fut pas payé."[64] Such references bolstered rather than undermined his cultural status as Author, underscoring not his lack of talent or deservedness, but the opposite, his disinterest and virtue, moral qualities that would then be laid by Brissot as the cornerstones of his autonomous authorial self: "J'ai toujours pris trop d'insouciance sur mes intérêts pour n'avoir pas été facilement trompé par les libraires."[65]

Brissot thus found both autonomy and exploitation in the Book Trade.

Indeed, the rethinking that transformed the Book Trade into a sphere of exploitation of writers was exactly the same reconceptualization that also allowed this commercial and artisanal sector to become, in the expectations of an ambitious and frustrated *homme de lettres* like Brissot, a field of moral and intellectual independence. In this contradiction, I would argue, lay the essence and the specificity of the Enlightenment "literary market," which existed not as an objective, pre-constituted professional field in which marginal writers, in particular, unsupported by more respectable means, could nonetheless eke out a living. Rather, the "literary market" was envisioned by such symbolically poor *gens de lettres* as a new cultural space in which new types of authorial identities might be constructed. These identities would be valorized and enriched precisely by the profound dearth of traditional distinction that, in eighteenth-century France, any dependence on revenues from the Book Trade was perceived to signify.

N O T E S

1. Georges d'Avenel and Maurice Pellisson emphasized the importance of manuscript sales and author/publisher transactions in their early studies of Enlightenment writers; see d'Avenel, "Les riches depuis sept cents ans: VIII Honoraires des Gens de Lettres," *Revue des deux mondes* 48 (Nov. 15, 1908): 335–367; and Pellisson, *Les hommes de lettres au XVIIIe siècle* [1911] (Geneva: Slatkine Reprints, 1970), 64–75. Michel Foucault's 1969 essay, "Qu'est-ce qu'un auteur?" (included in *Dits et Écrits*, 4 vols. [Paris: Gallimard, 1994], 1:789–821) has, of course, been extremely influential in situating the modern concept of "author" within the intellectual context of eighteenth-century debates about the proprietorship of literary works. See, in particular, Martha Woodmansee, "The Genius and the Copyright: Economic and Legal Conditions of the Emergence of the 'Author,'" *Eighteenth-Century Studies* 17,4 (1984): 425–448, which focuses on the German context; and Carla Hesse, "Enlightenment Epistemology and the Laws of Authorship in Revolutionary France, 1777–1793," *Representations* 30 (Spring 1990): 109–137.

2. Roger Chartier, *Les Origines culturelles de la révolution française* (Paris: Seuil, 1990), 77.

3. Julia Simon, "The Public Sphere, Alienation, and Commodification: Rousseau's Autobiographical Writings" and "The Public/Private Dialectic Revisited: Diderot's Art Criticism," in *Mass Enlightenment: Critical Studies in Rousseau and Diderot* (Albany, NY: State University of New York Press, 1995), 72–84, 147–168.

4. Robert Darnton, *The Literary Underground of the Old Regime*, (Cambridge, MA: Harvard University Press, 1982), 198; see also "The High

Enlightenment and the Low-Life of Literature in Pre-Revolutionary France," *Past and Present* 51 (May 1971): 81–115, and "The Life of a 'Poor Devil' in the Republic of Letters," in Jean Macary, ed., *Essays on the Age of Enlightenment in Honor of Ira O. Wade* (Geneva: Droz, 1977), 39–92.

5. John Lough, *Writer and Public in France from the Middle Ages to the Present Day* (Oxford: Clarendon Press, 1978), 209; and *An Introduction to Eighteenth-Century France* (London: Longmans, 1960), 231.

6. Darnton, *The Literary Underground*, 27.

7. Pierre Bourdieu, *Les règles de l'art: génèse et structure du champ littéraire* (Paris: Seuil, 1992), 86.

8. Darnton, *The Literary Underground*, 17–18.

9. Georg Lukács, *Studies in European Realism* (New York: Grosset and Dunlap, 1964), 51. Lucien is, of course, the central character of Balzac's 1837–1842 novel of Restoration literary life, *Illusions perdues*.

10. Lough's discussion of eighteenth-century authorship, for instance, gives considerable space to enumerating the actual sums paid to various writers for their works. See *An Introduction to Eighteenth-Century France*, 237–48.

11. See, above all, *The Literary Underground*, 1–40.

12. Daniel Roche, *Les Républicains des lettres: Gens de culture et lumières au XVIIIe siècle* (Paris: Fayard, 1988), 255.

13. See Henri-Jean Martin's short introduction to part 3, "Auteurs et libraires," in *Histoire de l'édition française tome II: Le livre triomphant*, ed. Martin and Roger Chartier (Paris: Fayard, 1990), 496.

14. I am, of course, greatly indebted to Robert Darnton and his chapter "A Police Inspector Sorts his Files: The Anatomy of the Republic of Letters," in *The Great Cat Massacre and Other Episodes in French Cultural History* (New York: Basic Books, 1984), 145–189, for having brought my attention to these documents. They are gathered in three registers, entitled "Historique des auteurs," in the *nouvelles acquisitions françaises* collections of the Bibliothèque nationale de France, 10781–3.

15. Darnton observes: "protection functioned as the basic principle of literary life. Its presence everywhere in the reports makes another phenomenon, the literary marketplace, look conspicuous by its absence" (*The Great Cat Massacre*, 168).

16. Joseph d'Hémery, "Historique des auteurs," BNF, nouv.acq.fr. 10782.

17. "Historique des auteurs," BNF, nouv.acq.fr. 10781. I am uncertain about the identification of the *libraire*, which in the manuscript appears to be "La Foliot" rather than "La Billiot." Darnton rendered the name as La Foliot in his reference to this passage in *The Great Cat Massacre*; however, no bookseller by that name appears in Augustin-Martin Lottin's *Catalogue chronologique des libraires et des imprimeurs-libraires de Paris, depuis l'an 1470, époque de l'établissement de l'Imprimerie dans cette Capitale, jusqu'à présent*, 2 vols. (Paris: chez Jean-Roch Lottin de St. Germain, 1789). It is possible that La Foliot was a provincial *libraire*, and thus not included in Lottin's catalog. This might seem unlikely, though, given her relatively prominent role in d'Hémery's

files, notably as an important source of information on the Parisian literary scene for the inspector. La Billiot, on the other hand, was the daughter of the early eighteenth-century *libraire* Esprit Billiot, and the widow of the bookseller Jean-Barthélemi Alix, whose business she took over at his death in 1740. In 1789, she was listed by Lottin as the "doyenne des veuves."

18. "Historique des auteurs," BNF, nouv.acq.fr. 10783. Though unsuccessful playwrights themselves, François and Claude Parfaict did, of course, produce a number of works that are still of great interest to historians of the theatre, including an *Histoire générale du théâtre français depuis son origine jusqu'à présent*, published between 1734–1749. Their 7-volume *Dictionnaire des théâtres de Paris* (1767) has recently been made available online at the *Calendrier électronique des spectacles sous l'Ancien Régime (CESAR)* electronic database, at <www.cesar.org.uk>.

19. "Historique des auteurs," BNF, nouv.acq.fr. 10783.

20. Louis-Sébastien Mercier, *Tableau de Paris* [1781–1789], ed. Jean-Claude Bonnet, 2 vols. (Paris: Mercure de France, 1994), 1:332, 363.

21. Louis Petit de Bachaumont, et al., *Mémoires secrets pour servir à l'histoire de la République des lettres en France depuis MDCCLXII jusqu'à nos jours*, 36 vols. (London: John Adamson, 1777), entry for 27 December 1769, 5:39. The anonymous pamphlet, *Avis aux gens de lettres* (Liège, 1770), was, in fact, written by the playwright Fenouillot de Falbaire de Quingey, as part of the polemic surrounding the case of Luneau de Boisjermain. Luneau had incited the anger of the Parisian guild of printers and booksellers by trying to publish and sell his own works. Eighteenth-century laws prohibited anyone but *libraires* from selling books.

22. "Historique des auteurs," BNF, nouv.acq.fr. 10783.

23. Friedrich Melchoir, baron von Grimm, et al., *Correspondance littéraire, philosophique et critique addressée à un souverain d'Allemagne depuis 1753 jusqu'en 1769*, ed. Maurice Tourneux, 16 vols. (Paris: Garnier frères, 1877–1882), 8:274.

24. Pidansat de Mairobert, *L'espion anglois, ou correspondance secrète entre milord All'Eye et milord All'Ear*, 10 vols. (London: John Adamson, 1779–1784), 3:44. Cited in Rémy Saisselin, *The Literary Enterprise in Eighteenth-Century France* (Detroit: Wayne State University Press, 1977), 78.

25. See, for instance, Darnton's discussion of the earnings of established *gens de lettres*, and particularly his account of the career of Jean-Baptiste Suard, which he considers as representative of this group of "High-Enlightenment philosophes," in *The Literary Underground*, 3–10. Darnton estimates that Suard enjoyed an income of somewhere over 10000 livres, consisting exclusively of pensions and other traditional kinds of revenue, such as income from his membership in the *Académie française*. See also Lough's survey of the various forms that State and aristocratic patronage could take, as well as of the amounts that typically went with each one, in *Writer and Public in France*, 227–234.

26. Pidansat de Mairobert, *L'espion anglois*, 3:43.

27. The entry on de la Porte in Hoefer's nineteenth-century *Nouvelle biographie générale* describes the *Voyage* as having "quelque succès." The partial bibliography makes mention of the 1751 re-edition. A 1753 edition can be found in the collections of the Bibliothèque nationale de France. See "de la Porte," in Hoefer, *Nouvelle biographie générale depuis les temps les plus reculés jusqu'à nos jours, avec les renseignements bibliographiques et l'indication des sources à consulter*, 46 vols. (Paris: Firmin Didot frères, 1852–66), 29:558–559. Although d'Hémery's dossier on de la Porte is initially dated January 1, 1748, the dossier's reference to the *Voyage au séjour des ombres* suggests that, as with many of the files, much of the information was added subsequently.

28. Jean-François de la Harpe, *Correspondance littéraire, addressée à son altesse impériale, Mgr le grand-duc, aujourd'hui, empereur de la Russie, et à M. le comte André Schowalow, chambellan de l'impératrice Catherine II, depuis 1774 jusqu'à 1789*, 5 vols. (Paris: Migueret, 1801–1807), 3:44.

29. Elizabeth Eisenstein, *Grub Street Abroad: Aspects of the Cosmopolitan Press from the Age of Louis XIV to the French Revolution* (Oxford: Clarendon Press, 1992), 135–48; and Rémy Saisselin, *The Literary Enterprise*. Roche also emphasizes the rising prices of manuscripts and the growing recognition of "le droit des auteurs" in *Républicains des lettres*, 225.

30. See Duclos's chapter on *gens de lettres* in his *Considérations sur les moeurs de ce siècle* [1750], ed. F.C. Green (Cambridge, UK: Cambridge University Press, 1946), 135–46. According to Duclos, *gens de lettres*, through their contacts with *le monde*, "ont trouvé de la considération; ils ont perfectionné leur goût, adouci leurs moeurs, et acquis sur plusieurs articles des lumières qu'ils n'avoient pas puisées dans des livres," 135–36.

31. "Historique des auteurs," BNF, nouv.acq.fr. 10781.

32. In "The Facts of Literary Life in Eighteenth-Century France" (in *The French Revolution and the Creation of Modern Political Culture*, ed. Keith Michael Baker, 4 vols. [Oxford: Pergamon Press, 1987], 1:262–91), Darnton underscores "the population problem in literature" as a decisive factor for the evolution of authorship in the late eighteenth century: "The literary market place would not support three thousand writers. It probably would not support three dozen. Authors who lacked an independent income lived from sinecures and pensions dispensed by protectors. But these remained in short supply while the demand for them kept increasing. Polite letters therefore became the preserve of a privileged few, while a growing population of hacks crowded into Grub Street, where they survived as best they could, often by producing seditious and salacious tracts," 268.

33. In the introduction to *A Field of Honor: Writers, Court Culture, and Public Theatre in French Literary Life from Racine to the Revolution* (New York: Columbia University Press/Epic, 2002), Gregory Brown calls for a similar shift in focus onto the exercise of active identity construction as central to the problem of authorship in this period. Analyzing the careers of late eighteenth-century playwrights, Brown emphasizes a process that he calls "self-fashioning,"

which is to be distinguished from Stephen Greenblatt's notion of an "artful process." Rather, "self-fashioning," for Brown, describes a more psychologically ambiguous process, according to which the individual constructs a self in an attempt to "reconcile his or her previous understanding of self to social experiences that seem to contradict that conception. Writers self-fashioned [...] not to get ahead, but to understand their own behavior, including their own writing, as deserving of recognition and respect," in the objective absence of such recognition. Electronic resource available at <www.gutenberg-e.org>. For Greenblatt's account of self-fashioning, see *Renaissance Self-Fashioning: from More to Shakespeare* (Chicago: University of Chicago Press, 1980), 1–9.

34. Louis-Sébastien Mercier, "Dissertation sur la littérature," preface to *Le génie, le goût et l'esprit: poëme en quatre chants dédié à M. le duc de *** (The Hague: 1756), iii–iv.

35. Mercier, *Tableau de Paris*, 2:804–807.

36. Mercier, *Tableau de Paris*, 2:804–807. Crébillon himself offers a somewhat different, geographic reading of the contrast, observing that the latter author is from Rouen whereas the former is from Toulouse: "Une expérience de plusieurs années m'a démontré que sur vingt auteurs qui arrivent du midi de la France, il y en a dix-neuf qui sont détestables; et que sur le même nombre qui arrive du Nord, il y en a la moitié au moins qui ont le germe du talent et qui sont susceptibles de perfection," 807.

37. Jacques-Pierre Brissot de Warville, *Mémoires*, ed. Claude Perroud, 2 vols. (Paris: Alphonse Picard, n.d.), 1:102–3.

38. Jean-Jacques Rousseau, *Confessions* [1765], 2 vols. (Paris: Gallimard, 1963), 1:185. Offering a surprisingly different image of Rousseau in salon society that, if nothing else, emphasizes the willful and strategic nature of the latter's self-deprecation, Françoise de Graffigny writes of his conversation in a letter to François-Antoine Devaux: "C'est une légèreté, une facilité, une gentillesse à comparer presque à celle de Voltaire. [...] Il vous jette mille petites louanges dans son espèce de volubilité que vous ramassez si vous voulez, mais que vous pouvez laisser tomber sans embarras. Il a un son de voix et une facilité de parler qui jette beaucoup d'agrément sur ses discours. Tout ce qu'il dit est bien écrit." Letter of 29 October 1751, in *Choix de lettres*, ed. English Showalter (Oxford: Voltaire Foundation, 2001), 211.

39. Claude Favre de Vaugelas, "Préface," in *Remarques sur la langue française utiles à ceux qui veulent bien parler et bien écrire* (Paris: éditions Champ Libre, 1981), 10.

40. Mercier, *Tableau de Paris*, 1:953.

41. Mercier, *Tableau de Paris*, 1:332, 744.

42. Brown discusses the centrality of a critique of established cultural institutions, notably of the *Comédie française*, in Mercier's self-representation as a dramatic author in the 1760s and 70s. See "Mercier, the Patriot Playwright," in *A Field of Honor*, chapter 3, section 2.

43. Simon-Nicolas-Henri Linguet, *L'aveu sincère, ou Lettre à une mère sur les dangers que court la jeunesse en se livrant à un goût trop vif pour la*

littérature (London: Louis Cellot, 1768), 45.

44. Jean-Baptiste Poquelin de Molière, *Le misanthrope* (II,4), in *Oeuvres complètes*, ed. Georges Couton, 2 vols. (Paris: Gallimard,1971), 2:169. Hélène Merlin traces the emergence of the concept of the "Public" as an institution of literary judgment in the course of the "Querelle du Cid," in *Public et littérature en France au XVIIe siècle* (Paris: Les Belles Lettres, 1994). See also Joan Dejean, "The Invention of a Public for Literature," in *Ancients against Moderns: Culture Wars and the Making of a Fin de Siècle*, 31–77, which, of course, focuses on a later part of the seventeenth century.

45. Linguet, *L'aveu sincère*, 43, 45–47.

46. Nicolas Gilbert, "Les plaintes d'un malheureux," included in Alphonse Séché's early twentieth-century collection, *Les "poètes-misère"* (Paris: Louis Michaud, n.d.), 69. Séché's collection positions Gilbert along with his contemporary Jacques-Charles-Louis Clinchamps de Malfilâtre as "les premières victimes littéraires dont nous allons voir croître le nombre avec le XIXe siècle," 15. In 1832, Charles de Saint-Maurice published an account of Gilbert's final days, "romanticized" as a period of religious repentance. See *Gilbert. Chronique de l'Hôtel-Dieu* (Paris: Dénain, 1832). This was, of course, two years before Vigny's sensational literary resuscitation of another eighteenth-century *homme de lettres*, Thomas Chatterton, as a Romantic hero.

47. Gilbert, *Le Genie aux prises avec la fortune, ou le poète malheureux, pièce qui a concouru pour le prix de cette année* (Amsterdam, 1772), 3.

48. Louis-Sébastien Mercier, *Virginie, Tragédie en Cinq Actes* (Paris: Duchesne, 1767). Cited in Brown, *A Field of Honor,* chapter 3, section 2.

49. References to marginalized eighteenth-century writers as constituting a literary or intellectual "proletariat" can be found in Darnton, *The Literary Underground,* 16; Martin, "Auteurs et libraires," 496; and Roche, *Républicains des lettres,* 254.

50. Mercier, *Tableau de Paris,* 1:332.

51. Linguet, *L'aveu sincère*, 47.

52. Linguet, *L'aveu sincère*, 24, 46.

53. Gilbert, *Le Génie aux prises avec la fortune*, 15.

54. Eisenstein's polemic with Darnton on the case of Brissot is one illustration of the problems that are raised by a seemingly systematic discrepancy between the images that self-designated outsiders construct of themselves in their own writings and those that might be gleaned from other kinds of sources. Eisenstein's more favorable reconstruction of Brissot's literary career in *Grub Street Abroad* emphasizes among other things his extensive travels, including to the United States where he met with George Washington: "To stroll along the banks of the Potomac is surely far from being trapped in the gutters of Paris," 148. For more on the Brissot debate, see Eisenstein, "Bypassing the Enlightenment: Taking an Underground Route to Revolution," and Jeremy Popkin, "Robert Darnton's Alternative (to the) Enlightenment," both included in *The Darnton Debate: Books and Revolution in the Eighteenth Century*, ed. Haydn Mason (Oxford: Voltaire Foundation, 1998), 157–77 and 105–28,

respectively. Darnton responds in his own contribution to the volume, "Two Paths Through the Social History of Ideas," 267–68. For Darnton's original argument about Brissot's revolutionary politics coming not from the high-minded principles of Enlightenment, but from an intense bitterness born of poverty and failure, see "The Grub Street Style of Revolution: J.-P. Brissot, Police Spy," *Journal of Modern History*, 40 (1968): 301–327, and "A Spy in Grub Street," in *The Literary Underground*, 41–70. Gilbert has inspired similarly contradictory appraisals of the conditions in which he lived his life, particularly in the last years. His entry in Michaud's *Bibliographie universelle, ancienne et moderne,* 52 vols. (Paris: Michaud, 1811–28) asserts that "[c]et infortuné, que ses protecteurs ne tiraient point de misère, tomba dans la démence, et fut conduit à l'Hôtel-Dieu. Dans un de ses accès, il avala la clef d'une petite cassette où il avait quelque argent, et mourut le 12 novembre 1780, âgé de vingt-neuf ans," 17:357–358. This account differs quite strikingly from that offered in the *Nouvelle biographie générale* (19:499), according to which Gilbert, in a "chemise fine," fell off a horse in late October 1780, sustaining fatal injuries to his head. This latter account, moreover, underscores Gilbert's relative affluence at the time, consisting of several pensions that came to "2,200 livres de revenus" in total. Whatever the reality of his earnings, or for that matter, of the circumstances of his final days, Gilbert clearly fostered an image of himself as an author wracked by the symbolic poverty, if not the economic poverty, of the "literary market."

55. Séché, Les *"poètes-misère,"* 10.
56. Brissot, *Mémoires*, 1:2.
57. Brissot, *Mémoires*, 1:2.
58. Mercier, *Tableau de Paris*, 2:1260.
59. Gilbert, "Les plaintes d'un malheureux," 69.
60. Pidansat de Mairobert, *L'espion anglois*, 3:43–44.
61. Analyzing Brissot's correspondence with his publishers at the Société typographique de Neuchâtel, Darnton offers a detailed account of how Brissot's ambitions of becoming an established *philosophe* repeatedly collided against the "hard facts of literary life" and the eighteenth-century Book Trade, in "J.-P. Brissot and the Société Typographique de Neuchâtel (1779–1787)," *SVEC* 2001:10, 7–47.
62. Brissot, *Mémoires*, 1:2.
63. Brissot, *Mémoires*, 1:103.
64. Brissot, *Mémoires*, 1:227. For a quite different rendering of this affair, see Darnton, "J.-P. Brissot and the Société Typographique de Neuchâtel," 28–36.
65. Brissot, *Mémoires*, 1:227.

Dreams of Stone: Femininity in the Eighteenth-Century Sculptural Imagination

CAROLINE WEBER

Je suis belle ô mortels comme un rêve de pierre . . .
Et jamais je ne pleure et jamais je ne ris.
—Charles Baudelaire

Scholars of eighteenth-century France need only glance at a handful of canonical images or texts to notice just how large the figure of the statue loomed in the cultural imagination of that time and place. Mysterious sculptures pepper the landscapes of Watteau, Boucher and Fragonard; Condillac develops a theory of sense-acquisition on the basis of an imaginary statue that gradually learns to see and smell; and Rousseau's works reference both a dilapidated Glaucus and a seductive Galatea.[1] Diderot, for his part, repeatedly describes his two moral and artistic touchstones, "Truth and Virtue," as twin monuments towering over a desert of petty human ignorance, while Sade reserves a rare moment of tenderness for a favorite statue lodged in Florence's Uffizi Gallery.[2] Historically speaking, the vast proliferation of sculptural imagery in the French arts and letters can be attributed to a host of factors. From the copying of antiquities undertaken by students at the French Academy in Rome to the passion for *tableaux vivants* that dominated fashionable parlors; and from the widely acclaimed and imitated findings of Graeco-Italian archaeological digs to the booming mass-reproduction of plaster figurines and antiquarian illustrations, the vogue for statuary infused virtually all areas of cultural activity.[3] But despite its massive scope, scholars of the period have largely ignored the deeper theoretical implications of this trend, implications for subjectivity and sociability that I would like to address in this essay through the lens of gender. For the specifically *feminine* sculptural imagery that dominates eighteenth-century French representational practices—be they visual or textual, rococo or libertine—time and again works to locate women in an erotically and ontologically restrictive subject position. For although later celebrated by the Goncourts as "the century of Woman," this was after all an age whose notions of virtue and freedom were still (like the Goncourts themselves) unabashedly patriarchal.[4] Accordingly, the era's iconic female figures derived their presumed personal "liberation" from an ability to regulate appearances, to *hold the pose* of modesty, through the strict disciplining of the body. As Nancy K. Miller has pointed out, this imperative of sexual self-effacement has as its most troubling effect the transformation of female subjects into "exquisite cadavers," and of their so-called lives into "the oxymoron of a living death."[5] In the literary sphere, a prime case in point is Rousseau's famously virtuous feminine ideal Julie, who combats her abiding desire for Saint-Preux by means of behavior that she likens to a kind of deathly self-mortification.[6] Another is Madame de T___ of Vivant Denon's *No Tomorrow* (1777), who hides her extramarital shenanigans behind a façade of requisite prudishness, and whose lover, admiring her success in keeping her conduct hidden from both her husband and the public eye, describes her as being "made of stone."[7] Taking my cue from this evocative phrase, as from Miller's critical qualification of feminine life as living death, I propose here to examine a range of eighteenth-century literary and visual representations where sculptural imagery collaborates in the production of a punishing—and today, all too familiar—ideology of sexual containment. This ideology, I want to argue, turns its female subjects into effectively paralyzed statues, dubiously exquisite corpses.

As an investigative and chronological starting point, Antoine Watteau's *fêtes galantes* have much to tell us. Despite their much-vaunted representation of "natural" eroticism[8] (amorous idylls occurring beyond the boundaries of urban and/or courtly society), these paintings by no means depict a world where unfettered sensual abandon functions as the norm, particularly as far as women are concerned. In this respect, Watteau's work inscribes itself in a longer artistic tradition wherein the space of erotic delight is structured around or by a female object of desire struggling to preserve her chastity.[9] In Guillaume de Lorris' portion of the *Romance of the Rose*, written in the early thirteenth century, the "embattled wall" that encircles the Garden of Mirth ("tout clos d'un haut mur bataillé" [v.131]) becomes both metaphor and metonym for the Rose's self-protective withdrawal from her male Lover's ardent grasp.[10] When Jean de Meun continues the text later in the thirteenth century, the strategic necessity of the Rose's stonewalling posture becomes retroactively apparent when the fortified Tower of Shame—organized around a beautiful female statue, no less (v.20797–20810)—is destroyed and the Rose herself brutally raped. With the *Rose*, first published in the eighteenth century, understood as an intertext,[11] it becomes evident that in Watteau's bucolic scenes too, the women who appear to inhabit a space of unmitigated delight must in fact assume a defensive, self-restrictive posture with respect to male sexual advances.[12] At first view, for instance, the *Fêtes vénitiennes* (1719) [fig. 1] presents a seemingly relaxed gathering of the sexes: men and women frolicking and lounging in close, casual contact on the garden grass; yet the key feminine figures in the gathering betray clear signs of erotic constraint. First and foremost among the women is the dark-haired beauty sitting between and behind the two dancers in the foreground, directly beneath an intensely elongated column of leaves. As it bears down on our heroine's head, this leafy, unmistakably phallic shaft implies a distinct physical menace, doubled by the forward-thrusting gesture of her male companion's wandering hand. As the man grabs somewhere between her bosom and her crotch, the woman checks his advance with both of her own hands, while visibly attempting to pull her head and torso out of his grasp. She is sustained in this effort by a vigilant female friend, who stares at the lovers' manual dueling as if to register any improprieties it might contain; in this way, the two women work together to regulate and deflect the disrupting forces of Eros expressed by their male companion.[13] These forces are sublimated, too, in the carefully orchestrated dance that occupies the painting's foreground: a configuration inherently artificial not only in its mincing, choreographed steps but in also the theatrical costumes of its participants (the man's curious Oriental turban and the woman's high-necked cape).[14] Tellingly, though, the male dancer's clothing is far less restrictive than his partner's; while he points not so subtly at the baggy folds of cloth between his legs, she grasps the edges of her skirt and, avoiding his gaze, primly concentrates on the footwork. At the same time, the man's provocative finger gesture is repeated in the background by another man's designation of a figure that art historians have tended to read as the dancing woman's polar opposite: a nude statue languorously posed with all her charms on unabashed display.[15] I would propose,

Figure 1. Watteau, *Fêtes vénitiennes* (c.1719). National Gallery of Scotland, Edinburgh.

however, that the relationship between the *danseuse* and the statue, between moving flesh and immobile stone, is structured less as an antithesis than as a chiasmus. As each female figure confronts the sexual advance betokened by a prurient male finger, the sensuality of the living woman is displaced onto the supine sculpture, which in turn imparts to its human counterpart the chilly stiffness of marble. Michel Serres has suggested that the statue marks the space of death.[16] Likewise, in the *Fêtes vénitiennes*, death makes its appearance in the form of the radical containment to which the female body must submit, the "economy of death" which Sarah Kofman has located at the root of eighteenth-century prescriptions for feminine modesty.[17] In this light, contrary to readings that emphasize the uncanny, almost lifelike quality of the voluptuous Watteauan statue,[18] I would offer an alternative interpretation: namely, that this figure evokes, as Slavoj Zizek has written in a different context, though echoing Miller, "the living dead, a life of disavowed, mortified desire."[19]

The morbid terminology of Kofman, Miller, Serres, and Zizek becomes more appropriate still when we juxtapose the *Fêtes vénitiennes* to a work that Watteau painted roughly a year beforehand, *Les Champs Elysées* (fig. 2). Initially, the presentation of eroticized femininity in this painting might strike the viewer as more straightforward and untroubled than in the later work. After all, with the exception of the girl in yellow, whose ramrod posture suggests successful training by an exacting dance-master, the ladies here lounge freely and easily in their cozy glade, preoccupied neither with suitors' untoward sleights of hand nor with the complex steps of a strictly regulated social dance. As carefree as the children playing next to them, this group of ladies seems to reap unmitigated the benefits of the *fête galante*: peaceful sociability untainted by the hassles of city life, not to mention the hazards of male desire. Thus liberated, they allow themselves to relax some of the restrictions conventionally imposed on their bodies in the name of modesty. The two women in the middle sit with open legs, distinctly unladylike and (thanks to the emphatic brushstrokes with which Watteau has rendered their laps) bordering on suggestive, and all three of the frontally painted ladies display casually enticing *décolleté*. Their gathering thus appears at first blush as a more or less uncomplicated, unblushing pastoral of free and easy feminine corporeality. Once again, however, the statue on the edge of the painting offers a subtler and less sanguine insight into the psychosexual dynamics that Watteau is articulating in his composition. The key here resides in the overdetermined resemblance between the sleeping female nude—on the surface an evocation of dormant sexuality or relaxed physicality—and an almost identical figure from an earlier work, Watteau's *Jupiter and Antiope* (1713) (fig. 3). For of course the encounter between Jupiter and the nymph Antiope (as between the god and virtually all his mortal conquests) culminates in a rape; the artist depicts the moment just prior to the violation, when Jupiter overtakes his prey in all her inviting vulnerability. Similarly, the women in *Les Champs Elysées* are wholly oblivious to the approach of a mysterious gentleman—his face shaded over by hat and ruff—just below the statue. And although the

Figure 2. Watteau, *Les Champs Elysées* (c.1717). The Wallace Collection, London.

statue's own hand reaches downward as if to pull off his hat, to reveal his identity or perhaps to block his passage altogether, the lurking outsider does not look as though he will take no for an answer.[20] A shadowy smile plays on his lips, not unlike the mustachioed smirk with which Jupiter initiates his unsolicited advances, and in moving forward the interloper steps directly on the closest woman's cape or train, a gesture of careless violence if not of outright violation. In this sense, the sculpture can be understood to function as a kind of warning to the unsuspecting women, a reminder that unguarded sexuality (uncrossed legs and uncovered bosoms) is never without its perils, and that the greatest safety may very well lie in the statue's supreme physical restraint.

Similar conclusions can be drawn from the work of Fragonard, in whose painterly celebration of the erotic, as in Watteau's idyllic vignettes, it is possible to detect a paradoxically cautionary attitude toward feminine sexual freedom. A prime case in point is Fragonard's series of panels, *The Progress*

Figure 3. Watteau, *Jupiter & Antiope* (1713). Musée du Louvre, Paris.

of Love, created for Louis XV's mistress, Madame Du Barry.[21] Painted between 1770 and 1773, this series depicts the progress of a love affair in four episodes, from the *Declaration of Love* (fig. 4) made by a hopeful admirer in the first panel to *The Lover Crowned*, in which the hero's lady-love seems at last to accept his affections.[22] In each of these and the two middle panels, *The Pursuit* and *Storming the Citadel*, a statue of Venus and/or a group of her attendants presides over the action, appearing like Watteau's outdoor sculptures to take an active interest in the courtship unfolding at her feet. More significantly, though, and also like the stone figure in *Les Champs Elysées*, the Venus of these paintings can be said to mirror and maybe even to dictate the living woman's responses to her suitor's advances. In *The Declaration of Love*, for instance, the lady allows her lover to rest his head on her shoulder, his lips hovering dangerously close to her neck, while she reads a letter that he, presumably, has written to her. At the same time, the act of reading provides her with a pretext to keep her eyes demurely downcast and her hands and attention elsewhere than on the young buck's anxiously poised body. This ambiguous gesture, which simultaneously encourages and rebuffs the eager gentleman, is echoed by the nearby Venus, who with one hand withholds a piece of fruit from a lustily begging cherub, while with the other hand lifting her toga high enough to reveal her leg to mid-thigh. The statue, then, might be said to provide the model for the go-away/come-closer dynamic that characterizes the "real" woman's flirtation. Such a dynamic requires the female party to exert, like the Marquise de Merteuil in *Dangerous Liaisons* (1782), the strictest control over her emotions and her body, even as she teeters on the brink of erotic abandon.[23]

But in Fragonard's panels as in Laclos' novel, sexual demise stands as one distinctly possible consequence of strategic coquetry, and humiliated virtue as the negative mirror image of feminine self-containment. The series' second panel, *The Pursuit* (fig. 5), gestures in this direction by representing an amorous interaction in which the threat of sexual aggression subtends the suave rococo surface. Here the man boldly brandishes a flower which may have been culled from between his mistress' legs, themselves spread wide over a metonymically suggestive patch of flowers as she flees his embrace. Two female friends, reminiscent of the watchful chaperone in the *Fêtes vénitiennes*, support the young woman in her escape, and present a gendered front of unity against the onslaught of male libido. Meanwhile the beleaguered beauty herself appears to derive little if any pleasure from the combat. Unsmiling, her arms extended stiffly for balance and her body tilted resolutely away from her pursuer, she looks almost as if, were it not for her companions, she would fall backward into the fountain: a fate with the most obvious Biblical implications for her presumed innocence. The fountain itself, not incidentally, gushes forth from the mouth of a stone dolphin, one of Venus' traditional attributes here abandoned by its patroness and ridden, if by no means bridled, by two ineffectual cherubim. One of them is quite literally asleep at the wheel, shut-eyed and slack-jawed as it holds onto the dolphin's central fin, while the other looks mainly concerned with extricating himself from the water spewing about his steed. Without a savvy Venus to direct the action, the force of nature over which the cherubim preside thus erupts unchecked, a proto-romantic reflection of the suitor's sexual daring or perhaps even of the erotic cataclysm soon to be experienced, if her resistance proves futile, by the woman herself.[24]
And as if the plucked flower and the threat of a fall were not sufficient in intimating just where this untrammeled libidinous frenzy might lead, the small still-life in the painting's bottom right-hand corner brings the point home. No longer brandished aloft to frustrate an overeager lover, the fruit designating the woman's favors is now eminently accessible—and even, if we read it in conjunction with the exposed apple and the overturned vase of Fragonard's later painting, *The Bolt* (1780) (fig.6), under threat of a direct assault. Indeed, the cliched visual metaphor (and, through physical

Figure 4. Fragonard, *The Declaration of Love* (1770–1772). The Frick Collection, New York.

Figure 5. Fragonard, *The Pursuit* (1770–1772). The Frick Collection, New York.

proximity to the female subject, metonym) of the fallen or broken vase that surfaces in *Storming the Citadel* (fig. 7) bespeaks, like the panel's titular reference to an overpowering invasion, the menace to womanly chastity that amorous games such as these imply. (The broken urn in Greuze's painting by the same name (fig. 8) likewise implies the loss of feminine virtue, echoed by the maiden's bared breast and strategically placed hands.) As if summoned to stave off her fleshly counterpart's imminent danger, an instructive Venus sculpture returns to the scene, almost naked this time but twisting forcefully away from the putto that grasps at her buttocks. Now displaying vehement defensiveness rather than coy seductiveness, the statue clings protectively not only to the shred of cloth that still covers her genitals, but also to an empty quiver that doubles, and conjures up the metaphorical associations of, the fallen urn. Her body positively strains with the effort, becoming almost grotesque in the process and thereby revealing the stresses involved in the protection of one's virtue.[25] Stripped of the flirtatious grace she enjoyed in *The Declaration of Love*, the stone goddess can thus be read here as a warning to women about the risks that attend the invitation to sensual pleasure.

That is not, of course, to say that sculptural femininity lacks seductive charms of its own; in fact the prospect of "mortified" female desire emerges in certain contemporary works as downright appealing to men with an overweening narcissistic investment in their own phallic powers. Undoubtedly the best example of this phenomenon is Rousseau's *Pygmalion* (1762), a one-act play in which the eponymous mythological sculptor falls in love with his female masterpiece, Galatea.[26] "How dear, how precious it will be to me, this immortal artwork!" Pygmalion exclaims in his opening monologue as he fawns over his new creation:

> When my spirit is extinguished, when I am no longer capable of producing anything great, anything beautiful, anything worthy of me, I will point to Galatea and say: This is my work. O my Galatea, when I have lost everything else, you will remain to me, and I will be consoled.[27]

With this outburst, the sculptor emphasizes the relationship between his feelings as a lover and his ambition as an artist: the former, in his single-minded estimation, derives quite directly from the latter. At the same time, Pygmalion's words sketch out a clear opposition between his status as a living, breathing mortal—one who risks disappearing as soon as his "fire goes out, [his] imagination goes cold" (1224)—and Galatea's position as an immutable, eternal piece of marble.[28] "Pygmalion," he reminds himself,

Figure 6. Fragonard, *The Bolt* (1780). Musée du Louvre, Paris.

"this is your work, this is a stone" (1226); if the female sculpture holds him in her thrall, this is because she stands as a reification of and a permanent testimony to his transitory passionate genius. Here too the relationship between the human and the sculptural operates as a chiasmus: Pygmalion envisions the lifeless stone woman as the embodiment of his true life, and imagines the death of his mortal body as the precondition for her immortalizing existence. "Ah!" he exclaims, "let Pygmalion die so that Galatea can live!" (1228) The paradox is of course that in order for the sculptor to attain eternal recognition (in both the colloquial and the Hegelian senses of the word) through his work, Galatea herself has to remain an inanimate object. Small wonder, then, Pygmalion should greet the phantasmagoria that catalyzes the play's denouement—the magical transformation of the statue into a woman—with an ambivalence verging on revulsion. "Good God! That's palpitating flesh I feel, pushing away my chisel! Vain terror, crazed blindness!" (1227) In expressing such horror at Galatea's humanization, the sculptor betrays the dubious nature of what he calls his "love" for her. If love it be, then Pygmalion's version of sentiment is, in his own words, both "vain" and "blind": blind because he is unwilling

Figure 7. Fragonard, *Storming the Citadel* (1770–1772). The Frick Collection, New York.

or unable to see Galatea as anything more than a ticket to immortal renown, and vain because his preoccupation with fame overrides any attractions that might be found in another person's urgently palpitating body. In the play's closing lines, Pygmalion finalizes this double negation of Galatea's fleshly independence by responding to her single, repeatedly uttered word, "Me," with an emphatic "Me" of his own (1230). Stressing that that Galatea's "me" should function solely as an extension and eternalizing reflection of his own ingenious self, he addresses to her the words with which Rousseau's text concludes:

> Yes, dear and charming object: yes, worthy masterpiece of my hands [and] my heart . . . it's you, you alone: I have given you my whole being, and I will no longer live but through you. (1231)

This apostrophe puts into effect yet another a chiasmic exchange between the person and the sculpture: on the one hand, Pygmalion dubs Galatea an "object" of his own making, while on the other hand he charges her with the perpetuation of his "whole being." Understood as performative utterances, these seemingly contradictory assertions share the common goal of turning Galatea back into stone—for only as a timeless "masterpiece," an "object" not vulnerable to the vicissitudes of mortality, can she properly assume the role of prolonging indefinitely the life of her creator. In this sense, no sooner does Galatea come to life than she is forced to die again—her corporeal quickening reduced to marmoreal stillness—so that Pygmalion might achieve everlasting life in the pantheon of celebrated artists.

Although less extensively treated, the myth of Pygmalion and Galatea also subtends the final sculptural vignette I wish to analyze, which appears in the Marquis de Sade's massive novel, *Juliette* (1797). As is well known, this book is a kind of libertine *Bildungsroman* whose title character decides to shake off the shackles of conventional womanly modesty and to embark on a life of sexual debauchery and criminal bloodlust. In essence, her story reads as an endless alternation between scenes of sexual torture—Juliette's erotic pleasure always requires unwilling, unhappy victims—and long philosophical discourses attempting to justify a libertine refusal of traditional social and moral behavior. This pattern, however, is interrupted by one significant passage: an account of the peripatetic heroine's visit to the Uffizi Gallery. Although consistently nonplussed even by the most extravagant of orgies, when faced with one the Uffizi's chief attractions, the Medici Venus, Juliette abandons for the first time her cold-blooded reserve. Invoking the rapture of Pygmalion to explain her own unprecedented feelings, she describes her reaction to the statue of Venus in the following terms:

> Upon beholding that stunning piece, a rush of emotion assailed me as surely must happen to any sensitive spectator. A Greek, they say, was smitten by passion for a statue . . . It is understandable; I could well have duplicated his distracted behavior, I trow: a survey of this work's wondrous features leads one to believe tradition says true in reporting that the sculptor resorted to no fewer than five hundred models before completing it; the proportions of this sublime effigy, the beauty of the face, the heavenly contours of each limb, the graceful curves of the breasts, of the buttocks, are touches attesting [to] a human genius rivaling Nature's own . . . I need not describe it at greater length, it has been copied often enough; but though a reproduction of it is within anyone's means to buy, nobody will ever appreciate it quite as I did.[29]

In the broader context of Sade's novel, Juliette's concession to emotion, sensitivity, and "distracted behavior" reads as an unmistakable red flag—an indication that something in the Medici Venus has moved and attracted our heroine in a way that an endless slew of delicious sexual conquests has never done.[30] The clue to this mysterious "something," I think, resides less in the work's "graceful curves" *per se* (virtually all of Juliette's sex partners have been endowed with these), than in the fact that Juliette identifies such qualities as "touches attesting [to] a human genius rivaling Nature's own." For a woman who endeavors constantly to defy Nature through her highly "abnormal" sexual excesses (thousands of victims violated in countless, unthinkable ways), the statue is enchanting because it too manages to exceed the limits of "normal" biological existence. By alluding to the legend whereby the Venus' sculptor used over five hundred women as models for its composite parts, Juliette emphasizes the fact that this is a work that has successfully outstripped Nature's habitual techniques for creation and has become instead an ideal translated, against all odds, into reality.[31]

And yet, the statue's inconceivable beauty is not at all the only indication of its ability to triumph over Nature's laws; the Medici Venus also benefits from the materially transcendent qualities proper to the sculptural medium—properties which constitute the key to Pygmalion's uncommon predilections as well. Juliette highlights this physically resilient aspect of her beloved artwork when, commenting on the partial vandalism to which it has been subjected, she cries:

> This marvelous piece was once broken by some vandals, led
> by their execrable piety to this act of madness. The boors,
> the fools! [They failed to understand that this] creation . . .
> inspires the imagination, [and that] contemplating it is one of
> the sweetest pleasures that can be derived from the sight of
> man-made things. (614)

In fact, if the Medici Venus "inspires the imagination" of an insatiable
libertine like Juliette, and if she deems foolish those who would try to
destroy it, we might say this is because the sculpture presents the possibility
of a body that can never be entirely annihilated. As Alenka Zupancic has
pointed out:

> The basic problem that confronts the Sadeian heroes/
> torturers is that they can torture their victims only until they
> die. The only regrettable thing about these sessions—which
> could otherwise go on *endlessly*, towards more and more
> accomplished tortures—is that the victims die *too soon,* with
> respect to the extreme suffering to which they might have
> been subjected . . . . In short, the problem is that the body is
> not made to the measure of [the libertines'] enjoyment. There
> is no enjoyment but the enjoyment of the body, yet if the
> body is to be equal to the task . . . of *jouissance*, the limits of
> the body have to be "transcended."[32]

In contrast to Juliette's multitude of human victims, then, the Medici Venus
represents what Zupancic calls a "sublime body," or what Miller would
term an "exquisite corpse": that is to say, a body that survives beyond all
natural constraints of mortality and matter, in order to gratify the people
who have pushed it past those limits. Consistent with this ideal, Juliette
herself dubs the sculpture a "sublime effigy": yet another figure of mortified
desire, of palpitating feminine physicality sacrificed on the altar of another's
desire, and transmuted into stone.

Still, Juliette's relationship to her sculptural ideal cannot be completely
assimilated to the one between Pygmalion and Galatea (because, unlike the
sculptor, she is a woman), nor to the one between Fragonard's and Watteau's
ladies and their stone counterparts (because, unlike these demure dames,
she actively seeks sexual gratification). In the heterogeneous field of Sade
scholarship, Juliette has been both decried as a traitor to feminist liberation
and celebrated as an early modern harbinger of a new sexual age,[33] and

either critical perspective could be plausibly brought to bear on the Uffizi chapter of the heroine's story. In her love for a "sublime effigy," Juliette would in these opposing narratives stand as either a self-hating anti-feminist who colludes in promulgating an ethics of misogynist subjugation, or an intrepid rebel who subverts patriarchy by daring to constitute herself as a subject at the expense of an object traditionally available to men alone. But in my view, neither of these readings fully accounts for the dynamic sketched out in the Medici Venus passages: a dynamic whose specificity derives, again, from the sculptural body that helps to define it. For Juliette, a self-proclaimed devotee of libertine eroticism, the goddess of love is a fitting patron saint . . . but only if she, Venus, figures forth the physical and mental resilience required of libertinage's acolytes. Apathy, numerous critics have noted, is the affective *sina qua non* of Sadean heroism: to feel pity or flinch at pain is to fall short of the categorical principle which Juliette's principal mentors, the spectacularly merciless *messieurs* Noirceuil and Saint-Fond, postulate as the basis of the libertine will to pleasure.[34] By the same token, as Juliette is well aware, the sexual system into which her two idols indoctrinate her does not tend to construe its requisite radical apathy as a stance that women would be willing or even able to adopt.[35] In her efforts to conform to this model, the protagonist of *Juliette* realizes that she is expected to leave the emotional tendencies of her sex—the tendencies to sympathize, fall in love, recoil at another's suffering and wish to relieve it—behind her. (More precisely, she leaves them to her younger sister Justine, who doggedly retains her sentimental "weaknesses" even when most brutally pressured to recant.) In this respect, Juliette's assertion that "nobody will ever appreciate [the Medici Venus] quite as I did" can be traced to the singular position that she occupies vis-à-vis both mainstream and libertine erotic paradigms. Unlike a prudish, well-behaved *femme comme il faut*, she can delight in the Venus as an exemplary victim: a body that will never fully succumb to the atrocities that Juliette and her debauched comrades practice ad infinitum. By the same token, Juliette marks her distance from these very comrades (the vast majority of them male) by singling out as her favorite work of art a sculpture that embodies an ideal to which she herself, and alone, might aspire. "Broken by vandals," the Medici Venus is to some extent physically deficient, just as Juliette is repeatedly taken to task for her lack of a male member[36] . . . but the statue also embodies the hardness that the Sadean heroine manages to cultivate, both mentally and physically, to an astonishing degree. The perfection of this hardness, and the libertine triumphs it enables, is the sole and singular goal of Juliette's trajectory; it *is* her *Bildung*. The paradox, however, is that at least on the surface of things, Juliette's identification with a frigid, unyielding statue bears no small resemblance to the sculpturally inspired, chiasmically effected "mortification" of Fragonard's and Watteau's modest misses. On either end of the eighteenth-century sexual spectrum, the result thus looks very much the same: the petrification of female flesh in a world where only male bodies enjoy unrestricted libidinal movement. Or to put the point in slightly subtler terms, it seems to me that by declaring her singular appreciation for the Medici Venus, Sade's libertine woman reveals herself to be a fundamentally split subject. On the one hand, like Pygmalion she strives to operate beyond the constraints of biological (and in Juliette's case, affective) nature, and so to assert a transcendental genius uncommon among mere mortals. On the other hand, like Galatea she consents to lead a life of unfeeling coldness, the paradigm for which she herself did not create, and which will keep her forever immobilized on a pedestal. It perhaps goes without saying that in general, the kind of split between that which the individual wants for him- or herself and that which an overarching symbolic order demands is not the unique province of the eighteenth-century feminine subject. But insofar as the ubiquitous female sculpture brings an "economy of death" to bear on her flesh-and-blood body double, we might say that the terms of the latter's negotiation with the society in which she is condemned to dwell appear especially restrictive, because set in stone.

NOTES

1.   To my knowledge, the statues that appear everywhere in these painters', and their contemporary imitators', work have almost never been studied as manifestations of an overarching aesthetic or theoretical phenomenon. The only two essays I have located on this topic are A.P. de Mirimonde's "Statues et emblèmes dans l'oeuvre de Watteau," in *Revue du Louvre*, no. 1 [1962], which is disappointingly superficial in its treatment of the subject, and Calvin Seerveld's "Tell-Tale Statues in Watteau's Painting," in *Eighteenth-Century Studies* 14 [Winter 1980–1981]: 151–180, which I discuss at length below. The same lacuna riddles the vast body of scholarship on Rousseau's work, which in addition to its well-known evocations of Glaucus and Galatea includes a more obscure, fragmentary text about a dystopia governed by a host of hideous statues. See Jean-Jacques Rousseau, "Fiction ou morceau allégorique sur la révélation," in

Oeuvres complètes, tome IV, ed. Bernard Gagnebin & Marcel Raymond (Paris: Gallimard/Pléïade, 1969), 1044–1054. The passage on Glaucus appears at the beginning of Rousseau's *Discourse on Inequality*, trans. Maurice Cranston (London & New York: Penguin, 1984); and I analyze the Galatea text in detail below.

2. See Denis Diderot, *Entretiens sur 'Le Fils naturel,'* in *Oeuvres complètes*, tome X, ed. Jacques & Anne-Marie Chouillet (Paris: Hermann, 1980), 122; as well as his "Lettre à Sophie ou reproches adressées à une jeune philosophe" (reproduced and glossed in Grimm's *Correspondance littéraire*, tome V, 366). Sade's praise for the Uffizi's Medici Venus is discussed at length later on in this essay.

3. Because the cultural history of the eighteenth-century French (or broader European) sculptural vogue has yet to be written, the sources I cite here are necessarily scattered and non-totalizing. That said, I can point the interested reader in the direction of a few prime catalysts of the trend: culture ministers Natoire and Madame de Pompadour's brother Marigny, who presided over the French Academy in Rome, where Fragonard and many other French artists trained in the rigorous pictorial reproduction of local antiquities; the great sculptor Falconet, who served (also thanks to Madame de Pompadour) as the director of the Sèvres factory from 1757–1766 and during his tenure supervised the production of decorative statuettes for wealthy French homes; Winckelmann, whose mid-century reflections on Greek sculpture were hugely influential in France and throughout Europe; Goethe, whose apologia of the *tableau vivant* in the *Elective Affinities* enjoyed a similarly broad influence, particularly in the salons of cosmopolitan Parisians; and the archaeologists whose discoveries of Herculaneum and Pompeii contributed greatly to the rise of the neo-classicizing Louis XVI style in all the arts, as well as to a more active European discourse on ancient sculpture.

4. The relative containment or curtailment of feminine social and sexual autonomy in eighteenth-century France is a vast issue to say the least, addressed at the time by political thinkers like Olympe de Gouges (*Déclaration des droits de la femme et de la citoyenne*) as well as by novelists like Isabelle de Charrière (*Lettres de Mistriss* [sic] *Henley*), Madame Riccoboni (*Lettres de Juliette Catesby*), and Choderlos de Laclos (*Dangerous Liaisons*). In addition to Nancy K. Miller, mentioned above, scholars from Madelyn Gutwirth to Joan B. Landes and from Aileen Ribeiro to Lynn Hunt have documented the phenomenon of women's paradoxical socio-cultural disenfranchisement in the age of Enlightenment and Revolution. (Carla Hesse's recent work, *The Other Enlightenment: How French Women Became Modern* [Princeton: Princeton University Press, 2001], argues, it should be remarked, against this line of historical inquiry.) For a more properly theoretical treatment of the problem, as manifested in Kant's and Rousseau's prescriptions for feminine modesty, see Sarah Kofman, *Le Respect des femmes* (Paris: Galilée, 1982).

5. Nancy K. Miller, *French Dressing: Women, Men, and Ancien Régime*

Fiction (New York: Routledge, 1995), 156. In fact, although it focuses almost exclusively on Choderlos de Laclos' *Dangerous Liaisons*, the chapter from which this citation is drawn is compelling in its entirety: "The Exquisite Cadavers: Women in Eighteenth-Century Fiction," 147–159.

6.   See Jean-Jacques Rousseau, *Julie or the New Heloise*, translated & abridged by Judith H. McDowell (University Park, PA: The Pennsylvania State Press, 1968). Most tellingly, see the letter Julie writes from her deathbed, in which she informs Saint-Preux that her apparently imperturbable virtue was in fact the product of a constant and exhausting struggle against sexual instinct. "What danger might there [have been] in a whole life spent with you! What risks I have run!… Every trial has been made, but trials could be too often repeated. Have I not lived long enough for happiness and for virtue? What advantage was left for me to derive from life? By depriving me of it, Heaven no longer deprives me of anything regrettable and instead protects my honor… After so many sacrifices, I consider as little the one left for me to make. It is only to die once more" (405).

7.   Vivant Denon, *No Tomorrow*, translated by Lydia Davis, in *The Libertine Reader*, ed. Michel Feher (New York: Zone Books, 1997), 745.

8.   This perception has its roots in the eighteenth-century reception of Watteau's work, exemplified by the painter's obituary in the *Mercure de France*, which praised him as an "exact observer of nature." (Cited in Michael Levey, *Rococo to Revolution* [New York: Praeger Publishers, 1966], 57.) For a more current expression of the same view, see, among others, Pierre Schneider, *The World of Watteau* (Alexandria, VA: Time-Life, 1977).

9.   Mussia Eisenstadt has persuasively argued for the importance of Watteau's painterly adaptation of the literary *locus amoenus*—as presented in Homer, Virgil, Milton, Lorris and de Meun, among many others. (See Eisenstadt, *Watteaus Fêtes Galantes und ihre Ursprünge* [Berlin: Bruno Cassirer Verlag, 1930]). In a more recent essay, referenced in note 1, Calvin Seerveld more or less endorses Eisenstadt's conviction and expands upon her focus on the *Romance of the Rose* in particular. Promisingly for my purposes, he even combines this emphasis on the *locus amoenus* with a close attention to how Watteau's statues function within the painter's erotic landscapes. But although Seerveld's aim is to show how Watteau's outdoor pleasure parties *critique* contemporary, codified practices of love and seduction, he does not consider the specifically vexed position of women within this system. On the contrary, he reads the statue of the rape victim Antiope—which I discuss in altogether different terms—as emblematic of female desire for male domination. "A quiet afternoon in the park is really a masquerade that hides one's secret desire to be a nymph asleep, waiting for a lover to take her by surprise" (172); according to this questionable formulation, Watteau's social critique would be understood as targeting women's duplicity and not their disadvantage.

10.   The topos of quasi-military fortification pervades not only Lorris' section of the *Rose* but also, and again with respect to female figures, much

eighteenth-century French fiction. On the latter subject, see Joan DeJean, *Literary Fortifications: Rousseau, Laclos, Sade* (Princeton: Princeton University Press, 1984).

11. I am grateful to Howard Bloch for informing me of the *Rose*'s eighteenth-century début as a published work, a fact that supports Eisenstadt's and Seerveld's claims about the importance of this text for Watteau.

12. As numerous critics have pointed out, the *fête galante* itself, was a highly civilized and codified, ergo still aristocratic, form of retreat from life at court, a form that valorized the gentlemanly ethos of *honnêteté*. On this topic, see Thomas E. Crow, *Painters and Public Life in Eighteenth-Century Paris* (New Haven & London: Yale University Press, 1985), 66–72; and Julie Anne Plax, *Watteau and the Cultural Politics of Eighteenth-Century France* (Cambridge: Cambridge University Press, 2000), Chapter Three, "The *Fête Galante* and the Cult of *Honnêteté*," 108–153. Significantly, the innovations in sociability presented by the cult of *honnêteté* had principally to do with men's comportment as "artless" leisurely elegance; as a result, it comes as little surprise that traditional expectations for women (modesty, reserve, passivity in the face of male erotic aggression) should remain unchanged. Indeed, psychoanalytic critics have long stressed the degree to which male *galanterie* or *courtoisie*, purportedly a testament to its practitioners' desire for their mistresses, in fact fucntions as a means of staving off feminine sexual difference. See for example Jacques Lacan, *Le Séminaire XX: Encore* (Paris: Seuil, 1975), 65; and Renata Salecl, "I Can't Love You Unless I Give You Up" & Slavoj Zizek, "'No Sexual Relationship'" in *Gaze and Voice as Love Objects: SIC 1*, ed. Renata Salecl & Slavoj Zizek (Durham: Duke University Press, 1996), 179–207 & 208–250, respectively.

13. In the work of sublimation that subtends much of Watteau's painting, see Norman Bryson's excellent *Word and Image: French Painting of the Ancien Régime* (Cambridge: Cambridge Univrsity Press, 1981), 84. Bryson, however, does not ascribe the effort "to take the greedy, raw material of Eros and transform it into a principle of social harmony" solely to Watteau's women, although the *Fêtes vénitiennes* clearly display such a gender divide. On a related note, it bears remarking that the united female front devised by a pair or group of friends to protect one woman's virtue foreshadows the campaign to protect Julie's "virtue" that Rousseau's aforementioned heroine undertakes with the assistance of her cousin Claire. Although it exceeds the scope of this essay, the idea of women banding together to reinforce one another's moral and sexual propriety suggests an interesting collective internalization of patriarchal ideology by its apparent "victims." As this variation on Stockholm Syndrome—the identification of a victim with his or her aggressor—surfaces with considerable frequency in the French novels of the eighteenth century, it invites further research.

14. On the dance in this painting—the elaborately technical and precise *danse à deux*—see JoLynn Edwards, "Watteau and the Dance," in *Antoine Watteau: The Painter, His Age, and His Legend*, ed. François Moureau & Margaret Morgan Grasselli (Geneva: Slatkine, 1987), 224; and Sarah Cohen, *Art, Dance,*

and the Body in French Culture of the Ancien Régime (Cambridge: Cambridge University Press, 2000). Whereas Edwards sees this dance as an analogy for the codification of erotic activity in Watteau's day, Cohen dismisses the question of eroticism and reads the structure of the *danse à deux* as conducive to (presumably sublimated) social "bonding" between male and female participants (201). As in the citation from Bryson provided in note 13, above, Cohen's concerns in interpreting Watteau focus less on gender-specific issues than on what, more broadly, an aristocratic "body [does] with itself to present a distinctive identity to the world" (208) in the face of dwindling political power.

15. See "Watteau and the Dance," 224: "Watteau purposefully sets up an opposition between the naked and clothed states, between natural passion and social convention, between abandon and restraint."

16. See Michel Serres, *Statues* (Paris: Flammarion, 1989) in its entirety, but especially "Erres dans les cimetières," 55–85; and Michel Serres, *L'Hermaphrodite* (Paris: Flammarion, 1989), 119. Similarly, in his commentary on Freud's commentary on the *Moses* statue, Michel de Certeau hypothesizes that sculptural "law is based on a death." See de Certeau, *The Writing of History*, trans. Tom Conley (New York: Columbia University Press, 1988), 340.

17. *Le Respect des femmes*, 77; my translation. It is not, I would submit, incidental that Kofman coins this phrase specifically à propos of Rousseau.

18. See René Vinçon, *Cythère de Watteau: Suspension et coloris* (Paris: Harmattan, 1996), 148; and Marie Roland Michel, *Watteau: An Artist of the Eighteenth Century* (London: Trefoil, 1984), 204; in direct opposition to the interpretation I am proposing here, Michel goes so far as to qualify the nude in the *Champs Elysées* as "far more of a woman than the young people seated on the grass, [far more of a] carnal presence" (204).

19. Slavoj Zizek, *The Plague of Fantasies* (London & New York: Verso, 1997), 123. Interestingly, such a lifeless life is also evoked in Lorris' half of the *Romance of the Rose*, and commences at the precise moment the Lover first drinks from "inside a marble stone" ["dedens une pierre de marbre"] whose reflective waters condemn him to love an elusive, impossible image (v.1432). From this moment on, Lorris' hero realizes that "Love will make a martyr" of him ["fera Amors de moi martir"], and that as such he would be better off dead than alive ["miex vousisse estre mors que vis"] (v.1835–1837). To be sure, such claims are characteristic of the *doux mal d'aymer* and cannot be said categorically to betray the altogether negative valence which Zizek or Miller might ascribe to them, although certain literary ancestors of Lorris, like Maurice Scève, insist on the unremitting destruction and indeed the paralysis wrought by love.

20. Here again, my interpretation parts company with Seerveld's, for whom the presence of this beumsed stranger "suggests that the formalized lovemaking of Watteau's day is a charade . . . of disguised and suppressed sensuality" (174), but who fails to consider the sexual etiology and ideology behind such "suppressions."

21. The royal favorite ultimately decided not to hang these panels in her

retreat at Louveciennes. The reasons for her decision remain shrouded in mystery to this day, though commonly given explanations are the personality clash between her and the painter, and the stylistic incongruity between the rococo paintings and the neo-classical style of the building in which they were to lodge. However, it seems to me equally possible that Du Barry's dissatisfaction could have had something to do with the interpretation I am proposing here: namely, that the paintings depict the bleak consequences of female physical abandon in an age that still valued at least the appearance of *pudeur*. Surely a woman who occupied the official position of royal mistress—a role not readily assimilable to a discourse of feminine virtue—would not have welcomed such a lesson on the walls of her love-nest.

22. The chronological order that I impose here on Fragonard's four panels is not, it should be noted, intrinsic to the works, nor was it ever specified by the artist himself; I suggest such an order in my reading for the sake of nominal narrative coherence and expositional convenience. For three different perspectives on the sequence that should or could be assigned to *The Progress of Love*'s composite images, see Pierre Rosenberg (ed.), *Fragonard* (New York: Metropolitan Museum of Art, 1988), 323; Mary D. Sheriff, *Fragonard: Art and Eroticism* (Chicago: University of Chicago Press, 1990), 82; and Thomas M. Kavanagh, *Esthetics of the Moment, Literature and Art in the French Enlightenment* (Philadelphia: University of Pennsylvania Press, 1996) 234–235.

23. See Choderlos de Laclos, *Dangerous Liaisons*, trans. P.W.K. Stone, in *The Libertine Reader*, ed. Michel Feher (New York: Zone Books, 1997), 937–1254; and within this text, the magisterial Letter LXXXI, in which Merteuil outlines to Valmont her lifelong "experiment in self-mastery" (1075) both moral and physical. The latter is exemplified by, and evokes statuary through, both "the power over my features at which I have sometimes seen you so astonished" (1074), and "[the] apparent frigidity [which] proved to be the unshakeable foundation of [men's] blind trust in me" (1076). Because Nancy K. Miller so brilliantly analyzes the figure of Merteuil in terms similar to the ones I am adopting, I have excluded from this paper any further consideration of a heroine whose eventual symbolic death, effected by her loss of "virtue," nevertheless exemplifies the dynamic of the living dead examined here.

24. For a summary, and a problematization, of the "symbolic diction" that dominated eighteenth-century European aesthetics—diction that posited an equivalence between the subject and his surroundings—see Paul de Man, "The Rhetoric of Temporality," in *Blindness and Insight* (Minneapolis: University of Minnesota Press, 1971), 187–228.

25. See Jacques Thuillier, *Fragonard* (Geneva: Skira/Rizzoli International, 1987), 106: "From the leafy branches a statue of Venus shoots out in a leap that stretches its shape to the point of ugliness. . . . "

26. In this instance too, the *Romance of the Rose* would appear to rear its ubiquitous head, given the pride of place which Jean de Meun assigns to the Pygmalion myth (v.20815–21194) in his ironic revision of Lorris' far more restrained

model of courtly love. (In fact, de Meun literally interpolates his telling of the myth into the aforementioned account of the Tower of Shame's destruction: a *mise en abyme* of the Tower's own encasement of a female statue.) To be sure, it is in Lorris' sublimating *ars amatoria* that Paul de Man locates the "ethos of renunciation" which governs the erotic space of Rousseau's *Julie*. See again, Paul de Man, "The Rhetoric of Temporality." That being said, it seems to me that a comparative reading of de Meun's and Rousseau's versions of the Pygmalion tale would also be fruitful, if only to demonstrate the degree to which the *philosophe*, faithful Lorris, refutes the other writer's apologia of gratified desire.

27. Jean-Jacques Rousseau, *Pygmalion: scène lyrique*, in Bernard Gagnebin & Marcel Raymond (eds.), *Oeuvres complètes de Jean-Jacques Rousseau*, tome II (Paris: Gallimard/Pléïade, 1961), 1225; my translation.

28. And yet, as Paul de Man points out in his analysis of artistic figuration in Rousseau, the figurative "coldness" of Pygmalion's imagination finds its literal reflection in the hard, cold marble of his creation. See Paul de Man, *Allegories of Reading: Figural Language in Rousseau, Nietzsche, Rilke, and Proust* (New Haven & London: Yale University Press, 1979), 178.

29. D.A.F. de Sade, *Juliette*, trans. Austryn Wainhouse (New York: Grove Press, 1968), 613–614.

30. For more on the centrality of apathy to Sadean philosophical and aesthetic discourse, see note 34, below.

31. This reading contrasts, deliberately so, with Winckelmann's breathless celebration of the Medici Venus' exemplary naturalness, which, he claims, taught Bernini to "discover the beauties [of] nature." Nevertheless, he remarks that Raphael conceived of none other than Galatea as a necessarily unnatural figure because of her extreme beauty. See Johann Joachim Winckelmann, *Reflections on the Imitation of Greek Works in Painting and Sculpture*, trans. Elfriede Heyer & Roger C. Norton (LaSalle, Illinois: Open Court, 1987), 19 & 15, respectively.

32. Alenka Zupancic, *Ethics of the Real: Kant, Lacan* (London & New York: Verso, 2000), 80–81.

33. Lynn Hunt, *The Family Romance of the French Revolution* (Berkeley: University of California Press, 1992), Chapter 5, "Sade's Family Politics"; and Angela Carter, *The Sadeian Woman* (New York: Pantheon, 1978), respectively, offer two prime examples of these opposing viewpoints.

34. Four monographs that discuss at length Sade's categorical imperative of apathy are: Pierre Klossowski, *Sade My Neighbor*, trans. Alphonso Lingis (Evanston: Northwestern University Press, 1991); Philippe Sollers, *Sade dans le texte: L'Écriture et l'expérience des limites* (Paris: Seuil, 1968); Gilles Deleuze, *Coldness and Cruelty* (New York: Zone Books, 1991); and Marcel Hénaff, *Sade: The Invention of The Libertine Body*, trans. Xavier Callahan (Minneapolis: University of Minnesota Press, 1999).

35. On the explicitly male gendering of apathetic discourse in Sade's work, see Caroline Weber, "Madame de Mistival's Differend: Animality and Alterity in

Sade's *Philosophie dans le boudoir*," in *The Utah Foreign Language Review* (Spring 1997): 49–61; as well as Caroline Weber, *Terror and Its Discontents: Suspect Words in the French Revolution* (Minneapolis: University of Minnesota Press, 2003), Chapter Four, "The Second Time as Farce," 233–305. See also Jacques Lacan, "Kant avec Sade," in *Écrits*, tome II (Paris: Seuil, 1971), 119–148, for an elliptical but extremely suggestive meditation on the relationship between the foreclosure of femininity (*qua* affective and corporeal difference) and the instantiation of paternal law in Sade's writing.

36. On the frequent denigration of female genitalia, and the concomitant valorization of the penis, in Sade's *oeuvre*, see *The Sadeian Woman*, 5 & 24. In this work, Angela Carter correctly identifies a connection between masculine physiology and libertine ontology: "In [Sade's] schema, [the] vagina might be regarded . . . as a speaking mouth, but never one that issues the voice of reason" (5).

SELECT BIBLIOGRAPHY

Bryson, Norman. *Word and Image: French Painting of the Ancien Régime.* Cambridge: Cambridge University Press, 1981.

Carter, Angela. *The Sadeian Woman.* New York: Pantheon, 1978.

Crow, Thomas E. *Painters and Public Life in Eighteenth-Century Paris.* New Haven & London: Yale University Press, 1985.

Cohen, Sarah. *Art, Dance, and the Body in the French Culture of the Ancien Régime.* Cambridge: Cambridge University Press, 2000.

DeJean, Joan. *Literary Fortifications: Rousseau, Laclos, Sade.* Princeton: Princeton University Press, 1984.

Deleuze, Gilles. *Coldness and Cruelty.* New York: Zone Books, 1991.

de Man, Paul. *Allegories of Reading: Figural Language in Rousseau, Nietzsche, Rilke, and Proust.* New Haven & London: Yale University Press, 1979.

———— *Blindness and Insight.* Minneapolis: University of Minnesota Press, 1983.

Denon, Vivant. *No Tomorrow*, trans. Lydia Davis in *The Libertine Reader*, ed. Michel Feher. New York: Zone Books, 1997: 721–747.

Diderot, Denis. *Entretiens sur 'Le Fils naturel,'* in *Oeuvres complètes*, tome X, ed. Jacques & Anne-Marie Chouillet. Paris: Hermann, 1980.

Edwards, JoLynn "Watteau and the Dance," in *Antoine Watteau: The Painter, His Age, and His Legend*, ed. François Moureau & Margaret M. Grasselli. Geneva: Slatkine, 1987: 220–229.

Eisenstadt, Mussia. *Watteaus Fêtes Galantes und ihre Ursprünge.* Berlin: Bruno Cassirer Verlag, 1930.

Hénaff, Marcel. *Sade: The Invention of The Libertine Body*, trans. Xavier Callahan. Minneapolis: University of Minnesota Press, 1999.

Hesse, Carla. *The Other Enlightenment: How French Women Became Modern*. Princeton: Princeton University Press, 2001.

Hunt, Lynn. *The Family Romance of the French Revolution*. Berkeley: University of California Press, 1992.

Kavanagh, Thomas M. *Esthetics of the Moment. Literature and Art in the French Enlightenment* . Philadelphia, University of Pennsylvania Press, 1996.

Klossowski, Pierre. *Sade My Neighbor*, trans. Alphonso Lingis. Evanston: Northwestern University Press, 1991.

Kofman, Sarah. *Le Respect des femmes*. Paris: Galilée, 1982.

Lacan, Jacques. *Écrits*, tome II. Paris: Seuil, 1971.

———— *Le Séminaire XX: Encore*. Paris: Seuil, 1975.

Laclos, Choderlos de. *Dangerous Liaisons*, trans. P.W.K. Stone, in *The Libertine Reader*: 911–1254.

Levey, Michael. *Rococo to Revolution*. New York: Praeger Publishers, 1966.

Lorris, Guillaume & Jean de Meun. *Le Roman de la Rose*, ed. Daniel Poirion. Paris: Garnier-Flammarion, 1974.

Michel, Marie Roland. *Watteau: An Artist of the Eighteenth Century*. London: Trefoil, 1984.

Miller, Nancy K. *French Dressing: Women, Men, and Ancien Régime Fiction*. New York: Routledge, 1995.

Plax, Julie Anne. *Watteau and the Cultural Politics of Eighteenth-Century France*. Cambridge: Cambridge University Press, 2000.

Rosenberg, Pierre (ed.). *Fragonard*. New York: Metropolitan Museum of Art, 1988.

Rousseau, Jean-Jacques. *Discourse on Inequality*, trans. Maurice Cranston. London & New York: Penguin, 1984.

———— *Oeuvres complètes*, 5 volumes, ed. Bernard Gagnebin & Marcel Raymond. Paris: Gallimard/Pléïade, 1959–1969.

Sade, D.A.F. de. *Juliette*, trans. Austryn Wainhouse. New York: Grove Press, 1968.

Salecl, Renata "I Can't Love You Unless I Give You Up," in *Gaze and Voice as Love Objects: SIC 1*, ed. Salecl & Slavoj Zizek. Durham: Duke University Press, 1996: 179–207.

Schneider, Pierre. *The World of Watteau*. Alexandria, VA: Time-Life, 1977.

Seerveld, Calvin. "Tell-Tale Statues in Watteau's Painting," in *Eighteenth-Century Studies* 14 (Winter 1980–1981): 151–180

Serres, Michel. *L'Hermaphrodite*. Paris: Flammarion, 1989.

———— *Statues*. Paris: Flammarion, 1989.

Sheriff, Mary D. *Fragonard: Art and Eroticism*. Chicago: University of Chicago Press, 1990.

Sollers, Philippe. *Sade dans le texte: L'Écriture et l'expérience des limites*. Paris: Seuil, 1968.

Thuillier, Jacques. *Fragonard*. Geneva: Skira/Rizzoli International, 1987.

Vinçon, René. *Cythère de Watteau: Suspension et coloris*. Paris: Harmattan, 1996

Weber, Caroline. "Madame de Mistival's Differend: Animality and Alterity in Sade's *Philosophie dans le boudoir*," in *The Utah Foreign Language Review* (Spring 1997): 49–61.

———— *Terror and Its Discontents: Suspect Words and the French Revolution*. Minneapolis: University of Minnesota Press, 2003.

Winckelmann, Johann. *Reflections on the Imitation of Greek Works in Painting and Sculpture*, trans. Elfriede Heyer & Roger C. Norton. LaSalle, Illinois: Open Court, 1987.

Zizek, Slavoj. *The Plague of Fantasies*. London & New York: Verso, 1997.

———— "'No Sexual Relationship'," in *Gaze and Voice as Love Objects*: 208–250.

Zupancic, Alenka. *Ethics of the Real: Kant, Lacan*. London & New York: Verso, 2000.

"'To Sing the Toils of Each Revolving Year': Song and Poetic Authority in Stephen Duck's 'The Thresher's Labour'"

JAMES MULHOLLAND

The eighteenth century marks a peculiar and difficult moment for the English pastoral tradition. For some scholars, exemplified perhaps by Frank Kermode, the pastoral, properly defined, does not survive into the eighteenth century.[1] Others argue that the changing conditions of the English countryside require unique generic transformations of eighteenth-century pastoral.[2] Responding to changes in the English countryside, particularly in agrarian labor, pastoral undergoes a redefinition throughout the century whose instability arises from both the adaptation and the persistence of its classical conceits.[3] One author who exemplifies this dual process of generic innovation and conservation is Stephen Duck. Duck, who worked as a thresher in England, composed and circulated "The Thresher's Labour" in 1730. He has received renewed critical treatment in the last decade, in part because the poem presents a detailed account of his rural labor, and also because its rapid success in the literary culture of England secured for him the patronage of Queen Caroline, which initiated his personal transformation from agrarian laborer to poet.[4]

Recent criticism considers "The Thresher's Labour" an important starting point for a poetry that describes rural labor and the English countryside more accurately, rather than portrays an idealized golden age. The meticulous description of the thresher's physical labor often is interpreted as a reflection of the larger social and economic changes precipitated by agrarian capitalism and by the continued enclosure of common land.[5] In addition, Duck represents one of the most visible origins of "plebeian" authorship during the eighteenth century. His dual identity as an agrarian laborer and a poet makes his career a fertile context in which to investigate changes in eighteenth-century authorship and its relationship to mass print.[6] In connection with all of these themes, this article examines "The Thresher's Labour" in relation to orality, one aspect of the poem that has been overlooked in recent studies. It argues that with "The Thresher's Labour" Duck modifies the convention that the pastoral poem is a song, and, in the process, engages with a broader type of pastoralism that encompasses what are typically seen as separate pastoral and georgic modes. Duck's reinvented pastoral song uniquely registers the conditions of his labor, and, therefore, reflects wider social and economic changes of the English countryside.

Singing also permits Duck to reconcile his dual status as an agrarian laborer and as a poet. The use of singing in "The Thresher's Labour" suggests, moreover, the roles that manuscript and print play in publicizing the conditions of the English countryside to a primarily urban and upper-class readership. The subtle acknowledgement of manuscript and print circulation isolates the relationship between orality and literacy in the poem, and reveals the ways that Duck differentiates singing from other types of orality—such as the speech of women laborers—that remain largely unrecognized by literate technologies. Finally, this article considers "The Thresher's Labour" within the larger context of Duck's poetic career, and demonstrates the significance of the metaphor of singing for contemporary responses to Duck's poetry by authors such as Jonathan Swift, Robert Dodsley, and George Crabbe.

The perception that pastoral originates with the song of shepherds makes singing fundamental to the artistry of the pastoral poem. In the early-eighteenth century, singing reflects pastoral's supposed origin in an ideal golden age. In *The Guardian* 22, the critic and author Thomas Tickell is explicit about the correlation between the abundance of nature and the presence of song in pastoral poetry. He claims, for example, that pastoral begins in "a state of ease, innocence and contentment; where plenty begot pleasure, and pleasure begot singing, and singing begot poetry, and poetry begot pleasure again."[7] The abundance of nature generates the conditions that make singing, and therefore poetry, possible. For Tickell, it is natural that pastoral poetry should "transport us to a kind of *Fairy Land*, where our ears are soothed by the Melody of Birds, bleating Flocks, and purling

Streams; our Eyes enchanted with flowery Meadows and springing Greens; we are laid under cool Shades, and entertained with all the Sweets and Freshness of Nature" (105). In Tickell's pastoral, the presence of singing signifies the ease, pleasure, and contentment of the golden age.

In "A Discourse on Pastoral Poetry" (1709) Alexander Pope also emphasizes pastoral's origin in song and in a pre-modern golden age. He declares that pastoral begins with the leisure of shepherds and that no diversion was more proper "to that solitary and sedentary life as singing, and that in their songs they took the occasion to celebrate their own felicity."[8] Singing emphasizes the felicity of shepherds and the leisure of their occupation so that pastoral poetry "consists in exposing the best side only of the shepherd's life, and in concealing its miseries" (120). Yet Pope's "Discourse" also suggests some of the latent possibilities for transforming the pastoral eventually taken up by authors such as Duck. The emphasis upon the leisure of rural laborers in "Discourse" encourages speculation about its opposite, and admits the possibility of investigating the conditions of rural labor. To depict the conditions of rural labor and the English countryside, Duck modifies the pastoral by exposing its antecedent preoccupation with the difference between leisure and labor.

That song serves as a means of political or social commentary is not new to the pastoral tradition or unique to the eighteenth century. Toward the end of the first of Virgil's *Eclogues*, Meliboeus, removed from his property and divested of his flock by civil unrest in Rome, abruptly states: "I'll sing no songs."[9] Meliboeus's forthright assertion that he'll no longer sing possesses both an aesthetic and a political purpose: his decision not to sing indicates both the conclusion of Virgil's first eclogue and the end of the stable political and prosperous economic conditions that make singing possible. To place it within Tickell's terminology from *The Guardian*, if plenty begets pleasure and pleasure begets singing, then Meliboeus demonstrates that the lack of leisure and plenty culminates with the cessation of singing. Even in the classical pastoral, therefore, singing acts as an interchange between the aesthetic realm and the social and political realm, and serves as a measure of social, political, and economic change.

In "The Thresher's Labour," Duck identifies the changing conditions of the English countryside and of the pastoral tradition in a way similar to Meliboeus at the conclusion of Virgil's first eclogue.[10] Though "The Thresher's Labour" does not describe the outright cessation of singing, early in the poem the speaker creates a vivid portrait of the thresher at work:

> Nor yet, the tedious Labour to beguile,
> And make the passing Minutes sweetly smile,
> Can we, like Shepherds, tell a merry Tale;
> The Voice is lost, drown'd by the louder Flail.
> But we may think—Alas! What pleasing thing,
> Here, to the mind, can the dull Fancy bring?
> Our eye beholds no pleasing Object here,
> No chearful Sound diverts our list'ning Ear.
> The shepherd well may tune his Voice to sing,
> Inspir'd with all the Beauties of the Spring.
> No Fountains murmur here, no Lambkins play,
> No linnets warble, and no Fields look gay.[11]

What's noticeable about this passage is the conscious contrast between the thresher and the shepherd. The description of the thresher differs remarkably from that of the shepherd, and this contrast extends to their experience of voice. Whereas the shepherd "well may tune his voice to sing / Inspir'd by all the beauties of the Spring," the thresher's "Voice is lost, drown'd by the louder flail" so that "no cheerful sound diverts [his] list'ning Ear" (13). In this instance, it is the relationship to *singing* voice that announces the difficulties of the thresher's labor, and the difference of his labor from that of the shepherd. The shepherd, surrounded by playful lambkins and murmuring fountains, finds ample means and subject matter for song, and through his song he cheerfully diverts himself from his labor. The thresher, by contrast, does not work in an environment conducive to song. Laboring when the outdoor work of harvest is complete, the thresher toils while closely confined within the barn.[12] But the techniques involved in threshing are even more important than the location of his work. The thresher's "louder flail" drowns out his voice; his song is overwhelmed by the tools involved in his labor, making it impossible for that song to be heard. The thresher, Duck laments, cannot "beguile" his labor and make the "passing Minutes sweetly smile" by hearing a "merry tale" (13).

The differentiation of the thresher and the shepherd signals Duck's revision of the artistic conventions of pastoral. In "The Pastoral Revolution," Michael McKeon organizes the value-laden oppositions of leisure and labor and of the bucolic and the georgic within the larger category of pastoralism. The "pastoral" and the "georgic," McKeon contends, "occupy alternative and partial positions on the pastoral continuum that is defined not by the dichotomous opposition of nature to art but by the fluidity with which the differential may be variously enacted."[13] He continues that pastoral "works both to affirm and to suspend such oppositions—to conceive of them, that is, not dichotomously but dialectically" (271). One of the most powerful and important separations occurs with Virgil's *Eclogues* and his *Georgics*, where the eclogues come to represent the bucolic impulse and the *Georgics* originate the georgic impulse. Yet the last line of Virgil's *Georgics* is the first line of his *Eclogues*, demonstrating a circularity that implies that pastoral and georgic are more continuous than separate (269). One might argue that the availability or unavailability of singing designates two different positions on this pastoral continuum. Duck's contrast of the thresher from the shepherd benefits from his sophisticated attention to the imbricated relationship between leisure and labor in pastoral. His representation of the thresher rather than the more traditional shepherd designates the difference between his own pastoral and the neoclassical pastoral of Tickell and Pope. In this way, the social and political potential of "The Thresher's Labour" relies not so much upon the difference between pastoral and georgic, but upon Duck's ability to transform pastoral by contrasting the shepherd's ability to sing with the thresher's inability to be heard while singing.[14]

The availability or unavailability of singing in "The Thresher's Labour" provides immediate access not only to formal issues of eighteenth-century pastoral, but also to social and economic changes in the English countryside. "The Thresher's Labour" presents a detailed depiction of one aspect of modern agrarian labor.[15] These working conditions differ substantially from those experienced by the shepherds of Tickell's and Pope's pastorals. Yet it is notable that Duck never specifies the historical moment of the thresher or the shepherd in the poem. Despite Pope's insistence that shepherds' song originates in the golden age, Duck does not explicitly associate threshers with the modern English countryside and shepherds with a pre-modern golden age.[16] Instead, it is the different rhythm of their labor rather than different historical periods that further distinguishes threshers from shepherds. At one point in "The Thresher's Labour," while addressing the peculiar rhythm of his work, the thresher states matter-of-factly that "No intermission in our Work we know; / The noisy threshal must for ever go" (12). It is the noise of the flail that marks out the thresher's time so that "in the Air our knotty Weapons fly, / And now with equal Force descend from high; / Down one, one up, so well they keep the Time" (12). By the end of the poem the thresher is even more explicit:

> Thus, as the Year's revolving Course goes round,
> No Respite from our Labour can be found:
> Like SISYPHUS, our work is never done;

Continually rolls back the restless Stone.
New-growing Labours still succeed the past;
And growing always new, must always last.
(27)

The final image of Sisyphus reinforces the unique rhythm of the thresher's labor. Whereas the shepherds of Pope's "Discourse" possess time for leisure, for the thresher "the threshal must forever go" so that "No Respite from our Labour can be found" (13, 27). The sound of the flail manifests materially the uniform temporality of threshing that "grow[s] always new" and therefore "must always last" (27). In this way, "The Thresher's Labour" does not differentiate the shepherd from the thresher through the temporal markers of pre-modern golden age and modern British agriculture—that is, through the past and the present—though these markers may be accurate. It is the thresher's mode of labor—noisy, mechanical, and repetitive yet "always new"—that differs so greatly from that of the shepherd. The noise of the thresher's flail and the thresher's song, moreover, represent two types of competing oralities and competing temporalities. The physical intensity of threshing, resulting from the noise of the thresher's tools and the uniform organization of his time, overwhelms both leisure and song. The way that the noise of the flail drowns out the thresher's song and efficiently organizes his time, therefore, demonstrates the evident difference between Duck's pastoral, grounded in the depiction of rural labor, and the idealized pastoral of Tickell and Pope.[17]

Yet one might ask who would hear the thresher's song if it could be heard over the noise of the flail? Considering Duck's meticulous attention to singing, it is unsurprising that he uses the metaphor of singing to answer this question. One of the most important features of the poem is its prominent dedication: "To the Reverend Mr. Stanley." Stanley was a local clergyman who noticed Duck while he was employed as a thresher, and the opening stanza of "The Thresher's Labour" figures Stanley's patronage as essential to the creation of the poem:

> The grateful tribute of these rural Lays,
> Which to her Patron's Hand the Muse conveys,
> Deign to accept: 'Tis just she Tribute bring
> To him, whose Bounty gives her Life to sing;
> To him, whose gen'rous Favours tune her Voice;
> And bid her, 'midst her Poverty, rejoice.
> Inspir'd by these, she dares herself prepare,
> To sing the Toils of each revolving Year;

Those endless Toils, which always grow anew
And the poor *Thresher's* destin'd to pursue:
Ev'n these, with Pleasure, can the Muse rehearse
When you and Gratitude demand her verse.
(10)

The opening stanza introduces Stanley as an important facilitator of the poem. It is significant, though, that Duck uses singing to relate Stanley's patronage to the overall operation of the poem. It is Stanley's "bounty" which permits the Muse to sing and his "generous favours" that "tune her voice." The metaphor of "tuning" the Muse's voice is particularly noteworthy. It suggests that the Muse possesses a wide vocal register, and that the attention of individuals such as Stanley allows the Muse to discover the appropriate tone and articulation with which to depict the specific labors of the thresher.

Yet if the addressee of the opening stanza is fairly clear, its speaker is not. Whereas the majority of "The Thresher's Labour" appears in the voice of a male thresher, the opening stanza involves the voice of a female Muse and creates a significant ambiguity about the relationship between the singing Muse and the thresher. One could interpret this as a typical image of inspiration by a Muse. Yet the opening stanza of the poem troubles the possibility of identifying an anonymous thresher, or even Duck, as the speaker of these lines. It is her voice that sings "the toils of each revolving year; / Those endless Toils, which always grow anew / And the poor Thresher's destined to pursue" (10). The stanza ends by arguing that Stanley and gratitude demand "her verse." About the multiple speakers of "The Thresher's Labour," Bridget Keegan claims that "the poem, as Duck creates it, is explicitly not originally the product of the laborer."[18] She continues that the "verbal exchange of the literary work between the Muse and patron frames the ensuing account of the exchange of labor—agricultural work— between the farmer and thresher" (553). The displacement of the thresher's poetic authority onto the Muse reinforces the thresher's alienation from the products of his own labor—both of his agricultural labor and of his "voice." The exploitation of the thresher's labor repeats itself in the framework of the poem, where the thresher cannot speak of his own labors without the mediation of a patron and a conventional Muse. Duck responds to this required mediation through his complicated use of pronouns; as Keegan states, throughout the poem Duck creates a "singular poetic 'I,' a speaking subject distinct from the threshing 'we'" (556). The "we" records the manual labor of the thresher and the "I" translates that labor into a more suitable figurative discourse (555).

While Keegan rightly points out the necessary mediation of the poem, one might add that Duck formulates the poem as the song of a female Muse and, in the process, partly replaces his own authorship of the poem with the image of a creative circuit between a generous patron and a singing female Muse. Yet one need not interpret Duck's separation of poetic authority in the opening stanza between a patron and a singing female Muse solely as a devaluation of the thresher's voice and of Duck's poetic authority. If one of the explicit questions of "The Thresher's Labour" concerns the possibility of the thresher singing, then Duck's separation of poetic authority between his patron and a singing female Muse demonstrates, at the level of the overall poem, one solution to Duck's anxiety about poetic authority. McKeon declares about pastoral in the eighteenth century that "when the customary objects of pastoral representation become also its authorial subjects, the contemporary revolution in status and gender categorization becomes quite explicit."[19] Duck's identification with both the unheard male thresher and the singing female Muse allows him to partly inhabit both the subject and the object of pastoral within the same poetic exercise, and the convention that the pastoral poem is a song creates one opportunity for Duck to negotiate his own ambiguous status both as subject and object. Singing supplies a solution to the problem of representing the conditions of modern agrarian labor both as a participant in those conditions and as an observer of those conditions–that is, as a thresher and as a singer. In effect, the separation of poetic authority in "The Thresher's Labour" recapitulates the entire occasion of the poem: the Muse sings of how the thresher's song cannot be heard over the noise of his own labor.

Duck's description of the entire poem as the song of a Muse suggests that the scribal or the printed poem succeeds in making the thresher "heard" when the thresher's song could not. The speaker, for example, asserts that the Muse's "rural lays" are conveyed to the patron's *hand*, which presumes a tangible, material form for the poem.[20] The seemingly contradictory image of the Muse's song being conveyed to the patron's hand subtly acknowledges the scribal and printed forms of the poem, and imagines the creation and circulation of "The Thresher's Labour" as a successful translation from song into manuscript and print. If the thresher's song represents an aesthetic form that cannot be recognized over the noise of his own labor, then the manuscript and printed versions of "The Thresher's Labour" preserve one account of that lack of recognition. William Christmas argues that Duck's poem "gives public, plebeian voice to rural laboring life."[21] One could further argue that the wide circulation of the poem in manuscript and print is the most tangible evidence of the degree to which the poem succeeds in publicizing the conditions of rural labor. The poem's ability to "give voice" is predicated upon the circulation, in script and print, of the thresher's inability to be heard while singing. Therefore, song contributes the essential metaphor that describes the poem's existence both as manuscript and print, and its potential to publicize the conditions of rural labor. In effect, the literate circulation makes the thresher's song "heard." In "The Thresher's Labour," however, singing is not simply a synonym for literacy, or for writing. As the opening stanza demonstrates, the poem conceives of its own creation as a translation from singing into manuscript and type–that is, from orality to literacy.

"The Thresher's Labour" did circulate quite successfully in the literary culture of England during the 1730s, and the popularity of the poem provoked a number of satires that raise additional questions about Duck's figuration of poetic authority.[22] Many of these satires scrutinize Duck's suitability as a poet by emphasizing his history as a thresher. One of the most acidic examples of this type of response is Jonathan Swift's "On Stephen Duck, the Thresher, and Favourite Poet" (1730). In his poem, Swift dismisses Duck's poetry by insisting upon its fundamental similarity to agrarian labor. Swift begins his poem:

> The Thresher Duck could o'er the Queen prevail.
> The proverb says, 'No fence against a flail.'
> From *threshing* corn, he turns to *thresh* his brains;
> For which Her Majesty allows him grains.[23]

Swift's image of Duck prevailing over the Queen refers to Duck's acquisition of a royal sinecure from Queen Caroline, largely due to the popularity of "The Thresher's Labour." But it is also significant that Swift claims Duck composes his poems by "thresh[ing] his brains." In Swift's image, the "rural lays" of "The Thresher's Labour" are more like an agricultural harvest than a song, and Duck merely threshes his brain in the same way that he once threshed corn. Swift's association of Duck's brain with nature's bounty—both of which can be threshed—realigns him with the object, rather than the subject, of the traditional pastoral.[24] While in "The Thresher's Labour" the unheard thresher and the singing Muse contribute to an image of Duck's ambiguous authorial identity, Swift attempts to conflate these two positions and to associate Duck with the bounty of nature rather than the artfulness of the singer. Swift's basic assertion is that Duck remains a thresher whether the final product is a harvest or a poem.

Yet the metaphor of singing suggests another possible interpretation of Duck's transformation from threshing corn to "threshing his brains." If one allows that he represents his ambiguous position as both subject and object of pastoral through the singing Muse and the unheard thresher, then these two positions may help describe his own transformation from agrarian laborer to working poet. In his "Epistle to Stephen Duck" (1732), the laboring poet Robert Dodsley addresses the issue of laboring-class authorship through the metaphor of singing. Dodsley is a footman (who would eventually become a renowned bookseller), and his position demonstrates some clear affinities to that of Duck:

> So you and I, just naked from the shell,
> In chirping notes, our future singing tell;
> Unfeather'd yet, in judgement, though, or skill,
> Hop round the basis of Parnassus' hill:
> Our flights are low, and want of art and strength
> Forbids to carry us to the wish'd for length.
> But fledg'd and cherish'd with a kindly spring,
> We'll mount the summit, and melodious sing.[25]

The optimism of Dodsley's figuration of himself and Duck as newborn birds—or even as "ducklings"—ready to ascend Parnassus derives from singing. While Duck and Dodsley remain "unfeather'd" in poetic judgment or skill, their "chirping notes" promise more able "future singing," and their ascent up Parnassus results from their "flights" of song. For Dodsley, occupying the position of singer indicates the success of their ascent. The ascent up Parnassus, moreover, denotes two material transformations: it signifies entry into the exclusive realm of polite literary culture and a corresponding elevation in social status.

Duck himself relies upon the identity of singer to evaluate his ambiguous status as a poet. A few years after the composition of "The Thresher's Labour," he again uses singing to detail his peculiar position as a poet who began as an agrarian laborer. In his lengthy "A Description of a Journey," Duck self-consciously considers his new identity as a poet and his increasingly distant identity as a thresher. At one point in the poem, he describes a feast held once a year in his honor in Wiltshire, the county in which he was born and where he worked as a thresher.[26] In the process of portraying the holiday, he employs song, and the concept of an oral tradition in general, to envision his newer status as a poet:

> Hence, when their children's children shall admire
> This Holiday, and, whence deriv'd, inquire;
> Some grateful Father, partial to my Fame,
> Shall thus describe from whence, and how it came.
>
> "Here, Child, a *Thresher* liv'd in ancient Days;
> Quaint Songs he sang, and pleasing Roundelays,
> A gracious QUEEN his Sonnets did commend;
> And some *great Lord*, one TEMPLE, was his *Friend*:
> And feast *the Threshers*, for *that Thresher's sake*."
>
> Thus shall Tradition keep my Fame alive;
> The *Bard* may die, the *Thresher* still survive.[27]

Written a few years after the enormous success of "The Thresher's Labour," in this passage Duck imagines himself as the thresher whose singing finally has been heard. The lines themselves shift between Duck speaking in his own voice about the holiday, and the voice of a thresher ("Some grateful Father") who recounts its origin. "A Description of a Journey" contains some ambitious self-figuration: the now singing thresher is an "ancient" whose song secures his own reputation for posterity through the reproduction of oral tales by other threshers such as the "grateful Father." Much like Dodsley's "Epistle," Duck's "A Description of a Journey" formulates his literary success as an ascent to the position of the singer, and the references to "Bard" and "Thresher" suggest his earlier separation of Muse and thresher. Even at this early point in his career as a poet, Duck represents himself as someone who has occupied the position of the singer which, paradoxically, preserves for posterity his fame as a thresher. That it is the oral tradition, rather than literate circulation, that perpetuates Duck's fame further accentuates the paradox, and reverses the idea from "The Thresher's Labour" that literate circulation makes the thresher's song "heard."

"A Description of a Journey" creates a sophisticated continuity between the artist and the laborer, though in a much different manner than the one that Swift proposes in his satire. It is telling that Duck declares that his *singing* secures for future threshers some momentary respite from their labors. He associates his role as a singer, and his labor as a poet more generally, with the alleviation of the threshers' conditions. Yet he also elevates himself to the position of singer by acting as a benevolent patron to the nameless threshers in the same way that Stanley acts as a patron to the

Muse in "The Thresher's Labour." Thus, "A Description of a Journey" reveals some of the implicit goals and contradictions of Duck's poetic career. If, as Christmas argues, Duck's verse publicizes the conditions of rural labor, then his success as a singer is an essential part of that publicity; in Duck's representation, the ability to "give voice" to rural laborers rests upon his skill as a singer rather than his authenticity as a thresher.

While Duck's self-characterization as a poet relies upon presenting himself as like the singing female Muse of "The Thresher's Labour," it is also important to distinguish the singing female Muse from Duck's fellow women laborers. At one point in "The Thresher's Labour," the thresher describes a group of women laborers at work:

> Our Master comes, and at his Heels a Throng
> Of prattling Females, arm'd with Rake and Prong;
> Prepar'd, whilst he is here, to make his Hay;
> Or, if he turns his Back, prepar'd to play:
> But here, or gone, sure of this Comfort still;
> Here's Company, so they may chat their Fill.
> Ah! were their Hands so active as their Tongues,
> How nimbly then would move the Rakes and Prongs.
> (19–20)

The description of the women's speech is even more severe. The thresher states that

> what they speak, the rest will hardly hear:
> Till by degrees so high their notes they strain,
> A Stander by can nought distinguish plain.
> So loud's their Speech, and so confus'd their Noise,
> Scarce puzzled ECHO can return the Voice.
> (20–21)

About this moment McKeon writes: "within the context of Duck's radicalized pastoralism, the speaking thresher should find a class ally in the women, who enforce custom and resist the regimentation of the work week by setting their 'tongues' against their 'hands,' their 'play,' against their work. . . . "[28] It is the thresher's posture as a poet, McKeon claims, that leads him momentarily to identify with the master and not acknowledge the possible identification with women laborers, and to make their speech unintelligible. Donna Landry suggests that the concept of the oral tradition is one way to understand Duck's depiction of the women's speech as unintelligible. Duck objects to women's speech because "such gatherings for gossip and other forms of exchange are an expression of community among these rural women, for whom there are so few opportunities for recreation and amusement. In a sense, these women have become custodians of the oral tradition to which their relative exclusion from print culture has increasingly relegated them."[29] In Landry's account, the oral tradition and print reinforces the sexual difference between women and men, and corresponds with the wide exclusion of women, especially laboring women, from access to print at this particular historical moment. Moreover, women's access to a community organized through orality provides one of the most effective means for them to resist the exploitation of their labor; that is, to set their "tongues" against their "hands."

Both McKeon's and Landry's accounts permit a further specification of Duck's reaction to the "prattling females." One of the reasons that the thresher identifies so readily with the master results from Duck's objection to the particular type of orality that women laborers come to represent in "The Thresher's Labour." Duck expresses his disinterest in female community by characterizing their speech in terms similar to that of the flail; for example, the thresher's claim about women laborers—that "so loud's their Speech, and so confus'd their Noise / Scarce puzzled ECHO can return the Voice" (21)—recalls the earlier description of the "noisy threshal" that "must forever go" and how the thresher's voice is "drown'd out by the louder flail." Duck's objection to the noise of women's speech indicates that his identification with the song of the female Muse does not extend to an equal identification with another readily available version of orality: that of women laborers. The thresher's criticism of the women's speech results, in part, from Duck's association of the unheard song of the thresher with the Muse's song, and the separation of each from the speech of women laborers. In this way, Duck's identification with the singing female Muse paradoxically reinforces sexual difference through the differentiation of orality. Much as he positions himself as a singer in "A Description of a Journey" by elevating himself to the role of beneficent patron, in "The Thresher's Labour" he elevates himself to the status of singer by separating song from the supposedly unintelligible speech of women laborers. And women's orality is not only unintelligible to the thresher but, as Landry suggests, it is also unintelligible to the literate techniques of the poem and print culture in general. Therefore, while singing in "The Thresher's Labour" provides access to important historical changes in the English countryside, Duck's deliberate valuation of a particular type of orality—one that can be reproduced in manuscript and print—obscures the existence of other types of orality that also substantiate, but resist, those historical changes.[30]

In "The Thresher's Labour," and throughout Duck's career, the trope of singing provides access to the conditions of the English countryside and describes his difficult negotiation of his status as a poet. George Crabbe's *The Village* (1783) is another eighteenth-century pastoral that uses singing, and Duck's ambiguous identity as an author and an agrarian laborer, to comment upon pastoral. Early in *The Village*, Crabbe characterizes his poetic endeavor as a song:

> On Mincio's banks, in Caesar's bounteous reign,
> If Tityrus found the golden age again,
> Must sleepy bards the flattering dream prolong,
> Mechanic echoes of the Mantuan song?
> From truth and nature shall we widely stray,
> Where Virgil, not where Fancy led the way?
>
> Yes, thus the Muses sing of happy swains
> Because the Muses never knew their pains[31]

The most striking feature of these lines is Crabbe's unabashed reconsideration of the classical pastoral. The references to "Tityrus" and Caesar demonstrate that the target of his reconsideration is Virgil's *Eclogues* and its imitators. Crabbe's question—"shall we widely stray / Where Virgil, not where Fancy led the way?"—imagines the imitation of Virgil, and perhaps the classical pastoral in general, as the mystification rather than the revelation of truth and nature. It is meaningful that Crabbe characterizes the imitation of the Virgilian pastoral as "mechanic echoes of the Mantuan song." His emphasis upon the capacity of mechanical echoes to obscure the truth and nature of pastoral suggests both that imitation of the classical pastoral is artificial and mechanistic, and that the nature of the English countryside requires a significantly transformed pastoral song rather than an echo of the classical.

Crabbe's reexamination of the Virgilian pastoral results in an unexpected alternative. Moments after describing the "mechanic echoes" of Virgil's modern imitators, Crabbe offers Stephen Duck as an example of an alternate pastoral. He asks "Save honest Duck, what son of verse could share / The poet's rapture and the peasant's care?" (27–28). It is significant that Crabbe establishes Duck as someone who participates both in the "poet's rapture" and in the "peasant's care"—that is, participates both as the subject and the object of pastoral. Duck's own negotiation of subject and object indicates the profoundly new demands of eighteenth-century pastoral, and his ability to feel the "poet's rapture" and the "peasant's care" makes him a unique origin for a pastoral tradition able to depict the English countryside more accurately. His simultaneous identification with "poet" and "peasant" constitutes the innovation of his verse, and it is instructive that the ambiguity of voice in "The Thresher's Labour" later becomes one criterion for truthfulness in *The Village*.

Yet it is the first stanza of *The Village* that most prominently reveals the characteristics of the new pastoral song that originates with Duck. Crabbe opens the poem by stating:

> The Village life, and every care that reigns
> O'er youthful peasants and declining swains;
> What labour yields, and what, that labour past,
> Age, in its hour of languor, finds at last;
> What forms the real picture of the poor
> Demands a song—The Muse can give no more.
> (1–6)

The reference to song recalls Duck's own use of singing to gain access to the social and economic history of the English countryside, and the first stanza of *The Village* continues to make explicit many of the concerns of "The Thresher's Labour." Much like Duck, Crabbe describes his own poetic project as an adaptation of pastoral song, which he imagines as the continuation of Duck's career. One of the most explicit political statements of *The Village* is that the empirical impulse of later eighteenth-century pastoral demands a particular type of song from the Muse, reflected not by imitations of Virgil but by Duck's ability to feel both the "poet's rapture" and the "peasant's care." Later in *The Village* Crabbe asks:

> Nor you, ye poor, of lettered scorn complain,
> To you the smoothest song is smooth in vain,
> O'ercome by labour and bowed down by time
> Feel you the barren flattery of a rhyme?
>
> Can poets soothe you, when you pine for bread,
> By winding myrtles round your ruined shed?
> Can their light tales your weighty griefs o'erpower,
> Or glad with airy mirth the toilsome hour?
> (55–62)

Much like the differentiation of orality in "The Thresher's Labour," Crabbe distinguishes between two types of song: between the "smoothest songs" of Virgil's imitators and a new type of song that originates with the "real picture of the rural poor." Crabbe's questions about the "smoothest song" of Virgil's imitators reveal equally profound questions about a song that originates in the "real picture of the rural poor": does his reinvented pastoral song succeed in soothing the rural poor in a way that the "smooth songs" of Virgil's imitators do not? The question is not rhetorical and Crabbe's answer is not obvious. Still, the opening stanza indicates a substantial transformation of the pastoral tradition because the emphasis upon a more empirical description of the English countryside requires fundamental changes to the Muse's song. Rather than "winding the myrtles round the ruined shed" the speaker claims to "paint the cot / As truth will paint it, and bards will not" (60, 53–54). Furthermore, the opening stanza establishes that the rural poor play a significant role in the Muse's song. While in "The Thresher's Labour," the patron serves as an important facilitator of the Muse's song, in *The Village* it is the real conditions of the rural poor that demand a new type of pastoral song from the Muse.

Yet, in many ways, *The Village* reconsiders the relationship between pastoral song and the alleviation of the conditions of rural laborers that Duck takes up years earlier in his "A Description of a Journey." In the latter poem, Duck imagines that the publication of his "quaint songs" momentarily alleviates the working conditions of rural laborers. *The Village*, by contrast, is less optimistic about the possibility that singing, or even literate publication, can alleviate the conditions of the poor. Though the speaker of *The Village* claims to create a pastoral grounded in the accurate description of the countryside, the poem also states that the Muse can give no more than a song, which suggests that a song, even one derived from the "real picture of the poor," has a limited effect. *The Village* does not represent the Muse's song as an artistic endeavor that ultimately compensates the rural poor. Rather, the speaker suggests, that song may only describe, rather than not alleviate, those conditions.

That Crabbe offers Duck as a representative figure of his rejuvenated pastoral song signifies Duck's continued importance within eighteenth-century pastoral, an importance that often remains unacknowledged. In many ways, Duck's verse creates a model for a new type of pastoral song indebted to a more accurate depiction of rural labor, and *The Village* exists in a much transformed pastoral tradition that begins with "The Thresher's Labour." Duck uses the idea that pastoral is a song to distinguish his representation of the thresher from the early eighteenth-century pastoral's representations of shepherds and of an idealized golden age. He adapts the pastoral convention of singing to comment directly upon the changing social and economic conditions of the English countryside, much as Virgil subtly commented upon the civil unrest in Rome in his first eclogue. The metaphor of singing, moreover, introduces one effective way for Duck to consider his ambiguous status both as the subject and the object of pastoral, and to explain his transformation from an agrarian laborer to a poet. It is his complicated negotiation of subject and object that makes him significant for *The Village*, and attracts the scrutiny of his contemporaries.

Duck also figures the creation of "The Thresher's Labour" as the translation from song into manuscript and type. The ways that he employs singing to elucidate the creation and circulation of his poem raises larger questions about the relationship between orality and the representation of poetic authority during the eighteenth century. His careful differentiation of the thresher's song from other types of orality, particularly from the speech of fellow women laborers, calls for further consideration of the ways that orality reinforces sexual difference, and of the ways that women authors utilize orality to construct their own poetic authority. The affinity between Duck's song and scribal and print circulation, and the more common exclusion of women's speech from literate reproduction, demonstrates the need for a more precise sense of the differences that exist in orality, and to what degree orality impacts upon poetic discourse of the eighteenth century. In a century often highlighted for the importance of print culture, Duck's complicated use of the metaphor of singing suggests the ways that orality remains an essential though still unacknowledged resource for authors.

NOTES

A shorter version of this paper was presented at the thirty-third annual meeting of the American Society for Eighteenth-Century Studies in Colorado Springs, Colorado. I would like to thank the panel chair, Mark Pedreira, and the participants: J. Douglas Canfield, Hueikeng Chang, and Michael Schwartz. I would also like to thank Michael McKeon and Paula McDowell for reading early versions of this essay, and the anonymous readers for *Studies in Eighteenth-Century Culture.*

1.   *English Pastoral Poetry: From the Beginnings to Marvell*, ed. with an introduction Frank Kermode (New York: Barnes and Noble, 1952). In his introduction, Kermode argues that after the seventeenth century the pastoral "live[s] in a quite different atmosphere, and in a quite different relationship to its readers" (42). The relationship and atmosphere are so different that Kermode

ends his collection with the poetry of Andrew Marvell.

2. For broad surveys of pastoral in the eighteenth century, see J.E. Congleton, *Theories of Pastoral in England, 1684–1798* (Gainesville, Florida: University of Florida Press, 1952); A. J. Sambrook, "An Essay on Eighteenth-Century Pastoral, Pope to Wordsworth (I)," *Trivium* 5 (1970): 21–35, and "An Essay on Eighteenth-Century Pastoral, Pope to Wordsworth (II)," *Trivium* 6 (1971): 103–15. Raymond Williams associates the eighteenth century with a counter-pastoral tradition in opposition to the aristocratic ideals of seventeenth-century pastoral; see, *The Country and the City* (New York: Oxford University Press, 1973), 13–35, 68–96. For an argument about how pastoral continues to enact aristocratic modes in the eighteenth century and the early nineteenth century, see Roger Sales, *English Literature in History, 1780–1830: Pastoral and Politics* (New York: St. Martin's Press, 1983), especially 13–18. For criticism that evaluates Duck within the pastoral tradition, see John Goodridge, *Rural Life in Eighteenth-Century English Poetry* (Cambridge: Cambridge University Press, 1995): 6–7, 12–15. John Barrell considers Duck's representation of farmworkers in the eighteenth century. See his "Sportive Labour: The Farmworker in Eighteen-Century Poetry and Painting," in *The English Rural Community: Image and Analysis*, ed. Brian Short (Cambridge: Cambridge University Press, 1992), 118–20; and also his argument about the changing relationship to pastoral in the visual arts in *The Dark Side of the Landscape: The Rural Poor in English Painting, 1730–1840* (Cambridge: Cambridge University Press, 1980). For a helpful discussion of women authors and pastoral, consider Ann Messenger, *Pastoral Tradition and the Female Talent: Studies in Augustan Poetry* (New York: AMS Press, 2001), especially 1–15.

3. See Michael McKeon, "Surveying the Frontier of Culture: Pastoralism in Eighteenth-Century England," *Studies in Eighteenth-Century Culture*, ed. Syndy M. Conger and Julie C. Hayes (Baltimore: Johns Hopkins University Press, 1998): 7–28. McKeon argues that the instability of the pastoral is not accidental, but rather "congenital and constitutive of the genre" so that pastoral "takes as its subject the problem of conventionality itself" (9).

4. Rose Mary Davis, *Stephen Duck, The Thresher-Poet* (Orono: University of Maine Studies, 1926). Davis's work, though dated, remains the most complete account of Duck's life. See also Joseph Spence, "An Account of the Author, in a Letter to a Friend." Written in 1730, Spence's account was published in 1731, with slight changes, as *A Full and Authentick Account of Stephen Duck, the Wiltshire Poet* (London, 1731) and as a preface to Duck's *Poems on Several Occasions* (London, 1736).

5. For different discussions of the radicalism of Duck's attention to the detail of rural labor, see Williams, 87–90; H. Gustav Klaus, *The Literature of Labour: Two Hundred Years of Working-Class Writing* (New York: St. Martin's Press, 1985), 11–14; McKeon, "Surveying the Frontier of Culture," 21–23. On the "rural realism" of Duck's poetry and its relationship to the actual practices of agrarian labor, see Goodridge, 15–17, 18–22, 30–32, 37–39, 44–49. For a good

summary of the changing practices of eighteenth-century agriculture, see E.L. Jones, "Agriculture: 1700–1800" in *The Economic History of Britain Since 1700. Vol. 1: 1700–1860.* ed. Roderick Floud and Donald McCloskey (Cambridge: Cambridge University Press, 1981), especially 70–82.

6. On Duck's place in plebeian authorship of the eighteenth century, see William Christmas, *The Labr'ing Muses: Work, Writing, and the Social Order in English Plebeian Poetry, 1730–1830* (Newark: University of Delaware Press, 2001), 20, 64–66, 75–76, 79, 84, 107–08. Also consider Bridget Keegan, "Georgic Transformations and Stephen Duck's 'The Thresher's Labour'," *Studies in English Literature* 41, 3 (Summer 2001): 546, 548–52. Keegan focuses upon how Duck transforms the georgic tradition to accommodate his position as an agrarian laborer producing georgic poetry.

7. *The Guardian*, ed. with an introduction John Calhoun Stephens, (Lexington: University of Kentucky Press, 1982), 105.

8. Alexander Pope, "A Discourse on Pastoral Poetry," *The Poems of Alexander Pope*, ed. John Butt (New Haven: Yale University Press, 1963), 119. Pope's "Discourse" was first published in Tonson's *Miscellanies* in 1709, though Pope insists in a headnote that it was composed in 1704.

9. Paul Alpers, *The Singer of the Eclogues: A Study of Virgilian Pastoral* (Berkeley: University of California Press, 1979), 15. Virgil's *Eclogues* were written around 40 B.C. The civil unrest in Rome at that time serves as an important context for the representation of song in the first eclogue, and for the *Eclogues* as a whole. Alpers claims, for example, that "it is essential to keep in mind that the *Eclogues* were written under the first triumvirate, when Octavian was young, Italy was torn by civil wars, and the political situation was at best uncertain" (3).

10. Duck was familiar with both Virgil's *Eclogues* and *Georgics*. Spence claims that Duck owned John Dryden's 1697 translation of Virgil, which contained both these works ("Account," xiii).

11. *The Thresher's Labour and The Woman's Labour*, ed. with an introduction Moira Ferguson, Augustan Reprint Society 230 (Los Angeles: William Andrews Clark Memorial Library, 1985), 13. Unless otherwise stated, all the selections from Duck's poetry refer to this edition and subsequent references appear parenthetically in the text. Ferguson's edition of "The Thresher's Labour" is based upon Duck's *Poems on Several Occasions*, published in London in 1736. Though this is the first authorized edition of Duck's poetry, "The Thresher's Labour" was published numerous times between 1730 and 1736, and those printings contain variations. For a discussion of these differences, and the merits of using the 1730 edition of "The Thresher's Labour," see the introduction to *The Thresher's Labour by Stephen Duck and The Woman's Labour by Mary Collier*, ed. E. P. Thompson and Marian Sugden (London: The Merlin Press, 1989); and Peter J. McGonigle, "Stephen Duck and the Text of *The Thresher's Labour*," *The Library* 4, Sixth Series (1982): 288–96. McGonigle observes that Duck's patrons, such as Spence, were involved in the revision of the poem—

though the evidence about exactly how is scant—and that the 1736 version reveals a "movement towards the polite Augustan literary mode" (291, 288). He argues (without judging its value) that the 1736 version provides a less authentic vision of the thresher (289). It is notable that the passages that deal explicitly with song remain largely unchanged between the 1730 and 1736 versions of the poem. I have selected from the 1736 version because it demonstrates the full extent of Duck's "literate" translation of song. Furthermore, it represents his final, authorized text, and since I argue that from the inauguration of the poem he self-consciously considers the role of the patron in the figuration of its creation, his patrons' involvement in the 1736 version does not necessarily represent an abdication of authority.

12. Goodridge points out that threshing occurs indoors, often during the winter when the summer work of harvesting has been completed (32, 44).

13. McKeon, "The Pastoral Revolution" in *Refiguring Revolutions: Aesthetics and Politics from the English Revolution to the Romantic Revolution*, ed. Kevin Sharpe and Stephen N. Zwicker (Berkeley: University of California Press, 1998): 271.

14. A number of recent critics argue that Duck is not a proper "pastoral" poet, but rather uses the georgic tradition. See, for example, Keegan's "Georgic Transformations," where she states that though "Duck's work should be seen in dialogue with contemporary pastoral as well as anti-pastoral satires. . . it should be analyzed primarily in its relations to the georgic" (548). Christmas articulates a similar position in *The Labr'ing Muses* when he states that Duck "counters the pastoral with a thoroughly modern rendering of the thresher's experience" that aligns Duck more closely with the georgic (82). Building from McKeon's insight, a pastoral continuum more adequately expresses Duck's contrast between shepherds and threshers, a contrast that suggests elements of what might be understood as both pastoral and georgic.

15. There are other types of agrarian labor present in the poem, particularly harvesting and haymaking. But, as Goodridge observes, the recurrence of threshing in the poem indicates that Duck saw threshing as his primary activity (44).

16. In his "Discourse," Pope claims that the shepherds' song originates from "that age which succeeded the creation of the world" (119).

17. For a description of the noisiness and physical intensity of threshing, see Goodridge, 44–46. The way that threshing, with its uninterrupted intensity, overwhelms song may not represent a general case for all manual labor, or even for all agrarian labor. See Bruce R. Smith, *The Acoustic World of Early Modern England: Attending to the O-Factor* (Chicago and London: University of Chicago Press, 1999). Examining primarily the acoustic "soundscape" of sixteenth-century and seventeenth-century England, Smith argues that "the sonic consequences of open-field farming were conversation, shouts, and song" that helped to create "a strong sense of community" (79). This differs from the type of enclosed field farming more prevalent in the eighteenth century and

most likely practiced by Duck, where, due to the dispersal of labor, it is not clear if "acoustic community" was as easy to create (79). For another case that relates the conditions of labor with the composition of poetry, see Keegan, "Cobbling Verse: Shoemaker Poets of the Long Eighteenth Century" *The Eighteenth Century: Theory and Interpretation* 42, 3 (Fall 2001): 195–217. Keegan specifically contrasts shoemaking and threshing (200–01), and focuses throughout upon the written composition of verse and its similarity to oral poetry.

18. Keegan, "Georgic Transformations," 553.

19. McKeon, "Surveying the Frontier of Culture," 21.

20. The two opening lines of the poem are as follows: "The grateful tribute of these rural Lays, / Which to her Patron's Hand the Muse conveys . . ." (13). It is also important to note that during this period the term "lay" can refer specifically to a song. One definition of "lay" in the *OED* is "a short lyric or narrative poem intended to be sung."

21. Christmas, 84.

22. For a detailed account of the circulation of Duck's "The Thresher's Labour" see Davis, 30–31. For an account of the reaction of his contemporaries, particularly satirical responses, see Davis, 45–52, 55–6, 59–60.

23. *The Complete Poems*, ed. Pat Rogers (New Haven: Yale University Press, 1983), 447, lines 1–4.

24. Swift's realignment of Duck with the object rather than the subject of pastoral is even more pronounced if one considers that "allow[ing] him grains" presents Duck as an animal of the same name, plucking stray grains from the ground. Puns on Duck's name are common in satires of him and his verse, and perhaps demonstrate the furthest extent of pastoral objectification.

25. Robert Dodsley, *A Muse in Livery: or The Footman's Miscellany* (London, 1732), 19. For a broader discussion of Dodsley's epistle to Duck, see Christmas, 107–108. On Dodsley's relationship to Duck, see Harry M. Solomon, *The Rise of Robert Dodsley: Creating the New Age of Print* (Carbondale and Edwardsville: Southern Illinois University Press, 1996), 19–28. Dodsley's identification with Duck's position is not representative of all responses from laboring authors, and not all laboring authors can be seen as allied along class lines. For an interesting example, see Robert Tatersal, *The Bricklayer's Miscellany: or, Poems on Several Subjects* (London, 1734), 23–5. Though Tatersal's consideration of Duck's value is more positive than that of Swift's satire, Tatersal imagines his own bricklaying trowel engaged in combat with Duck's flail, suggesting spirited competition among laboring authors.

26. See R. G. Furnival, "Stephen Duck: The Wiltshire Phenomenon, 1705–1756," *The Cambridge Journal* 6 (1953): 486–96. Furnival reports that land was set aside in Wiltshire, the county of Duck's birth, and the rent from that land was used to entertain local laborers each year (496). "Temple" is Henry Temple, first Viscount Palmerston, the benefactor of the feast, to whom Duck's "A Description of a Journey" is dedicated. For more information about Temple's

role in the creation of Duck's feast, see *Dictionary of National Biography*, s.v. "Temple, Henry, first Viscount Palmerston."

27. Duck, *Poems on Several Occasions* (London, 1736), 211–12. Davis suggests that the poem was composed in 1735, though this date cannot be verified (24).

28. McKeon, "Surveying the Frontier of Culture," 23.

29. Donna Landry, *The Muses of Resistance: Laboring-Class Women's Poetry in Britain, 1739–1796* (Cambridge: Cambridge University Press, 1990), 67.

30. One of the most eloquent and deliberate responses to "The Thresher's Labour" is Mary Collier's *The Woman's Labour* (London, 1739). In her poem, she both rebuts Duck's claims about women agrarian laborers, and depicts the conditions of women's rural work. For a discussion of the representation of women's labor in eighteenth-century pastoral and georgic, see Landry, 22–29. On the sexual division of agrarian labor, see Robert Shoemaker, *Gender in English Society, 1650–1850: The Emergence of Separate Spheres?* (London and New York: Longman, 1998), 150–59.

31. George Crabbe, *Selected Poems*, ed. with an introduction and notes Gavin Edwards (New York: Penguin, 1991), 3, lines 15–22. All selections from Crabbe's poetry refer to this edition and subsequent references appear parenthetically in the text.

Epistolary Relations:
Walpole and Cole

GEORGE E. HAGGERTY

The twenty-year epistolary relation between Horace Walpole and Rev. William Cole began in 1762 when Cole sent Walpole a detailed response to his *Anecdotes of Painting in England*, and it ended only with Cole's death in 1782. When W. S. Lewis began editing Walpole's correspondence for Yale University Press, the first two volumes to appear were those comprising the letters between Walpole and Cole. From early on these volumes were celebrated as a detailed account of the later-eighteenth-century fascination with English antiquities. Walpole and Cole share anecdotes, information, and discuss the exchange of various concrete objects that expand their collections of manuscripts, books, pictures and other kinds of architecturally impressive materials and ephemeral knick-knacks. Lewis and his co-editor Darryl Wallace argue in their preface to these volumes that in no correspondence is "the subject so uniform as this."[1] The lists of what interested these men and the depictions of their pursuit of desired objects make fascinating reading.

Even more fascinating, however, is a different subject that emerges in these letters, albeit indirectly. This is the subject of masculine friendship. In addition to this theme of collecting, that is, a special and increasingly idiosyncratic friendship between Walpole and Cole makes this correspondence constantly engaging. The relationship between them began when they were boys at Eton in the 1720s (Cole was three years Walpole's senior) and it reemerged when Cole wrote the letter mentioned above. As important as these letters are from the point of view of antiquarian studies, they are also valuable as examples of male epistolarity in the eighteenth century. Epistolary relations tell us a great deal about different versions of eighteenth-century masculinity and male-male interaction.[2] Indeed, they tell us more than we have been led to believe. Masculinity was a central preoccupation in the later eighteenth century, as critics like Helen Deutsch, Claudia Johnson and Andrew Elfenbein have argued.[3] The epistolary articulation of male relations that Horace Walpole develops in correspondences such as this one offers a valuable complement to these studies.

When Lewis's edition of Walpole's letters started to appear, it was greeted with enormous fanfare. Press releases and reviews appeared in dozens of newspapers and journals, and taken together they articulate the official line about Walpole that the editors were hoping to promulgate. In so far as they could control responses to these volumes, they did; and at the same time, in their preface they established the terms in which this correspondence would be discussed.[4] Some articles attempted to educate the public about Walpole and to explain why his letters would be interesting (William S. Ament's article for the *LA Times*, November 28, 1937, "Gouty Gentleman Discuss Antiquities"). Others were obsessed with Wilmarth Lewis himself (*Bridgeport Post*, October 24, 1937—"Son-In-Law of Mrs. Hugh Auchincloss of Fairfield, Owner of Finest Collection of Great Letter Writers outside of British Museum, to publish 50 volumes"). Some thought more directly about the correspondence (*New York Herald Tribune*, October 17, 1937: "It was a happy idea to begin the publication of the long-awaited Yale Edition of the Correspondence with the letters which passed back and forth between these two old friends.") Most of these accounts accept without question the assertion that Walpole selected Cole in order to have a correspondent to whom he could write about antiquities. While many see this as a landmark publication, few explore its full personal or cultural significance.

One reviewer, R. W. Chapman, writing in the *Times Literary Supplement* (October 30, 1937) claims that "If the [publishing] event is equal to its promise, it may well eclipse the Variorum Shakespeare as the greatest achievement of editorial scholarship in the United States." Chapman makes his review the occasion to theorize about British and American collecting, and private versus public ownership. He even has something to say about Cole, who was previously known as a diarist, and whose letters appeared here for the first time:[5] "Cole's [letters] are fuller, and in many ways better, than Walpole's, for Cole was the real master of his subject. [Throughout] the correspondence . . . the same things recur: the same books, pedigrees, and epitaphs, the same symptoms and the same remedies."[6] Such an account is perceptive about what the correspondence represented, and it is useful to have Chapman's celebration of Cole. Still, Chapman says relatively little about what brought these two men together. What does it mean for two men to talk about the same things all the time, the same people, the same books, the same symptoms? No one has seemed to care.[7]

Take for instance the question of personal health. These volumes are famous for their medical obsession with gout and its various effects, but what does that actually say about the men involved? Walpole and Cole share beliefs about the disease and its possible treatments; they list countless symptomatic physical details; and they offer each other endless accounts of the private suffering that gout entails.[8] A recent study by Roy Porter and G. S. Rousseau has begun to look more carefully at the role that gout played in eighteenth-century medical history. In their imagery, "crossing between mind and body in sickness remains a minefield," and it is this minefield that Walpole and Cole cross and re-cross in their attempt to share the experience of physical debility.[9] The intimacy suggested by their articulation of pains and bodily conditions is not unique in eighteenth-century letters. Authors as diverse as Johnson, Smollett, Cowper, [Benjamin] Franklin, and others, all write in great detail about their physical complaints. But the correspondence between Walpole and Cole, which sustains such a discussion over twenty years and develops it in several fascinating directions, can help us to understand how this illness functioned to construct a bond of intimacy.

As Porter and Rousseau point out, in the eighteenth century, "gout was framed within a natural teleology of healing. It was an 'effort of nature' to cope with indisposition by imparting a specific resolution. . . . [It] was viewed as one of nature's solutions to depravities of the humours."[10] They quote Walpole in this context: "I have so good an opinion of the gout that when I am told of an infallible cure, I laugh the proposal to scorn, and declare that I do not desire to be cured . . . I believe the gout a remedy and not a disease, and being so no wonder there is no medicine for it."[11] This comment, excerpted from a letter that Walpole wrote to Sir Horace Mann in 1785, suggests a perspective from which the detailed account of symptoms and anxieties that animate his letters to Cole can be viewed. It indicates how thoroughly fixated Walpole's concern with gout had become. Gout, not only his own but also that of his friends, haunts him throughout middle and old age. His own first attack of gout came when he was thirty-eight, and he was talking about it close to his death. He and Cole face this threat directly and admit their own fears in remarkably detailed terms.

Walpole does not sound sanguine when he first writes to Cole about gout in 1762, just a few months after their mature correspondence begins:

> I have not been at Strawberry Hill these three weeks. My maid is ill there, and I have not been well myself, with the same flying gout in my stomach and breast, of which you heard me complain a little in the summer. I am much persuaded to go to a warmer climate, which often disperses these unsettled complaints. I do not care for it, nor can determine till I see I grow worse: if I do go, I hope it will not be for long; and you shall certainly hear again before I set out. (1:33)

Flying gout, "where the pain flitted apparently at random around the body," was considered by George Cheyne, the theorist of eighteenth-century maladies, to be a nervous complaint: "The *Nervous* or Flying *Gout* (both which I take to be the same, and to differ from the Windy *Gout,* which is nothing but a *Hypochondriacal* or *Hysterical* Symptom) is owing to the Weakness, Softness, or Relaxation of the *Nerves* of those Persons who labour under it."[12] Walpole does seem to fret about his illness, and he often worries whether the gout will remain in his feet or travel to more central and dangerous locations, like his stomach or his head. The flying gout hovers over this correspondence with an uncanny force: this is the unknown that is truly feared, the only enemy that might be hiding in a darkened corridor. "Unsettled complaints" are truly unsettling for Walpole, and they remain a continual concern.

Cole, as preoccupied as Walpole with the state of his body, tends to portray himself as painfully convalescent in a way that leads him into discussing the other interests he shares with his wealthy and well-placed friend. He uses the intimacy of illness to introduce his antiquarian concerns:

> You are so kind as to mention my health as an excuse why I answered not your last kind letter. Thank God, notwithstanding the misery of the last four months, which have totally confined me to my parlour, not even stirring into the garden, it has been so wet and dirty, yet I have enjoyed a fireside as much as if it was better weather, nor have had the least complaint till about a fortnight ago, when I had a pretty sharp fit of the gravel, as they tell me it is, being a very violent pain across my loins, so as to disable me to sit or

stand upright, and not to turn myself in my bed. However, I am much better, and if I should tell you how I employed the last week in my convalescence, you would be surprised at anyone else, though not at me, who have done something like it at Strawberry Hill: in short, looking over my collection of prints, I found it would be very useful to have an easy alphabetical index to Mr. Ames's *Catalogue of English Heads* to recur to . . . . (1: 54; 8 February 1764)

Cole's complaints tend to be as complex and contradictory as this one. He likes to portray himself as homebound and unable even to visit his own garden. His fireside, and the warmth it provides, is a constant refrain in these letters. Periods of convalescence often function as periods of intense activity in writing or research; and he proposes "an easy alphabetical index" to justify and in a sense celebrate his convalescence. Cole is happy to talk about himself and his own bodily complaints. He has no compunction in referring to his ailments in a specifically physical way. He is happy to tell Walpole about "a very violent pain across my loins," and he is ready to insist on the physical effects, "so as to disable me to sit or stand upright, and not to turn myself in my bed." This only begins to seem worth remarking when we consider how little bodily detail Walpole engages in elsewhere. For Cole to write to his friend so expressively about the areas of his own body and their reaction to pain indicates a willingness to invite Walpole into the inner recesses of his private world.

In an intriguing discussion of Tobias Smollett as an illustration of the anxieties of eighteenth-century authorship, Helen Deutsch argues that "his anxiety about masculine integrity is written on and from the body in epistolary form. The epistolary mode is particularly suited to Smollett's project . . . because of its own dividedness between the private body to which the letter is linked and which it claims to transparently represent, and the disembodied mass-produced materiality of the printed page."[13] Anxieties about masculine integrity is at issue in this correspondence as well; and if Walpole and Cole do not have the immediately dividing force of the printed page to distract them, they do have the written page, written and rewritten in their cases, and a very thorough commitment to the private body. The letters themselves celebrate their private relations in a way that makes them more than the transparent representation of personal feeling. Walpole and Cole use their letters as a kind of courting that is different from the letters between other famous pairs of eighteenth-century letter writers, such as those between Richardson or Smollett and their personal physicians. Walpole and Cole use the rhetoric of illness to create a bond in this correspondence, a symptomatic correspondence to be sure; and this is a bond that sustains them for over twenty years of epistolary intimacy.

When Cole invokes a precarious state of health; when he announces "a troublesome sore throat" as an excuse for a visit, and mentions his intention of being "blooded" as treatment, he elicits a concerned response on Walpole's part. Critics who hold that these letters merely suggest that Walpole is "using" Cole for the mere purpose of extracting information from him are missing the touching friendliness of interchanges like these.[14] Like a dear old friend, fussy perhaps and concerned for his own health as immediately as he is concerned for that of his interlocutor, Walpole voices concern that grows in intensity over the years and starts to feel genuinely warm. "Pray write me one line to tell me how you are"—he says more than once: this is not the dispassionate single-minded antiquarian we have been led to expect.

At times the anxiety becomes palpable. Cole writes:

> I was desirous, very desirous to know how you fared in mind and body with your shocking companion the gout before I sent you this letter, but not hearing from, and as you have no reason to write to me directly, I despaired of a letter from you very soon to inform me of your situation in that respect. (1:289–90; 6 January 1773)

Cole dramatizes the situation amusingly, both by personifying gout and by making the correspondence itself a cause of his "despair." Their letters become a measure of health and Cole's urgent need to write to inquire after Walpole's gout even disrupts the protocol of correspondence. Cole is often "desirous, very desirous" to hear from his friend, as he says in one letter he is writing out of turn, and by repeating this desire urgently, he reminds us that desire is what these letters themselves represent. The letter itself becomes an object of desire; and the need to keep this line of communication open and alive to the personal needs of each writer becomes paramount. Their relationship takes on a special quality in the letters. It becomes its own kind of friendship, establishing new terms and working out ways of exploring even a physical relation. These men talk to each other about their bodies. They suggest treatments and recommend cures, to be sure, but for the most part they simply use all this talk as a way of constructing a special closeness. Two self-absorbed middle-aged gentlemen, solitary in their domestic lives (and committed to a circle of male friends), reach out to each other through the medium of bodily debility. As friends, at times giddy and at times ruminative, emotionally committed to each other and intellectually challenging, outrageous in their demands and touching in their concern, Walpole and Cole, sensitive and emotionally finely tuned as they are, extend our understanding of eighteenth-century masculine friendship.

Cole offers various self-diagnoses as if they were meant to interest Walpole or even to seduce him into attending on his suffering friend:

> I write now with the fever on me, and am much disposed to follow your prescription of James's Powder, for I have swallowed a load of bark, and all to no purpose. I am sorry to say that your sagacity lets nothing escape you: I own I am apt to fear colds, and may have nursed myself more than was necessary for them. However, I am convinced that no one can be a perfect judge of another person's constitution. Who, for instance, with your delicate frame of body, could at all conceive that in November, slip-shod in his slippers on the wet grass, without greatcoat, without hat or other covering for your head than the hair on it, you could walk about your garden as unconcerned as in July? Such an experiment I am certain would utterly demolish me, notwithstanding my seemingly robust make. The least cold gives me a sore throat and fever, and I am laid up for a month or two. (1: 338–39; 25 July 1774)

This amusing comparison of constitutions is as playful as it is arch. Cole appears to be crediting Walpole with sagacity in these matters, but then he turns round to chide him for his own wanton disregard of basic precautions. Cole is ready to feign shock at Walpole's own behavior and to wax poetic (and indeed almost incoherent) about Walpole's careless garden stroll. Cole is performing his role in Walpole's life as the one seemingly robust but timid in health, in comparison to Walpole the dashingly careless counterpart. The image of Walpole in his slippers is precious, and Cole's use of it in contrast to his own miserable make-up is diverting. The tongue-in-cheek tone of self-deprecation and barely veiled accusation can tell us a lot about Walpole and Cole, two solitary gentleman working out their physical frustrations in amusing missives back and forth. They describe these physical details as a way of reaching out from the recesses of privacy to cling to one another emotionally and physically. Their bed-scenes are sickbed-scenes, which is not only to say that they fetishize the bed and its role in their intimate lives, but also to suggest that such scenes emphasize the degree to which these men are emotionally committed to each other. If in the nineteenth-century the sick-bed becomes the erotically coded space for the romantic heroines; then in the eighteenth, such scenes as these suggest that men could eroticize the sick-bed too. Walpole and Cole are not objects of desire to each other per se, but they create an atmosphere of intimacy in order to pour out their physical anxieties to one another.

Another common concern extends this intimacy in interesting ways. As almost every one of these symptomatic letters demonstrates, Walpole and Cole take a constant delight in discussing gothic antiquities. There is an intense relation between their bodily intimacy and their exploration of things gothic, with the result that their intimacy gains an architectural solidity and their antiquarian passion a suggestive terminology. Two ailing antiquarians studying their catalogues: at times they can share information about this avocation when they can contemplate little else. Cole especially seems to conquer physical limitations when facing an antiquarian challenge, and Walpole turns from listing his symptoms to listing his requirements for an historical head or a gothic archway. Their mutual antiquarian obsessions complement their physical concerns with a range of shared passions that become central to both their lives. As collectors, they share many specific passions, and their ability to examine artifacts and architectural materials with a sense of common purpose brings them closer and closer together as the correspondence proceeds. If it were just their deeply realized avocation that brought them together, there would not be more to say than the *Correspondence* editors have offered. But something more is going on here. Their antiquarian interests become part of a private world that they construct for themselves in these letters, and more than any practical value for collecting, constructing, or construing materials, these epistolary explorations constitute a mutual relation that pushes beyond the isolated individualism that the letter form might be said to represent.

This happens most vividly when Walpole articulates for his friend the dream that inspired his novel, *The Castle of Otranto*. Let me quote in its entirety this section of the letter that Walpole wrote to Cole on 9 March 1765:

> Your partiality to me and Strawberry have I hope inclined you to excuse the wildness of the story. You will even have found some traits to put you in mind of this place. When you read of the picture quitting its panel, did you not recollect the portrait of Lord Falkland all in white in my gallery? Shall I even confess to you what was the origin of this romance? I waked one morning in the beginning of last June from a dream, of which all I could recover was, that I had thought myself in an ancient castle (a very natural dream for a head filled like

mine with Gothic story) and that on the uppermost banister of a great staircase I saw a gigantic hand in armour. In the evening I sat down and began to write without knowing in the least what I intended to say or relate. The work grew on my hands, and I grew fond of it—add that I was very glad to think of anything rather than politics—In short I was so engrossed with my tale, which I completed in less than two months, that one evening I wrote from the time I had drunk my tea, about six o'clock, till half an hour after one in the morning, when my hand and fingers were so weary, that I could not hold the pen to finish the sentence, but left Matilda and Isabella talking, in the middle of a paragraph. (1: 88)

Walpole begins with a self-conscious and even slightly apologetic gesture that sets the tone for what follows. His willingness to connect the details of the story to the architectural details of Strawberry Hill, his own gothic-inspired suburban abode, is not surprising. Cole had helped him define and indeed furnish many of the details of the place and Cole's interest in architecture was nearly as keen as his own. Walpole invites Cole to imagine scenes of the novel as if they were scenes set in his own home: it is almost as if Walpole is trying to play down his novel as a work of fiction and celebrate it instead as an evocation of his gothic abode. In doing this, he makes *Otranto* a personal gesture to Cole and makes the gothic story an experience that can be understood in more intensely private terms. The description that follows is as familiar as anything in Walpole, but as the letter turns to the dream ("I waked one morning in the beginning of last June from a dream"), Walpole privatizes the experience of the novel and places it in a special relation between them.

Walpole pulls a "gigantic hand in armour" out of his dream and offers it to Cole as a way of making that dream tangible for him. Those who have written about the dream have suggested that this grotesque body part has everything to do with Walpole's own psychological makeup.[15] *The Castle of Otranto* codifies the hand as representing the grasp that the legitimate past holds on the illegitimate present. It also suggests a threatening erotic presence that dismembers the poor, puny Conrad, the villain's son who is mangled by a gigantic helmet in the first scene of the novel. But the hand, for these men, is also the mechanism by which they can communicate with each other, and throughout their correspondence it has a magical presence. The interest in gothic materials provides a bond that reaches into the private experiences of each of these men, and they use it to invoke the world that *Otranto* represents: the world of desire, love, and loss. Whatever deeply rooted anxiety this hand is meant to allay, Walpole reaches it out to Cole, as it were, and offers it to him as a tangible-seeming antiquarian touchstone for an entire fictional world. In a sense this enables him to make *The Castle of Otranto* a personal gift to Cole, a book that represents the life that they share.

Because the intimacy between Walpole and Cole was grounded in the fascination with antiquarian pursuits, and because the friendship was more important to Walpole than biographers have allowed, Walpole's account of his dream can be read as a genuine act of intimacy on Walpole's part. It is his attempt to appeal to Cole by taking him into the world of his private fantasy. If Walpole could dilate on a gothic nightmare as a way of winning Cole's support for his fictional venture, then that was a measure of what they shared. Exaggerated enthusiasms and frantic searches for the right image or ornament suggest that the two men used their gothic interest as a short-hand for intimate feelings and shared desires.

When Walpole writes to Cole from Matson, the seat of his friend George Selwyn, about a mile southeast of Gloucester, he uses a tone of playful teasing that suggests more than academic interest in the materials at hand:

> As I am your disciple in antiquities, for you studied them when I was but a scoffer, I think it my duty to give you some account of my journeyings in the good cause. You will not dislike my date: I am in the very mansion where King Charles I and his two eldest sons lay during the siege, and there are marks of the last's hacking with his hanger on the window, as he told Mr. Selwyn's grandfather afterwards. The present master has done due honour to the royal residence, and erected a good marble bust of the Martyr in a little gallery. In a window is a shield in painted glass with that King's and his Queen's arms which I gave him,—so you see I am not a rebel, when Alma Mater Antiquity stands godmother. (1: 340–41; 15 August 1774)

Walpole plays on his dependence on Cole at the same time that he pays him an elaborate compliment. Walpole is not as devoted as Cole to the memory of the "Martyr"—King Charles the Martyr (Charles I)—but he tantalizes his friend with the details of the setting. Walpole calls himself "not a rebel" as a way of playing on the political differences between the two men, differences that are forgotten when "Alma Mater Antiquity" is present. If it seems that Walpole is writing tongue-in-cheek, then it is worth pointing out that he often uses this tone with Cole. He is willing to joke with his friend, and to let him know he is joking, precisely where their differences might be most intense. This is a private joke, one that Cole can cherish even as he clucks his tongue in response to Walpole's careless appraisal of what Cole would see as an almost holy spot; as such it brings the two men together at a place where they might remain distant, replacing potential discord with playful intimacy.

In many other ways collecting becomes a passion for Walpole and Cole, and they express that passion by conspiring together to bring the materials of the past into their lives and (equally importantly) into their correspondence. In this fairly typical request, Walpole asks Cole for help with Strawberry Hill:

> After gratitude, you know comes a little self-interest, for who would be at the trouble of being grateful, if he had no farther expectations? *Imprimis* then, here are the directions for Mr. Essex for the piers of my gates. Bishop Luda must not be offended at my converting his tomb into a gateway. Many a saint and confessor, I doubt, will be glad soon to be *passed through,* as it will at least secure his being *passed over.* . . . The width of the iron gates is six feet two, and they are seven feet ten high. Each pilaster is one foot wide: the whole width with the interstices, is eight feet ten. The ornament over the gates is four feet four to the point. Perhaps you will understand me from this scrawl. The piers should certainly, I think, be a little, and not much higher than the ornament over the gates, but Mr. Essex will judge best of the proper proportion. I would not have any bas relief or figures in the bases. The tops to be in this manner—nothing over the gates themselves (I have drawn these piers too wide.) (1: 178–79; 15 July 1769 [see figure 1])[16]

The degree of detail that Walpole provides, and the care with which he makes drawings to accompany the text, all mark the seriousness of his gothic enterprise. Walpole is precise in his desires here because he knows that Cole will be precise in his response. The detail offers a challenge to Cole, as playful a challenge as that above, and this is the kind of challenge that he is always ready to meet. More than sending a request for antiquarian aid, Walpole reaches out to Cole out of a sense of what they share. At the same time he offers Cole participation in his own careless plundering of gothic monuments for his own local effects. The gothic spirit of this enterprise suffuses the transaction with a seriousness of purpose; and if Walpole risks offending his antiquarian friend with this crazy plan, he also knows that by pushing Cole into these almost sacrilegious plunderings, both literal and figurative, he appeals to the desire for mischievous transgression that Walpole offers. If Walpole wants to use a tomb-gate for Strawberry Hill, Cole will not be the friend to stop him.

When Cole responds, barely two weeks later, his enthusiasm for the project is clear:

> This day I received from Mr. Essex the plan of your gateway. . . . Mr. Essex bids me tell you that he has done no design for the iron gates, on a presumption that you had prepared them yourself. If it is not so, on any notice to me or him, he will do these also. He desires me to tell you that he has some thoughts of putting all his collections toward a regular treatise on Gothic architecture together, in order to bring it into a system on that subject, but should be infinitely obliged to you to sketch out a little plan for him, which he will pursue according to your method. (1: 184: 3 August 1769)

The gothic enterprise becomes a concrete bond here, and Cole is delighted to be of service to Walpole. He proposes a large-scale gothic study as a way of appealing to his friend, and he manages to flatter Walpole in the process. If Walpole is using Cole, then Cole could hardly be more willing. His participation in the design of Strawberry Hill clearly brings him great pleasure. It is a great compliment to Cole that Walpole is willing to engage him in these private pursuits. Walpole's learning on the topic of gothic architecture is considerable, and his willingness to share it with his friend suggests the degree to which he expects him to be able to participate in his plans. By offering this delightful account of the various ways in which this "head" is useful to him, Walpole opens his world to Cole. The range of possibilities assumes that Cole is intimately familiar with Walpole's collections and that he can take pleasure in contributing to them. Walpole's exaggerated gratitude might also appeal to Cole, who asks for nothing in return for his gifts but such elaborately expressed thanks.

Walpole gives testimony to this intimacy as late as 1781, as the two men in their sixties look back on their epistolary relation. Cole has written in praise of Walpole's amazing accomplishment as an historian of art, and Walpole uses the occasion to talk about his own estimation of himself and his relation with Cole:

> But now, my good Sir, how could you suffer your prejudiced partiality to me to run away with you so extravagantly, as to

call me one of the greatest characters of the age? You are too honest to flatter, too much a hermit to be interested, and I am too powerless and insignificant to be an object of court, were you capable of paying it, from mercenary views. I know then that could proceed from nothing but the warmth of your heart. But if you are blind towards me, I am not so to myself. . . . What am I but a poor old skeleton, tottering towards the grave, and conscious of ten thousand weaknesses, follies, and worse! And for talents, what are mine, but trifling and superficial; and compared with those men of real genius, most diminutive! . . . We have been friends above forty years; I am satisfied of your sincerity and affection—but does it become us, at past threescore each, to be saying fine things to one another? Consider how soon we shall be nothing! (2: 269; 4 May 1781)

This letter commemorates the relation that this correspondence has revealed. In chiding his friend for momentary flattery, Walpole reminds him of the lack of pretense they share. Walpole's position is always a threat to their intimacy, and it takes constant reminders to both himself and Cole to bring their friendship onto the preferred ground of intimacy. Walpole offers Cole the image of himself as a "poor old skeleton, tottering toward the grave" because he wants to emphasize the forty years of friendship that earn them the right to be honest with one another. If Walpole never again pushes himself to such extreme self-exposure in his letters to Cole, then that is because this letter puts their relation on a new footing.

Walpole and Cole are not lovers, but the quality of their epistolary relation suggests that they are more than friends. They offer a prototype for a different kind of friendship: intense, personal, playfully erotic, and intellectually challenging. In their epistolary moments they exist only for one another, and it is the intensity of this bond that gives life to the correspondence. The expressions of epistolary desire that we encounter in their letters—the expressions of mutual respect, devotion to common concerns, celebration at similar discoveries, the intimate rehearsal of bodily affect, constantly addressing the state of their bodies in and among the intellectual and artistic interests—all these things begin to explain how this correspondence can expand our sense of the kinds of relations possible between two men in the later eighteenth century.

In Cole's last year the correspondence returns touchingly to questions of health, each man trying to soothe the pains of the other and accept whatever nostrums the other offers. Cole writes to Walpole:

> I write immediately, first to thank you for your kind letter and ready compliance with my request, and above all to recommend to you, in your complaint of a cough, to take ass's milk as soon as possible: it will do you more good than any medicine. I experience it at this instant for catching a bad cold near a month ago, going out for an airing in that detestable east wind which has been the bane of animals and vegetables. It was soon followed by a violent cough. As my gouty habit would not allow me to bleed, I took ass's milk, and it is in a manner gone. (2: 317; 16 May 1782)

And Walpole responds in kind:

> You are always kind to me, dear Sir, in all respects—but I have been forced to recur to a rougher prescription than ass's milk. The pain and oppression on my beast obliged me to be blooded two days together which removed my cold and fever, but as I foresaw, left me the gout in their room. I have had it in my left foot and hand for a week, but it is going. This cold is very epidemic; I have at least half a dozen nieces and great-nieces confined with it, but it is not dangerous or lasting. (2: 318; 24 May 1782)

Two old men sharing symptoms: what could be a more fitting conclusion to these forty-some years of symptom-sharing friendship? Cole seems persuaded of the efficacy of ass's milk, and Walpole is sure that the departure of his cold has brought on the gout. The bodies on display here are aged, infirm, even cut open in the pursuit of health. Cole's ass's milk is a weak (if suggestive) attempt to administer to his friend and to offer a gift in return for all that Walpole has done for him.[17] It is the kind of gift that Walpole can never really accept—Cole's home-spun remedies rarely suit the aristocratic invalid—but in not doing so he offers himself, his debilitated body, as a spectacle to Cole once more. He invokes the specter of gout yet again as a way of connecting with his friend, and he reminds him of his familiarity with its visitations. Cole always laments when gout invades the hands and makes it impossible to write, and Walpole knows that he will be moved by this suggestion. After all Cole treasures the missives that he receives from Walpole, and he does not want his friend's hands rendered useless.

Cole died on December 16, 1782. A little more than a month before his death, he sent Walpole advice and best wishes in terms that by now we might expect:

> I most heartily wish you the continuance of your health and
> use of your hands: you are too prudent to neglect any caution
> about them. My fingers are so numbed with cold, with the
> little snow we had last night, that I can hardly subscribe myself,
> dear Sir, Your ever faithful and most obliged servant, Wm.
> Cole (2: 338; 7 November 1782)

This communication cuts through many of the rigidities of old age to reach
out in a friendly gesture. Cole offers his own fingers, "numbed with cold,"
as a consolation to his long-suffering friend. He places himself as the solitary
scholar once more, writing from the confines of a snow-covered cottage;
and he writes in a valedictory tone to wish Walpole well. His first concern
is for Walpole's hands because it is as a writer—as a letter-writer—that
Cole most values his friend. He also dramatizes himself as a letter writer in
these lines, the writer who with difficulty subscribes his devotion to his
friend. This is a fitting conclusion to the correspondence, as Cole tries to
write out of his misery to send wishes for continued health to his friend.

Our crude attempts to talk about sexuality in the eighteenth century are
here challenged by a rich and varied relation that conforms to none of our
preconceptions about masculinity or male-male affection. At the same time,
I think, it can offer a valuable insight into the history of sexuality itself. For
if relations like these, intense personal epistolary relations, are not taken
into account, we are in danger of depriving ourselves of the complexity of
the past. If we have been able to see friendship at times as erotic friendship,
as between Walpole and Gray or Walpole and Conway, then we need also to
understand how two men can share more than simple friendship in
exchanging such intimate details about their collections, their fantasies,
their increasingly debilitated bodies.[18] The epistolary relation that we
encounter here defies our simple binaries for discussing male-male relations.
It establishes a standard for male intimacy that reaches beyond the eighteenth
century and reminds us how little we have really understood about all those
letters that we have been left.

NOTES

1. *The Yale Edition of Horace Walpole's Correspondence*, vols. 1–2, ed. W. S. Lewis; *Horace Walpole's Correspondence with The Rev. William Cole*, 1 and 2, ed. W. S. Lewis and A. Dayle Wallace (New Haven: Yale University Press, 1937), xxv. Further parenthetical references are to this edition.

2. Discussions of masculinity even in eighteenth-century epistolary narrative form are rare. As Amanda Gilroy and W. M. Verhoeven argue, in a recent collection of essays on this topic, "the epistolary form . . . was the eminently favored mode of moral instruction for women. . . . As the century progressed, the emerging middle-class ideology of affective individualism offered women the promise of romantic attachment and the choice of partner, but social stability continued to be predicated on the subjugation of women in marriage. The obsession with femininity and with the process of 'feminization' . . . spilled over into narrative fiction." See Amanda Gilroy and W. M. Verhoeven, "Introduction," *Epistolary Histories: Letters, Fiction, Culture* (Charlottesville: University of Virginia Press, 2000), 2.

3. See Helen Deutsch, "Symptomatic Correspondences: The Author's Case in Eighteenth-Century Britain," *Cultural Critique* 42 (Spring 1999): 37–80; Claudia L. Johnson, *Equivocal Beings: Politics, Gender, and Sentimentality in the 1790s* (Chicago: Chicago University Press, 1995); and Andrew Elfenbein, *Romantic Genius: The Prehistory of a Homosexual Role* (New York: Columbia University Press, 1999). See also, George E. Haggerty, *Men In Love: Masculinity and Sexuality in the Eighteenth Century* (New York, Columbia University Press, 1999). A recent intriguing study of male epistolary relations is that by Richard Hardack, "Bodies in Pieces, Texts Entwined: Correspondence and Intertextuality in Melville and Hawthorne," *Epistolary Histories: Letters, Fiction, Culture*, 126–51.

4. For a discussion of the politics of the Walpole Correspondence, see George E. Haggerty, "Walpoliana," *Eighteenth-Century Studies* 34.2 (2001): 181–202.

5. See Cole, William, *The Blecheley Diary of the Rev. William Cole, 1765–67*, ed. Francis Griffin Stokes, with an introduction by Helen Waddell (London, Constable, 1931).

6. This review was reprinted in R. W. Chapman, *Johnsonian and other essays and reviews* (Oxford, Clarendon Press, 1953), 214–233.

7. Only Virginia Woolf, writing about these volumes when they first appeared, expresses the difference between these two correspondents in more personal terms: "We have here, then, in conjunction, the Honourable Horace Walpole and the Reverend William Cole. But they were two very different people. Cole, it is true, had been at Eton with Horace, where he was called by the famous Walpole group 'Tozhy', but he was not a member of that group, and socially he was greatly Walpole's inferior. His father was a farmer, Horace's father was a Prime Minister. Cole's niece was the daughter of a cheese-monger;

Horace's niece married a Prince of the Blood Royal. But Cole was a man of solid good sense who made no bones of this disparity, and, after leaving Eton and Cambridge, he had become, in his quiet, frequently flooded parsonage, one of the first antiquaries of the time. It was this common passage that brought the two friends together again." Woolf understands how these two very different men can communicate so intensely for over twenty years. She is unique among early reviewers in finding something more than the mere subject of discussion in these letters. For Woolf, "They were two very different men. They struck unexpected sparks in one another. Cole's Walpole was not Conway's Walpole; nor was Walpole's Cole the good-natured old parson of the diary." Virginia Woolf, "Two Antiquarians: Walpole and Cole," *The Death of the Moth and Other Essays* , 66, 69; rpr. *The Collected Essays,* 4 vols (London: Harcourt, Brace, 1967). 3: 111–12, 113.

    8.   The editors said when the volumes first appeared: "gout is the remorseless enemy of Walpole and Cole. It stretched them on the rack, prevented their meetings, interrupted their studies and confused and mocked them by making them believe it was a specific against more serious enemies. The object of their never-ending warfare against it was to keep it on the ramparts, in the hands and feet, and out of the citadel, the stomach and head. Where once it was established, all was lost" (1: xxvii). This amusing account of the role of gout, succumbing as it does to its own rhetorical structure, stops short of assigning any further significance to the health issues that are articulated here.

    9.   Roy Porter and G. S. Rousseau, *Gout: The Patrician Malady* (New Haven: Yale University Press, 1998), 15.

    10. Porter and Rousseau, *Gout,* 75.

    11. *The Yale Edition of Horace Walpole's Correspondence; Horace Walpole's Correspondence with Sir Horace Mann and Horace Mann the Younger,* ed. W. S. Lewis, Warren Hunting Smith, and George L. Lam (New Haven: Yale University Press, 1971), 25: 597.

    12. George Cheyne, *Observations Concerning the Nature and Method of Treating the Gout; For the Use of my Worthy Friend, Robert Tennison, Esq.: Together with an account of the Nature and Qualities of the Bath Waters* (London: G. Strahan, 1720, 78; quoted in Porter and Rousseau, *Gout,* 55; see also, 50.

    13. Deutsch, "Symptomatic Correspondences," 49.

    14. Lewis and Wallace ask: "And what was there in it [the correspondence] for Walpole?" Their answer is simple: "He needed an antiquary among his correspondents, not only for his own researches but as a medium through which he could express a dominant interest" (1: xxix). Walpole may be writing to Cole to fulfill a need, but surely it is a much more personal need than this analysis implies.

    15. There are important exceptions. See, for instance, Robert L. Mack, "Introduction," Horace Walpole, *The Castle of Otranto* and *Hieroglyphic Tales* (London: Dent-Everyman, 1993): xi–xxvii; and Jill Campbell, "'I am no Giant':

Horace Walpole. Heterosexual Incest, and Love Among Men," *The Eighteenth Century: Theory and Interpretation* 39.2 (1998): 238–60.

16. W. S. Lewis and A. Darryl Wallace remind us that Bishop Luda was William de Luda (d. 1298), Bishop of Ely 1290–98. His tomb in Ely Cathedral is the basis of Walpole's designs. (1: 178, nn. 6 & 7).

17. Porter and Rousseau suggest that milk was often used as a "folk cure" for gout, but they do not mention the use of ass's milk for this purpose; see *Gout: The Patrician Malady*, 41, 56, 63, 91.

18. For a discussion of the erotics of these relationships, see George E. Haggerty, *Men In Love*, 116–18; 154–60.

Sea Tales: Nature and Liberty in a Seaman's Journal

APRIL SHELFORD

"**B**idding a final adieu to the distroyer of all constitutions," Antigua, H.M.S. *Sterling Castle* began the long voyage home to England on July 23, 1757, as part of a convoy of thirty vessels. William Milton, the ship's third lieutenant, may or may not have intended a pun with these parting words to the Caribbean. Nonetheless, they neatly encapsulate two of the concerns he expressed in his journal: his encounter with the Caribbean natural environment, still captivating despite deadly microbes and commercial exploitation;[1] and his encounter with the Caribbean social order, a slave society that challenged all of his expectations of what a healthy political constitution ought to be.

Milton did not keep his musings to himself, but shared them with at least one like-minded crewman, Midshipman Edward Thompson, who published his reflections nearly a decade later in *Sailor's Letters*.[2] What they wrote about their convoy duty early in the Seven Years' War should interest historians of the Caribbean, the war itself, and the Royal Navy.[3] Each work on its own rewards close scholarly attention. Safely stowed away in a special collection, Milton's journal has evaded scholarly notice until now.[4] In contrast, Thompson cut a very interesting figure in English letters and politics in the 1760s and 70s, though his earliest effort, the

Sailor's Letters, has received very little attention.[5] As we will see, the two texts are so closely related that it is both natural and illuminating to consider them together.

Here I introduce both texts as representative artifacts of the British imperial project, one in which colonies served as "a bulwark of trade and liberty."[6] After briefly describing the *Sterling Castle*'s mission and the relationship between the journal and the letters, I will analyze two of their central themes—nature and liberty—in light of the development of the British imperial identity during the eighteenth century. Unlike Linda Colley and Kathleen Wilson, I explore the issue of identity formation not from the metropolitan perspective of patriotic clubs and a boisterous, often bellicose print culture, but as it might unexpectedly emerge in encounters between seamen, European colonists, and enslaved Africans on the colonial periphery. The cases of Milton and Thompson show how a voyage could become "a quite painful moral journey of readjustment and revision of prejudgements," threatening to destabilize identities formed at home.[7] We will see how they responded by reconfiguring elements of that identity to neutralize the challenge Caribbean slavery posed to their own and what they considered their nation's moral integrity.

Thompson's and Milton's accounts also provide an instructive contrast to the South Sea voyages that fascinated the contemporary European public and that have drawn considerable scholarly attention recently.[8] Jonathan Lamb has written that, in the eighteenth century, "the voyage to a strange country is the standard model of the Utopian narrative in an age when the market was redoubling the needs of navigation and fantasy."[9] But Lamb was primarily concerned with European ventures into a *terra incognita* where, at least initially, inconvenient facts did not inhibit wishful thinking. In contrast, Thompson and Milton confronted a Caribbean long since transformed by its subjection to European consumerism, corrupted in the process by trivial tastes for sugar, coffee, and cocoa. Thus, they depicted not a Utopia, but a Dystopia haunted by memories of Eden, where the free play of unnatural cruelties and lusts disordered society and human souls.

*   *   *

On June 17, 1756, scarcely three weeks after Great Britain declared war on France, the *Sterling Castle*, a 64-gun man-of-war, set sail from England under the command of Captain Samuel Cornish.[10] According to Milton, she was transporting "169 chests of treasure amounting to one hundred and twenty thousand Pounds sterling" in the company of "16 sail of merchantmen, 11 of which had Troops and stores" (1v).[11] The ship's company fell short of her complement of 480 men, but the vessel was no doubt crowded enough with nearly 400 sailors and more than a hundred marines.[12] Few members of the crew would have known that their ultimate destination was the Caribbean, and some may well have shared Milton's reluctance to leave New York, "so beautiful a Country" (3v), after a brief three-day visit on August 24.

Upon reaching the Caribbean, the *Sterling Castle* was charged with protecting merchant shipping. She patrolled the Leewards, a necklace of islands arching eastward into the Atlantic, haphazardly strung with "neutral" islands as well as French, English, and Dutch possessions.[13] The *Sterling Castle* ranged from Barbuda in the north to Tobago in the south, her duties interrupted by frequent stops for repairs and reprovisioning. Theoretically, at least, she could expect to see a lot of action. While the waters windward of Barbadoes were relatively secure, those around Antigua were popular with privateers who hid in the abundant shelter provided by French Guadeloupe's and Martinique's sinuous coastlines. In time of war, the French navy was also a threat.[14] Yet, while Milton's journal gives the impression of crowded seaways and the *Sterling Castle* chased down promising ships with alacrity, she netted little plunder for her crew.[15] Indeed, Thompson complained that the entire voyage netted him a mere £3 (II, 41).

The voyage threw together Thompson, a newly minted midshipman, and Milton, a seasoned third lieutenant, but we know far more about the former's life than the latter's. Born around 1738, Thompson was one of the many young men of respectable, if undistinguished, social background who sought success in a naval career. He found it, steadily rising through the ranks during intermittent tours of duty and dying in 1786 as commodore of a small squadron in command of the *Grampus*. When not at sea, he wrote to support himself, supplementing the half-pay of an officer on inactive duty. Though undistinguished, his poetry and plays earned him the nickname "Poet Thompson" in the Navy, and "[o]ur captain seems to have always had one hand on the lyre, even if he were guiding the helm with the other."[16] He was also a prolific contributor to periodicals, though his entries appeared anonymously or under a variety of pseudonyms.[17] By contrast, we have only hints of Milton's achievements before his death in 1766: promotion to third lieutenant of the *Bedford* in 1747; tours of duty on the *Swan Sloop, Sterling Castle,* and *Edinburgh* from 1755 to 1757; a return to the *Sterling Castle* in 1758, this time as first lieutenant.[18]

One can infer from the striking similarities between Milton's journal and Thompson's letters that the two seamen knew each other well. Thompson's letters sometimes reproduce passages verbatim from the journal, and Milton's journal contains the transcription of a poem written by Thompson during the voyage and attributed to a "young gentleman of my acquaintance" (17r).[19] Milton's description of Thompson suggests some social distance between them; a comparison of the men's writing styles indicates other important differences. Milton's anarchic punctuation (when there is any at all) and shaky orthography confirm the impression that he possessed less formal education than Thompson. Thompson's grasp of the classical tradition was rather more secure than the lieutenant's, and, while Milton might have been an autodidact, he probably incorporated information relayed by Thompson.[20] It is even possible that Thompson encouraged Milton to prepare his journal as an exercise in self-improvement designed to make himself more "gentlemanly." The social tone of the higher ranks of the Royal Navy was rising during the eighteenth century,[21] a trend Thompson registered with approval in a letter written to a cousin on June 19, 1756, as the *Sterling Castle* made for open waters. His cousin aspired to a naval career, and Thompson encouraged him to pursue a demanding curriculum even at sea, writing:

> It is now the happy taste of the present age . . . to admire men of erudition and manners. . . . To say we did not navigate and fight our ships well in the reign of Queen ELIZABETH, would be an untruth; but from that age to this, we have been as unpolished and rough as the element. It will bear no kind of argument to advance, that ignorance can act better than accomplished knowledge. I will venture to say, that the gentlemen of the navy will bring more laurels to their country, than were ever brought in any former time. (I, 163–4)

Yet when Milton wrote, a seaman with a literary bent lacked no encouragement to put pen to paper, nor did he lack models. The buccaneer William Dampier revived the travel narrative with *A New Voyage Round the World* in 1697; by the beginning of the eighteenth century, travel literature rivalled theology in popularity.[22] "[T]he Relation of one traveller is an Incentive to stir up another to imitate him," John Locke aptly observed, "whilst the rest of Mankind, in their accounts without stirring a foot, compass the Earth and Seas, visit all Countries, and converse with all Nations."[23] Even so, Milton seemed to follow quite closely Thompson's advice on the preparation of a "historical journal," found in another letter to his cousin:

[Delineate in your journal] the head lands and coasts you see, — with their bearings and distances, and all other observations that may occur; for you cannot make too many, in order to acquire the character of an able seaman. Every day observe the ship's run on some mercator's chart, the variation of the compass, the setting of currents . . . besides taking off the common daily occurrences of the log-board, keep an historical journal, after the manner of our best voyages: in which insert the description of places, the manners, customs, habits, languages, worship, and policy of men; the produce, culture, and manufactory of each country; the curiosities, phoenomena, birds, beasts, fish, vegetables, and minerals of each place, &c. &c. From such observation, we have collected our histories of foreign countries, and tho' they be ever so puerile; you can correct and embellish them in maturer year; the observations which strike you will be ever good and true; for an elegance of writing must arise from polite converse, experience, and reading. (I, 159–60)

Accordingly, Milton's journal is a redacted version of the log every officer was required to keep. He compressed the *Sterling Castle*'s 16-month tour (June 17, 1756 to September 27, 1757) into an attractively designed leaflet of forty pages, graced with major headings, sub-heads, and more than 30 watercolors.[24] The journal reflects the process of self-education that every serious seaman undertook to familiarize himself with unknown waters, precisely noting wind direction, soundings, the nature of the sea floor, and the bearings of the islands the *Sterling Castle* passed. Milton fleshed out these bare-bones observations with gray-wash depictions of island coastlines from the vantage point of the *Sterling Castle*'s deck,[25] observations of the region's natural history, sometimes illustrated with watercolors, and descriptions of the local peoples' mores.

The layout of Milton's journal reflects considerable care and forethought, but also a certain self-sufficiency. He did not compose a manuscript for publication; he made a book, one he perhaps shared with friends and family, but one that he apparently designed chiefly to please himself. In contrast, Thompson wrote for a public audience, and what he believed that public wanted shaped the representation of his experience. Thompson's poetic and dramatic works have recently been described as calculated "to appeal to popular tastes for travel and history, sensationalism, lascivious allusion, and satirical gossip."[26] The same is no doubt true of his letters, extensively reworked before publication.[27] N.A.M. Rodger, historian of the Georgian navy, could have cited Thompson's depiction of the lower ratings in nearly bestial terms (I, 150–151) as an example of "offering the public the view of naval life which the author thought they wanted to read."[28] Similarly, Thompson's brief account of a white Creole woman torturing her slave to death skillfully combined moral outrage and sensationalism (II, 21–23, an incident that does not appear in Milton's journal). Thompson's letters also openly appealed to an English audience's chauvinism (see below).

Thompson was also willing to bend the truth to achieve his literary ends. For example, both he and Milton recounted the desertion of a group of sailors while the *Sterling Castle* was docked at New York. Milton's account is quite brief and factual: He commanded a party sent out on a fishing expedition; having secured "nearly 12 [dozen] fish," he ordered the company to return; several of the men refused and were willing to back up their resolve with murder; having no weapon, he yielded, returning to the ship with some difficulty as "having a narrow channel to pass on each side which ran two large surfs and a dark night with much lightning" (4r). Extant logs from the *Sterling Castle* confirm the mutiny and identify the poorly served officer as "the 3rd lieutenant."[29] Yet in Thompson's account, contained in a letter written from New York, *he* led the expedition, narrowly avoiding death thanks to the repentance of two mutineers. "[H]ad they perpetrated their villainy," Thompson concluded, "I should have died by the mouths of some thousands of sharks . . . . This is so striking an act of the hand of Providence, that had it happened to an atheistical person, it might have been the happy means of converting him" (II, 6–7).

Clearly Thompson lied about his involvement in the mutiny, but he also made it more dramatic and immediate with a first-person narrative that not coincidentally projected himself as a man of courage and piety. He also gave the mutiny a tidy, edifying moral. In contrast, Milton's account is spare and matter-of-fact, with neither sharks nor God putting in appearances. Indeed, while Milton was clearly a man of principle, he never attempted to present himself as a moral exemplar; for example, he recounted without embarassment his enjoyment of whatever transient pleasures presented themselves, including evening revels in the punch houses around English Harbour, Antigua, imbibing "the best and wholesomest liquor in the world" (5v).

Differences in background, education, and character made for subtle variations in how Thompson and Milton interpreted their Caribbean experience, even when they recorded their impressions in strikingly similar terms. But the ways in which they conceived themselves as Englishmen and in which they envisioned the business of empire ensured a common approach to the Caribbean's natural environment and to Caribbean slavery.

* * *

Unlike the European seamen who first set foot on Caribbean beaches centuries before—or who would explore the South Seas in years to come—neither Milton nor Thompson had the luxury of experiencing the Caribbean as wholly "new." The Caribbean's wealth accrued to Great Britain thanks to an intensive agricultural regime that profoundly altered the natural environment and that required the importation of tens of thousands of African slaves. Subjected to the demands of commerce, the Caribbean had been rendered "useful" to Europe. Milton and Thompson took it for granted that the region's utility should continue and even be increased.[30] The latter depended in part on the task of inventorying and classifying the region's resources, a daunting task because of the region's diversity, but one furthered methodically, if slowly, through well-established practices of observation. Thus, soon after arriving in the Caribbean, Milton began recording his observations about the tropical environment, satisfying Thompson's earlier injunction to record "the curiosities, phenomena, birds, beasts, fish, vegetables, and minerals of each place." Hence Milton's curiosity was never wholly idle. Curiosity was, rather, the "Mother of Improvement," making the voyage serve the greater good of increasing knowledge.[31]

Milton's efforts as a naturalist focused mostly on botany, a widespread passion in English society that furthered a variety of commercial, recreational, aesthetic, and scientific ends. Physicians sought new pharmaceuticals, colonial agents sought new commercial crops, and botanists sought new varieties of plants to taxonomize with new classificatory systems. Sketching and painting plants was as suitable an occupation for a lady as for a man like Milton, and securing exotic flora for one's garden or gathering became a sure sign of social distinction.[32]

Many of Milton's observations occur in the context of brief, general descriptions of particular islands. For example, he described Tobago's Courland Bay as "well cover'd with pelicans and all sorts of aquatick Birdes the woods abound with green Parrots, Cockatoes, Woodpickers Hawkes &c likewise Monkeys, Squirrel, Armadillios" (12r). He complained about the expense of supplies on Barbadoes, except for the "flying fish which are commonly call'd Barbadoes Pigeons and they are as plentiful as Mackarel when in season and an excellent fish as is also the Snapper & old Wife" (9r); he provided drawings of the latter two. Docked at English Harbour, one of the major sites for resupplying and repairing of naval vessels in the Leewards, he recorded how the "Negroes visit us every Day but especially on Sunday in great numbers bringing with them: Greens, Yams, potatoes, Oranges, Limes, Lemon, Guava's, Cucumbers in short the whole produce of the country—which they truck with the seamen for Bread and salt beef" (6v).

At two points, Milton offered his observations and illustrations in a more formal presentation. The first compendium begins with a rather proud summary of Antigua's varied produce: its commercial crops of sugar, coffee and cocoa, as well as "Tamarind, Guavas, Plaintains, Oranges, Lemons, pineapples, sugar apples, Limes, Coconuts, &c & shaddocks, [of which] no part of the world produces better" (6v–7r). But he singled out a dozen plants for special attention, five of which were noteworthy for their utility: the commercially valuable coffee, cocoa, and cotton, all three of which Milton illustrated, and the medicinal wild sage and aloe. Milton included plants that the slaves found useful, too: the calabash, "which the Negroes always convert [into drinking cups] by scraping the pith out," and the balsam, from which they "extract the liquid. . . . by breaking the leaves and squeezing the juice into a vial it has a fragrant smell." The other plants he recorded were noxious: The fruit of the Manzanillo, while "a most beautiful Apple pleasing to the Eye," was also a "rank poison"; fortunately, the White Cedar was nearly always found conveniently nearby "as tho' Nature design as an antidote the leaves, which grow & smell like our Nectarine."[33] The *Indicus ficus,* "by the Negroes call'd the prickly pear," was as troublesome in the islands as briars and nettles were at home in England.

Milton's second compendium appears near the end of the journal, where he devoted another page to illustrating and describing Caribbean flora and fauna (18v–19r). This list is less systematic than the earlier one. The gaulin (a bird), cabbage tree (probably the mountain cabbage palm), sea urchin, Indian corn, and armadillo—all caught his eye, and he illustrated the last three. As he abandoned system, so he despaired of comprehensiveness: "the various sorts of shells in these Islands are too numerous to be inserted here, and the many beautiful Trees too large to be delineated." Almost as an afterthought, on the last page, he painted a wild cat of indeterminate species, which accompanied them back to England along with "several curiosities for the Nobility, Amongst which was a beautiful Brassilian Vulture or Kings crow, whose feathers were worthy the imitation of the best of Pensilo" (20r).[34]

In contrast to Milton's obvious enthusiasm, Thompson's interest in the Caribbean's natural history was passing, but dutiful. He quoted many of Milton's botanical notes verbatim in one letter home, but this was more to satisfy his correspondent's curiosity than his own (II, 26–31). Thompson did not appear to appreciate, as Milton did, the sheer exuberance of the tropics, preferring his nature rather more domesticated. For example, while Milton thought that New York was beautiful, Thompson appears to have liked it precisely because of its orderly, cultivated appearance (II, 1–7). Similarly, for him, Barbadoes was "more like a christian country, than any of the Carribees: every spot of it is cultivated" (II, 21–25). He never expressed a sense of sheer wonder at the natural world; Thompson's letters offer nothing like Milton's paean to the cabbage tree:

> in Beauty height, and proportion [it] excells all the forest, even the tall Cedars of Lebanon, it justly claims that superiority amongst Vegetables as London does over it's neighbouring Hamlets. They grow generally as straight as an arrow and are in their prime at 30 years growth when wooding at Tobago, our seamen cut down numbers of these stately Trees for their cabbage, which when boiled would please the greatest Epicurean. . . . I almost thought it a sin to destroy a Tree which would be the greatest ornament to the most magnificent palace in Europe. (18v)

Whatever level of interest the two men brought to their observations, both possessed set ideas of how to record information about different flora and fauna and what information merited recording. While they could expect the natural environment of the Caribbean to be different from that of England, they also expected it to present commercial products like coffee; medicinal products like wild sage; and collectibles like the cat of indeterminate species. In other words, their shared "scientific" culture, however unsophisticated,[35] gave Thompson and the lieutenant a clearly defined and readily accessible set of intellectual tools with which to confront and interpret an environment that remained exotic, despite its having been made a profitable cog in the European mercantile machine.

Still, an older, less utilitarian view of Nature subtly informed Milton's and Thompson's accounts—a comparison between Eden and the postlapsarian world. Thompson wrote of the orchards of New York that they looked "so much like the golden age, and the first state of nature, that I could almost determine to spend the remainder of my life here" (II, 2). And he quite literally transposed the moment of the Adamic fall to the Caribbean in a moralizing treatment of the Manzanillo described in more pedestrian terms by Milton:

> One would imagine, from its delightful tempting appearance, and the bad consequence of the taste, that it was the tree so

fatal to our first mother,—which being of beautiful aspect, and a poisonous nature, *Adam* forbad her to eat thereof: — but EVE, having a *longing* inclination to gratify herself, where she was enjoined to forbear, plucked the fruit of that forbidden (poisonous) tree,—"whose mortal taste brought death into the world, and all our woe."—In short, I suppose it blistered her mouth, which *Adam* removed by the application of the WHITE CEDAR, a tree always growing near, and meant by the God of Nature as an immediate antidote to so fatal and so tempting a poison. (II, 29–0).

Milton never evoked the deity so readily. But, as his lament on the destruction of the cabbage trees makes clear, he was sufficiently alive to the wonders of Caribbean nature to consider the destruction of natural beauty for trivial ends sinful. Moreover, he clearly delighted in the Caribbean's fruitfulness, an abundance and fecundity that held out the promise of nourishment without effort. How powerful a contrast to the Caribbean's new social order governing new peoples that rewarded those who labored most with the most misery and want. How telling Thompson's choice of words to define Eve's sin in a world where the desires of those who labored least were gratified to surfeit.

*   *   *

While Eden is implicit in Milton's and Thompson's accounts of the Caribbean natural order, the hellishness of the Caribbean social order is quite explicit, and the cause of that hellishness was slavery. Slavery was present in New York, of course, but Milton and Thompson encountered it up close when the *Sterling Castle* docked in Antigua in September 1756.

Milton duly recorded the "manners, customs, [and] habits" of the slaves as he learned of them. We have seen how he noted the slaves' uses for various plants. He related, too, how one Dr. Hill of Barbadoes "told me [the slaves] was very superstitious especially those who have lately come from the coast of Africa," and he relayed the "eminent physician's" description of Obeah, a variety of African-Caribbean religious practice:

> For its a custom in the West Indies as in all other parts of the World for to fix raggs etc. to a Poll to keep birds from devouring new sown corn in the plantations. Now if a Negroe has stolen anything from his master or committed any crime and he should accidently meet with one of these scare crows

he will immediately fall into a malancholy declining way, immagining every thing he eats is poison and in a short time will expire looking upon it as sent by their God whom they call Obia. But should a Doctor or Priest of their Own tribe visit them in this situation, by his slight of hand or Legerdemain he'll perswade them he draws from their Bodye Birds, Toads, Snakes, etc., which he has conceal'd about him. And after this imposition, they recover, believing they're pardon'd. But all the medicines and advice that we can administer to them signifies nothing. (9r)

The sailors of the *Sterling Castle* frequently bartered with slaves, who offered fresh fruits and vegetables for meat and bread; they also found fugitive female companionship among the slaves. In very similar accounts, Thompson and Milton remarked the temporary liaisons the sailors established with local slave women, and both commented on the women's "constancy." Nevertheless, there is a certain snideness to Thompson's account, an impression heightened by his characterization of the sailors' romantic objects as a "charcoal seraglio" (II, 18). Thompson also made a point of mentioning the slaves' body odor, allegedly so great "that I have smelt, when the wind set from that quarter, a negro market a mile or more" (II, 15–20). Milton did not mention such details, and was more bemused than condescending when he remarked that the sailors with their temporary wives form a "pritty family" on a Sunday (6v).

Both men sympathetically described the slaves' miserable living conditions. The slaves of Antigua, wrote Milton, lived "in mean low thatch'd cottages and after their hard labour by day have nothing but a board to rest on at night their food is chiefly vegetables & have commonly their fires in the middle of the house by which they dress their victuals they go very meanly cloathed both men and women having nothing but a ragg round their middles which scarce covers what they pretend to hide and the boyes & girls til 8 or 9 go naked"—a marked contrast, of course, to the "Planters houses in the country where they enjoy themselves very happily" (5v). Thompson essentially repeated Milton's description of the slaves' living conditions (albeit more grammatically!), though he added an account of the physical sufferings and social ostracism of slaves who were afflicted with yaws, concluding "I am sorry I cannot say any thing pleasant of this place" (II, 19–20).

Their sensitivity to the contrast between miserable slaves and prosperous planters would probably have sufficed to inspire a harsh condemnation of Creole society.[36] Yet the very vehemence of their rebukes makes it clear that the planters did more than offend a sense of decency. Rather, it was as if Thompson and Milton recoiled in horror, asking: "How can *these* be Englishmen? How can *they* be *us*?" Their response indicates how deeply their sense of mission as British seamen was informed by a political culture that identified mercantile activity not just with national interest, but with virtue. As Kathleen Wilson has written, domestic publics passionately subscribed to a "view of the essentially fair-minded, just and paternalistic nature of the British, as opposed to the French or Spanish empire, and the former's ability to 'tame the fierce and polish the most savage.'"[37] Doing well was not good enough; one also had to do good. "*Trade*, gives fair *Virtue* fairer still to shine," declared *The Merchant* in 1741, "Enacts those Guards of Gain, the *Laws*; / *Exalts* even *Freedom's* glorious Cause."[38] The Navy was obviously essential to implementing this benevolent vision of expansion, her men ideally prompted by an ethos that linked a "commitment to the public good and subordination of individual or selfish interests," with the values of "liberty, Protestantism and trade."[39] Thus, as Englishmen, both Thompson and Milton believed themselves citizens of a polity unique in its possession of liberty, which was simultaneously a source of pride, moral integrity, and purpose, for they had both pledged their lives to defend it. But having traversed the Atlantic, having collapsed the distance between home with its fine sentiments and the Caribbean with its brutality, Thompson and Milton found their "universal principles," their belief in liberty and the "civilizing effects of commerce," profoundly challenged.[40]

For Thompson and Milton, the dissonance of virtuous ends and barbarous reality rendered moral opprobrium inadequate. So they sought to distance themselves as far as possible from the planters by making the Creoles radically "other"; they defined them as *un*-English. Identifying themselves as free and decent Englishmen, Thompson and Milton identified the slaveholders with moral opposites of themselves: tyrannous foreigners, both ancient and contemporary, Oriental and Occidental, continental and insular. With England as the model of social order, they located the source of this Caribbean tyranny in what they perceived to be the social disorder of colonial societies: People with no right to rule—those on the lower rungs of the social ladder, even criminals—had been given unlimited power over others. This "othering" of the Creoles required no great flash of originality, though both men had to deploy in an original way the constituent elements of English national identity. To understand the *bricolage* undertaken by them, let us begin with Milton's summary description of Creole society, which Thompson strongly echoed:

> The Creoles are an haughty ignorant people and look on the world in general and especially the English (whom they call Foreigners with all the contempt of Eastern Bashaws). They are the greatest Tyrants in an abject state in the Universe which partly arises from their despotick absolute government of their Slaves. A Planter in these Isles lives in the greatest luxury, in a word his every thing agreable to a Seraglio of charcoal Ladies. He imagines himself a petty King over his slaves he commands and inflicts such punishment on them as his weak imperious Fancy dictates . . . (15v)[41]

Full of ideologically loaded language, this passage clearly identifies liberty with "Englishness" and "despotism" with the Creoles.

Milton and Thompson took it for granted that their possession of liberty set them and other Englishmen apart. "More than any other component of English life or character," notes Jack P. Greene, "possession of this unique system of law and liberty was the most distinctive and important marker of the English people during the early modern period."[42] David Armitage recently reminded us of the integral role liberty played in British imperial ideology.[43] Prior to the Seven Years' War, the new anthem "Rule, Britannia" asserted that "Britons never will be slaves" and that "[Britain] shall flourish great and free."[44] The Marine Society, just one of many patriotic organizations, exhorted the young recruits whom they provided with clothes: "You are the sons of freeman. Though poor, you are the sons of Britons, who are born to liberty."[45] A sophisticated interpretation of the past provided English liberty with a historical pedigree and a forward momentum; xenophobia and paranoia threw up enemies who were detestable because they opposed the constellation of values associated with it. The end result was a reserve of public opinion that could be mobilized in support of domestic political agendas and foreign wars.[46]

In the eighteenth century, England's enemy became identified most consistently as the French. Thus, the Anti-Gallican Society, founded in 1745, linked patriotism with commerce, seeking to discourage French imports while encouraging English productions.[47] Milton clearly got the message. In his illustrations of colonial settlements, Union Jacks stake visual claims to Caribbean territory (12v, 15v). He noted with some chagrin how the French had so improved and cultivated one of the neutral islands, Dominica, that "in some year it will be the finest of the Leeward Isles . . . [and] a French one" (10v), predicting that the other neutrals would become French possessions, too. Comments towards the close of his journal indicate how potently French politics had become fused with popery in the English imagination. Lamenting that the *Sterling Castle* would be returning home without encountering the French navy (for Milton relished the chance to engage the enemy), he recounted how they pursued one ship for six hours until:

> the kind Goddess Night vail'd him with her sable mantle—I really think [the French are] more indebted to Her—than ever the Antients (Particularly the Romans) was to that crouded Pantheon of Agrippa's; for Night too often saves them from British Lodgings; if the polite Lewis was sensible how much he's indebted to Her, he would undoubtedly erect a statue to her honour, in every publick place; and doubtless but in time, she'd be rever'd by every Virgin in each Convent, and her image wore by every hoary Capuchin in a religous circle of Beads.

Yet he warned the French monarch not to trust too much to that "nocturnal caress," for "British vigilance" would supply "the Dawn of day," surprising and flushing the French out, whether at home or in America.

In English minds, the French monarchy had long been associated not just with a corrupt Catholicism, but with oriental despotism. "The Constitution of our English government (the best in the World) is no Arbitrary Tyranny like the Turkish Grand Seignior's," declared Henry Care in *English Liberties* (1685), "or the French Kings, whose Wills (or rather Lusts) dispose of the Lives and Fortunes of their unhappy subjects."[48] Living wholly in this ideological moment, our two seamen readily identified the arbitrary power of the slaveholder with Eastern tyranny, yet again signalling the Creole's dangerous "otherness." When the West Indian planter abused his slaves, he was like the French king against whom our seamen waged war, and the Turk, whose iniquity had been thoroughly if entertainingly deplored in popular literary works that had oriental slavery as their subject.[49]

Finally, both Thompson and the lieutenant identified the tyrannous slaveholder with an "other" quite close to home, an occupant of Great Britain no less—the Scotsman.[50] Their comments reflect a pervasive hostility towards Scots in contemporary English society, one that had grown stronger by the 1760s when Thompson published his letters.[51] Historically, there was little love lost between the two nations. Although the two kingdoms had united in 1707 and some effort made to forge a "Briton" identity, this did not prevent several Jacobite uprisings. In the final rebellion of 1745, the Stuart pretender to the throne, Charles Edward Stuart (a.k.a. "Bonnie Prince Charlie") led an insurrection in Scotland that was openly supported by the French Bourbons. By then, "Stuart" had become nearly synonymous with "despot" in the minds of many Englishmen, and its association with the Bourbon variety of despotism—not to mention Catholicism—only made it more repellent. Successfully suppressed, the '45 revolt became "the lens through which the components of the national identity were brought sharply into focus" through propaganda that was "anti-Catholic, anti-Caledonian, and anti-French"; the resulting nationalism, Wilson notes, "privileged conceptions of the nation that excluded a range of Britons and valorized a national and imperial identity that asserted England's political and cultural superiority over all competitors."[52]

A stereotype of the Scot was readily available, then, as a kind of cultural scapegoat for Thompson and Milton.[53] Thus, Milton characterized an escaped prisoner working in the Caribbean as "now a bonny Lad, especially should he have breath'd in the pure air of Scotland." A decade later in his published letters, Thompson pushed the identification of Caribbean slavery with things Scottish when he identified slave overseers with Scots. In addition, where Milton had written that "all the good living in the Island is at the Planters houses in the country where they enjoy themselves very happily," Thompson wrote, "All the good living is in the country, where, if you are a Scotsman, you may be well entertained" (12). Thompson made similar edits to a poem he wrote aboard the *Sterling Castle*, which Milton transcribed into his journal. In the original version, Thompson rhymed:

> Will not the ass, before the Monarch bray:
> Then cease vain Creole! for this Globe t'is true,
> Was form'd for Midas, but for Quaco too;[54]
> Are they not forc'd in chains from Gambia's shore,
> By you to taste sweet Liberty no more;
> But should we ask, how came Lycaon here!
> Mute rests the Tongue, and thunder strikes the Ear.

For the published version, Thompson reworked the passage in a way that reflected the "runaway Scottophobia in England" of the 1760s, a sentiment encouraged by the radical John Wilkes and his political followers, among whom Thompson figured:[55]

> Will not the ass before a CAESAR bray?
> O cease, vain reptile, give the black his due,
> "The world was made for Scots and NEGROES too!"
> Are they not forc'd in chains from Gambia's shore,

> By you to taste of LIBERTY no more;
> But should we ask, How came MacDuggle here!
> Mute rests the tongue, and thunder-struck's the ear.
> (II, 43–46)

In the revised version, classical allusions gave way to anti-Scottish specificity. The impious king of Arcadia, Lycaon, so repellent that Zeus transformed him into a wolf, now became MacDuggle. Later in the poem, Thompson reinforced the point with a couplet that deftly played on the prejudices of his readers: "Shame, like a whirlwind, swallow up your pride, / Or Heaven, from better men,—your clan divide."

The corruption of Caribbean tyranny worked on the body politic through the "despotick absolute government of their Slaves," and on the bodies of the tyrants themselves, who lived "in the greatest luxury," able to indulge whatever their "imperious Fancy dictates." At least since the struggles of the ancient Greeks with the Persians, political excess had been linked with immorality and with indulgence in sensuous luxury (we saw Henry Care lament the subjection of the French to their king's "lusts"). Thus, when both Thompson and Milton employed the word "seraglio" in their descriptions of Creole life, the term signified "oriental despotism," much as it had done in Montesquieu's *Lettres persanes*.[56] But Thompson and Milton meant it quite literally, too, referring to the planters' "amours with their ladie's slaves" (II, 46), while "the Ladies ogle where they please." Tyranny brought the means to gratify illicit longings, and it further disordered the soul by making pride its dominant passion.

A Caribbean slaveholder, the Jamaican Thomas Pinnock, acknowledged as much when he wrote to a friend in England at nearly the same moment our two seamen confronted Caribbean slavery:

> Our Journey in this Life is so short that I am astonished to see men wantonly destroy all happiness; this Island is healthy, pleasant, and fruitfull, and affords the Industrious Man a genteel and agreeable living for his labour, he may Live comfortably and enjoy his [illegible word] in great cheerfulness, provided he can curb his ambition; but as our Government over slaves is almost Absolute, so it intoxicates the brain, and creates in us a most notorious Desire to Lord it over our Equalls from whence great Men can bear no control, nor have they any bounds to their passions.[57]

Thompson and Milton similarly identified pride as the ruling sin of the slaveholders, whether male or female. With respect to the latter, Milton hesitated to be disrespectful, "But there is so sensible a difference between the English Ladies and the Creoles that if I don't set the latter in their proper light it will be doing injustice to the former. . . . They like the Gentlemen are puff'd up with a fulsome pride, carried to the greatest extravagancie" (17r). Both seamen also remarked the prickliness that made the Creole ready to challenge an offender to a duel—though, once taken up, the planter as readily and rapidly retired to his estates (16v; II, 41–45).

Just as violent lusts defined the planter personality, so violations of liberty defined planter society. Milton and Thompson tacitly acknowledged that tyranny in any form violated something fundamentally human. The lieutenant did not comment on slavery in New York, but Thompson did in revealing terms: "the laborious people, in general, are Guinea negroes, who lie under particular restraints, from the attempts they have made, to massacre the inhabitants for their LIBERTY, which is ever desired by those (you find) who never knew the enjoyment of it" (II, 4). He expressed similar sentiments in the same poem quoted above:

> Forbear ye Western Sons, nor thus despi[s]e,
> A race whose less the Brute, and quite as wise:
> In shape, in manners Modesty, nay Face:
> They far excell, altho' the Gambian race:
> With equal Eye, our Maker views us all,
> The Planter perish, or the Negroe fall. . . .
> Why then the wretched pride, in lifes short span,
> The slave in chains is much the better Man.
> The Welcome Zephyr that refreshes you,
> Visits the Hutt, and fans the Negroe, too. . . .
> Nature to man, does she obedience pay?
> Will not the ass, before the Monarch bray? . . .
> With an impartial Eye—behold the two,
> The Captive Negroes just; but what are you. . . .

In the published version, Thompson made his point even stronger: "O wretched pride! spun through life's wretched span; / Is not the slave, tho' black, a Heaven form'd man?" (II, 43–46).

The argument is clear: Although the black slave and white planter were equal before God, the slaveholder had deprived the slave of his liberty and kept him subject only through brute force. The consequences were likewise inescapable: Slavery invited insurrection, a familiar feature of Caribbean life noted by both seamen. Neither had probably ever read Charles Leslie's

1740 description of the Jamaican maroons, escaped slaves who successfully brought the British to terms, but they could well agree with Leslie's depiction of the Maroon insurrection as noble, because asserting a natural human right:

> Is it not natural here to observe how strongly the Love of Liberty prevails in the Breasts of Men, notwithstanding the most wretched Circumstances? These Runaways endured more for near the Space of a Century, than can be found on Record of any State or People. They struggled with a superior Force, went naked, exposed to the Inclemencies of the Air, fed on Roots and Fruits, and chearfully ventured their Lives to secure themselves free. Can the History of old *Rome* produce greater Examples? They, tho' unfortunate, held it out to the last, and made Terms not inglorious to themselves. The other, always successful, fell a Prey to one of its own Citizens.[58]

Yet while Thompson and the lieutenant clearly believed that all Englishmen were free (theoretically, at least), they certainly did not believe that all Englishmen were equal. They were not the radical seaborne egalitarians of the lower ranks described by Peter Linebaugh and Marcus Rediker.[59] One already an officer, the other aspiring to high rank, both Milton and Thompson found a basis for condemning Caribbean slavery not by believing that men were equal, but by asserting that they were profoundly and justly unequal.[60] If hierarchy were natural and just (not to mention, necessary for collective survival in the context of shipboard life), the disruption of hierarchy could be expected to have disastrous consequences. Both Milton and Thompson opined that, more than likely, the slave overseer was a criminal transported to another colony who, having escaped to the Caribbean, "stile[d] himself Swiney Esq." The Ancients needed prisons, Milton wrote, but not "Albion," for she possessed the Leewards. But perhaps the overseer had not been a criminal; perhaps he had been merely a laboring rustic at home in England. Nevertheless, "suddenly leaping into such a sea of Fortune, [he] forgets his birth & even himself; thus he becomes a tyrant in low life stock'd with an audacious pride, a pride so odious to the better World." He "becomes a *Monster* and takes upon himself to speak disrespectful of Men who are true patriots to their Country & of approv'd Courage, & Education" (16r; my emphasis). As Thompson asked the planter rhetorically in his poem, "Here Heav'n bestow'd you an imperial ray, / Would Heaven have hid it, in plebeian clay?" (17v). Obviously, the social distance Thompson and Milton interposed between themselves (gentlemanly patriots and officers) and the

Creoles (rustics, if not outright criminals) enhanced the latters' "otherness."

Authors writing before Thompson and Milton had already remarked the intemperate Creole mentality; the obnoxious extravagance of the Jamaican Beckfords and other Creoles who returned to England made a terrible impression and became cliché in eighteenth-century English literature.[61] But while many of these writers attributed the Creoles' coarseness to the effects of climate, Thompson and Milton never did.[62] They attributed Caribbean social disorder to absolute power wielded unwisely by the unworthy in a land that should have been marked by both utility and bounty. A terrestrial paradise had been made an all-too-human hell. In their case against the Creoles, social views and political ideology, class prejudice and contemporary xenophobias seamlessly combined. In their strategy of "othering," the parts—tyrannous Scots, Frenchmen, Turks and social inferiors—reinforced the whole. By making the Creole so unlike themselves, they remained unsullied, virtuous Englishmen, absolved of any culpability for the Creoles' acts.[63]

In an ironic twist, the objects of their criticism made it easy for Thompson and Milton to distance themselves, because the Creoles were indulging in some "othering" of their own. They labelled the English "Foreigners with all the contempt of Eastern Bashaws," wrote Milton, and the women of the slaveholding class regarded with contempt "those foreigners who pester the Isle" (16v–17r). "These light gentlemen treat us, who are come to defend their island, by the genteel appellation of alien and foreigner," Thompson remarked with disgust, "we, who defend them from the insults of the enemy" (42).

N O T E S

Many thanks to James Robertson, Andrew Lewis, Philip Katz, the readers of *Studies in Eighteenth Century Culture*, Miss Dunn of the West Indies Collection, the Social History Project at the University of the West Indies, to which I presented a very early version of this project in April 2001, and American University for the Senate Award that made additional writing and research possible.

1. Since Columbus's landfall, the Caribbean had become an even less salubrious environment, for European and African immigrants had brought their microbes with them. For example, yellow fever, an African disease, arrived in the Caribbean in the mid-seventeenth century, with epidemics becoming routine after the 1690s. John R. McNeill, "The Ecological Basis of Warfare in the

Caribbean, 1700–1804," *Adapting to Conditions: War and Society in the Eighteenth Century*, ed. Maarten Ultee (University, Alabama: University of Alabama Press, 1986), 26–42.

2. Edward Thompson, *Sailor's Letters written to his select friends in England, during his Voyages and Travels in Europe, Asia, Africa, and America. From the Year 1754 to 1759* (London, 1766), two volumes. I cite Thompson in this article in text as (volume, pages).

3. Thompson's and Milton's writings give insight into a little studied phenomenon of the war, the operation of a convoy, for example. Julian Corbett's *England in the Seven Years' War: A Study in Combined Strategy* (London, 1907) is the best source for information on the war at sea, but it is dated and in need of replacement according to N.A.M. Rodgers, *The Wooden World: An Anatomy of the Georgian Navy* (Great Britain: William Collins, 1986; New York: Norton Paperback, 1996), 13. They also supply information on life in the Leeward Islands during the mid-eighteenth century; Thompson even briefly described the indigenous peoples of Tobago (II, 32–40).

4. The manuscript journal, catalogued under the title *Journal of a Voyage from North America to New York in 1756 & of a Cruise around the West Indies in 1756 & 1757*, is held in the West Indies Collection of the University of the West Indies at Mona, Jamaica; no information is available on its provenance other than the fact that it was purchased from Sotheby's in 1963 for £90. The journal is anonymous. I have determined the author's identity by comparing extant officer logs from the voyage, especially the account of a desertion by some sailors on August 23, 1756, during a fishing expedition (see below). The logbooks of Lieutenant James Hume (ADM/L/S/445, National Maritime Museum, Greenwich, England) and Captain Samuel Cornish (ADM 51 / 934, Public Record Office, London, England) identify the third lieutenant as the officer in charge of the expedition; according to the *Sterling Castle's* Muster Books (ADM 36 / 6731, Public Record Office), this was William Milton.

5. For example, Clowes quotes Thompson's descriptions of shipboard life, including life in the lower ratings and the abusiveness of officers, the encounter with slave women in Antigua, and the poor state of health aboard ship. William Laird Clowes, *The Royal Navy: A History from the Earliest Times to the Present* (London: Sampson Low, Marston and Company; rpt., New York, 1966), III, 19–22. Rodger cites Thompson only twice and very reluctantly, stating that Thompson's "claims are never to be depended on." Rodger, *The Wooden World*, 171, 181. Thompson's literary efforts have received more attention (see below).

6. Bob Harris, "'American Idols': Empire, War and the Middling Ranks in Mid-Eighteenth Century Britain," *Past and Present* 15 (1996): 127.

7. Philip Edwards, *The Story of the Voyage: Sea-narratives in Eighteenth Century England* (Cambridge, UK: Cambridge University Press, 1994), 13.

8. Edwards, *The Story of the Voyage*, though he treats voyages to other geographic areas, too, briefly mentioning Thompson's *Sailor's Letters* in his

introduction; Jonathan Lamb, *Preserving the Self in the South Seas 1680–1840* (Chicago and London: University of Chicago Press, 2001); Neil Rennie, *Far-Fetched Facts: The Literature of Travel and the Idea of the South Seas* (Oxford: Clarendon Press, 1995); Glydar Williams, *The Great South Sea: English Voyages and Encounters 1570–1770* (New Haven and London: Yale University Press, 1997); Glyn Williams, *The Prize of All the Oceans* (New York and London: Viking, 2000).

9. Lamb, *Preserving the Self*, 45; for seventeenth-century precedents, see Williams, *The Great South Seas*, 70–72.

10. H.M.S. *Sterling Castle*, often rendered *Stirling Castle*, was built at the Chatham dockyard in 1742 and was originally classed as a 70-gun ship. She was lost in the British action at Havana in 1762. David Lyon, *The Sailing Navy List* (London: Conway Maritime Press, 1993), 41–43. The National Maritime Museum in England has a painting, "Reduction of Havannah 1762," in which she is depicted.

11. Milton's journal is unpaginated, so I have supplied references in text as (folio recto or verso). Also, I have made no changes to the text in orthography, grammar or punctuation, so the reader should keep "*sic*" always in mind.

12. ADM 36 / 6731, Muster Books, Public Records Office, London, England.

13. The "Neutrals," established by the Treaty of Aix-la-Chapelle (1748), were Tobago, Dominica, St. Lucia, St. Vincent, and a few of the Virgins. At the beginning of the war, European claims to the other Caribbean islands were: Spain: the Bahamas (though, according to Corbett, their occupation was "ineffective"), Puerto Rico, Cuba, Trinidad, and the eastern half of San Domingo; France: western half of San Domingo, Guadeloupe, Martinique; United Provinces: Curaçoa, St. Eustatius, St. Martin, a few of the Virgins; England: Jamaica, some of the Virgins, Antigua, St. Christopher's or St. Kitt's, Nevis, Montserrat, Barbuda, Barbadoes. Corbett, *England in the Seven Years' War*, I, 351–353.

14. For general information on Caribbean convoy duty during the Seven Year's War, see Corbett, *England in the Seven Years' War*, I, 351–370.

15. "You can't think how keen our men are," wrote Admiral Boscawen in the same year the *Sterling Castle* sailed, "the hopes of prize money makes them happy, a signal for a sail brings them all on deck." The lion's share went to the officers, of course. Rodger, *The Wooden World*, 136.

16. General information from the *Dictionary of National Biography*; see also *The Plays of Edward Thompson*, Catherine Neal Parke, ed. (New York: Garland Pub., 1980). Quotation from Anonymous, "The M.S. Journal of Captain E. Thompson, R.N., 1783–1785," *The Cornhill Magazine*, XVII (January–June, 1868): 614.

17. According to Pitcher, he followed the styles of "his declared mentors, the 'ancients' Horace, Juvenal, and, above all, Ovid, and the 'moderns,' Hudibras, Swift, Pope, Churchill, Lloyd and Wilkes." Thompson also prepared editions of the works of Andrew Marvell, John Oldham, and Paul Whitehead. For a very lengthy list of materials believed to have been published by Thompson, see Edward W. Pitcher, "Edward Thompson (1738?–86): The Contributions of a Satirist

to the *London Magazine* and the *Westminster Magazine*," *Papers of the Bibliographic Society of America* 92:2 (June 1998): 125–158. Pitcher has a rather higher opinion of Thompson than does Parke, writing that, in the 1770s, he "transcended his earlier reputation as a scandalizing, obscene wit whose minor contributions as a poet and editor might be ignored" (127). Parke, editor of a recently published anthology of Thompson's plays, considers his work imitative and derivative, but believes that "his career gives, as those of minor writers often do, a useful and interesting sketch of the tastes of the contemporary reading and theater-going public" (x–xi).

18. *The Commissioned Sea Officers of the Royal Navy, 1660-1815*, ed. David Syrett (Aldershot: Scolar Press for Navy Records Society, 1994).

19. Thompson never alluded to Milton by name, though he slipped once with an indirect reference. He began an account of a trip into the interior of Tobago as a solitary "I," but returned to the ship as a "we" (II, 32–40). The journal suggests that there were, in fact, at least three members of that party: Thompson, Milton, and a "young gentleman on board" with the initials S.E.E., who composed a poem about their encounter with a French hermit (12r). Thompson rewrote the poem and published it with the letter describing their Tobago excursion (II, 39–40).

20. For example, Milton explained that the origins of the shipboard ceremony of "crossing the line" (in this instance, the Tropic of Capricorn) lay in the ancient myth of Daedalus and Icarus, but Thompson was clearly more familiar with the classical source (4v; II, 8–9). Perhaps Thompson assisted the lieutenant in preparing his journal. At any rate, someone corrected the lieutenant's error of identifying the Palatine Hill as the site of Romulus's prison in ancient Rome, crossing it out and writing in "Capitolinus" (16v).

21. Rodger, *The Wooden World*, 261–262.

22. See Rennie, *Far-Fetched Facts*, 58–59; Edwards, *The Story of the Voyage*, 1–5.

23. Lamb, *Preserving the Self*, 49.

24. The paper appears to be that of a log book, folded in half and collated to make up a booklet of 20 folios with the approximate dimensions of 7.5 x 9.25 inches. The first and last pages are blank. The account is written in a highly legible hand with occasional corrections. The binding is unfortunate, sometimes making it hard to read words close to the gutter, and the text runs very close to the page's edge.

25. These illustrations are comparable to, though not as skilled as, those made by Robert Durand, a French merchant seaman making his first voyage to the slave coast of Africa in 1731. Robert Harms, *The Diligent, A Voyage through the Worlds of the Slave Trade* (New York: Basic Books, 2002).

26. Parke, *The Plays of Edward Thompson*, xv.

27. The *Sailor's Letters* "betray the reviser's hand in the fund of appropriate quotations from Milton and Shakespeare, in the evident selection of the most edifying scenes, and in the carefully phrased moralizings," according to Karl F.

Thompson, "Poet Thompson of the Navy," *Notes and Queries* 11:1 (1954): 300–302. See below for comparison of a poem written by Thompson as it appeared in Milton's journal and in its published version.

28. Rodger, *The Wooden World*, 422.

29. See note 4. Such incidents could hardly have been unexpected as 115 of the ship's complement had been pressed. Rodger, *The Wooden World*, 171.

30. "People came to the new societies of colonial British America not merely to better their economic situation but also with the complementary hope of transforming those new places into improved ones." Jack P. Greene, "Identity in the British Caribbean," *Colonial Identity in the Atlantic World, 1500–1800*, eds. Nicholas Canny and Anthony Pagden (Princeton: Princeton University Press, 1987), 228; for a more extensive discussion of the eighteenth-century "cult of improvement," see Richard Drayton, *Nature's Government* (New Haven and London: Yale University Press, 2000), 50–82.

31. "Mother of Improvement" is from the poem written by the unnamed companion who accompanied Thompson and Milton on their trek into the Tobago interior; the poem's subject was their encounter with a French hermit (12r). The Royal Society recognized the utility of voyages for securing new knowledge as early as 1666; one of its fellows, Tancred Robinson, anonymously listed the advantages of "judicious and accurate Journals ... as the Improvement of *Geography, Hydrography, Astronomy, Natural and Moral History, Antiquity, Merchandise, Trade, Empire*, &c." in *An Account of Several Late Voyages*, which might have inspired Dampier's more scientific content in *A New Voyage Round the World* (1697). Edwards, *The Story of the Voyage* , 26–28. For more on the eighteenth-century trinity of science, exploration, and empire, see Lamb, *Preserving the Self*, 76–113; Pratt, *Imperial Eyes*, 15–37; David Philip Miller and Peter Hans Reill, editors, *Visions of Empire: Voyages, botany, and representations of nature* (Cambridge, England: Cambridge University Press, 1996); John Gascoigne, *Science in the Service of Empire: Joseph Banks, the British State and the Uses of Science in the Age of Revolution* (Cambridge and New York: Cambridge University Press, 1998). For a discussion of the disciplining of curiosity during the eighteenth century, see Lorraine Daston and Katharine Park, *Wonders and the Order of Nature 1150–1750* (New York: Zone Books, 1998), 329–363.

32. Physicians played an especially important role in botanical investigations in the Caribbean, though searching for pharmaceuticals in exotic lands predated the eighteenth century. Harold J. Cook, "Physicians and Natural History," *Cultures of Natural History,* ed. N. Jardine, J.A. Secord, and E.C. Spary (Cambridge & New York: Cambridge University Press, 1996), 91–105. The division of roles I have indicated here was not hard and fast. For example, when Patrick Browne, an Irish physician, wrote *The Civil and Natural History of Jamaica* (1756), he was alert to the potential for commercial crops, whether indigenous or imported like coffee, as well as plants that could be used as pharmaceuticals. Beth Fowkes Tobin explored the "cult of botany" in eighteenth-century England and how upper-class women used New World plants as a sort of "cultural capital"

to impress their peers in "Connoisseurship and Collecting New World Plants in Smith's *Exotic Botany*," a paper presented at the conference *Bacon to Bartram: Early American Inquiries into the Natural World*, New York, March 23, 2002. The naturalist Mark Catesby spurred great interest in including New World plants in English gardens. Therese O'Malley, "Mark Catesby and the Culture of Gardens," and Mark Laird, "From Callicarpa to Catalpa: The Impact of Mark Catesby's Plant Introductions on English Gardens of the Eighteenth Century," *Empire's Nature: Mark Catesby's New World Vision*, ed. Amy R.W. Meyers and Margaret Beck Pritchard (Chapel Hill, N.C.: University of North Carolina Press, 1998). For the adoption of Linnaeus's classificatory system, see Frans Antoine Stafleu, *Linnaeus and the Linnaeans: The Spreading of Their Ideas in Systematic Botany (1735–1789)* (Utrecht: The International Association for Plant Taxonomy, 1971). Even before the eighteenth century, botanical illustration had been encouraged as a lady-like preoccupation, one pursued in Antigua by Lydia Byam, who published her botanical engravings in two collections at the end of the eighteenth century (my thanks to Norman Fiering of The John Carter Brown Library for indicating the existence of Byam's work to me). Also see Ann B. Shteir, *Cultivating women, cultivating science : Flora's daughters and botany in England, 1760 to 1860* (Baltimore, Md.: Johns Hopkins University Press, 1996).

33. Milton expressed the conventional belief that cures were always found in close proximity to the affliction's source. Thus, physicians were encouraged to seek out medicines for the diseases that affected colonists in the Caribbean. Karen Ordahl Kupperman, "Fear of Hot Climates in the Anglo-Colonial Experience," *William and Mary Quarterly*, 3d Series, 41:2 (1984): 213–240.

34. I speculate that "Pensilo" is a variant or corrruption of "pencel / pensile / pencill, etc.," which refers to pennons or banners used in a military context.

35. Neither, for example, appears to have been aware of the Linnaean system being applied in the Caribbean by visiting botanists such as Patrick Browne.

36. I use "Creoles" here as Thompson and Milton do, which is to say, they use the term to refer exclusively to Europeans, and they make no distinction between a colonist from Europe and one born in the islands.

37. Wilson, *The sense of the people: Politics, culture and imperialism in England, 1715–1785* (New York and Cambridge: Cambridge University Press, 1995), 157.

38. Citing Young's *The Merchant* (1741), David Dabydeen, "Eighteenth-century English literature on commerce and slavery," *The Black Presence in English Literature*, ed. David Dabydeen (Manchester, UK: Manchester University Press, 1985), 32.

39. Bob Harris, "American Idols," 119.

40. I have adapted the phrases of Seymour Drescher, who wrote that "the world was made safe for North-West European colonial slavery by the tyranny of distance rather than universal principles," and of Dabydeen on the "civilizing effects of commerce." Seymour Drescher, *Capitalism and Anti-Slavery* (London:

Macmillan Press, 1986), 24; Dabydeen, "Eighteenth-century English literature," 32.

41. Milton appears to have picked up Thompson's "charcoal Seraglio" and applied it in a different context.

42. Jack P. Greene, "Liberty, Slavery, and the Transformation of British Identity in the Eighteenth-Century West Indies," *Slavery and Abolition* 21:1 (April 2000): 2. In this article, Greene treats the paradoxical situation that resulted when colonial slaveholders claimed "this unique system of law and liberty" for themselves against metropolitan control. A 1757 pamphlet, *An Essay concerning Slavery*, charged, for example, that the home country "had effectively indulged colonial white settlers with a liberty based upon the slavery of others, a 'Liberty contrary to the Laws of God and Nature'" (15).

43. David Armitage, *The Ideological Origins of the British Empire* (Cambridge, England: Cambridge University Press, 2000). Also see J.C.D. Clarke, *The Language of liberty, 1660–1832: Political Discourse and Social Dynamics in the Anglo-American World* (Cambridge, England: Cambridge University Press, 1994); Jack P. Greene, "Empire and Identity from the Glorious Revolution to the American Revolution," *The Oxford History of the British Empire: Volume II, The Eighteenth Century* (Oxford and New York: Oxford University Press, 1998), 208–230.

44. Armitage, *The Ideological Origins,* 173.

45. Linda Colley, *Britons*, 97. A few years after the war, Arthur Young summed up this political ethos: "The 'birthrights and privileges of Britons' form a system of liberty, so happily tempered between slavery and licentiousness, that the like is not to be met with in any other country of the globe." Quoted by Greene, "Liberty, Slavery," 4.

46. See Wilson, *The Sense of the People*, 137–205; Bob Harris, "American Idols."

47. Colley, *Britons*, 89.

48. *The Boisterous Sea of Liberty*, ed. David Brion Davis and Steven Mintz (Oxford and New York: Oxford University Press, 1998), 83.

49. Sylie Sypher, *Guinea's Captive Kings: British Anti-Slavery Literature of the XVIIIth Century* (New York: Octagon Books, 1969), 25–29. Thompson contributed to the genre with the play, *The Seraglio*, produced in November 1776.

50. On the Scottish presence in the overseas empire, Colley, *Britons*, 138–142; Ned C. Landsman, "Nation, Migration, and the Province in the First British Empire: Scotland and the Americas, 1600–1800, *American Historical Review* 104:2 (1999), 463–475; *Scotland and the Americas, 1600–1800* (Providence: John Carter Brown Library, 1995); Alan L. Karras, *Sojourners in the Sun: Scottish Migrants in Jamaica and the Chesapeake, 1740–1800* (Ithaca: Cornell University Press, 1992).

51. Colley, *Britons*, 105–132.

52. Wilson, 174.

53. Ironically, their physical safety depended upon a vessel named after an ancient Scottish castle that had frequently been the site of English-Scottish conflict, the last time during the 1745 rebellion; moreover, the British Army very successfully recruited Scottish Highlanders during the Seven Years' War. Colley,

Britons, 103.

54. "Quaco" is one of several forms of a day name, in this case Wednesday, derived from the Akan African language. The practice of naming children after the day of the week was transported to the Caribbean sugar islands, where such names predominated particularly among the Maroons and other people of African descent in Jamaica. Maureen Warner-Lewis, "The Character of African-Jamaican Culture," *Jamaica in Slavery and Freedom*, ed. Kathleen E.A. Monteith and Glen Richards (Kingston, Jamaica: University of the West Indies Press, 2002), 91.

55. For Thompson's association with Wilkes, see Pitcher, "Edward Thompson," 131, 136, 140. For "runaway Scottophobia," see Colley, *Britons*, 105–117; Wilson, *The Sense of the People*, 206–236.

56. Suzanne Rodin Pucci, "The discrete charms of the exotic: fictions of the harem in eighteenth-century France," *Exoticism in the Enlightenment*, ed. G.S. Rousseau and Roy Porter (New York: St Martin's Press, 1990), 150.

57. June 26, 1756, MS 490, National Library of Jamaica, Kingston, Jamaica.

58. Charles Leslie, *A New History of Jamaica* (London, 1740), 288.

59. Peter Linebaugh and Marcus Rediker, *The Many-Headed Hydra* (Boston: Beacon Press, 2000).

60. Though Thompson did complain of the "too dispotick an authority" exercised over midshipmen, and he compared the lives of inferior officers in the Navy to a "state of vassalage" (I, 141–142). Yet this was to require a softening of authority, not its abolition, and he clearly regarded the lower ranks with contempt, portraying the pressed men as largely drawn from England's prisons. In this, he exaggerated yet again, according to Rodger. Rodger, *The Wooden World*, 171.

61. See Greene, "Identity," 233; Sypher, *Guinea's Captive Kings*, 86–90. One planter's house was even described as "a palatial Turkish affair." Michael Craton, "Reluctant Creoles: The Planters' World in the British West Indies," *Strangers within the Realm*, ed. Bernard Bailyn and Philip D. Morgan (Chapel Hill: University of North Carolina Press, 1991), 348.

62. For example, in *Natural History of Barbadoes*, Griffith Hughes qualified his general praise of the Creole character by noting that "Inhabitants of hot Countries are of a more volatile and lively Disposition, and more irascible in general, than the Inhabitants of the Northern Part of the World." Sypher, *Guinea's Captive Kings*, 87. Charles Devenant attibuted the "excess and luxury" of the Caribbean colonies to "rich soil, easy acquisition of wealth, and . . . warm climate." Greene, "Identity," 233. Such views had a long life, as Edward Long, author of *History of Jamaica* (1774), attributed the volatility of the Jamaican personality to a climate that made "the nervous system ... far more irritable than in a Northern climate." Michael Craton, "Reluctant Creoles," 342. Also see Kupperman, "Fear of Hot Climates."

63. The reader might well ask, did Thompson and Milton favor the abolition of slavery? Perhaps they did, but they never said so. If they had, they would have been decades ahead of the vast majority of their contemporaries, for abolitionist sentiment was very much in the future. Also, even in the 1770s,

many still believed that, however repugnant, slavery was essential to the wealth of the empire, that, indeed, slavery and empire were indissolubly linked. Christopher L. Brown, "Empire without Slaves: British Concepts of Emancipation in the Age of the American Revolution," *William and Mary Quarterly*, 3d Series, LVI:2 (1999): 273–306. Thompson's doggerel does appear to have been slightly ahead of the curve, though, as "[f]rom the 1770s onwards England was deluged with anti-slavery verse." David Dabydeen, "Eighteenth-century English literature on commerce and slavery," 44.

Wants and Goods: Advertisement and Desire in Haywood and Defoe

BARBARA M. BENEDICT

> In a word, as the whole relation is carefully garbled of all the
> levity and looseness that was in it, so it is all applied, and
> with the utmost care, to virtuous and religious uses. None
> can, without being guilty of manifest injustice, cast any
> reproach upon it, or upon our design in publishing it.[1]

So Daniel Defoe asserts in the preface to *Moll Flanders*. Reproach
nonetheless appeared aplenty, not only for this novel, but for much of
the fiction of the 1720s. Despite their moralistic rhetoric and didactic
structure, novels by Daniel Defoe and Eliza Haywood feature scandalous
titles advertising erotic contents, and dwell on the pleasures of sin and
crime. This ambiguity enraged contemporaries like Swift and Pope, who
in *Gulliver's Travels* and *The Dunciad* excoriated the authors for pandering
to the audience's basest desires from mercenary motives. Modern critics
have similarly interpreted it as a methodological error produced by
contradictions of point of view, authorial motive, or literary model.[2]
Scholars of Haywood have also blamed her "non-literary" speed of
composition—she completed fourteen novels, along with four other literary
works in the two years between 1722 and 1724 alone—and her attempt to

221

please an audience itself torn between a thirst for erotica and an insistence on narrative morality.[3] Clearly, both Defoe and Haywood wrote for profit: facile, commercially-oriented writers, they faced similar problems in managing their own beliefs and their audience's appetites in a market rife with publishers' lies, texts of ambiguous factuality, and confusions of morality and popularity.[4] The result is an unremitting and destabilizing ironic ambiguity, but this is not a formal failure. Rather, this ambiguity provides a way to negotiate the contradictions of value and meaning in a period of ideological change. These authors' moralism is not merely the trace of a discourse inherited from pre-Restoration religious models, Protestant or Anglican.[5] Rather, it is a transformative, new discourse patched together in order to sell commodities, including print, as greater "goods." Ironic ambiguity facilitates the transformation of desire into a commodity.

The commodification of desire is the fundamental method of a parallel, burgeoning new form: the printed advertisement.[6] Early advertisements employ a rhetoric that uses narrative plots and vague terms conventionally associated with morality—like "preservation," "benefit," "restoration," and "improvement"—in the service of materialism; this familiar rhetoric defuses the audience's resistence to the ideological clash between the physical and the spiritual, and between the promise and the performance. Readers may hold in suspension opposing desires or impulses: skepticism and belief, humor and moralism, advocacy of religious resignation or stoicism and thirst for passion, pleasure in orderliness and pleasure in chaos, care for the body and care for the soul. Similar tonal elisions characterize much prose and satirical poetry of the early eighteenth century, but Haywood and Defoe deliberately exploit it as rhetoric. By incorporating advertising discourse into their works, these authors invite readerly pleasure in a commodified world while condemning moral turpitude; moreover, they tout their own books without compromising their judgment. This irony, however, is more than a trick to sidestep conscience. It is a formal solution to the cultural problem of establishing a fabric of significance in a world crammed with shifting values, material things, and unproven claims: the new consumer world of the eighteenth century.[7] By accommodating the inconsistences of value in a society poised between the spiritual and the empirical, advertising established a rhetoric of desire for early eighteenth-century readers. This rhetoric grants both the comforts of commodified "goods," from sexual satisfaction to clothes and cures, and the simultaneous, implacable and contradictory force of indefinable, immaterial, insatiable desire.

The Want Ads, or "The sick may have advice for nothing":

Advertisement has a complex definition and a long history in English culture. Public advertisements—notices of news—as well as oral and visual solicitations to buy goods and experiences from a pint to a prayer for the King were a feature of Renaissance life. In the Restoration and eighteenth-century, as the populace grew wealthier and more literate, as the book trade arose, and as goods for sale became more varied and sophisticated, advertisements changed in form and cultural significance. Advertisement as announcement glided into advertisement as persuasion; "advertisement" became not just information but promotion in print. "Promise, large promise, is the soul of an advertisement," Samuel Johnson declared, and the promise was improvement or cure through consumption.[8]

The primary site targeted for consumption in the Restoration was the body.[9] The correctable body first stepped into popular print when the Royal Society was itself mounting a concentrated advertisement campaign, directed by Thomas Sprat, to legitimize an empirical, scientific methodology. While Sprat's *History of the Royal-Society of London, for the Improving of Natural Knowledge* (1667) supplied a moral justification for a concentrated attention to the physical world, Henry Oldenburg's *Philosophical Transactions*, by publishing experimental results, served to promote remedies, discoveries, and instruments, and above all the empirical motive: a voracious, curious, irrepressible desire to penetrate, dissect, and control the natural world. These publications represented nature, especially the human body, as the object of intellectual desire. In promoting concrete good through empirical cures, this scientific ideology stridently opposed the religious and mystical enterprise that had driven the Puritan regime even while members of the Society urgently asseverated a similar, absolute altruism. As physicians and virtuosi, they claimed they worked entirely for the common good, without personal interest.[10] The rhetorical assertion of a benevolent, elevating, mental desire—the desire to improve the sum of human knowledge—became linked to the quest to cure the body.

This contradiction between physical and metaphysical enterprises and "goods" was echoed in other aspects of Restoration culture. In newspapers and posters, the experiments of the Royal Society reappeared as magical cures. By featuring advertisements for rival scientific instruments, the *Philosophical Transactions* helped to commodify scientific processes and ideas, and further undermined scientific altruism.[11] While members of the Society stayed loftily above motives of profit, quacks happy to gain from their reputations proliferated: their bombastic claims of disinterest parodied not only the physicians of the Society, but the very language of disinterest.

Moreover, as Lisa Foreman Cody shows, they exploited the contemporary fad for investment and credit by mounting advertisements for patently useless medicines.[12] The correspondence between credit, a contradictory kind of invisible money, and magical cures mirrored the cultural confusion about the relationship of the physical to the ideational in the wake of the political shift from the Commonwealth to the Restoration.

Although ads for plague remedies flooded Restoration London, other advertising ventures did exist.[13] Imitating Newcombe's 1657 weekly *Public Advertiser*, featuring prices for various goods, shipping schedules, and new books, other papers increasingly bore advertisements. In 1692, John Houghton, a Fellow of the Royal Society, produced a *Collection for the Improvement of Husbandry and Trade*, endorsed by a coterie of Society members including Samuel Pepys, John Evelyn, and Hans Sloane, signed by "England's *hearty Well-Wisher*," and promising:

> to lay out for a large *Correspondence*: And for the Advantage of *Tenant, Landlord, Corn-Merchant, Mealman, Baker, Brewer, Feeder of Cattel, Farmer, Maulster, Grazier, Seller* and *Buyer of Coals, Hop-Merchant, Soap-Boyler, Tallow-Chandler, Wool-Merchant*, their *Customers*; &c. For these, I say, it was intended, *weekly* to give an account from the most *principal* places of the Kingdom, of the *Prizes* [sic] of *Wheat, Rye, Mault, Oats, Pease, Hay, Coals, Hops, Tallow* and *Wool*: To which I add, the Price, at *London*, of *Beef, Pork*, and *Mutton*.[14]

This disinterested enterprise floundered, but advertisement for profit soared.[15] By the 1720s, advertisement had become a pervasive aspect of culture, not only because of the popularity of newspapers but also because of the related crest in commodities and consumption during a decade dazzled by paper credit and soaring stock.[16] Newspapers increasingly relied on advertising revenue, and featured columns purveying goods and services, so that by the mid 1720s, readers were complaining about the overload of advertisements in newspapers.[17] By the 1730s, papers had revived the term for their titles: *The Daily Advertiser*, for example, hoped to monopolize advertising itself, and heaped coffee-house names in its imprint to help its distribution.[18] By 1759, Samuel Johnson could remark that, "The practice of appending to the narratives of public transactions, more minute and domestic intelligence, and filling the newspapers with advertisements, has grown up" so much that "Advertisements are now so numerous that they are very negligently perused."[19]

The physical placement of advertisements increased the instability of their reception. In the Restoration, censorship and printing limitations encouraged the placement of advertisements in public venues—doors, walls, taverns—and, as prints by William Hogarth and other artists reveal, this practice continued in the eighteenth century.[20] Some polemical scribblers play with their haphazard context, like the author of "The CRISIS upon CRISIS. A POEM. Being an ADVERTISEMENT Stuck in the LION's Mouth at Button's," which explains that, "I, in Nestor's wooden Mouth, / Am stuck, to tell the self-same Truth".[21] Before billboards, advertisers favored corners or large walls to post advertisements either serially or at the same time. These physical juxtapositions increased the instability of advertisements because they eliminated control over the audience and the immediate context.

Similarly, in newspapers, each advertisement juxtaposes rival print: other advertisements or news items that demand a different response from the reader. *The London Journal* for 21 January 1720, for example, lists an ad for the removal of Mr. Normand Curry's "fine Bed" from Somerset House and imminent display of it elsewhere above the account of Mr. William Mclean's six-year old son, who "languished with a violent Pain and Swelling in his Stomach" before the apothecary Mr. John Moore removed from his gut a nine foot, 3 ½ inch long "*Worm*" (also on display). Such juxtapositions imply an ironic equation between "goods" of widely different kinds and importance: luxury and death; life and facial complexion; health, houses, and hounds; books promising salvation and books promising sinful indulgence. Samuel Johnson comments on this dynamic in his essay on the fad for advertising marriages in the newspapers: "When the reader has contemplated with envy, or with gladness, the felicity of [bride and groom], his attention is diverted to other thoughts, by finding that Mirza will not cover this season, or that a spaniel has been lost or stolen, that answers to the name of Ranger."[22] Juxtapositions invite readers to make invidious comparisons: they create irony. In another number, Johnson comments:

> It has been remarked by the severer judges, that the salutary sorrow of tragick scene is too soon effaced by the merriment of the epilogue; the same inconvenience arises from the improper disposition of advertisements. The noblest objects may be so associated as to be made ridiculous. The camel and dromedary themselves might have lost much of their dignity between "The True Flower of Mustard" and "The Original Daffy's Elixir"; and I could not but feel some indignation when I found the illustrious Indian warrior immediately succeeded by "A Fresh Parcel of Dublin Butter."[23]

The irrelevance—or ironic relevance—of advertised goods to the surroundings in which they appear makes advertising discourse continually open to ironic deconstruction. In addition, advertising by its very nature always directs the reader to a subject—the touted commodity or service— that is absent, and thus possesses an ironic structure that refers to a private context, and simultaneously represents and denies satisfaction.[24]

The printed advertising of consumer goods, especially reading matter, by the early eighteenth century flooded every printed venue so much that literature and advertisement tended to merge. Advertisements appeared without differentiation in paragraphs of political news or disaster announcements since shareholding booksellers often placed them.[25] Many early journalistic writers like Tom Brown in *The London Spy* use the trope of the London tourist overwhelmed by the aggressive advertisements of tradespeople and performers in such public goods-fests as Bartholomew Fair. With the establishment of the first daily newspaper, *The Daily Courant*, in Queen Anne's reign, advertisement regularly juxtaposed other forms of information, partly because of the financial concerns of the 1712 Stamp Act, and partly because of the ferocious competition between papers.[26] Books boasted imprints touting booksellers and concluded with sometimes as many as eight pages of titles for other works. Posters and broadsides announced not merely political, but increasingly consumer-geared messages, and literature itself often constituted advertisements. Bernard Lintot's *Miscellaneous Poems and Translations* (1712), for example, contains poems by Gay and Pope that celebrate the miscellany itself, a self-promoting practice common in the period.[27] Jonathan Swift's *Verses on the Death of Dr. Swift* constitutes an ironic tout, like many of his satires. The distinction between the advertising of a product and the product itself blurred.[28]

The slippage between tout and text, promise and product, reflects the structural and rhetorical irony of advertising's juxtapositions. Advertisements address a great range of desires and topics, indiscriminately mixing announcements about people, places, and things. Late seventeenth-century ads often mingle several in a continuous string that compels readers, searching for pause, to finish the whole ad. *The City Mercury*, a free paper of advertisements that in the 1670s gave away a thousand copies a week to "booksellers, shops, inns, and coffee-houses" in London and provincial towns, announces that, "Any person that has anything to insert in it. As the *titles of books, houses* or *land* to be *lett* or *sold, persons removing from one place to another,* things *lost* or *stole*, for *places*, or for *servants*, &c., may bring or send them to the Publisher, *Tho. Hawkins* in *George Yard*, in Lombard Street, London, who will carefully insert them at reasonable rates"

(78). Even later advertisements, set off from each other, cannot control forced juxtapositions. Advertising levels conventional distinctions between palpable and impalpable goods.[29]

The incongruous format of advertisements was partly driven by the necessities of financing. Advertisements always profited the monopolizers of print, whether they helped the tradesmen selling goods or not. In the Restoration, the repressive Printing Act of 1662 (renewed in 1693) censored the contents of print, but in 1663, Sir Roger L'Estrange took on the authority to censor papers dealing with state issues, in return for the rights to "'all narratives or relacons not exceeding two sheets of paper and all advertisements, mercuries, diurnals, and books of public intelligence'."[30] Five years later, he began the *Mercury, or Advertisements concerning Trade*, although it died out quickly. After the Stamp Act of 1712, increasing freedom from censorship seems not to have affected the profitability of advertisements for newspapers, while allowing advertisers flexibility. Michael Harris points out that although many tradesmen used regularized advertisements with fixed rates, a "considerable number" of advertisements were "of unusual length or form for which charges were variable," while newspapers also offered cut-price advertisements to boost their number of advertisers.[31] Presumably, advertisers chose what they could afford, but before newspaper advertisement and cultural shifts made regularization in columns most effective, they could also experiment with length, format, font, and rhetoric.

Since advertisements could range widely in form by the early eighteenth century, advertisers encouraged readers to peruse them as artful works. Many run their prose horizontally, sometimes in thick columns, using spaces as well as words. Some texts constitute a paragraph, others a page, still others, particularly in the later eighteenth century, run for pages as mini-books.[32] For novelists and advertisers alike, the first task must be to win the reader's attention, and to do this, advertisers imitated the aural and gestural sensations of live touting—the pedlars, packmen, horn-carrying criers, and bellmen of Medieval and Renaissance days—by the use of a variety of fonts, ornaments, and type sizes, including capitals, italics, black letters, pointing hands, asterisks, and plain and decorative printer's lines.[33] In addition, they plunder and modify Renaissance stylistics to cobble together a style defined by repetition, ballooning synonyms, alliteration, assonance, symmetry, narrative progression, rapid shifts in fonts, paragraphs comprising long, single sentences, descriptive detail, and eye-witness testimony. These features stress narrative and novelty by making the most of every change of word or theme, and exploit the informal, oral, immediate rhetoric that Carey McIntosh finds characteristic of the first decades of the eighteenth century.[34] Both the novelists of the 1720s and Restoration medical advertisers rhetorically reflect psychological processes: their rhetoric emphasizes movement, instability, a wavering of fluids and feelings. The resulting linguistic ambiguity expresses the uncertain relationship between feelings and things in the early modern period.

Advertisement as printed persuasion is a form of classical oratory, itself essential to early-modern English self-representation, and shares its staple features.[35] Thomas Hobbes, in his translation of Aristotle's *Treatise on Rhetoric* in 1681, explains that "Rhetoric is an Art consisting not only in moving the passions of the Judge; but chiefly in Proofs. And...this Art is Profitable."[36] Advertisement, like classical rhetoric, uses as proof fictional examples, rather than only employing witnesses and evidences, designedly "*moving* the Judge to Anger, Love, or other Passion" (396). Aristotle isolates as key techniques repetition, amplification, and diminution, and differentiates three "modes of persuasion furnished by the spoken word," which parallel the ways in which printed persuasion works: "The first kind depends on the personal character of the *speaker*, the second on putting the *audience* into a certain frame of mind; the third on the proof, or apparent proof, provided by the *words* of the speech itself" (5–6). For Aristotle and for advertisers, the source's credibility, emotional manipulation, and the audience's perception of a truth are the means of persuasion.[37]

Primary among the rhetorical necessities of advertisements was thus the need to prove the reliability of the speaker. Samuel Johnson notes that, "In an advertisement it is allowed to every man to speak well of himself," and certainly quacks mimicked the altruistic rhetoric of Royal Society physicians in claiming benevolent motives.[38] In *The Tatler* for 1710, Joseph Addison famously mocked advertisers' bombastic rhetoric and cunning printing devices designed to entice readers into thinking themselves privy to a secret.[39] In his *Dictionary* in 1755, Samuel Johnson defines "advertisement" not as selling, but as "instruction" and "information," and advertisers in the Restoration consciously slide between the disinterested representation of knowledge, the altruistic dissemination of improvement, and the self-interested promotion of goods. Their pleas may well have intensified the contemporary skepticism concerning the possibility, or indeed utility, of this supposed disinterest. Much Restoration satire, notably Samuel Butler's *The Elephant in the Moon*, Aphra Behn's *The Emperor in the Moon,* and Thomas Shadwell's *The Virtuoso*, targets the self-deception or plain deceit behind virtuosi's claims of public utility, and this charge reappears centrally in Gay, Pope, and Arbuthnot's farce *Three Hours After*

Marriage (1717). These rhetorical features of deferred authenticity, self-promotion by prior narrative or public knowledge, and disinterested aim remain characteristics of the popular novelists of the 1720s.

Proofs are fundamental to medical advertisement. Many cite the testimony of sufferers and promise refunds. However, the central rhetorical ploy is narrative. In this one, for example, the advertiser catalogues the contract for cure in time:

> And it may be truly affirm'd, that in almost every Parish in and about the City of *London*, many of the inhabitants of all ranks have been cur'd by these medicines, in the use of which, with the blessing of God is such assurance of success, that if these diseases have not been render'd incurable by ill management, and other accidents the cure of them shall be undertaken according to the following proposals:
> 1. A certain time shall be agreed upon for the cure of the above-mention'd diseases before they are undertaken.
> 2. The sick shall know at first what the medicines will cost that are necessary for their cure, tho' they shall pay for them only as they use them.
> 3. Whatever is receiv'd for medicines of them as they use them, shall be faithfully return'd, if the cure be not perfected within the time present.
> 4. That they may be sure of having either their money or their health restor'd, they, or their friends for them, shall have a Note, if they desire it, under my hand and seal, with what witnesses they please to it, for the performance of these proposals.
>
> ☞ *Tis very well known, that many other diseases have been frequently cur'd at the* Angel *and* Crown *in* King-Street, *near* Cheap-side; *so that the sick may as probably find relief there, in most diseases, as any where else; and indeed* J. Pechey *that has practis'd there several years, has Authority, and an ample Testimonial of his ability to practise Physick, from the Colledge of Physicians in London.*[40]

The terms of the treatment are financial, but the terms of the cure are temporal: "a certain time" is allowed for change. Thus, cure is proved by a narrative, and, furthermore, by a narrative of restoration. The advertisement specifies that "either" the customers' "money or their health" will be "restor'd": money and health are figured as equal, exchangeable commodities in an ideal economy impervious to loss. Moreover, this definition of cure is guaranteed doubly in print: by the advertisement and by the promised "Note . . . under my hand and seal." The printer even represents this "hand"—this authorship and authority—typographically with the printer's ornament directing readers to the concluding assertion of time-tested reliability and professional authority.

A dental advertisement from the same period similarly illustrates the narrativity of cure. It begins with an announcement of the dentist's profession and location, with an italicized emphasis that these cures "*may be had any time*":

> *David Perronet*, Surgeon, his *Universal Dentrifice*, Or General Remedies against all Distempers afflicting the Teeth and Gums in Old or Young,
> *Which may be had at any time, at* Buckridge-street, *between* Dyot-street, *in* Bloomsbury *and* St. Giles*'s*-Church, *at the* Blue *and* White Ball*, the* Surgeons-Sign *being likewise over my door.*

The following rhetoric presents remedy as a logical sequence of illness:

> Whereas there is no vexatious Illness more common and frequent than the *Tooth-Ach*, for which there are various Remedies, but very few that prove serviceable; and likewise considering the many Accidents which daily happen by drawing them, as well as the Inconveniency in the loss of them, I thought fit to give this Information, that I have a sure and speedy Remedy for the Cure of the worse of *Teeth-Aches*, such as be hollow and rotten: For, be they never so raging or of long continuance, this Remedy presently cures it, by killing the Worm in it, or dispersing the sharp Humours that cause it. *Price One Shilling*

Subsequent paragraphs specify both the problems and the solutions:

> Another Remedy which absolutely cures any eating Ulcers, or Scurvy in the Gums, and fastens loose Teeth to admiration, tho' never so shaking, and that in a few times using. *Price One Shilling.*
> My *Salt of Cloves*, which wonderfully cleaneth and whitens the Teeth, and preserves them and the Gums from Putrefaction or Decay. *Price Six-pence.*
> *Lastly*, Considering the many fatal consequences hard

breeding of Teeth causes in little Children, some falling into
Fevers, others into Convulsions, and many into the Grace by
it, I have such an absolute Remedy, that being applied to the
Gum, (tho' never so sore, inflamed, and swelled) it presently
appeaseth the Anguish of it, and instantly removes all other
Disorders occasioned by it.

These advertisements portray the body from the time of birth (or at
least of teething) as a swelling, leaking, rotting hulk that repeatedly veers
away from its original wholeness, and must be reined back in to be restored
to perfection. Rhetorically, such advertisements feature colorful and plentiful
adjectives and nouns; very long, phrase-laden sentences that pull readers
along to the end, which is often the end of the paragraph as well; and
anaphoric phrasing. Visually, they use italics, capitals, frequent paragraphs,
and parentheses. Often, they include the personal testimonies of cured
sufferers, or a narrative recounting the professional's career. Always
prominently featured are the details of the location where the cures may be
found, and usually the credentials of the physician. Throughout, advertisers
tout newness, availability, immediacy, time. Their rhetoric combines the
religious discourse of the Fall and the Redemption with the scientific
discourse of empirical measurement and objectified improvement.

This rhetorical blend exploits two of the central sources of cultural
authority in the Restoration—science and religion—and presents the body
as a catalogue of separate, if painful, parts that nonetheless can be restored
to wholeness, as modeled by the narrative. Using this rhetoric, advertisers,
amateur and professional, by the 1720s identified physical symptoms with
luxury commodities, implying with various levels of subtlety the associations
between material and moral benefits. Most notorious, perhaps, is the ad
for the anodyne "NECK-LACE", containing a narrative recounting the
horrors of the plague and a woodcut displaying the necklace in a stylish
cartouche.[41] [See Plate 1] By innuendo, these advertisements work the
unstable relationship between commodity and narrative, real and promised,
parts and the whole. This rhetoric identifies the physical and the moral
even while, by bluntly underscoring the concrete, it acknowledges their
distinction. The resulting linguistic ambiguity keeps contradictory
interpretations in suspension.

Titles also serve significant rhetorical purposes for advertisements and
fiction. Advertisements, in a sense, are entirely title, as titles are entirely
advertisement. J. Paul Hunter has pointed out that the elaborate titles of
late seventeenth and early eighteenth-century novels invite a range of
readerly expectations that transgress strict generic boundaries. [42]

in raculti by the Abbot de Vertot of the Royal Academy
f Infcriptions, and tranflated from the laft Edition printed at
uris, by G. Rouffilleu of Merton College, Oxon. Price
ound 3 s.
IV. The Sequel to Henry the Fourth: With the Humours
Sir, John Falftaffe and Juftice Shallow. Alter'd from Shake-
ear by the late Mr. Betterton, Price 1 s. 6 d.
V. The 6th Edition, with large Additions of. The Gen-
tman's Recreation, in 4 Parts, viz. Hunting, Hawking, Fifh-
g and Fowling, &c. Adorn'd with Cuts proper to each Di-
vion. Price Bound 6 s.

Juft Publifh'd,

|* I. **Three Letters relating to the South
a Company and the Bank. The Firft written in March,
19-20. The Second in April, 1720. The Third in Sept.
20, Now firft publifh'd. By James Milner, Efq; The fe-
id Edition. (Price Six-pence.)
II. Confiderations on the prefent State of the Nation, as
Publick Credit, Stocks, the Landed and Trading Interefts.
th a Propofal for the fpeedy leffening the Publick Debts,
l reftoring Credit, in a Manner confiftent with Parliamen-
t Engagements. (Price One Shilling.)
II. An impartial Enquiry into the Value of South-Sea
ck: With fome Thoughts on the Occafion of the prefent
:ay of Trade and Credit; and fome Means propofed for
oring the fame. In a Letter to Sir Richard Steele, Kt.
:e Eight-pence. All printed for J. Roberts, in Warwick-
c.

** Whereas Mr. *Normand Carty* did advertife
Publick, in the *Daily Courant*, of the 8th of *October* laft,
t he was taking down his fine Bed, at *Somerfet-Houfe*;
:hat as foon as he could find a convenient Place for fetting
he fame, he would give Notice thereof to the Publick,
all Perfons may have the Pleafure of feeing the moft
ous, as well as the moft elegant Piece of Furniture that
was. This Bed is wrought with the moft beautiful Fea-
s of divers Colours, woven into a Stuff : fo that the Cur-
: are as light, and as manageable, as if they were of Da-
:. There are Six Curtains, which, together, take in the
pafs of Thirty Four Feet; and the Bed may be raifed
Sixteen to Eighteen Feet in Height. The feveral Parts
are diverfify'd by different Defigns; the Ground of
h refembles a white Damask, interfperfed with Silver;
each Defign is compofed of Ornaments, that fupport
s of Flowers and Fruits: Each Curtain has a Purple
:g of a Foot Broad, branched with Flowers clouded with
er: The Valences and Bafes are likewife bordered with
e, and flowered in the fame Manner, and enriched with
nge of tufted Feathers: The Cornifhes anfwer to the
in Borders: The Corners of the Bedftead, and the Four
, which alfo on the Tefter, are adorned with Feftoons
Flowers in Relief. In fhort, This is fuch a curious
of Workmanfhip, as cannot be paralelled by any Hand
oever. This, with feveral other curious and beauti-
tees of the fame Kind as the faid Bed, are to be feen at
Change, in the *Strand*, in that Part which Mr. *Brown*,

...ess, and effectual to the aged; Perfons in the
Country fending their Bignefs, and which Side
the Rupture is, may be fupplied with the Truffes, and proper Directions, by Peter Bartlet, at
the Golden-Ball in St. Paul's Church-yard, near
Cheapfide, London. His Mother Mrs. M. Bartlet at the Golden-Ball over-againft St. Bride's Lane in Fleet ftreet, is fkil-
ful in this Bufinefs to her own Sex. Her Steel Spring Truffes,
for Ruptures at the Navel, are not only more effectual, but
eafier than thofe made without Steel.

*** **Wright's Diuretick or Cleanfing Tincture,**
which Urinarily difcharges all the Faeces or putrid Relicks of the Lues Alamode, or Veneral Infections, and chafes
its Concomitants, the wretched Train of that complicated Di-
ftemper, as all mucous, filthy fanious Matter lodged in tho
Reins, or fpermatick Parts, which either caufe a Sharpnefs in
the Urine, or too frequently provoke it. This Relick is dif-
coverable, partly by fubfequent Symptoms, viz. by a Debili-
y, or Weaknefs of the Back, a faetid, mukous, and averting
Smell of the Urine, with a purulent Matter, or feculent Sordes
refiding at the Bottom, or flying in it, with variety of Figures.
Farther, this Tincture effectually carries off all Relicks of
the Veneral Difeafe, after ill managed Cures, not only cleanfing the Urinary Paffages of all Sand, Gravel, Films, or mem-
b anous Pellicles, &c, but after a fingular Efficacy, invigo-
rating the Reins, reftoring them, and all their Genital Parts,
their Original Tone and Ufe, tho' the Misfortune and Decay
be of the longeft Date, with an equal Succefs in each Sex.
To be had of Dr. Wright, for Ten Shillings per Bottle, with
Directions for its Ufe, only at his Houfe at the Golden Head
in Bell Savage Yard on Ludgate-Hill.

The late Dreadful PLAGUE at
Marfeilles compared with that in London,
Anno 1665, in which died above 100,000
Perfons, Carts continually going about London Streets to fetch away the Dead Bodies,
the Carmen crying out, Bring out your
Dead, Bring out your Dead. Together with
the Method of Cure ufed to thofe who Recovered in London,
not One having Died that ufed it; publifhed then by the College of Phyficians, by the exprefs Order of the King and Coun-
cil; with Rules for its Prevention and Cure. This Book is
given Gratis, (for the Prefervation and Benefit of all Perfons
who may at any Time be where this terrible Marfeillian Infection may reach) only up one Pair of Stairs, at the Sign of
the Celebrated Anodyne NECK-LACE, Recommended
by Dr. Chamberlain for Childrens Teeth without Temple-
Bar, and no other Place. And where, as long as they hold
out, every Family may have one to keep by them againft the
Day of Affliction and Time of Need. Note, 1. Thefe Books
will not be given to any Boys or Girls who may pre end to be
fent for them. Note, 2. If fuch a Book as this had but been
Given away in Marfeilles, that every Family might have had
one, fome Thoufands of Lives might have been faved, whereas now 'tis computed that out of every Eight in a Houfe, 7
have perifhed, moft for want of Help.

NDON: Printed for J. ROBERTS in *Warwick-Lane* : At which Place
Advertifements, and *Letters to the Author*, are taken in.

Plate 1. *The London Journal,* Oct. 1720; this advertisement was plentifully
reprinted juxtaposed with ads for various goods. By Permission of the British
Library

Advertisements similarly signal a range of different subgenres. Early printed advertisements often label themselves generically, yet the title "advertisement" indicates not merely something for sale, but a narrative of restoration or improvement. Many, indeed, fuse titles into the narrative itself, as in this 1710 example:

Advertisement.

> There is lately brought to this Place from *America*, a *Savage*: Being a *Canibal-Indian* or *Man-Eater*, who was taken in a Skirmish near *South-Carolina*, between the Natives of that Place and some of the Wild *Savage* men. Likewise an *Indian* Woman, a Princess of that Country, who gives great Satisfaction to all that have seen them, being the greatest Curiosity that ever was seen in these Parts.
> *N.B.* They are to be seen at any Time of the Day, at the *Black Horse* at *Charing-Cross* over-against the *Muse-Gate*, with their own Native Dress and Paint.[43]

This rhetoric echoes such early novel titles as "The Fortunes and Misfortunes Of the Famous Moll Flanders, &c. Who was Born in Newgate, and during a Life of continu'd Variety for Threescore Years, besides her Childhood, was Twelve Year a *Whore*, five times a *Wife* (whereof once to her own Brother) Twelve Year a *Thief*, Eight Year a Transported *Felon* in *Virginia*, at last grew *Rich*, liv'd *Honest*, and died a *Penitent*." In both title and ad, the descriptive clauses and variations of print sketch narrative while heaping emphasis on nouns, boasting the multiplicity of "goods" on sale for spectatorship or reading. Both fashion readers' desires for strangeness, possession, mystery, exoticism, adventure, violence, and passion into a series of defined items, specified times, places, and sights for sale.

This is also the formula Haywood uses. For example, the title *Love in Excess; or, the Fatal Inquiry* signals didacticism, eroticism, luxury, mystery, myth, and tragedy, among other themes. Such a multiplicity of signals not only expands the book's appeal, but also incorporates the philosophical irony of sexuality, reading, and human appetite—all variations of Eve's inevitable yet avoidable transgression.[44] These readers are themselves "inquirers," promised that they will encounter the libidinous delights that entail punishment.[45] Haywood's combination of overt exemplary morality and erotic appeal was a point to be advertised. At the end of *Letters from a Lady of Quality*, the publisher Chetwood touted her collection of stories as "a Book entitled the Danger of giving way to Passion in five Exemplary Novels."[46] These titles, like that of *Moll Flanders*, help to organize the text's reception by proclaiming simultaneously inconsistent or morally ambiguous notions. The semantic juxtaposition of Defoe's terms *"Whore"* and *"Wife'*, for example, hints at an equivalence that undermines the ostensible morality of Defoe's rhetoric; Haywood's "Love", conventionally a complete good, is paradoxically "in Excess," and so simultaneously a virtue and a vice; in the advertisement, the exotic *"Savage"* cannibal appears as urban spectacle for public ocular consumption. Titular rhetoric spectacularizes and undercuts moral categories.

Advertisements indicate the essential elements of the goods for sale, along with the moral or ending: cure. For example, at the end of the 1709 chapbook *Love in a Passion without Discretion, or the Young Merchants Sudden Bargain,* between ornamental printer's rules is printed:

ADVERTISEMENT.

At the *Pastry-School*, over again the *Compter* in *Shovel-Ally* in *Wood-street*, near *Cheapside*; is Sold, a never failing Oyntment that Cures the *GOUT*, altho' the Party be reduced to his Crutches, and that in two or three Days time; having often been found True by Experience, to the great Ease and Comfort of many: It also Cures *Rheumatick* Pains. Likewise a Cure for the *Tooth-Ach*, which Infallibly Cures without Drawing.[47]

Specific details of location open the paragraph; tucked within is the tale of the gout-crippled patient cured by this ointment. Like the novel, the advertisement presents a dramatic narrative of indulgence, repentance, and redemption or recovery both specifically placed in time and urban geography, and touted as universally applicable, both "real" and representational.[48]

Just as specificity of location pins "cure" to scientific concreteness, so the classical device of amplification enables advertisers and novelists to produce "goods."Amplification multiplies categories, creates distinctions, invents choice. At the same time, cataloguing, commonly used in scientific treatises and on title pages, classifies and orders tumultuous human nature into discernible symptoms; print regulates the body for treatment. For example, a typical quack's "ADVERTISEMENT" asserts that:

At the *Angel* and *Crown* in *King-Street*, near *Cheap-side*,

next door to the Ally that leads into *Ironmonger-lane,*
The sick may have advice for nothing.
   And approv'd medicines at reasonable rates, such as have
been found by many years experience successful to
admiration, in the cure of *Fevers, Agues, of the Cholic,*
Griping in the Guts, Bloody Flux, Vomiting and Looseness,
of Coughs, Chin-Coughs, Worms, Rickets, of the Jaundice,
Scurvey, Rheumatism, or Pains and Lameness in the Limbs;
of many of the Diseases peculiar to Women; of Swellings,
Ulcers, or Scabs, occasion'd by the French-Pox, and the
like.[49]

This rhetoric, like the title of *Moll Flanders,* specifies and differentiates
between symptoms and sensations, and thus produces what it promises to
destroy. The impression of multiplicity and fullness promotes consumption
itself—more is better, the more it cures the better it is—while also
differentiating between closely similar phenomena. In addition, the
redundancy of the language and information enforces importance. This
repetitiveness commodifies immaterial feelings into wants, each provided
by the advertiser with a purchasable cure. This repetitive rhetoric of
difference and similarity defines for the reader his/her own desire: a desire
for cures or commodities that are the same, yet not the same—a pattern of
consumption closely linked with Restoration and early eighteenth-century
depictions of sexual libertinism as the compulsive consumption of different
women. Both Haywood and Defoe employ this technique, not merely in
their prose, but by a structure that repeats the basic drama of the fall:
Love in Excess retells the cycle of looking, longing, falling, and punishment;
Moll Flanders replicates incidents of seduction, theft, and fear; *Roxana*
repeats seduction, acquisition, and remorse.
   In contrast to these concrete symptoms, this advertisement promises
that, *"the sick may have advice for nothing."* While capitalizing on the
notorious generosity of Royal Society physicians, this advertiser is also
playing on the ambiguous relationship between the material and the moral.
No thing is what advice—wisdom and instruction—is, indeed, for. Offered
as the cure for behavior, this advice addresses the impalpable with the
impalpable: moreover, unprinted, it remains words, breath, air—no thing
at all—whereas flesh, medicine, and print have substance. The advice, of
course, is to consume the concrete cure, but the rhetoric implies a moral
center beyond consumption. Precisely the same rhetoric marks the prefatory
moral justifications and passages of characters' remorse or advice—like
Roxana's adjuration to "Never, Ladies, marry a Fool"—in the fictions of

Haywood and Defoe.[50] This implicit moral guardianship of the consumer endows advertising with the authority to define desire—what Jean Baudrillard explains as the illusion that "somewhere there is an agency...which has taken upon itself to inform [the consumer] of his own desires, and to foresee and rationalize these desires to his own satisfaction."[51] For example, one quack in 1690 beckons *"Those that desire Health"* to his door:

> There be many Elixirs, but none compare with this, nor come close to it, for it is nearest to an Universal Medicine on Earth; for he hath practiced it near fifty years, and thirty since the Lord was pleased to reveal the Vertues of the same to him: and since that it hath been his Refuge to serve the Lives of all in distress (his own as well as others) curing all Diseases, when other medicines could not prevail: it seldom fails (only it is dear). It cures those Diseases which no other medicine can; and with this the Lord hath been pleased to do miracles, that all may know his Power: by helping abundance of despairing souls, being afflicted with Barranness and those direful and corroding cancers in the Breasts and Wombs; and by saving many women and children that were even lost by hard Travel: It expells all venemous Humours, and helps the Plague and all Pestilential Fevers and Agues...The Cause therefore of printing this is, to satisfie all People that there is now a medicine which our Fore-fathers sought for many Generations, but could not obtain it: God's time is the best...If People would believe, certainly by the use of this they will be preserved from many Diseases, and kept in Health; thereby disappointing many Doctors of getting great Estates, and themselves of having occasion to take those Mortal Potions that make a dark Massacre.
>
> I would teach it to all such as the Lord shall stir up to learn it....
>
> Leave Debauchery, and that Judgement, the *Pox*, will cease. Women, Women, love your Husbands, and be civil; the Lord is good; bring not Misery on your selves. Young Men, fear God and depart from Evil; Fools will babble: be sober, watch.[52]

This advertiser exploits the ambiguous rhetoric of improvement to elide moral and physical categories. Moreover, he commodifies his advertisement itself as a cure by concluding with the italicized directive: *"Keep this Bill, for it will help you, and save you money."* These elisions between body and soul, advertisement and commodity, run through Defoe's and Haywood's fictions of desire.

The Fictional Rhetoric of Goods:

Haywood asserts narrative disinterestedness both in her own voice in her prefaces, and in the voices of her idealized characters even while providing goods for her own profit. In her "Advertisement" to the reader in *The Tea-Table: or, A Conversation between some Polite Persons of both Sexes, at a Lady's Visiting Day* (1725), she denies alluding to any "particular Persons, or Families," protesting that altruism motivates her:

> The Design of [these Sheets of paper] being only to expose those little Foibles which disgrace Humanity, and render those who are guilty of them incapable of receiving that Admiration and Respect, which their other good Qualities and Accomplishments would else merit from the World. If I succeed in my Aim so far as to influence but one Person to correct any of these Solecisms in Humour, I shall think my self happy; and if I fail, have yet this Comfort, that it is less my Fault than my Misfortune.[53]

The author's good intentions assure readers of the speaker's moral authority, just as similar claims do for advertisers of cures. Yet the title advertises flaw: "Wherein are Represented The Various Foibles, and Affectations, which form the Character of an Accomplish'd *Beau*, or Modern *Fine Lady*. Interspersed with several Entertaining and Instructive Stories." The authorial promise is to cure these "Irregularities" through narrative: Haywood's speaker acts as a moral physician who will calm the desires she creates.

The Tea-Table, despite its brevity and dialogic frame, represents very well the rhetorical and structural techniques of Haywood's fiction. While advocating stoicism, it describes invitingly the inevitability of passion. This contradiction organizes all of Haywood's fiction of the 1720s. *The Tea-Table* contains two, separate stories, both illustrating love's torments and destructiveness, especially for women, framed within a rational and abstract discussion of its folly, conducted by four visitors and the narrator at the salon of Amiana. Presented as a philosophical debate, this frame licenses pleasurable narratives of chaotic feeling, although Haywood here eschews the erotic details of her longer novels of the 1720s. The four speakers are described by the narrator in the hyperbolic, general terms that mark advertising and romantic discourse. Philetus, for example, is a "Gentleman than whom there is scarce to be found on Master of more Accomplishments, a greater Capacity, or a Taste more refin'd and polite: he is just arriv'd at those Years, which look back with Shame on the Inadvertencies of Youth, and far from those which threaten a Decay of Vigour and Understanding" (10). This rhetoric represents the philosophe as a touchstone of truth. The others are similarly perfect, yet the setting of the tea-table emphasizes the association of fiction, gossip, and consumption, thus presenting the literary fare as a commodity for physical pleasure.[54] Indeed, at the end of *The Tea Table*, the philosophes' wise discourse on the morality of fiction is interrupted "by the coming in of Lady in a new Suit of Cloaths.—Her Appearance put an End to the Conversation we were upon, and it turn'd imediately on Dress" (33). Haywood ironically contrasts the morality of passion, recounted in the stories, with the immorality of vain consumption; further irony lies in the moral that passion itself leads to disgrace and despair; and a final destabilization of moral oppositions rests in the ostentatious presentation of this "tea-table" talk and love itself as a consumptible for the reader.[55]

Both the structure and the rhetoric of *The Tea Table* sketch a retelling of the Fall from rational stasis and self-possession into passion, loss of identity, disorder, and death. Haywood opens with Ciceronian anaphora and innuendo that deliberately echo advertising rhetoric:

> Where have the Curious an Opportunity of informing themselves of the Intrigues of the Town, like that they enjoy over a TEA-TABLE, on a Lady's *Visiting-Day*?—Can the Love-sick *Maid*, the Wanton *Wife*, or Amorous *Widow*, be guilty of the least false Step which falls not under the Observance of these *Criticks* in Fame?—Can the seemingly Uxorious *Husband*, who in all Company extols the Merit of his *Wife*, and talks of nothing but their mutual Fondness, keep from the prying Eyes of this Cabal, his Amour with her *Chamber-maid* undiscover'd?—Can the new wedded *Bride*, trembling and blushing at the approach of Night, prevent the inquisitive Fleerers from examining her past Conduct; and if her Modesty be real, or affected?—Can the *Beau*, with a splendid Equipage and no Estate, pass here without the most strict Scrutiny into the Means by which his Grandeur is supported!—is the false Hair, fine Cosmetick, or any other Assistant to Beauty, laid on with so much Art, that the Rival *Belle* cannot distinguish it from Natural?—In fine, is there any Irregularity in Conduct,

any Indecorum in Behaviour or Dress, any Defect in Beauty, which is not here fully expatiated on? Scandal and Ridicule seem to reign here with uncontested Sway, and but rarely suffer the Intrusion of any other Themes.—Sometimes, indeed, it does happen that more useful Topicks make the Conversation, but it is so scarce, and so little approv'd of by the Generality of the persons...that I never founds Wit and good Humour in fashion among them, except at AMIANA's . . . " (7)

This tout advertises *The Tea-Table* as an occasion simultaneously for and of satire. This ambiguity is fundamental to advertising since it enables consumers simultaneously to stand back from and fall for the tout.

The framing device of the salon dramatizes the ideal stasis of rational discourse as the five, idealized *philosophes* converse in abstract terms on passion. The periodical format allows repetition without narrative through inset, didactic tales, none of which changes the relationships of the five speakers. In contrast, characters who enter Amiana's salon, either as visitors or as figures in a narrative, bring with them the disruptions of passion, signaled both by their interruption of the conversation and by a descriptive diction emphasizing loss of control. When the narrator first arrives, for example, and "had just began [sic] to enter into a Conversation which would have been very Entertaining", she is interrupted by the intrusion of "a Titled *Coxcomb*" whose "Inundation of Impertinence put a Stop to every Current of good Sense" (8). Shortly following, a lady enters: "She was no sooner seated, than she began to complain of a most terrible Headake, rolled her Eyes wildly round the Room, wreath'd her Neck, and distorted a Face which Nature had made extremely lovely, into such Looks of Anguish, that one could never have imagin'd, without being assur'd it was so, that she should do it thro' Choice" (8). While the narrator marvels at a "supposed Disorder," she also perceives a real one: the social disorder of abandonment that this lady dramatizes by her psychosomatic illness. These instances of vanity, along with the spiteful comments of another lady, plunge the narrator into so deep a "*Resvery*" or reverie that she remains "altogether ignorant of what was said or done in the Room" (9). Social experience, like the narrative insets, thus provides the speaker with material for philosophical contemplation. Both visitors possess obtrusive and aberrant bodies. The chattering Coxcomb is nothing but his title; the twitching lady is body without control. As exemplars of the loss of integrity who supply food for thought, these characters and the narrator's contemplation of them model for Haywood's reader the moral uses of observing passion: reading enable morality.

The philosophizing of Amiana's companions further dramatizes the conflict between stasis and movement, morality and desire, the means of narrative and its ends. Philtetus defends "that which is called *Love,*" but his defense is as ironic as this ambiguous language (10). While ostensibly differentiating "*Love*" from revenge, anger, and ambition, he equates them as self-elevating impulses; their only difference lies in love's imperceptibility which makes it impossible to avoid. Love is lust, and like "lawless" Ambition, "corroding" Revenge, and "sudden" Anger, it destabilizes the self:

> new Desires play round the gently throbbing Heart, thrill through each swelling Vein, and make us all o'er Pulse!. . .The soft Inchantment steals upon us ere we are aware!— o'erwhelms the Sense with a Tide of Extasy, and we are lost before we see the Danger!... Vainly we strive to raise our sinking Reason, the Current flows too strong, and with a Force which only can be felt, drives us to Actions, such as one must be guilty of to pardon. (11)

Dorinthus adds that "True *Reason*, being utterly depos'd, the sweet Deceiver, *Love* usurps his Seat" (11). In language echoing the royalist-inflected poetic diction of the Restoration, Haywood characterizes passion as a disorder that must be cured for the restoration of reason and physical, emotional, and intellectual control.

The tales within this frame also dramatize the loss of self that passion entails. In the first fable in *The Tea Table*, the exemplary Arabella falls in love with Mr. Worthy, but their engagement is abruptly cancelled because of dowry disputes. Nonetheless, after three years of frustration, they wed, yet when Philetus, the tale-teller, visits her, he finds "instead of the Gaiety of a Bride, adorn'd with Blushes, and beautified with Smiles, . . . rather an Object of Condolence: a gloomy Melancholy sat upon her Brow!" (15). Her love has destroyed her integrity: "when the mischevious little Deity once enter'd into her Breast, all his Attendants, Hope, Fear, Distrust, restless Wishes, disorder'd Joy, and causeless Grief, rush after him: She grew immediately another Creature; and as before her Conversation was Affable, Sweet, and Entertaining, she now became Dull, Reserved, and sometimes Peevish" (15). Not only has she lost her identity and emotional integrity, but her symptoms are physical: "her lovely Eyes were swell'd with Tears! Her Voice faulter'd [sic], and sometimes was wholly stopp'd with Sighs!" (15). The exclamation marks and capitals underscore the objectification and commodification of feeling, presenting her body as the infected site that calls for a cure that will restore it to wholeness. The second tale of the seduction of the beautiful, innocent, illegitimate offspring of a Prince, Celemena, by the heartless rake Beraldus, replays Haywood's familiar story of the arbitrary, "Changeable," and fickle nature of men's passion, their antipathy for commitment, and the folly of giving in to love since possession destroys (male) desire (19). Again, Celemena's symptoms are physical: "She had not presently the Relief of Tears, and her wild Griefs, deny'd that most natural and less painful way of venting themselves, burst out in Cries and Exclamations so loud, so violent" that others could hear them from afar (26). When he denies their affair, "Her Words, and the Distraction which appeared in her Countenance, with the wild Confusion of her unregarded Dress" convinces "Beholders" of her cause, but her loss of integrity approaches "Madness" (30). Deliberately echoing Shakespeare's description of Ophelia, Haywood presents the body and mind infected by passion as suffering from illness that only death can cure. When Celemena regains her reason, she retires miserably to a monastery, but "Fate not permitting her to leave the World till she had seen her Injuries in full reveng'd," she finally learns that her betrayer Beraldus, poisoning his hated wife, was put to a "shameful" death. (30–31) When Celemena learns of this, "blessing the Justice of Providence, [she] expir'd soon after, as tho' she had no longer Business with the World" (31). Her physical breach is closed off: she is whole again, in death.

Haywood completes her frame with overt proselytizing. The philosophes comment on the style and meaning of the story of Celemena and Beraldus. Amiana complains that Celemena's "Character" is "faulty" since "She yields . . . with too much Ease, to create that Pity for her Misfortunes, which otherwise they cou'd not fail of exciting", while Dorinthus recommends that "a Woman, when she reads of such a Fate as Celemena's, will but give her self leave to reflect how very possible it is that the Man she is most inclin'd to favour, may be a BERALDUS," the villainous hypocrite with a fair face in the story, so that she should "inspect into his Behaviour with a Care and Watchfulness which cannot fail of discovering the *True* Affection from the *Counterfeit*" (31-32). Philetus further defends the moral of the story:

> these kinds of Writings are not so trifling as by many People they are thought.—Nor are they design'd , as some imagine, for *Amusement* only, but *Instruction* also, most of them containing Morals, which if well observed would be of no small Service to those that read 'em.—Certainly if the Passions are well represented, and the Frailties to which Humane

> Nature is incident, and cannot avoid falling into, of one kind
> or another, it cannot fail to rouze the sleeping Conscience of
> the guilty Reader to a just Remorse for what is *past*, and an
> Endeavour at last of Amendment for the *future* (32). . . . But,
> methinks . . . there is little occasion of Defence for writing of
> *Novels*, the very Authority of those great Names which adorn
> the Title-Pages of some large Volumes of them, is a sufficient
> Recommendation. (33)

Citing Madame D'Aulnoy, Georges de Scudéry, and other seventeenth-century romance writers, he argues that these authors dressed their morals in fictions to enforce them on the reader. This claim provides a theory to justify the felt disparity between the didactic teleology and the experiential libidinous pleasure of reading parallel to that of the narratives of plague advertisements: reading of the pain ensures the cure. Reading is presented both as the *process* of cure and the model for it.

Haywood's other novels are similarly structured as repetitive narratives of sin. *Fantomina: or, Love in a Maze* (1724) again shows narrative as a desire doomed by teleology by portraying a woman whose insatiable desire for a man causes her to become a different woman every night. In this version of *A Thousand and One Nights*, Fantomina driven by curiosity to learn about men, adopts the posture of a prostitute and falls in love with the gallant Beauplaisir. She is, in fact, in love with desire itself. This desire leads her into his arms, but men are fickle, and soon Beauplaisir bores of her. To retain his interest, she adopts a series of masquerades, becoming a country gentlewoman, a rustic servant, a widow—renewing herself and therefore his desire by a new costume, name, and identity in a rapid run-through of the victims of seduction depicted in the most popular Restoration dramas. She makes herself a commodity for male consumption, and in so doing displays the irony that the cultural lust for novelty is insatiable.

In structure, *Fantomina,* like most of Haywood's fictions, uses the advertizing technique of structural anaphora; incidents repeat themselves in increasingly abbreviated form as the plot spirals to its end.[56] In rhetoric, too, the novel uses the capitalizations and italics that make proper nouns—concrete objects—out of aspects of the body.

> She was young, a Stranger to the World, and consequently
> to the Dangers of it; and having no Body in Town, at that
> Time, to whom she was obliged to be accountable for her
> Actions, did in every Thing as her Inclinations or Humours

rendered most agreeable to her: Therefore thought it not in the least a Fault to put in practice a little Whim which came immediately into her Head, to dress herself as near as she could in the Fashion of those Women who make sale of their Favours . . . .[57]

Just as Beauplaisir, in common with his "Sex", cannot "prolong Desire, to any great Length after Possession", so Haywood, to renew desire in the reader, must vary the narrative (791). Like the sexual encounters that Haywood describes of titillation, arousal, climax, and a remorse that sours the pleasure, the narrative repeats episodes to keep the reader wanting more in search of a final ending. In her tout for the deaf-and-dumb seer Duncan Campbell, *A Spy Upon the Conjuror* (1724), Haywood repeats the formula: over and over again, Campbell astounds the narrator by foretelling the future. The pleasure of a final ending, of an ultimate restoration, never appears. Something is always wanting.

Defoe uses a similar structure. For Defoe, desire expresses the wayward will in opposition to the discipline demanded for social stability and for adherence to God's Providential design. The wandering Robinson Crusoe, the loose-willed Moll Flanders, and the commodity-mad Roxana all fail to discipline the appetite for experience and acquisition. While Defoe portrays desire as the human condition, he also depicts it as a power that can be channeled to bring about individual progress. Desire is *itself* narrative: the desire to go on, to reap what you have sewn and sow more, to resist conclusion, closure, ending, death, stability, stasis, stagnation. What compromises this desire is the fixation on things: money, clothes, men— commodities that bewitch the will but ultimately lead to the loss of self, and yet define identity in the modernizing world. Perhaps the two scenes that dramatize this most powerfully are Robinson's sermon on worthless gold followed by his life-hazarding dive to recover his sunken store, and Moll Flanders' impulse to murder a child for her pearl necklace, but Defoe's novels brim with lovingly detailed things that simultaneously represent sin. In a typical passage describing Moll's robbery of a drunken lover, Defoe echoes the cataloguing rhetoric of advertisements: "I took a gold watch, with a silk purse of gold, his fine, full-bottom periwig and silver-fringed gloves, his sword and fine snuff-box" (218). The anaphora of "gold" and "fine", the adjectival details, and juxtaposition of "sword" and "snuff-box" intensify the irony of the moral comparison between Moll's gift of her body and her narrative of acquisition.[58] As spurs to crime and hooks into the secular world, material things as "goods" remain ambiguous.

For Defoe, advertising models and rivals the narrative of becoming which is his main topic. In *A Journal of the Plague Year*, the narrator disgustedly reports on the exploitation of the fear-ridden poor by advertising quacks:

> it is incredible, and scarce to be imagined, how the posts of houses and corners of streets were plastered over with doctors' bills and papers of ignorant fellows, quacking and tampering in physick, and inviting the people to come to them for remedies, which was generally set off with such flourishes as these, viz.: "INFALLIBLE preventive pills against the plague." "NEVER-FAILING preservatives against the infection." "SOVEREIGN cordials against the corruption of the air." "EXACT regulations for the conduct of the body in case of an infection." "Antipestilential pills." "INCOMPARABLE drink against the plague, never found out before." "An UNIVERSAL remedy for the plague." "The ONLY TRUE plague-water." "The ROYAL ANTIDOTE against all kinds of infection;" and such a number more that I cannot reckon up; and if I could, would fill a book of themselves to set them down. (37–8)

Defoe reproduces in small capitals the boasting adjectives, many suggestively royalist: "Infallible," "Sovereign," "Only True," "Royal." Here, he links superstition, advertising, and a papist-tainted government: all exploit fear and shape it into forms that support tyranny. This tyranny, however, is the tyranny of the marketplace that makes the body an object of commerce (through advertising remedies) or of mystery, through transubstantiation and the notion of the divinity of the royal body. Certainly Defoe accepted the materiality of the body, even if it disgusted him.[59] He himself promoted cures when he wrote in the "*Mercure Scandale*: or, Advice from the Scandalous Club," in one case reporting that the publishers of *The Weekly Review* (1704–13) were summoned to the Club to justify printing a physician's advertisement "for the Cure of a Scandalous Distemper," i.e. syphilis, and the *Journal of the Plague Year* stringently describes the suffering of the confined and the dying.[60]

However, Defoe remains aware of the power of print to make the insubstantial into reality, spin truths from lies, and coopt authority. H.F., Defoe's narrator reproduces the false touts of quacks exactly, noting:

> Others set up bills to summon people to their lodgings for directions and advice in the case of infection. These had specious titles also, such as these:

An eminent High Dutch physician, newly come over from Holland, where he resided during all the time of the great plague last year in Amsterdam, and cured multitudes of people that actually had the plague upon them.

An Italian gentlewoman just arrived from Naples, having a choice secret to prevent infection, which she found out by her great experience, and did wonderful cures with it in the late plague there. Wherein there died 20,000 in one day.

An antient gentlewoman, having practised with great success in the late plague in this city, anno 1636, gives her advice only to the female sex. To be spoke with, &c.

An experienced physician, who has long studied the doctrine of antidotes against all sorts of poison and infection, has, after forty years' practice, arrived to such skill as many, with God's blessing, direct persons how to prevent their being touched by any contagious distemper whatsoever. He directs the poor gratis. (38)

Recognizing how these advertisements manufacture authority from print, Defoe outdoes them using the same techniques. His rhetoric and typography isolate these real advertisements from his own narrative, which is also a fictionalization of empirical truths. Claiming that he could provide dozens of examples, the narrator comments, "'Tis sufficient from these to apprise any one of . . . how a set of thieves and pickpockets not only robbed and cheated the poor people of their money, but poisoned their bodies with odious and fatal preparations; some with mercury, and some with other things as bad, perfectly remote from the thing they pretended to, and rather hurtful than serviceable to the body in case an infection followed." Whereas this advertising poisons, Defoe's narrative promises cure.

Ironically, the narrator isolates one "subtility" above all by which "one of those quack operators gulled the poor people to crowd about him, but did nothing for them without money":

He had, it seems, added to his bills, which he gave about the streets, this advertisement in capital letters, viz.: "He gives advice to the poor for nothing."

Abundance of poor people came to him accordingly, to whom he made a great many fine speeches, examined them of the state of their health and of the constitution of their bodies, and told them many good things for them to do, which were of no great moment. But the issue and conclusion of all was, that he had a preparation which if they took such a quantity of every morning he would pawn his life they should never have the plague; no, though they lived in the house with people that were infected. This made the people all resolve to have it; but then the price of that was so much, I think 'twas half-a-crown. "But, sir," says one poor woman, "I am a poor almswoman, and am kept by the parish, and your bills say you give the poor your help for nothing." "Ay, good woman," says the doctor, "so I do, as I published there. I give my advice to the poor for nothing, but not my physick." "Alas, sir!" says she, "that is a snare laid for the poor, then; for you give them advice for nothing; that is to say, you advise them gratis, to buy your physick with their money; so does every shopkeeper with his wares." (39)

Defoe condemns not the commodification of the body whereby health and hope are figured as desires no different from any other, subject to the same market, but rather the abuse of the market and the consumer held in the false promise of something for nothing. Where the doctor is a shopkeeper, the body is a shop, and desire itself becomes linked to material things—a point Pope made in his satire in *The Rape of the Lock* of women's eternal desires that shift the "moving Toyshop of their Heart" (Canto I, l. 100) [See Plate 2]. By reproving false science and false print, Defoe justifies his own empirical narrative cure, the *Journal* itself.

Conclusion:

Novels by Haywood and Defoe explore the motifs of medical advertising: the substantiality of desire; the fragmentation of the body and of identity; the closed economy of time and money whereby reading and being cured become equal and fungible; the power of print to produce authority. However, the two authors differ in their moral perspectives. As a Royalist and Jacobite sympathizer, Haywood projects an ideal restoration to a static, prelapsarian order: her "cure" echoes Restoration advertisements as well as Aphra Behn's conjuration of Edenic stasis.[61] The Dissenter Defoe promotes an endless fall and recovery, a constant movement toward Providential reward that resembles the developing rhetoric of the commodity-advertisements of the 1720s. These differences express historical changes in the views of health and the body. Whereas late-Stuart quacks promised physical restoration to a pure nature, Georgian physicians

Plate 2. "Thomas Willdey, at the Great Goldsmith Toy, Spectacle, China and Print Shop" 1720. By permission of the British Library. This advertisement depicts multitudinous items for sale above a narrative catalogue describing other goods.

described disease as a nervous sensibility, and touted cures for added energy.[62] Despite these differences, however, both authors portray the irony of wanting experiences and things that promote more desire through a narrative rhetoric that makes cure contingent on reading.

Early-modern advertisements provide this rhetoric by accommodating the contradictions between readers' resistence to and fascination with commodities and commodification in a period of ideological and social transition. Placed in incongruous places in unpredictable juxtapositions with other touts, advertisement developed a way to negotiate the conflicts of meaning, feeling, morality, and materialism in print. Borrowing the rhetoric of the Royal Society and interlarding it with moral terms, advertisers assert their disinterestedness, particularize places, symptoms, and qualities, and portray the process of restoration and improvement in a narrative about consumption. By visual and rhetorical devices, advertisers both create plenitude and establish differences between symptoms, benefits, and/or proofs. This rhetoric defines the reader's desire as the desire for cure yet constant consumption: a condition of contradiction that expresses the transition into a secular culture. Moreover, the dominant topics of early advertising are the body and books: historically advertising connects physical and representational or represented experience, and establishes the combination as desire itself for the reader. The negotiation of these contradictory pleasures of the physical and the virtual constitutes the method of early eighteenth-century fiction.

For Defoe and Haywood, advertising discourse, with its noun-heavy bombast, hyperbole, anaphora, synonyms, and typographical signals, provides self-promoting titles, moralistic prefaces, confessional narrative, and detailed descriptive prose. In the works of both authors, printed touts provide a rhetoric of improvement that projects a utopian restoration or redemption rationalized by consuming smaller delights along the way. By making desire itself a narrative commodity, they transfer the ideals of improvement and cure from the body to books. Theirs are the modern stories of the commodification of the self.

NOTES

1. Daniel Defoe, *Moll Flanders*, ed. and intro by Juliet Mitchell (Middlesex, England and New York: Penguin Books, 1983), 30. All citations refer to this edition.

2. Catherine Ingrassia explains the way her fictional topics and productivity

commodified Haywood in *Authorship, Commerce, and Gender in Early Eighteenth-Century England* (Cambridge: Cambridge University Press, 1998), esp. 77–83. See also Ian Watt, *The Rise of the Novel: Studies in Defoe, Richardson, and Fielding* (Berkeley: University of California Press, 1957); George A. Starr, *Defoe and Spiritual Autobiography* (Princeton: Princeton University Press, 1965) and *Defoe and Casuistry* (Princeton: Princeton University Press, 1971); J. Paul Hunter, *The Reluctant Pilgrim: Defoe's Emblematic Method and Quest for Form in Robinson Crusoe* (Baltimore: Johns Hopkins University Press, 1966) and *Before Novels: The Cultural Contexts of Eighteenth-Century English Fiction* (New York: Norton, 1990); Paula R. Backscheider, *Daniel Defoe: His Life* (Baltimore: Johns Hopkins University Press, 1989); Hal Gladfelder, *Criminality and Narrative in Eighteenth-Century England: Beyond the Law* (Baltimore: Johns Hopkins University Press, 2001); Michael McKeon, *The Origins of the English Novel, 1600–1740* (Baltimore: Johns Hopkins University Press, 1987).

3. Christine Blouch, "Biographical Introduction" to *Selected Works of Eliza Haywood* vol. 1, *Miscellaneous Writings 1725–43*, ed. Alexander Pettit (London: Pickering and Chatto, 2000), xxxv, xlv. See John Richetti, *Popular Fiction before Richardson: Narrative Patterns, 1700–1739* (Oxford: Oxford University Press, 1969). Some critics have modified this charge by identifying her tonal contradictions as deliberate irony directed at hypocritical audiences: Ros Ballaster explains Haywood's techniques as a response to the market in *Seductive Forms: Women's Amatory Fiction from 1684 to 1740* (Oxford: Clarendon Press, 1992), and see also Barbara M. Benedict, *Framing Feeling: Sentiment and Style in English Prose Fiction, 1745–1800* (New York: AMS Press, Inc., 1994), 26–30.

4. Bradford K. Mudge, *The Whore's Story: Women, Pornography, and the British Novel 1684–1830* (Oxford: Oxford University Press, 2000), 174.

5. John Richetti argues that Defoe stages a debate in *Robinson Crusoe* between secular and religious ideas that results in Crusoe's integration of the two; see "Secular Crusoe: The Reluctant Pilgrim Re-Visited" in *Eighteenth-Century Genre and Culture: Serious Reflections on Occasional Form*, ed. Dennis Todd and Cynthia Wall (Newark: University of Delaware Press, 2001), 58–78. However, I think the emphasis of the book and the reader's experience rests in the dynamic of suspended, contrary frames of reference that drives the book.

6. See T. R. Nevett, *Advertising in Britain: A History* (London: William Heinemann, Ltd., 1982) 17–22.

7. Laura Brown, *Fables of Modernity: Literature and Culture in the English Eighteenth Century* (Ithaca and London: Cornell University Press, 2001), 95–102; Neil McKendrick, John Brewer, and J. H. Plumb, *The Birth of a Consumer Society: The Commercialization of Eighteenth-Century England* (Bloomington: Indiana University Press, 1982); John Brewer, "'The most polite age and the most vicious': Attitudes toward culture as a commodity, 1600–1800" in *The Consumption of Culture, 1600–1800: Image, Object, Text*, eds. Ann

Bermingham and John Brewer (London and New York: Routledge, 1995), 345–6.

8. Samuel Johnson, *The Idler*, no. 12 (Saturday, 20 January 1759) in *"The Idler" and "The Adventurer"*, ed. W. J. Bate, John M. Bullitt, and L. F. Powell (New Haven and London: Yale University Press, 1963): 125. All citations refer to this edition.

9. Roy Porter, *Health for Sale: Quackery in England 1660–1850* (Manchester, NY: Manchester University Press, 1989), 44, 91–2.

10. Michael Hunter, *Science and the Shape of Orthodoxy: Studies in Intellectual Change in Late Seventeenth-Century Britain* (Woodbridge, Suffolk: Boydell Press, 1995), esp. 129-32; Steven Shapin, *A Social History of Truth: Civility and Science in Seventeenth-Century England* (Chicago: Chicago University Press, 1985); Steven Shapin and Simon Schaffer, *Leviathan and the Air Pump: Hobbes, Boyle, and the Experimental Life* (Princeton: Princeton University Press, 1985).

11. Joanna Picciotto documents the reverence according microscopes in the Restoration in "Optical Instruments and the Eighteenth-Century Observer," *SECC* vol. 29, eds. Timothy Erwin and Ourida Mostefai (Baltimore: The Johns Hopkins University Press, 2000), esp. 129.

12. Lisa Forman Cody, "'No Cure, No Money,' Or the Invisible Hand of Quackery: The Language of Commerce and cash in Eighteenth-Century British Medical Advertisements," *Studies in Eighteenth-Century Culture* 28, ed. Julie Candler Hayes and Timothy Erwin (Baltimore and London: The Johns Hopkins University Press, 1999), 103–30. I am greatly indebted to this article.

13. Blanche B. Elliott, M. B. E., *A History of English Advertising* (London: Business Publications Ltd., 1962), 44–49; Phillipe Schuwer provides an incomplete but provocative chronology of the development of European advertising in *History of Advertising*, trans. Joan White (Leisure Arts, n.d.), 107.

14. *The London Mercury,* Monday, Feb. 1, 1691: "Advertisement" by John Houghton, F.R.S., *Collection for the Improvement of Husbandry and Trade* for Wednesday, March 30, 1692.

15. Frank Presbrey argues that Houghton developed the single-line advertisement in *The History and Development of Advertising* (New York: Doubleday, Doran & Company, Inc., 1929), 59–60.

16. Elizabeth Kowaleski-Wallace, *Consuming Subjects: Women, Shopping, and Business in the Eighteenth Century* (New York: Columbia University Press, 1997), 6. Catherine Ingrassia, *op. cit,* esp. 17–39.

17. Michael Harris, *London Newspapers in the Age of Walpole: A Study of the Origins of the Modern English Press* (London and Toronto: Associated University Presses, 1987), 55–58, 207, n. 82; see R.B. Walker, "Advertising in London Newspapers, 1650–1750," *Business History* 15 (1975): 112–30.

18. Harris, *London Newspapers in the Age of Walpole*, 31.

19. Samuel Johnson, *The Idler*, no. 12 (Saturday, 20 January 1759): 124–5.

20. Henry Sampson, *A History of Advertising from the Earliest Times* (London: Chatto and Windus, 1874), 24–25.

21. "The Crisis upon Crisis. A POEM. Being an ADVERTISEMENT Stuck in the LION's Mouth at Button's: And Addressed to Doctor S—t." (London: J. Morphew, 1714), 1, ll. 5–6.

22. Samuel Johnson, *The Idler*, no. 12 (Saturday, 1 July 1758): 40–41.

23. Samuel Johnson, *The Idler*, no. 40 (Saturday, 20 January 1759): 126–7.

24. Amongst the standard analyses of the rival contexts irony invites, see Wayne C. Booth, *A Rhetoric of Irony* (Chicago and London: The University of Chicago Press, 1974), although Booth is concerned with ahistorical rhetorical ploys rather than cultural contexts, and Ronald Paulson, *The Fictions of Satire* (Baltimore MD: The Johns Hopkins University Press, 1967).

25. Sampson, *A History of Advertising from the Earliest Times*, 70; Harris, *London Newspapers in the Age of Walpole*, 59–60.

26. Jeremy Black, *The English Press in the Eighteenth Century* (London and Sydney: Croom Helm, 1987), 11; J. A. Downie, *Robert Harley and the Press* (Cambridge University Press, 1979), 150.

27. See Barbara M. Benedict, *Making the Modern Reader: Cultural Mediation in Early Modern Literary Anthologies* (Princeton: Princeton University Press, 1996), 119–35.

28. George Ritzer points out in his "Introduction" to Jean Baudrillard, *The Consumer Society: Myths and Structures* that,"Ultimately, what is being consumed in the consumer society is consumption itself...[which] is best exemplified by advertising. In watching or reading advertisements people are consuming them; they are consuming consumption" (London, Thousand Oaks, New Delhi: Sage Publications, 1998), 15.

29. The pervasive commodification produced by advertising was a common subject of satire by the mid-century. Samuel Johnson comments on the equation between "intellectual" and "material" wares in the discourse of advertising in *The Idler*, no. 40 (Saturday, 20 January 1759): 125. See also an entry in *The Public Advertiser* entitled "The Advertising Age" that satirically recommends advertising for showing a comedy or a pig, nursing children or vamping pamphlets, marrying or setting up a mistress, etc. (13 April 1785).

30. Qtd. in Black, *The English Press in the Eighteenth Century*, 3.

31. Harris, *London Newspapers in the Age of Walpole,* S9.

32. See, for example, the collection in B.L. C.116.i.4, especially no. 132, "An IMITATION of MODEL for WATER-Works, Contrived after the nearest Manner to save Friction, and likewise be made capable of draining the deepest Mine and greatest Quantity of Water that was ever done by any other Engine," a long broadside which contains an explanation of the problem, the refusal of the government to fund the plan, a sketch of the planned solution, and an appeal for financial support. See also no. 103, "PROPOSALS For Publishing by SUBSCRIPTION A COMPLETE COLLECTION of the WORKS Of the Honourable *ROBERT BOYLE* Esq; Printed from the Best EDITIONS . . ." (Dated May 1742 by Andrew Millar).

33. Sampson, *A History of Advertising*, 47–48.

34. Carey McIntosh, *The Evolution of English Prose, 1700–1800: Style,*

Politeness, and Print Culture (Cambridge University Press, 1998), vii.

35. Porter, *Health for Sale*, 92; Jean-Pierre Agnew, *Worlds Apart: The Market and the Theater in Anglo-American Thought, 1550–1750* (Cambridge: Cambridge University Press, 1986).

36. Thomas Hobbes, *A Brief of the Art of Rhetorick* (London, 1681), reprinted in the translation *Aristotle's Treatise on Rhetoric* (Oxford: D. A. Talboys, 1823), Book I, Chapter I: 307.

37. Richard E. Petty, *Attitudes and Persuasion: Classic and Contemporary Approaches* (Boulder, Colorado: Westview Press, 1996 [reprinted from 1981]).

38. Samuel Johnson, *The Idler*, no. 12 (Saturday, 1 July 1758): 127.

39. See Addison, *The Tatler* no. 224 for 14 September, 1710; also no. 228, the reply.

40. *Medical Advertisements*: B.L. 551.a.32 (1) also marked K.244.

41. See Francis Doherty, *A Study in Eighteenth-Century Advertising Methods: The Anodyne Necklace* (Lewiston: Edwin Mellen Press, 1992).

42. J. Paul Hunter, "Making Books, Generating Genres," forthcoming essay (13). I am grateful for permission to see this manuscript.

43. Unidentified. B.L. 1168.d.7.

44. The title of Haywood's later moralistic work "The Female Spectator" similarly gestures toward prurience.

45. For the moral ambiguity of inquiry in the eighteenth century, see Barbara M. Benedict, *Curiosity: A Cultural History of Early Modern Inquiry* (Chicago: Chicago University Press, 2001).

46. Blouch, "Introduction" to Eliza Haywood, *Miscellaneous Writings, 1725–43* (London: Pickering and Chatto, 2000), xxxii.

47. *Love in a Passion without Discretion, or the Young Merchants Sudden Bargain* (London: printed by Henry Hills, 1709?), 8.

48. John Bender notes the correspondence between the representational aspects of science and the novel in "Enlightenment Fiction and the Scientific Hypothesis" in *Eighteenth-Century Genre and Culture: Serious Reflections on Occasional Form*, ed. Dennis Todd and Cynthia Wall (Newark: University of Delaware Press, 2001), 236–60.

49. *Medical Advertisements*: B.L. 551.a.32 (1) also marked K.244.

50. Daniel Defoe, *Roxana*, ed. David Blewitt (Middlesex and New York: Penguin Books, 1987), 40.

51. Jean Baudrillard, *The System of Objects*, trans. James Benedict (London and New York: Verso Books, 1996), 167.

52. B.L. 85/LR 305 a 7 (2).

53. Eliza Haywood, *The Tea-Table: or, A Conversation between some Polite Persons of both Sexes, at a Lady's Visiting Day* (1725) in *Selected Works of Eliza Haywood* ed. Alex Pettit (London: Pickering and Chatto, 2000), I.5. All citations refer to this edition.

54. Beth Kowalesi-Wallace notes that "women's conversation runs scandalously free" at tea tables in contemporary writing in *Consuming Subjects*, 30.

55. Paula R. Backscheider points out Haywood's sophisticated awareness of the exchange value of commodities, including women, in her "Introduction" to Eliza Haywood, *Selected Fiction and Drama of Eliza Haywood*, ed. Paula R. Backscheider (Oxford and New York: Oxford University Press, 1999), xxxii.

56. Jennifer Thorn observes that many of Haywood's texts contain figures, "male and female, who see pregnancy as an obstacle to the achievement of a desired individualism" and self-determination. She argues that Haywood depicts as powerful those women who "resist being 'reduced' to their bodies, and do not deny the body" (122). See Jennifer Thorn, "'Althea must be open'd': Eliza Haywood, Individualism, and Reproductivity" in *Eighteenth-Century Women: Studies in their Lives, Work and Culture*, vol. I, ed. Linda V. Troost (New York: AMS Press, 2001): 96.

57. Eliza Haywood, *Fantomina: or, Love in a Maze* in *British Literature, 1640-1789*, ed. Robert DeMarina, Jr. (Cambridge, MA: Blackwell Publishers, 1996), 786-7. All citations refer to this edition.

58. Carey McIntosh argues that in *Moll Flanders*, "Defoe undermines suspense and expectations by coming to the end of major constituent structures" very often in a sentence, so that semantics are periodical but syntax is not, just repeated structures (82).

59. See Carol Houlihann Flynn, *The Body in Swift and Defoe* (Cambridge: Cambridge University Press, 1990).

60. *The Weekly Review*, p. 51: no. 9 (4 April, 1709).

61. Blouch, *The Works of Eliza Haywood*, lxxiv–v.

62. Porter, *Health for Sale*, 113–14. See also G. J. Barker-Benfield, *The Culture of Sensibility: Sex and Society in Eighteenth-Century Britain* (Chicago: Chicago University Press, 1992) and John Mullan, *Sentiment and Sociability: The Language of Feeling in the Eighteenth Century* (Oxford: Clarendon Press, 1988).

Prévost ou l'exotisme tragique: l'épisode américain dans *Cleveland*

LAURENCE MALL

Aujourd'hui, Antoine Prévost d'Exiles est d'abord et surtout l'auteur de *Manon Lescaut*. Pourtant, c'est *Le Philosophe anglais ou Histoire de Monsieur Cleveland* (1731–1739) qui, entre le *Télémaque* de Fénelon et *La Nouvelle Héloïse* de Rousseau, est le plus grand succès romanesque de l'époque.[1] Cet ouvrage considérable, autant en longueur[2] qu'en importance, tout à la fois plonge ses racines dans la tradition du grand roman baroque du dix-septième siècle[3], appartient au genre typique des Lumières qu'est le roman philosophique,[4] et présente (selon certains) des affinités avec le romantisme.[5] Le héros-narrateur Cleveland, fils illégitime de Cromwell, y raconte entre plusieurs récits intercalés en tiroirs la très riche série d'aventures de tous ordres, et le plus souvent malheureuses, qui lui sont arrivées depuis la tendre enfance jusqu'à la maturité, où il amorce une conversion à la religion chrétienne. De cette vaste somme, ce sont fréquemment les trois "micro-utopies" du texte qui sont étudiées: l'aventure sur l'île de Saint-Hélène vécue par Bridge, le frère de Cleveland (livre III), le séjour de Cleveland et de sa famille dans la tribu américaine des Abaquis (livres IV et V), que l'on verra ici; et enfin une suite de l'épisode américain, relatée rétrospectivement beaucoup plus loin par une amie de la famille de Cleveland, Mme Riding et qui décrit son passage chez les Nopandes, autre peuple américain (livres XIII et XIV).

Pourquoi, comment le héros Cleveland parvient-il en Amérique, et au milieu des sauvages? Elevé par sa mère dans une cave pour échapper aux violences de Cromwell, il y fait la rencontre de Lord Axminster (lui aussi menacé par Cromwell), devient son protégé et ami et tombe amoureux de sa très jeune fille Fanny, à qui il est bientôt promis en mariage. Axminster décide de partir en Amérique pour disposer les colonies anglaises en faveur de Charles II, le roi légitime en exil. A la suite d'un malentendu, Fanny et son père croient Cleveland infidèle et partent sans lui (90). Cleveland se lance à leur poursuite: "J'entre dans la mer immense de mes infortunes," annonce-t-il au début du livre III (85). Il les retrouve après six mois (181), pourtant, et sur l'invitation de son guide abaqui nommé Iglou tous décident de se reposer dans la tribu de ce dernier, dans une vallée au pied des Appalaches (177). Cleveland y restera quinze mois (217) en compagnie de Fanny, avec qui il se marie au milieu des Abaquis et dont une fille naîtra bientôt; de Mme Riding, une amie de la famille; et, initialement, d'Axminster qui les quitte bientôt. L'épisode se termine mal: gouvernés par Cleveland et menés par lui à la recherche d'Axminster, de nombreux Abaquis sont décimés par une épidémie ou s'enfuient avant qu'une féroce tribu ennemie ne s'empare du reste et de nos héros. Cleveland et Fanny, qui croient leur fillette et Mme Riding dévorées par les anthropophages, seront épargnés mais traînés, captifs, par monts et forêts pendant de longues semaines pour finalement être vendus à des trafiquants espagnols et ainsi retrouver la civilisation européenne.

Cet épisode participe tout à la fois de la tradition baroque du récit extraordinaire (avec attaques et enlèvements, fuites et errances en pays inconnus[6]) et de l'utopie ou plus certainement de la contre-utopie dans la lignée de l'*Histoire des Sévarambes* (1677–79) de Denis Veiras dont on sait que Prévost s'est inspiré d'assez près.[7] Il contribue également à faire de Prévost "le véritable créateur du roman exotique" selon Gilbert Chinard.[8] Au-delà de l'emploi évident d'un certain nombre de clichés d'époque sur les "Amériquains," l'épisode offre une perspective intéressante sur la notion d'exotisme, l'élargit, l'approfondit, la complique. Qu'entendre par ce terme d'exotisme? Dans *L'Amérique et le rêve exotique*, Chinard tend à en privilégier le sens ordinaire, soit l'exotisme géographique, l'évocation plus ou moins exacte d'un pays étranger, lointain et peu familier—ce qu'est encore certainement l'Amérique pour les lecteurs européens des années 1730. Cet exotisme géographique n'a pas de quoi surprendre chez celui qui sera d'abord aux yeux des philosophes de la seconde moitié du siècle l'auteur de l'immense *Histoire des voyages* (1746–1759).[9] Comme l'écrit Jean Sgard, "Le périple américain de Cleveland tient à la fois du voyage extraordinaire et de la relation géographique. Comme tout le roman, il procède en effet d'un mythe intérieur; mais il relate en même temps . . . une tentative de mission inspirée par les récits jésuites."[10] Cette "relation" sera donc suffisamment informée pour produire sur le lecteur de l'époque sinon l'effet d'un document ethnographique, du moins une impression de réalité relativement puissante.[11]

En littérature, l'exotisme intéresse "tout récit centré sur l'évocation d'un ailleurs: relations de voyages authentiques, utopies, voyages imaginaires, littérature 'sauvage' des Lumières."[12] De nombreuses productions du dix-neuvième siècle mèneront à favoriser une définition méliorative de l'exotisme, que Todorov explique comme une attitude "où l'autre est systématiquement préféré au même" en vue de "la formulation d'un idéal."[13] Prévost ne joue pas de cette préférence. D'une part le pittoresque évocateur à la manière de Bernardin puis de Chateaubriand est quasiment inexistant dans *Cleveland*.[14] D'autre part, dans l'économie du roman l'Amérique fonctionne certes comme un puissant instrument de révélation, selon sa vocation dans la production européenne jusqu'à aujourd'hui, mais ce qu'elle découvre soit au lecteur soit au héros n'entraîne aucune célébration. L'exotisme de Prévost romancier se situe davantage dans la lignée de celui des explorateurs de la Renaissance tels que Jean de Léry[15] pour qui le sauvage violent (cannibale en particulier) est d'abord une énigme, imprégné d'une inquiétante étrangeté, pris dans un "phénomène d'*Unheimliche* . . . sur le mode tragique",[16] on y reviendra.

C'est donc dans un paradoxe qu'on invoquera ici le petit *Essai sur l'exotisme* de Victor Segalen datant du début du vingtième siècle[17] pour enrichir la compréhension de l'exotisme dans *Cleveland*. Segalen exalte l'exotisme comme valeur esthétique première[18] et en fait une hyperbole de l'altérité, saisie par une sensibilité exacerbée à la différence comprise comme "la perception aiguë et immédiate d'une incompréhensibilité éternelle."[19] Le paradoxe s'impose puisqu'à première vue l'exaltation segalenne est totalement étrangère à Prévost, mais il s'atténue lorsque l'on considère à quel point cette "perception" exacerbée de l'incompréhensible domine l'épisode américain et à travers lui tout le roman. Célébration ici; là, déploration, mais Prévost comme Segalen a porté à son plus haut point d'intensité le sens d'une distance, d'une étrangeté profonde entre les hommes, entre les hommes et le monde, distance que le voyage loin d'abolir maintient et amplifie. Que l'on considère en effet la définition en apparence si simple du terme d'exotisme chez Littré: "qui n'est pas naturel au pays." Les habitants mêmes de l'Amérique—*topos* parce que *locus* par excellence de la nature—sembleront parfois inadaptés au lieu, étrangers sur leur propre sol. Serait-ce que, dans un geste subtil, dans un mouvement original Prévost ait conçu les sauvages non pas comme exotiques par rapport aux Européens mais comme les porteurs obliques de sa vision de la condition humaine dominée par l'anxiété de l'incompréhension?

J'ambitionne ici de déployer les composantes de la notion d'exotisme afin de montrer comment dans *Cleveland* cette notion prend une ampleur et une profondeur exceptionnelles à partir de l'épisode américain chez les Abaquis et les Rouintons. On devra considérer d'abord comment les effets de ressemblance autour d'une barbarie commune comblent d'un côté et creusent sur un autre plan le fossé ostensible entre Européens et sauvages. On observera ensuite la façon dont l'Amérique et ses habitants sauvages sont peints négativement, en rupture avec la tradition déjà bien en place du Bon Sauvage.[20] Mais on devra souligner que cette dévalorisation n'entraîne en rien une valorisation de la civilisation où l'étrangeté et la violence règnent également, sous d'autres formes trompeusement plus familières. L'épreuve exotique possède une densité de significations et une multiplicité de dimensions qu'il nous appartiendra d'explorer. On pourra y voir une source essentielle de la fascination exercée par un roman qui, par la qualité particulière de son exotisme américain, ôte à l'imagination la vision facile d'un paradis lointain pour suggérer la souffrance d'un dépaysement intérieur.

*   *   *

L'extrême proximité de l'Autre; l'extrême altérité du tout proche

De la part de Cleveland chez les Abaquis, aucune tentative d'assimilation; une adaptation aménagée suffira, et elle est purement instrumentale. Tout ce que le héros reçoit des sauvages est pour son confort et celui de sa famille; tout ce qu'il observe en eux ou apprend d'eux, leurs mœurs, leur religion, leur langue, ne l'intéresse que parce qu'il peut s'en servir pour agir sur eux et les dominer. Cleveland n'a rien de l'ethnologue, encore moins d'un esthète; le savoir sur l'Autre n'est pas une fin en soi. Son orientation n'est pas non plus œcuménique; ce n'est pas chez lui que l'on trouvera de ces élans de *caritas* envers ces "frères" que seraient tous les hommes sur terre. Certes, il est reconnu que "ce bon peuple" (220) forme "une nation douce, et beaucoup plus humaine que la plupart des autres sauvages" (182). Mais les rapports de l'Européen avec les Américains sont hiérarchiques, distants, souvent condescendants.

Lors de son séjour chez les Abaquis, Cleveland parvient à se faire nommer leur chef afin, dit-il, de leur inculquer des rudiments de religion et d'ordre social et de leur apprendre à se défendre efficacement contre leurs cruels ennemis les Rouintons (196).[21] On a souvent remarqué une grave équivoque éthique dans ce projet d'apparence altruiste. Sans même prendre en compte les méthodes plus que douteuses de Cleveland—il fait assassiner le chef de l'opposition abaquie en déguisant le meurtre sous les apparences d'un miracle (207–210)—, on rappellera que son but ultime est d'enrôler les Abaquis "militarisés" au service d'Axminster, lui-même soucieux de gagner les colonies anglaises à la cause du roi Charles (193; 220). De ce point de vue, l'humanité des sauvages, donc l'humanité tout court est sacrifiée à l'intérêt d'un groupe restreint. Que l'on compare l'attitude de Cleveland à celle que formulera Montesquieu dans ses *Pensées*: "Si je savois quelque chose utile à ma patrie, et qui fût préjudiciable à l'Europe, ou bien qui fût utile à l'Europe et préjudiciable au Genre humain, je la regarderois comme un crime."[22] L'instrumentalisation de l'Autre, acceptée sans états d'âme par le héros de Prévost, exclut tout échange dans l'égalité. L'altérité est préservée jusqu'au bout, et paraît négative; l'écart est un échec de l'humanité.

Mais c'est justement cette menace commune de chute dans l'inhumanité qui dans une banale ironie rapproche sauvages et Européens. Depuis la page immensément fameuse de Montaigne dans "Des Cannibales", l'idée est certes immensément commune que la barbarie n'est pas toujours où l'on croit.[23] Le roman de Prévost fait la démonstration de cette vérité d'ailleurs expressément reprise: par rapport à la norme qu'est la raison, "l'on trouverait peut-être autant de sauvages et de barbares en Europe qu'en Amérique." (212). Les Abaquis, rapporte Cleveland horrifié, tuent les nouveaux-nés mal formés (200). Mais Cromwell, dont la "barbarie" est proprement inimaginable selon Mme Riding (26), aura lui aussi cherché à se débarrasser de ses deux fils illégitimes Cleveland et Bridge, et Cleveland lui-même, en pleine crise de dépression, sera tout près de tuer ses propres fils (291). Que le barbare est d'abord européen, Cleveland le montre dans l'assassinat politique qu'il commet pour maintenir sa dictature chez les Abaquis, si bien qu'un critique a pu le nommer "le double exotique de Cromwell,"[24] son féroce père. Contribuant au climat lourd, pénible, de tout l'épisode américain, les incertitudes, les menaces de retournements soudains culminent dans la boucherie anthropophagique de la tribu des Rouintons. Les tortures atroces que ces derniers font subir à leurs ennemis sont comme l'image naïve du mal, des violences que les hommes ne cessent de s'infliger mutuellement—du côté des Européens, combien de meurtres dans tout le roman, combien de sang versé, celui des femmes en particulier,[25] alors que les plus barbares des sauvages ne tuent pas les femmes, cela est marqué explicitement.[26]

Quant aux Abaquis, finalement jugés "capricieux et inflexibles" (222)[27] lorsqu'ils fuiront devant l'ennemi, n'est-il pas ironique que Cleveland ait voulu leur faire servir Charles II, qui se révélera lui-même "faible et inconstant" (621), indigne de confiance, déloyal? Tous les hommes sont "exotiques" les uns pour les autres, potentiellement dangereux et impénétrables. C'est par la sauvagerie ou l'irrationalité qu'il porte en lui que l'Autre est tout proche.

Inversement, et c'est ce qui donne à l'épisode sa densité romanesque, le tout proche va se révéler tout autre. En effet, c'est au cœur du séjour abaqui qu'achèvent de se nouer les nœuds d'équivoques dont naîtront les "événements les plus tragiques et les plus sanglants" (205) du roman. On parlera ici d'exotisme moral et, suivant Segalen, d'exotisme des sexes. Sans entrer dans un impossible détail qu'il faudrait étendre à plusieurs épisodes du roman dans son ensemble, on peut ici définir ces deux formes psychologiques de l'exotisme pour ne faire qu'en repérer la naissance dans l'épisode américain. La première consiste à se déguiser, à s'altérer sous le regard d'autrui, à se présenter autre que l'on est, à se faire lointain. Paradoxalement, c'est dans le milieu "naturel" de l'Amérique et au milieu des sauvages simples et sans art que Cleveland décide d'adopter une stratégie permanente de dissimulation vis-à-vis de Fanny, de soutenir un personnage: "la résolution que je pris. . . de me rendre maître de tous les témoignages extérieurs de ma peine devint une règle que j'ai suivie depuis avec une incroyable constance" (219). Souvenons-nous, en contraste, de Montaigne dans le fameux avis "Au lecteur" des *Essais*: ". . . si j'eusse esté entre ces nations qu'on dict vivre encore sous la douce liberté des premieres loix de nature, je t'asseure que je m'y fusse très-volontiers peint tout entier, et tout nud."[28] Dans le roman de Prévost, le héros non seulement n'adopte pas la naïveté transparente des "natifs" mais se fait opaque, étranger aux autres et bientôt à lui-même. L'altérité se marque ici par l'altération.

Segalen écrit: "*L'Exotisme des sexes. Et là toute la Différence, toute l'incompatibilité, toute la Distance, surgit, s'avère, se hurle, se pleure, se sanglote avec amour ou dépit.*"[29] Que l'on songe à Manon, bien sûr, ou à Théophé la Grecque moderne, on sait que "le caractère incompréhensible des femmes"[30] est une évidence pour les narrateurs de Prévost.[31] L'aimante Fanny se montre mystérieusement inquiète près de Cleveland; pourtant "la crainte de lui déplaire m'empêchait de l'interroger d'une manière trop pressante: mais sa peine n'en passait pas moins jusqu'au fond de mon cœur; et j'étais d'autant plus à plaindre que n'en connaissant point la cause ni même la nature, je ne pouvais donner d'explication ni de bornes à la mienne" (198). Fanny de son côté se fait à elle-même subir une "violente dissimulation" en cachant à son mari qu'elle est jalouse d'une amie et compagne du voyage de Cleveland vers l'Amérique, Mme Lallin. Le malentendu est à la source d'une bonne partie des aventures et surtout des malheurs du narrateur. On notera ici encore que l'Amérique, lieu de la simplicité, de la nudité des êtres non seulement ne communique en rien ces qualités—dans leur version morale—aux héros, mais qu'au contraire c'est en cette même Amérique que se noue la véritable complication du livre: l'incompréhension entre Cleveland et Fanny, qui chacun se distancient profondément l'un de l'autre au moment de leur suprême rapprochement (le mariage). La proximité, la familiarité, l'intimité réelle entre homme et femme est fausse, illusoire; Prévost a fait en sorte que ce soit en terre étrangère, en terre lointaine que s'enracine cette vérité jusqu'ici encore neuve mais que le reste du roman amplifiera jusqu'à la rendre quasi mortelle.

Leur mariage a lieu "dans le fond de l'Amérique, au milieu d'un peuple barbare" (187), suivant une "fête ridicule" (188) ou ce que Sgard nomme "une sorte de mômerie exotique."[32] "Hélas! me dit-elle [Fanny à Cleveland], quelle bizarre destinée! Quels auspices pour les suites de notre amour et de notre mariage! Elle prononça ces quatre mots en me serrant la main et en laissant tomber quelques larmes. Je frémis moi-même d'un si triste présage" (187). Le plus "naturel" des mariages, loin de toute pompe à l'européenne, se révèle être le moins transparent, le moins harmonieux — distant comme l'endroit où il a lieu. L'exotisme du cadre fait surgir l'*Unheimliche*, la conscience d'un secret étrange et (déjà) familier. Ce secret est celui de la violence sauvage de la haine qui surviendra entre les époux, et des excès de souffrance qu'ils se préparent l'un à l'autre— "Quelle étrange familiarité ai-je contractée avec la douleur", écrira le narrateur (359). Bien plus tard aussi, Cleveland appelera Fanny "barbare" (375); elle parlera du "barbare Cleveland" (379). Il est ainsi remarquable que la cérémonie abaquie sous les yeux attendris du père et de Mme Riding, dans sa simplicité apparente possède un caractère *heimlich* dans ses deux sens: familier, et "'caché, 'ténébreux', 'dissimulé'". L'*Unheimliche* défini comme "tout ce qui devait rester un secret, dans l'ombre et qui en est sorti"[33] sera au cœur du mariage barbare célébré par les Européens, le lecteur le comprendra progressivement. A mesure que l'exotique est rendu familier, le familier devient exotique.

*   *   *

Exotique: qui n'est pas naturel au pays

Il est un paradoxe plus large qui atteint dans cet épisode le traitement de notre question envisagée sous son aspect extensif. Il nous faut ici reprendre le sens originel d'exotisme donné par Littré: qui n'est pas naturel au pays. A lire la description des Abaquis, et suivant les propos appuyés de Prévost, on en conclut aisément que les sauvages ne sont pas des hommes de la nature.[34] Ils sont sortis de la nature, ils en sont exilés. Certes, Cleveland loue certaines de leurs pratiques telles que la nudité en été ou encore leur nourriture (grossière) et leurs maisons "commodes, sans être belles ni régulières" (199). Mais les Abaquis ne possèdent aucunement ce goût naturel de la liberté que Rousseau, après bien d'autres, attribuera aux hommes primitifs, se laissant au contraire aliéner, sans défense contre l'étranger—c'est très facilement que Cleveland les subjugue, ce dernier "admirant" "l'inclination qu'ont tous les hommes à flatter ce qu'ils regardent comme supérieur à eux," le "penchant des hommes à la soumission et à la dépendance" (195). On observera ensuite que les sauvages prennent fort mal soin de leur propre conservation—soit ils s'autodétruisent, soit ils déciment les autres tribus. La "plupart de ces misérables peuples," rapporte Cleveland, "en viennent aux mains et s'égorgent brutalement sur les moindres démêlés" (214). Les Abaquis lui parlent ainsi de "la guerre presque continuelle qu'ils entretenaient avec leurs voisins, et qui ne finissait ordinairement que par l'extinction presqu'entière de l'une des deux nations. Il fallait quelquefois plus d'un demi-siècle aux vaincus pour réparer leurs pertes. J'ai appris dans la suite qu'il en est de même à peu près de tous les autres peuples de l'Amérique" (194). Considérons encore qu'ils sont d'une déconcertante fragilité en dehors de leur étroit territoire—c'est lors de leur excursion hors de leur vallée sous la direction de Cleveland qu'ils sont presque tous emportés par une épidémie, dont les causes possibles (et énigmatiques) sont commentées ainsi par le narrateur: "soit qu'ils ne fussent point aussi endurcis à la fatigue que les sauvages vagabonds, . . . soit que la chaleur et le changement d'air pussent contribuer à les affaiblir" (221).

Examinons enfin la curieuse propension des Abaquis à se perdre. Ils semblent entièrement dépourvus de cet exquis sens de l'orientation que les voyageurs se plaisent à reconnaître aux Indiens. Sortis de leur vallée ils sont déplacés, complètement perdus dans le gigantesque territoire américain.[35] Ces égarements incompréhensibles disent plus que tout discours que même dans les lieux naturels par excellence *la nature est perdue* . Les sauvages sont *dépaysés dans leur propre pays*: ce n'est pas une des moindres étrangetés de la description de Prévost. De fait dans *Cleveland* l'Amérique, "labyrinthe inextricable" (221) sans charme ni beauté, est le continent des errances douloureuses et massives. On ne s'étonnera pas que les seuls êtres qui semblent y vaguer tout à leur aise soient les anthropophages. Les inhumains Rouintons dans des périples de cauchemar entraînent les héros des semaines durant à marcher comme prisonniers dans de vastes espaces stériles:[36] sans description, sans valeur, sans présence. L'évocation suivante des "habitants vagabonds du grand désert de *Drexara*," "les plus cruels de l'Amérique" et qui "n'habitent proprement aucun lieu" (218), fait de l'Amérique un enfer pour tout autre que les "bêtes cruelles" (219) qu'ils sont: " Ils sont sans cesse errants, à la chasse des bêtes et des hommes, qu'ils regardent comme leur plus friand gibier"; "cherchant les montagnes et les bois comme les lieux les plus propres à la chasse, ils aiment ce grand désert, qui est rempli de bêtes féroces parce qu'il est couvert de forêts d'une immense étendue" (218).

Nel mezzo del cammin di nostra vita/mi ritrovai per una selva oscura,/ ché la dirrita via era smarrita.[37] La qualité mythique ou allégorique de ce désert[38] américain et de ses immenses forêts confère à "l'épopée de l'homme moderne" la dimension d'une "descente aux enfers."[39] Dans la représentation sans pittoresque de Prévost l'Amérique, plutôt que de satisfaire la soif d'un ailleurs, renvoie à un exotisme métaphysique, c'est-à-dire au sens d'une altérité fondamentale non seulement entre les hommes, mais entre l'homme et sa nature et entre l'homme et l'univers. Les sauvages ne sont pas chez eux dans ce milieu "naturel" de l'Amérique, ou pourquoi n'y cessent-ils de se détruire? Par eux Cleveland apprend qu'il n'est pas ou plus de juste mesure de la condition naturelle de l'homme.[40] Prévost ici ôte à l'esprit européen (et d'abord à son héros) la possibilité de penser une harmonie à la fois spontanément et historiquement réalisée entre l'homme et le monde, entre la nature et la nature humaine. Les Abaquis stupides, inadaptés et désorientés au sortir de leur vallée, malades et torturés, décimés presque, ne sauraient en aucun cas inspirer un idéal de bonheur à l'homme civilisé. En eux la nature est faible, lacunaire, elle leur *fait défaut*: "Rien ne marque mieux la stupidité des sauvages de l'Amérique que de voir qu'ils manquent d'industrie même pour leur conservation, quoique la nature seule dût suffire pour leur en inspirer" (198).

Mais si les sauvages ne sont finalement même pas des hommes, comme semble le conclure brutalement Cleveland au moment de son départ,[41] nous savons que beaucoup d'Européens ne le sont pas davantage d'après la proposition selon laquelle n'appartient pas à l'humanité "tout ce qui est

opposé à la raison, ou qui s'en écarte par quelques excès" (212). Le lecteur
de *Cleveland* sait combien il est difficile d'établir les rapports entre raison
et nature tels que dans ses nombreuses méditations le héros s'efforce de
les préciser.[42] Les sauvages ont perdu les lois naturelles, n'en possèdent
plus que des *restes*.[43] Dans une vertigineuse ironie, c'est l'Européen
Cleveland qui prétend les leur enseigner ("je leur expliquai les devoirs de la
nature. . . ," 200) alors qu'il ne cessera de les enfreindre précisément
parce qu'il les méconnaît, parce qu'il les cherche sans jamais les trouver.
Où donc les trouverait-il, puisque les hommes naturels eux-mêmes les ont
perdues, depuis toujours semble-t-il?

Il importe donc ici de ne pas voir dans la description des sauvages que
fait Prévost le classique procédé de miroir inversé par lequel le blâme de la
vie sauvage peut simplement être retourné en éloge symétrique de la
civilisation. L'homme nulle part n'est naturel au pays; nulle part il n'est
pour lui de juste demeure. Fanny le dira éloquemment:

> "La plupart des nations de l'Europe s'écartent des bornes de
> la raison par leurs excès de mollesse, de luxe, d'ambition,
> d'avarice: celle [*sic*] de l'Amérique, par leur grossièreté et
> leur abrutissement. Mais dans les unes et dans les autres, je
> ne reconnais point des hommes. Les unes sont en quelque
> sorte au-delà de leur condition naturelle, les autres sont en
> dessous; et les Européens et les Amériquains sont ainsi de
> vrais barbares par rapport au point dans lequel ils devraient
> se ressembler pour être véritablement hommes" (212).

Ils sont barbares par rapport au lieu théorique qu'est le genre humain dans
sa plus juste *mediocritas*, dans son plein accomplissement. Mais alors,
c'est la condition humaine naturelle elle-même qui devient tout entière
exotique: étrange parce qu'incompréhensiblement étrangère aux hommes,
distante jusqu'à leur être inaccessible. Entre Européens et sauvages situés
non pas diachroniquement mais synchroniquement de chaque côté de ce
"point," la séparation est poreuse: arbitraire et non hiérarchique, excès et
défaut s'annulant en regard de la règle d'or.[44]

Les Abaquis s'étaient momentanément ouverts à la raison, raison que
les Européens, eux, sont susceptibles de perdre à tout moment. Si on pose
comme Hayden White que les deux modes d'appréhension de la relation
entre Européens et "natifs" sont la continuité ou la contiguïté,[45] alors Prévost
choisit la continuité.[46] Pourtant aucune perspective historique et
anthropologique ne dirige le regard de Cleveland sur les sauvages—ce qu'ils
peuvent révéler à l'Européen sur l'homme n'intéresse ni le passé ni l'avenir

de la civilisation occidentale. Point ici de cette attitude propre au primitivisme des Lumières que la formule suivante résume admirablement: "C'est donc, pour ainsi dire, l'ignorance des sauvages qui a éclairé les peuples policés."[47] Michelet avait pu déceler une sûre continuation entre les *Dialogues* de La Hontan[48] et Rousseau: La Hontan montrait "la noblesse héroïque de la vie sauvage, la bonté, la grandeur de ce monde calomnié, la fraternelle identité de l'homme. C'est Rousseau devancé de plus de cinquante ans."[49] Prévost, malgré l'extrême goût que Rousseau avait pour son œuvre, et pour *Cleveland* en particulier, n'est certes pas un des maillons de cette chaîne.[50]

*   *   *

L'épreuve exotique

L'épisode américain illustre ce que Prévost avait lui-même annoncé dans sa préface: "Un ouvrage de cette nature peut être regardé comme un pays nouvellement découvert, et le dessein de le lire comme une espèce de voyage que le lecteur entreprend" (9). Celui qui deviendra le célèbre auteur de l'*Histoire des voyages*, celui qui fut exilé à plusieurs reprises, grand traducteur, grand aventurier, grand voyageur lui-même ne pouvait manquer de faire voyager ses héros; pour eux comme pour leur auteur les pays nouvellement (et imparfaitement) découverts se prennent dans les deux sens, littéral et figuré, ce dernier désignant un paysage intérieur.[51] C'est bien pour cette raison que la lectrice ou le lecteur d'aujourd'hui s'aventure encore dans le voyage immense que représente "un ouvrage de cette nature."

Numa Broc, qui nomme Prévost "maître du roman géographique," demande s'il est aussi l'un des créateurs du roman exotique, comme l'affirment certains critiques, et répond: "Oui sans doute, si 'exotique' signifie simplement extra-européen; non, s'il implique une idée de compréhension des pays lointains,"[52] qui ne seraient qu'un cadre commode (et, en ce sens, indifférents) au déploiement des aventures du héros. Il est vrai que *Cleveland* est un roman d'aventures qui, présentent les parcours forcenés de ses héros à travers le monde, ne fait guère de place à une description de type ethnographique des lieux visités. L'épisode chez les sauvages a pu légitimement attirer la moquerie indulgente de Xavier de Maistre, la raillerie de Chinard, par exemple.[53] Il est des évocations confinant à un exotisme naïf qui pour le lecteur moderne est lui-même devenu exotique: venu d'un autre temps et inassimilable. Un certain comique émane des descriptions de ce type: "Ces impitoyables sauvages [les Rouintons] se regardèrent les uns les autres en riant, ou plutôt en grinçant les dents d'une manière effroyable. Leurs regards étaient vifs et brillants, mais de cet air cruel et malin qu'on représente ordinairement dans les yeux d'un tigre. Leur taille était courte et ramassée, et presque tous avaient la bouche d'une grandeur démesurée" (226).

L'épisode cependant n'aurait pas retenu l'attention de lecteurs tels que Voltaire ou Sade s'il se réduisait à de maladroits clichés sur les sauvages ou même à l'ébauche d'utopie (ratée) tracée par Cleveland dans son plan pour les Abaquis.[54] Ce qui en fait la force et l'originalité me paraît pouvoir être centré sur la notion d'épreuve exotique, celle que tout le roman va renouveler, au fond, sous des formes diverses—épreuve de la séparation, de la distance, de la défamiliarisation, de la méconnaissance. Cleveland en effet ne fait pas tant l'*expérience* que l'*épreuve* de l'Amérique sauvage, et cette épreuve est d'abord celle de la violence et de l'incompréhension. On ne le verra pas tel un voyageur classique diffuser ou utiliser les connaissances que son voyage en Amérique lui aurait permis d'acquérir. A l'exception évidemment des retrouvailles avec Mme Riding, qui mènent à celles de Cécile avec ses parents Cleveland et Fanny et qui entraînent un récit rétrospectif replongeant dans le monde américain, l'épisode ne suscite que très peu de réminiscences. Voici la principale, alors que Cleveland se laisse distraire de son étude de la philosophie: "Dans le temps que j'avais les yeux attachés sur un livre, insensiblement mon attention s'en éloignait pour se transporter dans tous les lieux où s'était passée la scène de mes pertes et de mes malheurs. Elle se fixait sur le spectacle sanglant de ma fille et de Mme Riding, égorgées à mes yeux et dévorées par des tigres revêtus d'une figure humaine; sur mes horribles souffrances dans les déserts de l'Amérique. . . " (280). Mais justement, le quasi refoulement de l'épisode dans la suite de cet énorme roman entraîne en retour un débordement de la vérité qui s'y était dramatiquement dévoilée: la perte de l'idée (la mort du rêve) d'une nature familière, facile, juste et heureuse. R.A. Francis a raison de juger que l'épisode des Abaquis est situé tôt dans le roman "comme une sorte de critique de la notion même de nature."[55] Cela signifie que très tôt le héros ne peut plus songer à un *ailleurs* où serait miraculeusement préservée cette nature (paix, bonheur, innocence). Presque d'emblée, il n'y a plus d'ailleurs; presque d'emblée, l'horizon est fermé: comme dans *Manon Lescaut* le voyage américain qui devait permettre un élargissement produit au contraire pertes et repliement désemparé, désorienté sur soi. Cleveland au milieu des Amériquains découvre l'étrangeté de l'humanité en ses retournements soudains et ses paroxysmes de violence, mais il *se* découvre aussi fondamentalement étranger à Fanny, et elle, à lui. Etranger chez les sauvages, il le sera partout, et à lui-même.

Quelques belles lignes de F. Lestringant sur l'*Histoire d'un voyage* de Léry peuvent éclairer ce qui fait l'essence de l'épreuve exotique:

> . . . . c'est sans doute de Léry que date ce trouble, ce tremblement lié à la découverte d'une vérité bouleversante entre toutes, vérité seulement entraperçue à ce stade, que l'exotisme n'est pas ailleurs, dans les objets du monde, mais en soi, au plus intime de l'être.
>
> C'est en cela que consiste 'l'épreuve exotique': elle entraîne l'exhaustion d'un passé enfoui, que le récit de voyage en pays lointain permet, par le plus long détour qui soit, de retrouver non sans effroi ni souffrance.[56]

L'exotisme "au plus intime de l'être," c'est cette "perception aiguë et immédiate d'une incompréhensibilité éternelle," soit le sens de l'obscurité en soi, que Prévost de tous les écrivains du siècle a porté à son point le plus profond. Le détour chez les sauvages désigne en la figurant la voie d'un cheminement intérieur qui ne conduit pas à la lumière (illumination d'un idéal qu'aura produite la vision d'un paradis vrai) mais à un univers d'ombres qui ne feront que s'épaissir. C'est pour cela que *Cleveland* n'est pas tant un ancêtre du *Bildungsroman* qu'un *Prüfungsroman*: un roman de l'épreuve.

La dimension religieuse de l'œuvre de Prévost n'est plus à souligner, notamment depuis les magistraux travaux d'Alan Singerman qui écrit que "l'augustinisme constitue en quelque sorte un moule dans lequel Prévost a coulé sa matière romanesque."[57] Pour le croyant irrégulier et inquiet qu'est Prévost, l'homme déchu est la proie de ses passions, et qu'importe qu'elles naissent ou meurent au cœur des déserts américains, dans un sérail turc ou en plein Paris. On pourrait plus largement poser que l'exotisme est une spécialité chrétienne dans la mesure où pour le chrétien dans l'attente d'un plus clair séjour la terre est terre étrangère. Jésus n'est pas de ce monde, il n'est pas naturel au pays, et le chrétien non plus qui chemine dans le monde en quête d'épreuves qui le fortifieront dans sa volonté d'obtenir une place dans la maison du Père. Mais l'image très ancienne du *peregrinus* chrétien est ici plus troublée que vivifiée par l'arrière-plan politique et romanesque qui fait des déplacements de Cleveland une nécessité tout immanente, toute pratique. De fait, la quête est d'abord existentielle, quête du bonheur avant tout.

Or ce que trouve le "pélerin," c'est l'étrangeté qui l'habite. Prévost en effet retrouve, pour sous un autre angle l'anticiper, l'idée de "l'autre en soi:" entre les frissons d'horreur ou de fascination des premiers explorateurs de la Renaissance, et la découverte de l'inconscient.[58] Son héros est frappé de voir "combien nous devenons obscurs et impénétrables à nous-mêmes" (575), et aux autres.[59] Les contacts avec les Abaquis et surtout les Rouintons figurent dans l'hyperbole la menace, la peur, l'infinie distance ou la transgression (Cleveland après tout s'y fait meurtrier) que tant de scènes ultérieures mettront de nouveau en acte. L'altérité profonde et implacable de l'Amérique, la déception et la perdition, la violence et les tortures, les blessures et la mort qui la hantent renvoient non seulement à l'exil des héros en Europe même, mais à une anxiété face à un monde véritablement indéchiffrable, imprévisible, souvent hostile et finalement incontrôlable. L'homme prévostien, comme Cleveland en arrivant dans les déserts à la recherche d'Axminster, peut à tout moment dire: "tout était en effet si obscur et si désespérant dans la conduite que je devais tenir que je n'y voyais pas le moindre jour" (178). L'exotisme américain *donne lieu* à la représentation de cette horreur et de cette terreur soudaines qu'éprouvent tant de héros de Prévost, aveugles, perdus et seuls au seuil d'un immense bouleversement, selon la comparaison de des Grieux dans *Manon:* "je frémissais, comme il arrive lorsqu'on se trouve la nuit dans une campagne écartée: on se croit transporté dans un nouvel ordre de choses; on y est saisi d'un horreur secrète, dont on ne se remet qu'après avoir considéré longtemps tous les environs,"[60] . . . jusqu'au prochain dépaysement intérieur.

L'exotisme des Lumières et avec lui ses plus beaux fleurons, le Sauvage (bon ou mauvais) et le voyageur, ont pour fonction bien définie de fournir une arme critique aux philosophes en quête de modèle ou d'anti-modèle théorique, dans la fiction d'une distance. Cleveland est-il un de ces "raisonneurs pérégrinants"[61] dont fourmille le siècle? La figure de l'étranger au dix-huitième siècle est l'alter ego du philosophe, comme le remarque J. Kristeva qui écrit: "l'*étranger* devient. . . la figure en laquelle se délègue l'esprit perspicace et ironique du philosophe, son double, son masque."[62] Or Cleveland est à la fois le voyageur, le philosophe et l'étranger (anglais), et ceci littéralement. Il est donc doublement étranger. Après l'Amérique, il vit en exil, et dans l'éloignement de la philosophie: étranger à sa patrie géographique et intellectuelle. C'était comme étranger qu'il avait quitté l'Europe: il traverse l'Atlantique pour retrouver les siens (Axminster, Fanny) qui, se croyant trahis par lui, étaient pour lui devenus lointains en Europe même. L'Amérique alors, curieusement et perversement, est presque sa patrie: le pays qui lui est naturel est le lieu où les hommes sont exilés au sein d'une terre hostile, où les rapprochements (le mariage avec Fanny) sont illusoires, où la raison naturelle (sur laquelle se fonde la philosophie) est introuvable. *Cleveland* appartient aux Lumières en cela que Prévost a cru à l'épreuve exotique: au choc de la vérité sur soi révélée dans un Ailleurs au contact de l'Autre. Néanmoins ce qu'il en rapporte, une méditation indirecte mais récurrente sur le mystère sombre de l'autre, la brutalité bestiale du plus fort, la nécessaire injustice du pouvoir, la terrible vanité des projets systématiques, la dégradation par la souffrance et l'affaiblissement par le malheur, la solitude aussi, tout cela ne sera guère d'usage aux philosophes. Au demeurant le héros Cleveland ne célèbre que peu la différence, sinon la sienne ("je suis tout différent des autres hommes," 58), égalisant l'ensemble de ses expériences dans ce qu'il nomme une "masse uniforme de douleur" (241).

L'exotisme dans *Cleveland* se distingue de l'exotisme baroque purement ancillaire de l'intrigue comme de l'exotisme romantique plutôt privilégié pour sa valeur esthétique.[63] Il diffère aussi de l'exotisme philosophique qui est d'abord instrument polémique.[64] Il participe sans doute des trois sans s'y réduire, mais est plus proche, au bout du compte, de l'exotisme au sens large de Segalen: la conscience (ou "perception") d'une étrangeté au cœur du monde et des êtres, ici quintessenciée par le séjour américain mais inhérente à l'existence humaine.

*   *   *

Dans *Cleveland* l'altérité du Sauvage n'est pas polarisée en positive ou négative comme elle le sera dans la seconde moitié du siècle. Chez Prévost, par rapport à l'Européen cette altérité désigne d'abord une autre sorte de manque, une autre façon de ne pas être pleinement au monde. Le "philosophe" apprend qu'il n'est pas d'accueil, pas d'asile, pas d'harmonie originaires sur terre. Parcourant les déserts d'Amérique, il ne découvre pas un paradis nouveau mais prend au contraire conscience de ce que le monde tout entier est pour l'homme *terra incognita*, terre étrangère, et c'est la dramatique étendue de cet exotisme généralisé qui chez Prévost le rend tragique.

NOTES

1.   Michel Delon et Pierre Malandain, *Littérature française du XVIIIe siècle* (Paris: PUF, 1996), 204

2.   Le roman faisant près de 2500 pages dans l'édition originale a "les dimensions d'un continent," écrit Jean-Michel Racault dans *L'Utopie narrative en France et en Angleterre, 1675–1761. Studies on Voltaire and the eighteenth century* 280 (Oxford: The Voltaire Foundation, 1991), 603. Les quinze livres de *Cleveland* occupent environ 640 grandes pages dans l'unique édition moderne, utilisée ici. Il s'agit de l'édition de Philip Stewart, dans *Œuvres de Prévost* sous la direction de Jean Sgard, 8 vols (Grenoble: Presses de l'Université de Grenoble, 1977–1986), vol. II. Toutes les références de pages dans le texte renvoient à cette édition.

3.   Voir Carol M. Lazarro-Weis, le chapitre *"Cleveland as Romance"* de *Confused Epiphanies: l'abbé Prévost and the Romance Tradition* (New York: Peter Lang, 1991). Cf aussi Jean Sgard: "Prévost puise à pleines mains dans le vaste fonds d'aventures ou de sentiments des Amadis ou du roman héroïque," *Prévost romancier* (Paris: Corti, 1968), 155.

4.   English Showalter estime que *Cleveland* "was in fact one of the first truly philosophical novels," *The Evolution of the French Novel 1641–1782* (Princeton: Princeton U.P., 1972), 301.

5.   Dans son étude classique *L'Amérique et le rêve exotique dans la littérature française au XVIIe et au XVIIIe siècle* (Paris: Librairie Hachette, 1913), Gilbert Chinard n'hésite pas à tracer un parallèle entre Cleveland et le René de Chateaubriand: "tous deux, en effet, apportent dans les forêts de l'Amérique la même inquiétude, le même pessimisme, le même désir du bonheur insaisissable et les mêmes motifs intérieurs de désespoir" (300).

6.   ". . . le sentiment de malédiction et la fuite dans l'exotisme, dans les déserts . . . appartiennent à l'univers baroque . . . ," Sgard, *Prévost romancier*, 159.

7.   Voir J. Sgard, *Prévost romancier* 201 et 208–9. Racault signale l'ouvrage de Veiras comme la "source vraisemblable de Prévost pour l'épisode des Abaquis," *L'Utopie narrative* 627n. Voir cette même étude pour une très éclairante analyse de "l'utopie désenchantée" (601) dans *Cleveland*. Voir aussi Philip Stewart, "Utopias That Self-Destruct," *Studies in Eighteenth-Century Culture* 9 (1979): 15–24.

8.   *L'Amérique et le rêve exotique*, 280. Chinard ajoute: "Il n'est peut-être pas un écrivain du XVIIIe siècle, qui ait plus contribué à la vogue des pays lointains ou simplement étrangers" (280–1).

9.   Michèle Duchet rappelle le lien entre l'ouvrage de Prévost et l'*Encyclopédie* : "pour toutes les matières 'exotiques', l'un est d'ailleurs la source obligée de l'autre," *Anthropologie et histoire au siècle des Lumières* (Paris: Maspéro, 1971; Albin Michel, 1995), 91.

10.   *Prévost romancier*, 203.

11. Selon Chinard, la documentation de Prévost n'est pas très étendue: "les Abaquis ne peuvent représenter que les Abénaquis, mais ces derniers vivaient au nord du continent et non en Floride; quant aux Rouintons, je n'en ai trouvé trace nulle part" (*L'Amérique et le rêve exotique*, 300). Mais Paul Vernière a montré que Prévost, qui a travaillé sur des cartes, "n'invente que lorsque les sources sérieuses lui font défaut," " l'Abbé Prévost et les réalités géographiques, à propos de l'épisode américain de 'Cleveland'," *Revue d'histoire littéraire de la France* 73 (1973): 635. Philip Stewart a complété cet article pour conclure que "dans *Cleveland* la liberté de l'imagination est loin d'être totale", "L'Amérique de l'abbé Prévost: aspects documentaires de *Cleveland*," *The French Review* 49:6 (Mai 1976): 882.

12. Jean-Michel Racault, "Instances médiatrices et production de l'altérité dans le récit exotique aux 17e et 18e siècles," *L'Exotisme*, Cahiers CRLH-CIRAOI 5 (1988): 33.

13. Tzvetan Todorov, *Nous et les autres: la réflexion française sur la diversité humaine* (Paris: Seuil, 1989), 297.

14. Voir René Pomeau, "Voyage et lumières dans la littérature française du XVIIIe siècle," *Studies on Voltaire and the eighteenth century* 57 (1967):1287.

15. Le voyage de Jean de Léry a eu lieu en 1556–1558 et est relaté dans *Histoire d'un voyage fait en la terre du Bresil, autrement dite Amérique*, éd. Michel Contat (Lausanne: Bibliothèque romande, 1972).

16. Frank Lestringant, "L'exotisme en France à la Renaissance de Rabelais à Léry", *Littérature et exotisme XVIe–XVIIIe siècle*, éd. Dominique de Courcelles (Paris: Ecole des chartes, 1997),14.

17. Le véritable "essai sur l'exotisme" que Victor Segalen désirait publier n'a jamais dépassé le stade de notes, commencées en 1908 et continuées au long de la vie de l'auteur. Les *Notes sur l'exotisme* sont "publiées d'abord dans le *Mercure de France*, mars-avril 1955, puis en volume chez Rougerie (1972)," écrit Henri Bouillier dans son "Introduction" au "Cycle des ailleurs et du bord du chemin" où figure l'*Essai sur l'exotisme*, dans Victor Segalen, *Œuvres complètes*, éd. Henri Bouillier (Paris: Robert Laffont, 1995), 737.

18. Segalen définit l'exotisme d'abord "comme une Esthétique du Divers," *Essai* ,749.

19. *Essai*,751.

20. Sur cette tradition déjà bien en place au XVIIe siècle, voir le chapitre "Le Bon Sauvage" de Geoffroy Atkinson, *Les Relations de voyages du XVIIe siècle et l'évolution des idées: contribution à l'étude de la formation de l'esprit du XVIIIe siècle* (Paris: Champion,1924): 63–81.

21. Je ne reprendrai pas ici l'analyse, faite plusieurs fois, de l'entreprise civilisatrice (réticente) de Cleveland. Voir par exemple Jean-Paul Sermain, *Rhétorique et roman au dix-huitième siècle: l'exemple de Prévost et de Marivaux (1728–1742)*, *Studies on Voltaire and the Eighteenth Century* 233 (1985), 88–94; le livre déjà cité de Racault et, dans sa lignée, celui de Guillaume Ansart qui nomme l'épisode des Abaquis une "robinsonnade utopique,"

Réflexion utopique et pratique romanesque au siècle des lumières: Prévost, Rousseau, Sade (Paris-Caen: Lettres modernes-Minard, 1999), 84.

22. *Mes Pensées* dans *Œuvres complètes* vol. I, éd. Roger Caillois (Paris: Gallimard, 1949), 981.

23. "Nous les [les cannibales du Brésil] pouvons donq bien appeller barbares, eu esgard aux regles de la raison, mais non pas eu esgard à nous, qui les surpassons en toute sorte de barbarie," Montaigne, *Essais* I, XXXI, dans *Œuvres complètes*, éd. Albert Thibaudet et Maurice Rat, (Paris: Gallimard, 1962), 208. Jean de Léry, qui avait lui-même assisté à des scènes de cannibalisme chez ces Indiens du Brésil, avait déjà écrit: "Pourquoi qu'on n'abhorre plus tant désormais la cruauté des sauvages anthropophages ... car puisqu'il y en a de tels, voire d'autant plus détestables et pires au milieu de nous qu'eux qui ... ne se ruent que sur les nations lesquelles leur sont ennemies, et ceux-ci se sont plongés au sang de leurs parents, voisins et compatriotes, il ne faut pas aller si loin qu'en leur pays, ni qu'en l'Amérique pour voir choses si monstrueuses et prodigieuses," *Histoire d'un voyage* chap. XV, 186–7.

24. J.-P. Sermain, *Rhétorique et roman*, 92.

25. Axminster, croyant sa femme infidèle, l'avait percée "de plusieurs coups d'épée" (44) dans un "transport barbare" (48); le duc de Monmouth enfonce "son épée dans le sein" de la traîtresse Cortona (598), ce que le narrateur qualifie de "barbarie" (600).

26. C'est ce que rapporte Madame Riding: "Je ne doutai point que leur usage ne fût d'épargner les femmes dans leurs barbares et sanglantes exécutions, et j'ai su depuis plus certainement que les sauvages les plus inhumains de l'Amérique ont cette espèce de respect pour la nature," 446.

27. Buffon s'étendra sur l'instabilité des tribus sauvages d'Amérique décrites comme "un assemblage tumultueux d'hommes barbares et indépendants, qui n'obéissent qu'à leurs passions particulières, et qui, ne pouvant avoir un intérêt commun, sont incapables de se diriger vers un même but et de se soumettre à des usages constants, qui tous supposent une suite de desseins raisonnés et approuvés par le plus grand nombre," *De l'homme* (1749), éd. Michèle Duchet (Paris: Maspéro, 1971), 296.

28. Montaigne, *Essais*, 9.

29. *Essai sur l'exotisme* ,753, en italiques dans le texte.

30. *Histoire du Chevalier des Grieux et de Manon Lescaut*, éd. Henri Coulet (Paris: GF-Flammarion, 1967), 37.

31. Voir là-dessus James P. Gilroy, "Prévost's Théophé: A Liberated Heroine in Search of Herself," *The French Review* 60:3 (February 1987): 317, et Pierre Hartmann, "Femme étrangère/femme étrange: le personnage de Théophé dans l'*Histoire d'une Grecque Moderne* d'Antoine Prévost d'Exiles,"*Revue francophone* 8:2 (automne 1993): 50–61.

32. *Prévost romancier*, 141.

33. Sigmund Freud, "*L'Inquiétante Etrangeté" et autres essais* (Paris: Gallimard, 1985) 215, cité par Julia Kristeva, *Etrangers à nous-mêmes* (Paris:

Fayard, 1988), 270.

34. Plusieurs critiques ont noté la démarcation clairement opérée par Prévost entre sauvage et homme naturel. Voir par exemple René Démoris: "en ces sauvages, il [Cleveland] se garde bien de reconnaître l'homme naturel," *Le Roman à la première personne, du Classicisme aux Lumières* (Paris: Armand Colin, 1975), 436. Sgard parle d'"un humanisme tragique avant la lettre" chez Prévost: "Abandonnés à eux-mêmes, les sauvages ne sont ni bons ni méchants; ils ne connaissent ni le péché ni la grâce. La parfaite nature n'est pas donnée; elle se définit comme un équilibre idéal, lentement atteint et toujours compromis, un composé de bons instincts et de lois, aussi difficile à créer qu'à maintenir," *Prévost romancier*, 597.

35. Par exemple les Abaquis envoyés à la recherche de Lord Axminster "avaient erré longtemps sans être assurés de leur route" (204) et "s'étaient prodigieusement égarés" (221). L'un d'eux précise "avoir erré deux mois dans des pays qui lui étaient inconnus" (218).

36. "... tous les environs [de la vallée des Abaquis] étaient sablonneux et stériles" (195).

37. Dante, *Inferno*, canto I, 1–3. "Au milieu du chemin de notre vie/je me retrouvai par une forêt obscure/car la voie droite était perdue," *La Divine Comédie: L'Enfer*, éd. et tr. Jacqueline Risset (Paris: Flammarion, 1985), 27.

38. On comprend que "désert" n'a pas le sens moderne de lieu désertique, privé d'eau. Terme de la langue classique, il signifie lieu écarté, peu fréquenté; le désert dans ce sens n'exclut pas la végétation. Sur l'emploi de ce mot aux XVIIe et XVIIIe siècles, voir Pierre Naudin, *L'Expérience et le sentiment de la solitude dans la littérature française de l'aube des Lumières à la Révolution* (Paris: Klincksieck,1995), 501–502.

39. "*Cleveland*, dont le héros, ayant vu s'effondrer ses certitudes et ses systèmes, doit faire une longue descente aux enfers avant de retrouver ses raisons de vivre, est l'épopée métaphysique de l'homme moderne," Henri Coulet, *Le Roman jusqu'à la Révolution* (Paris: Armand Colin, 1967), 355.

40. "Par leur grossièreté et leur abrutissement," même les excellents Abaquis, supérieurs aux autres peuples américains, sont "au-dessous de la qualité d'hommes" (212).

41. "Je reconnus les matelots pour des Espagnols. De quelque nation qu'ils pussent être, c'était des hommes; ce n'étaient plus de stupides et impitoyables sauvages" (234).

42. Démoris appelle *Cleveland* l'"épopée de la raison naturelle," *Le Roman à la première personne*, 433. Voir ses pages 433–440 sur les complications et incohérences attachées aux concepts de nature et de raison dans *Cleveland*.

43. "Quoique les Abaquis ne fussent point dans le même degré de grossièreté et d'ignorance que plusieurs autres peuples de l'Amérique, et qu'il leur *restât* du moins quelques sentiments d'humanité et quelque connaissance de la loi naturelle..." (200; mes italiques).

44. Déjà la possibilité d'une confusion au plan physique est marquée à

plusieurs reprises: Youngster, l'écuyer d'Axminster, est d'abord pris pour un sauvage par Cleveland ("cet homme nu, que je prenais pour un sauvage ...," 179); celui-ci et Fanny, en fin de périple avec les sauvages, seront pris pour des "Amériquains" par les Espagnols ("la fatigue nous avait tellement changés qu'à la réserve d'un peu plus de blancheur, nous n'étions guère différents de nos compagnons d'esclavage," 235); Mme Riding enfin sera prise par les sauvages "pour une fugitive de quelque nation voisine" (543).

45. "On the one hand, the natives were conceived to be *continuous* with that humanity on which Europeans prided themselves; and it was this mode of relationship that underlay the policy of proselytization and conversion. On the other hand, the natives could be conceived as simply existing *contiguously* to the Europeans, as representing either an inferior breed of humanity or a superior breed, but in any case as being essentially different from the European breed; and it was this mode of relationship which underlay and justified the policies of war and extermination which the Europeans followed throughout the seventeenth and most of the eighteenth century," Hayden White, "The Noble Savage Theme as Fetish" dans *First Images of America: the Impact of the New World on the Old*, éd. Fredi Chiappelli, 2 vols (Berkeley, Los Angeles, London: U. of California Press, 1976), vol. 1, 132.

46. Cleveland mentionne ostensiblement le "sentiment d'humanité" qui lui fait refuser les vêtements personnels qu'Iglou, son serviteur indien, lui propose lors d'une nuit froide: "Je ne voyais point que ma qualité de maître lui fît perdre celle d'homme, ni qu'elle pût lui ôter par conséquent le droit naturel qu'il avait à des secours qui lui étaient aussi nécessaires qu'à moi" (177).

47. *Histoire des deux Indes* IV (éd. de 1772) cité par Yves Benot, *Diderot: de l'athéisme à l'anticolonialisme* (Paris: Maspéro, 1981), 228. Et encore: "Sans doute il est important aux générations futures de ne pas perdre le tableau de la vie et des mœurs des sauvages. C'est peut-être à cette connaissance que nous devons tous les progrès que la philosophie morale a faits parmi nous," *Histoire des deux Indes* VI, cité par Benot, 227.

48. La Hontan, *Dialogues avec un sauvage*, éd. Maurice Roelens (Paris: Editions Sociales, 1973).

49. Jules Michelet, préface à *La Régence*, vol. XIV de *Histoire de France* dans *Œuvres complètes de J. Michelet* (Paris: Flammarion, 1881), 7.

50. Chinard avait très tôt signalé, avec raison, que "Prévost n'est en aucune façon le prédécesseur de Rousseau, au moins du Rousseau que le *Discours sur l'Inégalité* et le *Contrat Social* nous révèlent," *L'Amérique et le rêve exotique*, 299. C'est le Rousseau futur romancier et autobiographe qui fait "avec fureur" "la lecture des malheurs imaginaires de Cleveland," *Les Confessions* V dans *Œuvres complètes* I (Paris: Gallimard 1964), 220.

51. Cf M. Duchet: "les héros de Prévost sont eux aussi des 'voyageurs errants' à la découverte d'eux-mêmes, dans un espace aux dimensions du rêve, où les chemins, les ports, la mer semée d'écueils, les îles, les forêts et les déserts figurent un paysage intérieur," *Anthropologie et histoire*, 88

52. Numa Broc, *La Géographie des philosophes: géographes et voyageurs français au XVIIIe siècle* (Paris: Ophrys, 1975), 262.

53. Xavier de Maistre écrit: "Combien de fois n'ai-je pas maudit ce *Cleveland*, qui s'embarque à tout instant dans de nouveaux malheurs qu'il pourrait éviter! Je ne puis souffrir ce livre et ses enchaînements de calamités, mais si je l'ouvre par distraction, il faut que je le dévore jusqu'à la fin. Comment laisser ce pauvre homme chez les *Abaquis*? que deviendrait-il avec ces sauvages? ... je m'intéresse si fort à lui et à sa famille infortunée, que l'apparition inattendue des féroces *Ruintons* me fait dresser les cheveux: une sueur froide me couvre lorsque je lis ce passage, et ma frayeur est aussi réelle que si je devais être rôti et mangé par cette canaille," *Voyage autour de ma chambre* (1795) (Paris: Editions Bibliopolis, 1998), 71. Chinard, lui, se moque (entre autres) de la bruyère "qui me paraît plus anglaise qu'américaine," *L'Amérique et le rêve exotique*, 300.

54. Voltaire s'en inspire en partie pour ses Oreillons anthropophages dans *Candide*. Voir R.A. Francis, "Prévost's *Cleveland* and Voltaire's *Candide*," *Studies on Voltaire and the eighteenth century* 208 (1982): 295–303. Dans *Aline et Valcour* Sade imagine un parcours en deux étapes pour Sainville, le royaume de cauchemar où le cannibalisme règne en maître, Butua, puis l'île idyllique de Tamoé. Michel Delon commente: "Prévost avait déjà imaginé les aventures de Cleveland chez les bons sauvages Abaquis, puis chez les féroces Rouintons . . . ," Notice, *Aline et Valcour* dans *Œuvres* de Sade, éd. Michel Delon, vol. 1 (Paris: Gallimard, 1990),1205.

55. Richard A. Francis, "Le *Cleveland* de Prévost: sensibilité ou critique de la sensibilité?" *La Sensibilité dans la littérature française au XVIIIe siècle*, éd. Franco Piva (Schena-Didier Erudition, 1998), 84.

56. "L'exotisme en France à la Renaissance," 15.

57. Alan J. Singerman, "L'abbé Prévost et la quête du bonheur: lecture morale et philosophique de l'*Histoire de M. Cleveland*," *Studies on Voltaire and the eighteenth century* 228 (1984): 195. Voir du même auteur *L'Abbé Prévost. L'Amour et la morale* (Genève: Droz, 1987).

58. Voir la conclusion de l'ouvrage de Tzvetan Todorov, *La Conquête de l'Amérique: la question de l'autre* (Paris: Seuil, 1982): "L'instauration de l'inconscient peut être considérée comme le point culminant de cette découverte de l'autre en soi," 250.

59. Que l'on considère le désir érotique du narrateur envers Cécile, la jeune fille dont il tombe amoureux après la trahison (apparente) de Fanny et qui est sans qu'il le sache leur propre fille "américaine" (qu'il avait cru tuée par les Rouintons). Cleveland s'avoue à lui-même qu'il souhaite "peut-être" se trouver dans des occasions où la vertu de Cécile soit "exposée au dernier péril": "ce désir était un monstre qui n'osait se produire, qui ne se nourrissait que dans les replis les plus ténébreux de mon cœur, et que ma raison eût encore suffi pour étouffer s'il eût parlé assez haut pour se faire entendre" (337); "il y avait dans mon cœur des obscurités que je n'osais démêler"; "... tout me paraissait obscur

au-dedans et autour de moi . . ." (344)

60. *Manon Lescaut*, 60.

61. Pomeau, "Voyage et lumières", 1276.

62. *Etrangers à nous-mêmes*, 196 (en italiques dans le texte).

63. Pierre Naudin écrit à propos de Cleveland: "*Homo viator*, frère en malédiction du voyageur romantique, il a vécu lui aussi la longue errance de tous les sans-patrie, l'émigration intérieure de ceux qui ne sont nulle part à leur place ici-bas," *L'Expérience et le sentiment de la solitude*, 282. Mais il marque ensuite d'importantes différences entre l'auteur de *Cleveland* et les écrivains romantiques.

64. G. Atkinson écrit qu'"On peut même dire que chaque livre de voyage est, en quelque sorte, un livre de critique" et que "le terme 'exotique' est donc en quelque sorte intimement lié au terme 'critique'," *Les Relations de voyages*, 187. Prévost n'utilise pas l'épisode américain pour nourrir directement une critique de l'Europe.

Casanova, the Novel, and the Woman as Desiring Subject: The Case of Bettina

TED EMERY

It is no accident that Casanova's *Histoire de ma vie* presents the first of his many loves as a great reader of novels.[1] The eighteenth-century novel has often been called a women's genre, not only because its readership was thought to consist predominantly of women, or because many prominent novelists were women, but because novels were nearly always concerned to some degree with women's behavior and with their proper position in society.[2] In setting out to write an autobiography in which women will play an unusually important role, Casanova is aware that his reader's expectations of female characters will have the novel as an almost inevitable point of reference. In the story of his precocious affair with Bettina Gozzi, Casanova plays with these expectations in order to propose a model of female behavior in which the woman will be not the object of male desire, but instead herself a desiring subject.[3]

During the course of its evolution, the novel's critics attacked the new genre for both its supposed lack of verisimilitude and its dangerous moral effects.[4] Novels were considered immoral because the examples of female behavior they provided appeared to challenge patriarchal order. As early as the mid-1660's, Boileau attacked Scudéry for her effeminizing view of love which weakened male vigor and allowed women to assert dominance over the domestic space.[5] A generation later, in treatises by Père Porée (*De*

Libris qui vulgo dicuntur romanenses, oratio, 1736) and the Abbé Jacquin
(*Entretiens sur les romans*, 1755) novels were still being attacked for their
reversal of the "natural" relations of power between the sexes and their
"corruption" of female readers.[6] Young women were commonly thought
to run the greatest risk of corruption, a view shared even by many liberal
thinkers such as the Marquise de Lambert, who advises her daughter that:

> La lecture des romans est plus dangereuse: . . . ils mettent du
> faux dans l'esprit. Le roman n'étant jamais pris sur le vrai,
> allume l'imagination, affaiblit la pudeur, met le désordre dans
> le cœur ; et pour peu qu'une jeune personne ait de la
> disposition à la tendresse, hâte et précipite son penchant.[7]

This fear of the premature sexualisation of the reading girl is so common
that it is often inscribed within the plots of novels themselves, as in Mme
Meheust's *Histoire d'Emilie* (1732), where the narrator tells us that as a
young woman she had surreptitiously read the novels her mother kept
under lock and key, and that they had given her "une envie extrême d'avoir
un Amant."[8]

Objections to the novel's lack of verisimilitude are less and less common
after mid-century, but concerns about their moral effects remain strong.
Rousseau vehemently condemned novel reading as perilous for young
women, insisting polemically in the first preface to *La Nouvelle Héloïse*
that "Jamais fille chaste n'a lu de Romans."[9] His disciple, Bernardin de
Saint-Pierre, continues in the last decades of the century to draw the
connection between novel reading, the vicarious experience of sexual
passion, and female discontent with the patriarchal order of the world as it
is:

> Si on vient à examiner l'effet que les livres produisent en
> particulier sur l'esprit des femmes, il s'en trouvera peu qui
> leur soient utiles, même parmi ceux que l'on croit bons. Dans
> les romans, les uns mettent la vertu en parole, et le vice en
> action. Ceux-ci, plus dangereux, montrent la route des
> passions comme la seule que nous enseigne la nature. Les
> meilleurs les jettent dans un monde imaginaire, et leur font
> haïr celui où elles doivent vivre.[10]

Such critics of the novel implicitly view the adolescent girl as defined by a
double lack: herself without desire, she is potentially the object upon which
masculine desire will be written; lacking agency, the power to produce,

change, or contest her position within phallogocentric culture, her function within society and indeed her very identity are "written" for her by the discourses upon which that society depends. The novel is considered perilous because it is thought to awaken sexual desire in the adolescent girl, and by so doing to offer her, at least in the vicarious experience of an alternative world, a position as a sexual and social subject.

In the two chapters of *Histoire de ma vie* in which Casanova describes his affair with Bettina, he repeatedly evokes the novel. He calls Bettina a "grande liseuse de romans," compares his secret, nocturnal meeting with her to a scene in a novel (*HV*, 1:34), and when he explains how she is able so easily to stir his sympathy, he says she learned the human heart by reading novels (*HV*, 1:43).[11] Casanova is clearly hinting that we should view this episode against the models of female behavior that novels propose.

The beginning of the story reflects elements of the sentimental novel and of what Peter Brooks called novels of worldliness, both of which usually have as protagonists young people who are entering the social world at the same time they reach sexual maturity, and both of which follow their young characters as they negotiate (or fail to negotiate) their position as subject or object of desire. In sentimental novels, this negotiation is presented from the point of view of the woman, whose femininity is coded "in paradigms of social vulnerability."[12] The story generally begins with a confrontation between female innocence and male lust. The man's attempts at seduction are initially cautious, involving ambiguous compliments and physical touching that can be easily disavowed as non-erotic. The young woman's response, as she begins to understand his intentions, is one of "confusion"; when the sexual invitation later becomes explicit the heroine often falls into a fever, her physical state mirroring her emotional one.[13]

By underscoring Bettina's youth at the same time he identifies her with the novel, Casanova leads us to expect that she will occupy this position of vulnerability, but the beginning of the episode overturns those expectations completely. As an intellectually precocious but sexually inexperienced eleven-year-old, Casanova is sent to Padua to study with Dr. Gozzi, a young priest who boards his pupils in his own home. Gozzi's fourteen-year-old sister, Bettina, becomes very attached to the boy, who in his innocence does not understand her advances:

> Elle venait me peigner tous les jours, et souvent lorsque j'étais encore au lit me disant qu'elle n'avait pas le temps d'attendre que je m'habillasse. Elle me lavait le visage, le cou, et la poitrine, et elle me faisait des caresses enfantines qu'en devoir

de juger innocentes, je me voulais du mal de ce qu'elles m'altéraient. Ayant trois ans moins qu'elle, il me semblait qu'elle ne pût pas m'aimer avec malice, et cela me mettait de mauvaise humeur contre la mienne. Quand assise sur mon lit elle me disait que j'engraissais, et que pour m'en convaincre elle s'en rendait sûre par ses propres mains, elle me causait la plus grande émotion. . . . Après m'avoir débarbouillé, elle me donnait les plus doux baisers m'appelant son cher enfant ; mais malgré l'envie que j'en avais, je n'osais pas les lui rendre. Quand enfin elle commença à mettre en ridicule ma timidité, je commençais aussi à les lui rendre, même mieux appliqués ; mais je finissais d'abord que je me sentais excité à aller plus loin. . . Après son départ j'étais au désespoir de n'avoir pas suivi le penchant de ma nature, et étonné que Bettine pût faire de moi sans conséquence tout ce qu'elle faisait tandis que je ne pouvais m'abstenir d'aller plus en avant qu'avec la plus grande peine. Je me promettais toujours de changer de conduite. (*HV*, 1:32)

Aroused by Bettina, but unable to understand her intentions or her apparent lack of desire, Casanova is caught in a confusing emotional bind. Then some older boys join Gozzi's school. Within a month, Bettina is on the best of terms with Candiani, an ignorant farmer's son whose only advantage over Casanova is that he is sexually mature. Casanova begins to lose his esteem for Bettina, who responds with an act of sexual aggression. Claiming that she needs to wash his thighs before he can try on a pair of new stockings, she carries her zeal for cleanliness so far that "me causa une volupté qui ne cessa que quand elle se trouva dans l'impossibilité de devenir plus grande" (*HV*, 1:33). Casanova's immediate apology for his ejaculation surprises Bettina, and her response implicitly denies that she had felt any desire: "me dit d'un ton d'indulgence que toute la faute était d'elle, mais que cela ne lui arriverait plus" (*HV*, 1:33). Distraught, and believing that he has dishonored Bettina, Casanova falls into a "black melancholy."

The story of Casanova's first sexual encounter repeats several of the characteristics of vulnerability Miller has noted in "heroine's texts"—the ambiguous compliments and touching, the victim's confusion, the move to more straightforward advances, and the victim's reaction of illness—but it attaches them to the male character. This is pure parody: Casanova is turning the sentimental novel on its ear. At the same time, however, the episode evokes a different model, that of the libertine novel of worldliness, which often begins with a young man's social and sexual initiation at the hands of an older woman.

In the novel of worldliness, Brooks suggests, erotic relations are seen as a metaphor for social relations, in that both are based on power and the will to dominate. They are the site of a struggle in which one partner must establish ascendancy over the other. Dominance is established through an act of "penetration," as one character succeeds in reading the other's true motives while concealing his or her own, and uses that knowledge to manipulate the other's feelings and actions. Male libertines penetrate women figuratively as well as literally: in pursuing, seducing, and breaking off relations, they remain unfixed and free, while they deprive their victims of freedom by controlling their psychological movements.[14] This is the role in which we initially see Bettina, but her behavior also bears a strong resemblance to the older women of the novels of worldliness, who assert their dominance over men in a different way. To establish mastery, a woman must maintain a public façade of virtue, while in private she "manipulates and controls men for her pleasure, and disarms them so they cannot publicize their exploits." The older woman's domination, intended to "undermine an established order of male domination," thus depends on an act of dissimulation.[15] Characters such as Crébillon's Mme de Lursay and Laclos' Mme de Merteuil do not arrogate to themselves the libertine position as desiring subject; instead they cancel their desire from public (and even private) view.

From the beginning of their relationship, Bettina controls and limits Casanova's ability to understand her by producing ambiguous meanings that conceal her desire. When her interest in Candiani threatens to loosen her hold on Casanova, Bettina proceeds to a deliberate act of aggression, explicitly characterized as her revenge, that allows her to manipulate the young man's emotions while at the same time disavowing any sexual attraction. In part, what is at stake is control over the male or dominant role in their relationship. Just as Crébillon's Meilcour, lacking sufficient penetration to understand his older lover, finds himself in a feminized position vis-à-vis Mme de Lursay, so Casanova is initially feminized by Bettina. And the narrator underscores this relation with a striking image: Bettina proposes attending a masked ball with Casanova, she dressed as a boy and he as a girl, and when the young man refuses, she tries to force him to go, threatening to show him a sight that will make him cry (*HV*, 1:39). On one level, this proposed cross-dressing would be a public admission of Casanova's feminine role and lack of power with respect to Bettina, and an equally public demonstration of her ascendancy over him. But as Terry Castle has shown, the transgressive power of masquerade allows a much profounder challenge to the fundamental binary oppositions upon which patriarchal culture is based.[16] In donning masculine costume, Bettina would deploy an alternative language—the sartorial code—to create a symbolic reversal of her gender, and a consequent repositioning of herself from feminine object to masculine subject. What is more, her masquerade would incorporate into a single, contradictory sign both her "true" female body (covered by men's clothes but still evident) and its carnivalesque Other, subverting the distinction of fixed, "natural" genders, and suggesting that male and female roles are not biologically given, but instead socially created.[17] As the episode continues, it becomes increasingly clear that Bettina's transgressiveness is not limited to her premature sexual activity, nor to her attempt to impose a feminine role on her young lover, but instead involves a broader challenge to patriarchal authority. As Casanova gradually becomes aware of this, his view of Bettina becomes more sympathetic.

On his way to a nocturnal meeting with Bettina, Casanova is assaulted at her door by his rival. He is sure that she is sleeping with Candiani, and later finds a compromising letter that confirms his suspicions. Now he holds power over Bettina, but before he can expose her to her family she begins to have attacks of violent, almost orgasmic fits: "je la vois dans le lit de son père en convulsions effroyables . . . se tournant à droite, et à gauche. Elle s'arquait, elle se cambrait donnant des coups de poing et de pied au hasard . . ." (*HV*, 1:35). Casanova is the only member of the household who can read the sexual nature of Bettina's illness (a "penetration" that marks his acquisition, for the first time, of a masculine identity). He stands off to one side, coldly observing the scene, sure that "la maladie de cette fille ne pouvait dériver que de ses travaux nocturnes, ou de la peur que ma rencontre avec Candiani devait lui avoir faite" (*HV*, 1:36). He soon realizes that her fits are faked, and that she is using them to delay the revelation of her sexual activity by either Casanova or Candiani. Bettina's family understands nothing of this, and when she begins to shout words in Greek and Latin during her bouts of feigned delirium, they conclude that she has been possessed by the devil.

As in her project of a cross-dressing masquerade, Bettina here deploys a non-linguistic code to communicate a transgressive meaning: in the language of the body, her convulsions are a clear, metaphorical representation of sexual climax. Moreover, her verbal ejaculations not only parody the languages of the Church Fathers, but fragment and disintegrate these privileged signs of patriarchal authority.[18] Her challenge to the masculine domain of the Symbolic continues in the "insane" ravings that allow her, temporarily, to arrogate to herself a masculine authority and agency, besting Fra Prospero, the most celebrated exorcist in Padua, in a comic contest of will and intelligence:

> Bettine à son apparition lui dit en éclatant de rire des injures sanglantes, qui plurent à tous les assistants, puisqu'il n'y avait que le diable d'assez hardi pour traiter ainsi un capucin ; mais celui-ci à son tour s'entendant appeler ignorant, imposteur, et puant commença à donner des coups à Bettine avec un gros crucifix disant qu'il battait le diable. Il ne s'arrêta que lorsqu'il la vit en position de lui jeter un pot de chambre à la tête, chose que j'aurais bien voulu voir. *Si celui qui t'a choqué,* lui dit-elle, *par des paroles est le diable, frappe-le avec les tiennes, âne que tu es ; et si c'est moi apprends butor que tu dois me respecter ; et va-t-en.* J'ai vu alors le docteur Gozzi rougir. (*HV*, 1:38).

The "raving" Bettina is able to use this fiction of possession and the expressive freedom it confers to challenge, in turn, all the male figures of authority by whom she is surrounded: her priestly brother, who unsuccessfully attempts an exorcism, her literal father, a drunkard who tries to exorcise her while so inebriated he can barely stand, and two institutional representatives of the Father's law in the persons of Fra Prospero and Father Mancia.

It is precisely Bettina's "unnatural" ability to challenge men in the domain of language that marks her, to all save Casanova, as possessed. The onlookers cannot accept such a powerful ability to manipulate language in the figure of an adolescent girl, who "should" be defined by the lack of just such agency. The only explanation they can accept for such a transformation is her possession—the total overwriting of her identity and her gender—by a demon they presume to be male. Bettina strikes at the heart of this comforting fantasy by instructing Fra Prospero that he is wrong to address her demon as male, for "un diable est un ange qui n'a aucun sexe," while she, on the contrary, is a woman (*HV* 1:38). Bettina's words amount to a castration of the onlookers' fantasy demon: she projects onto it/him the sign of female lack, deprives the concept of agency of its male association, and reassigns to herself as woman a power to use language that her audience can see only as male. In effect, Bettina has reproduced at a different level the strategy of her proposed masquerade: conflating male and female opposites in the same body-sign, she breaks down not only the polar distinction of gender, but the related distinctions (male agency, female lack) that are associated with gender in patriarchal discourse.

As Casanova begins to see Bettina's behavior as an act of resistance to authority, his view of her changes. He approves of her behavior toward the priests, whom he regards as superstitious buffoons, and praises her as an "Inconcevable fille remplie de talent" (*HV*, 1:38). He especially admires her facility as a performer, and his wording suggests that he sees her pretence almost as a poetic effort, that is to say one in which "wild" and abnormal language is deployed in a deliberate challenge to normal language and logic: "Rien n'était si joli que le désordre de Bettine le lendemain. Elle commença à tenir *les propos les plus fous que poète pût inventer*" (*HV*, 1:42; emphasis mine).[19] He is struck, too, by her ability to keep a straight face even when her audience is laughing, a trait the narrator elsewhere ascribes to himself (*HV,*1:41 and 1:313). Earlier in the *Histoire* Casanova had made a point of his precocious intelligence, his ability to out-argue his tutor, and his unwillingness to accept Gozzi's religious superstitions. Bettina's mocking resistance to Fra Prospero and Father Mancia has much in common with Casanova's own attitude to intellectual authority. Understanding that he and Bettina are fundamentally alike in their deployment of superior intelligence to resist domination, Casanova can now perceive and approve the desire she masks: "L'esprit de cette fille lui avait gagné mon estime ; je ne pouvais plus la mépriser. Je la regardais comme une créature séduite par son propre tempérament. Elle aimait l'homme ; et elle n'était à plaindre qu'à cause des conséquences" (*HV*, 1:40).

Though I have been unable to find a specific source for Bettina's feigned demonic possession in any novel, the attitude of overt and extravagant resistance to figures of patriarchal authority that is expressed here may draw loosely on a model of female behavior well-known to Casanova: the type of adventure novel with female protagonists popularized in the late 1600's by Mme de Villedieu, and still widely imitated in the eighteenth century.[20] In the next move of the episode, however, Bettina's actions return again to the paradigm of the sentimental novel, and the rest of her story may be seen as an extended comment on that novel's model of female subjectivity.

The central feature of Bettina's behavior to this point has been her duplicity, whether directed toward Casanova or toward her family and her would-be exorcists. The next move of the story foregrounds and subtly redefines the problem. Casanova tells Bettina how much he admires her intelligence, despite having been its "dupe," and asks her to deal honestly with him from now on. Yet in his narrator's voice, several pages previously, Casanova had already stressed the impossibility of honesty in love. Despite the excellent schooling he received from Bettina, he tells us, he would continue to be the dupe of women until the age of sixty (*HV*, 1:40). Indeed, he argues in his preface that reciprocal deception is impossible to avoid between men and women: "Pour ce qui regarde les femmes, ce sont des tromperies réciproques qu'on ne met pas en ligne de compte, car quand l'amour s'en mêle, on est ordinairement la dupe de part et d'autre" (*HV*, 1:3). The problem, then, is not that men and women in love deceive each other. What is unacceptable is Bettina's particular manner of deception, derived from the novel.

Bettina attempts to convince Casanova that she has not had an affair with Candiani. Casanova explicitly links her deception to novelistic models: "Cette fille me paraissait plus étonnante que toutes celles dont les romans que j'avais lus m'avaient représenté les merveilles. Il me semblait de me voir joué par elle avec une effronterie sans exemple" (*HV*, 1:43). The novelistic source of Bettina's behavioral model becomes clearer during the course of their conversation. Bettina claims not only that she had never loved Candiani, but that he had been blackmailing her. Having seen her masturbating Casanova through a hole in the ceiling, Candiani had threatened to expose her to her family unless she eloped with him. Bettina's deception requires her to assume the pose of the non-desiring victim of unwanted male attention, attempting to rewrite her behavior according to the paradigm of the sentimental heroine. Bettina gives a narrative performance that like the letters in a sentimental novel seeks to (re)constitute virtue and create a morally authentic self.[21] But Casanova does not see her performance as authentic, any more than skeptical eighteenth-century readers automatically accepted the authenticity of Richardson's Pamela or Rousseau's Julie. Indeed, the Pamela/Anti-Pamela debate revolved around a disagreement over precisely the same problem posed here. Pamela's supporters saw her language as a totally transparent representation of her feelings and her motivations, while Richardson's critics read his heroine's letters "as a performance of deceit, with Pamela's language . . . cunningly hiding her true self."[22]

Like the anti-Pamelists, Casanova strongly underscores the artfulness of Bettina's language in this part of the episode. Her diction is hyperbolic, repeatedly stressing the key terms of "honor" and "virtue" and describing her "martyrdom"; the actions she recounts have a strong stamp of the novelistic about them (for example, she says she waited for her blackmailer with a stiletto in her pocket); and she twice uses tears as an instrument of emotional manipulation, a "well-documented tactic for the innocent heroine."[23] Casanova recognizes the "literariness" of Bettina's narration, underscores it by glossing her tale with a famous tag-line from Ariosto's *Orlando furioso* ("Forse era vero, ma non, però, credibile / A chi del senso suo fosse signore"),[24] and concludes: "L'esprit délié de cette fille, qui ne s'était pas raffiné par l'étude, prétendait à l'avantage d'être supposé pur et sans art ; il le savait, et il se servait de cette connaissance pour en tirer parti, mais cet esprit m'avait donné une trop grande idée de son habileté" (*HV*, 1:48).

Bettina's language is thus seen not as transparent expression, but as a form of deceit in which she uses narrative to position herself as object rather than subject of desire. It is precisely this deceptive use of narrative that the anti-Pamela writers criticized in Richardson: the "modesty" of her letters was seen as a sham, hiding the reality of her own desire and of her wish to be desired.[25] Skeptical readers of Rousseau's *La Nouvelle Héloïse* had a similar reaction to Julie's suppression of her desire for Saint-Preux, and to the pretension to virtue by both of these characters. In his highly polemical *Lettres sur la Nouvelle Héloïse*, Voltaire sneers that "Jamais catin ne prêcha plus, et jamais valet suborneur de filles ne fut plus philosophe," while Fréron, in a review of 1761, remarks that "ses principaux personnages sont vicieux dans la pratique, et vertueux dans la spéculation."[26] The same sentiments are repeated almost word for word in an anonymous review in the *Annales typographiques* in 1762.[27] Like the anti-Pamelists, these critics of Rousseau object to his characters' use of the language of virtue (that is, of non-desire) hypocritically to conceal the desire they feel, and act upon. For Casanova, too, the sentimental heroine's project of engendering desire while never expressing it herself constitutes the ultimate mark of inauthenticity. Bettina's deception, modeled now on the sentimental heroine rather than the older women of the novels of worldliness, is no longer just a matter of control, but a fundamental *self*-deception about, and a distortion of, the nature of female sexuality.

The contrast between the transgressive, "possessed" Bettina and this imitator of sentimental novels could not be more stark. In the first instance, Bettina uses alternative languages (masquerade, body language), fragmentary language (disconnected bits of Latin and Greek), and poetic language ("insane" ravings) to contest the masculine domination of the Symbolic, to perform a carnivalesque reversal of its constitutive binary oppositions, and to seize for herself a position as subject. In the second, she accepts the position provided for her in novels that, despite the danger they were felt to represent, did more to confirm women's position in patriarchal culture than to contest it.

Casanova's implied criticism of the sentimental novel becomes more pointed in the concluding section of the episode, which I suggest must be read as a comment on *La Nouvelle Héloïse*.[28] Bettina's fiction of demonic possession has by now become untenable, and Casanova tells her that her obvious preference for the handsome Father Mancia may expose the real nature of her malady. Bettina takes to her bed with violent chills, but this time her illness is real: she has smallpox. As her condition worsens, her body becomes monstrous, her head, face, and throat swollen by a third, her body exuding pus and stinking sweat. Casanova is the only member of the household who can stand to remain at her bedside. The heroic scene of the young man's faithfulness is quickly turned to comedy, however, as the narrator says that he saved Bettina's beautiful face by continually telling her that if she were to scratch herself, she would be so ugly no one would ever desire her again. Casanova is infected with eight or ten pustules. Since he has already had smallpox, they are not seriously dangerous, but they convince Bettina that he alone is worth her love. When she recovers, they enjoy a blissful but platonic relationship until, after Casanova's departure from Padua, she marries a shoemaker named Pigozzo, a "base scoundrel" who married her only for her dowry and then abandoned her in poverty (*HV*, 1:51, 406). The narrator tells us that she died in his presence, many years later.[29]

This entire, concluding section of the Bettina episode is carefully modeled on a sequence in *La Nouvelle Héloïse* (Part III, letters 12-14) in which Julie, torn between her desire for Saint-Preux and her filial duty, falls ill with smallpox. As she lies in delirium, Saint-Preux secretly comes to her bedside, embraces her and covers her with kisses in an attempt to infect himself with her disease. This occurs at a crucial moment in the novel: Julie's bout with smallpox marks her separation from her lover, the point after which she represses her desire for him, and instead accepts integration into the order of the Father by marrying Wolmar. Casanova's re-evocation of the episode is clearly deliberate, repeating several of its key elements, though developing them in a comic tone: like Julie, Bettina comes down with smallpox at the moment her resistance to patriarchal order becomes unsustainable; Bettina's lover is also present at her bedside, and is infected by her; Julie's concern about the disease's effect on her face (letters 13 and 14) is re-expressed in Casanova's urging that Bettina not scratch herself; and the episode *appears* to provide a resolution to the problem of the heroine's illicit desire by substituting a platonic relationship for a sexual one.

Yet while Casanova repeats enough elements of *La Nouvelle Héloïse* to make the reference recognizable, he evokes the novel only to attack its ideological presuppositions. In his second preface, Rousseau explicitly tells us that the novel is to be a model of a happy marriage ("J'aime à me figurer deux époux lisant ce recueil ensemble . . . Comment pourraient-ils y contempler le tableau d'un ménage heureux, sans vouloir imiter un si doux modèle?)"[30] However, such an idealization can be accomplished only if the chaste wife completely represses the desire she felt as guilty lover. Indeed, Julie erases not only her desire for Saint-Preux, to whom she can offer only platonic friendship, but *all* desire, dwelling in part three, letter 20 on an idea of marriage where passion is neither present nor necessary.[31] And when desire for Saint-Preux again begins to surface at the end of the novel, Julie gladly accepts her death as the final, necessary repression that protects her virtue.

Rousseau's domestic social contract thus requires, as its most basic condition, the exclusion of women from the position of desiring subject and the forcible erasure of their sexuality. Unlike modern readers of the novel, Rousseau's contemporaries were not much struck by the *loss* to the woman entailed in such a contract. Casanova's development of the Bettina episode, by contrast, underscores the price that the woman is required to pay. As the episode draws to a conclusion, it appears to promise what Miller has called a euphoric ending: Bettina has successfully avoided the consequences of her premature sexuality, substituting for it a platonic relationship, and in the end she is successfully reintegrated into society through marriage. But there are two jarring elements here. First, the transformation costs Bettina her voice. In her feigned possession, Bettina had created an identity that allowed her to criticize and to resist domination by the representatives of patriarchal society; once she has given up her sexuality, she falls mute in Casanova's text, spoken about but never again speaking for herself. And far from integrating her into society, Casanova stresses, Bettina's marriage brings her only poverty, suffering, and death. In Rousseau, the connection between the repression of desire, marriage, and death, remains implied, and it is unlikely that he or any of his readers would have been aware of it in those terms. In the Bettina episode, however, Casanova appears deliberately to underscore the disturbing implications of Rousseau's novel. Unlike his contemporaries, Casanova sees the implied violence in the sentimental novel's suppression of female desire, and rejects it utterly.

I noted earlier that the novel was thought to be dangerous for its potential to sexualize young women in a way that would threaten their acceptance of their place in the social order. Casanova, however, suggests that far from constituting female readers as desiring subjects, the novel actually objectifies them, providing models of female behavior in which sexual feeling is at best dishonestly dissembled, and at worst cruelly repressed. The Bettina episode does not end with the author's counter-proposal of a different kind of feminine subjectivity, for at this point Casanova is still too young and inexperienced to imagine such a thing. But by showing in the first, precocious love-affair of his *Histoire de ma vie* the tragic example of a woman who allows her identity to be written by the sentimental novel, he prepares us for the very different women who will follow: Henriette, M.M., Pauline, and others who, by employing some of Bettina's transgressive strategies, will succeed in becoming desiring subjects whose sexuality is enjoyed outside the repressive realm of patriarchal order, and, often, as a means of resistance to it.

N O T E S

An earlier version of this paper was delivered at the 2002 Annual Meeting of the American Society for Eighteenth-Century Studies, in Colorado Springs, CO.

1. Giacomo Casanova, *Histoire de ma vie, suivie de textes inédits*, ed. Francis Lacassin, 12 vols. in 3 (Paris: Laffont, 1999), 1:28. Subsequent references will be given parenthetically, abbreviated as *HV*. This edition reproduces the text of the Brockhaus-Plon *édition intégrale* of 1960–62, which was the first to respect the author's original manuscript. All others reprint the first edition (Brockhaus, 1826–38) in which Casanova's text was heavily edited and altered by Jean Laforgue.

2. However, Françoise Weil, *L'interdiction du roman et la librairie 1728–1750*. Collections des mélanges de la Bibliothèque de la Sorbonne 3 (Paris: Aux Amateurs de livres, 1986), 15–17, goes a long way toward exploding the notion that novels were read primarily by women. The largest collections of novels she lists were owned by men, many of them prominent in government, finance, and law.

3. Though Casanova's biographers have often compared his autobiography to a novel, there are very few scholarly studies of the novel's impact on the narrative strategies of *Histoire de ma vie*. Marie-Françoise Luna, "L'univers du romanesque" in *Casanova mémorialiste* (Paris: Champion, 1998), 451–77, traces a great many superficial resemblances between Casanova's self-presentation and the construction of the hero in adventure novels, sentimental novels, and libertine novels. Cynthia Craig, in her very interesting "Gender, Genre, and Reading in the Texts of Giacomo Casanova," *RLA: Romance Languages Annual* 7 (1995): 227–33, studies the links between the novel and the *Histoire de ma vie* in the context of what she sees as the feminization of Casanova's text. Neither examines Casanova's use of the Bettina episode to critique the novel's construction of feminine subjectivity.

4. Georges May, *Le Dilemme du roman au XVIIIe siècle : Étude sur les rapports du roman et de la critique (1715–61)* (New Haven: Yale Univ. Press; Paris: Presses Universitaires de France, 1963), 8–11.

5. Joan De Jean, *Tender Geographies: Women and the Origins of the Novel in France* (New York: Columbia Univ. Press, 1991), 91.

6. DeJean, 91–92, 179–80.

7. *Avis d'une mère à sa fille,* quoted in May, 25.

8. Quoted in Jenny Mander, *Circles of learning: narratology and the eighteenth-century French novel,* Studies on Voltaire and the Eighteenth Century, 366 (Oxford: Voltaire Foundation, 1999), 177.

9. Jean-Jacques Rousseau, *Julie, ou la Nouvelle Héloïse*, 2 vols., ed. Henri Coulet (Paris: Gallimard, 1993), 1:71.

10. "Discours sur l'éducation des femmes," in Jacques Henri Bernardin de Saint-Pierre, *Oeuvres complètes de Jacques-Henri-Bernardin de Saint-Pierre,* ed. Louis Aimé Martin, (Paris: Méquignon-Marvis, 1818–1826), 12: 150.

11. Casanova's language here mimics familiar defenses of the novel as a "tableau de la vie" by authors such as d'Argens, Desfontaines, d'Arnaud, Laclos, and Sade (May, 112–113, 148–149, 230; DeJean, 187). The autobiographer writes, "dans quelle école avait-elle appris à si bien connaître le cœur humain? En lisant des romans. Il se peut que la lecture de plusieurs soit la cause de la perte d'une grande quantité de filles ; mais il est certain que *la lecture des bons leur apprend la gentillesse, et l'exercice des vertus sociales.*" (*HV*, 1:43). As my reading of the Bettina episode will suggest, this comment is best understood as ironic.

12. Nancy Miller, *The Heroine's Text: Readings in the French and English Novel 1722–1782* (New York: Columbia Univ. Press, 1980), x–xi.

13. Miller, 4–10, 23, 54.

14. Peter Brooks, *The Novel of Worldliness: Crébillon, Marivaux, Laclos, and Stendahl* (Princeton: Princeton Univ. Press, 1969), 16–17, 21–22.

15. Brooks, 180.

16. Terry Castle, *Masquerade and Civilization: The Carnivalesque in Eighteenth-Century English Culture and Fiction* (Stanford, CA: Stanford Univ. Press, 1986), 1–109, and especially 75–77.

17. On the challenge to heterocentric culture represented by such performances of drag, see Judith Butler, *Gender Trouble: Feminism and the Subversion of Identity* (London and New York: Routledge, 1990), 128–141.

18. I am indebted for this insight to an anonymous peer reviewer, whose careful reading and cogent advice has been very helpful in the final elaboration of this article.

19. One cannot help but be reminded of Julia Kristeva's view of poetic language as similar to psychosis, and of her appreciation of its potential to disrupt and subvert paternal law. On this aspect of Kristeva's thought, see Butler, 79–93.

20. The novels of Mme de Villedieu (Marie-Catherine Desjardins, 1640–1683) describe the highly-colored sexual adventures of their heroines: the protagonist of her *Mémoires de la vie de Henriette Sylvie de Molière* (1671–74) kills the adoptive father who attempts to rape her, seduces her mother's lover, violates the rule of cloister of the convent in which she is placed, and later

dresses as a man in order to make love to women. For DeJean, "Villedieu's novel is simultaneously a celebration of women bold enough to challenge the social order and a defense of those it presents as victims of this system" (P. 133). Similar episodes of cross-dressing and of seduction *en travestie* are found in d'Aulnoy's *Mémoires des Avantures singulières de la Cour de France* (1692) and in many popular novels of the eighteenth century, such as d'Auvigny's *Mémoires de Madame de Barneveldt* (1732). Casanova knew Villedieu's work, or at least her reputation, and he praises her "gentilissime . . . storie romanzeggiate*"* in the preface to his translation-adaptation of Riccoboni's *Lettres de Juliette Catesby*.

21. The use of narration to create authenticity has been noted as a fundamental feature of the sentimental novel in Christine Roulston, *Virtue, Gender, and Authentic Self in Eighteenth-Century Fiction: Richardson, Rousseau, and Laclos* (Gainesville: Univ. Press of Florida, 1998), xvi–xvii. Roulston suggests that letters, in the sentimental novel, are structured around "the loss of female virtue, which the act of writing is repeatedly seeking to reconstitute. . . . In the sentimental novel . . . virtue becomes the locus of a new writing self, a self that may not be 'real' but that is morally authentic and that, in this sense, has the authority to reverse the relationships between the real and the fictional."

22. Roulston, 2.

23. Miller, 28. Miller goes on to note that tears are "An effective means of non-verbal communication, they deliver a message while temporarily suspending dialog. Tears also have the advantage of reversing the balance of power." Curiously, Moll Flanders refers to tears as "Womans Rhetorick"; and immediately after his second reference to Bettina's tears Casanova underscores the falsity of rhetoric in general: "Après avoir essuyé ses larmes, elle fixa ses beaux yeux dans les miens, croyant y discerner les marques visibles de sa victoire ; mais je l'ai étonnée lui touchant un article que par un artifice elle avait négligé dans son apologie. *La rhétorique n'employe les secrets de la nature que comme les peintres qui veulent l'imiter. Tout ce qu'ils donnent de plus beau est faux*" (*HV*, 1:48).

24. Ludovico Ariosto, *Orlando furioso* I, 56. At this point of the poem, Angelica has just tried to convince Sacripante that she is still a virgin, despite having been abducted by the love-struck Orlando and brought by him from Cathay to Europe. By using the quotation here, Casanova in effect allows the cultured reader to see Bettina's similar action through the prism of a well-known literary situation, comically heightening the episode's sense of literariness.

25. Roulston, 7

26. Raymond Trousson, *Rousseau et sa fortune littéraire* (Saint-Medard-en-Jalles: Ducros, 1971), 25–26.

27. Anna Attridge, "The Reception of *La Nouvelle Héloïse*," *Studies on Voltaire and the Eighteenth Century* 120 (1974): 245. On the reception of *La Nouvelle Héloïse*, see also Daniel Mornet's extensive preface to his edition of the novel (Paris: Hachette, 1925).

28. Casanova commented on *Julie, ou La Nouvelle Héloïse* and on the

sentimental novel several times prior to writing his *Histoire*. Initially, in his *Confutazione della Storia del Governo Veneto d'Amelot de la Houssaie* (1769), and in the pamphlet *Lana caprina, epistola di un licantropo* (1772), his incidental remarks on Rousseau's novel echo the moralistic pronouncements of most of the French literary establishment. However, Casanova's surprising moral conservatism in these works is probably due less to conviction than to his expectations of his audience. The *Confutazione* was written to convince the Venetian State Inquisitors to pardon Casanova and allow him to return from exile to his native city, while *Lana caprina*, though not directly addressed to the Inquisitors, was published while his actions and publications were still subject to close scrutiny by the conservative authorities of his homeland. Casanova's mature views on the sentimental novel, and in particular his skepticism regarding Platonic love, are most clearly expressed in his unfinished manuscript *Examen des* Études de la nature *et de* Paul et Virginie *de Bernardin de Saint-Pierre*, composed at Dux in 1788–89, roughly a year prior to beginning the *Histoire*. See Giacomo Casanova, *Casanova et Bernardin de Saint-Pierre*, eds. Marco Leeflang and Tom Vitelli, Documents Casanoviens, 1 (Utrecht: n.p., 1985), 73–86.

29. Casanova intended to recount the episode of his reunion with Bettina in 1776. Unfortunately, the *Histoire de ma vie* breaks off before his return to Venice in 1774.

30. *Julie, ou la Nouvelle Héloïse*, 2:407.

31. "Ce qui m'a longtemps abusée et qui peut-être vous abuse encore, c'est la pensée que l'amour est nécessaire pour former un heureux mariage. Mon ami, c'est un erreur ; l'honnêteté, la vertu, de certaines convenances, moins de conditions et d'âges que de caractères et d'humeurs suffisent entre deux époux . . . On ne s'épouse point pour penser uniquement l'un à l'autre, mais pour remplir conjointement les devoirs de la vie civile, gouverner prudemment la maison, bien élever ses enfants." *Julie, ou la Nouvelle Héloïse*, 1:441–42.

"What Do You Think Laws Were Made For?": Prison Reform Discourse and the English Jacobin Novel

ALEXANDER H. PITOFSKY

> I sink beneath a torrent, whose resistless waves overwhelm alike in a common ruin the guiltless and the guilty.
> —Mary Hays, *The Victim of Prejudice*

> Prepare a tale however plausible, or however true, the whole world shall execrate you for an impostor. Your innocence shall be of no service to you.
> —William Godwin, *Caleb Williams*

The novelists of eighteenth-century Britain staged a remarkable number of episodes in which innocent characters are imprisoned. The catalogue of novels published during the period in which at least one character is wrongfully jailed includes Samuel Richardson's *Pamela* (1740) and *Clarissa* (1747–48); Henry Fielding's *Jonathan Wild* (1743), *Tom Jones* (1749), and *Amelia* (1751); Tobias Smollett's *Roderick Random* (1748), *Peregrine Pickle* (1751), and *Humphry Clinker* (1771); Oliver Goldsmith's *The Vicar of Wakefield* (1766); William Godwin's *Caleb Williams* (1794); and Mary Hays's *The Victim of Prejudice* (1799). British novels published before the 1790s frequently portray wrongful imprisonment as a blessing in disguise. In *Pamela*, for instance, Parson Williams turns a substantial profit as a result of his confinement for debt. After the young clergyman is released,

293

Mr. B. apologizes for orchestrating his arrest, offers him a well-paying living, and hands him a £100 bank-note. In Book XII of *Amelia*, William Booth claims to experience a religious epiphany during his incarceration in Bailiff Bondum's sponging house. Booth is astonished by the corruption and disorder of a London prison in the novel's opening chapters,[1] but when Dr. Harrison visits him in the sponging house Booth insists that his latest confinement has been a stroke of good fortune: "I rejoice in this last Instance of my Shame, since I am like to reap the most solid Advantage from it. . . . Since I have been in this wretched Place, I have employ'd my Time almost entirely in reading over a Series of [Isaac Barrow's] Sermons . . . and so good Effect have they had upon me, that I shall, I believe, be the better Man for them as long as I live."[2] Even Clarissa Harlowe perceives a melancholy kind of benefit in her confinement—in a letter to Belford, she characterizes the prison room in Officer Rowland's house as a refuge in which she can remain "safe and uninterrupted for the short remainder of [her] life."[3] In several English Jacobin novels of the 1790s, by contrast, wrongful imprisonment is portrayed as an unconscionable miscarriage of justice. The prison episodes produced by Godwin, Hays, and other Jacobin writers are fraught with merciless jailers and nightmarish dungeons. Some of the prisoners these novelists imagine are hanged. Others die in prison before their accusers' charges can be refuted in court. Those who survive their prison-house tribulations suffer unremitting physical and emotional distress. This essay will discuss the wrongful imprisonment episodes of the 1790s and suggest that the English Jacobins set the novelistic representation of imprisonment on a new foundation by modeling their prison episodes on John Howard's exhaustively detailed reformist discourse in *The State of the Prisons* (1777), not on depictions of imprisonment which had appeared in previous works of fiction.

Over the last twenty-five years, a number of commentators—most notably John Bender and W. B. Carnochan—have discussed the representations of prison experience in the imaginative literature of eighteenth-century Britain.[4] During the same period, Mona Scheuermann, Marilyn Butler, Gary Kelly, Eleanor Ty, and other cultural historians have investigated the ways in which British writers of the late eighteenth century employed the novel as an instrument of social protest and political activism.[5] My purpose in this essay is to elaborate on these lines of inquiry in two ways. First of all, I want to call attention to the frequent recurrence of wrongful imprisonment episodes in eighteenth-century British novels, a curious phenomenon that has not been addressed in any critical study published to date. Second, by examining the relation between prison reform discourse and the novel in the 1790s, I hope to complement Bender's analysis in *Imagining the Penitentiary*. Bender's central argument is that prison episodes fashioned by Daniel Defoe, John Gay, Henry Fielding, and other eighteenth-century writers may have altered the course of the British prison reform movement by disseminating "the penitentiary idea," *i.e.*, the concept that prison experience can give rise to a "revolution of conscience" in which "errant personality is reconstituted . . . by solitary reflection."[6] By the last quarter of the eighteenth century, Bender observes, Parliament initiated the process of replacing the nation's notoriously corrupt prisons with penitentiaries designed to engender the kind of "revolution of conscience" that had been foregrounded in popular works of imaginative literature. This argument is strikingly cogent and original, but it may create the impression that while eighteenth-century novelists had much to say to prison reformers, prison reform discourse made no corresponding impression on eighteenth-century fiction. By highlighting the ways in which the prison episodes in Jacobin novels draw on Howard's commentaries, I want to suggest that the period's novelists and prison reformers were engaged in an ongoing dialogue, marked by a mutually beneficial exchange of ideas.

I

The wrongful imprisonment episodes in English Jacobin novels insistently emphasize the inhumanity of the British criminal justice system.[7] In *Caleb Williams*, seventeen-year-old Emily Melville dies of fever after her cousin Barnabas Tyrrel has her imprisoned on the pretext that she owes the Tyrrel family £1100 for fourteen years of "board and necessaries."[8] Mr. Falkland arranges to have Emily released, but she dies within hours after he pays her bail. A few pages later, a farmer named Benjamin Hawkins and his son Leonard are hanged after they are wrongly convicted of murdering Tyrrel. Falkland's steward Mr. Collins points out that the elder Hawkins allegedly confessed during the interval between his trial and his execution, but the audience never doubts that the Hawkinses are innocent victims of what Godwin defines in the novel's preface as the "unrecorded despotism by which man becomes the destroyer of man" (3).[9] During his own wrongful confinement, Caleb Williams is outraged by the death of Brightwel, a young prisoner who had been falsely accused of petty theft: "In a few days he would have been acquitted, his liberty, his reputation restored; mankind perhaps, struck with the injustice he had suffered, would have shown themselves eager to balance his misfortunes, and obliterate his disgrace. But this man died" (171). And in *The Victim of Prejudice*, Mary Raymond is tormented by illness and despair during her incarceration for debt:

> [T]he damp and unwholesome air of my [prison] has communicated rheumatic pains to my limbs; the vigour of my frame begins to yield to the depredations of grief, the inactivity of my situation and the mephitic vapour that surrounds me. . . . A deadly torpor steals over my faculties; principles loosen in my clouded mind; my heart, formed for tender sympathies, for social affections, withers in joyless, hopeless solitude . . . the current of life creeps slowly, wasted by inanity and clogged by disease. Why should I drain the embittered cup,—why exhaust life's wretched dregs,—why shiver, like a dastard, on the brink of dissolution,—when enjoyment, activity, usefulness, hope, *are lost for ever*?[10]

As these passages suggest, the "happy prisons" Carnochan discerns in *Moll Flanders*, *Tom Jones*, *Roderick Random*, and other early to mid-eighteenth-century novels are nowhere to be found in the narratives of the English Jacobins.[11] The wrongfully jailed characters of the 1790s do not become richer, wiser, or more devout as a consequence of their prison experiences. Instead, they invariably find horror and desolation in their places of confinement. Williams, for instance, recalls that he plunged into "inexpressible agony" after Falkland arranged to have him wrongfully jailed:

> I regarded the whole human species as so many hangmen and torturers . . . confederated to tear me to pieces; and this wide scene of inexorable persecution inflicted upon me inexpressible agony. I looked on this side and on that; I was innocent; I had a right to expect assistance; but every heart was steeled against me; every hand was ready to lend its force to make my ruin secure. No man that has not felt in his own most momentous concerns justice, eternal truth, unalterable equity engaged in his behalf, and on the other side brute force, impenetrable obstinacy, and unfeeling insolence, can imagine the sensations that then passed through my mind. I saw treachery triumphant and enthroned; I saw the sinews of innocence crumbled into dust by the gripe of almighty guilt. (163)

Godwin stresses throughout *Caleb Williams* that prison experience in eighteenth-century Britain is a life-threatening ordeal and every Briton knows it. When Tyrrel announces his intention to persecute Emily Melville, his steward Barnes warns that the community will view the scheme as tantamount to murder: "Pray, your honour, think the better of it. Upon my life, the whole country will cry shame . . . I have heard as how that Miss Emily is sick a-bed. . . . You do not mean to kill her, I take it" (72). (This prediction proves to be accurate: as soon as reports of Emily's death began to circulate, Tyrrel "looked round and saw sullen detestation in every face. . . . His large estate could not purchase civility from the gentry, the peasantry, scarcely from his own servants" [81].) Similarly, when Leonard Hawkins is arrested for a trumped-up violation of the Black Act, his father worries that Leonard may be killed by a fellow prisoner: "Who can tell what may hap in a jail?. . . there is one man in the same quarter of the prison that looks so wicked! I do not much fancy the looks of the rest . . . come what will, I am determined he shall not stay among them twelve hours longer" (103). For Godwin's characters, then, the notion that prisoners in an eighteenth-century British jail could sit contentedly with their children like Thomas Heartfree in *Jonathan Wild*, engage in leisurely conversations with friends like Roderick Random, or reflect in solitude on past indiscretions like Tom Jones would seem absurd. Godwin compels his audience to see imprisonment for what it is—a devastating *physical* hardship that precludes the tranquil, undisturbed meditation that is commonplace in previous novelistic prison episodes.

In *Anna St. Ives* (1792), Thomas Holcroft appears to share Godwin's determination to illustrate that all Britons are keenly aware of the dangers of their society's prisons. After Frank Henley is rewarded by Sir Arthur St. Ives for fending off a highwayman, he rescues a young man who has been arrested for debt. While Frank looks on in amazement, the prisoner's wife implores a crew of bailiffs not to seize her husband: "The horrors of a jail were so impressed, so rooted in her fancy, that she was willing to sell anything, everything; she would give them all she had, so that her [husband] might not be dragged to a damp, foul dungeon; to darkness, bread and water, and starving. Thou canst not imagine the volubility with which her passions flowed, and her terrors found utterance . . . "[12] Frank liberates the prisoner by offering to pay his debts, but the feelings of dread expressed by the prisoner's wife reverberate long after the conclusion of this brief episode. As Mona Scheuermann points out in *Social Protest and the Eighteenth-Century English Novel* (1985), Holcroft emphasizes that "the woman's terror for her husband . . . is well-founded."[13] The prisoner would almost surely have been "dragged to a damp, foul dungeon" and afflicted by "darkness, bread and water, and starving" if not for a chain of contingencies which includes the highwayman's attack, Sir Arthur's decision to compensate Frank for his intervention, Frank's presence at the scene of the arrest, and Frank's empathetic sensibility. "It is only chance," Scheuermann notes, "that [the prisoner] was not condemned to slime and starvation; it is only chance that Frank happened to be where he was and that he happened to have the money with him."[14] The prison episodes in British novels published before the 1790s frequently suggest, as Dr. Harrison posits in *Amelia*, that the innocent can rely on providence to redeem them with "the Justice . . . which it will, one Day or other, render to all Men."[15] The narratives of the English Jacobins, on the other hand, unfold in a world devoid of providential justice. If the period's innocent prisoners survive, the source of their deliverance will be a stranger's altruism or some other form of happenstance.

The wrongful imprisonment episodes in English Jacobin novels also diverge from previous novelistic prison episodes in that they usually contain extended descriptions of the penal facilities in which innocent characters are detained. Williams's account of his confinement, in particular, is so meticulously rendered that it often appears to have been excerpted from an eighteenth-century prison reform tract:

> The only furniture [in my dungeon] was the straw that served me for my repose. It was narrow, damp and unwholesome. The slumbers of a mind, wearied like mine with the most detestable uniformity, to whom neither amusement nor occupation ever offered themselves to beguile the painful hours, were short, disturbed, and unrefreshing . . . To these slumbers succeeded the hours which, by the regulations of our prison, I was obliged though awake to spend in solitary and cheerless darkness. Here I had neither books nor pens, nor any thing upon which to engage my attention; all was a sightless blank . . . Cruel, inexorable policy of affairs, that condemns a man to torture like this; that sanctions it and knows not what is done under its sanction. (164)

The wrongful imprisonment episodes in *Clarissa* and *Amelia* are more elaborately developed than those in other British novels published before the 1790s, but they seem cursory when juxtaposed with Williams's narrative. While Richardson and Fielding devote a series of paragraphs to the physical characteristics of the prison room in Officer Rowland's house and Booth's various places of confinement, Godwin devotes a series of chapters to a comprehensive record of everyday life in his narrator's prison. Williams specifies that his fellow prisoners included five men accused of stealing livestock, two highwaymen, two burglars, a shoplifter, and a counterfeiter. We learn a great deal about his attitudes toward the prison staff, a corps of sadists who took "a barbarous and sullen pleasure in issuing their detested mandates, and observing the mournful reluctance with which they were obeyed" (160). When Williams recounts his confinement in an underground "strong room," he inventories the ways in which he was tortured, from the handcuffs, fetters, and padlock he was forced to wear to the "mouldy" bread and "dirty stinking water" (178) delivered to him by the jailer. No detail, it seems, is too insignificant to be noted in this episode—Williams even pauses to describe the dirt on the floor of the prison, a substance that "speaks sadness to the heart, and appears to be . . . in a state of putridity and infection" (158). One of the most striking features of Williams's prison narrative is the way it blends realistic, strictly empirical discourse with the portrayals of confinement in "gloomy passages" behind "massy doors" (158) commonly associated with gothic fiction. While the scenes of horror fashioned by Ann Radcliffe, Horace Walpole, *et al.* are generally set in periods and cultures far removed from eighteenth-century British society, however, Godwin holds that comparable scenes routinely erupt in British towns of his own time. The prison episodes in *Caleb Williams* seem to pose an unsettling question: if innocent characters such as Williams, Emily Melville, and Benjamin and Leonard Hawkins can be imprisoned with so little difficulty, how many Britons can assume that they are not at risk? This sense of ineluctable danger is heightened by the fact that the innocent prisoners in *Caleb Williams* are destroyed by the ordinary protocols of the British criminal justice system, not by an apparition, an ancient curse, or any other supernatural gothic phenomenon.

The prison episodes in *The Victim of Prejudice* are also replete with details that bring the destructive power of imprisonment into sharp, detailed focus. Near the conclusion of the novel, Mary Raymond is committed to

> a house large and gloomy, the windows defended by bars of iron. . . . [I followed the sheriff's officer] through long and dark passages, up a narrow stair-case, into a small back-room wretchedly furnished, the windows of which, obscured by dirt, shed, as the twilight shut in, a glimmering, uncertain light, according with the melancholy desolation of the place. Sinking into an old-fashioned armchair, worm-eaten and tottering, I resigned myself to reflections, that succeeded each other in long and mournful trains.   (147)

The narrow stairway, barred windows, and tattered furnishings of this prison resemble those described in the prison episode in *Clarissa*, but Hays does not follow Richardson by intimating that her heroine's confinement might prove to be a salutary experience.[16] To the contrary, Mary's narrative suggests that the ferocity of her victimization is *increasing*. Sir Peter Osborne—the Lovelace-like villain who has confined Mary in his London residence, raped her, and demanded that she become his mistress—is determined to compel her obedience. If she resists, he warns, she will suffer "the squalid miseries of famine and destitution" and "mix in the loathsome gaol with the refuse of mankind" (150). Thus, unlike Clarissa, who welcomes her confinement because it seems to indicate that her ordeal has nearly run its course, Mary views her imprisonment as yet another phase in an elaborate, ongoing process of coercion. (In *The Wrongs of Woman* [1798], Mary Wollstonecraft also rejects the idea that confinement can provide refuge and security for persecuted women by underscoring the bleak realities of the period's private madhouses. Maria Venables is unnerved by virtually every aspect of her place of confinement, from the "groans and shrieks" she hears at night to the manacles chained to her body.[17] She finds temporary solace in borrowed books, but her husband's cruelty and the rigors of confinement eventually convince her that it would be futile to hope for relief: "The lamp of life seemed to be spending itself to chase the vapours of a dungeon which no art could dissipate."[18])

The most salient difference between the wrongful imprisonment episodes of the 1790s and those in previous works of fiction is the fact that the Jacobin novelists attribute injuries suffered by innocent prisoners to the failings of the British criminal justice system and British society *as a whole*, not to what Scheuermann defines as "the depredations of individuals upon one another."[19] When Williams recalls his prison experience, for example, he spends very little time railing against Falkland's ruthlessness and hypocrisy. Instead, he denounces his British contemporaries and the code of criminal justice they have formulated:

> Thank God, exclaims the Englishman, we have no Bastille! Thank God, with us no man can be punished without a crime! Unthinking wretch! Is that a country of liberty, where thousands languish in dungeons and fetters? Go, go, ignorant fool! and visit the scenes of our prisons! witness their unwholesomeness, their filth, the tyranny of their governors, the misery of their inmates! After that, show me the man shameless enough to triumph and say England has no Bastille! Is there any charge so frivolous upon which men

are not consigned to these detested abodes? Is there any villainy
that is not practised by justices and prosecutors? . . . I looked
round upon my walls, and forward upon the premature death I
had too much reason to expect; I consulted my own heart, that
whispered nothing but innocence, and I said "This is society.
This is the object, the distribution of justice, which is the end of
human reason. For this sages have toiled, and midnight oil has
been wasted. This!" (161–62)

This passage delivers the moment of explicit, unqualified political protest
that previous British novelists had excluded from their wrongful
imprisonment episodes. Godwin's innocent prisoner does not bother to
demonize Falkland because he understands that his nemesis could not have
orchestrated his imprisonment without the complicity of a criminal justice
system enforced by corrupt "justices and prosecutors," tyrannical prison
officials, and a nation of "ignorant fools" who assume that all is well in the
nation's prisons because Britons have traditionally boasted of their
unsurpassed commitment to "liberty." A few pages later, Williams describes
British society as a dystopian arena in which the guilty annihilate the innocent
with impunity: "My resentment was not restricted to [Falkland], but extended
itself to take in the whole machine of society. I could never believe that all
this was the fair result of institutions inseparable from the general good"
(163). The contrast between Williams's response to his imprisonment and,
say, Fielding's characters' responses to the imprisonment of Tom Jones
after he wounds Mr. Fitzpatrick in self-defense could hardly be more
pronounced. No one contends that the justice who committed Jones to the
Gate-House was a tyrant or that Britain's laws should have prevented the
kind of injustice Jones has suffered. In Godwin's England, on the other
hand, the prisoner's most powerful impulse is to condemn "the whole
machine of society" and its "distribution of justice."

It would have been more than understandable for Williams to place the
blame for his imprisonment squarely on Falkland. Like Mr. B., Jonathan
Wild, Mr. Blifil, and other villains in novels published before the 1790s,
Falkland deliberately injures an innocent victim to serve his own dubious
interests. Indeed, if not for Falkland's psychological instability and
extravagant concern for his reputation as a "man of honour," it seems
likely that Williams would never have been accused of a serious criminal
offense. In contrast with previous British novelists, however, Godwin does
not represent wrongful imprisonment as a corrupt individual's attempt to
misuse the power of a fundamentally sound criminal justice system. Instead,
he proposes that Williams's ordeal is representative of "things as they are"

because the system itself is corrupt to the core, an apparatus designed to perpetuate what E. P. Thompson has called "the hegemony of the eighteenth-century gentry and aristocracy."[20]   When Benjamin Hawkins sues Tyrrel for breach of contract, Williams likens the farmer's attempt to construct an effective legal strategy to "a fawn contending with a lion . . . Wealth and despotism easily know how to engage . . . [the] laws as the coadjutors of their oppression" (40). In other words, affluent Britons do not merely write the laws—they *own* them, and do not hesitate to use their property to overpower plebeians who dare to contest their social, economic, and political supremacy. Tyrrel manifestly shares Williams's opinion of Britain's criminal justice institutions; when Barnes admonishes his employer not to have Emily Melville imprisoned, Tyrrel exclaims "Scoundrel! . . . The law justifies it.—What do you think laws were made for?" (72). Similarly, as soon as Tyrrel discovers that Emily has died, he begins to defend his actions on the ground that they did not violate the letter of the law: "I did nothing but what the law allows. If she be dead, nobody can say that I am to blame" (85). (The squire's attempt to exculpate himself through legal reasoning is, of course, wholly unpersuasive. As Barnes recognizes from the moment he learns of his employer's scheme, the arrest was illegal because Emily was not "of age" to be committed to prison and did not in fact owe Tyrrel "a brass farthing" [72].) The point I want to emphasize here is not that Godwin invites his audience to excuse Falkland and Tyrrel for the injuries they inflict. To the contrary, he leaves little room for doubt that their wrongdoing consumes Williams, Emily Melville, Benjamin and Leonard Hawkins, and ultimately themselves. What I do want to stress is that the wrongful imprisonment episodes in *Caleb Williams*, unlike those in previous British novels, do not confront readers with inequities and then suggest that they can be ascribed to what Bender refers to as "the petty tyranny of a few individuals acting outside the law on impulses essentially foreign to the British spirit."[21] Godwin concerns himself with wrongful imprisonment to cast a critical eye on his nation's legal system. It is not coincidental that his prison episodes are laced with politically charged terms—"tyranny," "despotism," "justice," "governors," "oppression"—that seldom appear in the narratives of his early to mid-eighteenth-century precursors. While previous novels focus on benefits drawn from private epiphanies, *Caleb Williams* highlights the destructive effects of public policies.

The prison episodes in *The Victim of Prejudice* mirror Godwin's narrative by repeatedly indicting the British criminal justice system and British society as a whole. In his account of the imprisonment and execution of Mary's mother, for instance, Mr. Raymond maintains that the prisoner "forfeited her life on a scaffold . . . to the sanguinary and avenging laws of her country" (62). Raymond, the devoted guardian of an abandoned child, performs a role in Hays's novel that often resembles that of Mr. Allworthy in *Tom Jones*. Nonetheless, Raymond (unlike Allworthy) does not denounce one dishonorable individual when he learns that a character he cares for has been wrongfully jailed. Instead, he reserves his invective for the criminal code that allowed her no opportunity to make amends for her errors of judgment. Similarly, in a letter to Raymond, Mary's mother underscores the mercilessness of the law, not the criminality of the aristocratic rake whose misconduct was the proximate cause of her arrest. In particular, she contends that Britain's legal institutions "completed" the process of seduction, poverty, and desperation that has culminated in her death sentence: "*Law* completes the triumph of injustice. The despotism of man rendered me weak, his vices betrayed me into shame . . . a sanguinary policy precludes reformation, defeating the dear-bought lessons of experience, and by a legal process, assuming the arm of omnipotence, annihilates the being whom its negligence left destitute, and its institutions compelled to offend" (68–69). Accordingly, although Hays does not attempt to explain away the wrongdoing of Sir Peter Osborne and the rake who seduced Mary's mother, the primary function of *The Victim of Prejudice*'s prison episodes is, as Eleanor Ty has observed, to "use tragic events to illustrate the injustice of late eighteenth-century social customs and laws," not to censure individual villains.[22]

Viewed together, the wrongful imprisonment episodes in *Caleb Williams*, *The Victim of Prejudice*, and other Jacobin novels mark a turning point in the novelistic representation of prison experience. In British novels published after the 1790s—Charles Dickens's *Oliver Twist* (1837) and *Little Dorrit* (1857), W. M. Thackeray's *Barry Lyndon* (1844), and George Eliot's *Adam Bede* (1859) are among the first that come to mind—no one suggests that imprisonment can be beneficial. Like British novels of the 1790s, post-eighteenth-century narratives highlight the trauma and despair suffered by prisoners and include explicit declarations of what J. M. S. Tompkins has characterized as "the ethical, social, and political views of the authors, streamed through the novel as through a well-worn channel of access to the public."[23] Thus, although novelistic representations of imprisonment have been commonplace since the episode in which Moll Flanders is arrested for theft and compelled to return to her birthplace, British novelists did not begin to portray confinement in their society's prisons as a harrowing, endlessly destructive ordeal until Godwin published *Caleb Williams* in 1794.

II

It seems to me that the English Jacobins' representations of wrongful imprisonment are fundamentally different from those in previous British novels for two reasons. First, the Jacobins, unlike their early to mid-century precursors, were among the most militant, outspoken social critics of their time. As Gary Kelly points out, it would be difficult to drape a single definition over the English Jacobin movement, but it would be reasonably accurate to refer to Godwin, Hays, *et al.* as a group of reformist writers who

> took the motto *écraser l'infâme*, often because they . . . had direct personal experience of social, moral, or legal oppression, be it domestic, national or international, spiritual or temporal; they were against all distinctions between men which were not based on moral qualities, or virtue; and they were utterly opposed to persecution of individuals, communities, or nations for their beliefs on any subject. Most important of all, they saw history, both past and present, as an account of the efforts of some men to establish a rule of reason against its enemies, which were not imagination and feeling, but error and prejudice.[24]

Godwin was continually monitored by agents of the Pitt administration; accordingly, after the administration suspended *habeas corpus* and initiated the Treason Trials in 1794, he reluctantly agreed to withdraw the politically inflammatory preface he had intended to include in the first edition of *Caleb Williams*.[25] (In light of the ministry's untiring harassment of London's radicals in the mid-1790s, Godwin would likely have faced charges of sedition had he published the preface, which asserts that his narrative of legally sanctioned persecution is "no refined and abstract speculation; it is a study and delineation of things passing in the moral world" [279].) Hays's indictments of the legal and economic oppression of women in *The Victim of Prejudice,* her first novel *Memoirs of Emma Courtney* (1796), and *An Appeal to the Men of Great Britain* (1792) shaped her reputation as one of the period's most forceful and inventive feminist writers.[26] And Holcroft was not merely threatened with prosecution as a consequence of his political convictions—he spent eight weeks in Newgate before he was acquitted of sedition in September 1794. One could go on at length about the radical activism of the Jacobin novelists, but no more evidence is necessary to substantiate the point I want to emphasize here. In short, the wrongful imprisonment episodes of the 1790s diverge from those in previous novels because the Jacobins' representations of criminal justice were informed by their revolutionary politics and their firsthand experience of official surveillance and intimidation. Previous British novelists had exposed social inequities, but their narratives seldom include eruptions of political protest, largely because they were more concerned with private relationships and crises than with critiques of public policy. The Jacobins, by contrast, repeatedly assail their government by portraying the British criminal justice system as a weapon powerful Britons use to oppress innocent victims.

The wrongful imprisonment episodes in Jacobin novels also differ from those in previous British fiction because they show the influence of *The State of the Prisons* (1777), John Howard's commentary on the penal systems of Britain, Ireland, and several continental nations. Howard began his prison inquiries shortly after he was appointed sheriff of Bedfordshire in 1773. When he presented his initial findings to a panel of magistrates, Howard insisted that the county could improve local prison conditions by paying jailers a salary and abolishing the practice of requiring prisoners to pay exorbitant "gaol fees" for food, bedding, delivery of legal documents and so on. The magistrates, he explains, "were properly affected with the grievance . . . but they wanted a precedent for charging the county with the expense."[27] Howard answered this challenge by embarking on a prison inspection tour that encompassed nearly every county in England and Wales. Then he enlarged the scope of his inquiries by studying prison conditions in France, the Netherlands, and Germany. Six months after he returned to Bedfordshire, Howard published *The State of the Prisons in England and Wales*. The book was an immediate, resounding success; it went through numerous editions in Britain and French, Spanish, and German translations were circulated throughout Europe. Two of England's most eminent legal theorists, William Eden and William Blackstone, found Howard's commentaries so convincing that they drafted a statute intended to establish the first English penitentiaries. The *Gentleman's Magazine* reflected the initial public response to Howard's reformist project by rhapsodizing about "the reward which this true and faithful servant will receive from that King of Glory whom in the person of the poor and destitute he visited and comforted when sick and in prison."[28] The writings of James Oglethorpe, Moses Pitt, and other late seventeenth- and early eighteenth-century British prison reformers had offered little more than anecdotes chronicling the most inhumane practices of a few jailers and the most grievous hardships suffered by a few prisoners. Howard, on the other hand, confronted his audience with a minutely detailed study of conditions in every prison he had inspected. In Section VII of *The State of the Prisons*, for instance, he presents the data he had collected in London and in the Home, Norfolk, Midland, Oxford, Western, Northern, Chester, North Wales and South Wales circuits by advancing methodically from county to county, prison to prison, and room to room:

COUNTY BRIDEWELL

PETWORTH. This bridewell has two rooms: one, seventeen feet by ten, the other eighteen by nine, six feet high: too small for the general number of prisoners. No chimney: no glass or shutters to the windows: no court: no water: no employment.

YORKSHIRE

COUNTY GAOL, YORK CASTLE. . . . The day-room for men is only twenty four feet by eight: in it are three cells: in another place nine cells: and three in another. The cells are in general about seven and a half feet by six and a half, and eight and a half high; close and dark; having only either a hole over the door about four inches by eight, or some perforations in the door of about an inch diameter: not any of them to the open air . . . In most of these cells three prisoners are locked up . . . in winter from fourteen to sixteen hours . . . (194–95; 229)

Whenever they concern themselves with prison experience, the Jacobin novelists draw on Howard's writings. Caleb Williams's prison narrative, for instance, echoes *The State of the Prisons* by carefully attending to precise measurements, administrative details, and prisoners' daily routines: "Our dungeons were cells, 7 ½ feet by 6 ½, below the surface of the ground, damp, without window, light or air, except from a few holes worked for that purpose in the door. In some of these miserable receptacles three persons were put to sleep together. . . . [We] were thrust in here at sun set and not liberated till the returning day. This was our situation for fourteen or fifteen hours out of the four and twenty . . . " (161). Nearly everything Williams mentions about his place of imprisonment, from the unwholesome food delivered to him in the "strong room" to the texture of the dirt strewn on the floor, bears the unmistakable stamp of Howard's writings. In fact, Godwin acknowledges his debt to Howard by inserting a footnote to *The State of the Prisons* in Williams's narrative. Scheuermann contends that the purpose of this citation is to indicate that the narrative is a realistic account of conditions in an ordinary British jail, not the product of a radical novelist's imagination: "Godwin's descriptions of [Williams's confinement] . . . are factual if we judge by Howard's descriptions in *The*

State of the Prisons . . . In some cases, Godwin did not even use the worst examples [cited by Howard], perhaps feeling that the reader might reject these darkest truths as unlikely imaginings."[29] While I agree that the footnote underscores the verisimilitude of *Caleb Williams*'s prison episodes, this does not fully explain why Godwin imitates the precision, the scope, and even the prose style of Howard's writings in his fictional representations of wrongful imprisonment. The answer, it seems to me, is that Godwin recognized that Howard had introduced a new and fundamentally different mode of prison reform discourse. Howard occasionally alluded to the practices of individual jailers, but he was primarily concerned with the physical characteristics of prisons, not the ethics of prison officials. He discarded the anecdotal approach of previous prison reform advocates by describing the cells, day-rooms, dungeons, windows, walls, and floors of the nation's prisons in voluminous detail. And by contrasting his domestic findings with data he had collected overseas, Howard persuaded his contemporaries that Britain's prisons had become inferior to those of France, the Netherlands, and other nations in continental Europe.

The Jacobin novelists incorporate all of these features of Howard's writings in their wrongful imprisonment episodes. As I have suggested, the novels of the 1790s highlight the failings of the British criminal justice system rather than focusing on the wrongdoing of corrupt individuals. The Jacobins also follow *The State of the Prisons* by constructing prison episodes that are more elaborately rendered than those in previous novels. As a consequence of this heightened attention to detail, representations of prison experience perform a more central role in the fiction of the 1790s than they had in previous British novels. The Jacobins do not stage cursory prison episodes that occupy a few pages and are never mentioned again; to the contrary, several of their novels (most notably *Caleb Williams*, *The Victim of Prejudice*, and *The Wrongs of Woman*) could be described as prison fiction, narratives in which characters are seized by predatory villains and never recover their autonomy. Moreover, Godwin follows Howard's example by insisting that Britain's prisons have become no less inhumane than those of France and other continental nations. Shortly after Williams is committed to prison, he ridicules his fellow Britons' assumption that only "foreigners" torture prisoners: "We talk of instruments of torture; Englishmen take credit to themselves for having banished the use of them from their happy shore! Alas! he that has observed the secrets of a prison, well knows that there is more torture in the lingering existence of a criminal . . . than in the tangible misery of whips and racks!" (160). Similarly, when a fellow servant sees the prison in which Williams has been confined, he protests that British prisoners are tortured "under our very noses . . . and a parcel of fellows with grave faces swear to us that such things never happen but in France, and other countries the like of that" (180).

In one significant respect, however, the English Jacobins chose not to adopt Howard's mode of prison reform discourse. In spite of his unrivaled degree of expertise, Howard insists in *The State of Prisons* that he wishes to be viewed as a nonpartisan investigator, a public servant whose function is to *adduce* empirical data, not to interpret them or to counsel his audience to take any particular course of action in response to them. "As to what is still wrong," he writes, "I set down matter of fact without amplification; which would in the end rather impede than promote the object of my wishes; that is, the correction of what is really amiss" (3). When Howard indulges in a few sentences of what he calls "amplification," he immediately pauses to apologize: "The writer begs his reader to excuse the frequent egotisms; which he did not know how to avoid, without using circumlocutions that might have been more disgusting" (3). And in the third section of *The State of the Prisons*, Howard asserts that he should not be deemed an authoritative commentator on questions relating to prison management; to the contrary, his role is merely to facilitate the reformist projects of "persons of superior abilities": "I do not pretend to be qualified for drawing up a perfect system of this difficult business; but in order to assist persons of superior abilities in their researches . . . I have added, at the end of the volume, a table of such general heads and particulars as seem to me most deserving of attention" (43). Accordingly, *The State of the Prisons* is, among other things, highly paradoxical: a reformist manifesto in which the reformer's views are overshadowed by a dispassionate recitation of the facts. The Jacobin novelists, by contrast, are anything but dispassionate and refuse to limit themselves to the collection of empirical evidence. Their wrongful imprisonment episodes infuse the raw data presented in *The State of the Prisons* with emotion, narrative energy, and radical ideology and suggest that prison reform discourse has been transformed. It is no longer adequate to confine representations of imprisonment, whether fictional or non-fictional, to anecdotes regarding individual misconduct. In the wake of *The State of the Prisons*, prison experience has become a subject worthy of comprehensive, subtly nuanced examination and the Jacobin novelists who examine it concur that the British criminal justice system is deeply flawed and in urgent need of reform.

NOTES

1. As Booth and a pickpocket named Robinson wander around the prison, they encounter convicts "laughing, singing, and diverting themselves with various kinds of . . . Gambols." Henry Fielding, *Amelia* (1751; Oxford: Oxford Univ., 1971), 27. They see a grief-stricken prisoner who has just learned that his pregnant wife has attempted suicide. They are harangued by a young prostitute who "discharge[s] a Volley of Words, every one of which was too indecent to be repeated" (33). Then they recoil as a man rumored to be a homosexual is savagely attacked by a gang of fellow prisoners. These early passages suggest that *Amelia* will offer an unambiguous indictment of the British criminal justice system, but as the narrative progresses, Fielding begins to convey a profoundly different message. Booth is redeemed, not destroyed, by prison experience. If not for his wrongful confinement in Bondum's house, it seems, he would not have experienced his religious awakening and the series of crises that torments Booth and his family throughout the novel would have continued indefinitely.

2. Fielding, *Amelia*, 510. The title characters of *The Vicar of Wakefield* and *Humphry Clinker* provoke religious epiphanies in others by preaching to their fellow inmates after they are wrongfully jailed. Dr. Primrose observes that after one week of his impromptu sermons "some were penitent, and all attentive." Oliver Goldsmith, *The Vicar of Wakefield* (1766; London: Oxford Univ., 1974), 148. And after Clinker is committed to a prison in Clerkenwell, a turnkey complains that there has been "nothing but canting and praying since the fellow entered the place.—Rabbit him! the tap will be ruined—we han't sold a cask of beer, nor a dozen of wine, since he paid his garnish." Tobias Smollett, *The Expedition of Humphry Clinker* (1748; London: Oxford Univ., 1979), 148.

3. Samuel Richardson, *Clarissa; or, The History of a Young Lady* (1747–48; New York: Viking, 1985), 1070.

4. See John Bender, *Imagining the Penitentiary: Fiction and the Architecture of Mind in Eighteenth-Century England* (Chicago: Univ. of Chicago, 1987) and W. B. Carnochan, *Confinement and Flight: An Essay on English Literature in the Eighteenth Century* (Berkeley: Univ. of California Press, 1977). For broader discussions of law and literature in eighteenth-century Britain that occasionally focus on literary representations of prison experience, see John Zomchick, *Family and the Law in Eighteenth-Century Fiction: The Public Conscience in the Private Sphere* (Cambridge: Cambridge Univ., 1993) and Ian Bell, *Literature and Crime in Augustan England* (London: Routledge, 1991).

5. See, e.g., Mona Scheuermann, *Social Protest in the Eighteenth-Century English Novel* (Columbus: Ohio State Univ., 1985); Marilyn Butler, *Romantics, Rebels and Reactionaries: English Literature and its Background, 1760–1830* (London: Oxford Univ., 1981); Gary Kelly, *Women, Writing, and Revolution, 1790–1827* (London: Oxford Univ., 1993) and *The English Jacobin Novel, 1780–1805* (Oxford: Clarendon, 1976); and Eleanor Ty, *Unsex'd*

Revolutionaries: Five Women Novelists of the 1790s (Toronto: Univ. of Toronto, 1993).

6. Bender, *Imagining the Penitentiary*, 47, 54.

7. The roster of Jacobin novels which contain wrongful imprisonment episodes includes *Caleb Williams*, *The Victim of Prejudice*, Thomas Holcroft's *Anna St. Ives* (1792), and Elizabeth Inchbald's *Nature and Art* (1797). A number of the period's representations of prison experience are more complex and ambiguous than those in previous British novels. While Godwin's Caleb Williams, Emily Melville, and Benjamin and Leonard Hawkins are unequivocally innocent, Mary Raymond in *The Victim of Prejudice* and the unnamed young husband arrested for debt in *Anna St. Ives* are, strictly speaking, guilty of punishable offenses (respectively, failing to pay for lodgings in a boarding-house and signing a note on which the debtor has defaulted). Nonetheless, it would be difficult not to conceive of the punishments of these "guilty" characters as miscarriages of justice—Mary's crime is largely attributable to the misconduct of the aristocratic rake who has seduced and abandoned her and the young husband's sole offense is an attempt to help a relative secure a loan.

8. William Godwin, *Things As They Are; or, The Adventures of Caleb Williams* (1794; London: William Pickering, 1992), 71. Subsequent references to *Caleb Williams* are from this edition and will be cited parenthetically in the text.

9. Godwin also signals his intention to underscore the predatory impulses of his contemporaries in the novel's epigraph: "Amidst the woods the leopard knows his kind;/The tyger preys not on the tyger brood:/Man only is the common foe of man" (4).

10. Mary Hays, *The Victim of Prejudice* (1799; Petersborough, Ontario: Broadview Press, 1996), 167–68. Subsequent references to *The Victim of Prejudice* are from this edition and will be cited parenthetically in the text.

11. Carnochan, *Confinement and Flight*, 19.

12. Thomas Holcroft, *Anna St. Ives* (1792; London: Oxford Univ., 1970), 34–35.

13. Scheuermann, *Social Protest in the Eighteenth-Century English Novel*, 94–95.

14. Scheuermann, *Social Protest in the Eighteenth-Century English Novel*, 95.

15. Fielding, *Amelia*, 327.

16. Richardson's persecuted heroine describes her place of confinement as follows: "A horrid hole of a house, in an alley they call a court; stairs wretchedly narrow, even to the first-floor rooms: and into a den they led me, with broken walls, which had been papered, as I saw by a multitude of tacks, and some torn bits held on by the rusty heads. . . . The floor indeed was clean, but the ceiling was smoked with a variety of figures, and initials of names, that had been the woeful employment of wretches who had no other way to amuse themselves. . . The windows dark and double-barred; and only a little four-

paned eyelet-hole of a casement to let in air . . . in a dark nook stood an old broken-bottomed cane couch, sunk at one corner, and unmortised by the failing of one of its worm-eaten legs, which lay in two pieces under the wretched piece of furniture it could no longer support." Richardson, *Clarissa*, 1064–65.

17. Mary Wollstonecraft, *The Wrongs of Woman; or, Maria, A Fragment* (1798; London: Oxford Univ., 1980), 75.

18. Wollstonecraft, *The Wrongs of Woman*, 79.

19. Scheuermann, *Social Protest in the Eighteenth-Century English Novel*, 232.

20. *Whigs and Hunters: The Origin of the Black Act* (New York: Pantheon Books, 1975), 262. Similarly, William St. Clair observes that Godwin described "how easy and common it was for an unscrupulous landowner to manipulate the law to dominate and oppress his tenants, explaining the links in the mechanisms whereby greater tyrants use economic power (and the associated ties of gratitude and obligation) to create a structure of lesser tyrants obedient to their will." *The Godwins and the Shelleys* (New York: W. W. Norton, 1989), 119.

21. Bender, *Imagining the Penitentiary*, 110.

22. Ty, *Unsex'd Revolutionaries*, xxiv.

23. J. M. S. Tompkins, *The Popular Novel in England, 1770–1800* (Lincoln: Univ. of Nebraska, 1961), 296.

24. Kelly, *The English Jacobin Novel*, 7.

25. St. Clair observes that Godwin believed that he would have been prosecuted for publishing his *Enquiry Concerning Political Justice* (1792) had the volume been less expensive and therefore more easily available to working-class Britons: "In later years, Godwin liked to tell the story that William Pitt personally advised the [Privy Council] that 'a three guinea book could never do much harm among those who had not three shillings to spare' . . . Compared with the *Rights of Man* which was available to farm labourers and factory workers for sixpence in every town and village *Political Justice* could not be regarded as a direct threat to social peace." St. Clair, *The Godwins and the Shelleys*, 85.

26. Hays began to write *Emma Courtney* in 1795 after Godwin urged her to "set out her ideas on the restrictions society imposed on women in the form of a novel." Caroline Franklin, Introduction to *The Victim of Prejudice* (London: Routledge/Thoemmes, 1995), viii. In her *Appeal to the Men of Great Britain*, Hays asserts that her society's oppression of women is especially harmful because it is authorized by law. In particular, she writes that "in forming the laws by which women are governed . . . have not men . . . consulted more their own conveniency, comfort, and dignity, as far as their judgment and foresight served them than that of women?" Mary Hays, *Appeal to the Men of Great Britain in Behalf of Women* (1798; New York: Garland, 1974), 158–59.

27. John Howard, *Prisons and Lazarettos, vol. 1, The State of the Prisons in England and Wales*, ed. Ralph W. England, Jr. (Montclair, N. J.: Patterson

Smith, 1973), 1. Subsequent references to *The State of the Prisons* are from this edition and will be cited parenthetically in the text.

28. Quoted in Martin Southwood, *John Howard, Prison Reformer: An Account of his Life and Travels* (London: Christopher Johnson, 1958), 73.

29. Scheuermann, *Social Protest in the Eighteenth-Century Novel*, 159.

Learning from Experience, or Not: from Chrysippus to Rasselas

JEFFREY BARNOUW

In *Reflections on the Revolution in France* Edmund Burke "appeal[s] to what is so much out of fashion in Paris, I mean to experience . . . . By a slow but well-sustained progress, the effect of each step is watched; the good or ill success of the first, gives light to us in the second; and so, from light to light, we are conducted with safety through the whole series."(281).[1] What is meant by 'experience' in this context involves the continuity suggested by 'slow but well-sustained' and 'through the whole series', but it hinges on the light to be gained from good or ill success of our efforts at each step. More about this 'light' can be gleaned from the passages leading up to this appeal to experience, where Burke emphasizes the value of difficulty. This suggests that we learn more from ill than from good success. Burke argues that the untested rationalist schemes of the French revolutionaries have abandoned "the public interests . . . wholly to chance; I say to chance, because their schemes have nothing in experience to prove their tendency beneficial" (277).

> Their purpose every where seems to have been to evade and slip aside from difficulty. This it has been the glory of the great masters in all the arts to confront, and to overcome;

> and when they had overcome the first difficulty, to turn it into an instrument for new conquests over new difficulties; thus to enable them to extend the empire of their science . . . He that wrestles with us strengthens our nerves, and sharpens our skill. Our antagonist is our helper. This amicable conflict with difficulty obliges us to an intimate acquaintance with our object, and compels us to consider it in all its relations (278).
>
> It is this inability to wrestle with difficulty which has obliged the arbitrary assembly of France to commence their schemes of reform with abolition and total destruction (279).
>
> No difficulties occur in what has never been tried. Criticism is almost baffled in discovering the defects of what has not existed; and eager enthusiasm, and cheating hope, have all the wide field of imagination in which they may expatiate with little or no opposition (280).

Particularly the last passage sounds Johnsonian in resonance, but the principle which Burke is setting out is itself pervasive in Johnson's writing. But, as here in Burke, it is more often observed in the breach in Johnson, that is, observed or dramatized in its absence in others' ways of acting. I want eventually to pursue aspects of the idea of 'learning from experience, or not' in writings of Johnson. Let me first turn to a writer who seems to me to have had seminal subliminal influence on Johnson in this respect, Francis Bacon, and then to a key antecedent of Bacon.

Bacon was a main (if largely unrecognized) source of a moral psychology flourishing in eighteenth-century Britain, exemplified in Johnson and Burke, but also Hume and others, which drew at the same time on a form of Stoicism and on the experimentalist frame of mind of the New Science. This psychology, with its strong moral implications, is a significant component of what is coming to be recognized as a distinctive English Enlightenment, or, if we were to co-opt the well-established Scottish Enlightenment, a distinctive British Enlightenment.[2] The present paper is meant as a contribution to this recognition.

Bacon understood his idea of experimental science as a discipline, a self-disciplining of the mind. The human mind is prone to project its own wishes on what it perceives, both within perception itself and as it makes the world over imaginatively, for example in poetry and in metaphysics.[3] Two aphorisms from the *New Organon* spell this out.

> XLV. The human understanding is of its own nature prone to suppose the existence of more order and regularity in the

world than it finds . . .[4]

> XLVI. The human understanding when it has once adopted an opinion (either as being the received opinion or as being agreeable to itself) draws all things else to support and agree with it. And though there be a great number and weight of instances to be found on the other side, yet these it either neglects and despises, or else by some distinction sets aside and rejects; in order that by this great and pernicious predetermination the authority of its former conclusions may remain inviolate. And therefore it was a good answer that was made by one who when they showed him hanging in a temple a picture of those who had paid their vows as having escaped shipwreck, and would have him say whether he did not now acknowledge the power of the gods,—"Aye," asked he again, "but where are they painted that were drowned after their vows?" . . . With far more subtlety does this mischief insinuate itself into philosophy and the sciences . . . . It is the peculiar and perpetual error of the human intellect to be more moved and excited by affirmatives than by negatives; whereas it ought properly to hold itself indifferently disposed toward both alike. Indeed, in the establishment of any true axiom, the negative instance is the more forcible of the two (472).

Bacon made this point with regard to the established presuppositions that guide scientific inquiry in an earlier aphorism of the *New Organon*,

> XXV. The axioms now in use, having been suggested by a scanty and manipular experience and a few particulars of most general occurrence, are made for the most part just large enough to fit and take these in: and therefore it is no wonder if they do not lead to new particulars.
> And if some opposite instance, not observed or not known before, chance to come in the way, the axiom is rescued and preserved by some frivolous distinction; whereas the truer course would be to correct the axiom itself (466).

Bacon's moral philosophy, as presented in the *Advancement of Learning*, defines itself by opposition, among other tendencies, to the Stoicism of Epictetus, "which presupposeth that felicity must be placed in those things which are in our power, lest we be liable to fortune and disturbance" (322). "It censureth likewise that abuse of philosophy which grew general about the time of Epictetus, in converting it into an occupation or profession; as if the purpose had been, not to resist and extinguish perturbations, but to fly and avoid the causes of them, and to shape a particular kind and course of life to that end" (323). Thus he agrees, as he says, with Diogenes, who commended, not those who abstained, but those who sustained.

Bacon's difference from and with Epictetus becomes clearer where he appropriates that late Stoic's initial distinction for his own moral philosophy. "First therefore, in this, as in all things which are practical, we ought to cast up our account, what is in our power and what not; for the one may be dealt with by way of alteration, but the other by way of application only" (333). Things of nature or fortune which we cannot control or change must be dealt with by application; they are to be overcome by being suffered and endured. This may at first sound 'stoic' in the most traditional sense, but a qualification makes the difference evident.

> But when we speak of suffering, we do not speak of a dull and neglected suffering, but of a wise and industrious suffering, which draweth and contriveth use and advantage out of that which seemeth adverse and contrary; which is that property which we call Accommodating or Applying. Now the wisdom of application resteth principally in the exact and distinct knowledge of the precedent state or disposition unto which we do apply: for we cannot fit a garment, except we first take measure of the body" (334).

In other words, we can only learn from the failure of our efforts if we determine exactly what expectations were disappointed, that is, which assumptions or convictions were shown to be mistaken by the result. Then we try to 'correct the axiom' to the extent it is in our power, using what we have learned from the resistance provided by the event. 'Industrious suffering' draws use and advantage out of what seems adverse and contrary by taking it as 'negative feedback'. Being able, from experience, to anticipate the consequences of contemplated actions allows us to guide our actions successfully by enlisting the support and avoiding the opposition of 'nature' or reality.

This is neither a manipulative 'instrumental reason' bent on dominating nature, reducing it to the mere raw material of human purposes, nor passive acquiescing in external causal necessity, but rather something beyond the grasp of this simple-minded opposition, the sort of experience that builds character and achieves wisdom. When Johnson praises Shakespeare as "the poet of nature," it is for the knowledge of life expressed in his works, gained through experience of the sort Bacon intends. Johnson rejects the idea that Shakespeare's capacity to capture life derives from nature (i.e.

genius) rather than art and attributes it to cumulative experience not unlike the collective judgment that gradually established Shakespeare's reputation.

> [T]he power of nature is only the power of using to any certain purpose the materials which diligence procures, or opportunity supplies. Nature gives no man knowledge, and when images are collected by study and experience, can only assist in combining or applying them. Shakespeare, however favoured by nature, could impart only what he had learned; and as he must increase his ideas, like other mortals, by gradual acquisition, he, like them, grew wiser as he grew older, could display life better, as he knew it more, and instruct it with more efficacy, as he was himself more amply instructed.[5]

Bacon's moral philosophy is closely tied up with the moral implications of his psychology of the scientific enterprise, which allies it to the Christian principles of faith, hope and charity, opposing it to pride. In the concluding words of "The Clue to the Maze," "The supposition of the sufficiency of man's mind hath lost the means thereof " (402). Pride in supposed knowledge led the Aristotelian-Scholastic tradition to present 'science' as a perfected whole, not as something to be critically built on and improved, and conversely presupposed impossibilities for human enterprise "tending to the circumscription of man's power, and to artificial despair; killing in men not only the comfort of imagination, but the industry of trial"(394). In a later version this becomes: "to the unfair circumscription of human power, and to a deliberate and factitious despair; which not only disturbs the auguries of hope, but also cuts the sinews and spur of industry, and throws away the chances of experience itself" (507, Aphorism LXXXVIII). The chances of experience, which include taking advantage of what happens without our intending or expecting it, would be lost if we did not try, and we would not try without "the auguries of hope." It may be such "auguries of hope," and not wish-fulfilling fantasies (about which Bacon wrote tellingly with regard to poetry and metaphysics), which are meant by "comfort of imagination."

The "industry of trial" is an active version of "industrious suffering". There is a related sense of openness to negative feedback implicit in Bacon's maxim, "nature to be commanded must be obeyed," where obedience to nature is a matter of observing (in both senses, taking note of and following, as one follows or observes a law) cause and effect relations or consequences. The full context in Aphorism III of the *New Organon* shows this, "Human knowledge and human power meet in one; for where the cause is not known the effect cannot be produced. Nature to be commanded must be obeyed; and that which in contemplation is as the cause is in operation as the rule" (462). Cause-and-effect relations in nature are the basis of means-and-end relations in human practice, which renders the results of our efforts crucial to cognition.

It is possible that the early Greek Stoics (as distinguished from Epictetus) meant something akin to Bacon's position when they defined virtue as 'living in accordance with nature'. The Stoic founder, Zeno, "represented the end as: 'living in agreement'," but Cleanthes, supposedly taking this for an incomplete predicate, added 'with nature'. "Chrysippus wanted to make this clearer and expressed it thus: 'living in accordance with experience of what happens by nature.'"[6] Here 'things that happen' (*sumbainonta*) has the sense of consequences, just as Zeno thought of causes as causes of events (*sumbebêkos*). Chrysippus saw man as defined by the capacity for a kind of synthesizing (in fact predicative) perception which other animals did not have, which, he added, "amounts to his possessing the conception of 'following' and directly grasping, on account of 'following', the idea of sign. For sign is itself of the form 'if this, then that.' Therefore the holding true of the sign follows from man's nature and constitution."[7] The human capacity for grasping consequences is providential, demonstrating our fitness for this *logos*-ordered cosmos.

Realizing fully its intrinsic inclination, a mind that cognitively mirrors the consistency and necessity of the cosmos comes to have the same character. As Emile Bréhier points out, "it is the same word, *akolouthia*, which designates the consistent conduct [*conséquente avec elle-même*] of the sage, the concatenation of causes which defines will or destiny, and finally the link that unites the antecedent to the consequent in a true proposition." He adds that Epictetus "repeated it many times: one cannot have the conduct of a sage if one has not learned 'what thing is the consequence of another thing'."[8]

Diogenes Laertius also cites the emendation of Chrysippus, quoted above from Stobaeus, but with an explanatory gloss. "Further, living in accordance with virtue is equivalent to living in accordance with what happens by nature, as Chrysippus says in *On Ends* book 1: for our own natures are part of the nature of the whole." "The nature consequential upon which one ought to live is taken by Chrysippus to be both the common and, particularly, the human."[9]

The reference to human nature recalls the Stoic doctrine of *oikeiôsis* which Diogenes has just outlined. Fully developed, this doctrine is a psychobiological grounding of the ethical character of human motivation, epitomized in a formula: "According to Chrysippus, the impulse of man is reason prescribing action to him; he has written thus in his book *On law*."[10]

> They [the Stoics] say that an animal has self-preservation as the object of its first impulse, since nature from the beginning makes it congenial to itself [*oikeiousês*], as Chrysippus says in his *On Ends*, book 1. The first thing congenial [*oikeion*] to every animal, he says, is its own constitution and the consciousness of this . . . . This is why [or how] the animal rejects what is harmful and accepts (pursues) what is congenial to it.[11]

When Chrysippus says the impulse of man is reason prescribing action to him, he means that man recognizes imperatives directed to him by his own nature on the basis of insight into causes and the anticipation of consequences in the cosmos and in his relation to it. It may help us to understand how imperative reason can develop from the fundamental level of *oikeiôsis*, the self-preservative drive or orientation to one's own interest, if one compares it to the continuity established by Hobbes between *jus naturale*, 'right of nature,' and *lex naturalis*, 'law of nature.' The latter is "a precept or general rule, found out by reason, by which a man is forbidden to do that which is destructive of his life or taketh away the means of preserving the same."[12] This 'forbidden' is the germ of an ethical human constitution that must develop and be developed.

In *On Ends* Cicero has his Stoic representative Cato say, "We are left with the conclusion that the final good is a life in which one applies knowledge of those things that happen by nature, selecting those in accordance with nature and rejecting those contrary to nature, that is—a life in agreement and consistent with nature."[13] The blending of the prudential and the ethical which we find in Bacon and Hobbes is already clearly established in Chrysippus. "They say that the good man experiences nothing contrary to his desire or impulse or purpose on account of the fact that in all such cases he acts with reserve and encounters no obstacles which are unanticipated."[14]

The Stoic ethical stance was originally an openness to experience, not inward withdrawal from it. It was linked to intellectual curiosity and a confidence in that reason which is oriented to experience and reality or 'nature'. Bacon's sense of man as the servant and interpreter of nature, observing its cause-and-effect 'rules' and anticipating particular consequences, was the key to his "*Plus Ultra!*," his motto for the New Science, which he likens to the New World discovered by daring to go beyond the Pillars of Hercules. No longer clinging to the shores of what we think we already know, but, armed with the 'compass' of the New Method, we should commit ourselves "to the waves of experience," (432) "to the uncertainties and difficulties and solitudes." (434) "A new world beckons . . . Not to try is a greater hazard than to fail."[15] Trying is crucial because we learn most from our mistakes and because we can never know what is possible without trying.

Trying is an essential element of experience. This is evident in its Greek root *peira*, which suggests trial and risk, related etymologically not only to 'empirical' but to 'peril' and 'pirate'. One must venture something in experience in order for it to be profitable even in failure, because the element of real disappointment informs our learning from it. Another important point about experience as understood by Bacon is that pleasure attends not only the accomplishment, the end result, but the progress toward that. Bacon gives priority to what he calls Active Good in light of

> the consideration of our estate to be mortal and exposed to fortune . . . the pre-eminence likewise of this Active Good is upheld by the affection which is natural in man towards variety and proceeding . . . .[I]n enterprises, pursuits, and purposes of life, there is much variety; whereof men are sensible with pleasure in their inceptions, progressions, recoils, reintegrations, approaches, and attainings to their ends: so as it was well said: *Vita sine proposito languida et vaga est* [life without an objective is languid and tiresome]. (324)

Not only in the enterprise of the New Science but in life too, not to try is a greater hazard than to fail. We must make efforts and risk failure in order to know what is possible, what we are capable of. We learn through meeting resistance to our wishes and will. Finally, in a main aspect of the Protestant Ethic, life without effort and endeavor is unworthy. The moral importance of trying reverberates in Johnson's essay, *Adventurer* 111,

> To strive with difficulties, and to conquer them, is the highest human felicity; the next, is to strive, and deserve to conquer: but he whose life has passed without a contest, and who can boast neither success nor merit, can survey himself only as a useless filler of existence; and if he is content with his own character, must owe his satisfaction to insensibility. (Y 2,451)[16]

His essays are consistently dialogical, approaching their object successively from various angles to bring out different aspects. This makes it risky to cite passages without their context as if we could be sure to have Johnson's own views. He had mastered this characteristic mode of dialectic by *Rambler* 2. It begins by picking a topic, that is, introducing a *topos* or commonplace, which must initially have something to be said for it simply because it is common or established.

> That the mind of man is never satisfied with the objects immediately before it, but is always breaking away from the present moment, and losing itself in schemes of future felicity; and that we forget the proper use of the time now in our power, to provide for the enjoyment of that which, perhaps, may never be granted us, has been frequently remarked; and as this practice is a commodious subject of raillery to the gay, and of declamation to the serious, it has been ridiculed with all the pleasantry of wit, and exaggerated with all the amplifications of rhetoric. (Y 3,9)

Johnson enjoys himself in this vein for several paragraphs, exposing (and exemplifying) the practice of "wantoning in common topicks," then turns to serious examination of the issue.

> This quality of looking forward into futurity seems the unavoidable condition of a being, whose motions are gradual, and whose life is progressive: as his powers are limited, he must use means for the attainment of his ends, and intend first what he performs last; as, by continual advances from his first stage of existence, he is perpetually varying the horizon of his prospects, he must always discover new motives of action, new excitements of fear, and allurements of desire.
>
> The end therefore which at present calls forth our efforts will be found, when it is once gained, to be only one of the means to some remoter end. The natural flights of the human mind are not from pleasure to pleasure, but from hope to hope. (Y 3,10)

The psychology put forward here owes something to that of Hobbes, whose point in denying a *summum bonum* was much the same as Johnson's.

> [T]he felicity of this life consisteth not in the repose of a mind satisfied. For there is no such *Finis ultimus* (utmost aim) nor *Summum Bonum* (greatest good) as is spoken of in the books of the old moral philosophers. Nor can a man any more live, whose desires are at an end, than he whose senses and imaginations are at a stand. Felicity is a continual progress of the desire, from one object to another, the attaining of the former being still but the way to the latter.[17]

A corollary of this is Hobbes's recognition of what Bacon called 'pleasure in proceeding' or 'the felicity of continuance and proceeding.'[18] Still, auguries of hope, anticipations of the goal, are essential to motivating efforts to get there. In *Rambler* 2 there are hints that hope may work to undermine pursuit, if it leads to the mind's "losing itself in schemes of future felicity."

The function of hope should be to motivate action. According to *Rambler* 67, hope "begins with the first power of comparing our actual with our possible state, and attends us through every stage and period, always urging us forward to new acquisitions." (Y 3,354) Not as itself a source of pleasure, but only by urging us forward to and in action can hope contribute to lasting happiness, because then it must lead either to its fulfillment or to the sort of disappointment that is crucial to learning from experience and coming to hope and strive for something attainable.

In *Ramber* 129 Johnson starts from the topic (*topos*, commonplace) of warning against temerity. "But there is likewise some danger lest timorous prudence should be inculcated, till courage and enterprize are wholly repressed, and the mind congealed in perpetual inactivity by the fatal influence of frigorifick wisdom." (Y 4,322) He says moralists should give equal time to "the folly of presupposing impossibilities and anticipating frustration." Vain man may be ignorant of his own weakness, but "man is no less ignorant of his own powers, and might perhaps have accomplished a thousand designs, which the prejudices of cowardice restrained him from attempting." (Y 4,324)

Johnson, or 'the Rambler' (in *Rambler* 25), finds rashness preferable to its counterpart, cowardice, or presumption preferable to despondency, or "heady confidence, which promises victory without contest, [to] heartless pusillanimity, which shrinks back from the thought of great undertakings, confounds difficulty with impossibility, and considers all advancement towards any new attainment as irreversibly prohibited." "Presumption will be easily corrected," he writes. "Every experiment will teach caution, and miscarriages will hourly show, that attempts are not always rewarded with success." (Y 3,137)

> It is the advantage of vehemence and activity, that they
> are always hastening to their own reformation; because they
> incite us to try whether our expectations are well grounded,
> and therefore detect the deceits which they are apt to
> occasion. But timidity is a disease of the mind more obstinate
> and fatal; for a man once persuaded that any impediment is
> insuperable, has given it, with respect to himself, that strength
> and weight which it had not before. He can scarcely strive
> with vigour and perseverance, when he has no hope of gaining
> the victory; and since he never will try his strength, can
> never discover the unreasonableness of his fears. (138)

This text echoes Bacon as it goes on to the intellectual cowardice proper
to "men devoted to literature," which tends "to depress the alacrity of
enterprise, and, by consequence, to retard the improvement of science."
The debilitating influence of others is no excuse, however, for "it is the
business of every man to try whether his faculties may not happily co-
operate with his desires; and since they whose proficiency he admires,
knew their own force only by the event, he needs but engage in the same
undertaking, with equal spirit, and may reasonably hope for equal success."
(139) The essay concludes, "Every man, who proposes to grow eminent
by learning, should carry in his mind, at once, the difficulty of excellence,
and the force of industry; and remember that fame is not conferred but as
the recompense of labour, and that labour vigourously continued, has not
often failed of its reward." (140)

The same dynamic that corrects presumption also attaches to other
passions. *Rambler* 47 makes a fundamental distinction among the passions
in this regard.

> Of the passions with which the mind of man is agitated, it
> may be observed, that they naturally hasten towards their
> own extinction by inciting and quickening the attainment of
> their objects. Thus fear urges our flight, and desire animates
> our progress; and if there are some which perhaps may be
> indulged till they out-grow the good appropriated to their
> satisfaction, as is frequently observed of avarice and ambition,
> yet their immediate tendency is to some means of happiness
> really existing, and generally within the prospect. (Y 3,253)

One exception is sorrow, because it "dwells upon objects that have lost or changed their existence." It is nonetheless unreasonable to try to avoid the possibility of sorrow, that is, "not to gain happiness for fear of losing it." (257) We must have recourse to antidotes, the best of which is employment, activity motivated by some other passion, since sorrow cannot meet its object.

In another variation on this pervasive theme, or more properly, this complex of interrelated topics, and opposing stoicism (or the convenient cliché of it), he writes in *Rambler* 32,

> Patience and submission are very carefully to be distinguished from cowardice and indolence. We are not to repine, but we may lawfully struggle; for the calamities of life, like the necessities of nature, are calls to labour, and exercises of diligence. When we feel any pressure of distress, we are not to conclude that we can only obey the will of heaven by languishing under it, any more than when we perceive the pain of thirst we are to imagine that water is prohibited. (Y 3,177)

Johnson examines the precept "not to take pleasure in any thing, of which it is not in our power to secure the possession to ourselves," and asks, "is it not like advice, not to walk lest we should stumble?" (179) In much the same spirit in his 'Georgics of the Mind' Bacon supported the Sophist who places felicity "in much desiring and much enjoying" against a 'stoic' Socrates, judging that "to abstain from the use of thing that you may not feel the want of it; to shun the want that you may not fear the loss of it; are the precautions of pusillanimity and cowardice."[19]

These same interrelated themes can be encountered throughout the writings of Hume, but we will limit the comparison to a single essay, "The Stoic." Subtitled, "Or the man of action and virtue,"[20] its opening theme is that man is distinguished from beast by an obligation or imperative derived from his constitution. Nature "allows not such noble faculties to lie lethargic or idle; but urges him, by necessity, to employ, on every emergence, his utmost *art* and *industry*." Humans should become the objects of their own industry, not only improving their bodily powers and faculties, but those of the mind, which requires even greater "industry and application." Hume's Stoic understands virtue as the art practiced in pursuit of "the great end of all human industry, [which] is the attainment of happiness," and the key to this art is learning from our mistakes. "If mistakes be often, be inevitably committed, let us register these mistakes; let us consider their causes; let us weigh their importance; let us inquire for their remedies."[21]

The second theme of Hume's essay is "that this labour itself is the chief ingredient of the felicity to which [man aspires], and that every enjoyment soon becomes insipid and distasteful, when not acquired by fatigue and industry." Implicitly correcting a conventional view of the Stoic position, Hume then insists the sage does not preserve himself in "philosophical indifference, and rest contented with lamenting the miseries of mankind, without ever employing himself for their relief," since "he knows that in this sullen *Apathy,* neither true wisdom nor true happiness can be found." The antidote to *apatheia* which Hume proposes here is the deliberate development of the social passions, a venerable Stoic exercise.[22]

Experience is something continual and cumulative. Since it works by self-correction, each increment builds on the last because it interacts with it. *Rambler* 41 contrasts the instinct of animals with the reason of humans. The former have "scarce any power of comparing the present with the past, and regulating their conclusions from experience." (Y 3,222) Johnson identifies this capacity with reason, and exemplifies it with the ability to participate in an ongoing technology.

> The sparrow that was hatched last spring makes her first nest the ensuing season, of the same materials, and with the same art, as in any following year. . . . [H]e that contemplates a ship and a bird's nest, will not be long without finding out, that the idea of the one was impressed at once, and continued through all the progressive descents of the species, without variation or improvement; and that the other is the result of experiments compared with experiments, has grown, by accumulated observation, from less to greater excellence, and exhibits the collective knowledge of different ages, and various professions. (Y 3,223)

Bacon deliberately modeled his new experimental science on practical arts, that is, the craft knowledge which is concerned to make something that works. The value of experimentation is owing in part to its replicating the contact with the workings of things that is essential to *technê*, the technological application of knowledge. The importance of feedback from failure in such a setting is evident. In this connection one should recall *Adventurer* 99, on projectors and the significance of their failures and of how others regard these failures.

It has always been the practice of mankind, to judge of

actions by the event. The same attempts, conducted in the same manner, but terminated by different success, produce different judgements: they who attain their wishes, never want celebrators of their wisdom and their virtue; and they that miscarry, are quickly discovered to have been defective not only in mental but in moral qualities. ... (Y 2,429)

This Species of injustice has so long prevailed in universal practice, that it seems likewise to have infected speculation. ... By this unreasonable distribution of praise and blame, none have suffered oftener than projectors, whose rapidity of imagination and vastness of design raise such envy in their fellow mortals, that every eye watches for their fall, and every heart exults at their distresses. (430)

Though he brings up negative aspects of ambitious projectors, particularly political, and refers to Rowley's attempts at perpetual motion and Boyle's at transmutation, this essay is more univocal and straightforward than most, in criticism of those who disparage projectors. Johnson singles out for vindication the species of projectors

who are searching out new powers of nature, or contriving new works of art [i.e. technology], but who are yet persecuted with incessant obloquy, and whom the universal contempt with which they are treated, often debars from that success which their industry would obtain, if it were permitted to act without opposition.

They who find themselves inclined to censure new undertakings, only because they are new, should consider, that the folly of projection is very seldom the folly of a fool: it is commonly the ebullition of a capacious mind, crowded with variety of knowledge, and heated with intenseness of thought; it proceeds often from the consciousness of uncommon powers, from the confidence of those who, having already done much, are easily persuaded that they can do more . . . .(Y 2,433)

That the attempts of such men will often miscarry, we may reasonably expect; yet from such men, and such only, are we to hope for the cultivation of those parts of nature which yet lie yet waste, and the invention of those arts which are yet wanting to the felicity of life. (434)

This essay, in its entirety, can (and should) be taken as a gloss on chapter 6 of Rasselas, the "Dissertation on the Art of Flying." *Adventurer* 99 continues,

> Men unaccustomed to reason and researches think every enterprise impracticable which is extended beyond common effects, or comprises many intermediate operations. Many that presume to laugh at projectors, would consider a flight through the air in a winged chariot, and the movement of a mighty engine by the steam of water, as equally the dreams of mechanic lunacy . . . .
>
> Those who have attempted much, have seldom failed to perform more than those who never deviate from the common roads of action: many valuable preparations of chemistry, are supposed to have risen from unsuccessful inquiries after the grand elixir; it is, therefore, just to encourage those, who endeavour to enlarge the power of art, since they often succeed beyond expectation; and when they fail, may sometimes benefit the world even by their miscarriages.

At the outset of Chapter 6 of *Rasselas* we are told that the 'artist' was eminent for having "contrived many engines both of use and recreation," and various examples are given of his skill and success. The Prince knew of these and so was "willing to fancy that he could do more; yet resolved to enquire further before he suffered hope to afflict him by disappointment."[23] He tells the experimenter, "I am afraid that your imagination prevails over your skill... Every animal has his element assigned to him." The mild satire attaching to these standard objections should not be allowed to obscure the telling correlation that precedes them: hope should be avoided because it exposes one to possible disappointment. The artist's response is also standard, "Nothing will ever be attempted, if all possible objections must first be overcome," but it is a point which Johnson followed Bacon in thinking important, along with the indispensability of hope for endeavor.

The artist tries and fails. The next chapter begins, "The prince was not much afflicted by this disaster, having suffered himself to hope for a happier event only because he had no other means of escape in view." (29) He is not much afflicted because he did not really hope. His relative lack of disappointment is an important reaction the reader should note along with the terror and vexation of the experimentalist. A similar relation obtains in the encounter with the stoic in Chapter 18, who breaks down emotionally at the death of his daughter. This shows the failure of an extreme form (and cliché) of stoicism, not unlike the failure of the mechanical artist.

Again, the response of Rasselas is more telling. "'Sir,' said the prince, "mortality is an event by which a wise man can never be surprised." As the philosopher says, he speaks "like one who has never felt the pangs of separation." (75) Since he can go on spouting such 'stoicism', what in fact has Rasselas learned from this encounter? "The prince, whose humanity would not suffer him to insult misery with reproof, went away convinced of the emptiness of rhetorical sound, and the inefficacy of polished periods and studied sentences." (76)

In each case he could have learned something, from the experience of others, about the power of passion. But the experience of both the artificer and the stoic remain foreign and closed to Rasselas. Failing to share in their experience, he cannot profit vicariously from it. This is a fundamental configuration, repeated and varied throughout *Rasselas*. Before we turn finally to Rasselas there is a related strain in the *Life of Mr. Richard Savage* that should be pointed out, his insulation from experience or, more particularly, from the 'negative instances' it afforded him.

Of the beginning of his public career Johnson writes, "as whatever he received was the gift of chance, which might as well favour him at one time as another, he was tempted to squander what he had, because he always hoped to be immediately supplied."[24] An epitome of his attitude: he would go to the tavern trusting "for the reckoning to the liberality of his company," often people he did not know, and so charm them that "this conduct indeed very seldom drew upon him those inconveniences that might be feared by any other person." (95)

With regard to the reception of his work, he was unable to take criticism or neglect as a reflection on his own efforts but found external explanations for it that amounted to excuses.

> By arts like these, arts which every man practises in some degree, and to which too much of the little tranquility of life is to be ascribed, Savage was always able to live at peace with himself. Had he indeed only made use of these expedients to alleviate the loss, or want, of fortune or reputation, or any other advantage which is not in man's power to bestow on himself, they might have been justly mentioned as instances of a philosophical mind. . . .
>
> But the danger of this pleasing intoxication must not be concealed; nor indeed can any one, after having observed the life of Savage, need to be cautioned against it. By imputing

none of his miseries to himself he continued to act upon the same principles, and to follow the same path; was never made wiser by his sufferings, nor preserved by one misfortune from falling into another. He proceeded throughout his life to tread the same steps on the same circle; always applauding his past conduct, or at least forgetting it, to amuse himself with phantoms of happiness which were dancing before him; and willingly turned his eyes from the light of reason, when it would have discovered the illusion, and shown him, what he never wished to see, his real state. (103)

Johnson extracts from this pattern the judgment that "the reigning errour of his life was that he mistook the love for the practice of virtue." (103–4) But his narrative suggests another 'reigning error', in an unfamiliar guise. In context it is praise when Johnson says, "His distresses, however afflictive, never dejected him," (118) yet his buoyancy, resilience, cheerfulness, comes to seem a liability, shielding him from experience. He bore his misfortunes "not only with decency, but with cheerfulness, nor was his gaiety clouded even by his last disappointment." (124) Johnson considers this "the insurmountable obstinacy of his spirit," but in insistent variations on the theme he insinuates the negative aspect of Savage's inveterate cheerfulness.

"It is observable, that in these various scenes of misery, he was always disengaged and cheerful; he at times pursued his studies, and at others continued or enlarged his epistolary correspondence, nor was he ever so far dejected as to endeavour to procure and increase his allowance by any other methods than accusations and reproaches." (131) He declared "his resolution to publish a pamphlet, that the world might know how 'he had been used' [in his final imprisonment]. The pamphlet was never written, for he in a very short time recovered his usual tranquility, and cheerfully applied himself to more inoffensive studies. . . . He seemed to resign himself to that as well as to other misfortunes, and lose the remembrance of it in his amusements and employments." (134)

Overtly Johnson praises this trait, but his justification takes the praise back. "Surely the fortitude of the man deserves, at least, to be mentioned with applause, and whatever faults may be imputed to him, the virtue of 'suffering well' cannot be denied him. The two powers which, in the opinion of Epictetus, constituted a wise man are those of 'bearing' and 'forbearing', which cannot indeed be affirmed to have been equally possessed by Savage, but it was too manifest that the want of one obliged him very *frequently* to practice the other." (135) The same fatal balance of traits reappears in a further judgment: "He had the peculiar felicity that his attention never deserted him; he was present to every object, and regardful of the most trifling occurrences. He had the art of escaping from his own reflections, and accommodating himself to every new scene." (139) The avoidance of feedback reinforces a false openness to experience, false because the present has no future as a meaningful past. Savage "disregarded all considerations that opposed his present passions. . . . Whatever was his predominant inclination, neither hope nor fear hindered him from complying with it, nor had opposition any other effect than to heighten his ardour and irritate his vehemence." (137) Johnson's praise here and his use of the term 'felicity' may not be ironic. But absorption in the disconnected present is brought back two paragraphs later in a moralistic context. "It cannot be said that he made use of his abilities for the direction of his own conduct; an irregular and dissipated manner of life had made him the slave of every passion that happened to be excited by the presence of its object. . . . He was not master of his own motions, nor could promise anything for the next day." (139–40) The capacity to be taken up by things present is part of Savage's cheerfulness; it is an indifference to the future, the possible consequences, implicit in things present.

In the same way, for Rasselas, hope is not a future-regarding passion, but a state he can be comfortable in, a self-satisfying self-sufficient condition. This is a key to the psychology of the prince and to the structure of the satire which generates and shapes the work, *the History of Rasselas*. It is a cautionary tale for those "who listen with credulity to the whispers of fancy, and pursue with eagerness the phantoms of hope; who expect that age will perform the promises of youth, and that the deficiencies of the present day will be supplied by the morrow." (7) The fact that hope provides them with phantoms and not real objects to pursue is a reflection of their own passivity: they expect that things will be provided without the need for real pursuit.

The not at all paradoxical effect of Happy Valley conditioning and treatment, in which supposedly nothing is left to be desired, is that Rasselas is discontented. But his lament about how is he burdened with himself and his capacity to fear pain not felt, shrink at evils recollected and "start at evils anticipated," becomes a mode of self-satisfaction. "With observations like these the prince amused himself as he returned, uttering them with a plaintive voice, yet with a look that discovered him to feel some complacence in his own perspicacity." (14) "If I had any known want, I should have a certain wish; that wish would excite endeavour....I fancy that I should be happy if I had something to persue." (16) Wishes are of value because they excite endeavor, yet Rasselas's wishes become self-sufficient mental surrogates for endeavor.

In Chapter 4, 'The Prince Continues to Grieve and Muse,' "this first beam of hope that had been ever darted into his mind" becomes "a secret stock of happiness," (17) and Rasselas begins to indulge himself royally in wish-fulfillment phantasies. This self-gratifying turn sets the pattern for his future non-development.

For twenty months "he busied himself so intensely in visionary bustle that he forgot his real solitude; and, amidst hourly preparations for the various incidents of human affairs, neglected to consider by what means he should mingle with mankind." (18) He could neglect to consider the means because he still had no ends or purposes that actually moved him. His incessant musing is finally halted by recognition that he is musing his life away, but the "consciousness of his own folly" (19) merely replaces the musing as another self-sufficient state of mind. "These sorrowful meditations fastened on his mind; he passed four months in resolving to lose no more time in idle resolves, and was awakened to more vigorous exertion by hearing a maid who had broken a porcelain cup remark that what cannot be repaired is not to be regretted." (20) In the next chapter we read that Rasselas, "having now known the blessing of hope, resolved never to despair." (21)

Hope is a blessing if it leads to efforts at realization; at best a mixed blessing if it provides solace and contentment that replaces and undercuts any sense of the need to act. And is resolving never to despair an idle resolve? Certainly, Johnson has done what he can to make us sensitive to the possible emptiness of 'resolve', when it is taken as a mental act or state apart from a particular effort.[25] It then becomes a supposed preparation for action which can indefinitely postpone it.

He continues in the next sentence, "In these fruitless searches he spent ten months. The time, however, passed cheerfully away: in the morning he rose with new hope, in the evening applauded his diligence, and in the night slept sound after his fatigue." Here too, as in the psychology of Savage, a simulacrum of hope sustains cheerfulness because it never commits itself to any chance of disappointment. The attempt with the flying machine comes at this point, and its failure does not really matter, to Rasselas, because he does not really give in to hope.

Rasselas's relation to all the endeavors he observes later is detachment; he is merely the observer, and Imlac supports and frames this abstraction of 'looking on'. "Whatever be the consequence of my experiment," Rasselas tells him before they know how to escape, "I am resolved to judge with my own eyes of the various conditions of men, and then to make deliberately my *choice of life*." (56) Detached observation does not lead us know the conditions of men; for that we must experience them, at the very least by participating sympathetically in them. At the end of chapter 15, after they have escaped and are approaching Cairo, we read, "They had no pretensions to judge for themselves, and referred the whole scheme" to the direction of Imlac. He tells Rasselas, "you will see all the conditions of humanity, and enable yourself at leisure to make your *choice of life*." (63) They study the language for two years, "while Imlac was preparing to set before them the various ranks and conditions of mankind." (65)

Rasselas says, "I have here the world before me; I will review it at leisure: surely happiness is somewhere to be found." (68) But the next chapter informs us, "The prince soon concluded that he should never be happy in a course of life of which he was ashamed. He thought it unsuitable to a reasonable being to act without a plan, and to be sad or cheerful only by chance. 'Happiness,' said he, ''must be something solid and permanent, without fear and without uncertainty." (69)

Rasselas has taken the 'hap' out of 'happy'. For that reason, nothing ever really happens to him. He remains external even to events that supposedly involve him; they do not touch him. He has found a psychological equivalent of the cliché of 'stoic' indifference. That is also why what he observes and contemplates never has any life in it for him. Risk and trial and the possibility of disappointment are intrinsic to experience. By his attitude Rasselas deprives himself from the outset of the possibility of learning from experience. Imlac provides indispensable assistance.

Let us conclude with 'the Conclusion in which Nothing is Concluded'. A great deal has been written about this, but it seems to me that the point of the title of the concluding chapter still has not been grasped. That the protagonists have made any progress in the course of the tale is not apparent. Yet it seems that readers are still intent on finding something positive in the ironic conclusion and fail to see that the point or the moral, like the position from which the satire must be construed, is one which is not represented in the tale at all. It depends essentially on what they as readers bring to the text themselves, their sense of human life and their moral judgment.[26]

The princess "desired first to learn all sciences, and then purposed to found a college of learned women, in which she would preside." "The prince desired a little kingdom, in which he might administer justice in his own person, and see all the parts of government with his own eyes." (175–6) But the final paragraph informs us, "Of these wishes that they had formed they well knew that none could be obtained. They deliberated a while what was to be done, and resolved, when the inundation should cease, to return to Abissinia." (176)

That they are still capable of spending their time forming wishes which they know are unobtainable is a terrible thing. The cause is not to be sought in the world and what it might offer but in the attitude which has informed their 'approach' to the world and its possibilities. Readers should not be at a loss what to conclude from this. The satire has consistently underscored the pernicious attitudes keeping Rasselas from ever trying anything, taking a risk, making an effort.

The last sentence of *Rasselas* has proved a crux within the conundrum of the conclusion. Geoffrey Tillotson wrote in an article that "the party returns to the happy valley" in the end, deriving his sense of their experience or lesson from this conclusion. Reworking the article for publication in a book, he corrected himself, "the party returns to Abyssinia," and credited the change to George Sherburn's article, "Rasselas returns—to what?" According to Tomarken, Sherburn's discovery that they cannot and do not return to the happy valley is "one of the most important moments" in the reception of *Rasselas*. It "altered almost all future interpretations of the tale," in that "it altered the conception of the structure of the text."[27]

Unfortunately, Sherburn's discovery is a red herring. His view that they return to Abyssinia is wrong. If one reads the conclusion attentively, it is clear that what they did was deliberated and then resolved. If Johnson's efforts to render the term 'resolve' suspect have proved unsuccessful, one cannot say it was because they were subtle. Nothing is concluded by the characters because they have been moving in a void. They are motivationally hollow, and the human world they "look upon" (111) seems to have no possibilities of meaningful activity as a result of the mutually reinforcing perspectives Imlac and Rasselas have brought to it.

The tale does not reflect Johnson's view of the prospects for human happiness in the world. The bleak prospects are those of characters who will not commit themselves to the chances of experience and accordingly manage to turn any effectual motive to try something (be it hope or discontent) into a self-sufficient state that is the opposite of motivation. Their lack of initiative, of real desire, is projected onto the world. This renders learning from experience impossible.

The prevailing error of readings of this work replicates the error of its protagonists. The meaning of what is presented is taken as objective possibility already given in the presentation, whereas a world or a text only has real possibilities through the participation of those who invest their feelings and passions in it. Such participation is needed to put the events and responses within the text into proper perspective, to bring the characters to (even schematic) life.

In the first generation of reactions to *Rasselas* there were notable critical condemnations of its general tenor, its ending and its moral, based on sound ethical or social practical instincts and mistaken readerly judgment. John Hawkins was concerned about the practical effect of the work.

> I wish I were not warranted in saying, that this elegant work is rendered, by its most obvious moral, of little benefit to the reader. We would not indeed wish to see the rising generation so unprofitably employed as the prince of Abyssinia; but it is equally impolitic to repress all hope, and he who should quit his father's house in search of a profession, and return unprovided, because he could not find any man pleased with his own, would need a better justification than that Johnson, after speculatively surveying various modes of life, had judged happiness unattainable and choice useless.[28]

It is, of course, not Johnson who has speculatively surveyed and judged in this way, but his main characters. He was counting on his readers to have the sound sense and initiative critically to judge the judgments of the characters. In her 1810 evaluation Anna Letitia Barbauld notes the abstraction of the characters from any real practical life context, and links it to their indecision. But she attributes this to Johnson's view of the world rather than his conscious artistry. Her reading is wrong but based on grounds that are right according to Johnson's actual worldview.

> Such is the philosophical view which Dr. Johnson and many others have taken of life; and such indecision would probably be the consequence of thus narrowly sifting the advantages and disadvantages of every station in this mixt state, if done without that feeling reference to each man's particular position, and particular inclinations, which is necessary to incline the balance. If we choose to imagine an insulated being, detached from all connexions and all duties, it may be difficult for mere reason to direct his choice; but no man is so insulated: we are woven into the web of society, and to each individual it is seldom dubious what *he* shall do.[29]

Rasselas has avoided having to strive with difficulties and, in the words of *Adventurer* 111 quoted earlier, "can survey himself only as a useless filler of existence; and if he is content with his own character, must owe his satisfaction to insensibility." His insensibility, tied up with the attitudes that are satirized, is indeed part of Johnson's satiric premise, but those critics who, not seeing this, are nonetheless content with the character of Rasselas and Imlac, show a different kind of insensibility, a lack of Mrs. Barbauld's "feeling reference" to concrete life. The inner distance to life

N O T E S

1. Edmund Burke, *Reflections on the Revolution in France*, ed. Conor Cruise O'Brien, (Harmondsworth: Penguin, 1968), p. 281. Subsequent references to this volume given in parentheses in the text.

2. On the question of the English/British Enlightenment see note 22 below.

3. See Jeffrey Barnouw, "Active Experience vs. Wish-Fulfilment in Francis Bacon's Moral Psychology of Science." *The Philosophical Forum*, vol. 9, no. 1, (Fall 1977), 78–99; "Bacon and Hobbes: The Conception of Experience in the Scientific Revolution." *Science/Technology and the Humanities*, 2 (1979), 92–110.

4. *Selected Writings of Francis Bacon*, ed. Hugh G. Dick, (New York: Random House Modern Library, 1955), p. 471. Subsequent references to this volume given in parentheses in the text.

5. Johnson, *Preface to Shakespeare*, in *Johnson on Shakespeare*, ed. Arthur Sherbo, (*The Yale Edition of the Works of Samuel Johnson,* vol. VII*)*, (New Haven: Yale University Press, 1968), pp. 87–88.

6. Stobaeus, *Eclogues* 2.77, in A. A. Long and D. N. Sedley, ed. and tr. *The Hellenistic Philosophers*. 2 vols., (Cambridge: Cambridge University Press, 1987), I, 394. For further support and elaboration of this reading of the Stoics, see Jeffrey Barnouw, *Propositional Perception*. Phantasia, *Predication and Sign in Plato,* Aristotle *and the Stoics.* (Lanham, Maryland: University Press of America, 2002), pp. 154–64.

7. Sextus Empiricus, *Against the Professors* 8.275–6, Long and Sedley, I, 317–8, translation altered.

8. Emile Bréhier, Introduction to Antoinette Virieux-Reymond, *La Logique et l'épistemologie des stoïciens. Leurs rapports avec la logique d'Aristote, la logistique et la pensée contemporaines* (Lausanne: Librairie de l'Université, n.d.), p. v.

9. Diogenes Laertius, *Lives and Opinions of Eminent Philosophers* 7.87; 89, in Long and Sedley, I, 395.

10. Plutarch, *On Stoic Self-Contradictions* 1037F, Long and Sedley, I, 317. Reason is impulse (*hormê*) in the character of an imperative, and its opposite, repulsion (*aphormê*), works as a prohibition.

11. Diogenes Laertius, 7.85, in Long and Sedley I, 346, translation altered.

12. Hobbes, *Leviathan*, ed. Edwin Curley, (Indianapolis: Hackett, 1994), p. 79, chap. 14, § 3.

13. Cicero, *On Ends* 3.31, Long and Sedley, I, 401. Gisela Striker, "Following Nature: A Study in Stoic Ethics," and "The role of *Oikeiôsis* in Stoic Ethics," in Striker, *Essays on Hellenistic Epistemoilogy and Ethics* (Cambridge: Cambridge University Press, 1996), 221–80, 281–97, provides a penetrating analysis of this matter. She suggests that when Stobaeus says Zeno proposed 'living in agreement', meaning 'living in accordance with a single harmonious principle' because those who live in conflict (*machomenôs*) are unhappy, this may "indicate the conflicts that arise when a man's expectations are frustrated by nature because

they are false" (pp. 223, 288n). "It is agreement with nature's will, or observation of the natural order, that provides consistency" (p. 230) of the sort Zeno prescribed. Such agreement with nature "offers a basis for an account of how one should live by the guidance of reason—namely, as Chrysippus expressed it most accurately, by adhering to what experience shows to be the natural course of events" (p.231).

14. Stobaeus 2.155,5–9, Long and Sedley, I, 419. Johnson seems to treat this doctrine in chapter 22 of *Rasselas* as mere verbiage: "To live according to nature, is to act always with regard to the fitness arising from the relations and qualities of causes and effects." This does not mean he was unaware of or neglected the moral importance of relating effect to cause in the process of learning from experience.

15. "Thoughts and Conclusions," in *The Philosophy of Francis Bacon*, ed. Benjamin Farrington, (Chicago: University of Chicago Press, 1966), p. 98. Cf. *Novum Organum*, Aphorism CXIV.

16. Johnson's essays from the periodicals, *The Rambler, The Adventurer*, and *The Idler* will be cited according to the Yale Edition, vols. 2–5, in parentheses within the text in this format: Y2.451.

17. Hobbes, *Leviathan*, p. 57, chap. 11 § 1.

18. See the discussion of 'the happiness of pursuit' in Jeffrey Barnouw, "The 'Pursuit of Happiness' in Jefferson, and its Background in Bacon and Hobbes," *Interpretation. A Journal of Political Philosophy*, 11 (1983), 225–248, pp. 235–40.

19. *Selected Writings of Francis Bacon*, p. 327.

20. Note the proviso attached to the preceding essay, "The Epicurean," Hume, *Essays Moral, Political, and Literary*, ed. Eugene F. Miller, rev. ed., (Indianapolis: Liberty Classics, 1987), p. 138, "The intention of this and the three following essays is not so much to explain accurately the sentiments of the ancient sects of philosophy, as to deliver the sentiments of sects, that naturally form themselves in the world, and entertain different ideas of human life and of happiness. I have given each of them the name of the philosophical sect, to which it bears the greatest affinity."

21. *Essays*, pp. 146, 148–9.

22. *Essays*, pp. 149, 151. The affinities of Johnson and Hume have been nicely brought out by Adam Potkay, *The Passion for Happiness. Samuel Johnson and David Hume* (Ithaca: Cornell University Press, 2000), who says, p. 6, that he was "inspired" in pursuing their conjunction and its relevance to a conception of the Enlightenment in England by my essay, "Johnson and Hume considered as the core of a new 'period concept' of the Enlightenment." *Transactions of the Fifth International Congress on the Enlightenment*, I. (*Studies in Voltaire and the Eighteenth Century*, vol. 190.) (Oxford: Voltaire Foundation, 1980), 189–196. Potkay stresses the moral philosophical orientation both writers derived "from the eclectic Stoicism of Cicero's dialogues" (p. 5). I pursue the question of an English (British) Enlightenment that would centrally include Johnson—and

Burke—in "Britain and European Literature and Thought," in *The Cambridge History of English Literature, 1660–1780*, (Cambridge: Cambridge University Press, forthcoming).

23. Samuel Johnson, *Rasselas and Other Tales (The Yale Edition of the Works of Samuel Johnson*, vol. 16.), ed. Gwin J. Kolb, (New Haven: Yale University Press, 1990), p. 24. Further page references to this edition will be given in parentheses within the text.

24. Samuel Johnson, *Lives of the English Poets*, ed. L. Archer-Hind, (London: Dent/Everyman's Library, 1925), II, 87. Further page references to this volume will be given in parentheses within the text.

25. Johnson used 'resolution' in a positive sense, not as a mental act or state, but as a quality of active endeavor, as in *Rambler* 178, "Many of the blessings universally desired, are very frequently wanted, because most men, when they should labour, content themselves to complain, and rather linger in a state in which they cannot be at rest, than improve their condition by vigour and resolution." "No man has a right . . . to consider himself as debarred from happiness by such obstacles as resolution may break or dexterity may put aside." Such resolution is like dexterity a character of real acts or efforts.

26. I presented a reading of *Rasselas* and analyzed previous readings in a chapter of my dissertation, *'Action' for Johnson, Burke and Schiller* (Yale 1969), and in abbreviated form in "Readings of *Rasselas*. 'Its Most Obvious Moral' and the Moral Role of Literature," *Enlightenment Essays*, 7 (1976), 17–39, where I discuss the early views of John Hawkins, Hester Chapone, William Hazlitt and Anna Letitia Barbauld, who all to my mind respond soundly (in a Johnsonian moral sense) to what they mistakenly take to be Johnson's point of view and point, where most later critics, making the same mistake, find that point more acceptable. Among modern critics I consider Paul Fussell, Sheldon Sacks, Bertrand Bronson, Mary Lascelles and others. I find support for my approach in Martin Price, Clarence Tracy, Alvin Whitley, Robert Voitle and John Aden. See Edward Tomarken, *Johnson,* Rasselas, *and the Choice of Criticism* (Lexington: The University Press of Kentucky, 1989) for a different construing of the history of readings of *Rasselas*. His compendious list of *Rasselas* criticism, 1759–1986, pp. 194–202, does not include my article or dissertation, though he does mention my grandfather's "*Rasselas* in Dutch."

Among recent interpretations three may be mentioned. Duane H. Smith, "Repetitive Patterns in Samuel Johnson's *Rasselas*," *Studies in English Literature* 36 (1996), 623–39, holds that "the repetition of a pattern of unfulfilled expectations so permeates the narrative that it extends to and applies to any final answers" (p. 626). But this leads him to trivialize the tale. "If Johnson's *Rasselas* affirms neither a traditional Christian otherworldliness nor a 'proper occupation,' what prevents it from being essentially nihilistic? Johnson asserts the value of his work as entertainment even as he denies its value as a moral tale." The narrative suggests "that while our attention, Rasselas's attention, or Johnson's attention, is temporarily absorbed in these diversions, it is possible to forget about failure, hopelessness, and boredom" (p. 637). More rewarding is Oscar Kenshur, "Authorized Experience: Narration and Moral Knowledge in *Rasselas*," the final chapter in *Dilemmas of Enlightenment. Studies in the Rhetoric and Logic of Ideology* (Berkeley: University of California Press, 1993). He starts from the thesis "that the overall project of *Rasselas* is an inductivist experiment in which moral knowledge is supposed to be obtained through systematic observation and experimentation" (p. 196). But the way the tale proceeds throws "a somewhat different light on Rasselas's inductivist project since it renders experience both necessary and superfluous" (p. 199). A "shift from the mediation of eloquence to the immediacy of experience is precisely what the reader of *Rasselas* does not encounter." Where Kenshur judges that "while Johnson, like Voltaire [in *Candide*] wishes to appeal to the prestige of inductivism, he is less willing to play the narrative role of an inductivist—he is less willing to (appear to) step aside and let the facts speak for themselves" (p. 205), I would rather say that that is precisely what Johnson does do, but that the facts in question are not about the chances of happiness in the world but about the psychological liabilities of characters incapable of trying those chances. Kenshur is right about some readers when he says, *a propos* of Bate's 'satire manqué', "The various people who make bad moral choices tend to escape satiric treatment, not because Johnson is too close to them but because the reader is too far away." But that distance is not the work of Johnson's tale so much as of the mindset of his 'sympathetic' critics, who fail to judge moral failure in the tale. Most valuable of all is the final chapter of Potkay, *The Passion for Happiness*, "The Spirit of Ending," which brings out a factor I have not taken account of in this essay, namely that many readers read the penultimate chapter, on the nature of the soul, as the real conclusion of *Rasselas*. But, as Potkay says, "Johnson follows his defense of the soul's immortality with a conclusion that's quite adrift" (p. 197). "Are we therefore to read *Rasselas*'s final chapter as undercutting Imlac's metaphysical consolations? The tale's end would seem both to ironize the otherworldly sentiments of the penultimate chapter and to highlight their incongruity with the strong and vivid account of our world that fills out the bulk of *Rasselas*" (p. 201). "In *Rasselas* to leave the question of our proper course in life undecided is, for all of Johnson's reasoned arguments for belief, to acknowledge the limited effectiveness of rational enquiry." (p.215) Does the tale truly leave *our* proper course in life undecided? The tale is inconclusive in a thematically consistent way, both in its formal lack of closure and in the indecisiveness of the characters represented, but Johnson has given *us* sufficient direction and freedom to reach our own conclusions from that not at all inconclusive ending.

27. Tomarken, *Johnson,* Rasselas, *and the Choice of Criticism*, p. 22.

28. Hawkins, *The Life of Samuel Johnson LL.D.*, ed. Bertram H. Davis, (New York, 1961), p. 156.

29. *The British Novelists*, with an Essay, and Prefaces Biographical and Critical, by Mrs. Barbauld, vol. XXVI (London, 1820), p. iii.

The Ecliptic of the Beautiful

TIMOTHY ERWIN

I must be careful not to suffer the misfortune which
happens to people who look at the sun. . . during an eclipse.
— Plato, *The Phaedo*

To hear you have to see clearly.

An absolute knowledge [*savoir*] will never accept this
unique separation, that in the veiled place of the Wholly
Other, nothing should present itself.
— Hélène Cixous and Jacques Derrida, *Veils*

Early modern astronomy has a word for the way the beautiful is eclipsed by novelty and sublimity during the Enlightenment in Britain. When the new moon passes between the earth and sun its shadow occasionally blots out the solar disk entirely. A total eclipse is visible only from the umbra, that narrow band of shadow which arcs across the globe at more than twice the speed of sound before passing into space. If we imagine the path of the lunar shadow as a curtain hung from the solar orbit the points from which the curtain is suspended are its ecliptic. The celestial metaphor is meant to suggest different ways in which the dark veil of the sublime— shifting in its several phases from the rhetorical elevation of Longinus and

Boileau towards the novelty and perspicuity of Addison, through a Burkean psychology of fear, and then into the Kantian imaginary—obscures a traditional view of the beautiful during the long eighteenth century. Just as the dark glow of the corona reflects the light of day the unstable attributes of the sublime obliquely acknowledge the continuing presence of classical beauty. The instrumental causes of the sublime open onto the deep mystery of human creation. Its fearsome asymmetry invokes the secret harmony of the whole. And the primacy of the word suggests that a persistent if unrecognized composite beauty be traced across literary history in the intersection of word and image. None of these interdisciplinary crossroads need place us in the path of a totalizing darkness. Ancient notions of beauty comprised of symmetry, proportion, and completeness have always been central to the academic discourse of painting, and they remain at least as much with us today as the weak and diminished beauty of empiricism. If we are unaware of their presence in eighteenth-century writing it is largely because we are still standing in our own shadow, still caught in the dim penumbra of disciplinary complacence.[1]

What I want to propose is a skeptical look at what might be called, after Butterfield's famous Whig view of history, a Whig view of aesthetics. I want to look beyond the discourse of novelty and sublimity for a glimpse of the theory it was meant to challenge, the classicizing linear design promoted by the French *académie royale* and the *scuola Carracci*. Academic design aimed at the creation of the beautiful in history painting primarily through linear arrangement. And because the canvas often depicted biblical or mythological narrative, design also addressed the *pictura-poesis* doctrine of Aristotle and Horace. When we speak about the image-text relation in early modern Britain we can easily conflate two opposed historical metaphors. The discourse of design promoted during the Restoration likens perspective and arrangement to narrative emplotment. Not only does it imagine that common formal artifice may take place across the boundaries of space and time, it celebrates the labor of overcoming obstacles to the process as a *difficulté vaincue*. The discourse of the image or of novelty developed by empiricism redefines beauty in natural or practical rather than artificial terms. It qualifies the pictorial analogy by replacing the correctness of outline and plot with the novelty of coloring and verbal imagery. Both paradigms are ultimately grounded in the rhetorical triad of *inventio*, *dispositio*, and *elocutio*, in the three-part process of inventing, designing, and coloring or adding the figural elements of a work. They once formed part of a unified field theory of the imagination on that basis, before falling into the quarrel between the *rubénistes* and the *poussinistes* in the French academy, a skirmish important to the quarrel of the ancients and moderns in France and England alike, and then into the further separation enforced by empiricism. A civic-humanist discourse, design views the aesthetic realm as a reliable vehicle for public-minded sentiment suited to the higher genres of epic and history painting. In literature it typically affirms the values of space rather than time. Supplanted only gradually in the poetics of the period, the discourse of design persists even longer in the theory of painting, where it is associated with a Stuart taste in the arts, and above all with the vogue for the school of the Carracci. Not until Henry Fuseli invents his sublime poetical painting, as the artist called his dreamlike canvases to distinguish them from history painting, is extreme novelty much at home in the academy of Sir Joshua Reynolds. What remains today of the tradition for literary criticism is mainly the practice of gesturing in a vaguely visual way towards something called *imagery* in poetry. The *pictura loquens* of rhetorical tradition has likewise long since been replaced by what Hans-Georg Gadamer calls the speechlessness of the modern image, meaning its mute dependence upon the beholder.[2]

Where the discourse of design stresses the central term of the rhetorical triad, *dispositio*, *disegno*, or *dessin*, the discourse of the image defers any comparison to the third term, coloring, even as it redefines invention as the direct observation of nature. The novel discourse of the image sketched out in Joseph Addison's *Spectator* papers on the pleasures of the imagination likens coloring to the vividness of language. An emergent aesthetic, the discourse of the image is most visible in the graphic art of Hogarth and the privatized realm of the novel.[3] In voicing it tends toward a personal utterance harking back to the Puritan revolution. It typically asks space to submit to the demands of time, often on commercial grounds, and dispenses with artifice as potential deception. Although art historians are familiar with the discourse of design, literary scholars tend not to be. When interdisciplinary theory devises methods based in either the spaces of reading or structural linguistics it can replicate at a distance longstanding differences between design and the image.[4] Let's look briefly into three period contexts of aesthetic controversy, each offering a contest of word and image, for the lingering traces of classical formal beauty. The early history of C. A. Du Fresnoy's *De arte graphica* in English reveals a commitment on the part of Alexander Pope to the tradition of linear design, a commitment that serves in turn as backdrop for the way Addison's colorist aesthetics of the great, uncommon, and beautiful redefine the linear beauty of the formal analogy. For Richardson, Fielding, and their illustrators the future of the mid-century novel is contested on the grounds of language and vision.

While illustration cannot in and of itself make a text visual, it may well point to the kind of visuality a text either refuses or embraces. And although it had become attenuated during the course of her career, visual-verbal conflict informs Jane Austen's last novel, *Persuasion*, a novel that closes by opposing the constant word to the fickle image.

I. Bold Designs

Wendy Steiner among others has recently welcomed back into cultural criticism an ambitious concept of the beautiful, an idea that may be either real or ideal, male or female, and that represents "an intense experience of value" available in "a thousand guises."[5] When Pope opens *The Rape of the Lock* by telling us that the bright gaze of his heroine must eclipse the day he claims a bold ambition for beauty in the guise of linear design. The scene from canto one beginning "And now, unveil'd, the *Toilet* stands display'd"[6] is among other things a sustained ekphrasis describing the creation of a *beau idéal*. Its prime visual analogue is the frontispiece engraving (fig. 1), at once formal and also ruefully funny. In tracing three episodes upward through a vertical axis—the scene of adornment, the fateful game of ombre, and the apotheosis of the lock—the image anticipates the disappointment and eventual commemoration of Belinda's ambitions. The verses unfolding beyond the image meanwhile recount the destruction of an ideal form, a narrative pointed by Clarissa as a defense of the visual imagination: "Nor could it sure be such a Sin to paint" (*TE* 2: 201; canto 5, line 24). The iconography of the frontispiece recalls in a self-consciously inept way a linear seated Venus painted time and again by Annibale Carracci and his followers. The most interesting of several versions after Annibale is Francesco Albani's *Toilette of Venus*, the third painting in a cycle of four now in the Louvre (represented here by a late engraving; fig. 2).[7] The formal affinities between the plot of the poem and Albani's image are highly suggestive. According to Catherine R. Puglisi, the Louvre cycle involves an Ovidian contest between the loves of Venus and the chastity of Diana. The four paintings treat individually of the four elements, the image of Venus adorned addressing the element of the air.[8] In an English context these themes might well metamorphose into the conflict between the false chastity urged by Ariel and the innocence of the visual. More central to Carracci-school *disegno* is the way it binds the gaze of the beholder through the power of the line. As canto two opens the tensile attraction of design is evoked in the series of linear metaphors ending "And Beauty draws us with a single Hair" (*TE* 2: 161; canto 2, line 28). The passage announcing

Figure 1. Claude du Bosc, after Ludovico du Guernier, Frontispiece,
The Rape of the Lock (1714). Photo: William Andrews Clark Memorial Library,
University of California, Los Angeles.

Figure 2. Etienne Baudet, after Francesco Albani, *Toilette of Venus* (1672). Photo: The Metropolitan Museum of Art, Gift of Mr. Giorgio Sangiorgi, 1958 (58.555.2)

Belinda's appearance on the Thames ends in a meditation on the power of beauty to bind the eye by means of outline and arrangement. The passage places the discourse of design well inside aesthetic discussion. The lock symbolizes among other things a symmetrical ideal just assuming full aesthetic powers when it is destroyed. French neoclassical discourse fused literary and visual design into a visual-verbal whole. If we follow the thread of this strong beauty far enough it leads us to superimpose the turning point of narrative onto the vanishing point of perspective. Such a power to fascinate is light years away from Burke's weak beauty.[9]

In a syncretic commentary on Aristotle's *Poetics* the influential humanist René Rapin defines design in language by likening it to the organization of history painting. Among the particulars of the art of poetry, writes Rapin, the subject and design ought to have the first place, because it is, as it were, the first production of the wit; and the design in a poem is what they call the *ordonnance* in a picture. The great painters only are capable of a great design in their draughts, such as a Raphael, a Julius Romanus, a Poussin; and only great poets are capable of a great design in their poetry . . . . For 'tis necessary that the same spirit reign throughout,that all contribute to the same end, and that all the parts bear a secret relation (*un raport secret*) to each other . . . ; and this general design is nothing else but the form (*la forme*) which a poet gives to his work . . . . The most perfect design of all antiquity, is that of Virgil in his *Aeneids*. But the sovereign perfection of a design, in the opinion of Horace, is to be simple, and that all turn on the same centre (*tout aille au même but*).[10]

Design is finally the metaphorical quality that reconciles the classical unity of plot to a larger harmony of parts. A poem designed correctly might revolve at once around both a narrative and a rhetorical turning. Arguably, all of Pope's verse from the *Pastorals* to *The Dunciad* may be read as a formal composite of verbal emplotment and visual figuration, as the bold design of a beautiful whole. He was certainly committed to the tradition.

The story of the connection between Pope and the linear tradition of the Carracci actually begins with Dryden's workmanlike recasting of a long Latin poem by the French artist Charles Alphonse Du Fresnoy into the English prose of the *Art of Painting* (1695). Already engaged in his translation of the *Aeneid*, Dryden allowed the translation of Du Fresnoy's *De Arte Graphica* a mere two months. In his haste he came upon a controversy that meant little to him. A disagreement of two decades' standing, the quarrel of the French academy between the *rubénistes* and the *poussinistes* pitted the party of design, led by academy chancellor Charles Le Brun, against the party of coloring led by Roger de Piles. The *De arte graphica* leaves no doubt about the crucial importance of design. The title-page of the lengthy Latin poem praises Annibale Carracci for fostering a new restoration in art, and the poem concludes by returning to praise *sedulus Annibal*, the "laborious and diligent" Annibale of the Dryden translation, for bringing together all that is admirable in painting and making it his own.[11] But Dryden followed the French of the colorist de Piles instead of the Latin original. Where Du Fresnoy characterizes coloring simply as "*complementum graphidos* (*mirabile visu*)," the complement of design and wonderful to see,[12] de Piles bends the Latin to his side of the controversy. He promotes coloring to "*l'ame & dernier achevement de la peinture*."[13]

In Dryden coloring becomes "the Soul of Painting and its utmost perfection" (36). Assisted by Pope, the painter Charles Jervas offered English readers a new edition of the *Art of Painting* correcting de Piles and restoring Du Fresnoy to himself. In dedicating the new translation to Burlington the connoisseur Richard Graham makes it clear that unlike de Piles (and also, presumably, Dryden) Jervas had not been misled: "the French translator has frequently mistaken the sense," writes Graham in a preface to Burlington emended by Pope, so "Mr. Jervas . . . has been prevailed upon to correct what was found amiss."[14] And once again Du Fresnoy is heard to commend the ancient party of arrangement and perspective, of outline and design, qualities long associated with the measured heroic style of the Carracci academy.

The new frontispiece (fig. 3) likewise endorses the party of design by repeating a story after Le Brun that takes us back to the *poussiniste* response to the first *rubéniste* challenge in the academy in 1672, when the chancellor was compelled to correct a serious intellectual confusion. The academy had always taken the primacy of design for its founding doctrine. Now a dissident intramural faction was militating for the equal importance of coloring. From Le Brun's perspective the colorists were arguing for the crude substitution of artistic means for artistic end. No less an authority than Aristotle had considered plot the soul of tragedy, and neoclassical theory after him had always considered *disegno* or *dessin* the soul of painting. Le Brun understood the colorist challenge to involve a categorical confusion of theory and practice where the final stage of the rhetorical triad becomes the highest achievement of the art of painting. For Le Brun the colorists had stolen the soul of painting through the linguistic alchemy of mistaking a finishing touch for a final aim. Le Brun responds with a typical Augustan appeal to historical origin, defending the primacy of design by asserting its priority. He reminds his audience of the story from Pliny of the Corinthian maiden Dibutade, the shepherdess who traced the silhouette of her lover on the wall for solace during the season of loneliness:

> If we return to what the ancients tell us of painting
> we will see that it didn't originate in colouring; because
> it's said that the shepherdess who made the portrait of
> her lover had only a stylus for her palette and brush; or
> at best a pencil, with which she traced the image of the
> one she loved, and yet all antiquity has not failed to
> name this first portrait the origin of painting, though
> the maiden used no colour at all in drawing it.[15]

Figure 3. Simon Gribelin, Frontispiece, *The Art of Painting* (1716).
Photo: William Andrews Clark Memorial Library, University of California, Los Angeles.

Le Brun enjoyed the story well enough to see it engraved, and for more than a century afterwards the scene was closely associated with academic design.[16] Norman Bryson has shown that the royal academy was never at a loss for discursiveness,[17] and for Le Brun the point of the legend, not calculated to hearten opposition, is that only design can make the artist. Where coloring is an accident of lighting, design is graphic substance; where coloring is pigmented matter, design is spirit. Painting requires above all a certain ability to fix a mental image firmly enough that it may be copied onto the canvas as a meaningful, symmetrical whole according to ancient standards of beauty. Adapting the ramified analytic of the academy to the distinction, Le Brun points out that there are actually two sorts of design, intellectual or theoretical design, which depends upon the imagination and which may be expressed in words as well as images; and practical or external design, which depends upon theoretical design and which through the master's hand expresses form, proportion, and every passion of the soul. Regarding coloring Le Brun concedes only that it contributes to the final perfection of painting, just as a fine complexion lends perfection to the most beautiful features (*beaux traits*) of the face.[18] Punning upon the word *traits* as *features* composed of *lines,* Le Brun practices a linguistic alchemy of his own, putting coloring in its place by asking his audience to remember that the prime element of drawing is the individual line. Dibutade recalls her lover not through his seasonal coloring but through the flowing outline of his profile.[19] Casting the image in high relief as if viewed in the mirror of art, the Pope-Jervas frontispiece tells the same story, lending narrative emphasis by making the shepherd's departure appear imminent, and adding a decorous cupid to guide the hand of Dibutade to show that painting began in chaste love.

Classical rhetoric had long supplied the poetic imagination with a three-part schema also adopted by painting. Each part—invention, design, and coloring—named a regulated stage of creation. In poetry as in painting the artist first canvassed representational history. The searching of literary or iconographic precedent was termed invention. Next the poet or painter structured the parts according to the principles of the whole. For the charcoal sketch proportioned to classical standard as for the marvelous or probable shaping of narrative event the middle stage was called design. And finally in the verbal coloring of the poem the artist set down a metaphorical gloss to unify the work and to convey it memorably to posterity. Of the trio of terms *design* was allotted the lion's share of commentary. The modernist departure of Addison like that of de Piles grants a new priority to the third stage of the analogy, coloring. In the *Spectator* papers on the pleasures of the imagination, Addison distinguishes between two sorts of the beautiful, the beauty that attracts sexual desire and the beauty that inspires in the beholder a "secret Delight."[20] Color is the prime feature of both. It is inscribed in the mating rituals of birds as an instinctual attraction to the particular "Tincture of a Feather" (3: 543). In art and nature alike the various delights that color presents to the beholder are superior to those of either symmetry or arrangement. We enjoy the beauty of coloring as a secondary pleasure best through the vividness of language:

> Words, when well chosen, have so great a Force in them, that a Description often gives us more lively Ideas than the Sight of Things themselves. The Reader finds a Scene drawn in stronger Colours, and painted more to the Life in his Imagination, by the help of Words, than by an actual Survey of the Scene which they describe. In this Case the Poet seems to get the better of Nature; he takes, indeed, the Landskip after her, but gives it more vigorous Touches, heightens its Beauty, and so enlivens the whole Piece, that the Images, which flow from the Objects themselves, appear weak and faint, in Comparison of those that come from the Expressions (3: 560-61).

Addison proposes a contest of descriptive word and image in which verbal description triumphs so well that it permits the signifier of language to see through and nearly to replace the signified of vision. A new three-part schema is devised in the interest of aesthetic perception and imaginative novelty—the great, uncommon, and beautiful—and in the interest of Lockean liberty the term *image* comes to supplant the *design* of formal discourse. The composite ideal of the painter in which the separate parts of beauty are assembled into a whole ("the joint Force and full *Result* of *all*," Pope calls the beautiful in the *Essay on Criticism*; *TE* 1: 267, line 246) is atomized into a readerly process of poetic selection and combination. Appeals to classical proportion are replaced by the promise of macrocosmic and microcosmic discoveries situating mankind in worlds yet unknown. The least particle of life contains within it "a Heaven and Earth, Stars and Planets, and every different Species," writes Addison, and all of these elements are capable of being "spun out into another Universe" (3: 575–76).[21] Where the humanist discourse of design brings the visual metaphor under the sway of form to arrive at a mysterious harmony of the whole, in other words, the empiricist discourse of the image dissolves the formal object into verbal description to uphold the power of language to inspire vivid novelty and a powerful sublimity. One pictorial discourse tends to naturalize culture for the sake of a renewed classical tradition, the other to textualize nature for the sake of heightened individual perception, occasionally to the point of iconoclasm.

II. Deconstructing and Reconstructing Neoplatonism

Richardson's *Pamela* provides a case in point. Pamela absolutely refuses ekphrasis and the composite beauty it imagines.[22] She remains faithful to the symbolic word even when she enters the visual field. The engraving after Joseph Highmore where she proposes to correspond with Parson Williams by placing letters beneath the sunflower, symbol of fidelity (fig. 4), inclines more toward still life than toward history painting. Well before the episode Pamela embodies the ethical superiority of the strict word. In letter twenty-three the artless young servant is visited by a number of great ladies from the neighborhood who come to see for themselves this paragon of beauty, as they call her. The phrase recalls the *paragone* or representational contest of Leonardo da Vinci. Warned beforehand of their arrival, Pamela preempts their worldly gaze by hiding in a closet, a vantage from which she captures each of her visitors in a diffident but devastating verbal portrait or character. Pamela is particularly severe on one Miss Towers, who both embodies and subverts baroque neoplatonism. "Miss Towers is well-shaped," Pamela tells us, "and has no one ill feature, taken separately: yet I know not how it is; but they seem as if they were not well put together, if I may so say."[23] The neoplatonic doctrine of ideal beauty, the *idea della bellezza* of Giovanni Bellori (a commentator translated by Dryden by way of preface to his *Parallel betwixt Poetry and Painting*), was founded upon a symmetrical whole amounting to more than the sum of its composite parts. The fine features of Miss Towers paradoxically amount to less than the sum of their parts. The episode offers a remarkably iconoclastic moment in a genre not much disposed to classical iconography in the first place. (When Moll Flanders tells us that as a girl she absolutely loved to hear anyone speak of her beauty she hints that she was too young to know her own interest.) Pamela's visitors travesty language with their unseemly wit and *double-entendre*, and Pamela views them as the very image of falsehood. At last emerging from hiding as the picture of formal perfection, Pamela denies her own visual dimension. When Miss Towers asks "Can the pretty Image speak?" she asks her to appear as the living proof of a baroque conceit. Pamela dissents with civil equivocation. She refuses to appear as an image that in any sense defiles the word. "The Sense I have of my Unworthiness," she replies, "renders me unfit for such a Presence." More is at stake here than mere politeness. Pamela recalls the

Figure 4. Antoine Benoist, after Joseph Highmore, *Pamela, Being Now in the Custody of Mrs. Jewkes, Seizes an Occasion to Propose a Correspondence with Mr. Williams* (1745;1762). Photo: Yale Center for British Art, Paul Mellon Collection.

remark of the centurion in Matthew 8: 5, a prayer that ends with the request that Jesus say the word and the centurion's servant will be healed. To reply to her visitors as a speaking image would be to deny an inner truth and symbolically to risk her soul. The episode is a test of the scriptural faith that grants the young servant the strength to resist the foreign discourse of the gentry, and it depends upon a progressive concept of virtue that refuses the imitation of aristocratic standards of conduct. Because such imitation was associated with the visual field, it also posits an unbridgeable gap between language and one sort of textual vision. Her visitors hardly notice Pamela's intense verbal subjectivity. Even as she takes her leave they continue to view her as an all-too-tempting formal outline. "See that shape!" is their hissing valediction (1801; 1980, 86).[24]

At a greater distance, the contest also corrects those classical texts that had woven vision into the textual fabric.[25] Lucian's second-century dialogue *The Images* describes the beautiful as an ekphrastic composite of inner and outer beauty. When Lycinus glimpses an unknown woman whose beauty strikes him nearly dumb Polystratus asks him to "describe her Person" as exactly as possible. Lycinus replies that her beauty is beyond words. "Not Apelles, nor Zeuxis, nor Parhassius, those most famous Artists are sufficiently qualified for this Work, no nor even Phidias or Alcamanes, were they now living."[26] Simply by calling to mind the excellence of these and other artists, Lucian suggests, Lycinus enters willy-nilly into ekphrasis. Polystratus then reminds him that external beauty is diminished when it fails to answer to inner virtue. In *Joseph Andrews* Fielding borrows from Lucian the notion of ekphrasis as a *difficulté vaincue* while in *Tom Jones* he follows the Greek author in representing the beautiful as an all-encompassing virtue.

When Joseph disappoints Lady Booby by speaking of his virtue when she would have him speak of love, the narrator conducts an iconographic inventory of the shocking image. Not the statue of surprise, not the onstage appearance of ghosts in tragedy, not the classical artists Phidias or Praxiteles, not even "the inimitable Pencil of my Friend Hogarth" says Fielding, could convey the "Idea of Surprize" the reader would find on the face of Lady Booby.[27] The tribute tactfully recognizes that while Hogarth is more than qualified to reject traditional iconography, Fielding's own readers may enjoy the latitudinarian freedom of consulting the visual record in assaying the accuracy of a verbal representation. The verbal portraits of his heroines Fanny Andrews in *Joseph Andrews* and Sophia Western in *Tom Jones* form an elaborate defense of visual beauty in the early novel. Like Pope's Belinda, Fanny attracts the gaze of all who surround her. Unlike Pope, Fielding feels that he must warn the reader against the idolatry of Pygmalion and the frustration of Narcissus before drawing her portrait. Fielding describes Fanny's beauty in terms of form ("the shape of her Arms, denoted the Form of those Limbs which she concealed"; 152) as well as of color ("her Hair was of a chestnut Brown"; 152), and he is careful to separate her natural beauty from any artfulness on her part. He asks readers to imagine her as the quintessence of the beautiful, a being superior to any sublunary attempt to capture her in the fallen vessels of either pigment or language but whose person might be approached in the union of both. The beauty of her skin, Fielding says, was such that "the finest *Italian* Paint" (152) could not capture it. To complement her visual elusiveness, Fielding makes Joseph unaware of her presence and has him intone a lovely pastoral song from the next room. As the song has it, a mental picture of Chloe troubles the young swain Strephon until the maiden herself arrives to embody the promise of her image. The passage imagines two representational halves of an ekphrasis seeking their union in a shared whole. The dying notes of the melody trace a narrative ending in an embrace, and when Fanny understands that it is the voice of her lost lover singing them, she promptly faints. An ideal almost beyond language to describe is united through a mimetic *mise-en-abîme* to the song of an image nearly beyond reach. Not until each utters the name of the other ("'Are you *Joseph Andrews?*'" "'Art thou my *Fanny?*'"; 153) do the young lovers fall back from their neoplatonic spell through the elevated realm of pastoral into the relative realism of the novel. The point of joining verbal melody to visual ekphrasis here, I take it, is to welcome the sister-arts analogy of epic and history painting back into the fictive narrative from which Richardson had banished them.[28] Even so their composite representation only approximates the otherworldly idea of the beautiful in Fielding, a visual ideal that fallen human language must seek to recognize and complete. The pointed hyperbole of the episode is heightened by a skeptical awareness of the worldly attraction that Richardson had found so dangerous. Fielding in fact lampoons the association of visual beauty and bawdy language in the person of Mrs. Slipslop. "If Prudes are offended at the Lusciousness of this Picture, they may take their eyes off from it," is his closing remark (153).

In *Tom Jones* Fielding presents Sophia as a paragon of beauty, and more importantly of the judgment and humanity that combine to form wisdom. Sophia is represented in a 1784 engraving after John Hoppner as the very incarnation of womanly charm (fig. 5). She appears much as Fielding describes her, as a vision almost beyond the reach of verbal art. Fielding frames his description by saying of Sophia much as he had done before of Fanny that "the nice Proportion of her Arms promised the truest Symmetry in her limbs."[29] Her hair, he writes, was "curled so gracefully in her Neck, that few could believe it to be her own" (1: 156). Her brows were "full, even, and arched beyond the Power of Art to imitate" (1: 156). "Her Nose," he goes on, "was exactly regular, and her Mouth, in which were two rows of Ivory, exactly answered Sir John Suckling's Description in those Lines,"

> Her Lips were red, and one was thin,
> Compar'd to that which was next her Chin,
>
> (1: 157)

"Her Cheeks," he continues, "were of the oval Kind" (1:157). Hoppner expands extravagantly upon the slight formal hint. He not only outlines her cheeks as two ovals, but includes those ovals within the larger oval of her face; superimposes upon her face the oval of her hat and its ribbon tie; and then drops from those intersecting ovals yet another oval described by the scarf tied at her bosom. With the *carpe diem* touchstones and comparison of Sophia to the Medici Venus, Fielding risks trivializing his heroine from any point of view other than an aesthetic one. He quickly reminds readers that her finest quality was her character and adds a long verbal pendant to his imaginary painting by telling the story of Sophia's reaction to the loss of Tom's youthful gift to her of a songbird at the hands of Blifil. The episode and its discussion by Allworthy, Square, and Blifil lend narrative counter-weight to the description of Sophia. As Martin C. Battestin points out, the episode is a sophisticated meditation on liberty, property, and *contra* Locke on a concept of conscience that includes innate agency (1: 171, n.1). The elaborate episode culminates in the gathering admiration of Sophia and Allworthy for the hero.

III. First Impressions vs. a Sublime Stoicism

From the vantage of the next century we are able to look back with some nostalgia at the long contest of visual metaphor we have been tracing. At the same time visual-verbal antagonism can assert itself in response to the pressure of history. Jane Austen entertains both ways of talking about texts as pictures, the discourse of design in *Pride and Prejudice* and the discourse of the image in *Persuasion*. Elizabeth Bennett and Fitzwilliam Darcy are from their first meeting textually bound by the gaze, unpromisingly so to begin with. Stuart Tave reminds us that the dark eyes of Elizabeth are the first thing Darcy notices about her.[30] Their "beautiful expression," as Darcy puts it, renders her face "uncommonly intelligent."[31] At the time the observation is almost extorted from him but he returns to it again and again. He tells Caroline Bingley that he has been meditating "on the very great pleasure which a pair of fine eyes in the face of a pretty woman can bestow" (*PP* 2: 27). A few pages later he silently admires the "brilliancy" that Elizabeth's exercise lends her complexion after she has walked all the way to Netherfield to look after Jane (*PP* 2: 33). When Caroline asks him further along whether the adventure has affected his admiration of her fine eyes, he answers, "Not at all, they were brightened by the exercise" (*PP* 2: 36). Later the narrator tells us that Darcy refuses to join in the general censure of Elizabeth prompted by Caroline's sarcasm. We learn as much

Figure 5. John Raphael Smith, after John Hoppner, *Sophia Western* (1784). Photo: Yale Center for British Art, Paul Mellon Fund.

for ourselves when in crossing over into the realm of representation and then drawing back from it, Caroline Bingley asks Darcy whether he would like to see portraits of Elizabeth's relative hanging at Pemberley: "As for your Elizabeth's picture," she goes on to ask teasingly, "what painter could do justice to those beautiful eyes?" (*PP* 2: 53). Darcy's reply has a formal wit of its own and looks forward to the dramatic irony of Elizabeth's visit to Pemberley. Austen links design with coloring in the common aim of raising portraiture, the typically British artform, to the level of an inexpressible ideal. "It would not be easy, indeed, to catch their expression," Darcy answers, "but the colour and shape, and the eye-lashes, so remarkably fine, might be copied" (*PP* 2: 53). We are given to understand that Darcy is not too proud to imagine Elizabeth memorialized at Pemberley by a family portrait despite the prejudice of Caroline Bingley that her appearance there would be out of place. Darcy is evidently something of a painter himself, indulging himself in constructing a mental picture or *disegno interno*, and in the process blurring any sharp divide between aesthetic reception and the visual imagination.

Then in the novel's crucial episode the unthinkable happens. Elizabeth visits Pemberley in the absence of Darcy and after a long and winding tour of the grounds and house finds him captured in a portrait upstairs. As she engages his portrait in a steady gaze she finds the painting to speak truthfully of his character where the self-interested slander of Wickham had beforehand misled her. The portrait answers in every civic-humanist detail the description of the housekeeper, who describes Mr. Darcy as responsible for the happiness of hundreds of people, all of whom consider him the best and most amiable of masters. The picture represents what Elizabeth punningly calls his "regard" for her (*PP* 2: 251) in that it recalls the smile that "she remembered to have sometimes seen, when he looked at her" (*PP* 2: 250). Memory briefly makes the heroic image surprisingly at one with the word about Darcy, as if dreamwork had somehow brought back a forgotten connection. The episode is set off from countless others throughout the text when Elizabeth literally cannot look at Darcy; more immediately, it is set apart by his sudden and embarrassing appearance on the scene. The fine eyes motif abruptly enters the plot at its central narrative juncture, when Darcy's likeness projects a new understanding and his subsequent presence confirms it, and becomes part of the formal narrative design as what Derrida calls a *parergon* or visual framing device.[32] The thread that sets Lockean striving and sisterly affection against the jealous pride of rank finally provides the two principals with an occasion for the recognition of mutual admiration. In the history of the eighteenth-century novel the episode suggests the cultural return of a long-repressed visual field, as if a pictorial line of action running beneath the events on the page had unexpectedly broken the surface of the text and then just as unexpectedly been cathected, returned to subtext. Darcy expresses something of the mystery when he confesses to Elizabeth that he cannot fix on either the look or the word with which he first fell in love with her. He admired her for what he calls her "liveliness of . . . mind" (2: 380). The remark reprises as epilogue a textual motif that begins in intelligence, is heightened by exertion, and is further prompted by rivalry. The sequence comes full circle when Elizabeth's rival perversely forces Darcy to complete his portrait by describing Elizabeth as one of the handsomest women of his acquaintance. Austen's working title was *First Impressions*, of course, and the novel remains among other things a critique of empirical observation, of the errors in judgment that Lockean sense impressions can mistakenly cause unless they are allowed to deepen and resonate through the visual field, to pass from the primary impression of the dismissive gaze into the secondary corrective of portraiture, and beyond to the exemplification of virtue.

In *Persuasion* the subject is the long-delayed romance of Anne Elliot and Frederick Wentworth, an interrupted courtship finally completed against the backdrop of the Napoleonic wars. Throughout the narrative the discourse of design flies the enemy flag. It is only a slight exaggeration to say that Austen's call for a more supple and understanding courtship ritual depends on the fragile Quadruple Alliance of November 1815 guaranteeing the stability of the French frontier. Two passages invoke the discourse of the image by endorsing novelty and the sublime. When Admiral Croft pauses to contemplate a print he sees in the window of a Bath print shop he appears so completely fascinated by the image that Anne must touch him to get his attention. "Here I am, you see, staring at a picture," he tells her. "I can never get by this shop without stopping. But what a thing here is," he goes on to say, looking as it were through representation at the object itself, "by way of a boat."

> Did you ever see the like? What queer fellows your fine
> painters must be, to think that anybody would venture their
> lives in such a shapeless old cockleshell as that . . . .
> I wonder where that boat was built! (5: 169)

The easy answer to the question is France. It would be more correct to say that the boat was imagined against the calm horizon of a formal aesthetic and was never meant to sail the choppy seas of verbal imagery. The utilitarian gaze of the Admiral offers a gentle parody of the aesthetics of linear fascination, in other words, even as it promotes the perspicuity of the empiricist image.

The second passage is drawn from the closing chapters. Anne and Frederick are brought together through the opposition of word and image as Anne and Captain Harville engage in a sustained closing discussion. In the drawing room of the Musgrove apartments at Bath the two examine a portrait miniature of Captain Benwick originally commissioned for one woman, Benwick's sister Fanny, now being made over to another, Louisa Musgrove. An emblem of the fickleness of imagery, the miniature launches a conversation regarding the relative constancy of men and women. Because inconstancy was considered a greater failing among women than men Austen levels the playing field of gender here before arranging an amicable standoff. Harville proposes an analogy between bodies and minds to argue that just as men's frames are stronger than women's, so also are their affections. Anne counters by noting that the analogy actually speaks to the greater tenderness of women's emotions. "We certainly do not forget you, so soon as you forget us," she says (5: 232). Anne takes the empiricist view that while men may be constant so long as the object of their affection remains in view, their business takes them into the world where occupation and change naturally "weaken impressions" (5: 232). Women by contrast "live at home," the prey of their emotions (5: 232). The abstract distinction provides an excruciating glimpse of what Anne fears may have become of Frederick's affections during their years of separation. The way *Persuasion* stirs our passions approaches rational apostasy, and its striving sublimity is unknown elsewhere in Austen.[33] Frederick meanwhile appears occupied in drafting paperwork consigning the keepsake to Louisa; in fact, he is eavesdropping on the conversation and drafting a love letter. When Anne says that she hopes she has done justice to men of feeling like Harville, Frederick quickly jots down an afterthought to his passionate declaration. "Too good, too excellent creature! You do us justice indeed," he writes, "You do believe that there is true attachment and constancy among men" (5: 237). The immediacy of writing within the moment of the utterance redoubles the verbal nature of the text and grants the declaration unique emotive power. (There is nothing like this in the cancelled closing of *Persuasion*, where Austen quickly clarifies Anne's "confusion of images and doubts" [5: 253] with the assurance of longstanding mutual affection.) "Unjust I may have been," he writes, "weak and resentful I have been, but never inconstant" (5: 237). The triumph of the word is felt all the more deeply for it.

When a nation is at war romantic and patriotic constancy must collaborate with difficulty. Austen brings them together through the medium of sound. Where *Pride and Prejudice* appeals to the eye, *Persuasion* is scored for the voice. Speech here is finely modulated or accompanied by sound effects. In the passage we have been considering Anne is annoyed by Mrs. Musgrove's "inconvenient tone of voice" because it is perfectly audible but pretends to be "a whisper" (5: 230). Harville speaks of the portrait miniature in a "deep tone" (5: 232) that modulates to "a tone of strong feeling" when he speaks of a sailor's devotion to those "treasures of . . . existence" that are his family (5: 234–35). Just before he calls her excellent and good Frederick writes to Anne that he can distinguish the "tones" of her voice "when they would be lost on others" (5: 237). In granting the couple the privacy of indirect discourse with which she always takes leave of her lovers Austen sends them down a "gravel-walk" (5: 240) where intimate discussion might be further masked by the white noise of footsteps. *Persuasion* is all about finding a private language. It seeks a new discourse to counter and replace the haughty reserve of the past. The title regrets the "over-anxious caution" that once convinced Anne not to marry (5: 30). Persuasion is also the general aim of rhetoric, the first three stages of rhetoric are the basis for the sister arts, and the novel creates its counter-rhetoric in part by isolating the heartfelt word from imagery. To the wrong-headed advice of her elders Anne firmly opposes an "early warm attachment, and a cheerful confidence in futurity" that places its trust in Providence (5: 30). The language recalls the neo-stoic *De Constantia* (1584) of Justus Lipsius, a dialogue that commends philosophic patience in the face of the swirling emotions generated by wartime. The three prime qualities that Lipsius lists as central to constancy—

> (1) An upright unmoved strength of the mind, neither elevated nor depressed by external or accidental occurrences.
> (2) A voluntary and complaintless endurance of all those things whatsoever they be, that fall out to, or fall upon a man from elsewhere.
> (3) A true apprehension and judgement of human and divine matters, as far as they appertain to us[34]

—reinforce the difficult lessons of *Persuasion* and temper the strains of the narrative. Remarkably enough, while she departs from *pictura-poesis* doctrine in nearly every other way, Austen locates her counter-rhetoric in a classical idea revisited by Renaissance humanism.

As sublime agitation is transposed into the resolute calm of relative closure, and as the pain of separation and doubt gives way to sublime delight, we might expect Austen to strike a complementary Burkean note of weak beauty. The beautiful on the face of it is not a strong value in *Persuasion*. From the outset the idea of male beauty is ridiculed as unwarranted self-regard if not outright effeminacy. When Anne once again sees Frederick she notices only that "the years that had destroyed her youth and bloom" had given him "a glowing, open, manly look" (5: 61). Here and elsewhere the word that Austen uses to describe the state of her heroine's appearance is *bloom*. On first meeting Anne we learn that "her bloom had vanished early" (5: 6) as a result of disappointment. "Attachment and regrets had . . . clouded every enjoyment of youth" and "early loss of bloom and spirits had been their lasting effect" (5: 28). In fact, Anne's bloom comes and goes, like the seasons. At Lyme Frederick notices that the brisk weather has restored her bloom. When she meets her former classmate Mrs. Smith, on the other hand, she is said to possess "every beauty except bloom" (5: 153). The word represents a certain aesthetic potential actualized by events. Anne's beauty is not the cause of Frederick's attachment but rather its lasting effect, *pace* Burke, and its full expression comprises a remarkable power and generosity of mind. And though her late blooming appears to reflect the empirical novelty of Addison, who defines the aesthetic quality he calls the uncommon in terms of "the opening of . . . Spring" (3: 542), Anne herself tells us that it is woman's nature to be less subject to new sense impressions than man's. Throughout the narrative Frederick has been "constant unconsciously" (5: 241), he says, captured in Anne's orbit not so much by her undiminished charm as by what he finally understands to be a character equally mixed of "fortitude and gentleness" (5: 241).

With his admission the narrative anguish of protracted separation is referred to history. Anne and Frederick ought now be able to look beyond the delight of reunion to the prospect of happiness and security. For readers of *Persuasion*, however, history is Janus-faced. "The dread of a future war," Austen says by way of returning us to our celestial metaphor, is "all that could dim her sunshine" (5: 252). Readers know what Anne cannot, that the False Peace of early 1815 will offer the couple uneasy respite from French conflict. The note of foreboding precludes any far-reaching classical harmony or completeness. "Beauty," Elaine Scarry observes in a wide-ranging study of the idea, "is pacific."[35] Until now I have been speaking about design either as the implicit antithesis of novelty and the sublime or else as an explicit perpetuation of ancient tradition, but there is another way of glimpsing the idea in play. Austen usually reconciles the ideological oppositions of her novels. In *Persuasion* we arrive at partial closure through a gendered discussion that is represented almost exclusively in auditory terms, and that at the same time makes a shared constancy the hidden final cause of events. The narrative, in other words, draws upon the features of modernist and classical discourse alike. In terms of its emplotment, mutual constancy is confirmed by the overcoming of such obstacles as Frederick's flirtation with Louisa Musgrove. With pained agitation Anne overhears her beloved and her rival speak about their mutual admiration for characters of "decision and firmness" (5:88) so ostensibly unlike her own. In a sequence of dramatic scenes, notably on the Cobb at Lyme Regis where she administers first aid to Louisa, Anne selflessly demonstrates that in fact the opposite is true. In the intersection of spatial description and temporal event with which this crucial episode is represented—and the verbal sketch of the sweeping bay of Lyme and its environs, "with the very beautiful line of cliffs stretching out to the east of town" (5: 95), leading up to the incident is among the most elaborate of the novel—Austen touches lightly upon design. The last plotful obstacle to be overcome, the resumption of conflict, takes place in an unnarrated space offstage. Any full discursive compromise is suspended in the open form of the ending. Yet Austen clearly understands war, and by implication the dark resolve it requires of nations and individuals, to be historical anomaly. She leaves her muted idea of the beautiful standing for the moment in an uncertain light, to be sure, but the reawakened bloom of her heroine awaits the poetic justice of more than one brief day in the sun.

NOTES

1. What Lawrence Lipking wrote twenty years ago remains all too true today: "The vast majority of modern readers are blind to eighteenth-century poetry. We do not see poems well; we do not make the pictures in our minds that the poets direct and excite us to make; and we are often so complacent about our ways of reading that we blame the poem for our own failure to notice its signals." Lawrence Lipking, "Quick Poetic Eyes: Another Look at Literary Pictorialism," in *Articulate Images: The Sister Arts from Hogarth to Tennyson*, ed. Richard Wendorf (Minneapolis: University of Minnesota Press, 1983), 5. The comment is even more true of eighteenth-century fiction. Among the reasons Lipking gives is the inherent logocentrism of Enlightenment thought, and particularly the intellectual and cultural revolution waged in the name of John Locke.
More recently, in "Sleeping Beauties: Are Historical Aesthetics Worth Recovering?", J. Paul Hunter has challenged readers to recover in detail forgotten

standards of beauty by way of introducing a special issue of *Eighteenth-Century Studies* [34 (2000): 1–20]. Two admirable responses to the historicist challenge are Alison Conway, *Private Interests*: *Women, Portraiture, and the Visual Culture of the English Novel, 1709–1791* (Toronto: University of Toronto Press, 2001); and David L. Porter's *Ideographia: The Chinese Cipher in Early Modern Europe* (Stanford: Stanford University Press, 2001).

2. "The Speechless Image" in *The Relevance of the Beautiful and Other Essays*, trans. Nicholas Walker, ed. with an introduction Robert Bernasconi (Cambridge: Cambridge University Press, 1986), 83–91: "If we consider the rich, colorful, and resplendent eloquence that speaks to us so clearly and fluently from the classical periods of painting represented in our museums, and compare it with the creative art of our own time, we certainly have the impression of speechlessness" (83).

3. Ronald Paulson has explored the aesthetics of novelty in *Breaking and Remaking: Aesthetic Practice in England, 1700–1820* (New Brunswick: Rutgers University Press, 1989), which sets forth the iconoclastic paradigm; and in *The Beautiful, Novel, and Strange: Aesthetics and Heterodoxy* (Baltimore: Johns Hopkins University Press, 1996), which charts the influence of Addisonian novelty through Hogarth into Fielding, Sterne, and others. The controversy of the ancients and moderns is treated in historical detail by Joseph M. Levine, *The Battle of the Books: History and Literature in the Augustan Age* (Ithaca: Cornell University Press, 1991). Prof. Levine's *Between the Ancients and the Moderns*: *Baroque Culture in Restoration England* (New Haven: Yale University Press, 1999) briefly discusses C. A. Du Fresnoy in connection with Dryden's translation (101–05).

4. I have in mind modern theories of representation drawn from spatial form or structural linguistics. My concern is not so much that they reify the values of one version of the analogy or another as that they may suggest the exclusive formulation of a period contest better viewed as historical dialectic. See Joseph Frank, *The Idea of Spatial Form* (New Brunswick: Rutgers University Press, 1991); and Wendy Steiner, *The Colors of Rhetoric*: *Problems in the Relation between Modern Literature and Painting* (Chicago: University of Chicago Press, 1982).

5. *Venus in Exile: The Rejection of Beauty in Twentieth-Century Art* (New York: Free Press, 2001), 241. The major focus of this brilliant study is the situation of the "female subject" (xix) in modern and postmodern discussions of art.

6. Refs. to the poetry are to *The Twickenham Edition of the Works of Alexander Pope*, gen. ed. John Butt et al., 11 vols. (London: Methuen, 1939–69), here to 2: 155; canto 1, line 121, and cited further as *TE* by volume and page, canto and line.

7. The connection is noticed in Timothy Erwin, "Alexander Pope and the Disappearance of the Beautiful," *Eighteenth-Century Life* 16, 3 (November 1992): 46–64; repr. with additions in *So Rich a Tapestry: The Sister Arts and Cultural Studies*, ed. Kate Greenspan and Ann Hurley (Lewisburg, PA: Bucknell University

Press, 1995), 88–115.

8. *Francesco Albani* (New Haven: Yale University Press, 1999), 19–23. During the early seventeenth century, Puglisi explains, Albani designed four separate but related allegorical landscape cycles for four different patrons. The Louvre cycle is the second of these. The earlier cycles treat of Venus and Diana and represent a contest based upon Ovid's *Metamorphoses*, while the later cycles involve the four elements of earth, air, fire, and water. The cycle now at the Louvre eventually became part of the royal collections of Louis XIV.

9. Edmund Burke, *A Philosophical Enquiry into the Origin of our Ideas of the Sublime and Beautiful*, ed J. T. Boulton (London: Routledge and Kegan Paul, 1958). Where the absence of pain produces delight, a kind of negative pleasure, the beautiful for Burke is experienced as a positive pleasure arising from six qualities: smallness, smoothness, variety in direction of the parts, integration of the parts, delicacy, and clarity of color. Burke is throughout interested in efficient rather than formal or final causes.

10. Translated in the same year by Thomas Rymer as *Reflections on Aristotle's Treatise of Poesie*. See the commentary of Curt A. Zimansky in his edition of *The Critical Works of Thomas Rymer* (New Haven: Yale University Press, 1956). The edition of the *Reflections* quoted here is from *The Whole Critical Works of Monsieur Rapin* (London: H. Bonwicke, 1706), 2 vols., 2: 150–51. Emile Audra pointed out that the formula in the *Essay on Criticism* according to which the rules are nature methodized comes directly from Rapin. E. Audra, *L'Influence française dans l'oeuvre de Pope* (Paris: Champion, 1931), 208. See also the introduction of Audra and Williams to the *Essay on Criticism* and 'The Design of the Essay' (*TE* 1: 219–20, 223–32). The Twickenham editors also cite several other parallels between the *Reflections* and the *Essay on Criticism* (*TE* 1: 248, 256, 258–59, 269, 273, and 314). The influence of Rapin's *Discourse of Pastorals* on Pope's *Pastorals* is documented by the Twickenham editors in the introduction to the *Pastorals* (*TE* 1: 13–20).

11. Caroli Alfonsi Du Fresnoy, *De arte graphica* (Paris, C. Barbin, 1668); C. A. Du Fresnoy, *The Art of Painting*, trans. John Dryden (London, J. Heptinstall, 1695), 75, cited hereafter in the text.

12. Du Fresnoy, *De arte graphica* (1668), 37, line 262.

13. C. A. Du Fresnoy, *L'art de Peinture*, trans. Roger de Piles (Paris: N. Langlois, 1673), 43.

14. *The Art of Painting*, 2nd ed. (London, B. Lintot, 1716), n.p.

15. André Fontaine, ed. *Conférences inédites de l'académie royale de peinture et de sculpture* (Paris: A. Fontemoing, n. d.), 38. The story is repeated in Henri Testelin, *Sentimens des plus habiles peintres sur la pratique de la peinture et sculpture* (1680; Paris: Mabre-Cramoisy, 1696), in the last lecture, on coloring, 36.

16. Daniel Wildenstein, "Les oeuvres de Charles Le Brun d'après les gravures de son temps," *Gazette des Beaux Arts*, 6th ser., 66 (1965), 47, item 251, "L'Invention du Dessin." Robert Rosenblum surveys later images of the Dibutade legend in "The Origin of Painting: A Problem in the Iconography of Romantic

Classicism," *Art Bulletin* 39 (1957): 279–90.

17. Norman Bryson, *Word and Image: French Painting of the Ancien Regime* (Cambridge, Cambridge University Press, 1981). See especially Bryson's distinction between "discursive" and "figural" discourse (6), and also his treatment of Le Brun and bureaucratic style (29–57).

18. Fontaine, ed., *Conférences inédites*, 35–38.

19. As the chief mechanical means to excellence in design, the line attracts an unusual amount of discussion. In the first lecture of Testelin in his *Sentimens des peintres* on the uses of design, for example, *le trait* is "nothing but a physical line, or mechanical demonstration, which always has sizable dimension, no matter how slim; which begins and ends the extent of the exterior surface of a subject, and which marks off the diverse parts which it contains; the task of lines is to express the forms of bodies according to their different aspects and situations" (9).

On the history of the French Royal Academy and the controversy of *dessin* and *coloris* see Nikolaus Pevsner, *Academies of Art, Past and Present* (Cambridge: Cambridge University Press, 1940), 82–110; and Bernard Teyssèdre, *Roger de Piles et les débats sur le coloris au siècle de Louis XIV* (Paris: Bibliotheque des arts, 1957). On colorist theory see Thomas Puttfarken, *Roger de Piles'Theory of Art* (New Haven: Yale University Press, 1985); and Jacqueline Lichtenstein, *The Eloquence of Color: Rhetoric and Painting in the French Classical Age* (Berkeley: University of California Press, 1993).

20. Joseph Addison and Richard Steele, *The Spectator*, ed. Donald F. Bond, 5 vols. (Oxford: Clarendon Press, 1965), 3: 543, and cited afterwards in the text.

21. One might well want to ask to what degree these competing frameworks are genuinely related, and whether their continental drift in opposed directions reflects a common geographical origin. While the discourse of design is based in rhetoric and the discourse of the image in perception, both frameworks articulate forms of critical discrimination. Although one discourse is associated with connoisseurship and the other with a polite print culture, both sponsor the appreciation of the aesthetic object in the public sphere. Both frameworks moreover take ancient authority to exemplify their prime qualities. For Pope in the *Essay on Criticism* the chief exemplar of invention or originality is Homer, of design Virgil, and of striking verbal coloring or metaphorical elaboration Longinus. For Addison the chief exemplar of the great is Homer, of the uncommon Ovid, and of the beautiful Virgil. A thoroughgoing comparison of the two triads would pursue implicit parallels between invention and greatness, and between design and the beautiful, as well as between the rhetorical sublime of Longinus and its empirical reconfigurations. A contextual analysis of the critical rivalry of Pope and Addison would further clarify the degree of aesthetic affinity and difference between the two.

22. On the long history of the term see James A. W. Heffernan, *Museum of Words: the Poetics of Ekphrasis from Homer to Ashbery* (Chicago: University of Chicago Press, 1993). Heffernan defines *ekphrasis* as a literary mode centered in

the verbal representation of a visual representation, including those imaginary visual representations such as Marvell's gallery or Keats's Grecian urn (3). "Ekphrasis," he adds helpfully, "commonly reveals a profound ambivalence toward visual art, a fusion of iconophilia and iconophobia, of veneration and anxiety" (7).

23. Samuel Richardson, *Pamela, Or, Virtue Rewarded*, ed. Peter Sabor with an introduction by Margaret Doody (Harmondsworth: Penguin, 1980), 85. The passage appears in abbreviated form in the two-volume first edition of *Pamela* (London: C. Rivington and J. Osborn, 1740). During the 1750s Richardson revised Pamela extensively, and though the revisions would wait until 1801 to be incorporated into the novel, they have good authority. Many of the later changes refine the language of the heroine. When the ladies visit her in the first edition, for example, Pamela asks simply, "Why can't they make their game without me?" (1740; 1: 59). After 1801 her lament reads, "Why should they make me the subject of their diversion?" (1801; 1980, 82). In general the later revisions to letter 23 only heighten the opposition of word and image. In the first edition the letter simply reports a brief but pointed dialogue between Pamela and her visitors; the revised edition interpolates paragraphs of damning verbal description, one for each of the ladies. Pamela explains to her parents that she draws these characters because "when I was hardly twelve years old, you used not to dislike my descriptions" (1801; 1980, 82–83). If Pamela makes her sketches for idle amusement, Richardson clearly gives them a social and aesthetic spin that represents the view from downstairs, where certain modes of art and architectural appreciation are the privilege of social rank. For more information about Richardson's revisions see the prefatory "Note on the Text" in Sabor's 1980 edition of *Pamela* (21–22); and T. C. Duncan Eaves and Ben D. Kimpel, "Richardson's Revisions of Pamela," *Studies in Bibliography* 20 (1967): 61–88.

24. On the visual reception of the novel see James Grantham Turner, "Novel Panic: Picture and Performance in the Reception of Richardson's *Pamela*," *Representations* 48 (1994): 70–96. Turner provides a loosely lexical account of the way the haptic, plebeian, and internalized visuality of the novel—notably its paradoxical use of scenographic terminology to frame incidents that refuse depiction—finds commercial expression in the "raucous public trading" (73) of its imitations and successors. Turner quotes Aaron Hill as wondering whether textual illustration would not damage the "inward Idea" (77) that readers entertain of Pamela. In *Licensing Entertainment: The Elevation of Novel Reading in Britain, 1684–1750* (Berkeley and Los Angeles: University of California Press, 1998), 176–230, William B. Warner argues convincingly that *Pamela* is an allegory of novel reading, an "overwriting" (193) or intertextual correction of the early novel of amorous intrigue. Richardson borrows from mid-century painting the

strategy of representing a virtuous innocence absorbed *à la* Chardin in its own quotidian interiority, according to Warner.

On the close association of Richardson and the painter, actor, and illustrator of *Pamela* Francis Hayman, see further an excellent article by Janet E. Aikins,

"Picturing 'Samuel Richardson': Francis Hayman and the Intersection of Word and Image," *Eighteenth-Century Fiction* 14, 3/4 (2002): 465–506.

25. On ancient ekphrasis and related *topoi* in a wide variety of cultural forms, from wall paintings to monuments as well as poems, see the collection edited by Jas Elsner, *Art and Text in Roman Culture* (Cambridge: Cambridge University Press, 1996). "The problems of the relation of word and image—of two kinds of representation which at the same time require different modes of apprehension—are among the oldest and most fruitful in the history of art," he writes by way of introduction (2). Classical discussions of the beautiful need not involve verbal description, as a glance at *The Phaedo* will show, nor is classical ekphrasis limited to the topic of the beautiful. I am grateful to Dr. Elsner for kindly pointing me to Lucian's *Images* as a consciously ekphrastic consideration of ideal beauty.

26. Lucian, *The Works of Lucian, translated from the Greek, by Several Eminent Hands, with the Life of Lucian, a Discourse on his Writings, and a Character of Some of the Present Translators, Written by John Dryden, Esq.*, 4 vols. (London: Samuel Briscoe, 1710–11), 2: 383 (1710). Dryden was responsible only for the biography of Lucian, written many years earlier.

27. *Joseph Andrews*, ed. Martin C. Battestin (Middletown, CT: Wesleyan University Press, 1967), 41, and cited hereafter in the text.

28. In *Richardson and Fielding: The Dynamics of a Critical Rivalry* (Lewisburg, PA: Bucknell University Press, 1999), Allen Michie remarks that nineteenth-century critics, especially, employ metaphors drawn from art to make distinctions of style between the two (112–14).

29. *The History of Tom Jones*, ed. Martin C. Battestin (Middletown, CT: Wesleyan University Press, 1975), 2 vols., 1: 156. Battestin notes that Fielding said that he formed his own style after Lucian, and that he admired him enough to plan a new translation, later abandoned (2: 686, n. 1)

30. In *Lovers, Clowns, and Fairies: An Essay on Comedies* (Chicago: University of Chicago Press, 1993), 63.

31. Jane Austen, *The Novels of Jane Austen*, ed. R. W. Chapman, 3rd ed., 6 vols. (Oxford: Clarendon Press, 1933), 2: 23, and quoted afterwards by title, volume, and page.

32. Jacques Derrida, *The Truth in Painting*, trans. Geoff Bennington and Ian McLeod (Chicago: University of Chicago Press, 1987). "A parergon comes against, beside, and in addition to the *ergon*, the work done [*fait*], the fact [*fait*], the work, but it does not fall to one side, it touches and cooperates within the operation from a certain outside" (54).

33. On the multiple permutations of the sublime in the novel, see Lorrie Clark, "Transfiguring the Romantic Sublime in *Persuasion*," in *Jane Austen's Business: Her World and Her Profession*, ed. Juliet McMaster and Bruce Stovel (New York: St. Martin's Press, 1996), 30–41. For a broad contextual treatment of nationalist discourses of masculinity influenced by the sublime, including that of Austen in *Persuasion*, see Tim Fulford, "Romanticizing the Empire: The

Naval Heroes of Southey, Coleridge, Austen, and Marryat," *Modern Language Quarterly* 60, 2 (1999), 161–96.

34. Justus Lipsius, *A Discourse of Constancy in Two Books, Chiefly Containing Consolations against Publick Evils*, trans. Nathaniel Wanley (London: J. Redmayne, 1670), 19–20, 21, 22. Like Erasmus a Dutch humanist, Lipsius advocated constancy as a means of withstanding political turmoil by reconciling stoic doctrine and Christian teaching. See further Adriana McCrea, *Constant Minds: Political Virtue and the Lipsian Paradigm in England, 1584–1650* (Toronto: University of Toronto Press, 1997); and Mark Morford, *Stoics and Neostoics: Rubens and the Circle of Lipsius* (Princeton: Princeton University Press, 1991).

35. *On Beauty and Being Just* (Princeton: Princeton University Press, 1999), 107. The Enlightenment diminution of the beautiful in favor of the sublime, Scarry argues, has separated the classical idea from its proper power to symbolize vitality, symmetry, and equality. Yet in the symmetry of weighted scales, in the ancient etymology of being *fair*, and in a joint promise of security, she goes on to say, classical beauty and justice have always shared an abiding association.

Pygmalion's "*Wanton Kind of Chace*": Hogarth, Rowlandson and the "Line of Beauty"

ADAM KOMISARUK

This is an essay about a dirty picture, made around 1800 by a leading practitioner of that art, Thomas Rowlandson. In recent years, although major social histories of pornography have emerged,[1] this artist's voluminous *oeuvre* has attracted little systematic analysis. His erotic works remain in disparate collections with no *catalogue raisonné*.[2] Thirty years have elapsed since Ronald Paulson's "new interpretation" of Rowlandson;[3] theory, especially feminism, has been virtually silent on the subject. An atmosphere of either sheepish evasion or smirking insinuation can attend the occasional critic who takes Rowlandson seriously. While I will not pretend to redress this situation at a stroke, I would like to delineate, by way of a single work, some aspects of Rowlandson's aesthetic as they relate to the conception of the erotic self. The picture (fig. 1) is variously titled "Pygmalion and Galatea", "The Modern Pygmalion" or simply "The Ancients." Pygmalion, his sculpting tools fallen by his side, reclines naked on a cloth-draped couch. He stares adoringly at the newly animated Galatea, who clambers up to mount him sexually. She grasps his right hand with her right while steadying his penis with her left. The assignation takes place in what appears to be a classical rotunda. Nude and seminude females in antique attire stare down at the lovers from the gallery. The pedestal of the enormous dolphin-handled urn to the right depicts the rape of the Sabine

Figure 1. Thomas Rowlandson, *Pygmalion and Galatea* (c. 1800?). Etching and Watercolor. Courtesy of the Victoria and Albert Museum, London.

women; the erection sported by the Roman male literally parallels Pygmalion's.

The bodies of Pygmalion and Galatea, both individually and jointly, form an S-shaped curve that dominates many of Rowlandson's satirical illustrations. The *Exhibition Stare-Case*, for example, depicts a mishap at Sir William Chambers' Somerset House, a Royal-Academy venue with a serpentining, notoriously steep stairwell. In *The Life Class*, the female model's S-shaped pose emphasizes her serene insouciance toward the ill-proportioned oglers.[4] In what may be his most important observation about Rowlandson, Paulson traces this motive to William Hogarth's *Analysis of Beauty, Written with a View of Fixing the Fluctuating Ideas of Taste*[5] — a 1753 essay that distills as the fundamental principle of art the S-shaped curve, the line of variety, or as Hogarth dubs it the "Line of Beauty" (fig. 2).[6] The *Analysis* includes two large fold-out prints, one of a statuary yard and the other of a courtly dance; each principal scene is framed by smaller numbered figures which Hogarth uses as examples in his text. Thus the muscled human thigh is beautiful but the tubular wooden leg is not; the sinuous pose of the Antinous is beautiful but that of the stiff-backed fop is not; the gentle dancers are beautiful, but not the Henry VIII who stares down at them from the wall, with his knees locked and hands on hips; and the twisted cornucopia is beautiful but becomes less so as it approaches the simple cone. The beauty of every one of these forms is in proportion to how much or how little it employs the serpentine line.

Despite an absoluteness in "fix[ing] the fluctuating ideas of taste" that might make the young Edmund Burke grin, the *Analysis* has as its fundamental theme the encounter with flux and difference. I would like to explore how Hogarth's valorization of "variety" destabilizes the aesthetic object and, in turn, the perceiving subject in ways for which psychoanalysis provides a vocabulary. Moreover, although Hogarth seems at first to welcome such a destabilization, his confrontation with female sexuality leads him to desire not difference but homogeneity. The line of beauty measures both the artist's solicitude to trammel sexual difference and the futility of such an effort. I will argue that Rowlandson the satirist is fundamentally more honest about the self-defeating quality of the line of beauty than Hogarth.[7] Bradford Mudge—an able critic of Rowlandson and reconstructor of the social contexts on which this largely theoretical essay will touch only in part—finds the "Pygmalion" image

> the closest thing we have to a comprehensive statement of Rowlandson's aesthetic. Not only does it depict the transformative powers of the Romantic imagination—one

THE
ANALYSIS
OF
BEAUTY.

Written with a view of fixing the fluctuating I D E A S of
T A S T E.

BY *WILLIAM HOGARTH.*

So vary'd he, and of his tortuous train
Curl'd many a wanton wreath, in fight of Eve,
To lure her eye.-------- Milton.

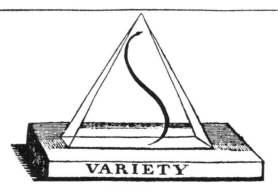

L O N D O N:

Printed by *J. REEVES* for the *AUTHOR,*
And Sold by him at his Houfe in LEICESTER-FIELDS.

MDCCLIII.

Figure 2. William Hogarth, *The Analysis of Beauty* (1753), title page.
© Copyright The British Museum, London.

cannot help but think of Keats's account of "Adam's dream"—
it also suggests that artist and artwork, artwork and viewer
participate equally in pleasures inescapably corporeal . . . .
The graphic representation of sexual intercourse was for
Rowlandson philosophically, aesthetically, and morally
justifiable precisely because it depicted three consummations
in one: that of the body, that of the mind, and that of the
market.[8]

I shall try a more anti-Romantic approach to Rowlandson, for I would
question whether his eroticism is best served by a millenarian vocabulary
of transubstantiation, incarnation and consummation. That eroticism, I
believe, is one not of immanence but of absence, not of the "comprehensive"
statement but of insufficiency, not of the Adamic waking dream but of the
elfish deception exposed. In Rowlandson's vision, both sexual partners
discover the impossibility of selfhood and, perhaps, of artistic representation
itself.

I

The pyramid-encased serpentine line as the essence of beauty, says
Hogarth in his preface, was a secret guarded by the ancients. Like most
secrets of its kind, it safeguarded not an intrinsically dangerous knowledge
but the authority of the priestly caste. The eighteenth-century aesthetic
treatise continues this trend by confining the true judgment of taste to
academicians. Hogarth's approach is a decidedly modern one that throws
the Eleusinian mysteries of beauty open to public view. His "anti-academic
treatise" begins not with abstractions but with particular observations: "We
can imagine Hogarth during the years 1745–1753 strolling around London,
observing as always expressions and movements, the way light plays on a
surface, the form shadows take as he passes beside a wall—collecting
aspects of Nature, but now looking more selectively, seeking examples to
fit his thesis" (Paulson 1993: 65, 57). The artist merely concretizes what
every layman already knows: "no sooner are two boxers stript to fight,
but even a butcher, thus skill'd, shews himself a considerable critic in
proportion; and on this sort of judgment, often gives, or takes the odds, at
bare sight only of the combatants. I have heard a blacksmith harangue like
an anatomist, or sculptor, on the beauty of a boxer's figure, tho' not perhaps
in the same terms" (Hogarth 67). Werner Busch summarizes: "Hogarth
attempts to separate artistic form and the expression of social rank from
each other."[9]

Without stretching the metaphor too much, we might say that Hogarth's analysis of the individual form exhibits a similar democratizing tendency. He asks us to imagine each object in a manner akin to the "wire mesh" mode of current computer-modeling programs,

> its inward contents scoop'd out so nicely, as to have nothing of it left but a thin shell, exactly corresponding both in its inner and outer surface, to the shape of the object itself: and let us likewise suppose this thin shell to be made up of very fine threads, closely connected together, and equally perceptible, whether the eye is supposed to observe them from without, or within; and we shall find the ideas of the two surfaces of this shell will naturally coincide (21).

This method surmounts the division between inside and outside, front and back, visible and invisible, part and whole. It unifies as instantaneous what would otherwise be a succession of mutually exclusive perceptions:

> in the common way of taking the view of any opake object, that part of its surface, which fronts the eye, is apt to occupy the mind alone, and the opposite, nay even every other part of it whatever, is left unthought of at that time: and the least motion we make to reconnoitre any other side of the object, confounds our first idea, for want of the connexion of the two ideas, which the complete knowledge of the whole would naturally have given us (21–2).

Hogarth repeatedly affirms his desire to "acquir[e] . . . a more perfect knowledge of the whole", to "view the whole form", to "retain the idea of the whole" (21). His metaphor of the transparent shell, however, introduces a disjunction in spite of itself. That the inside and outside surfaces "coincide" means that they must differ; they are, moreover, not copies but inversions of one another. Inside and outside are each *doppelgängers* to the other, each exposing what is lacking in the other and in itself, touching each other not in mutual completion but in mutual lack.

Hogarth's construction of inside and outside as a unity recalls the illusion of the child at Lacan's mirror stage.[10] The child forms an *imago* in an effort to position as ideal, coherent and *spatial* a self that is in fact powerless, premature and *temporal*. Because the specular "I" is detached, miniaturized and inverted, however, it mirrors this fragmentation of the self. The reliance of the *Innenwelt* upon a projection into the *Umwelt* to know its own nature affirms that nature as an irreducible exteriority. Hogarth's infantine dream of the all-at-once in a shell whose "two surfaces will naturally coincide" eventually reminds us of the heterogeneity of our perception, in which "the least motion we make to reconnoitre any other side of the object, confounds our first idea." By positioning himself inside a hollowed-out object, Hogarth does not penetrate to some essential and secure center—Lacan refers to the troping of the "I" as a "fortress", a "stadium", a "castle"—but rather observes through its crosshatched threads the operations of the *Umwelt* upon which the *Innenwelt* is contingent (the mother?). What Hogarth wants is to be in two places at once, to project his imagination "into the vacant space within this shell" while his eye performs its surveillance from without, and so "makes us masters of every view" (21). His panoptical terminology is a confession of impotence.

What saves Hogarth from inauthenticity is that he contradicts himself. He finally decides that simultaneity is neither achievable nor desirable.

> . . . in the example of the sphere given above, every one of the imaginary circular threads has a right to be consider'd as an out-line of the sphere, as well as those which divide the half, that is seen, from that which is not seen; and if the eye be supposed to move regularly round it, these threads will each of them as regularly succeed one another in the office of out-lines . . . and the instant any one of these threads, during the motion of the eye, comes into sight on one side, its opposite thread is lost, and disappears on the other (22).

Hogarth goes on in his chapter "Of Intricacy" to points out that the eye never takes in an entire visual field—in this case, a row of letter "A"s—in an instant, but darts back and forth. Naturally we could deconstruct the field further; even the single "A" has its component parts, and so forth. Thus when one part is in focus, another will be out of focus; but by alternating rapidly among them the eye, abetted by memory, suppresses this fact. Hogarth attempts to restore the temporality of perception. The successive play of visible and invisible, moreover, forms the core of his aesthetic theory. The serpentine line (line of grace) surpasses the waving line (line of beauty), even as the waving line surpasses the curved, and the curved the straight. Hogarth exemplifies the line of grace by a wire wrapped around a cone, or by the thread of a cornucopia "which, as it dips out of sight. . .in the middle, and returns again at the smaller end, not only gives play to the imagination, and delights the eye, on that account; but informs it likewise of the quantity and variety of the contents" (50). Such a line *"leads the eye a wanton kind of chace"*, fulfilling our natural "love of pursuit": "Wherein would consist the joys of hunting, shooting, fishing, and many other favourite diversions, without the frequent turns and difficulties, and disappointments, that are daily met with in the pursuit?—how joyless does the sportsman return when the hare has not had fair play?" (33, 32; emphasis Hogarth's). We can sympathize with the desire to place Hogarth in the empiricist pantheon:

> Attempting, from the Preface on, to demystify beauty and its would-be unaccountable "*je-ne-sais-quoi*", Hogarth, on the contrary, claims to be the proponent of an aesthetics of the "*je-sais-quoi*", based on a strong belief in a world understandable by reason. The perception of beauty proceeds from a careful sensorial observation of the world and its "particulars", as Locke called them, far and free from elitist, connoisseur or abstract prejudices, "without a pair of *double-ground* connoisseur spectacles."[11]

Such a revelatory posture, however, would seem to miss Hogarth's point. To subsume any form within a system of total knowledge would neutralize its grace—much as, true to form, Hogarth's own expository line must undulate from knowing to unknowing and back again, in a series of contrary movements where even self-contradiction prolongs the thrill of the chase. The "imaginary circular thread" that "divide[s] the half [of an object] that is seen, from that which is not seen"—even the syntax is asymmetrical—has "a right to be consider'd" a true outline; indeed, it may be the truest outline, since it alone takes the measure of the non-self-identicality that is constitutive of that object. "[T]here is", insists Hogarth, "only one precise serpentine line" (51).

Hogarth's game metaphors will by this time have called to mind the sexual implications of the serpentine line, which the *Analysis* amply considers. Hogarth returns again and again to the beauty of the female form, calling it generally preferable not only to the male but to the most finely wrought sculpture. The title-page to the *Analysis* prepares us for this theme. Its vignette shows an upstanding S-curve with a serpent's head, and an inscription from *Paradise Lost* describing Satan in his new serpentine guise. To quote a bit more of the passage than Hogarth does:

>   . . .With tract oblique
> At first, as one who sought access, but feared
> To interrupt, sidelong he works his way.
> As when a ship by skilful steersman wrought
> Nigh river's mouth or foreland, when the wind

Veers oft, as oft so steers, and shifts her sail
So varied he; and of his tortuous train
Curled many a wanton wreath, in sight of Eve
To lure her eye . . . .[12]

It is Satan's movement, not his shape, that really embodies variety; we can see the appeal for Hogarth, who finds the S-curve more interesting if it moves, and more interesting still if the path of movement is itself S-shaped. The line of beauty in motion is the line of grace, as in the Miltonic lines that Mary Wollstonecraft always resented—"For contemplation he and valor formed,/For softness she and sweet attractive grace" (4.297–8)—which makes Eve *l'allegra* to Adam's *il penseroso*. Indeed, Eve's capacity for varied movement, action, perhaps even social change as against Adam's less decisive philosophizing, establishes a well-known parallel between her and Satan.[13] The serpent-inhabiting fiend "curl[s] many a wanton wreath, in sight of Eve/To lure her eye", just as the "serpent" Eve wears her hair in "wanton ringlets" and is later ordered "out of [the] sight" of Adam—and, in turn, Hogarth's line of beauty will "lead the eye a wanton kind of chace."

The combination of attraction and danger in these wanton lines is clear from the famous passage about Eve's hair, which may appeal to Hogarth for the same reason that it is a deconstructive *locus classicus*:

She as a veil down to the slender waist
Her unadorned golden tresses wore
Disheveled, but in wanton ringlets waved
As the vine curls her tendrils, which implied
Subjection, but required with gentle sway,
And by her yielded, by him best received,
Yielded with coy submission, modest pride,
And sweet reluctant amorous delay (4.304–11).

What is it, exactly, about Eve's hair that implies subjection? Is it the fact that she wears it long, that she leaves it "disheveled", that it is "unadorned", all of the above? If the passage tries to pinpoint the reason for Eve's subjection, the subject remains elusive, slipping through the wanton folds of Milton's undulating syntax, and entangling the reader along with it. The word "subjection" itself offers little authority, since it does not clarify whether Eve is the subject or the object of the subjection. Indeed, she may be both, as Milton repeatedly asserts Eve's subjective autonomy, but also attributes this power paradoxically to her willingness to render herself subject to Adam's dominion. Satan tempts her by catalyzing the Satanic impulse that already dwells within her—the impulse to affirm her subjectivity in the face of authority, albeit by "tract oblique", "gentle sway", "coy submission, modest pride,/And sweet reluctant amorous delay." Because Eve's status as subject is semantically and actually ambiguous, her subjection cannot be accomplished, only "implied." Whether we read this crux of a passage as feminist, anti-feminist, or anti-anti-feminist, the idea of Eve's and Satan's mutual wantonness makes a fitting introduction to Hogarth's pursuit of the variegated subject that lures him. This epigraph, however, is merely an epitaph for the self-identicality of the text within. Hogarth suggests that the power of his own oblique tract to "fix the fluctuating ideas of taste," as his Satanically subtle subtitle puts it, may be a power of suggestion at best.

Hogarth's engagement with feminine difference seems well enough, but soon develops signs of anxiety. Taken out of context and carried to extremes, he explains later, variety will counterproductively collapse into "sameness", a "confused heap." For this reason he balances it with "character", the obedience of the harmonious line to universal categories. We recall Pope's axiom that "most women have no characters at all," by which he means they lack not moral fiber but distinguishing marks.[14] If the same female model can be painted on one occasion as "sweet [St.] Cecilia", and on another as "Fannia, leering on her own good man", Pope reasons, then she must have no fixed identity whatsoever (13, 9). Her "overdone" line of variety thus paradoxically becomes "uniform and confin'd", and reduces to two "general characteristick"s: "the love of pleasure and the love of sway" (210). This overabundance of female energy, however, exists alongside "man's oppression" in a kind of feedback loop or chicken-and-egg relationship (213). Pope addresses woman as

> Wise wretch! with pleasures too refined to please,
> With too much spirit to be e'er at ease,
> With too much Quickness ever to be taught,
> With too much thinking to have common thought:
> You purchase pain with all that joy can give,
> And die of nothing but a rage to live (95–100).

For Pope, as for Hogarth, the physical and mental voracity by virtue of which women lack character, is both a cause and an effect of men's ill-equipment to sate it. The line of beauty becomes nothing so much as a measure of its own incapacity.

The limitations to Hogarth's comfort with the "wanton kind of chace" become even more pronounced in the transition from art to life. His examples of femininity must remain carefully circumscribed by eighteenth-century bourgeois fashion. For example, the untressed lock of hair—a nod to Milton—has "an effect too alluring to be strictly decent, as is very well known to the loose and lowest class of women", even though "being pair'd in so stiff a manner, as they formerly were, they lost the desired effect" (39)—"they" presumably referring to the locks, although the unpaired pronouns point equally to the women, whom Hogarth finds paired in varying degrees of stiffness. Hogarth's objection to the errant curl is that it "break[s] the regularity of the oval" of the female face (39). The latter form figures in his chaste revision to *Boys Peeping at Nature* (fourth state, 1751); instead of lifting the skirt of the *Diana multimammia*, a putto now covers her pudenda with a small drawing of a female face, bisected with crosshatches and enclosed by an oval (Paulson 1993: 122). Paulson's attempt to resolve the loss of symmetry dialectically—"Both the uniformity of the Grecian Venus and the unenclosable variety of the living woman are required" (1993: 80)—portrays Hogarth as more untroubled by the female form than I think accurate.

In the *Analysis* Hogarth makes his point about the ideal S-curve in terms of the stay or stomacher, which supposedly pulls into the proper shape a female form that ordinarily is improper (fig. 3). The array is not of body types but of corset types; the moderate ideal at the center applies universally. It assures a women that is modest; fecund enough to have the single child that will recompense her alleged castration, but not so intimidating as the *Diana multimammia*; eminently available for male aesthetic delectation. Hogarth's presentation of the corset as empty and in profile—absolving him of bodily and facial confrontation respectively—complements this one-size-fits-all approach. He thus avoids confirming her as a subject—or, more likely according to Irigaray, as a site of perpetual flux:

> Woman is neither open nor closed. She is indefinite, in-finite, *form is never complete in her.* She is not infinite but neither is she *a* unit(y) . . . . This incompleteness in her form, her morphology, allows her continually to become something else, though this is not to say that she is ever univocally nothing. No metaphor completes her. Never is she this, then that, this and that . . . . But she is becoming that expansion that she neither is nor will be at any moment as definable universe . . . . And for her the risk of maternity is that of limiting (herself and her desire) to the world of *one* child . . . a femininity that conforms and corresponds too exactly to an idea—Idea—of woman, that is too obedient to a sex—to an

Figure 3. William Hogarth, *The Analysis of Beauty* (1753), pl. 1, fig. 2.
© Copyright The British Museum, London.

> Idea of sex—or to a fetish sex has already frozen into
> phallomorphism . . . . Whereas what happens in the jouissance
> of women exceeds all this . . . . The fullness of their coming
> into being is hinted, is proclaimed as possible, but within an
> extension swelling outward without discernible limits.
> Provided that . . . it has not already submitted . . . to a logos
> that claims to lead the potency of the maternal back into the
> same—to Sameness—in itself and for itself.[15]

What better device than a girdle to impose closure on woman and thereby
invite man to rend her apart? As one of Hogarth's shells, the compassing
threads here made of whalebone, it serves her up as a volumetric solid all
of whose surfaces coincide. Difference is brooked insofar as it can be
gracefully aestheticized. "[T]he whole stay, when put close together behind,
is truly a shell of well-varied contents, and its surface of course a fine
form" (49).[16]   The serpentine line doubles as a surgical slice across the
entire body, whose resemblance Paulson has noted to the dissected criminal
in *The Reward of Cruelty*: "if a line, or the lace were to be drawn, or
brought from the top of the lacing of the stay behind, round the body, and
down to the bottom peak of the stomacher; it would form such a perfect,
precise, serpentine-line, as has been shewn, round the cone" (Hogarth
49). An elusive object necessitates a circuitous path of penetration:
"Everything, then, has to be rethought in terms of curl(s), helix(es),
diagonal(s) spiral(s), roll(s), twirl(s), revolution(s), pirouette(s). Speculation
whirls round faster and faster as it pierces, bores, drills into a volume that
is supposed to be *solid* still. Covered with a hard shell that must be fractured,
trepanned, split open, explored in its hidden heart. Or belly" (*Speculum*
238).
  What is on the inside of woman, what are her contents, in what is she
content? It cannot be seen.

[T]he subject of women's sexuality is still very "obscure". . . .
female sexuality can be graphed along the axes of visibility of
(so-called) masculine sexuality. For such a demonstration to
hold up, the little girl must immediately become a little boy . . .
Inevitably, the trial of "castration" must be undergone. This
"little boy," who was, in all innocence and ignorance of sexual
difference, *phallic*, notices how ridiculous "his" sex organ
looks. "He" *sees* the disadvantage for which "he" is
anatomically destined: "he" has only a tiny little sex organ,
no sex organ at all, really, an almost invisible sex organ. The
almost imperceptible clitoris. The humiliation of being so badly
equipped, of cutting such a poor figure, in *comparison* with
the penis, with *the* sex organ can only lead to a desire to
"have something like it too," and Freud claims that this desire
will form the basis for "normal womanhood" (*Speculum* 48–
9).

Man responds to the inscrutable difference of woman by construing her
as the same, the same as herself and as him, the "not-one", the
"indifferent",[17] a closed volumetric solid that he can penetrate—not to
restore her primordial difference but to sheath himself, to find a receptacle
that reassures him of his identity. For the mirror that he makes of woman
to project the dream of his totality, in fact, reflects his own fearsome
heterogeneity. It is his own selfhood that is at stake in totalizing hers.
Hogarth makes this point clear in his treatment of the male torso, perhaps
the mirror-image of the girdled female. He asks us to imagine such a torso
made of wax, with thin wires drawn through it at right angles to one
another (fig. 4). These wires may then be painted up to the surface of the
wax figure. If the wires are then withdrawn from the wax and rearranged
at evenly spaced right angles, their unpainted area will describe the volume
of the torso. The original may thus be recreated at any scale. This body—
dismembered, pierced like the St. Sebastian that has become a gay male
icon—thus participates in a potentially endless act of reproduction of the
sort that Irigaray calls "hom(m)osexual." It enacts not a surrender but an
assertion of control, a fantasy not of perforation but of absolute closure—
a male self penetrated by the male self.

The conventional wisdom is that male homosexuality is at odds with
Hogarth's idea of beauty.[18] His preference for working from live female
models (a controversial practice in the contemporary academy because it
supposedly stimulated prurient interests [Paulson 1993: 77]) rather than
classical male statuary (or, more likely, its plaster facsimiles [105]) not

Figure 4. William Hogarth, *The Analysis of Beauty* (1753), pl. 1, fig. 53. © Copyright The British Museum, London.

only disparages the homosexual but associates him with the servile copyist. This apparent welcome of the female will is a welcome of the other in whom reproduction can be different every time, or who sometimes might not consent to reproduction at all. His decision to conduct his reproductive experiment on the male torso, however, suggests an aesthetics of the hom(m)osexual. His desire for the thing itself is rather a desire to "infus[e]" it with new meaning as Paulson says, to "fill" it, not to reproduce with it (always a chance operation), but to reproduce himself within it and by virtue of it (1993: 109, 107). The image in which he will remake it, of course, is never the same. The attempt at reproduction through total self-penetration reproduces only the insufficiency of the self, the masochistic *thanatos* that the sadistic drive for domination directs outward.

II

When Rowlandson employs the line of beauty he inherits a tradition, stretching from Hogarth back to Pope and Milton, of the male artist's desperate attempt to stabilize the difference traditionally symbolized by female wantonness but equally resident in himself. The self-defeating tendency of the line, the ultimate impossibility of "arraigning heterogeneity in a pose", as Derrida puts it, is central to Rowlandson's eroticism. Returning to the Pygmalion drawing, we find numerous kinds of impossibility that the seemingly perfect S-curve of the lovers' bodies cannot resolve. That Galatea goes from traditional object of the artistic gaze to sexual aggressor is the least of my concerns here. Her pose, for example, cannot be comfortable: in order to clasp Pygmalion's right hand, she twists her left hand around the inside of her left knee; illogically, her thumb faces outward. Alternatively, we might assume that it is her right hand that is holding his, but the positions of her upper arms do not support this interpretation. The only solution is for us to collapse the depth of field, finessing the awkwardness of Galatea's pose by eliminating the z-axis (relative to the viewer) across which her arm moves. To be sure, Rowlandson knew how to draw; he had been to the Royal Academy. The fact is that this fanciful foreshortening is a technique to which his erotic drawings often return, perhaps inspired by Hogarth's engraving *A Satire upon Perspective*.[19] For instance, in a print titled *The Jugglers* (fig. 5), leaving aside for the moment the ridiculous male figure to concentrate on the bare-bottomed woman on the left, we see that the coins she is catching in her apron are being thrown from the balcony a good distance in the background.

In most cases, the mutual exclusivity of figure and ground is essential to the integrity of an image. Kant implies as much when he repeatedly invokes the metaphor of the "ground" in positing the hierarchy of judgment: the ground of delight is desire; the ground of interest is want; the ground of experience is universal law; the law of nature is the ground of causality in the things of nature; the form of an object is the ground of aesthetic pleasure; *a priori* knowledge is the ground of judgment. The ground upon which Rowlandson builds, however, is shifting ground, and uses sexuality to deconstruct the idea of groundedness itself. At first sight, Galatea's limbs exemplify the line of grace which dips in and out of view, leading the eye a wanton kind of chase. Her arms disappear on one side of her raised left leg to reappear on the other side. If we eliminate the depth of field as Rowlandson seems to require, however, and read the composition as flat, then we must interpret her limbs as truly discontinuous. Her crooked right leg does not occlude her arms but bisects them. Unlike Hogarth's lines, which can presumptively be controlled as parts of a simultaneous whole, Galatea's come with no assurance that once they are interrupted they will pick up where they left off; their nature is to be broken from one another and by one another. They also break Pygmalion in four spots—his left wrist, his waist, his penis and his left thigh—and carve a gap into his chest that her left arm supplements, just as his right knee supplements a gap in her right knee. The lovers thus form what M.C. Escher calls "recursive figures," each of whose "ground can be seen as a figure in its own right."[20]

Figure 5. Thomas Rowlandson, *The Jugglers* (n.d.). Etching and watercolor. Courtesy of the Victoria and Albert Museum, London.

Barbara Johnson comments, "The dream of psychoanalysis is of course to represent sexual difference as a recursive figure, a figure in which both figure and ground, male and female, are recognizable, complementary forms. This dream articulates itself through the geometry of castration in Freud, in which the penis is the figure, or positive space, and the vagina the ground, or negative space. But there are limits to how recursive Freud wishes this figure to be", as he ultimately posits a hom(m)osexual model (19). Rowlandson's is more elaborate recursivity of mutual lack; each figure is drawn in drawing the other, because each has a gap waiting to be filled by the other. The ground collapses into the heterogeneous figure without the two ever becoming one.[21]

Is the relationship truly reciprocal? Is not Galatea destabilized by both the other and herself, but Pygmalion only by the other? Tranquil, with both feet on the ground, does he affirm a male selfhood that would remain intact if not for his partner, in whom he anticipates his own castration and consumption? No: he has enough anxiety on his own, something to which the antiquarian paraphernalia in the picture alludes. Rowlandson's figures are, of course, grounded, though not by one another: the true ground of the picture lies in the mythological allusions that specifically establish a male sense of ineffectuality. At the rear and center, the enthroned woman's exposed breasts, distended belly and twin lions on which she rests her hands associate her with the deity variously called Anath, Ishtar, Astarte, Cybele, Rhea, Ops—goddess of ferocious procreation whose priestesses, like the one on the far left, expose their loins in order to be impregnated by the spouting blood of men. Finally, the abduction of the Sabine women, portrayed on the pedestal to the right, was ordered by Romulus at the festival of the Consualia after the neighboring tribe had refused a depopulated Rome's request to intermarry. When the Sabine men avenged the rape by attacking Rome, the women interceded to make the peace again. Women's procreative power thus appears as the lynchpin of civilization, but the glowering presence of Cybele at back, combined with the violent reaction of the Roman men, suggests that this beautifying narrative exists only as an aspect of male solicitude to harness that procreative power.

More important still may be the role that antiquarianism itself played in Rowlandson's day. To place this movement in context, an historical interlude will be necessary. Much as they admired the antiquities of Europe, steadily imported by connoisseurs on the Grand Tour, eighteenth-century British artists felt anxious about the lack of an indigenous artistic tradition. Accordingly, there was much talk of setting up a national academy to nurture, and publicly exhibit the fruits of, such a tradition. The institutional history of art in the period, however, is rife with factionalism, infighting and political maneuvering.[22] The story begins at the founding of the St. Martin's Lane Academy in 1735 with the help of Hogarth, who envisioned it as egalitarian and emphatically un-French; he believed "the academy would never succeed if it aped the royal attitudes of a club of discerning gentlemen or was an adjunct of the royal court."[23] It was somewhat to his chagrin that, during a 1753 meeting at the Turk's Head Tavern, subscribers to the Academy made plans for converting it into a more regimented institution, although it was to be publicly chartered without resorting to royal patronage. The polite connoisseurs who comprised the Society of

Dilettanti (est. 1734) offered to contribute, provided they would retain control of the academy's administration and appointments; when the artists themselves refused this condition, the Dilettanti withdrew, leaving the scheme in disarray.[24]

There was William Shipley's drawing-school for the young at 101 Strand, which was also founded in 1753 and in the following year begat the Society for the Encouragement of Arts, Commerce, and Manufactures in Great Britain.[25] The "Society of Arts"—which resided at Charing Cross, then Little Denmark Court, then the Brothers Adam's Adelphi Buildings where it stands today—was populist in its conception. Its membership cut across class lines; it did not have a charter; it allowed open competitions; its product was intended for public rather than private consumption; and it emphasized the applied rather than the fine arts. One commentator noted that the founders' "objects were national, and the members gave their money and their time not for their own private advantage, nor for the increase of their personal knowledge, but in an attempt to raise the productive powers of the nation itself."[26] It would take advantage of the industrial revolution to decrease, rather than increase, factory-worker exploitation, awarding prizes for a steam central-heating system, a chimney-cleaning device, respirator-masks and fire-escapes.[27] Furthermore, once the rival Royal Academy began siphoning off Britain's finest talent, the Society of Arts would survive as something of a left-wing haven, boasting such members as John Hamilton Mortimer[28], George Romney[29] and James Barry.[30] Hogarth was elected to the Society of Arts in 1755 but withdrew in 1757, apparently finding it, despite its best efforts, insensitive to the needs of the poor (Paulson 1993: 200).

In 1760, artists from the Foundling Hospital (chartered 1739, with Hogarth becoming governor the following year) used the Society of Arts' Great Room in the Strand for what proved London's first-ever public art exhibition. A breakaway group founded the Society of Artists [sic] of Great Britain (chartered in 1765, one year after Hogarth's death, as the Incorporated Society of Artists) and moved to Spring Gardens, Charing Cross in 1761. When dissention broke out in its ranks, another splinter group sought and, in 1768, obtained a charter from George III as the Royal Academy. Joshua Reynolds served as its first president until 1792, followed by Benjamin West until 1820 (with an 1805–6 hiatus). Its school was housed in Pall Mall, the exhibitions in Somerset House. Rowlandson— freshly polished in a drawing-academy of Paris, where he had traveled at the age of sixteen—enrolled at the Royal Academy and exhibited there on several occasions in the 1770s and '80s, being "set up as a friendly rival to

Mortimer" and proving "highly popular with the two sections of academicians and students" (Grego 1.53).

Rowlandson "had the undoubted genius to reflect a lustre on the Academy", Grego scolds, "if he had exerted his talents in the recognized channels, and withstood the impulse of his notoriety for producing irresistibly droll novelties, which . . . must infallibly prove pernicious to the practice of sober portraiture" (1.14). As it turned out, there was another line of descent from Shipley's original drawing school that would prove more hospitable to the caricaturist. In 1763 the school at 101 Strand had passed into the hands of his student (and Blake's future teacher) Henry Pars. Later it was used frequently for political lectures by John Thelwall, the fiery Jacobin radical and prominent member of the London Corresponding Society for parliamentary reform. In 1794, when the government endeavored to silence Thelwall for sedition, the lease was purchased by the bookseller/inventor/philanthropist Rudolph Ackermann, who re-opened it as an academy.[31] In 1795 he also opened a print shop down the street at 96 Strand, then in 1796 consolidated the two operations at 101 Strand. The latter space became Ackermann's celebrated "Repository"—a place of *"conversazione"* and even employment for sundry intellectuals and elites, many of them *ancien-régime* refugees from the French Revolution.[32] Allen Samuels gives us its flavor:

> It was, in effect, something akin to a combination of fashion house, design center, private club, circulating library, art gallery, museum, and bookshop. There was a large stock of fine art materials through which customers could browse. They could acquire artists' materials, or drawing books by masters, inspect caricatures or hire folios of prints; they could discuss the latest art fashions in everything from medallions to country house interiors, private carriages to new developments in watercolor technique; they could discover the most recently designed textures for fabrics for the use of wall and furniture decoration; or examine the latest in transparencies with which their lighting could be adorned. The repository was a fine shop in an age of elegance, but it spread its messages wider than the metropolis. Those who wished to follow fashion in the newly prosperous emergent industrial cities, as well as those secluded in English country houses, could draw on it for ideas (246). [33]

Ackermann and Rowlandson would become one another's most valuable collaborators. Their long-lasting association produced such popular works as the *Microcosm of London* (1806), the three *Tours of Dr. Syntax* (1812, 1820, 1821; published jointly 1823) and *The English Dance of Death* (1815–16).

Complicating this story further, however, is Paulson's hypothesis that the erotic prints such as the Pygmalion were produced not for Ackermann but for the Cheapside bookseller Thomas Tegg.[34] Tegg's specialty was to issue abridgements and cheap reprints of books whose remainder and copyright he had bought at a fraction of the original price; Carlyle, in fact, complained about him in his Parliamentary petition for the Copyright Bill. From 1807 Tegg also published the *Caricature Magazine or Hudibrastic Mirror*, volumes 2–3 of which bear Rowlandson's name (Paulson 1972: 132n35). A grocer's son, Tegg grew wealthy at his trade but was less inclined to associate with the Dilettanti than with the likes of Bewick and Paine; he sponsored Hone and once paid a £30,000 surety for Hunt.[35] Grego criticizes the Tegg prints primarily for their technical inferiority, but with such animus (he cannot even bear to call Tegg by name) that one suspects he has their indecent subject-matter in mind as well:

> There is an amazing contrast between the plates issued from the Repository, worked out like elaborate water-color drawings, and the lurid chromatic daubs which pass current to the present day, as Rowlandson's caricatures were issued from Cheapside *'price one shilling colored'*, after a school of vulgarity . . . . We are not inclined to offer uncharitable reflections on Rowlandson's City publisher. . . it is the bad taste of his customers, the respectable dealer evidently stooped to flatter, with which we are inclined to disagree, and we think justifiably . . . [they are] abominable to the sight of modern purchasers, and ruinous to the fair fame of the designer . . . [they have an] undiluted garishness, which utterly confuses the mind as to the meritorious qualities of the subjects so bespattered, and has the sinister effect, deplorable in itself, of compelling persons of chaste dispositions to dread caricatures as being on the surface something worse than scarlet abominations, fiendishly aggravated with additional lurid iniquities of a depraving tendency . . . (1.34–5).

This, then, was the trajectory of Rowlandson's career. He came of age artistically in a conservative offshoot (the Royal Academy) of an offshoot (the Society of Artists) of a fairly progressive body (the Foundling Hospital).

He then walked away from it to work for an Anglophile expatriate German (Ackermann) whose shop had once been a nursery for some persons with anti-establishment proclivities (future members of the Society of Arts) and a forum for another (Thelwall) but, two generations later, had become an oasis for the elite (the Repository). Moreover, when it came time to produce his erotica, he turned to a bookseller of marginal reputation and legality (Tegg) who consorted primarily with radicals.[36] We could attribute these inconsistencies to Rowlandsonian caprice were it not for the ease with which the different, often antagonistic elements of the contemporary art scene—connoisseurs, academicians, anti-academicians, entrepreneurs—bled into one another. The connoisseurs, prizing art as an marker of material status, mistrusted artists as vulgar tradesmen; academicians, seeing art as an instrument of moral edification, mistrusted connoisseurs as sensualists. Yet the two groups were linked both genealogically and, in their fetishization of antiquity, ideologically. Rowlandson and Hogarth share a skepticism of the tendency to venerate the dead object at the expense of breathing creatures: the Pygmalion print brings to life the precept in the *Analysis of Beauty* that a real woman exceeds a sculpted Venus. We may admire the consistency of Hogarth, who never found an institution that was sufficiently anti-institutional to his tastes. Yet his resistance to antiquarianism runs the risk of becoming a totalizing position that deprives him of the motility he seeks. Rowlandson, a product of the contemporary art scene and a trimmer among its institutions, knows its pretensions. He can therefore perform the ultimate stroke of the satirist, which is to implicate himself in his critique.

What is missing, once again, is "the sex." An important aspect of contemporary antiquarianism, which Rowlandson is likely to have known through his continental sojourn and residence in Ackermann's Repository, was the excavation of pagan fertility-cults. Starting in 1738, phallic totems were unearthed at Pompeii and Herculaneum under the supervision of Charles III, king of the Two Sicilies. It was observed that they continued to be employed in contemporary Neapolitan festivals and, in sublimated form, throughout Christian symbolism. This knowledge found its way to England by way of the archaeological grand tours sponsored principally by the Dilettanti.[37] Many of the passers-through were entertained by Sir William Hamilton, envoy to Naples since 1764, whose personal collection of erotic artifacts informed such tracts as Richard Payne Knight's *Discourse on the Worship of Priapus* (1786).[38] Emma Lady Hamilton—the quintessential woman of no character at all—regaled guests at her famous salons by assuming attitudes from classical statuary and paintings in her husband's archive.[39] In his dabblings among the tombs, Rowlandson frequently invokes Emma to advance his thesis that the antiquarians who contemplate the line of beauty are as precarious as the line itself. In *Modern Antiques*, for example, a decrepit Sir William inspects the Antinous while Emma makes carnal embrace with Admiral Nelson in a sarcophagus. Ann Bermingham argues that gender as well as social caste defines this vulnerability of the connoisseur, that the penises thrusting up from the Dilettanti's pages serve to "stiffen their masculine image" amid the prospect of "infertility or impotence", that their "collective gazing at antiquity" is itself a kind of ritual "intended to promote virility and therefore to secure the production of feminine pleasure in marriage."[40] Where Hogarth replaces one fetish (the classical simulacrum) with another (the living woman), Rowlandson stresses how risky a strategy this inflated masculinism can be. In Rowlandson's *The Jugglers*, a portly clown sports an enormous erection on which he balances a stack of china-ware. What destabilizes the scene is not just the frangibility of the china (these are not skittles, after all) or the insufficient balancing surface (the juggler is not using his back, after all): it is the fact that the behavior of the balancing-instrument is unpredictable, subject to tumescence or detumescence at any moment. In most cases its own excitement or performance anxiety will be its undoing.

We come then at length to Pygmalion himself, that notorious misogynist who carved in ivory the epitome of virtue that he could find in no living woman. A lifelong celibate, he then asked Aphrodite to animate the statue. Some writers after Ovid turn Pygmalion into an idolater by making Aphrodite herself the love-object; others give us a sequel to suggest that Pygmalion's marriage may fall apart after the statue comes to life.[41] In all these cases, his story is one not of mutual love consummated but of consummate male narcissism. Assigning Galatea an independent agency accomplishes little, of course, if she recapitulates Pygmalion's domineering behavior.[42] Rowlandson's female-superior composition may seem merely to shift the locus of selfhood; Galatea can even be read as sculpting Pygmalion, if the penis in her hand recalls the shape of the hammer lying by his right foot. Rowlandson's triumph, however, is to capitalize on the feminine difference implicit in the line of beauty to offer a critique of the male artist's selfhood. Such a critique goes as far as it may be possible to do without omitting to create altogether.[43] The alterity of self and other, to each other and to themselves, paradoxically unifies them at the moment that art ceases. Pygmalion, having laid down his tools, lies naked and surrounded by drapery as if he were one of his own statues. His status as "naked I" complements the vulnerability that his "naked eye" enjoys in the presence of a woman who stubbornly resists objectification. The very phrase "naked eye"—or as Hogarth modifies it, "bare sight"—vacillates between activity and passivity, for "nakedness" may be a matter either of ornamentation or of self-reliance, marginality or centrality, as Adam and Eve found out. "Naked eye" as an idiom first appeared in Henry Power's *Experimental Philosophy* of 1664, and well suits that tract's delineation of "new experiments microscopical, mercurial, magnetical" (*OED*); for empirical observation may disclose nothing to us so much as the vastness of things still invisible, as well as our naked helplessness in the face of them. As naked "I", Rowlandson's Pygmalion—artist, scientist, narcissist—embraces the alterity that he resisted while he still had hammer and chisel in hand. If this marriage can be saved, it is by virtue of the happy accident that one cannot make art and make love at once.

NOTES

My thanks to those who assisted me in the many versions of this project, especially Fred Burwick, Kathleen McConnell, Anne Mellor, the members of the NASSR-L, Ronald Paulson, Katy Ryan and Judith Thompson.

1.   The tip of the iceberg would include Iain McCalman, *Radical Underworld: Prophets, Revolutionaries and Pornographers in London, 1795–1840* (New York: Cambridge UP, 1988); Peter Wagner, *Eros Revived: Erotica of the Enlightenment in England and America* (London: Paladin, 1990); Lynn Hunt, ed. and intro., *The Invention of Pornography: Obscenity and the Origins of Modernity, 1500–1800* (New York: Zone, 1996).

2.   Bradford Mudge is currently at work on two books of Rowlandson criticism. In the mean time, the most nearly comprehensive study is still Joseph Grego, *Rowlandson the Caricaturist: A Selection from His Works, with Anecdotal Descriptions of His Famous Caricatures and a Sketch of His Life, Times, and Contemporaries* (London: Chatto and Windus, 1880); other valuable resources for the non-erotic works include *Drawings by Thomas Rowlandson in the Huntington Collection*, ed. Robert Wark (San Marino, CA: Henry E. Huntington Library and Art Gallery, 1975) and *The Drawings of Thomas Rowlandson in the Paul Mellon Collection*, comp. John Baskett and Dudley Snelgrove (New York: Brandywine P, 1978). For good compilations of the erotic works, see *The Amorous Illustrations of Thomas Rowlandson*, introd. Gert Schiff (New York: Cythera Press, 1969) and *The Forbidden Erotica of Thomas Rowlandson*, introd. Kurt von Meier (Los Angeles: Hogarth Guild, 1970). There

is a descriptive catalog of some 122 erotic Rowlandson images in Pisanus Fraxi (Henry Ashbee), *Centuria Librorum Absconditorum* (1879), rpt. as vol. 2 of *Bibliography of Prohibited Books* (New York: Jack Brussel, 1962), 346–98; on the image under discussion here see pp. 371–2, where it is not identified with Pygmalion and Galatea.

3.   Ronald Paulson, *Rowlandson: A New Interpretation* (New York: Oxford UP, 1972).

4.   An almost identical composition by Rowlandson is titled "R.A.'s [sic] of Genius reflecting on the true line of Beauty at the Life Academy Somerset House"; the onlookers here are not lascivious types but the likes of Benjamin West and Benjamin Robert Haydon, identified by initials on the corners of their drawing-pads. The picture illustrates Bernard Blackmantle (Charles Molloy Westmacott), *The English Spy: An Original Work, Characteristic, Satirical, and Humorous, Comprising Scenes and Sketches on Every Rank of Society, being Portraits of the Illustrious, Eminent, Eccentric and Notorious*, 2 vols. (London: Methuen, 1907).

5.   William Hogarth, *The Analysis of Beauty*, ed. and intro. Ronald Paulson (New Haven: Yale UP, 1997).

6.   In addition to Paulson's Rowlandson study and the introduction to the *Analysis*, see his *Representations of Revolution, 1789–1820* (New Haven: Yale UP, 1983); and *Art and Politics 1750–1764*, vol. 3 of *Hogarth* (New Brunswick: Rutgers UP, 1993). If Paulson's half-dozen books dealing with Hogarth in whole or in part suggest that the artist eludes pinning down, they would be consistent with Hogarth's own skepticism about the self-identical and reproducible self, as I discuss below.

7.   The technique of the artists' lines also suggests this difference, although I will not be able to pursue the issue in detail here. For the most part, Hogarth's designs were line-engraved onto the plate itself; Rowlandson's were etched through a wax ground previously laid on the plate, then bitten with acid into the exposed metal. In Ackermann's shop and perhaps in Tegg's (see below), Rowlandson would then turn the print over to a team of assistants who added aquatint tones to the plate and color to the copies according to his specifications. Since wax yields to the stylus more easily than does copper, Rowlandson's etchings more closely resemble the freehand sketch than do Hogarth's more deliberate productions; nevertheless, they conceal beneath a semblance of spontaneous "genius" what was, in fact, a process of collaboration and deferred gratification. James Grantham Turner posits Hogarth's attempt to maintain self-identical authority over his burin, "its image-forming pressure a deliberate but cruel stimulus giving speed and direction" to the chronicle of a loose woman ("'A Wanton Kind of Chase': Display as Procurement in *A Harlot's Progress* and Its Reception", *The Other Hogarth: Aesthetics of Difference*, ed. Bernadette Fort and Angela Rosenthal (Princeton: Princeton UP, 2001), 41).

8.   Bradford Mudge, "Romanticism, Materialism and the Origins of Modern Pornography", *Romanticism on the Net* 23 (August 2001), December

2002 <http://users.ox.ac.uk/~scat0385/23mudge.html>.

9. Werner Busch, "Hogarth's *Marriage A-la-Mode*: The Dialectic between Precision and Ambiguity", *Hogarth: Representing Nature's Machines*, ed. David Bindman, Frédéric Ogée and Peter Wagner (New York: Manchester UP, 2001): 202.

10. Jacques Lacan, "The Mirror Stage as Formative of the Function of the I as Revealed in the Psychoanalytic Experience", *Écrits: A Selection*, trans. Alan Sheridan (New York: Norton, 1982): 1–7.

11. Frédéric Ogée, "*Je-sais-quoi:* William Hogarth and the Representation of the Forms of Life", *Hogarth: Representing Nature's Machines*: 80.

12. John Milton, *Paradise Lost, The Oxford Authors—John Milton* (New York: Oxford UP, 1990), 9.510–18.

13. On the political implications of "grace" and "character", see John Barrell, *The Political Theory of Painting from Reynolds to Hazlitt: "The Body of the Public"* (New Haven: Yale UP, 1986).

14. Alexander Pope, "Of the Characters of Women", *Poetical Works* (New York: Oxford UP, 1989), 2.

15. Luce Irigaray, *Speculum of the Other Woman*, trans. Gillian Gill (Ithaca: Cornell UP, 1985), 229.

16. If we associate the girdle's lines of beauty collectively with the specular "I", we might associate them individually with what Derrida in his reading of Kant calls the *parergon*, the frame or ornament upon the work proper. The girdle, for example, constitutes a pure form that stimulates sensuous interest in the work but not in itself. Yet Derrida describes the *parergon* as guarding "against the impossibility of *arresting différance* in its contour, of arraigning *différance* in a pose…of making it come back, equal or similar to itself…to its proper place, according to a proper trajectory" (Jacques Derrida, *The Truth in Painting*, trans. Geoff Bennington and Ian McLeod (Chicago: U of Chicago P, 1987), 80). The effort to differentiate inside from outside merely confesses the fact that the inside always already differs from itself. I take up these issues in my "Mortal Frames: Desire, Disgust and the Grotesque Body", *Journal of the Association for the Interdisciplinary Study of the Arts* 3.1 (1997): 17–31.

17. Luce Irigaray, *This Sex Which Is Not One*, trans. Catherine Porter (Ithaca: Cornell UP, 1985).

18. Paulson argues that the French dancing-master seems to be "indecently propositioning Antinous" in the first plate (1993: 106); Richard Meyer adds that Hogarth satirizes both the excessive curve of the statue's body and the inadequate curve of the fop's ("Nature Revers'd: Satire and Homosexual Difference in Hogarth's London", *The Other Hogarth*, 171). Peter Wagner says that "the macho and xenophobic irony works against Frenchmen, homosexuals and the received ideas of beauty" in one fell swoop; Hogarth performs a "progressive shift…toward associating beauty with the female" ("Hogarthian Frames: The 'New' Eighteenth-Century Aesthetics", *Hogarth: Representing Nature's Machines*, 38–9).

19. The *Satire* alludes to a powerful female agency, as the old crone leaning

out the window can still "light the fire" of the pipe-smoking young man on the hill; she does so right above a tavern sign depicting an upward-curving crescent moon, an ancient emblem of female fertility.

20. The statement is doubly deferred—quoted by Douglas Hofstadter, who is in turn quoted by Barbara Johnson, "Is Female to Male as Ground Is to Figure?", *The Feminist Difference: Literature, Psychoanalysis, Race and Gender* (Cambridge, MA: Harvard UP, 1998), 18.

21. Timothy Morton calls this phenomenon "ambience." See his "'Twinkle, Twinkle, Little Star' as an Ambient Poem; A Study of a Dialectical Image, with Some Remarks on Coleridge and Wordsworth", *Romanticism and Ecology*, ed. James McKusick, Romantic Praxis Series (2001), May 2002 <http://www.rc.umd.edu/praxis/ecology/morton/morton.html>.

22. A good introduction is David Solkin, *Painting for Money: The Visual Arts and the Public Sphere in Eighteenth-Century England* (New Haven: Yale UP, 1993). On the related issue of the politics of the book trade, see Tim Clayton, *The English Print, 1688–1802* (New Haven: Yale UP, 1997).

23. John Brewer, *The Pleasures of the Imagination: English Culture in the Eighteenth Century* (London: Farrar Straus & Giroux, 1997), 213.

24. See Jenny Uglow, *Hogarth: A Life and a World* (London: Farrar Straus & Giroux, 1997), 569–70; also Brewer 259; Paulson 1993: 188.

25. It was alternately known as the Society of Arts, the Society of Arts and Sciences, or the Premium Society. In 1908, King Edward VII allowed "Royal" to be added to its full title (Henry Trueman Wood, *A History of the Royal Society of Arts* (London: John Murray, 1913), 18).

26. H.B. Wheatley, quoted in Wood 28.

27. Derek Hudson and Kenneth Luckhurst, *The Royal Society of Arts 1754–1954* (London: John Murray, 1954), 106–7.

28. Mortimer remained loyal to the Society until the winter of 1778, three months before his death, when financial hardship finally impelled him to join and exhibit in the Academy. He dedicated to Reynolds his fifteen debut etchings, a series "which may be interpreted as much as criticism as praise" of the Academy's president (John Sunderland, *John Hamilton Mortimer: His Life and Works,* The Volume of the Walpole Society 52 (1986): 92). The fifteen include, among four classical allegories and four of Mortimer's trademark *banditti*, two contrasting pairs of images depicting the artists Salvator Rosa and Gerard Lairesse. "Rosa appears as unacademic, following the dictates and urges of his own heart, drawing direct inspiration from the rocky landscape in which he sits and from depictions of bandits rather than from the accepted subject matter of art. If Mortimer is contrasting the anti-academic with the academic, the romantic with the classic, then he could also be contrasting his own art with that of Reynolds, or at least the Reynolds of the *Discourses*" (92). Reynolds himself had been a member of the Society before defecting to the Academy; it was probably due to his intervention that in 1763 the General Meeting awarded second prize to Mortimer's anti-royalist *Edward the Confessor Stripping His Mother of Her Effects*, after the customary preliminary ruling by

the Committee of the Polite Arts had recommended Romney's *Death of General Wolfe* instead (17).

29. Romney refused persistently to contribute to the Academy. Later a supporter of the French Revolution, he incurred the ire of the Academy's president who was, moreover, his single greatest competitor for patronage: "All the town," Lord Thurlow would comment, "is divided into two factions, the Reynolds and the Romney" (*DNB* 17:195).

30. Barry's fallings-out with Reynolds, possibly stemming from the anti-royalist and anti-RA remarks Barry inserted into his lectures and publications, led to his expulsion from the Royal Academy in 1799 after seventeen years as Professor of Painting. He appears to have done much of his best work for the Society, whose members helped alleviate the financial misery of his final days (Wood 72).

31. Sources conflict on this point. Some have Thelwall speaking at the 101 Strand address used by Shipley, Pars and Ackermann (see S.T. Prideaux, *Aquatint Engraving: A Chapter in the History of Book Illustration* (London: Foyle, 1968), 111–12; and Allen Samuels, "Rowlandson, Ackermann and the Art Scene", *Trivium* (1997): 245); others, at 2 Beaufort Buildings, which was leased by the leather-merchant George Williams and known as the British Forum (see Gregory Claeys, "Introduction", *The Politics of English Jacobinism: Writings of John Thelwall* (University Park, PA: The Pennsylvania State UP, 1995), xx–xxi). To be sure, so controversial a speaker as Thelwall would have had to change venues frequently.

32. "It is said that [Ackermann] had seldom less than fifty nobles, priests, and ladies engaged upon screens, and racks, flower-stands, and other ornamental work" (Grego 1.91).

33. After 1806, Ackermann discontinued the school to focus on selling book and print subscriptions. He also began publishing the *Repository of Arts, Literature, Commerce, Manufactures, Fashions, and Politics* (4 series: 1809–15, 14 vols.; 1816–22, 14 vols.; 1823–8, 12 vols.; 1829, 9 vols.). This monthly miscellany celebrated the glories of the British nation and, especially, of polite British consumerism. Typical issues might include serial essays on the progress of the arts, epistles both real and fictional, poems, accounts of scientific innovations and medical oddities, political retrospectives (regularly decrying French barbarity), agricultural and meteorological reports, swatches of cloth, fashion illustrations, music reviews, descriptions of local wild game, obituaries.

34. Personal communication.

35. Henry Curwen, *A History of Booksellers, the Old and the New*, introd. Leslie Shepard (London: Chatto and Windus, 1873; rpt. Detroit: Gale Research Co., 1968), 388–9.

36. Paulson argues that by the time of Rowlandson the line of beauty becomes associated with revolutionary energy as embodied in the Wilkites and the *sans-culottes* (1983: 132). A full accounting of Rowlandson's politics will have to wait for another time, but I would suggest that the line of beauty is more accurately a limit (realistic or not) of such energy.

37. The Dilettanti sent the painter William Pars (Henry's brother and, like him, Shipley's protégé) to Asia Minor in 1764–6 with the classicist Richard Chandler and the architect Nicholas Revett. Their findings were published as *Antiquities of Ionia* (London: T. Spilsbury and W. Haskell, 1769; vol. 2, London: W. Bulmer and Co., 1797).

38. As I argue at length in "Private Persons: Class and the Construction of Sexuality in British Romanticism" (Ph.D. diss., U of California, Los Angeles, 1998), Knight's Priapic *Discourse* reveals the political prejudice of the connoisseurs. Its principal message is not one of political and clerical reform through sexual liberation, as has often been claimed; see, e.g., Shearer West, "Libertinism and the Ideology of Male Friendship in the Portraits of the Society of Dilettanti", *Eighteenth-Century Life* 16.2 (1992): 76–104; G.S. Rousseau, "The Sorrows of Priapus", *Perilous Enlightenment (Sexual, Historical)*, vol. 3 of *Pre- and Post-Modern Discourses* (New York: Manchester UP, 1991): 65–108; and essays in *The Arrogant Connoisseur: Richard Payne Knight, 1751–1824*, ed. Michael Clarke and Nicholas Penny (Manchester: Manchester UP, 1982). Rather, Knight articulates the bourgeois preoccupation with sexual respectability, mediated by a healthy reverence for spiritual and temporal authority. When Blake, for instance, adorns the manuscript pages of *Vala* with flying phalluses of the sort that his contemporaries were digging up in Italy, he symbolizes the sterile hermaphrodism of man's fallen consciousness, not only in the ancient world but among the eighteenth-century antiquarian hirelings who postured as subversives.

39. The "attitudes" are illustrated in Friedrich Rehberg, *Drawings Faithfully Copied from Nature at Naples* (London, 1794). Rowlandson himself alludes to the practice in works such as *Lady Hxxxxxxx Attitudes* and *Lady Hamilton at Home or A Neapolitan Ambassador*. A contemporary observer, as if to stress the necessity of spectralizing Emma, calls her "coarse and ungraceful in common life"—less so in her performances, although she sings "frequently out of tune . . . . she has no flexibility and no sweetness" (Mrs. St. George, qtd. in Grego 2.312). Jeffrey Cox discusses Rowlandson's Pygmalion in the light of Emma and the "fair attitude" of Keats' urn in *Poetry and Politics in the Cockney School: Shelley, Keats, Hunt and Their Circle* (New York: Cambridge UP, 1998).

40. Ann Bermingham, "The Aesthetics of Ignorance: The Accomplished Woman in the Culture of Connoisseurship", *Oxford Art Journal* 16.2 (1993): 17.

41. See Geoffrey Miles, ed., *Classical Mythology in English Literature* (New York: Routledge, 1999), ch. 6.

42. This is, I believe, the error of Ellen Peel's otherwise wide-ranging "Galatea: Rewritten and Rewriting", *He Said, She Says: An RSVP to the Male Text*, ed. Mica Howe and Sarah Appleton Aguiar (Madison, NJ: Fairleigh Dickinson UP, 2001): 176–93.

43. J. Hillis Miller notes that this irony does not spare critical writing: "We must think of Pygmalion, Galatea, Cinyras, Myrrha, and even Venus to some degree as if they were real persons, not just black marks on the page. This does

not bode well for the hope that the reader of these stories can be exempt from the error the tales describe"; *Versions of Pygmalion* (Cambridge, MA: Harvard UP, 1990), 11–12.

A Wanton Chase in a
Foreign Place:
Hogarth and the Gendering of
Exoticism

DAVID PORTER

Popular conceptions of beauty today most clearly betray their eighteenth-century origins in their emphatic insistence on disinterestedness as a precondition of artistic value. Theorists from Shaftesbury to Kant argued that a pure experience of the beautiful required a state of transcendent aloofness from the yearnings of the flesh and the pull of ideological attachments.[1] Aesthetic experience is meant to be a chaste, strictly non-partisan affair; the depth of pleasure it can afford is owing precisely to the freedom it offers from the merely contingent and material. The fact that for many modern viewers erotic art always teeters precariously on the edge of pornography and that patriotic art hovers dangerously close to propagandistic kitsch suggests the lasting power of this conception. We are skeptical of the aesthetic value of images suggestive of sexuality or national pride because the desires and attachments conjured up by such images would seem to preclude the disinterested experience of the formal qualities of the work.

The line from Shaftesbury to Kant, however, is not without its serpentine twists and detours. Edmund Burke struggles mightily in his *Philosophical Enquiry* to sustain a clear distinction between a pure aesthetic love for beauty and an animal lust for the attractive women in whom he found beauty most frequently incarnate. One reason, however, that we hear so much less about his account of the beautiful in the *Enquiry* than about his theory of the sublime is that he is embarrassingly unsuccessful at sustaining this distinction. Whereas Kant has the good sense to limit his examples of beauty to such unproblematic objects as flowers and arabesque designs, Burke severely compromises his credibility as an impartial arbiter of aesthetic value by basing his catalog of the empirical attributes of beauty on his close observation of sexually attractive young women, invoking their lisps, tottering steps, and even feigned distresses as emblems of a universal aesthetic ideal. In his discussion of the importance of "gradual variation" as a formal quality of beauty, for example, he writes with the air of a seasoned connoisseur, "Observe that part of a beautiful woman where she is perhaps the most beautiful, about the neck and breasts; the smoothness, the softness; the easy and insensible swell; the variety of the surface, which is never for the smallest space the same; the deceitful maze, through which the unsteady eye slides giddily, without knowing where to fix, or whither it is carried."[2]

To corroborate his argument, Burke cites the opinion of "the very ingenious Mr. Hogarth," pointing to Hogarth's famous line of beauty as if to vindicate his otherwise perhaps too obvious delectation of the female form.[3] But Burke's more important debt to Hogarth goes conspicuously unacknowledged, and that is precisely the invocation of the beautiful, living woman as the cornerstone of an empiricist aesthetic theory. Hogarth's *Analysis of Beauty*, more than any other aesthetic treatise of the period, rejects the Shaftesburian requirement of disinterestedness as a precondition of the experience of beauty, and indeed revels in the possibilities of sensuality and eroticism as components of aesthetic pleasure. According to Ronald Paulson, "Hogarth is attempting to create an aesthetics that acknowledges that if we place a beautiful woman on a pedestal we will inevitably and appropriately desire her and may discover, moreover, that she is not strictly virtuous." It is an aesthetics of "novelty, variety, intricacy, [and] curiosity" that foregrounds the pleasures of the chase and the tantalizing deferral of discovery, an "aesthetics of seeing under or into" that vindicates the natural wantonness of the wandering gaze.[4]

Not surprisingly, this aspect of Hogarth's theory has troubled not only adherents of the doctrine of disinterestedness, but also students of the artist's famous moral satires, which often convey a decidedly more somber tone. As Paulson points out, "an aesthetics in which sensation and pleasure replace moral judgment apparently contradicts the tenor of [Hogarth's] major works." Thus Wallace Jackson dismisses the *Analysis of Beauty* as "a strangely eccentric document," while other art historians have attempted to neutralize its radical eccentricity by reading it merely as a "rationalization of observed rococo principles."[5]

Joseph Burke, who produced the first scholarly edition of the *Analysis* in 1955, likewise tries to redeem the text from the unsettling charge of voyeuristic licentiousness by proposing a reassuringly chaste reading of one of the most pivotal and suggestive phrases in the work. Formal intricacy, Hogarth famously asserts, gives rise to the pleasurable experience we know as beauty by leading the eye on "a wanton kind of chase." Burke suggests that the word "wanton" here is without moral or sexual connotations, and rather means simply "free and frolicsome."[6] Certainly this would appear to be true much of the time, as when the eye wanders over an intricately carved rococo ornament. But it is disingenuous to deny the sexually charged overtones of the phrase itself and of the imagery Hogarth deploys in illustrating and explaining it. The *OED* quotes Shakespeare, Arbuthnot, and Samuel Johnson, among others, using the word "wanton" in the sense of lascivious or given to amorous dalliance. And the intricate objects that most frequently catch the eye, in Hogarth's account, are not ornamental carvings, but beautiful women. Nor are these the idealized beauties of classical statuary, held safely aloof from the realm of earthly desire by their transcendence of the particularities of actual bodies, but rather the living women of Southwark Fair and Covent Garden. "Who but a bigot," Hogarth famously asks, "will say that he has not seen faces and necks, hands and arms in living women, that even the Grecian Venus doth but coarsely imitate?" These women, moreover, are consistently presented as the objects of an explicitly eroticized gaze. Like the wanton ringlets of Milton's Eve, "the many waving and contrasted turns of [their] naturally intermingling locks ravish the eye with the pleasure of pursuit." The fashionable adornments of Eve's post-lapsarian progeny serve only to heighten the effect: while a naked body soon satiates the eye, Hogarth says, "when it is artfully cloath'd and decorated, the mind at every turn resumes its imaginary pursuits concerning it."[7]

The unabashed eroticism that informs Hogarth's conception of aesthetic experience poses a problem for those who would preserve the phenomenology of beauty from the tyranny of desire. Within the context of Hogarth's text, however, it also presents a second, less frequently considered conundrum. Not the least of Hogarth's radical departures from the established norms of contemporary aesthetic theory is his insistence on the universal accessibility of the aesthetic experience he describes. Whereas Shaftesbury and later Hume depict a sanctified realm of high art whose full enjoyment is limited to an elite cadre of cultivated men of taste, Hogarth insists "that no one may be deterr'd, by the want of . . . previous knowledge, from entring into this enquiry." This anti-academic, populist gesture is clearly intended primarily to undercut the monopoly on taste held by that wealthy class of connoisseurs that was the consistent object of Hogarth's disdain. But Hogarth appears sensitive to the exclusions of gender as well as class implicit in the received ideal of the man of taste: he holds out the promise of aesthetic edification to all readers of his book, "ladies, as well as gentlemen."[8] Given this conspicuous commitment to inclusiveness, it is striking that women are entirely absent as aesthetic subjects throughout the remainder of the text. When the gaze is gendered in the *Analysis*, it is inevitably gendered male. And when a human body figures as the object of aesthetic contemplation, it is, without exception, female. The hegemony of the male gaze is, obviously, an all-too-familiar dynamic in any number of contexts. Within the specific context of an iconoclastic work, however, that claims to present a universally valid theory of beauty to readers of both sexes, an aesthetic so closely modelled on the dynamics of an exclusively heterosexual male desire seems especially problematic. Where, we are left to wonder, do the eyes of Hogarth's women turn in their own pursuit of aesthetic pleasure? And how can one account for Hogarth's silence on this point?

Though the well-documented excesses of male foppery in the eighteenth century suggest that the beaux of the period expected a certain reciprocity in aesthetic desire between the sexes, Hogarth's adjudication of the human physique according to the serpentine line of beauty rules out a strict equivalency of pleasure. A simple comparison of the relative appeal of a series of increasingly curvaceous lines illustrated in one of the two plates accompanying the text proves for Hogarth "how much the form of a woman's body surpasses in beauty that of a man."[9] Should the female reader be disheartened by this revelation, she will find in the same plates no shortage of suitably curvaceous alternatives—including corsets, table legs, candlesticks, fingers, and leg bones—provided for her delectation (fig. 1). As captivating as some of these emblems of the line of beauty surely are, one can't escape the conclusion that those readers who don't share Hogarth's lusty delight in the spectacle of a consummately attractive woman are somehow getting the short end of the stick.

If Hogarth is silent on the question of women's aesthetic proclivities in *The Analysis of Beauty*, a review of his visual oeuvre suggests that it is not for a lack of information. Not surprisingly, the attractive woman figures prominently as an aesthetic object in many of his paintings and engravings. What is surprising is the number of women Hogarth depicts as aesthetic agents and the uniformity, in one crucial respect, of their aesthetic preferences. The most important literary source for popular conceptions

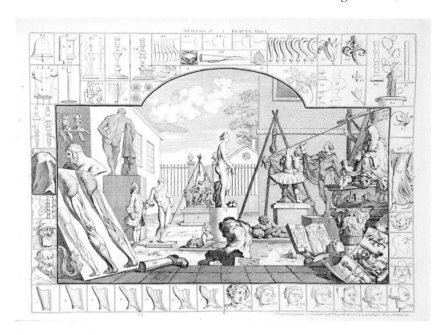

Figure 1. William Hogarth, *Analysis of Beauty, Plate I,* 1753. Courtesy of the British Museum.

of female taste in the early eighteenth century is, without a doubt, *The Rape of the Lock.* Hogarth's early illustration of the poem, showing a distracted Belinda seated with her companions at tea, reminds us that the taste of wealthy women, at least, tended toward the foreign and the exotic. (fig. 2) Within the poem, Belinda's tea-drinking habit is associated with vanity, extravagance, and luxury, to be sure, but it is also the mark of a particular aesthetic sensibility privileging rare foreign commodities that tend, according to Pope, to glitter, glow, and shine. The historical context of the reference to tea drinking is the rapidly expanding China trade of the East India Company, a trade which by the 1720 had established the tea party as the preeminent site for the conspicuous display of a woman's taste and social status.[10] Hogarth's early conversation pieces conspicuously illustrate the importance of both tea drinking as a social ritual and of the tea service itself as a marker of wealth and refinement. But imported porcelains and other examples of the fashionable Chinese taste crop up regularly in the satirical works as well, most frequently as a symbol of corrupted taste and, by implication, debauched morality, as in the second plate of *Marriage à la Mode* (Fig. 6), or as an exemplar of the absurd excesses of modern fashion,

Figure 2. William Hogarth, A Scene from *The Rape of the Lock,*
engraving for the lid of a snuff box, date unknown. Courtesy of the
British Museum

as in *Taste in High Life.*

So if Hogarth was clearly aware of a widely held belief in the affinity of
female taste for a particular class of exotic commodities, why is there no
mention of this taste in *The Analysis of Beauty*? One might have thought
that a shapely Chinese vase or teapot would have provided a more visually
appealing exemplar of the formal principles he describes than a human leg
bone, and that it would have offered the added advantage of being a familiar
object that many of his readers would have readily recognized as reflecting
their own decorative tastes.

Indeed, Chinese import wares of the period perfectly exemplify many of
the aesthetic values Hogarth champions in the *Analysis*. The unique qualities
of porcelain itself—purity, smoothness, translucence, delicacy—bespeak
the refined elegance and gentility that, as Paulson argues, are at the very
center of Hogarth's creed. Many of the shapely objects into which Chinese
potters fashioned this magical material likewise demonstrated the truth of
Hogarth's claims for the visual power of the serpentine line of beauty. Even
the imaginative exercise he advocates as a means of recognizing the lines of
beauty in complex three-dimensional objects would seem to be modelled on

the visual experience of a thin, translucent porcelain vessel: "Let every object under our consideration, be imagined to have its inward contents scoop'd out so nicely, as to have nothing of it left but a thin shell, exactly corresponding both in its inner and outer surface, to the shape of the object itself."[11]

One might expect, moreover, that as a champion of the rococo style, Hogarth would have found in chinoiserie more generally a set of decorative principles much in accord with his own. The designers of the Chinese and Chinese-styled silks, firescreens, wall hangings, furniture, and even garden buildings that were colonizing English sitting rooms and country gardens adhered fastidiously to the rules of intricacy, variety, asymmetry, and non-linearity he would promote in the *Analysis*. While these compositional attributes guaranteed the formal complexity necessary to engage the eye in its wanton wanderings, Chinese goods in their inescapable exoticism also invited imaginative play on another level entirely. The radical unfamiliarity of their visual language, the obscurity of their local meanings and cultural points of reference would have presented to the Hogarthian viewer an occasion for imaginative pleasure every bit as alluring as its surface design. For Hogarth, after all, it is not only the eye that seeks diversion in art but the mind as well. "The active mind is ever bent to be employ'd. Pursuing is the business of our lives; and even abstracted from any other view, gives pleasure. Every arising difficulty, that for a while attends and interrupts the pursuit, gives a sort of spring to the mind, enhances the pleasure, and makes what would else be toil and labour, become sport and recreation."[12] The essence of exoticism as an aesthetic attribute, I would argue, is that it erects precisely such a pleasing barrier to the immediate assimilation of a visual spectacle, a teasing sense of alienation from the familiar every bit as captivating as the wanton ringlets of a lover's flowing hair.

For a whole host of reasons, then, one would reasonably expect Hogarth to recognize and acknowledge the considerable aesthetic appeal of the Chinese goods his readers purchased and admired. And indeed, scholars have established that he owned a number of decidedly chinoiserie pieces himself.[13] Yet in *The Analysis of Beauty*, when the Chinese style is mentioned at all, it is summarily dismissed as an absurd and foolish taste unworthy of the least serious consideration. In a passage about the ubiquity of his line of beauty in depictions of the deities of classical civilizations Hogarth remarks on the contrast presented by the Chinese case. "How absolutely void of these turns are the pagods of China, and what a mean taste runs through most of their attempts in painting and sculpture, notwithstanding they finish with such excessive neatness."[14] Hogarth's manuscript notes on academies and the Society of Arts confirm this disparaging view of Chinese artistic production: in a discussion of the appropriate education for young artists, he praises English fabric designers for copying "the objects they introduce from nature; a much surer guide than all the childish and ridiculous absurdities of temples, dragons, pagodas, and other fantastic fripperies, which have been imported from China."[15]

In light of the logical reasons Hogarth should have looked more kindly on these fantastic fripperies and the circumstantial evidence that, in fact, he sometimes did, why does he lash out with such uncompromising fury against the popularity of the Chinese taste? A number of possible explanations immediately suggest themselves. To begin with, Hogarth's criticism of Chinese art on the grounds that it did not adhere to conventions of naturalistic representation was a commonplace one at the time. Although Hogarth rejected a classicist conception of nature as idealized form, he believed strongly that nature in its infinite variety was the artist's most trustworthy guide. To the extent, then, that Chinese art seemed to flout any standard of verisimilitude, it was beyond the pale of even Hogarth's post-classicist sensibilities. Furthermore, the popularity of the Chinese style surely grated on Hogarth's keenly developed sense of aesthetic nationalism. While perhaps weakening the claims of the highbrow connoisseurs to being the sole arbiters of fashionable taste, Chinese imports, like old Italian paintings, nonetheless threatened the livelihood of the native-born English artists Hogarth saw it as his mission to promote. To the extent that Chinese art seemed to replicate the rococo stylistics he espoused, there was all the more reason forcefully to repudiate it as a foreign usurper of English artistic glory.

I am more intrigued, however, by a third, less immediately obvious explanation for his disdain, an explanation that returns to the problem in the *Analysis* I raised at the beginning of this essay. Hogarth's repeated insistence on the worthlessness of the Chinese style, I would like to suggest, is intimately bound up with his perplexing silence on the question of female aesthetic agency. A closer look at some of the many contemporary literary and visual representations of Chinese goods and their domestic consumption will help to elaborate this connection. As in *The Rape of the Lock*, Chinese import goods figure prominently in these works as emblems of female vanity and extravagance. More intriguingly, though, their physical qualities are often compared to those of the women who collect them. Both fine ladies and fine porcelain, the familiar simile goes, are prized for their smooth surfaces and radiant splendor, but they are equally fragile as well, and are soon despised for the appearance of a crack or flaw. The analogy could, at times, appear so compelling as to elide any remaining differences between them. In *Royalty, Episcopacy, and Law*, for example, Hogarth imagines a courtly lady as a pastiche of exotic commodities, including a fan for a body and a teapot for a head (fig. 3); in a contemporary poem entitled "Tea, or Ladies into China-Cups" the anonymous poet effects a like transmutation of English women into the porcelain vessels of which they are so enamored.[16]

From the perspective of female aesthetic agency, the implications of an imagined identity between female consumers and the objects of their consumption are suggestive, to say the least. If women, in their pursuit of beauty, turn to objects that either resemble or are understood as synecdochical extensions of themselves, the result is an entirely self-contained, self-reflexive economy of female desire. Whether this economy is figured as narcissistic or homoerotic, it inevitably leaves male participants in the drama in the unaccustomed role of passive, powerless spectators. And indeed, those writers who imaginatively pursue the consequences of women's infatuation with Chinese goods invariably figure men as frustrated and jealous rivals, deprived by porcelain vases and teapots of attentions that might otherwise have been theirs. An enigma-solving contest in an issue of the *Woman's Almanack* of 1741 features a intricate, rhymed riddle about a Chinese teapot.

> Here the fair Nymphs with each becoming Grace,
> And studied Art, my varied Charms embrace;
> Oh! what wou'd Lovers give, cou'd they command
> So warm a Pressure from their fair one's Hand.

John Gay's poem, "To a Lady on her Passion for Old China," similarly laments a lover's displacement by imported exotica:

> What ecstasies her bosom fire!
> How her eyes languish with desire!
> How blessed, how happy should I be,
> Were that fond glance bestowed on me!
> New doubts and fears within me war:
> What rival's near? A China jar.[17]

This dynamic of displacement is taken to its logical conclusion in a long pornographic poem called "A Chinese Tale" published in 1740 (fig. 4) Described as "a tale in the Chinese taste," the mock-heroic fantasy recounts the adventures of the coy and beautiful maid-of-honour Cham-yam as she repels the advances of legions of desperately adoring mandarins. One of these suitors bribes a maid to conceal him in his tormenter's private

Figure 3. William Hogarth, *Royalty, Episcopacy and the Law,* 1724.
Courtesy of the Royal Pavilion Art Gallery, Brighton.

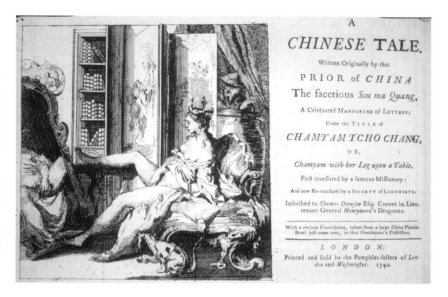

Figure 4. Frontispiece and title page to *A Chinese Tale,* 1740. Courtesy of the Institute for Sex Research.

chambers, where he watches from inside a large China jar as she masturbates in front of a mirror. The sight sets his soul ablaze, and he bursts from his jar to rape her. What is most interesting to me about the poem, apart from its rather remarkable frontispiece, is the setting Cham-yam chooses for her self-pleasuring and the state of mind the decor seems to induce. The room is furnished in the height of the Chinese taste, with motifs of dragons and gilt flowers adorning the ceiling and, as we see here, the furniture. These are juxtaposed with the lavishly described lewd paintings lining the walls, cabinets full of erotic curiosities, and bookshelves lined with novels and romances. Reclining on a sofa amidst all this splendor, Cham-yam's mind wanders over scenes of the triumphs of her sex.

> All languishing, supine she lay,
> Revolving over all that's gay:
> The Charms of Woman, and her Pow'r,
> From the Creation to that Hour:
> What Ravages! what Devastations!
> What Havoc caus'd among the Nations!
> What Slaves they made of lordly Man!
> When sudden thus the Dame began.[18]

While the theme of women's sexual power is a commonplace one, its triangulation here with vivid spectacles of chinoiserie and autoeroticism suggests a powerful and deeply resonant association between the aesthetics of Chinese exoticism and the potentially unsettling specter of female autonomy and self-determination.[19]

A more familiar and genteel locus of male anxiety about the wantonness of women's taste and power was the tea table itself. In an engraving called "The Tea Table" and published in 1710, the social consumption of tea is depicted as a site of viciously malignant female gossip (fig. 5). The theme here is homosocial rather than autoerotic self-indulgence, but the iconography is familiar: just as in "The Chinese Tale," male observers appear only as exiled, marginal figures, while a prominent display of Chinese porcelain suggests the aesthetic context of the women's transgression. The porcelain cabinet also draws our eyes to the devilish figure chasing Justice from the room. Justice appears to have dropped her sword, which lies broken on the floor next to a curiously intact china teacup. This pair of objects conspicuously inverts the iconic cliché of feminine china meeting its ruin at the hands of an impetuously phallic masculinity and provides a striking commentary on the reversal of roles enacted in this scene.

The same pair of icons appears again in the second plate of Hogarth's *Marriage à la Mode* (fig. 6). The broken sword on the floor at the husband's feet figures all the more obviously here as a sign of languid, frustrated masculinity; the wife's tea service, elevated and intact, provides a contrasting echo of her own wantonness and excess. It echoes as well the debauched taste revealed by the collection of Chinese figures on the mantlepiece above her head. Here Hogarth graphically illustrates his principal charges against the Chinese taste: that it is absurd, inelegant, and unnatural. But this plate, read in the context of the period's rampant associations between Chinese goods and an extravagant, wanton femininity also suggests an answer to the question of female aesthetic agency in the *Analysis* with which we began. Hogarth rejected the Chinese style as an alternative to classicism, I would propose, not so much out of a considered repudiation of its underlying aesthetic values, but rather out of a sobering recognition that to grant the validity of the Chinese taste would be to legitimate a regime not only of female aesthetic self-determination, but also of the autonomy of female desire more generally conceived. As a theorist of art, Hogarth radically asserted the emancipatory power of a spontaneous aesthetic experience unconstrained by classicist pieties. But his gestures of inclusiveness notwithstanding, he stopped short of extending this freedom to women. While beauty could henceforth be safely admired in English as well as Italian paintings, it was still to remain the exclusive preserve of European artists and of a predominantly masculine gaze. To accommodate the errant wanderings of the wanton female eye would have been to invite a wholesale defection from the Western artistic tradition and from the social and sexual order of which it was a well established part. And this was a travesty that our hero, canon-busting iconoclast and aesthetic libertine though he surely was, finally proved unable to countenance.

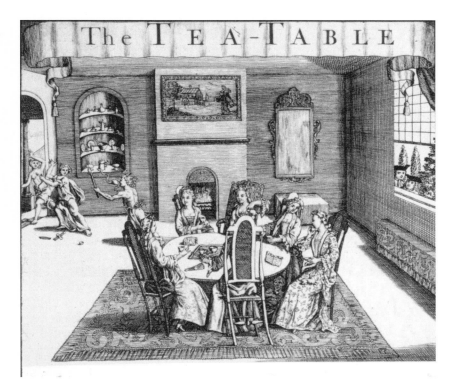

Figure 5. *The Tea-Table*, 1710. Courtesy of the British Museum

Figure 6. William Hogarth, *Marriage à la Mode, Plate II,* 1745.
Courtesy of the British Museum.

NOTES

    1.   On the history and implications of disinterestedness as a component
of the aesthetic attitude, see Jerome Stolnitz, "On the Origin of Aesthetic
Disinterestedness," *Journal of Aesthetics and Art Criticism* 20 (1961): 131–43,
and Elizabeth Bohls, "Disinterestedness and the Denial of the Particular: Locke,
Smith, and the Subject of Aesthetics," in Paul Mattick, ed., *Eighteenth-Century
Aesthetics and the Reconstruction of Art* (New York: Cambridge University
Press, 1993).
    2.   Edmund Burke, *A Philosophical Enquiry into the Origin of our Ideas
of the Sublime and Beautiful,* ed. James T. Boulton (Notre Dame: University of
Notre Dame Press, 1968), 115.
    3.   Ibid.

4. Ronald Paulson, ed., Hogarth, *The Analysis of Beauty* (New Haven: Yale University Press, 1997), xxxiii, xxxvii, xlix.

5. William Paulson, ed., Hogarth, *The Analysis of Beauty*, xi; Wallace Jackson, "Hogarth's *Analysis*: The Fate of a Late Rococo Document," *SEL* 6 (1966): 543–50; Joseph Burke, ed., Hogarth, *The Analysis of Beauty* (Oxford: Clarendon Press, 1955), xlvi–xlvii.

6. Joseph Burke, li.

7. William Hogarth, *Analysis of Beauty*, ed. Paulson, 59, 34–35, 40.

8. Hogarth, *Analysis*, 18.

9. Hogarth, *Analysis*, 49.

10. See the chapters on tea in Elizabeth Kowaleski-Wallace, *Consuming Subjects: Women, Shopping, and Business in the Eighteenth Century* (New York: Columbia University Press, 1997), 19–72; and James Walvin, *The Fruits of Empire: Exotic Produce and British Taste, 1660–1800* (New York: New York University Press, 1997), 9–31.

11. Hogarth, *Analysis*, 21.

12. Hogarth, *Analysis*, 32.

13. Lars Tharp, *Hogarth's China: Hogarth's Paintings and Eighteenth-Century Ceramics* (London: Merrell Hoberton, 1997), 49.

14. Hogarth, *Analysis*, 12.

15. William Hogarth, *Anecdotes*, ed. J.B. Nichols (London, 1833), 37.

16. *Tea. A Poem. Or, Ladies into China-Cups; A Metamorphosis* (London, 1729).

17. "The Prize Aenigma," *The Woman's Almanack* (London, 1741), 20; John Gay, "To a Lady on her Passion for Old China" (London, 1725).

18. *A Chinese Tale* (London, 1740), 16.

19. This argument is elaborated at more length in David Porter, *Ideographia: The Chinese Cipher in Early Modern Europe* (Stanford: Stanford University Press, 2001), 181–192.

The Return of Beauty.
Purity and the Neo-classical
Foundation of Modern Art

PETER C. SONDEREN

Introduction

I t was winter in Amsterdam when this essay was being prepared for an American conference on the exquisite theme of *Beauty*. The famous canals, in which all kinds of ships usually move around, were covered with a thick layer of ice and snow. The fluidity of the water had apparently stopped. The clear geometrical, off and on curved white lines operated as a kind of artistic *passe-partout*, as a unifying grid for the beautiful heterogeneity of the architecture. The aesthetic experience of a cultural phenomenon that was singled out by a pure natural cause is not unfamiliar to peoples of the northern hemisphere. Going further to the north, the whiteness of the grounds even increases in intensity and in durableness. Going to the south, however, to Greece for example, it is quite uncommon to come across a landscape that is completely white by heavy snowfall. This does not imply that these southern regions do not know snow. On the contrary, to them it is a well-known phenomenon, but it has a different appearance, status and even function. The snow is not known as a touchable substance but as a distant happening, a visual play. It hides itself permanently and impeccable in distant places, at the slopes and peaks of mountains, where it only shows its visibility and luminosity. Its actual temperature and tactility, however, remains remote. Its magnificent and purist outlook manages to overwhelm the distant perceiver by its inaccessibility and timelessness. It is therefore hardly surprising that the down-to-earth stable equivalence of it, white marble, became the cornerstone of both Greek art and architecture. Today we know—in contrast to eighteenth century and earlier writers—that ancient sculptures did not shine white at all, but appeared with a cover of colorful paint like so many sculptures from the Middle Ages. The Greek predilection for taking the white pureness of the stony material as the firm underground of their sculptures and buildings nevertheless reflects their love for the ideal remoteness and pureness of the visual and untouchable white that shone from above. Not from heaven, but from the unreachable peaks that housed the gods. White marble reflects the spotless eternity of untouchable snow, at least from the Renaissance on, when ancient whiteness had become a reality.

As this reflection shows there seem to be in nature two ways to achieve aesthetic purity. The first one acts by removing objects from sight in order to accentuate and emphasize others; it acts consequently by *exclusion*. The second way runs by displaying the idea of eternal remoteness and untouchability by itself; it acts therefore by *exclusiveness*. If we turn to the history of art we can easily recognize the same points of view; they are rather traditional but all the same modern oppositions. They represent two views on art: art as a self-containing unit without any relationship with or dependency on the reality outside of it; and second, art as a means to point at a certain content that is not necessarily restricted to its self-proclaimed domain of art. This dualism within the history of art seems strongly related to the recent return to beauty in art, which was the general starting-point of the congress mentioned above. The attention to beauty had apparently gone, so it was suggested, but at the turn of the millennium it had returned unexpectedly with a renewed vigor. The organizers did not, however, give any precise (historical) localization of beauty's comeback nor did they provide a clear view on its figure and form. The how and what of the return seems therefore still negotiable, just like for instance the exact moment of the arrival of postmodernism.

I therefore start this essay with the observation that, firstly, beauty never has been a reliable partner of art, and secondly, that their relationship is in fact rather young. The earliest contact of beauty with art can not be traced back in antiquity, as so many still suppose by pointing at the history of aesthetics with its petrified look back at Plato & sons. The first meeting only took place somewhere in the eighteenth century.[1] Beauty and art are therefore modern notions and it is only in this quality that they could and can be separated or joined again. It is my intention to shed some light on the historical connection of beauty and art, on their subsequent disjunction, and finally on the presumed return of beauty.

1

In contrast to the coupling of beauty with art, the concept of beauty itself can be convincingly traced back in remote times, as the many histories of art and aesthetics indefatigably show every time again and again with a soporific cadenza. Although the modern academic disciplines of aesthetics and the history of art co-originated in the early nineteenth century—albeit they did not stay together very long—, they both found it necessary to look back in remote history, or for that matter, to construct a long history in order to find a legitimization for their delivery. Beauty and works of art consequently can be found back in times when people like us liked to draw, mould or discuss their aesthetic needs in the darkness of caves and woods, or in the shadows of their early stylized imitations.

Beauty's deliberate turn towards art, however, is only a relatively recent step in the history of objects and ideas, because it is strongly related to the emergence of the modern, judging subject that emerged in the course of the eighteenth century. The *mutual* history of art and beauty could start its course during the same period, when beauty, instead of being awakened her self, tried, for the first time in history, to open up the eyes of art. Beauty became for a while so overwhelmed by art that she even became convinced that only the latter could rouse her tender feelings. Only art was meant for an exclusive liaison with her.

In our eyes this exclusivity looks, however, paradoxical, for we can list so many beautiful art-objects that are of a much earlier date, that a previous relation between art and beauty can hardly be denied. This is true. Of course we like all kinds of older objects, no matter if they are natural or artistic objects. We embrace them wholeheartedly with our feelings of beauty, by attributing them excellence, sublimity, fineness, picturesqueness, smoothness, warmth, essentialness, quintessence-ness, et cetera. We seem to forget, however, that this sense of beauty in its *pure* form first could show up when we started to judge art exclusively in aesthetical terms. That is, when our first motive for looking at art had become purely aesthetical, and not something else.

The aesthetic attitude is modern for it presupposes a sound theoretical connection of art and beauty. Prior to the eighteenth century this relation seems to have been almost absent, because the writings and images of eighteenth century writers, philosophers and artists, display—unlike earlier times—a continuous search for establishing a connection between art and beauty. Why would one look for this, when it already existed? To put it even more radical: the eighteenth century can not only be regarded as the age of reason, but can also be seen as the age of the beautiful becoming art and the art becoming beautiful. It is curious, however, that this happened without the simultaneous production of an awesome corpus of works of art to prove it. The seeming general lack of really great works of art in a great part of the eighteenth century—a problem that was at least felt and pronounced in the period itself—was possibly part of the problem, and, perhaps, also its cause.[2] The general rejection after 1750 of Rococo and Baroque art was not simply a change of style, but was a fundamental reorientation on the purpose of art. After 1750 the great ship of modernization accelerated only very slowly. It would take years to reach a temporary summit in David's *Oath* (1784–85).[3]

2

During the eighteenth century many factors were responsible for the preparation of the underground for the aesthetical turn towards art. A very important one was that the visual arts became increasingly public. They did not only become public for the very first time in modern history, but they also received a whole new apparatus that would give their products a structural textual comment: art criticism. It was in Paris, in the so-called Salons, that art-objects were displayed in public space. 'The Salon was the first regularly repeated, open and free display of contemporary art,' as Crow remarks, 'to be offered in a completely secular setting and for the purpose of encouraging a primarily aesthetic response in large numbers of peoples.'[4] This process finally led to the regular exhibition of contemporary art in a special section of the Louvre.

The public art show did not remain unnoticed.[5] The written comments on the exhibitions testify of a growing critical interest in art. The first art critiques did not please the artists very much, however, because the critics, such as the much-discussed La Font Saint-Yenne, did not speak for themselves, but in the name of the public.[6] Moreover, most critiques were written as anonymous pamphlets. Despite this unwelcome anonymity and the growing voice of the people, and despite the subsequent artists' threat to withdraw completely from public space in 1749, the public exhibition and its loyal companion, art criticism, were phenomena that have not disappeared since then.

When it was decided to organize a *Salon* every two years, art criticism could develop into a real and mature genre, with a personal style and touch. It was Denis Diderot, who led, in the sixties, the new genre of art criticism to a temporary climax. We must, however, not exaggerate the size of his audience, for the critiques that he wrote at the request of Melchior Grimm, circulated only in a few European courts, although copies of his manuscripts seemed to have found also other readers. After Diderot no real great art critics appeared at the art stage anymore. Only in the course of the nineteenth century, when writers like Charles Baudelaire dived into 'public art' again, art criticism could gain an important and autonomous status, not in the least by referring to Diderots groundwork. The emergence of public exhibition and public discussion of objects of art were therefore important prerequisites for the appearance of an aesthetical attitude. The public who read art critiques and not only they, were more and more forced and seduced to give themselves a judgment of what they saw.

Another closely related factor is obviously the *philosophical* connection of beauty with art, which settled down in the neologism of *aesthetics*. The writings of its name-giver, the German philosopher Alexander Baumgarten, were one of the many clear signs that visual experience became a very important focus point.[7] Baumgarten emancipated—within the realm of epistemology at least—the so-called inferior knowledge of the senses to a higher level; that is, sensual knowledge had to be taken more seriously.[8] He coined the term aesthetics in Latin (meaning visual knowledge), which was immediately translated in German. It arrived in France only in 1776, in a supplement to the *Encyclopédie*. More than 100 years after its conception, in 1843, it was by Théodore Jouffroy's *Cours d'ésthétique* that it first received its letter of honor in France, as Saint Girons has shown.[9] Baumgarten's ideas seem, however, to have been rather unimportant for the beautification of the *visual* arts, because he was mainly focused on poetry. It is therefore not necessary to look for the first signs of a philosophical legitimization of the visual arts in his works, solely because he gave birth to the term aesthetics.

How did beauty become the object of a growing serious philosophical approach in the eighteenth century, and why did beauty become all of a sudden interested, so to speak, in the special capacities of the visual arts? To get a clear view on this occurrence it proves to be very useful to take an unusual road. Instead of following the direction that histories of aesthetics generally take, which is mostly primarily motivated by shaping and retaining its own history, it is better to turn to the writings of two amateurs of art, the German archaeologist Johann Joachim Winckelmann (1717–1768) and the Dutch philosopher Frans Hemsterhuis (1721–1790).

In the history of aesthetics both authors mostly play a minor role. Their writings are merely used as an illustration, and considered as a side effect of the general development of beauty. This image—the image of a one road beauty—changes, however, when we accept more than one (mainstream) aesthetics in the eighteenth century, like Saint Girons recently proposed;[10] it changes also when we turn to the unwritten history of beauty *and* art, which is not the same as a simple addition of the history of beauty and that of art. Winckelmann and Hemsterhuis represent a turn to art that was in a certain way radically new; moreover, their writings are crucial for a (visual) understanding of the return of and to beauty, or better, for the first systematic connection of beauty with art. This does not imply that theorists like Abbé Du Bos, Pierre Crousaz, Charles Batteux, and Francis Hutcheson will lose their importance for the development of the notion of beauty. They are, however, less significant for the connection of beauty with the visual arts in the second part of the eighteenth century. Beauty in their hands remained a rather free-floating general concept, that hardly touched upon the visual work of art.[11]

3

Hemsterhuis and Winckelmann uncovered a completely new field of interest with regard to art and beauty through their fascination for Greek sculpture. If we want to summarize their positions, we could say that Winckelmann gave Greek sculpture its first, indigenous aesthetic territory in both space and time; Hemsterhuis, on the other hand, gave eternal Greek beauty a modern, scientific explanation and a new role. Winckelmann tried to surpass his fellow antiquarians by looking for the essence of art ('das Wesen der Kunst'). His intention was not to write a history of the art of antiquity as a pure tale of chronology with all its inherent changes, but he understood history ('Geschichte') in a broader sense, that is, as a means to offer artists and society an educational system ('Lehrgebäude').[12] By showing the origin, the growth, the change and the decline of art, but also the different styles, times and artists, he tried to teach his own time a moral lesson.[13]

His search for the essence of art brought him in contact with the beauty of Greek art, although the other way round is also plausible. In his enthusiastic pursuit of the essence of art, he postulated that beauty was both the ultimate goal and the center of art.[14] He was, however, at the same time unable to find a satisfying explanation of beauty's power, that he tried to catch in his new artistic language.[15] In his *Geschichte der Kunst des Althertums* of 1764 he tries to explain why:

> "For beauty is one of the big secrets of nature, whose effect we all see and experience; a universal and distinct concept of its essence, however, belongs to the yet undiscovered truths. If this concept were *geometrical* [PS] distinct, people's judgment with regard to the beautiful would not diverge. . . "[16]

In other words, Winckelmann, felt a little frustrated that the beauty he experienced so vehemently in his very close, almost corporal encounter with sculpture, could not be founded on a clear mathematical basis. He was not able yet, or better theory was not ready yet to give his aesthetical feelings, that he considered to be universally valid, a firm and steady basis.

Put in these terms it might seem as if Hemsterhuis, who shared Winckelmann's enthusiasm for Greek art and culture—'je suis né Grec'[17]—tried to give Winckelmann's plea a direct answer by his own sculptural theory, in which he arrived at a quasi *geometrical* definition of beauty. Any factual bond between Winckelmann and Hemsterhuis is, however, uncertain. They never met and they both wrote independently their views on the history of the art of sculpture in the same years.[18] More important, however, is their shared deep interest in sculpture and beauty, which led to the same question: what about beauty and what about sculpture?

While Winckelmann developed a whole new temporal, or more precise, *spatial* environment for the remaining artifacts of antiquity, Hemsterhuis's main focus lay at discovering the laws underlying our sense of beauty with regard to art, and to sculpture in particular. He was in fact the first philosopher to give sculpture a really important, fundamental place within the system of the arts; and what is even more important, he attached the art of sculpture directly and exclusively to the notion of beauty.

In his analysis of sculpture in his small but influential *Lettre sur la sculpture* (*Letter on sculpture*) of 1765, that was published in 1769, Hemsterhuis came to the following definition of beauty: man experiences that as beautiful that gives him the greatest amount of ideas in the shortest amount of time.[19] He called this description *geometrical* because it was composed of a minimum and a maximum-component. If an art object costs a lot of time to be perceived, that is: if a clear image does not originate in the mind or only fragmentary in viewing an art object, the feeling of beauty does not emerge, but only the feeling of disgust. When an art object gives the viewer an instant image, that is to say when its form can be internalized within a second of time, beauty appears immediately. This means that the speed of perception is directly related to the aesthetical view. Hemsterhuis's analysis of our sense of beauty is an original version of the well-known idea of unity and variety, because he prefers an art object whose heterogeneity is reduced to a minimum. His reductionism can even be related to the essence of much modernist design (less is more). Even some modern musicians took his maximum and minimum-idea as their motto.[20]

If we take a closer look at Hemsterhuis's ideas, we discover that his variant connects human desire for unification with the compactness and smoothness of artistic, sculptural form. A sculpture that refrains from the expression of form-distorting passions, and that attracts by a fluent, regular and slightly twisting outline, becomes the archetype of *Hemsterhusian* beauty. Basic to this idea is that Hemsterhuis views nature as incapable to satisfy the aesthetic need of mankind. Nature only produces by chance objects that do meet our expectations.[21] Only art, in particular sculpture or its exact counterpart: the hardly material sketch, is able to give this desire a visual and tactile satisfaction.[22] Beauty therefore becomes exclusively reserved for art. Only art provides beauty; beauty can only be experienced through the way of art. In the analysis of sculptural form beauty and art are forged together.

4

It becomes clear that the reflection on sculpture played a key role in the establishment of the relation between art and beauty in the second half of the eighteenth century. This implies that the traditional leading couple of *painting* and *poetry* becomes less important in this regard. Poetry did not loose its importance, however, but painting became much less normative. Does this imply a new *Paragone*, a repetition of the artistic discussion on the precedence of painting or sculpture? In a way, this is definitively the case. If we take a closer look at the archaeology of the discussion, however, also something else becomes apparent, which makes this traditional competition even a bit old-fashion. Hemsterhuis, for instance, does not at all seem to be really interested in the question which art is better equipped for imitation, although this aspect does not disappear completely. It takes rather another form and different direction. By way of his conscientious examination of sculpture and of our sense of beauty, he arrives almost by chance at the question which art suits best man's universal longing for unification. For this is what he connects to the arts: their capability in fulfilling a basic moral need of man.

In his *Lettre sur les désirs (Letter on Desires)*, the direct follow-up of the *Letter on Sculpture*, it becomes clear how Hemsterhuis views man's longing for unification with a desired object:

> "When I contemplate some beautiful thing, a beautiful statue, I am in truth only seeking to unite my being, my essence, with this heterogeneous being; but after much contemplation I become disgusted with the statue, and this disgust arises uniquely from the tacit reflection I engage in about the impossibility of a perfect union."[23]

He finally concludes:

> "One will love a beautiful statue less than one's friend, one's friend less than one's lover, one's lover less than God."[24]

It looks as if these quotations are implied as a deliberate degradation of (sculptural) art, because the other objects of desire are more immaterial and therefore more valuable than the work of art. Hemsterhuis makes this comparison in the context of the development of one of his basic philosophical ideas, namely that the human soul strives eternally to unite with the world around it. It constantly tries to break through its material bounds and chains, in order to reach the essential immaterial world of the other. It is clear that this perfect detached state is, however, hard to achieve in daily life. The (non physical) love for the lover knows after all its own imperfections. Also other possible human relations have their own restrictions and problems. To prove the essential qualities of the workings of the human soul, art unexpectedly appears as the perfect means to show the original and constantly recurring striving towards unification and unity of the soul.

Our perception of beauty is caused by the 'dematerialized' representation in art. Art is capable of showing a composite of ideas that are grouped in such a way that an instant internalization and therefore unification, takes place. A real human being is also a heterogeneous amalgam of ideas, but only sporadically shows up in a perfect balance and thus in a beautiful unity. An art object combines a maximum of ideas in a minimal form and connects the world of morality with that of causality.

At this point it is important to look more in detail into the general nature of Hemsterhuis's unique aesthetical experiments with the perception of works of art, as he described them in his *Letter on sculpture*. This experimentation not only shows the working of the soul but it also seems an answer to another Winckelmannian problem, namely that it was impossible to find in nature or in art perfect ideal beauty.[25] Hemsterhuis's experiment— he showed two different drawings of different vase-forms with the same amount of visual quantities to an audience of connoisseurs and laymen in art, and asked them about their preference; on the basis of the results[26] and his subsequent geometrical analysis he came to the conclusion that man always chooses that form that can be internalized in the fastest way—, was a new approach in the world of art. It was not only new because it concluded that nature in itself is aesthetically neutral, that we only experience it as being beautiful on account of our own artistic perceptiveness, but also because it was a definition or theory based predominantly upon concrete and specific experimentation. Just as Newton had based his natural philosophy and his optics upon experimental investigations, so Hemsterhuis was now drawing general conclusions from the ways in which specific persons react to vases, sculptures and sketches. The inner world of the human mind, man's longings and the search for beauty, were being opened up to rational enquiry by a scientific method which was only to come into its own in the field over a century later, when Gustav Theodor Fechner embarked on his experimental work in psychology and aesthetics.[27]

Ideal beauty does not exist in nature nor can it be realized or effectuated. Art can, however, give a short illusion, a temporary fulfillment of man's desire. Hemsterhuis's Newtonian experiment gives a metaphysical explanation for man's longing for beauty and the new artistic way to achieve this. By using simple vase-forms Hemsterhuis abstracts from sculptures and paintings alike but he did not choose for meaningless geometrical forms to do his experimenting, but used 'minimal' art objects.[28] His visual statement is therefore more than only a concept, a mere thought, to prove that only art had become capable of providing real beauty.

Hemsterhuis showed thus two major effects of art: beauty and disgust. Beauty arises from the quickness with which a certain artistic form can be internalized by the perceiver. Disgust results from the realization that this artificial unification is only temporary or unreachable. Beauty and its counterpart are consequently born simultaneously. This very ambiguous quality of art, its openness to our desires and its refusal or incapability to fulfill these, makes art the important playground and arena of beauty. This new quality points at a radical modern vision and shows in fact the first real manifestation of beauty and art's relationship. No hidden traditional geometrical or other order in the objective world is responsible for beauty anymore; only human desire is basic to our longing for beauty that found her partner in art.

5

What effect did Hemsterhuis's approach have on the view on classical art that Winckelmann had created with his history, or story, of ancient art? This is a difficult question, because many scholars have noted already that Winckelmann not only brought Greek art to life, but that he also buried her at the same time.[29] He sung ancient times back in his new artistic prose, but it was a mourning too. This nostalgia, that found expression in his call for a genuine imitation of inimitable Greek art, can be seen as a last attempt to recover something that in its (re)creation or (re)conception had gone already.

Viewed from this point of view, Hemsterhuis's aesthetics and vision on art go exactly the other way. In his writings we find no nostalgia into the past. Instead, we discover a strongly felt longing that is pointed at a distant future. This becomes apparent in his *Letter on sculpture* in his (implicit) advices for contemporary sculptors, but also, and in particular, in his platonic dialogue *Alexis, ou de l'âge d'or* (Alexis, or on the golden age), that was published in 1787 by Immanuel Kant's publisher, Hartknoch, in Riga.

In Hemsterhuis's concept of history, in which his idiosyncratic idea of the *Golden Age* plays a crucial role, the development of the faculty of feeling occupies a central place. How did morality come to life, when did its power fade away; can we still see and recognize a glimmer of its existence and how can this be regained again? How to develop a future Golden Age in which humanity becomes more complete than it has ever been? Hemsterhuis's answer to these questions is that the original, primitive state of mankind, in which feeling was strong, is able to return in the future, in a higher state, filled with a much richer content.

If we want to have an idea of this future we need art, Hemsterhuis's text seems to assume, because this human activity is accomplished to represent the future fusion of morality and causality. If this fusion will finally be historically achieved, however, we will not need art anymore. This is not because art had by then become useless or superfluous, but because man will then be able of viewing everything in perfect harmony. By the continued development of feeling everything will become aesthetized, that is: everything will be viewed as art.

In all of Hemsterhuis's writings, the attention for moral feeling is central. His early close examinations of the perfect fluent contours in objects of art in the *Letter on sculpture*, for instance, are also strongly related to this presumed weakened faculty. That is, feeling in the sense of both morality and touch. The touchability of art becomes the complement of the moral content of the work of art. Central to this awareness of and concentration on feeling implies of course the loss of feeling in modern times. Against this deficit Hemsterhuis uses art and its new born ally beauty: it must restore the nearly lost faculty. A return towards, or an imitation of art that shows the peculiarities of a truly moral society like the Greek one, is no serious option any more, as Winckelmann could still hope for. History has moved us already in another direction.

The changing role of history appears from Hemsterhuis's characterization of modern times as the geometrical or symmetrical era, in which reason prevails. All sciences and arts that are based on mathematical thinking are favored. Real (fine) art, however, and therefore feeling, suffer from this predominance, which is proved by the lack of fluent outlines in contemporary art, sculpture in particular. The heyday of feeling that preceded in ancient times, in which the fine arts could flourish but in which the exact sciences could not fully develop, can not, according to Hemsterhuis, be regained. Man is consequently only left with a (ideal) future in which reason and feeling can be merged. Ancient and modern times have to return on a higher level. Art therefore gets a new, modern mission, for only this branch of human activity, and sculpture in particular, can give us a hint of the reality and probability of the future Golden Age. [30] The aesthetization of the world by art had begun. Hemsterhuis connected beauty and art in order to give humanity an optimistic look into the future. We can see what Winckelmann's back could see.

6

The connection of beauty and art has led to an aesthetics of a strong formal and sensible *purity*. Hemsterhuis's sculptural ideas, which show a predilection for visual and tactile qualities in art, are very important for a sound understanding of the new classicism (neo-classicism) that spread its wings at the end of the eighteenth century. Antonio Canova's *Amor and psyche* symbolizes, or better: represents this *modern* classicism. Modern, because it is only in appearance that it shows a return towards classical ideas. It can not be denied that the ideas of love and the interest in human's psyche are symbolized by personifications, by recognizable gods. The way they are displayed and assembled, however, shows a clear and definitive break with the past. The continuous form of the sculpture in both time and space, in which both bodies float around an unconsummated kiss, was unknown to history. The formal simplicity, the turning screw-like form, the ultimate concentration on outline, the purist whiteness, all these elements contribute to a new form of beauty, that is no longer classic or reducible to a nostalgic or restorative classicism. This does not mean that Greek sculpture has lost its role as a point of reference. On the contrary: it is a reference-point but only at a far distance, in a far away time; it has definitively lost its real normative power. Greek art had become exclusive.

7

Beauty and art had thus become very close partners. In the nineteenth century this situation hardly changed, although what was felt as beauty differed of course from time to time. Only a few quarrels showed up, that did not harm, however, the belief in the essential quality of, mostly feminine, beauty. It was Manet's *Olympia* of 1863 that opened up a new and different view on the ideal image of female beauty that had become the petrified hallmark of artistic beauty. Picasso's *Les demoiselles d'Avignon* of 1907 scrambled the feminine image even a little further.[32] Beauty and art's relationship started to crack.

The final divorce of art and beauty took place with the arrival of the historical avant-garde in the early twentieth century. Marcel Duchamp, for instance, who followed the general redefinition and repositioning of beauty and art by Dada, decided to turn his back towards beauty.[33] The disappointment in his own failure to give painting a new content in order to combat its presumed meaninglessness is connected to his questioning and ridiculing traditional forms of beauty. His *Mona Lisa* with the curly moustache is of course well known. This reaction to the petrifying musealization of beauty, led to his exhibition of the famous urinal (*Fountain*, 1915).

The whiteness of the porcelain urinal can hardly be coincidence. It is related to the other forms of whiteness that I mentioned earlier. Duchamp's whiteness or pureness, is, however, not based on the idea of exclusion that strives for aesthetic amplification, or on the idea of exclusiveness, because it is not a white that wants to remain untouched. His whiteness points at a new category, that strives for *inclusion*. The unchanged common object, dressed in optical, brilliant white, enters the realm of art. By this inclusion beauty was excommunicated and had to leave by the backdoor. The later musealization of the *Fountain* finally led to a beautification of the urinal. This was something Duchamp deplored, but which he was unable to prevent. The power of beauty seems to be unexpectedly big.

8

Pureness and whiteness were often used as aesthetical categories in twentieth century art. The pureness that we experience in Barnett Newman's paintings, for instance, was supposed to be the opposite of beauty, just like Duchamp's whiteness. Newman stated that art had nothing to do with beauty at all, but that it was strongly related to the sublime, the very opposite of beauty. In his essay 'The Sublime is Now,' published in *Tiger's Eye* in 1948, he described the liberation of the tradition of beauty, and proclaimed that some American artists already completely denied '. . . that art has any concern with the problem of beauty and where to find it.'[34] This sort of statement turns up again and again in the writings of modern artists. Beauty was blamed for its conservativeness, for its prejudiced view on women, for its pretended essentialism, in short: beauty was condemned for being deeply suspicious. The fact that aesthetic considerations were no longer essential to art was probably the main conceptual discovery in twentieth-century art.[35]

9

At the turn of the new millenium there are many signs that beauty tries to find her way back, both in the scholarly environment and in public art shows.[36] Three art exhibitions in the Netherlands, in the United States, and in France, testify of the renewed artistic interest in beauty.[37] The why of beauty's return does not get, however, a clear answer yet. One of the main attractive aspects of beauty is probably the fact that she had become a real *taboo*, a strictly forbidden concept in most of twentieth century art. Artistic interest in (formal) beauty had become completely inappropriate. The tabooing of beauty in art—which was accompanied by beauty's immediate entrance in the culture of common goods and, of course, fashion—might be explained by the recurrent Western need to research every taboo.

That some artists have become (or: still were) interested in this very aspect of modern art hardly surprises. What intrigues perhaps more is the fact that beauty's power or attraction, had remained so strong, despite, or maybe, because of beauty's absence.[38] The absence seemed to have been more powerful with regard to the setting of artistic norms than any other *positive* category. The fear for beauty had become deeply rooted and has, in the negative, structured in fact various developments in modern art.

Beauty also changed her look. Albert Speer's Nürnberg Rally, Francis Bacon's paintings and Stanley Kubrick's *A Clockwork Orange*—the enumeration derives from Ronald Jones—, changed her face enormously. This is not so much related to a change of form, but is based on our changed expectations of beauty. Andy Warhol made this point very visible by his half-done painting *Do it yourself* of 1962, in which the traditional concept of the *picturesque*—which is a close relative of beauty—is ridiculed. The pictorial has been reduced '. . . to a formula, reproduced at will and can thus no longer continue as a pretender to beauty's power. His [Warhol's] picture is emblematic of the weight of beauty's influence in its own disappearance.'[39] This turning down of a relative of beauty as well makes the power of the whole family of beauty even more intelligible. Also other forms of beauty emerged in art; 'traditional' beauty, however, remained at home in fashion and the likes, but it also got a new home in computer aesthetics.[40]

Dave Hickey, who is said to have restarted the recent discussion on beauty in his 'Enter the Dragon', made a good point about the renewed function of beauty in his analysis of the photographs by Robert Mapplethorpe.[41] This artist reintroduced a specific aesthetics in photography by making repulsive subjects look very attractive although the subjects were rather difficult to the eye (e.g. fist fuckers). The effect of his work, his aesthetics means, was not simply '. . . to produce awe, but to awe and then negotiate that awe,' as Jones puts it. Hickey: 'The task of these figures of beauty was to enfranchise the audience and acknowledge its power—to designate a territory, to argue the argument by valorizing the picture's problematic content.' Beauty lost its power here to be just beautiful. It can, besides other things, also be highly contaminated.

In recent years, beauty seems thus to have regained some of her 'old' vitality. We encounter this in 'multimedia'-installations also. One impressive example of such an installation was the room that the Italian—*Arte Povera* —artist, Giuseppe Penone, made in the papal rooms in Avignon at the aforementioned, very beautiful exhibition 'La beauté in fabula' in 2000. He had covered the walls of the very huge room with thousands of bay leaves that were grouped in the form of large bricks (hold together by hardly visible iron strands). The walls did not only make a strong esthetical impression on the eye by their 'renatured' outlook, but also on the nose, and not to forget on the tactile senses. In the middle of the room Penone had placed the famous bronze *Hypnos* of the British Museum. For the rest only a gilded bronze cast of lungs and bronchial tubes were hung at the wall. This overall, and therefore sculptural approach played with beauty with a new vigor. Penone not only made the notion of sculpture all-inclusive, but even a different smell of beauty emerged.

Another room of the Avignon-exhibition was reserved for a work by James Turrell. He managed to create a very sensualistic experience with the traditional *awesome* aspect, which was connected to beauty. By the placement of a very subtle and pure light he arranged a space in which the perceiver lost all his daily references in the entering of a pure sensation. The perceiving eye almost turned white by the immediacy of this endorsement of light.

That beauty gives a flickering in art again sometimes, and particularly but not only in the broadened area of modern sculpture—sculpture seems to encompass almost every branch in art now—is not a surprise; at least, when we keep the *late-eighteenth century* sculptural birth of art and beauty in mind.

NOTES

1. That the actual age of aesthetics is still not fixed appears for instance from Trottein, Serge, ed. *L'esthétique naît-elle au XVIIIe siècle?* Paris: Presses Universitaires, 2000, in which is discussed if aesthetics really was born in the eighteenth century, if it was much older, or if it happens to be born again and again.

2. The general rise of new academies of art after 1750 is one important sign that art had to be ameliorated. For 'post-Pevsner' research on academies, see for instance Boschloo Anton W.A. et al., ed. *Academies of Art between Renaissance and Romanticism.* 's-Gravenhage: SDU uitgeverij, 1989 [Leids Kunsthistorisch Jaarboek].

3. Cf. Honour, Hugh. *Neo-Classicism.* Harmondsworth: Penguin, 1968.

4. Crow, Thomas E. *Painters and Public life in Eighteenth-Century Paris.* New Haven: Yale University Press, 1985, p. 3.

5. For the rise of the public as consumer in the eighteenth century, see Van Horn Melton, James. *The Rise of the Public in Enlightenment Europe.* London: Cambridge University Press, 2001.

6. La Font de Saint-Yenne. *Réflexions sur quelques causes de l'état présent de la peinture en France avec un examen des principaux ouvrages exposés au Louvre.* La Haye, Néaulme, 1747. Not only artists were not amused, also officials like Cochin blamed the negative critique to be the nonsense of an

'ignoramus'. See Crow, *Painters and Public life* p. 8. It is not unimportant to realize that the critics did not belong to the circle of artists and art officials. It was therefore critique from the outside.

7. Becq shows in her *Genèse de l'esthétique française moderne*, that the use of the term aesthetics appears for the first time in 1735 in Baumgarten's *Meditationes philosophicae de nonnullis ad poema pertinentibus*. In 1750 he publishes his *Aesthetica*. Becq, A. *Genèse de l'esthétique française moderne.1680–1814*. Paris: Albin Michel 1994, p. 5. For the visual interest and the use of visual metaphors, see Jay, Martin. *Downcast Eyes, the Denigration of Vision in the Twentieth-Century French Thought*. Berkeley etc.: University of California Press, 1994.

8. The eighteenth century catches the eye with regard to the visual. The use of visual metaphors to make human thinking both visible and understandable is enormous. The inspection of the ideas by the mind or the minds eye is the basis of the rationalistic and the sensualistic philosophy. Speculative and sensualistic ideas on vision coexisted in the eighteenth century. See Jay, *Downcast Eyes,* p. 80. For a very inspiring description of the visual aspect in the Enlightenment, see Starobinski, Jean. *L'invention de la liberté, 1700–1789*. Genève: 1964 and his *Les emblèmes de la raison*. Paris: 1973.

9. Saint Girons, B. *Esthétiques du XVIIIe Siècle, le Modèle Français*. Paris: Philippe Sers, 1990, p. 8.

10. Saint Girons, 'Avant-propos' in *Esthétiques du XVIIIe Siècle*.

11. Du Bos was in fact one of the most important (but often neglected) theorists, because he was the first continental author to introduce John Locke's empiricism in art theory. He opened up the autonomous, theoretical field of the receptive experience of art in general. See Saint Girons, *Esthétiques du XVIIIe Siècle,* p. 17–23 and Désirat, Dominique. 'Préface' in: Abbé Du Bos. *Réflexions critiques sur la poésie et sur la peinture*. Paris: École nationale supérieure des Beaux-Arts, 1993, p. X. To Du Bos, however, sculpture was much less important as it was to Winckelmann and Hemsterhuis.

12. Winckelmann's chronology must not be confused with the modern, nineteenth century art historical idea of linear development. His idea of temporality was founded in a cyclical system.

13. Winckelmann, J.J. *Geschichte der Kunst des Altertums*. Darmstadt: Wissenschaftliche Buchgesellschaft, 1972 (Sonderausgabe, unveränderter reprografischer Nachdruck der Ausgabe Wien 1934), p. 9.

14. In general theorists only mention 'imitation' as the ultimate goal of the arts. Winckelmann, p. 139: 'Die Schönheit, als der höchste Endzweck und als der Mittelpunkt der Kunst, erfordert vorläufig eine allgemeine Abhandlung ...' .

15. Apart from Winckelmann's 'new' writing it is equally important to point at his innovative parallels between words and images, or, to be more precise, between literary and artistic style. See Potts, A. *Flesh and the Ideal, Winckelmann and the origins of art history*. New Haven/London: Yale University Press, 1994, p. 96 ff.

16. Winckelmann, *Geschichte der Kunst des Altertums*, p. 139: 'Denn die Schönheit ist eins von den großen Geheimnissen der Natur, deren Wirkung wir sehen und alle empfinden, von deren Wesen aber ein allgemeiner deutlicher Begriff unter die unerfundenen Wahrheiten gehört. Wäre dieser Begriff geometrisch deutlich, so würde das Urteil der Menschen über das Schöne nicht verschieden sein . . .'

17. 'I was born Greek.' See his letters to Diotima, princess Amalia von Gallitzin: [14–08-1780] [Royal Library, The Hague] and [28–02–1786] [University Library of Münster]. Frans Hemsterhuis was a philosopher, who also made designs for monuments and medals. He was responsible for the antique collection of the Stadtholder, but he also had a private collection of (presumed) ancient gems that were highly admired by Goethe. Hemsterhuis can be considered as the most outspoken representative of the new classicist vision on art that was very influential, that is to say basic, to the modern look on art. See my own book: Sonderen, Peter C. *Het sculpturale denken. De esthetica van Frans Hemsterhuis.* [*Sculptural thinking. The aesthetics of Frans Hemsterhuis.*] [Diss. University of Amsterdam] Leende: Damon, 2000.

18. Although contemporary readers of Hemsterhuis like Denis Diderot, Immanuel Kant, Herder, Jacobi, August and Friedrich Schlegel, and especially Novalis, never mistook Hemsterhuis for Winckelmann, actual scholars, Dutch ones in particular, seem to refuse the idea that Hemsterhuis was an independent thinker; they still see him as a slavish follower, who only spread Winckelmann's news. See, for instance, the exhibition catalogue *Edele eenvoud. Neo-classicisme in Nederland 1765–1800.* Zwolle (Frans Halsmuseum and Teylers Museum in Haarlem) 1989.

19. His definition of beauty reads literal: 'Ne s'ensuit-il pas, monsieur, d'une façon assez *géométrique*, que l'âme juge le plus beau ce dont elle peut se faire une idée dans le plus petit espace de temps?' [*PS*] And a few lines further on: 'L'âme veut donc naturellement avoir un grand nombre d'idées dans le plus petit espace de temps possible . . .', in: *Wijsgerige Werken van Frans Hemsterhuis.* Edited, introduced and commented by Petry, M.J., Budel: Damon, 2001, p. 500– 502. Hemsterhuis's definition is rather unique, although many scholars have tried to play it down by pointing at the various sources of its ingredients. (See Sonderen, *Het sculpturale denken*, p. 24 ff.) Hemsterhuis's introduction of (physical) time as a basic idea for the experience of beauty, can be directly related to the idea of 'immediacy' or 'instantaneity' in modernism. The implied psychological and metaphysical purpose of the reducing of time was still unimportant for theorists like Diderot; Romanticists, like Novalis, however, immediately recognized it. Hemsterhuis's definition therefore points at the future, not at the past.

20. Richard Boursy of *Yale University* writes for instance about the Pullitzer-pricewinner, the American jazz-musician and composer of atonal music, Mel Powell, that he '[. . .] liked to quote Frans Hemsterhuis's definition of the beautiful as "the greatest number of ideas in the shortest space of time."'

Register to the Mel Powell Papers: http://webtext.library.yale.edu/xml2html/music.MelPowell.nav.html 1998. [Cited 5 April 2002.]

21. See *Lettre sur la sculpture*, 1769, in: Petry, *Wijsgerige Werken van Frans Hemsterhuis*, p. 496.

22. The sketch activates the mind maximally by its minimal materialness. The mind finishes that what in fact is only suggested. Hemsterhuis therefore prefers Italian art above Dutch art because the latter does not make the viewer active. He remains a passive reflector of what he sees. The unfinished-ness of Italian art makes the perceiver active. Cf. Guentner, W. A. "British Aesthetic Discourse, 1780–1830, The Sketch, the *Non Finito*, and the Imagination." *Art Journal*, 52, 2, 1993, p. 40–47.

23. 'Lorsque je contemple une belle chose quelconque, une belle statue, je ne cherche en vérité que d'unir mon être, mon essence, à cet être si hétérogène; mais après bien des contemplations, je me dégoûte de la réflexion tacite que je fais sur l'impossibilité de l'union parfaite.' (*Lettre sur les désirs*, 1770, in: Petry, *Wijsgerige Werken van Frans Hemsterhuis*, p. 540).

24. Idem.

25. Winckelmann, *Geschichte der Kunst des Altertums,* p. 148. See also Potts, *Flesh and the Ideal*, p. 155.

26. All of them, except one, preferred the Greek like vase-form. The so-called Dutch vase did not show any unity because it was regarded as an amalgam of parts. See Sonderen, P.C. "Beauty and desire: Frans Hemsterhuis' aesthetic experiments." *British Journal for the History of Philosophy*, 4, 2, 1996, p. 317–345.

27. Fechner tried to combat the high-flown aesthetics of German Idealism by his own 'aesthetics from below', which implied a return to the experience itself. The idealist ('high') philosophy took general ideas and concepts as starting-point; real art objects and experiences merely functioned as the filling of abstractly constructed frames. Like Hemsterhuis Fechner took the direct experience of lust and disgust as his basis in order to develop a system of concepts. See Van der Schoot, Albert. *De ontstelling van Pythagoras. Over de geschiedenis van de goddelijke proportie*. [The Pythagorean disposition]. [Diss.] Zwolle: Kok Agora 1998, p. 246 ff. Fechner categorized his own aesthetics as a part of psychophysics (his own term), a science that categorizes the measurable relationship between an external stimulus and the inner experience. His research on meaningless forms is strikingly similar to what Hemsterhuis called 'visible quantities' to describe visual stimuli in art. See Sonderen, *Het sculpturale denken, * p. 86.

28. In one of his unpublished letters he compared his vase-experiment with the ideas of the first geometrician, who considered the square and triangle as the most simple object that could give a glimpse of truth. His own drawings of the two vases should be regarded as the most simple object that would let feel beauty in its complete nudeness. 'De même que le premier Géomètre a considéré un carré ou un triangle comme l'objet le plus simple qui fait apercevoir des vérités toutes nues, afin de mener par la les hommes à la connaissance de

vérités cachées & plus compliquées & même à celle du vrai; de même nous devons considérer les vases comme l'objet le plus simple qui fait sentir la beauté toute nue, afin de mener par-là les hommes à la connaissance de beatités cachées & plus compliquées & même à celle du beau.' [28–09–1783] [University Library of Münster].

29. See for instance Potts, Alex. "Vie et mort de l'art antique: historicité et beau idéal chez Winckelmann", in: *Winckelmann: la naissance de l'histoire de l'art à l'époque des lumières*, Paris 1991, p. 9 ff.: 'il proclame à la fois son existence et sa disparition au sein de la culture moderne. ... [il] considérait que l'art de la Grèce antique était presque entièrement perdu à jamais.'

30. Hemsterhuis saw this future as a real ontological possibility, but he also acknowledged its remoteness. Art and beauty could function therefore in the meantime as important stand-ins; Hemsterhuis's idea of the future Golden Age was very influential in Germany (Novalis, the Schlegels, Hölderlin et cetera). See Sonderen, *Het sculpturale denken*, p. 237 ff.

31. It is no chance that the arrival of the new classicism of Antonio Canova coincided with the rise of genuine academism. Modern art and academism were twins.

32. Cf. Steiner, Wendy. *Venus in Exile. The Rejection of Beauty in 20-th Century Art.* New York et cetera: The Free Press, 2001.

33. Ronald Jones observed in a recent review 'Regarding Beauty' in *Artforum* (Jan 2000, www.artforum.com), that it was Duchamp who flipped the beauty switch to Off.

34. Regarding Beauty. A View of the Late Twentieth Century. (Hirshhorn Museum and Sculpture Garden, Smithsonian Institution, Washington, D.C., 7 Oct 1999–17 Jan 2000, and Haus der Kunst, Munich, 11 Febr–30 Apr 2000), p. 28.

35. This statement is Arthur Danto's. See Ronald Jones, 'Regarding Beauty' in *Artforum* (Jan 2000, www.artforum.com).

36. See for instance: Lambert, Craig. "The Stirring of *Sleeping* Beauty. After decades in scholarly eclipse, beauty rears its beautiful head." *Harvard Magazine*, Sept.–Oct. (1999), and Noël Carroll, "Art and the Domain of the Aesthetic." *British Journal of Aesthetics.* Vol. 40, no. 2, April (2000), p. 191–208.

37. The Power of Beauty, De terugkeer van schoonheid in de hedendaagse kunst. (Municipal museum of Helmond, 3 Oct 1999/9 Jan 2000) Eindhoven: Gemeentemuseum Helmond, 1999. *Regarding Beauty*: see note 34. In the summer of 2000 a couple of exhibitions on beauty were organized in the papal city of Avignon. The central exhibition was called: 'La beauté en fabule' [Beauty in Fabula], with works by Bill Viola, Jeff Koons, Luciano Fabro, Anish Kapoor and James Turrell to name only a few.

38. Ronald Jones, "Regarding Beauty" in *Artforum* (Jan 2000, www.artforum.com): 'Beauty is as powerful in our culture in its very absence as it was in earlier times, when present and deployed as the spellbinding agent of church and state.'

39. Ronald Jones, "Regarding Beauty" in *Artforum* (Jan 2000,

www.artforum.com).

40. Lev Manovitch. "The Engineering of Vision and the Aesthetics of Computer Art." *Computer graphics*, vol. 28, nr. 4, (1994): p. 259–263.

41. See also his "Enter the Dragon: On the Vernacular of beauty." Uncontrollable Beauty. Toward a New Aesthetics. Bill Beckley and David Shapiro (eds.) New York: Allworth Press, 1998, p. 15–25.

Contributors to Volume 33

Jeffrey Barnouw is Professor of English and Comparative Literature at the University of Texas at Austin. He has published three or more essays on Bacon, on Hobbes, On Leibniz, on Vico, on Schiller, and on Charles Sanders Peirce. His book, *Propositional Perception. Phantasia, Predication and Sign in Plato, Aristotle and the Stoics*, was brought out by the University Press of America in 2002.

Barbara Benedict is Charles A. Dana Professor of English Literature at Trinity College, Hartford, Connecticut. She is author of *Framing Feeling: Sentiment and Style in English Prose Fiction, 1745-1800* (AMS Press, 1994), *Making the Modern Reader: Cultural Mediation in Early Modern Literary Anthologies* (Princeton University Press 1996), and *Curiosity: A Cultural History of Early Modern Inquiry* (The University of Chicago Press, 2001). She has also edited *Wilkes and the Later Eighteenth Century,* a volume of eighteenth-century erotica (Pickering and Chatto, 2002) and is currently editing Jane Austen's *Northanger Abbey* for Cambridge University Press.

Melissa K. Downes received her Ph.D. in Comparative Literature from the University of Iowa. She is an Assistant Professor of English at Clarion University of Pennsylvania. Her current research focuses on representations of the Caribbean in early eighteenth-century British literature.

Ted Emery is Assistant Professor of Italian at Dickinson College. He is author of *Goldoni as Librettist* (Peter Lang, 1991) and of articles on Goldoni, Casanova, Carlo Gozzi, and Pietro Chiari. With Albert Bermel, he is editor and translator of plays by Gozzi, under the title *Five Tales for the Theater* (University of Chicago Press, 1989).

Timothy Erwin is Associate Professor of English at the University of Nevada, Las Vegas. The present essay, on beauty, was read at the 2001 MWASECS meeting in Iowa City. Along with recent essays on Hogarth in the *Huntington Library Quarterly* and on Johnson in *The Age of Johnson,* it belongs to an ongoing study of pictorial metaphors during the Enlightenment.

Susan C. Greenfield is Associate Professor of English at Fordham University and the author of *Mothering Daughters: Novels and the Politics of Family Romance, Frances Burney to Jane Austen* (Wayne State, 2002). She is co-editor (with Carol Barash) of *Inventing Maternity: Politics, Science and Literature, 1650-1865* (Kentucky, 1999). Her articles have appeared in *PMLA, ELH,* and other journals.

George Haggerty is Professor and Chair of English at the University of California, Riverside. His books include *Gothic Fiction/Gothic Form* (Penn State, 1989), *Unnatural Affections: Women and Fiction in the Later Eighteenth-Century* (Indiana, 1998) and *Men in Love: Masculinity and Sexuality in the Eighteenth Century* (Columbia, 1999). He has also edited *Professions of Desire: Lesbian and Gay Studies in Literature* (MLA, 1995) and *Gay Histories and Cultures: An Encyclopedia* (Garland, 2000). At present he is at work on a longer study of the life and work of Horace Walpole.

Adam Komisaruk is Assistant Professor of English at West Virginia University. His publications include articles on Mary Shelley and on Matthew Gregory Lewis. He is at work on a book-length study of sexuality and the middle class in British Romanticism; and on *The Blake Model*, a virtual-environments project. He delivered a version of this essay at the 2001 Northeast American Society for Eighteenth-Century Studies/Atlantic Society for Eighteenth-Century Studies conference in Halifax, Nova Scotia.

Laurence Mall is Associate Professor of French at the University of Illinois at Urbana-Champaign. She is the author of two books on Rousseau, *Origines et retraites dans* La Nouvelle Héloïse (1997) and Emile *ou les figures de la fiction* (2002), and she has written articles on various French eighteenth-century authors. Her current research includes the preparation of a book on the subject in Diderot's *Salons* and his later works.

James Mulholland is a doctoral candidate in English literature at Rutgers University, New Brunswick. His dissertation, from which this article is drawn, examines tropes of orality in relation to voice in eighteenth-century poetry.

Alexander H. Pitofsky is Assistant Professor of English at Appalachian State University. His publications include articles on Frances Burney's *Evelina,* James Oglethorpe's prison reform writings, and Theodore Dreiser's *The Financier*. His book-in-progress studies links between prison reform discourse and the novel in eighteenth-century Britain.

David Porter is Associate Professor of English and Comparative Literature at the University of Michigan. He is the author of *Ideographia: The Chinese Cipher in Early Modern Europe* and numerous articles on the reception of Chinese art and culture in eighteenth-century Europe.

Neil Saccamano is an Associate Professor of English and Comparative Literature at Cornell University. He has published various articles on eighteenth-century saitre, aesthetics, political philsosphy, and critical theory. He is currently at work on a book devoted to the conflicting functions and values of force in eighteenth-century aesthetics and political theory, and he is also co-editing a collection of essays on *Politics and the Passions* from Descartes to Hegel to be published by Princeton University Press.

Laura Schattschneider holds a Ph.D. in Comparative Literature from the University of California, Berkeley. From 2001–2003 she was Andrew W. Mellon Postdoctoral Fellow at the Humanities Consortium of the University of California, Los Angeles. She is completing work on a book manuscript entitled *Foundling Narratives: Fictions of National Kinship in England, France, and Germany, 1740-1840.*

April Shelford is Assistant Professor of History at American University in Washington, DC. Her work focuses on the intellectual history of early modern Europe. She is currently writing a book on the Republic of Letters in late seventeenth-century France and investigating networks of botanical exchange in the eighteenth-century Atlantic World.

Peter C. Sonderen is Director of the AKI, Academy of visual arts and design, Enschede (The Netherlands). He received his Ph.D. in Art History at the University of Amsterdam. He wrote *Het sculpturale denken. De esthetica van Frans Hemsterhuis (Sculptural thinking. The aesthetics of Frans Hemsterhuis),* Leende: Damon, 2000. His research focuses on the relation between modern art and the eighteenth century.

Geoffrey Turnovsky is Assistant Professor of French at Ohio State University. During 2002-03, he was a Mellon Postdoctoral Fellow at the Penn Humanities Forum, University of Pennsylvania. He has published articles on Rousseau and Diderot. His current research explores the formation of the literary market as a modern cultural field of authorship in eighteenth-century France.

Caroline Weber is Assistant Professor of Romance Languages at the University of Pennsylvania. She is the author of *Terror and Its Discontents: Suspect Words in Revolutionary France* (University of Minnesota Press, 2003) and the editor of *Fragments of Revolutions*, a special isssue of *Yale French Studies* (Yale University Press, 2002). Her current research interest is the *drame bourgeois* of mid-eighteenth-century France.

Executive Board 2003-2004

President: **Joan B. Landes**, Professor of Women's Studies and History, Pennsylvania State University

First-Vice President: **Margaret Anne Doody**, Professor of Literature, University of Notre Dame

Second-Vice President: **Sarah Maza**, Professor of History, Northwestern University

Past President: **John Bender,** Director, Stanford Humanities Center, Stanford University

Treasurer: **William F. Edmiston,** Professor of French, University of South Carolina

Executive Director: **Byron R. Wells,** Professor of Romance Languages, Wake Forest University

Members-at-Large

Kevin Berland, Professor of English and Comparative Literature, Pennsylvania State University

Ann Bermingham, Professor of History of Art and Architecture, University of California, Santa Barbara

Isobel Grundy, Professor of English, University of Alberta

Julie Candler Hayes, Professor of French, University of Richmond

Ann B. (Rusty) Shteir, Professor of Humanities and Women's Studies, York University

Larry Stewart, Professor of History, University of Saskatchewan

Administrative Office

Office Manager: **Vickie Cutting,** Wake Forest University

For information about the
American Society for Eighteenth-Century Studies, please contact:
ASECS
P.O. Box 7867
Wake Forest University
Winston-Salem, NC 27109-7867
Telephone: (336) 727-4694
Fax: (336) 727-4697
E-mail: asecs@wfu.edu
Web Site: http://asecs.press.jhu.edu

441

American Society for Eighteenth-Century Studies

Patron Members 2003-2004

Hans Adler
Paul Alkon
Mark S. Auburn
James G. Basker
Barbara Becker-Cantarino
R. Bernasconi
Kevin Binfield
Theodore Braun
Fritz Breithaupt
Peter M. Briggs
Morris Brownell
Michael Burden
Joseph A. Byrnes
Michael J. Conlon
Brian A. Connery
Kevin L. Cope
Margaret Mary Daley
Marlies K. Danziger
Joan DeJean
Roland Desne
Margaret Anne Doody
Julia Douthwaite
William F. Edmiston
Frank H. Ellis
Roger J. Fechner
Jan Fergus
Riikka Forsstrom
Christopher Fox
Bernadette Fort
Scott Gordon
Sayre Greenfield
Monika Greenleaf
Joan R. Gundersen
Phyllis Guskin
Wolfgang Haase
Martha Hamilton-Phillips
Karsten Harries
Robert H. Hopkins
Robert D. Hume

Lynn A. Hunt
Malcolm Jack
Margaret Jacob
Regina Mary Janes
Annibel Jenkins
Claudia L. Johnson
Gary Kates
Shirley Strum Kenny
Charles A. Knight
Paul J. Korshin
David H. Koss
Isaac Kramnick
Thomas W. Krise
Susan Lanser
J. Patrick Lee
Meredith Lee
Nancy M. Lee-Riffe
Elizabeth Liebman
Roger D. Lund
Robert P. MacCubbin
Marie E. McAllister
Christie McDonald
George C. McElroy
Alan T. McKenzie
James C. McKusick
Donald C. Mell Jr.
John H. Middendorf
Earl Miner
Dennis Moore
Melvyn New
Mary Ann O'Donnell
John H. O'Neill
Frank Palmeri
Virginia J. Peacock
Ruth Perry
Jane Perry-Camp
R.G. Peterson
J.G.A. Pocock
Adam Potkay

John Valdimir Price
Ruben D. Quintero
Ralph W. Rader
John Radner
Gary Richardson
James Rosenheim
Treadwell Ruml II
Roseann Runte
Peter Sabor
Steven D. Scherwatzky
Harold Schiffman
William C. Schrader
Richard Sher
Eleanor F. Shevlin
Kazuko Shimizu
John Sitter
Douglas Smith
Patricia Meyer Spacks
Barbara Stafford
Susan Staves
Ann T. Straulman
Mika Suzuki
Masashi Suzuki
Ruud N.W.M. Teeuwen
Diana M. Thomas
Linda Troost
Randolph Trumbach
Raymond D. Tumbleson
Bertil Van Boer
David F. Venturo
Joachim Von der Thusen
Howard D. Weinbrot
Byron R. Wells
Lance Wilcox
James A. Winn
Karin E. Wolfe
James Woolley
William J. Zachs
Lisa Zeitz

Sponsoring Members 2003-2004

Joseph F. Bartolomeo
Jerry Beasley
Carol Blum
Thomas F. Bonnell
Martha F. Bowden
Leo Braudy
Leslie Ellen Brown
Andrew H. Clark
Stephen P. Clarke
Brian Corman
Pierre Deguise
Alix S. Deguise
Robert DeMaria
JoLynn Edwards
A.C. Elias, Jr.
Antoinette Emch-Deriaz
Robert A. Erickson
Timothy Erwin
Clarissa C. Erwin
Carol Houlihan Flynn
Brandon Brame Fortune

Jack Fruchtman, Jr.
Anita Guerrini
Basil Guy
Roger Hahn
Phillip Harth
Donald M. Hassler
Julie C. Hayes
Daniel Heartz
Charles H. Hinnant
Mark Holland
Donna M. Hunter
J. Paul Hunter
Adrienne D. Hytier
Catherine Ingrassia
Thomas Jemielity
George Justice
Alan Kors
Thomas W. Krise
Colby H. Kullman
Joan Landes
Lawrence Lipking

April London
Devoney K. Looser
Cynthia Lowenthal
John A. McCarthy
Heather McPherson
Linda E. Merians
Maureen E. Mulvihill
Felicity Nussbaum
Suzanne L. Pucci
Walter E. Rex
Larry L. Reynolds
Albert J. Rivero
Wendy Wassyng Roworth
Barbara B. Schnorrenberg
Ann B. Shteir
Frank Shuffelton
Jeffrey Smitten
Dennis Todd
Peter Wagner
Myron D. Yeager

Institutional Members 2003-04

American Antiquarian Society
Arizona State University
Auburn University, *English Department*
    Paula Backscheider
Brown University,
    John Carter Brown Library
College of the Holy Cross, *Dinand Library*
Colonial Williamsburg Foundation
    John D. Rockefeller, Jr. Library
Florida Atlantic University
    Wimberly Library
Folger Institute
Fordham University
    History Department
Fordham University Library
Gale, *Mary Mercatante*
George Washington's Mount Vernon
Harvard University Library
Indiana University, *Kokomo Library*
Johns Hopkins University,
    Milton Eisenhower Library
McMaster University
Metropolitan Museum of Art
    Thomas J. Watson Library
The Newberry Library
Ohio State University
Omohundro Institute for Early American
    History - *Kellock Library*

Rutgers University, *Alexander Library*
Smith College, *Neilson Library*
Smithsonian Institute, *AA/PG Library*
Southern Illinois University, *Morris Library*
Thomas Jefferson Memorial Foundation
    Research Center
Towson University, *English Department*
University of Evansville, *Library*
University of Kentucky, *Young Library*
University of North Carolina,
    Davis Library
University of Notre Dame
University of Pennsylvania, *Libraries*
University of Rochester, *Library*
University of Tennessee, *Library*
University of Texas at Austin
    General Library
University of Tulsa, *McFarlin Library*
University of Victoria, *McPherson Library*
University of Wisconsin,
    English Department
Waddesdon Manor Collection Department
Washington University
    Olin Library
William Andrews Clark Memorial Library
Yale Center for British Art
    Reference Library
Yale University Library

Index

Every effort has been made to include references to all identifiable persons living before or during the long eighteenth century, as well as to often cited twentieth-century critics and commentators, and to provide a selective listing of relevant concepts and keywords. Readers may also wish to consult the endnotes of each essay for more comprehensive information.